Production Management

Fresno Valley California food processing company has need for aggressive individual to join our production management group. We are seeking a self-starter with appropriate college degree, and a minimum of 2 years food processing supervisory experience. Excellent opportunity for advancement. Salary open. Send resume to:

BOX 639D, THE WALL STREET JOURNAL
Equal Opportunity Employer M/F

PRODUCTION MANAGER

Fabricating business has an opportunity for a production manager.
The position entails complete responsibility for the fabrication of orders including plant management of 40 man shop, customer liaison, and cost analysis.
Applicant must have experience in mild steel, stainless and aluminum including welding and forming of plate and structurals.
This is an opportunity to grow with a well established company. Please forward your reply with resume of experience and salary required.
Box 573 B, Wall Street Journal

SYSTEMS ANALYST

We seek a qualified individual to develop a Bill of Material System and a Material Requirements Planning System for multi-plant manufacturing operations. Bachelor's degree in a technical/financial field with two years programming experience in Ansi-Cobol, and at least one year systems analyst experience in a manufacturing environment preferred. Knowledge of IBM 370 DOS/VS and CICS highly desirable. Please send resume indicating background, experience and salary requirement in complete confidence to:

Personnel Department
Heartline Corporation
Gainesville, Florida 30436

Heartline and the Pursuit of Excellence

An Equal Opportunity Employer Committed to Affirmative Action —
A Heartline Corporate Policy!

MANAGER PRODUCTION CONTROL

We are expanding our manufacturing operation in Oregon & have immediate opening for a seasoned Production Control Manager who has a working knowledge of computerized systems.
The ideal candidate will have a degree & manufacturing experience in fabricated metals & assembly.
For confidential consideration send resume including salary requirements to:
Box 923B, Wall Street Journal

Production Superintendent

ABC FAIR, INC. is a recognized leader in the world of sporting goods, and we are seeking a recognized leader for our production management team.

The position of Production Superintendent Athletic Division, will coordinate and direct some 400 P&M employees engaged in the manufacture, assembly and packing operations of such products as basketballs, footballs and swim & dive equipment.

Your experience should include a high volume production environment involving a unionized work force under an incentive wage system.

ABC FAIR, INC. is headquartered in Division County with plant and sales offices located throughout the country. Our compensation and benefit programs are highly competitive, offering a broad base of coverage.

Should you possess a degree in Engineering, Production Management, or the equivalent, five to ten years of direct manufacturing experience and look forward to a challenge and the opportunity for personal growth, we invite you to submit your confidential resume, including salary history to:

ABC Fair

Bill Roark
2913 So. Shore Blvd.
Englewood, Fl. 33439

PRODUCTION CONTROL MANAGER

We are seeking an energetic and capable individual from an electronics-based corporation with 5-10 years experience in production and inventory control techniques.

The successful candidate will be responsible for all aspects of production & material control including Spare Parts, Stockroom, and Receiving Departments. A college degree, a solid MRP background, inventory levels & inventory turns ratio are required.

This is a key position in our Manufacturing Group where your management skills will be fully utilized in the maintenance, initiation and organization of new systems to meet our increased sales and production schedules.

We offer a competitive salary & benefits package, excellent working conditions, and an attractive rural living environment.

CALL COLLECT (203) 693-5211

or send resume with salary requirements to: MR. P. A. BROWN

RAMSES

ONE OF THE S.P.T. COMPANIES
11 Bartlesville Road, Southfield, CT 06493

VICE PRESIDENT MANUFACTURING

A new, well financed manufacturer of capital equipment for the semiconductor industry is seeking a bright, experienced individual who can help us become a major factor in our industry. Minimum 5 years experience covering assembly operations for electro-mechanical equipment, installation of inventory and material control systems, dealing with primary component suppliers, and front-line production management. Base salary $27K to $32K. Profit incentive bonus. Equity participation. Send resume to:

JONES MANUFACTURING
Box G
5312 Colorado Drive
Santa Ana, CA 92704

Production / Operations Management

Production/Operations Management

Thomas E. Hendrick, Ph.D.
Professor of Production/Operations Management
and Management Science
College of Business and Administration
University of Colorado—Boulder

Franklin G. Moore, Ph.D.
Professor Emeritus
Graduate School of Business
The University of Michigan—Ann Arbor

1985 Ninth Edition

RICHARD D. IRWIN, INC.   Homewood, Illinois   60430

ISBN 0-256-03032-4

Library of Congress Catalog Card No. 83-82967

Printed in the United States of America

1 2 3 4 5 6 7 8 9 0 K 2 1 0 9 8 7 6 5

To
Kathleen
and
Laura

Foreword to Students _____

The purpose of a course in production/operations management is to provide you with insight into how goods and services are provided. And that is the purpose of this book. It has been designed to describe the conditions through which production takes place and the part managers and workers play in performing production activities. Through these descriptions, you will also see the kind of work that production/operations managers do, and the career opportunities which exist in production and purchasing management.

The book will also call your attention to many of the problems faced by managers and to the merits of the different courses of action open to them. Emphasis is on the role of managers as decision makers who continually face alternatives, each having certain advantages, yet at the same time having disadvantages. In addition, emphasis is also placed on the ways in which production/operations decisions must be considered in relation to other functional areas of organizations—marketing, finance, personnel, data processing, accounting, and engineering.

This book supplies descriptive material to provide you with the background necessary for understanding the concepts and appreciating the managerial problems presented. Quantitative materials and problems are introduced frequently. These follow the trend in the recent years toward quantifying more and more of the areas of decision making in production and operations management. The problems illustrated, however, are confined to small ones of the kind that can be presented and solved in the text. Difficult mathematical calculations have been avoided.

At times you may wish for a definite answer and recommendation to a problem, and find none in the text. This may not be fully satisfying, yet this is how it often is in the real world. The text frequently points out the good and bad things about alternative actions without categorically choosing one as best.

This is the way the world operates. Sometimes it is hard for a manager, even with a considerable array of facts before him or her to choose which action will prove to be the best. So don't feel annoyed if the text sometimes weighs pros and cons and does not recommend a choice. Often the matter being discussed is a little like trying to answer such questions as, "Should I buy a house or rent one?" or "Should I choose this college or that college?" There isn't any one answer which is best for everyone. There are two or more sides to many problems and being aware of them can promote our understanding and help us make better decisions, even if it does make decision making more difficult.

At the end of every chapter you will find several aids that will help you to understand what was presented in the chapter. First, there are review questions. These questions are about matters which you should be able to answer from having read the chapter. If you cannot answer them, it may be well to reread the text discussion on the subject.

It is well to familiarize yourself with new terms introduced in the chapter. If there is any question about the meaning of certain terms, you should consult the index at the end of the book. There you will find references to the pages where the terms are discussed and explained. By referring to the text discussion you will get a better explanation of the term than could be supplied in an abbreviated glossary.

Next are questions for analysis and discussion. These questions relate to the subject of the chapter but often they go beyond it. They relate to difficult problems and usually require the application of the ideas presented in the chapters. Many of these questions have been taken from executive training programs and consulting assignments and are questions that mature managers have asked to be answered in terms of the ideas presented.

Following the discussion questions are problems or cases or both, depending on the chapter. The problems allow you to apply the techniques introduced in the text to other similar problems to help you fix the method in your mind. The cases are like the analysis and discussion questions in that they relate to the subject of the chapter in a general way, although they are frequently more far-reaching. These cases, too, are often real-life cases developed from discussions in executive training programs and consulting assignments of the authors.

Students as well as instructors may want to do further research on the subject of a chapter. For this purpose, selected additional supplemental readings are provided in Appendix H, at the end of the text. These are sources where you will often find a more thorough treatment of the material. Sometimes these sources will bring up points of view different from those expressed in the text and sometimes they will deal with different aspects of the subjects.

All of these study aids are presented to help you learn. In a very real sense, a text does not teach, it only helps you to learn.

T. E. H.
F. G. M.

Preface

Production and operations management deals with the *supply* side of all types of organizations—manufacturing, service, private, public, profit, and nonprofit. In this ninth edition of *Production/Operations Management,* we continue to bring this concept into sharper focus through numerous examples, yet we have retained as our major thrust the management of production of products by manufacturing organizations. We have retained this emphasis for three reasons. First, in the past few years, the field of production/operations management has undergone a near-revolution brought about by the increased use of computer-based production and inventory planning and control systems. Not only do these new systems (which can be used by small, medium, and large firms alike) aid in bringing long-overdue order to the jungle of production and inventory planning and control, but by their nature, they provide for a more logical coordination of production activities with marketing (through master scheduling), finance (through capacity requirements planning and cash requirements planning), personnel (through labor requirements planning), engineering (through structured bills of materials), and data processing (through computer-based systems).

We have prepared the current edition with this integration in mind and believe it is important that students who are studying to become specialists in finance, accounting, marketing, personnel, information systems, and engineering gain this integrating perspective. Of course, for those students who plan professional careers in production and operations management, this book will introduce them to the kinds of activities they will do and the decisions they will face.

You will note, for example, that Section Three of the text is organized to include the five main areas covered by the American Production and Inventory Control Society's Certification Examination program—capacity planning, master planning, material requirements planning, inventory management, and production activity control. The chapters in this section introduce the student to these areas and can aid (with more advanced study) in their preparation for taking these examinations. Both APICS and NAPM and their certification programs are also discussed briefly in the text.

The second reason we have maintained much of our focus on the production of products is that the manufacturing firm has been found to be a particularly useful model to represent production and operations activities in all kinds of organizations. It not only represents a large segment of our working population but it also represents one of the most complex types of organizations. Generally, if a student understands the way production activities are designed, planned, and controlled in these organizations, it is not difficult to transfer these concepts to the operational activities of banks, cities, insurance companies, airlines, and fast-food chains. While we illustrate these transfers throughout the text, we have attempted not to go overboard, because we believe that operations planning and control systems that are developed for manufacturing organizations are generally more transferable to service organizations than vice versa.

Third, we focus upon this segment because of the critical challenges facing U.S. manufacturers from foreign competition. We must get better at manufacturing (in terms of quality and productivity) if we are to remain a world economic power and maintain our high standard of living.

The ninth edition has also been thoroughly updated to reflect current practices in the field and to give greater emphasis to the problems facing managers in the last half of this decade. The entire book has been reorganized and material cut or added to reflect this changing field. Quality management is introduced early in the text because of the growing challenge from foreign competition and from consumers to improve quality of products and services. Likewise, production and inventory planning and control is presented earlier in the text as it forms the backbone of the field's focus. Also, we have integrated discussions of Japanese production methods and philosophies throughout the text and have added a major section on just-in-time production and inventory management and the *kanban* technique of job and vendor order control.

This edition continues to put quantitative methods into perspective. We have, for example, changed the emphasis of waiting lines and simulation from "techniques" to that of methods to aid in the *design of service capacities*. Similarly, we direct our discussion of linear programming toward scheduling output and capacity planning and give examples from the public sector (fire station location) and process industries (oil refining and blending) to illustrate the generality of the method. Emphasis is on problem formulation and graphic solution, and the simplex method and related topics are placed in an appendix for those interested.

To enhance student interest, we have added a few complete (and abridged) articles from current trade and professional literature (*Fortune, Business Week, The Wall Street Journal, Industry Week,* etc.) throughout the text to illustrate what is happening in the industry.

As in the previous edition, end-of-chapter review questions, questions for discussion, problems, short cases, and suggested supplemental readings are included, and all have been updated and related more directly to chapter material. A complete instructor's manual is also available.

ACKNOWLEDGMENTS

We continue to receive positive and constructive feedback from users throughout the United States and from foreign countries. These comments are always welcome and are appreciated. Particular thanks should be given to William R. Sherrard (San Diego State University), Mildred Golden Pryor (Stephen F. Austin State University), and Gene R. Simons (Rensselaer Polytechnic Institute) for their thorough reviews and useful suggestions to improve this ninth edition.

Finally, we wish to thank our families for providing a creative and helpful environment to complete this project.

Thomas E. Hendrick
Franklin G. Moore

Contents _____

Section Three
Production and Inventory Planning and Control

Section Four
Special Planning and Control Techniques

Models. Monte Carlo Simulation. Truck Replacement Example. Machine Setup Mechanic Example. Car Wash Example. Denver Fire Department Example: *Static Analysis of Station Location Alternatives. Dynamic Analysis of Location Analysis, Using Monte Carlo Simulation.* Validation of Simulation Results. Use of Computers in Simulation.

Section Five
Designing Production and Service Facilities

Section Six
Managing Productivity

Safety Equipment. Accident Prevention: The Human Element. The Occupational Safety and Health Act. Noise: *Noise Control Methods*. Health Impairment: *The Costs of Health Impairment Protection. Financial Liability.*

27   Work Measurement and Standards   **610**

Concept of a Production Standard. Number of Cycles to Time. Need for Timing Jobs by Elements. Performing the Study. Setting the Standard. Machine Time within Work Cycles. Setup and Change Time: *Pay Hourly. Incentive Pay Plan. Pro Rata Basis Pay.* Problems in Setting Production Standards. Limitations to Use of Time Study. Work Sampling: *A Work Sampling Example. Determining the Accuracy of the Estimate.* Other Ways to Set Production Standards. Standard Data: *Macroscopic Methods. Microscopic Methods. Implementing Standards.*

Appendixes

Production / Operations Management

Section One

Overview

Production and operations managers carry on their work in a social and economic environment. Society puts restrictions on them as they strive to produce products and services. Their jobs are multifaceted and require managing the organization's resources, people, money, physical property, and the production of products and services.

In this section, Chapter 1, "The Domain of Production and Operations Management," presents a brief view of what production and operating managers do, why it is an important topic of study, career opportunities in the field, and the societal constraints placed on managers relating to product safety and environmental protection. Chapter 2, "Basic Economic Concepts," deals with fundamental relationships which managers need to know to be effective. Chapter 3, "Capital Investment Productivity Analysis," deals more specifically with the financial consequences of investment decisions.

Chapter 1

The Domain of Production and Operations Management

Students beginning a course of study in production and operations management are doing so during a time when we are undergoing a "second industrial revolution." Productivity issues, automation with robots, unprecedented pressure from consumers for improved quality, competition from Japan, and the computer age all make this topic extremely relevant and exciting to examine. Students may want to know how this subject relates to the rest of their college courses and to their career objectives. They may have a major interest in manufacturing and production, or it may be in marketing, finance, accounting, information systems, personnel, or engineering. They may be planning to manage their own small organization or to work in a manufacturing company, such as IBM, or in a retailer, such as Sears. Or they may work for a transportation company, such as United Airlines, for the government, or for some other kind of service organization, such as a bank, hotel chain, hospital, insurance company, or recreational facility.

The purpose of this book is to provide students with an overview of production and operations management, what production and operations managers do, why they do it, and how what they do is related to other areas, such as marketing, finance, accounting, personnel, engineering, and computer-based information systems.

SCOPE OF PRODUCTION AND OPERATIONS MANAGEMENT

Production and operations management activities are not confined to the manufacturing of products. It is true that the production activities carried on in manufacturing companies form the backbone of our consumer society through the production of a broad array of products. (Nearly 20 million people work in manufacturing activities or at other activities in manufacturing companies in the United States.) But people also perform production activities in organizations which provide services. In fact, in recent years, more and more effort has been directed toward the management of productive effort in the service sector of our economy.

Service organizations, such as banks, hotels, restaurants, and transportation and insurance companies, produce services much as manufacturing companies produce automobiles, furniture, and microcomputers. Furthermore, within the service sector, the management of the operations of governmental organizations is receiving more and more attention. The costs of municipal services for schools, police protection, fire protection, trash collection, and so on are outstripping cities' revenues. Costs of health services are also increasing rapidly and are receiving much attention.

In general, however, production and operations management deals with the *supply* side of the work of organizations, and marketing deals with the *demand* side. Other functional areas of responsibility include finance, which is concerned with supplying enough equity and debt capital at the right time to pay for labor, materials, and facilities. Other functional specialists are accountants, who are more or less "scorekeepers," controllers, and budget makers; personnel specialists, who recruit and train workers, develop pay plans for them, and aid in their performance evaluation; and engineers, who design products and services, determine the best ways to manufacture them, and control their quality. Yet the work of all of these functional specialists is intertwined, and a great deal of communication and coordination is required.

Perhaps a helpful way for a reader to gain insight into the kinds of activities, problems, and decisions in the domain of production and operations management would be to look at some items in the "in-baskets" of some typical production and operations managers. Accordingly, we will present some sample in-basket items for the production manager of a manufacturing company, an assistant city manager, an operations manager for a commercial bank, and an assistant hospital administrator.

IN-BASKET FOR LANCE REDFORD

Lance Redford is the production manager for Midget Microcomputers. Midget sells a variety of hand-held microcomputers worldwide through wholesalers and a variety of retail stores. Redford has just returned from a three-week vacation trip and finds the following items in his incoming mail basket:

1. A letter from the U.S. Labor Department's Occupational Safety and Health Administration (OSHA) informs him that the company is in violation of federal rules regarding permissible noise levels on certain machines in the factory. The letter also reports that the company is not providing adequate safety devices to keep machine operators' hands out of the machines during their "stamping" cycles. The company is also cited for inadequate control of the fumes and dust associated with the vinyl chloride plastics used in the manufacture of the cases for their Midget micros. The letter from OSHA specifies fines which will have to be paid by the company if these conditions are not cleared up by certain deadlines mentioned in the letter.

2. A memorandum from the director of marketing reads, "As you know, Lance, our market in the West has been increasing substantially, and we should be thinking about building a new warehouse somewhere in the western states so that we can give better service out there. Would you please lead a special study group to consider where we might best locate such a warehouse and how its operations might be correlated with those of our Chicago and Atlanta warehouses?"

3. A note from the supervisor of the machine shop reads, "Lance, I think that the layout and locations of our machines could be improved substantially. We seem to be spending too much time moving parts from machine to machine. I'd like to talk this over with you and see if we could reduce these costs by relocating some of our machines and improving the flow."

4. Bill Hernandez, supervisor of plant maintenance, has written Redford a note asking if he could meet with Redford soon to discuss some ideas he has regarding the preventing of machinery breakdowns of equipment in use. Hernandez noted that in the past, "We have followed a policy on most of our machinery of repairing machines only when they break down. Lately this has been causing numerous interruptions to production."

5. Shirley Hopkins, the materials control manager, has just returned from a weeklong seminar where she learned about materials requirements planning (MRP), a computer-based approach to production and inventory control. Her report of these meetings strikes Redford's interest. She reported that, "Some companies are implementing MRP systems on relatively

inexpensive minicomputers which are used exclusively for 'online real time' control of production, customer orders, and inventories." Redford has been concerned recently about several orders being delivered late because necessary materials and/or subassemblies were not available when they should have been. He wonders if this MRP approach might be of help there.

6. Ryan Cochran, manager of quality control, asks in a note to meet with Redford concerning the growing proportion of defective Midget micros which inspectors have been finding through their statistical sampling procedures. Cochran says that he is not sure whether the problem is in the use of substandard purchased parts, inadequate training of machine operators, sabotage, or just what. Redford has heard from some of the supervisors that recent changes in certain manufacturing operations have made some of the current time standards inaccurate, which in turn has caused considerable worker discontent. It may be the proper time to review the work methods and job standards in these areas. This would also be a necessary first step for his other plans to "rebalance" the Midget micro final assembly line.

7. Tadeo Shimamoto, an electronics engineer with the company, has left a book in Lance's basket titled *Japanese Manufacturing Techniques: Nine Hidden Lessons in Simplicity,* by R. J. Schonberger. He attached a note which said: "This may be of interest to you. Perhaps we can apply some of these concepts to our manufacturing activities. As you know, I used to work for Zony in Japan and was able to observe some of these approaches to decreasing inventories, increasing quality and productivity, and smoothing the flow of production. Please let me know if you would like me to share these experiences with you."

Since Lance knew that Japanese manufacturers were beginning to have a strong competitive impact on the American microcomputer industry, he should see what might work for Midget Micro. He immediately scheduled a meeting with Tadeo.

8. The research and development department has completed its testing of two new products—a Midget micro that produces synthesized voice output and one that monitors and records vital signs of runners, swimmers, and other athletes. Redford must now begin to integrate these new products into existing manufacturing operations. A note in his in-basket reminds him of a meeting next week with engineering, purchasing, personnel, and marketing to finalize market forecasts, engineering design specifications, and questions as to which component parts of the new Midget micros should be manufactured internally and which parts should be purchased from outside suppliers.

9. The last item in the in-basket was a stack of nearly a dozen applications from college students who are looking for jobs in the production operations management area. Since he had two openings, Redford thumbed through the stack quickly. One application struck his eye. It was from Mark Hoffmann, who was about to graduate from the university. Hoffman had majored in production and operations management (P/OM) and information systems. From his resume, Redford could see that Hoffmann had a well-balanced education in this area. His courses included production and inventory planning and control (PIPC), computer-based information systems, physical distribution management, and purchasing. In the summer between his junior and senior years, he worked (and was paid) as an "intern" at a local computer manufacturer. He also had a "live case" study course with a local tennis racket manufacturer near the university. Here he was able to apply what he had learned in his course work to some specific production planning and inventory control problems the company was facing.

He also noted that Hoffman was planning to take the Certification Examinations sponsored by the American Production and Inventory Control Society and that he was active in the university's student chapter of APICS. Redford, a member of this group himself, had heard that the examinations were tough but designed to examine students' knowledge of academic material and its practical application to the real world of production and inventory management.

Even though Hoffmann had little experience, Redford decided to invite him for an interview to see if he might fit into one of his openings in the manufacturing division. One opening was for an "assistant production supervisor." Here a new person would be responsible, after a training period, for the management of one of the Midget micro assembly lines. The second opening was in production and inventory planning and control. This job entailed the coordination of the master production schedule with material purchases, subassembly manufacture, and machine center loading. Redford thought that a person with Hoffmann's background might be quite helpful in installing an MRP system in the company, if it proved feasible.

Redford looked at his watch and noticed that it was time for him to attend this month's budget meeting with other top managers of Midget. He got out his file which contained his recommendations for capital expenditures for new machinery and additions to plant and warehouse capacity for the next three years. Included were proposals for four robots to replace some simple repetitive (and boring) subassembly tasks, and a new computer-automated parts picking system. He knew Ron Miller, director of finance, would ask about the expected costs and benefits of his recommendations. And he knew that Darcy O'Neil, head of engineering design, would be there to present her proposal for a new computer-aided design (CAD) system to improve the productivity of her design engineering staff. Since money was scarce, he was glad that he had prepared his proposals in detail before going on vacation.

7/2/85

7/2/85

IN-BASKET FOR KRISTEN THOMAS

Kristen Thomas is the assistant city manager for Rocky Springs, a city with a population of 250,000. She has a staff of eight budget and management analysts, whose job is to help vari-

ous city departments manage their operations. This staff of eight has a balanced mix of administrative skills: two were trained in political science and public administration; one is a statistician; one is an economist; two were trained in urban planning; and two were graduates of business schools with training in finance and production and operations management.

These last two individuals reflect the growing trend of public organizations' need to improve the operations which deliver services to the public. Interestingly, Ms. Thomas's own background was also in production and operations management. She has an M.B.A. in this field and moved into city administration after a number of years in the aerospace industry. In fact, she is currently a part-time instructor in production management at Rocky Mountain University. The items in her in-basket are:

1. A memo from the city's fire chief reads, "Kristen, I am becoming increasingly concerned about the current locations of our fire stations. As you know, our city has grown rapidly over the past few years, and we have really never done a citywide comprehensive analysis of whether our stations are located correctly in relation to the fire hazards which we must protect. Some of our stations are clustered too closely in the downtown area, while many of our new outlying areas are protected only by distant fire stations. Could you assign someone from your staff to work with us on these location problems?"

2. The telephone rings, and it's the director of public works, who says, "Kristen, we are having real problems with controlling our inventories here at Public Works. As you know, we carry spare parts for street lights, for water systems, street paving equipment, and so on. In total we carry more than 10,000 separate items valued at well over $2 million.

"I have been reading a book, *MRP: The New Way of Life in Production and Inventory Control,* by Joseph Orlicky, and I wonder if we could use our computer to help us control our inventories." Kristen, having read the book and lectured on it at Rocky Mountain University, told him that she thought it was worth looking into and that although her staff was loaded right now with current projects she would see what she could do.

3. An article titled "Work Measurement in Municipal Government" has been sent to her by the director of parks and recreation for Rocky Springs. The article, by Jerry Bethel of the city of Los Angeles, related how they applied methods-time-measurement (MTM) time standards to work management programs in the Los Angeles Parks Department. She reads: "The department has over 300 facilities located on 217 separate sites which cover 14,000 acres of land and utilize 600 separate buildings. Among these facilities are 144 recreation centers, 71 large parks, 52 swimming pools, 14 senior citizen centers, 13 golf courses, 11. . . '." Kristen notes that they are using MTM time standards to schedule and control the large range of maintenance activities of these facilities.

A note in the corner of the article says, "Kristen, while Rocky Springs certainly does not have the range of facilities that Los Angeles has, nevertheless, I think we should consider the use of some of these methods. Can you give us some help in this area?"

4. The telephone rings again, and it is a city councilman who has a complaint. He says, "I know that we have private companies which pick up our trash here in Rocky Springs, but doesn't it seem rather wasteful to you, Kristen, for each of the six different companies which are licensed to pick up trash in Rocky Springs to serve the whole city? Yesterday, for example, I noticed that four separate trucks came through my neighborhood, and each stopped at only one or two houses which were their customers. This seems terribly inefficient to me since the trash trucks must surely spend 80 percent of their time driving around and 20 percent of their time picking up trash. Besides, these trucks are noisy, and they probably get only about six miles per gallon of gasoline. Would you please look into this routing problem, and see what you can do about it?" Kristen said she would.

5. A memo from the policy chief of Rocky Springs reads, "I have just returned from a meeting of police chiefs where I heard about some new police patrol scheduling methods which have been used successfully in cities about the size of Rocky Springs. These methods would, according to reports, allow us to schedule our patrol beats more efficiently so that they match the 24-hour patterns of calls for police assistance.

"As you know, our budget is extremely tight this year and we have been asked to reduce our force by 5 percent. I want to make sure that I schedule our patrol activities in such a way so that we provide the best coverage possible for the citizens of Rocky Springs, considering our resources. We have a small grant through the Law Enforcement Assistance Act which we can use to implement these methods, but assistance from your office will be appreciated."

Kristen knew of these methods (which were developed under the sponsorship of the U.S. Department of Housing and Urban Development) and knew that complete users' manuals and computer programs were available at a nominal cost to any city which asked for them. She immediately dictated a letter to HUD requesting these materials.

6. A letter from the city manager requests assistance in a "make-buy" decision about parking control in the city. The city manager writes: "As you know, 'Proposition 13 Fever' continues to threaten our state and city, and we may have to shift some of our activities to the private sector. One area is parking control. Enclosed is a proposal from Binkerton's Security Service where they offer to issue parking tickets and collect money from the meters for us.

How do their proposal's costs and revenue projections compare with our experience with our own metermaid and coin collection program? What do you recommend?" Kristen, having managed similar analyses which led to the "contracting out" for garbage collection, for the food service at City Hospital, and for professional management of the city's data processing center, immediately assigned the project to a three-person team in her office.

7. A telephone call from the director of the city's skiing facility asks for help in evaluating the capital investment economics of three competing chair-lift systems which are under consideration to replace one of the older (and troublesome) lifts.

8. A stack of applications from people who wanted to join the staff came last. Since one of her operations management specialists, Henry Stevens, was leaving to join the Valley National Bank as assistant operations manager, she was looking for someone to replace him. One application from Mark Hoffmann interested her. She could see that his academic background would be a good foundation for the kinds of operational problems which faced the city of Rocky Springs, so she decided to invite him for an interview.

IN-BASKET FOR BART BAKER

Bart Baker is the operations manager for the Valley National Bank. Valley is a commercial bank located in Paradise City and has 40 branches throughout the state. Bart Baker supervises the operations of the 41 facilities of the organization. In his capacity he is responsible for planning and controlling many of the "production" aspects of the bank. His major responsibilities are in the areas of teller scheduling and performance, facilities maintenance, bank security, new branch construction, and inventory control. Baker finds the following items in his in-basket after returning from a two-week "Executive in Residence" program at Midstates University.

1. A note from Jim Jones, one of Baker's assistants who has been working on methods and job standards for the bank, says that he would like to meet with him and review his progress to date. Jones has been trying to improve the layout of tellers' windows so that they will be more effective in the serving of customers. Hand in hand with this, he has been trying to develop reasonable job standards for tellers so

that by determining the capacity of tellers to serve customers their work schedules could be arranged to coincide with arrival patterns of customers.

Jones is also working on how to improve waiting-line arrangements at drive-up windows. He would like, of course, to develop something like the single waiting lines used inside the bank but is hampered by the lack of adequate outside parking space.

2. A notice announces a meeting with the capital budget committee next week. Pulling his file from his drawer, Baker saw that he was ready to justify the costs and benefits of several capital items. They were:

a. A new ultrasonic intrusion detection system. The slightest unusual motion within the bank jars the system's normal sound pattern, and a disturbance of this pattern activates an alarm.

b. The installation of plastic card-activated deposit and cash dispensers in 10 satellite areas around the city.

c. The installation of a telecommunication system between the bank's central computer and the 40 branches.

d. A new coin wrapping machine which would replace the two machines they currently have and would eliminate the need for one machine operator.

3. A final report from Tom Todd outlines the plans to open a new branch in the next county. Tom had utilized the scheduling technique called PERT (program evaluation review technique) to coordinate and "time phase" all of the activities which must be completed before opening day. Included in these activities are the hiring and training of personnel, furnishing the bank, and the promotional campaign.

4. A letter from OSHA tells Valley that the dimensions of the stalls in the lavatories are in violation of the law.

5. An article has arrived entitled "Designing a Work Measurement Program for Maximum Usability" by Terry J. Abbott of the Seattle First

National Bank. In this article, Abbott described the application of MTM-based work measurement in the development of over 14,000 time standards for clerical operations in the bank's 140 branches. Baker sends the article on to Jim Jones, who is working on this subject.

6. A note from the bank's marketing director asks Baker to evaluate the cost of personnel, facilities, and the like, if bank teller service is extended to 6:00 P.M. on weekdays and until noon on Saturdays. This proposal needs to be evaluated in terms of its possible effects on the other services of the bank.

7. A job application from Mr. Mark Hoffmann.

IN-BASKET FOR JOAN REDFORD

Joan is Assistant Administrator for Operations at Fairmont General Hospital. Her responsibilities are broad and include such "production" areas as nurse scheduling, custodian service, capital investment analysis, inventory control, food service, and laundry. Her Monday-morning in-basket items are:

1. A letter from a computer manufacturer requesting her to let them demonstrate their newly designed system which automates patient and nurse scheduling. This system is based on current and forecasted patient load, bed and operating room capacities, and nurse-type and -time requirements for the current and forecasted "patient profiles" (services patients are likely to need and for how long). (Joan, whose husband is production manager for a microcomputer manufacturer, is always amazed at how much she and her husband have in common in their respective jobs.)

Since nursing salary costs are the largest item in the budget, and because good progress has been made in developing nurse-service time standards (called *acuity standards*), she decided to invite the computer representative, and also makes a mental note to have her husband Lance sit in on the demonstration.

2. A memo from the hospital's administrator asks: "Joan, as you know, we have been consid-

ering the decentralization of some of our outpatient and emergency room services to several locations in the county. We hope this might provide less congestion here and better service to the community. We think, on a trial basis, we should start with two of these neighborhood clinics. Would you and your staff please recommend where they should be located?

3. The telephone rings, and it is Greg Wood, administrator at a local private hospital. He asks: "Are you still interested in consolidating the laundry facilities of our two hospitals? Or, as an alternative, would you consider jointly contracting with National Laundry to have them provide our laundry service for us? As we have discussed, we both think we might be able to obtain economies of scale or reduce costs through combining our facilities—or by getting out of the laundry business altogether. Of course, there are drawbacks too."

Joan sets a lunch date with Greg to discuss the proposals. She recalls that their "brainstorming" analysis of their food service operations had led to FGH's subcontracting out this activity to Metropolitan Community College's food service, which had excess capacity and a newly installed minicomputer that allowed them to use an MRP approach to planning their menus, ordering materials (food, paper, and dishes), managing inventories, scheduling food production, and cost control.

4. A brochure from Central Hospital Supply strikes her attention. Central is an international manufacturer and distributor of hospital supplies and equipment. Their brochure describes their inventory management service program, which requires the installation of a small terminal which hooks up to an ordinary telephone and is connected to Central's computer in Chicago. As items are placed in or drawn from inventory, the inventory clerk enters the transactions into the terminal (usually once a day). Central's system monitors on-hand amounts, and when quantities get too low, it generates an order for the items. They are then picked from Central's stock and sent out by the appropriate transport mode within

24 hours. Central argues that their system would allow FGH to carry less investment in inventories, provide better service, and take advantage of Central's bulk buying and high-volume manufactured items.

Joan writes for more information, as she has been recently chastized by Jim Rush, FGH's financial director, for having too much invested in inventory and by Fred Spinetto, the head nurse, for running out of blood tubing sets for the operating room.

5. A note from the hospital's architect requests a meeting with her to discuss the layout of the new intensive-care wing which is being designed. She wants Joan to aid her in analyzing alternative room configurations and nurse station layouts which will allow visual observation and rapid travel rates to the rooms. She also wants Joan to determine the correct number of nurse station desks to incorporate into the design to match peak nursing-service demand with the number of nurses on duty. She thinks that "waiting-line" analysis or "Monte Carlo" simulation might be useful here but isn't sure.

6. The chief resident physician calls and says, "Joan, I have been thinking about your proposal to schedule our four operating rooms more efficiently. I realize that our doctors rarely operate on Fridays, and, of course, Wednesday is golf day; and afternoons are used for making rounds . . . etc., but perhaps we can give them some incentive to 'level the load'—as you call it—on these expensive and often idle facilities. Perhaps we could even convert one of the operating rooms to better use and sell the equipment. With rising health care costs, we have to try to squeeze out as much service as we can from our investment in these facilities. Now, what do you suggest we do next?"

7. A telegram arrived from OSHA requesting that an OSHA inspector be allowed to visit the facility without obtaining a court-ordered search warrant. Last Friday, a laundry employee severely burned himself in their sheet ironer and had to be rushed upstairs to their burn center for treatment. Joan immediately called OSHA

and invited them to inspect their facilities. She hoped her newly installed safety program would be acceptable to the inspector.

8. A memo from Jim Young, head of the hospital's laboratory, asks that Joan help him in preparing his capital-budget request for next year. At the top of his list is a new microcomputer-based blood analyzer—manufactured by Midget Microcomputers—which is expected to improve the efficiency of medical technologists enough so that one or two of them can do the work of their present force of three per shift. Joan decides that she will help but mentally notes that there may be a conflict of interest in purchasing this machine as it is manufactured by her husband's company.

9. The last item in her in-basket is a resume from Mark Hoffmann. She thinks a person with his background and training might be able to help her with her backlog of projects.

INTERRELATIONSHIPS

The diversity and yet commonality among the items in these four people's in-baskets give an insight into the role of production and operations management in many kinds of organizations. Many more illustrations could have been included. In-basket items could have been presented for other managers, such as for a production manager of a furniture factory, a steel mill, an office manager of an insurance company, or the manager of a fast-food franchise, such as McDonald's.

The common thread is that production and operations managers have to administer a great variety of activities. In order to do this, they assemble appropriate resources and direct the use of these resources—be they people, machines, or processes—in transforming materials and labor into products or services. They direct the inputs so that they produce outputs. Figure 1–1 suggests the universality of production operations activities.

As Figure 1–1 also shows, successful organizations also have reporting systems which pro-

FIGURE 1-1
Universality of Production and Operations Management: Inputs Are Transformed into Outputs

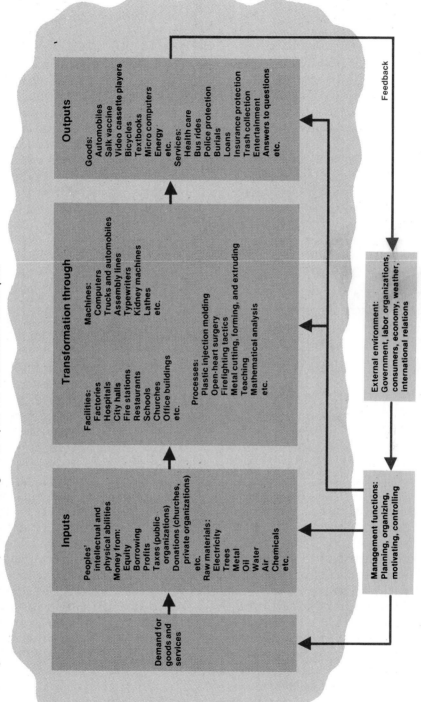

vide current *feedback* information so that the managers can see whether or not they are meeting customer demands. If they are not, then, at least in the private sector, they will lose customers. Consequently, in order to survive, they must redesign their products and services. Such changes are likely, in turn, to necessitate changes in internal operations and in the way resources are used.

Managers also have to respond to forces from the external environment, such as government regulations, labor union demands, and local, regional, national, and world economic conditions. Keeping in tune with current conditions is a continuous and dynamic process.

WHY STUDY ABOUT P/OM?

Questions occasionally asked by students with little business experience are: "Why do I need to know about production and operations management, since I am an accounting (or finance or marketing or personnel or information systems) major?" "Wouldn't my time be better spent studying more about my specialization?" These are good questions and deserve a good response, as education is expensive and time-consuming.

P/OM Deals with the Supply Side of Organizations

The first reason, as mentioned earlier, is that the topics studied here relate to the design, operation, and control of the *supply* side of organizations. All organizations exist to meet demand through their production functions. With a basic understanding of what it takes to build and operate production systems, *marketing managers* can better serve their markets and manage their sales forces if they understand the capabilities and limitations of their total demand-supply system; *financial managers* can better plan for capacity expansion and will be better able to understand the purposes of inventories before they demand their wholesale reduction. Financial managers also can utilize modern requirements

planning systems both in determining future capital requirements through capacity planning activities, and in forecasting *cash* requirements to pay for new machines, labor, materials, energy, and overhead—just as though *cash* were another raw material.

Accountants and controllers also need to learn about the capabilities of modern computer-based production and inventory control systems. These systems can provide cost accounting information, capacity utilization ratios, inventory valuation, cost of good sold, and other information for internal control, auditing, and financial reporting. Furthermore, internal accountants simply need to understand these activities in order to perform their jobs. Public accountants, too, would be severely hampered in their auditing of a manufacturing company if they did not know about EOQ, ROP, MRP, cycle counting, WIP control, ABC analysis, methods for determining labor standards, or other P/OM terms and tools, all of which are covered in this book.

Personnel managers can also gain an appreciation for the complexities of job design, the functions performed by P/OM managers and other workers, and the skills required to perform their jobs. This understanding can aid in the design of training programs, compensation systems, and in recruiting and selection functions.

Computer and information systems specialists perhaps have the most to gain from a thorough understanding of this material. They, most likely, will be charged with developing, implementing, or operating such P/OM-related systems as inventory control, job scheduling and order control, customer order entry, automated bills of materials, and labor cost reporting. *Engineers* will learn to appreciate the difficulty of translating their designs into production and the complexity of the coordination of materials, labor, and machine capacity to finished output.

Asset Concentration Controlled by P/OM

The second reason for studying P/OM is that approximately 70 percent of the assets in manufacturing and processing organizations are in inventories, plant, and equipment . . . which are directly or indirectly under the control of production or operations managers, materials managers, maintenance managers, and production supervisors—all members of the P/OM organization. With this concentration of assets, one should know what these people do, how they do it, and if they are using the most modern scientific methods for managing their operations.

In service organizations, direct labor often accounts for the majority of operating expenses. Scheduling of this resource is the responsibility of operations managers. One should know if this is being done effectively.

(3 / 2 / 84

16 (2 (84

Career Opportunities in P/OM and Purchasing

The third reason for studying P/OM is that there are excellent career and job opportunities for creative individuals who wish to pursue a professional career in production/operations management and purchasing management. Understanding the material covered in this book and course is the first step toward preparing for such a career.

(It is suggested that the reader check the Job Mart section of *The Wall Street Journal* for a few weeks to obtain a sampling of the kinds of positions available in these fields. The endpapers of this book also show examples of the kinds of jobs available in P/OM and in purchasing management.)

An excellent way to evaluate career opportunities in P/OM and in purchasing management is to become involved with a professional organization. APICS (American Production and Inventory Control Society), mentioned earlier, has a growing national membership of over 50,000 men and women. Their purposes are to educate members in modern P/OM methods, to promote professionalization of the field, and to certify the competence of individuals through a series of five written examinations given across the nation twice a year.

These examinations[1] cover inventory management, production activity control, capacity planning, master planning, and material requirements planning— all topics which are introduced in this book. Certification, along with a bachelor's and/or M.B.A. degree, virtually guarantees a person a chance to work as a professional in this field, but good jobs can also be obtained without certification if the person has the right combination of education and experience.

Most large cities have local APICS chapters and they openly welcome student participation in their educational seminars and monthly dinner meetings. Some chapters sponsor student APICS chapters on local campuses, promote intern job programs, offer scholarships, and aid in job placement of P/OM graduates.

Excellent career opportunities also exist in the purchasing and materials management field. People well educated and experienced in purchasing procedures, contract negotiation, legal aspects of purchasing, value and make-or-buy analysis, international trade, inventory control, and MRP, as well as purchasing's interfaces with production, marketing, engineering, and finance will find that they are in high demand by business and public organizations.

This demand is caused by the increasing problems of internal productivity (it often becomes cheaper to buy than make), by the material shortages, and by the high costs of investing in idle inventories brought about by high interest rates.

Career advancement in the purchasing and materials management field can often be achieved more quickly by becoming a certified purchasing manager (CPM). This certification program, sponsored by the National Association for Purchasing Management (NAPM), requires that candidates pass examinations in the fields of purchasing, materials management, business management, and quantitative methods, and by combinations of other things, including college

---

[1] For more information contact APICS, Certification Department, 500 W. Annandale Road, Falls Church, VA. 22046–4274.

course work and experience.[2] Students seriously interested in a career in the purchasing and materials management field should try to join their local chapter of NAPM and begin their preparation for taking these examinations.

P/OM and Strategic Business Decision Making

Strategic planning and decision making requires the simultaneous consideration of the markets targeted and the production and operations service systems required to produce these goods and services—the fourth reason for studying P/OM.

For example, McDonald's manufactures hamburgers "to stock." That is, when you walk in and ask for a Quarter Pounder, they almost always have it "in stock" and can provide it to you within seconds. Burger King, on the other hand, manufactures hamburgers "to order." At Burger King you can "have it your way," while at McDonald's "[they] do it all for you."

McDonald's market *strategy* is to provide standard finished products with broad appeal *very* quickly. Burger King's *strategy* is to provide products with enough perceived variability to meet people's particular tastes . . . also quickly, but not quite as quickly as McDonalds.

These market strategies severely dictate the way the production systems are designed and managed to make these fairly similar competing products. McDonald's manufactures *finished* products and puts them into stock. If a finished hamburger is not sold in 10 minutes, it is scrapped. It is thrown out! (No, not even eaten by employees!)

Burger King manufactures and stocks a small stock of subassemblies—cooked hamburger patties, toasted buns—and then adds the options (cheese, tomatoes, onions, mustard, and so on) when you place *your* specific order.

Both are fast-food companies, but each has its unique manufacturing systems. McDonald's cooks their burgers in batches on a grill, dresses them alike, and sends the batch to finished goods bins. They have found this system to work the best for their market strategy. Burger King uses a continuously moving gas-fired broiler that cooks both sides of the hamburger patty at once. Raw patties enter one end and emerge cooked at the other end. Each burger is then assembled according to the specific order and sent to the customer. They heavily market the concept that broiling "tastes better" than grilling. It takes longer, but Burger King has bet that customers will wait a little longer for a "customized" product.

In this case, the product and the service strategies have had a large impact on the design of the production process. Similar examples can be made where financial strategy or personnel strategy dictate production and operations system design. Thus, understanding P/OM is a necessary requirement for the total analysis of an organization's strategic options.

P/OM and Our "Productivity Crisis"

While the United States is still the most productive nation in the world, other countries, namely Japan, West Germany, and France are gaining rapidly. C. Jackson Grayson, chairman of the American Productivity Center, wrote that "If present trends continue, Japan will become the world productivity leader on May 14, 1992 at 3:45 in the afternoon. The United States will drop to second place."[3]

Obviously, this statement was meant to get our attention, but nonetheless, the challenge is real. The United States needs to streamline the way it manages the *supply side* of its industries. Meeting this challenge is clearly the job of everybody in manufacturing and service organizations, but much of the burden for increasing

---

[2] For more information about this program, write to National Association for Purchasing Management, P.O. Box 418, Oradell, New Jersey, 07649.

[3] C. Jackson Grayson, "The Japanese Productivty Challenge: A Modern Rashomon," in *Productivity Brief, # 1,* American Productivity Center, April 1981, p. 1.

productivity is placed squarely on production and operations managers. Everyone in the organization should have empathy for this challenging task, and thus the fifth reason for studying P/OM.

P/OM and Social Responsibility

The sixth reason for studying P/OM is to gain an appreciation for the kinds of pressures the managers of these functions are under as they attempt to meet their responsibilities to society (or are forced to by law).

Our picture so far of production managers in operation has been confined largely to *internal* organizational matters. This is proper because this is where most of them operate. Usually only top managers deal with broad social matters.

But high-level production and operations managers are in a dual position. They try to serve *their* employers, who are a company's stockholders or legislative bodies. But at the same time they operate in a social system and have certain obligations to society. Many of these obligations to society are written into laws, but others in the production area, such as trying to maintain stable employment, to pay fair wages, produce quality and safe products, to serve customers well, and to maintain or increase productivity, are less formal.

Social obligations are rarely stable and are often quite dynamic. Recent years have seen a shift, and the emergence of a strong consumer consciousness, particularly as it concerns the design of products and services so that they are safe for customers to use and so that working conditions will be safe for employees. Besides this, environmental considerations have also become very important.

Only a few years ago, an enterprising organization could design a product or provide a service in accord with its managers' views of whether or not the market would want it and whether the company could make a profit doing it. The primary considerations were economic, and, so far as quality and safety were concerned,

all that was required was to satisfy customers. If they were satisfied, they bought the product or service, and, if they were dissatisfied, they didn't buy it a second time.

Today this has changed. Managers, in both private and governmental organizations, have to pay more attention not only to what their customers might buy, but also to increasing governmental regulation and to consumer and environmental protection groups. Such groups take them to task if their products or services are unsatisfactory, or if they cause people to get hurt, or if people have their health impaired, or if they do harm to the environment by polluting the air or water, or if they waste scarce natural resources.

Nowadays there are frequent newspaper accounts about lawsuits against manufacturers, doctors, accountants, and transportation companies. And there are frequent stories about bans on the use of drugs or food preservatives or about the recall of a product from the market on orders from the Food and Drug Administration, the Federal Trade Commission, or the Consumer Product Safety Commission.

Much of the criticism in such actions is related to the quality of the product or of the service being rendered. These are areas where the remedial actions to correct the unsatisfactory conditions are often in the domain of production/operations managers and their staff.

PRODUCT SAFETY AND CONSUMER PROTECTION

The majority of organizations provide us with goods and services which perform as expected, are of good value, and are safe in use. However, there will always be some goods and services which are unsatisfactory and possibly unsafe in certain applications.

In the 1960s, people became increasingly concerned about injuries resulting from automobile accidents. There was a new awareness of the need for accident *prevention.* As a result new safety laws were passed which required considerable redesign of automobiles.

This interest in consumer safety quickly spread in many directions. Soon people were calling attention to hazards in the use of any number of other products. Instances were found where toys which children often put in their mouths and chewed on were painted with lead-based paint, which could give them lead poisoning. Other toys were found to have sharp edges which could cause cuts, and realistic toy cookstoves were found which could burn children.

The food industry also came under fire. Questions were raised over the possible health hazards of artificial coloring matter, of sweeteners, and of preservatives put into foods. Ecologists and environmentalists joined in with their interest in reducing air and water pollution and in the preservation of wildlife.

The new laws also gave existing regulatory agencies more power. The Food and Drug Administration, for example, can now ban or recall drugs and food items from the market; the Environmental Protection Agency has the power to set standards for vehicle exhaust emissions; and the Occupational Safety and Health Administration has the authority to prohibit the use of equipment and manufacturing processes which it regards as unsafe.

The point to these examples is that the design of products and services is no longer a matter of an organization's managers responding to the needs of the marketplace as they see them. They have to manage within the framework of the requirements that society imposes on them through government regulations and pressures from consumer and environmental groups.

Negative Aspects of Regulation

From a managerial point of view, there are two serious negative aspects to the consumer protection movement. First is the cost of complying with the regulations. General Motors reports that today's automobiles each cost nearly a $1,000 more to make because of all of the extras required by emission and safety regulations. Electric power companies spend many millions of dollars for "scrubbers" to keep smoke out of the air. All of these costs are, of course, passed on to consumers—and increase the cost of living for everyone. We are indeed getting cleaner air and water, and safer products and services—but we, the consumers, are paying for these improvements, and inflation is being spurred by them.

In the early days of the consumer protection movement, government regulations were often made unnecessarily strict. This caused production costs and prices to increase considerably. However, in recent years, attempts have been made to apply cost/benefit analyses to regulations to make them more reasonable. The very last ounce of safety or cleanliness has been found to come only at an exorbitant price.

A second negative aspect resulting from the consumer/environmental protection movement has been the increase in lawsuits claiming damages from injuries from products and services which are claimed to be faulty. These have multiplied in recent years, and juries and judges have been awarding large claims which were not awarded before the consumer protection wave. Today it often seems that courts and juries take the view that if an accident can happen it is the fault of the maker of the product or provider of the service.[4]

This means that makers of products and service organizations are obligated to do their best to keep the users of their products or services from having accidents, even though it may be unfair to blame the product manufacturer or service organization for most of the accidents. *People* cause accidents far, far more often than products or services cause accidents. According to the National Safety Council, unsafe practices by people are involved in perhaps as many as 90 percent of all accidents.[5]

---

[4] For an excellent discussion of some "horror stories," see Walter Guzzard, Jr., "The Mindless Pursuit of Safety," *Fortune,* April 9, 1979, pp. 54–64.

[5] See *Accident Facts,* National Safety Council, annual.

People don't get their brakes fixed and then have accidents from faulty brakes; they drive their cars too fast or after drinking too much alcohol; they smoke in bed; they leave open bottles of aspirin around children; they go away and leave the electric iron turned on; people ski in unsafe ways; people misuse a product, or use it for purposes for which it was never intended, and then if it fails or injures them, they blame the manufacturer or the server.

None of these acts of carelessness, however, excuse organizations from providing the safest product or service that they can. In some cases this means that cheaply made products will have to be discontinued even if they are in demand since such products are likely to be dangerous in use.

Thus, manufacturers need to do their best to be sure that their products are safe to use, just as service people must try to render good service. Product designers need to use safe materials and to put in appropriate safety guards. Both designers and lawyers should probably decide upon warning labels and review advertising claims to be sure that they are not misleading and that they include appropriate warnings of dangers. Records also need to be kept of complaints and of responsive actions, and appropriate liability insurance should be carried, if it can be obtained.

ENVIRONMENTAL CONSIDERATIONS

The 1970s developed into a decade of concern over the impact of our industrialized nation upon our environment. This concern continues into the 1980s. The 1974 Arab oil embargo and the 1979 Iranian revolution heightened this concern (it focused attention on our limited oil resources) and caused greater pressure on Detroit automobile manufacturers to design smaller and more efficient automobiles. The 1970s also produced more widespread support for ecological and environmental protective measures than in earlier years. These concerns also continue in the 1980s.

Like most controversial issues, these pressures have two sides. On the one side, environmentalists fight strongly for the preservation of our natural resources and clean air, but occasionally without regard for the costs which are being incurred along the way, and without regard to our needs for self-sufficiency in oil, coal, steel, copper, and other natural resources.

It is true, of course, that some organizations have damaged our environment by dumping harmful wastes into rivers and emitting smoke and fumes into the air. Strip-mining land for coal and leaving it denuded of trees and with unsightly mounds of unleveled overburden used to be common. "Brown clouds" caused by auto emissions are real health hazards. Today's regulations seek to eliminate these abuses.

In fairness, it should be said that managers of most organizations try to do everything economically and technically possible to protect the environment. By no means are they unsympathetic with the objectives of those who want to improve the quality of our lives. It is just that they have to decide how to do it, pay the bills and then, of course, raise the prices of products and services to cover these costs.

Everything comes at a cost, and sometimes two or more desirable goals conflict with each other. For example, automobile engines which minimize harmful air pollutants use gasoline wastefully at a time when we are all trying to reduce gasoline consumption. "Scrubbers" on smokestacks to reduce air pollution are costing electric utility companies (and subsequently their customers, the public) many millions of dollars. Filtering equipment for cleaning liquid wastes is also costly. Cities, as well as companies, have to spend large amounts of money to meet the new regulations. Furthermore, much of this extra activity requires extra energy.

Undoubtedly, these socially desirable goals which conflict with resource scarcity will continue to have important effects on the design of products and services. And, again, the burden of achieving the goals falls largely on production and operations managers in both industry and government. If the managers do not do enough voluntarily, even though doing these things drives prices up, then governmental agencies and nongovernmental pressure groups will be taking them to task. The mandate from the public seems to be confused. Some say "shape up and if it costs more, we will pay." Others seem to say, "We're being strangled by high prices and governmental regulations . . . give us a break!"

These *external* issues form the backdrop for *internal* activities which are continuously being performed by production and operations managers—and which must be considered as decisions are made.

Review Questions

1. Why does the domain of production and operations management include, to some extent, all organizations?

2. What problems and issues do Lance Redford, Kristen Thomas, Bart Baker, and Joan Redford have in common? What are the differences?

3. What are the purposes of the APICS and NAPM Certification Programs? (You might contact local members of APICS and NAPM and ask them.)

4. How does production and operations management generally fit in with other functional activities in organizations, and why should you study them?

5. Why are more and more graduates of business schools finding careers in public organizations as well as private organizations?

6. What kind of social pressures are P/OM managers facing these days, and what impact do they have on the way they do their jobs?

7. What are the six major reasons for studying P/OM? Are there other reasons?

8. Review the Job Mart section of *The Wall Street Journal* for a week to see what jobs are available in P/OM and purchasing management.

Questions for Discussion

1. Do cities and banks produce things? What do they produce?

2. Write a short description of the production activities of a manufacturing, service, and public organization.

3. Pick a specific organization (large or small) and identify its inputs, processes, and outputs, similar to those in Figure 1–1.

4. Why is it important to study P/OM?

5. What career opportunities exist for people who specialize in P/OM?

6. Why get the government into the area of product design? Wouldn't society be better served by letting the marketplace settle the question of quality and safety? Discuss.

7. Almost everyone favors the general objective of cleaning up our air and water. And we are all aware of the need to conserve energy. Yet, it takes extra energy to clean up the air and water. What should managers do? Discuss.

8. How can a company's market strategy affect the way they design their manufacturing facility or service delivery system?

Case 1–1

According to Peter Drucker, consumerism means that the consumer looks upon the manufacturer as "somebody who is interested, but who doesn't really know what consumer realities are, and who has not made the effort to find out." Perhaps Drucker is right, so far as what many consumers think. But whether this is what consumers think or not, consumerism seems to have gone even further. Manufacturers are often held liable for injuries even when consumers use products incorrectly.

A woman bothered by bugs bought a can of insecticide, but instead of spraying it on the furniture or in the air, she sprayed herself. She had a violent allergic reaction and sued and collected from the manufacturer.

In another case, a man who was injured in an accident while riding in a 13-year-old car sued the manufacturer. When he was thrown against the gear shift, the knob on top broke apart, and he was impaled on the shaft. The knob was made of white plastic, which over the 13 years had oxidized and developed hairline cracks. The man sued the company, claiming that the company had made the car with faulty materials, and won his suit. So did the woman who plugged a 115-volt vacuum cleaner into a 220-volt plug, causing the sweeper to "blow up." It is hard to see how a motor burning out could "blow up," but somehow the woman was injured in the process.

In all three of these cases there seems to have been no negligence on the part of the manufacturers. These accidents did not occur because the manufacturers were remiss in their concern for consumer needs.

In another case, a man was injured when the steering wheel of the car he was driving came off in his hands in an accident. The car was so badly damaged that it was not clear whether the steering wheel had been faulty or not. Nonetheless, the manufacturer was held liable. Today's consumerism seems almost always to hold manufacturers liable regardless of their culpability.

Hundreds of cases of extreme consumer protectionism can be quoted. In the vacuum cleaner case the court said the label should have warned that plugging it into a 220-volt line would be disastrous.

Since manufacturers have only one source of income from which to pay for both greater safety and liability claims, these costs must be added to the costs of products for everyone.

What really should the answer be? How far should a manufacturer have to go to protect everybody against highly unlikely accidents? How much should *all* consumers to required to pay for such protection for the few who have trouble?

Chapter 2

Basic Economic Concepts

General Motors makes automobiles and parts in over 100 factories in the United States, and K mart sells merchandise through about 1,500 outlets.

All of these facilities require that risks be taken and that money be invested, and the wisdom of making such investments rests on economic concepts and economic analyses. In the cases of GM and K mart, their total investments in buildings, machinery, and equipment exceeds $10 billion.

In both of these cases the company's managers decided, at some time in the past, to make these investments of money. Obviously, they did this only after making a careful economic analysis of each investment: How well would it pay off? How soon? What risks were involved? What alternative investments were available? And what would be their returns?

Such decisions of an economic nature have to be made in all of the areas of production and operations management listed in Chapter 1. The choices made rest on benefit/cost economic analyses.

PRODUCTIVITY

A person preparing accounting statements with the aid of a computer can perform more work than if forced to do it with an adding machine. His "productivity," the amount of work he gets done in that hour, is greater. A farmer who puts fertilizer on his fields gets a greater yield, both on a per-acre basis and on a person-hour basis. His productivity is increased even after counting the time he spends putting on the fertilizer. A student who has a calculator is able to solve analytical problems more quickly. And, in a factory, an employee driving a power-driven forklift truck can move far more material at less cost than he can when he uses a nonpowered hand-pulled lift truck.

In all of these examples there is a money cost—an investment—required in order to make the operator more effective. If this cost is too high it will not pay to substitute capital investments for labor. As a generalization, however, it usually pays to mechanize if any substantial volume of production is forecasted. The productivity per person-hour will be increased by more than enough to pay for the machine.

In many cases, productivity per person-hour can be increased just by doing things in different ways—ways which may not cost any more at all. Skilled typists use all of their fingers, and they are so skillful that they don't have to look back and forth from their manuscript to the keys. The rest of us who use the "hunt and peck" system and use only two or three fingers are much slower and get less done. Our productivity is lower. We turn out less production per hour.

As mentioned in Chapter 1, one of the pervasive and enduring objectives of production and operations managers is to improve productivity, thus reducing the costs per unit of output, or to increase output with a stable amount of inputs of people, capital, and energy. This in turn allows for price reductions or higher wages for people, or both, and so increases the standard of living in our economy.

During the early 1970s in the United States, productivity per person-hour, after many years of annual increase, not only stopped going up but actually went down. This, combined with continued wage increases, contributed to severe inflation. Productivity increased again in the late 1970s but only at about 1.2 percent per year, until 1979, when it was again negative. Productivity growth is predicted to stay below 2 percent per year through the 1980s. Most of these meager gains have come from increased efficiency in the production area in factories and the better use of resources in business operating in service industries. But some of the improvement came from the more economical use of facilities and resources in the public sector, in schools, and in other governmental service departments and agencies.

This low performance in productivity gains has continued to help fuel inflation and is therefore a problem of national importance. Trying to improve it is a challenge to all managers, especially to those who work in production/operations jobs. Chapter 24, The Management of Productivity, will treat this topic in greater depth.

ECONOMIES OF SCALE

Whenever anything has to be done over and over again and in large volumes, it is usually possible to become more productive. We learn how to do work at lower cost. This is particularly so where it is possible to mechanize any part of the work.

The economies of large-scale operations make it possible to "mass produce" products or services. Manual tasks can be cut into small tasks to which employees can devote full time, thus becoming proficient and more productive and consequently reducing costs. This can be observed in any factory or office. People specialize and can spend their full time at a single task because it has to be done so often. An offset to these gains in the form of boredom and dissatisfaction, however, often results from too much specialization.

The opportunities for economies from mass production are usually greater in operations which are mechanized than in those which are people-intensive. Large, costly, special-purpose machines can produce goods at very low unit costs if their investment can be spread over the production of millions of items over the course of time.

This is why it is possible for Ford Motor Co. to spend $50 million for an automobile assembly plant, or Pacific Gas & Electric to spend $50 million for a power plant, or Exxon Corporation to spend $50 million for an oil refinery. These initial costs will be charged off against a million or more cars, or against billions of kilowatt-hours of electricity, or hundreds of millions of gallons of gasoline. The cost per unit is only a few dollars a car, or a few tenths of a cent for a kilowatt-hour, or a few cents per gallon.

The economies of scale are not, however, confined to manufacturing activities. Large research expenditures, for example, are not at all onerous where the volume of the end product runs into large quantities. Years ago RCA Corporation spent $75 million developing color television before any sets were sold. But now that hundreds of millions of sets have been sold, and with RCA being one of the largest manufacturers, its original R&D expenditure is now less than a penny per set.

Similarly, economies of scale operate in advertising. Procter & Gamble spends several hundred million dollars a year advertising its products, principally soap, detergents, and personal consumer goods. But with P&G's enormous volume, the advertising cost per tube of toothpaste is very low.

DISECONOMIES OF SCALE

Economies of scale are available, however, only if large sales volumes are forecasted and only after large investments of money have been made in manufacturing facilities. Several disadvantages are immediately apparent. First, there is the need to invest large amounts of money, some of which will be at risk for some time. Evaluating this risk means investigating the question of how much the volume will be during the prospective investment recovery period and how long that period will be.

These forecasts of volume and time are also related to selling price since, at a low price, the volume of sales may be high but the investment recovery per unit of product may be low. A higher price might reduce sales volume but allow for a greater investment recovery per unit.

The disadvantage here is the great dependence on the accuracy of the forecasts—which, in fact, often prove to be wrong. Texas Instruments, Atari, Timex-Sinclair, and Mattel all overestimated the demand for home computers and as a result lost several hundred million dollars.[1]

Another disadvantage, or diseconomy, is that a "locked-in" investment in plant and equipment makes the company sluggish in responding to changing processes and to changing demand.

American manufacturers of steel, for example, did not adopt the "basic oxygen" process developed in Europe until the 1970s, 10 years after its use became common in Europe and Japan. Instead they stuck to their old "open-hearth" process, which was considerably more costly, because of their heavy investments in open-hearth equipment.

Something similar occurred in automobiles. American companies in the early 1970s were

reluctant to change to making smaller cars and moved slowly in developing good mileage and low air-pollution engines. In part, this was caused by their enormous investments in equipment to make larger models and in existing engine-making facilities.

Finally, when organizations become so large, they often become unmanageable and inefficient. But since they are so large, they usually dominate their market and can charge higher prices to offset these inefficiencies. One of the important jobs of production/operations managers is to strike a balance between the advantages and disadvantages of economies of scale by designing and operating production systems which are correctly "sized."

COSTS

All economic analyses and all economic concepts deal with costs. They are concerned with money being spent, how it can be spent in the most economical way, and how and when it will be recovered from revenues, sales, or other money inflows, such as tax receipts flowing to governments.

Fixed Costs

Fixed costs are those where amounts cannot be changed in the short run. If an organization signs a five-year lease on a building, the rental costs are fixed for that period of time. If a company buys a plastic injection molding machine on a monthly payment plan, the monthly payments are fixed whether the company finds any plastic injection molding business or not.

Similarly, annual charges made within a company for depreciation are usually fixed. So are many administrative and financial costs, such as bond interest and insurance costs. Administrative salaries, contributions to pension funds, and utility bills are also relatively fixed.

The important thing about fixed costs is that they do not fluctuate with levels of activity. If business goes down, the fixed costs, expressed

[1] "Home Computer Field Baffles Manufacturers and Many Buyers, Too," *The Wall Street Journal*, July 26, 1983, pp. 1, 14.

on a per-unit-of-output basis may become so high that they cannot be recovered from sales income. But if business volume goes up, the fixed costs *per unit* go down.

Fixed costs thus are very "sticky"—hard to control and reduce. "We are being killed by our overhead" is a common complaint of P/OM managers and a problem they must continually deal with.

Variable Costs

Variable costs are costs whose total amount goes up or down when volume goes up or down. The total cost of the meat that goes into Big Mac hamburgers in a month depends upon how many hamburgers are sold. So does the cost of the buns. And so, to some extent, does the cost of labor.

Variable costs, sometimes called direct, incremental, or marginal costs, vary in total with volume. Their costs per individual unit of production, however, remain almost constant unless economies or diseconomies of scale appear at higher or lower volumes. The cost of the meat in one hamburger is just about the same whether few or many are sold. The way in which fixed and variable costs relate to each other lies behind "break-even" analyses, which are discussed later in this chapter. Furthermore, the discovery of ways to reduce variable costs by increasing productivity or improving production or service methods is a major P/OM activity.

Opportunity Costs

Opportunity costs are the profits which a "foregone" choice of actions would have earned but which are lost because another choice is made. Obviously, the profits from the choice made should be greater than the foregone profits or else the choice is probably a poor one.

A person who keeps money in a mattress instead of investing it in a savings account or in some other investment may incur an opportunity cost from having made this choice. He or she has foregone the earnings the investment might have brought.

In 1983, IBM introduced their "XT" personal computer which was one of the first to have a built-in hard disk (rather than just floppy disks). The demand was greatly in excess of the company's anticipations, and the systems supplied to the dealers promptly sold out. Dealers estimated that they lost several million dollars of sales to competitors before adequate supplies became available. Had the company initially invested more in manufacturing capacity, it would not have lost these sales and incurred these opportunity costs.

It is rarely possible to put an accurate monetary value on an opportunity cost because one can rarely know what might have been. For example, what is the opportunity cost of not going to college? If people invest several years of their life and several thousand dollars of money in an education, they are forgoing the opportunity to earn a wage or salary during those years. On the other hand, if they do not invest in a college education, their lifetime earnings will probably be substantially less. The logic is easy to follow, but the numbers needed for comparisons and their probabilities can never be reduced to exact numbers. Opportunity costs should, nevertheless, be considered in almost every economic analysis made by production/operations managers in spite of this difficulty.

Sunk Costs

Sunk costs are investments made in projects from which the money normally cannot be recovered except gradually—by their costs being charged to continued production and operations.

Sunk costs are not at all synonymous with lost investments. They are money tied up and illiquid except as it may be possible to release it by means of continued operations or by a bargain sale. If, however, it proves impossible to recover the money in the future, then sunk costs are sunk in the most literal sense. A wildcatter who drills for oil and comes up with no oil, only salt water, has lost the money he spent drilling the well.

The importance of the sunk cost concept lies in the fact that sunk costs are permanent irrevocable investments which were made in the past. In most economic analyses of future projects, money spent in the past on a related project and which is now a sunk cost is *irrelevant to future decisions*. "What's done is done." P/O managers must remember this concept so they can avoid "throwing good money after bad," even though it may be a difficult and often embarrassing decision.

Relevant Costs

In contrast to sunk costs, "relevant costs" are those costs which *change* as a result of some action (investment in a new machine, change in a work method, redesign of a product or service, and so on) which is under consideration. Our interest is in the *impact* that the proposal is expected to have on costs, sales, volume, and profits. For example, if a Nautilus exercise center is considering staying open an extra two hours each day, the relevant costs are the costs that *change* from those of their current hours of operation—direct labor, some heat and light expenses, and more wear and tear on the facilities and equipment. These costs are then compared with an estimate of the extra revenue they expect to make before a decision is made on the change. This approach is sometimes called incremental or marginal benefit/cost analysis.

18 | 2 | 85

9 | 4 | 85 **TIME VALUE OF MONEY**

The concept of the time value of money is related directly to the concept of opportunity costs, presented above. This concept, the time value of money, says that $1 on hand today is worth more than $1 to be received at some time in the future. How much more? The amount that today's dollar could earn, if invested, between today and the date in the future when the promised dollar would be received.

Conversely, the present value of $1 to be received in the future is less than $1. These differences are the "opportunity costs" of *not* investing the $1 we have today, or *not* being able to invest the $1 now because we don't have it yet. Both values, the future worth of today's money and the present value of future money can easily be calculated.

The Future Value of Present Money

If we were to invest $100 today at a rate of 10 percent a year and let the interest earnings accumulate and let *them* also earn interest ("compounding" the interest), the total value at the end of any given time period can be found by using the following formula:

$$F = P(1 + i)^n$$

where:

$F =$ Future value
$P =$ Present amount
$i =$ Interest rate as a decimal per period
$n =$ Number of periods

For our example, and assuming a period of three years,

$$F = \$100(1 + .1)^3 = \$133.10$$

The opportunity cost of not investing our $100 is $33.10.

The Present Value of Future Money

If we expect to receive $100 at the *end* of three years and if we require a return of 10 percent, the present value of that $100 can be found by using this formula:

$$P = \frac{F}{(1 + i)^n}$$

For our example,

$$P = \frac{\$100}{(1 + .1)^3} = \$75.13$$

The opportunity cost of not having $75.13 now

to invest for three years is $24.87. Or, $75.13 $(1 + .1)^3 = \$100$.

The need to calculate the present value of money (or to "discount" it to today's value) to be received at different times in the future will become apparent in the problems on capital investment analysis methods in Chapter 3.

BREAK-EVEN ANALYSIS

Break-even analysis is a helpful tool used in analyzing managerial economic problems. It shows how much sales volume (in units or dollar sales) a company needs to have in order to break even financially. It also shows how much profit the company would earn or the loss it would suffer at various volumes above and below the break-even point.

Most manufacturing companies must operate above 60 percent of their capacity in order to break even. Normally most companies operate at a little more than 85 percent of their capacity, although they would like to operate at about 92 to 93 percent. Above 92 to 93 percent, efficiency usually drops off due to the disappearance of slack capacity. Holdups in one department are likely to hold up other departments right away, and congestion multiples rapidly. (This is a "diseconomies of scale" situation.)

In order to calculate break-even points, it is necessary to estimate fixed and variable costs for various sales volumes. This can be done for overall operations or for individual projects.

When break-even analysis is used in machinery buying decisions, the fixed costs are the machine's depreciation (which estimates its amortized capital cost) and such other fixed costs as insurance and installation costs. Variable costs are almost entirely made up of materials and direct labor costs and are "incremental" in that each additional unit of production causes an added increment of cost.

Break-even analysis also allows us to ask "What if?" questions. For example, *if* the selling price of a new solar heating panel is $100 per unit, and direct materials and labor costs are

$80 per unit, and fixed costs per month are $20,000, *then* break-even analysis will show how many units will have to be sold in a month in order to break even. This occurs when the *total revenue* equals the *total cost*. In formula form this becomes:

$$P \times Q = F + (V \times Q)$$

where:

P = Price per unit
Q = Quantity
F = Fixed costs
V = Variable costs per unit

Since Q, the quantity, is the unknown we want, we can use algebra[2] to restate this formula as follows:

$$Q = \frac{F}{P - V}$$

In our example, which is shown graphically in Figure 2–1, the unit sales required to break even would be:

$$Q = \frac{\$20,000}{\$100 - \$80} = 1,000 \text{ units}$$

"Contributions" to Overhead or Profits

The Term $(P - V)$ is called tne "contribution." It is the amount by which the selling price per unit exceeds the variable cost per unit (or total revenues exceed total variable costs). In our example, the sale of one solar heating panel contributed $20 toward offsetting fixed costs up until the break-even point, 1,000 units, was reached. Above 1,000 units this $20 would be a pretax profit.

These relationships can be used by managers in their planning. They can determine, for example, the effects on profits (or losses) of changes in sales quantities. If they want to know at what volume the profits would amount to

---

[2] $PQ = F + VQ$; $PQ - VQ = F$; $Q(P - V) = F$; $Q = F/(P - V)$.

FIGURE 2–1
Break-Even Chart

ERROR.
NOT TO SCALE!

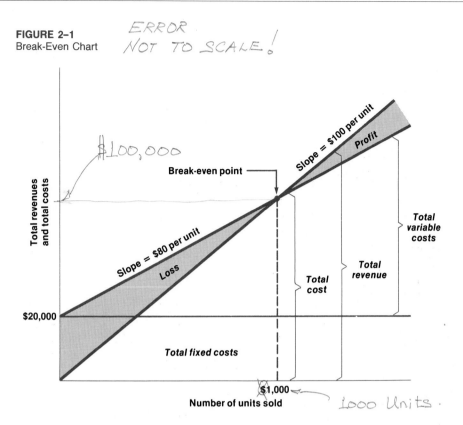

$100,000

Break-even point

Slope = $100 per unit

Profit

Total revenues and total costs

Total variable costs

Slope = $80 per unit

Loss

Total cost

Total revenue

$20,000

Total fixed costs

$1,000

1000 Units.

Number of units sold

$5,000, all they have to do is to divide $5,000 by $20 and find that 250 more units, or 1,250 in total, would have to be sold.

The total number of sales needed, put in formula form is:

$$Q = \frac{F + \text{Desired profits}}{P - V}$$

$$= \frac{\$20,000 + \$5,000}{\$100 - \$80} = \frac{\$25,000}{\$20}$$

$$= 1,250 \text{ units}$$

To be realistic, however, the company's managers should allow for income taxes because all profits generated by sales above the break-even point are taxed. The tax rate is something a little less than 50 percent, the exact figure depending on how much profit the company earns. If, in our example, it is 40 percent, then each $20 of profit will shrink to $12. Therefore,

in order to earn $5,000 after taxes, 417 units ($5,000 ÷ $12) above the break-even point, or 1,417 units in total, will have to be sold instead of 1,250.

The formula for the total number needing to be sold now becomes:

$$Q = \frac{F + \dfrac{\text{Desired profit}}{1 - \text{Tax rate}}}{P - V}$$

$$\frac{\$20,000 + \dfrac{5,000}{1 - .4}}{\$100 - \$80} = \frac{\$20,000 + \$8333}{\$20}$$

$$= \frac{\$28,333}{\$20}$$

$$= 1,417 \text{ units}$$

One can see that by manipulating the variables in the equations many "What if?" questions can be answered. What if, for example, direct material costs were to increase by 12 percent? What would happen to the break-even point? Or, what if competition forced us to cut our price from $100 to $90? Answers to such what-if questions can be calculated.

CONTRIBUTION RATIOS

For some purposes it is useful to know the "contribution ratio" or, as it is sometimes called, the "profit variation" for individual products. This ratio measures the product's relative contribution as a percent of its price per unit. The formula for its calculation is:

$$\text{Contribution ratio} = \frac{P - V}{P} \times 100$$

Using our earlier example:

$$CR = \frac{\$100 - \$80}{\$100} \times 100 = 20\%$$

Low contribution ratios often result from labor and material costs being high relative to the prices which can be charged. Changes in total volume do not affect profits or losses very much if the variable costs are high relative to the selling price. Conversely, if fixed costs are a bigger part of total costs, then the contribution ratios of individual products need to be larger, and volume changes cause greater swings in profits and losses.

These relationships are important since, once a manager knows the contribution ratios of products, he or she can promote the sale of those which contribute the most and perhaps remove those from the product line which have low CRs, and thus high opportunity costs. These ratios can also help a manager to decide whether or not to take on jobs at prices which cover variable costs but only part of fixed costs.

BREAK-EVEN ANALYSIS AND DECISION MAKING

Break-even concepts can be applied as an aid to managerial decision making in a number of

areas. The few examples presented here are intended only to provide a "flavor" for the use of this tool.

Mechanization Decisions

Suppose that a new glass-cutting machine would decrease the amount of glass breakage and labor required in the manufacture of our solar heating panel. What minimum volume (Q_m) is necessary to allow us to break even on this new investment; and what would happen to the break-even volume if such a machine were purchased? It would have a monthly fixed charge of $3,000 and would reduce variable costs by $5 to $75 per unit.

Since existing equipment is in place, the fixed costs relevant to this decision are the additional $3,000 and the $5 increase in contribution.

The minimum volume question is answered by:

$$Q_m = \frac{\$3,000}{\$5} = 600 \text{ units}$$

Thus, if volume is expected to be at or above 600 units per month, we should invest in the new machine.

To answer the second question, the new break-even volume—if the machine were added—would be:

$$Q = \frac{\$20,000 + \$3,000}{\$100 - \$75} = 920 \text{ units}$$

An interesting question now arises: The answer to our first question said that we should invest if volume is at or above 600 units per month. Yet, the new total break-even point is 920 units. Why? If the fixed costs are truly fixed and cannot be changed in the short run, then it would still be to our advantage to invest in the machine if volumes are above 600, even if they are below 920. This is because it is better to have *some* additional contribution to covering fixed costs ($5 per unit) rather than none. And, for that matter, in the short run it generally pays to operate at even lower volumes (below 600) as long as there is a positive contribution until the fixed costs are no longer fixed obligations.

Choices among Processing Alternatives

Break-even analysis can also be used to aid in making choices among alternative processes by comparing the relative advantages of each. In a manufacturing situation, for example, processes requiring simple machines which are easy to set up are usually slow and costly to operate. On the other hand, larger volumes of output may allow the use of faster machines which are costly to set up but which, once set up, are less costly to operate. Often there are several alternative methods, each of which may be the most economical for certain ranges of output. The method which should be used depends upon the expected volume of output.

The making of a small metal part illustrates such a choice from among alternatives. This part can be made on an ordinary general-purpose lathe which is easy to set up but not very efficient in production. The part can also be made on a turret lathe which is more costly to set up but which produces at lower unit costs once it is set up. Neither of these machines can compete, however, with automatic screw machines when volume begins to count. Setup costs are much higher, but operating costs, are much lower.

In the case of the part, it costs $2.50 to set up an ordinary lathe, after which the operating, material, and scrap cost is 45¢ per unit; turret lathes cost $5.00 to set up and 20¢ per unit; and automatic screw machines cost $15.00 to set up but only 4¢ per unit.

The cost formulas for making this part on these three kinds of machines are (with x being the quantity to be made each time the machine is set up):

Lathes	$ 2.50 + \$.45x$
Turret lathes	$5.00 + .20x$
Automatic screw machines	$15.00 + .04x$

Figure 2-2 shows graphically how the costs of making the part on these machines compare. Lathes are the least costly for very small quantities, then turret lathes, and then automatic screw machines for all large quantities.

Sometimes a chart is all that a manager would need for deciding which method to use because the size of the order is not near a cross-over point on the chart. But if it is necessary

FIGURE 2-2

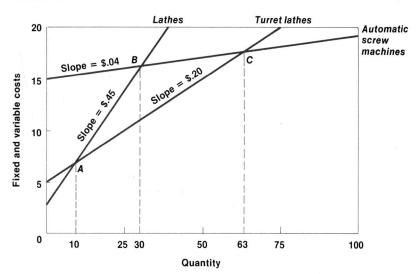

to know the exact crossover points (points *A, B,* and *C* in Figure 2–2), these can be calculated very simply. It is only necessary to set the equations for the two methods being compared equal to each other and solve for *x.* The comparison of lathes to turret lathes, for example, is:

$$\$2.50 + \$.45x = \$5.00 + \$.20x$$
$$.25x = \$2.50$$
$$x = 10$$

Thus, point *A* on the chart, the point of indifference between these two methods, is at a volume of 10 units. Similar calculations comparing automatic screw machines to lathe and to turret lathes show that points *B* and *C,* the other crossover points in Figure 2–2, are at 30 units and at 63 units.

So, for orders under 10 units, a lathe should be used, for 10 to 63, a turret lathe, and above 63, an automatic screw machine. If the turret lathes are all tied up on other work and not available, then a lathe should be used up to 30 units, and automatic screw machines for orders of more than 30. Crossover points among machines which perform similar functions are useful to know when alternate product routings are needed because the most efficient machine (for the size of the order) is busy.

Crossover charts can also be used in new-equipment purchase choices. The lines on the chart would compare the costs of doing the work in the present way against what they would be if a new machine (a new truck, for example) were purchased or leased.

Make-Buy Decisions

The break-even concept can also be useful in "make-buy" decisions when a company's managers are choosing between making a part themselves or buying it from an outside supplier.

Make-buy questions can come up at any time. Should the company have idle capacity when such a question comes up then, at least for the moment, the decision to make is almost automatic since the cost of machines does not need to be considered (the cost of idle capacity continues whether the choice is to make or buy).

The difficult make-buy questions are those which would involve the purchase of more equipment to make the item. It is here that break-even analyses can help. To illustrate, we will suppose that our solar panel manufacturer is making a decision about whether to make or buy a part.

If we invest $3,500 in a new die, we will be able to make this part ourselves for an added cost of $1 per unit in variable costs. If, however, we buy the part, the vendor has quoted two prices to us, $1.55 each for quantities up to 10,000 units and $1.30 each for all orders over 10,000.

Because of the price discount, if we purchase over 10,000 units, we need to calculate two break-even crossover points, one comparing each purchase price with our internal manufacturing costs:

$$\$1.55x = \$3,500 + \$1x$$
$$\$.55x = \$3,500$$
$$x = 6,364 \text{ units}$$
$$\$1.30x = \$3,500 + \$1x$$
$$\$.30x = \$3,500$$
$$x = 11,667 \text{ units}$$

Because there is no start-up cost involved and no machine to buy, buying the part would always be less costly for all small quantities. But our analysis tells us that although buying would be less costly up to 6,364 units, making is less costly thereafter.

The volume-price discount at the 10,000 mark complicates matters. For quantities just over 10,000, again it pays to buy but only up to 11,667 units, after which it again is profitable to make. All of these relationships are depicted in Figure 2–3.

CAUTIONS IN THE USE OF BREAK-EVEN ANALYSIS

Break-even analyses should be used with discretion because of the many assumptions which

FIGURE 2–3
Make-Buy Decisions

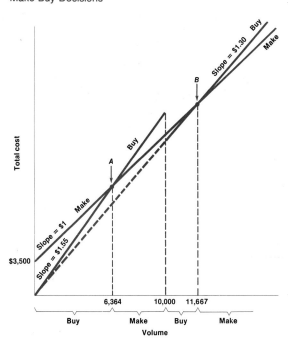

are made. First, it is difficult to separate fixed costs from variable costs in many operations; often these are only rough estimates. Second, variable costs per unit are not always as constant over a range of volumes as the straight lines on break-even charts indicate. Sometimes economies of scale cause variable costs to be less per unit as the volume increases. At other times, diseconomies of scale work the other way and cause variable costs per unit to increase as volume increases. Fixed costs, too, may not stay constant over the full range of volume under consideration. And, finally, greater volume may be in prospect but only at reduced prices, which affects contribution margins.

These several interacting relationships are depicted in Figure 2–4. Fixed costs may rise as volume increases because of the need to add to capacity in a "lumpy" sort of way. This might be caused by the need to buy more machines to support the added volume. Similarly, the addi-

tion of a second shift increases the salaries of supervision and other indirect labor which are relatively fixed costs.

Nor is the variable costs line a straight line. Because of the economies of scale, their total may go up more slowly than volume until near capacity. Then total variable costs are likely to rise faster than does volume because of congestion, the inefficiencies of second and third shifts, and other diseconomies of scale.

Finally, the total revenue line is rarely a nice straight line as we have depicted. As a firm tries to increase its volume, it may have to cut prices on some items in order to sell more. This has the effect of flattening out the total revenue line on the right side of the chart.

If, however, one were to look at Figure 2–4 and accept the cost and revenue figures shown there at face value, the volume which would produce the greatest profits would be just below point A. That is the point of greatest spread between total revenues and total costs. However, a manager looking at this chart, and knowing the inexact nature of the figures that went into its makeup, would probably conclude that it would be most profitable to produce at a volume somewhat above point B but somewhat less than point C, but not necessarily just below point A.

TRADE-OFF ANALYSIS

Many managerial decisions rest on another managerial economics concept, "trade-off analysis." "Waiting-line" problems are of this sort. If a large airport had only one landing strip, then airplanes coming in would have to queue up and fly around in the air waiting their turn to land. Similarly, airplanes wanting to depart would have to wait their turn. This would be costly. But more landing strips would be costly, too, and would likely result in idle landing strips, and that too would be costly (and result in higher landing fees for the airlines). Somewhere there is a proper trade-off point between the cost of more landing strips and the cost of airplanes waiting.

Figure 2–5 depicts the way these opposing

FIGURE 2–4
Break-Even Chart with Irregular Changes

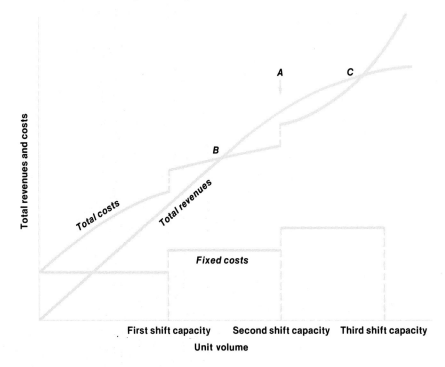

costs are related and depicts the point of minimum combined cost. As the cost of airplane idleness goes down, the cost of idle landing strips goes up. When these two costs are added together, we develop a "total incremental cost curve" whose low point is the most economical trade-off point, and the airport managers can determine how many landing strips to provide.

This concept, of there being an optimal trade-off point between two or more opposing

FIGURE 2–5
Trade-Off Relationships

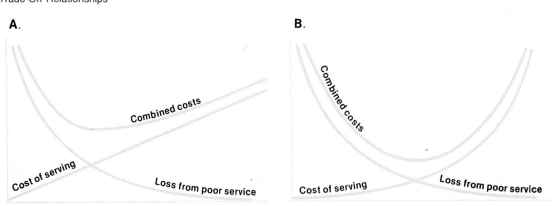

FIGURE 2–6
Some Important Trade-Off Decisions in Production/Operations Management

Decision Area	Decision	Alternatives
Plant and equipment	Span of process	Make or buy
	Plant size	One big plant or several smaller ones
	Plant location	Locate near markets or locate near materials
	Investment decisions	Invest mainly in buildings or equipment or inventories or research
	Choice of equipment	General-purpose or special-purpose equipment
	Kind of tooling	Temporary minimum tooling or "production tooling"
Production planning and control	Frequency of inventory taking	Few or many breaks in production for buffer stocks
	Inventory size	High inventory or a lower inventory
	Degree of inventory control	Control in great detail or in lesser detail
	What to control	Controls designed to minimize machine downtime or labor cost or time in process, or to maximize output of particular products or material usage
	Quality control	High reliability and quality or low costs
	Use of standards	Formal or informal or none at all
Labor and staffing	Job specialization	Highly specialized or not highly specialized
	Supervision	Technically trained first-line supervisors or nontechnically trained supervisors
	Wage system	Many job grades or few job grades; incentive wages or hourly wages
	Supervision	Close supervision or loose supervision
	Industrial engineers	Many or few such engineers
Product design engineering	Size of product line	Many customer specials or few specials or none at all
	Design stability	Frozen design or many engineering change orders
	Technological risk	Use of new processes unproved by competitors or follow-the-leader policy
	Engineering	Complete packaged design or design-as-you-go approach
	Use of manufacturing engineering	Few or many manufacturing engineers
Organization and management	Kind of organization	Functional or product focus or geographical or other
	Executive use of time	High involvement in investment or production planning or cost control or quality control or other activities
	Degree of risk assumed	Decisions based on much or little information
	Use of staff	Large or small staff group
	Executive style	Much or little involvement in detail; authoritarian or nondirective style; much or little contact with organization.

Source: Wickham Skinner, "Manufacturing-Missing Link in Corporate Strategy," *Harvard Business Review,* May–June 1969. Copyright © 1969 by the President and Fellows of Harvard College; all rights reserved.

sets of costs, has many applications. The scales along the two axes of the two diagrams in Figure 2–5 could be for a retail store where the attempt would be to trade off the costs of idle clerks against the loss of customers from having too few clerks. Or it could be the costs of carrying larger inventories balanced off against the loss of business from being out of stock of certain items. The diagram would be the same. Only the labels would change.

In a factory, a trade-off diagram could depict the waiting time of maintenance employees against the costs of production delays from having to wait for machine repairs when there are too few maintenance people. Or it could be the question of material order sizes. Large infrequent order quantities hold down setup and paperwork costs—but at the expense of having larger average inventories and the holding costs that these inventories entail.

Figure 2–5 shows two types of trade-off relationships. Diagram A reflects the relationships when the cost of providing services varies on a straight-line basis as would occur in the case of carrying larger inventories in order to reduce the losses from being out of stock. The same relationship might occur in a retail store where the number of clerks is traded off against the prospective losses from customers leaving when the clerks are all busy.

Sometimes, however, the costs of providing the service or expanding capacity are curvilinear, just as are the possible savings. This situation, depicted in diagram B, would often occur where quality is concerned. In this case, the horizontal scale would be measures or degrees of quality. Not only does better quality cost more in almost all cases, but almost without exception higher and higher degrees of quality cost disproportionately more. This is indicated by the cost of the quality line curving upward to the right.

Although the concept of trade-off analysis is quite useful in conceptualizing problems, it is sometimes hard to estimate the numbers. We have spoken of "the cost of idle clerk time," "the cost of lost business," "the cost of idle maintenance people," "the costs of waiting machines," and so on. These costs are real; yet it is difficult and sometimes impossible to get these numbers to use in the trade-off analyses.

Nonetheless, the concept and even the numbers which can be estimated do provide managers with a starting point as they try to answer the questions, "Which costs will go up or down and how much if I do more or less of something? What is the point of least cost when two or more variables are concerned?" The curves which result represent an accumulation of changes in cost behavior of several variables which change with volume.

Figure 2–6 depicts the wide range of trade-off decisions which face the P/O manager.

Review Questions

1. What is "productivity," and has the United States been keeping pace in their productivity in recent years?
2. What are economies and diseconomies of scale? Give examples.
3. There are several different classifications of cost. What are they?
4. Why is it difficult to estimate "opportunity" costs?
5. How does the interest rate affect the future value of present money? The present value of future money?
6. Explain how the contribution ratio and the break-even point are related.
7. List the ways that managerial decisions might change the break-even point and show how it would be changed.
8. What are some trade-offs in P/OM decision-making?

Questions for Discussion

1. How can the break-even volume be calculated for specific products?
2. The president looks at the break-even chart which the controller has just constructed and asks: "How can we lower the break-even point?" How should the controller answer?
3. Is a break-even chart reliable enough as a manage-

rial tool for a manager to rely on it in making a major business decision? Discuss.

4. Would the cost line on a break-even chart provide a reliable projection of costs if volume decreased by, say, one third? Justify your answer.

5. Suppose that some variable costs prove not to be entirely variable, particularly as volume decreases and some fixed costs prove not to stay entirely fixed, particularly when volume goes up. What would this do to break-even analyses? How often are either of these possibilities factors in real situations?

6. How do income taxes affect break-even points?

7. Discuss the limitations and precautions which should be taken in using break-even analysis.

Problems

1. What is the value of $1,000 invested today at the end of two years if the interest rate is 10 percent?

2. What is the present value of someone's promise to pay $1,000 at the end of two years if we value money at 10 percent per year?

3. Farnsworth Manufacturer has $50,000 in fixed costs assignable to a new electronic pest repeller designed for backyard use which utilizes high frequency sound. It will wholesale for $20.00 and has a variable cost of $12.43. What is the break-even point?

4. Farnsworth (see Problem 3) wishes to have a profit of $25,000 this year on the pest repeller, and their tax rate is 46 percent. How many units must they sell?

5. At a sales volume of $125,000, Fred's Income Tax Service has variable costs of $60,000, fixed costs are $50,000, and profits are $15,000. What is its dollar sales break-even point? (Hint: $X = F + (V/\text{Sales})\, X$. How much sales volume does it take to produce profits equal to a cost reduction of $500? (Hint: $500 = CM \cdot X$).

6. Variable costs are 40 percent of the sales price of $10 per unit for Modern Products, Inc. With fixed costs of $200,000, what is the break-even point? Assuming that sales have been exactly at the break-even volume, should Modern cut the price to $8 if this would boost sales volume to 50,000 units?

7. Superior Western's fixed costs are $20,000, and variable costs are $50 per unit. In order to improve profits, it has been proposed that the company increase fixed costs $30,000 plus $50 per unit to improve the product and change the price as well. The marketing staff has made the following estimate of the effects of these actions:

Price per Unit	Annual Sales without Improvement	Annual Sales with Improvement
$400	5	40
350	15	125
300	40	200
250	100	375
200	250	600
150	500	1,000
100	900	2,000

What action and at what price will there be the greatest profit for Superior? (Hint: Profit = Revenues − Costs)

8. The Atlanta plant has a capacity of 50,000 units per year, has fixed costs of $240,000, and variable costs of $3 per unit. The Boston plant makes the same products. It has a capacity of 75,000 units per year, fixed costs of $260,000, and variable costs of $4 per unit. The present production rates are for Atlanta, 22,000, units, and for Boston, 45,000 units a year.

a. What are the per unit average costs of production in each plant at present production levels?

b. What would they be at capacity?

c. For most economical production costs, how should the present volume of 67,000 units be divided between the two plants?

d. Assuming that sales will, in the future, be 75,000 units a year, how should this production be divided between the two plants?

9. Using a one-shift operation, Joyce, Inc. is selling its maximum capacity output (except for overtime) of 4,000 units at $175 each. Fixed costs are $300,000, and variable costs are $360,000 for at-capacity operations.

It would be possible, however, to boost sales to 4,500 units at current prices by using overtime. This would increase variable costs to $400,000. (Some of the variable costs do not go up and down in direct proportion to output.) It is also possible to raise prices to $180 and still sell 4,000 units.

For greatest profit, which of the two alternatives is best?

10. For the past period, Bishop Recreational Products has operated at capacity with the following distribution between products:

Product	Volume (units)	Contri-bution per Unit	Labor-Hours	Contri-bution
A	10,000	$10	10,000	$ 30,000
B	12,000	12	20,000	35,000
C	6,000	20	20,000	30,000
D	4,000	10	15,000	20,000
E	3,500	25	17,500	30,000
			82,500	$145,000

Business is expected to increase 10 percent in the next period, but it will not be possible to expand labor beyond 85,000 hours. What products should Bishop emphasize? What should the product distribution be to use the 85,000 hours to best advantage? (Hint: Calculate contribution per labor-hour and use it to aid in your analysis.)

11. Downing Press's plant has a capacity of 200,000 books per year with fixed costs of $450,000 and variable costs of $3 per unit. It can probably sell 100,000 units in its home market at $13 each. It can probably sell the other 100,000 books it could print in foreign markets at $7 per unit. What are the profits prospects from the home market alone? What might they be if the company produced at capacity and sold the second 100,000 abroad?

12. The Link Company, a large chain of stores, makes the following proposal to a vendor. Link proposes to pay $4 for each product. Labor and machine costs are $7.50 per hour for the vendor. Factory overhead is 125 percent of labor and machinery costs. General and administration costs are equal to 20 percent of factory costs. Materials cost will be $.50 per unit. The cost of tooling may be neglected since Link will pay separately for it.

For small quantities, the total production time for labor and machines is 10 minutes per unit for up to 1,000 units. This production time will be reduced by 10 percent by the time 5,000 are produced, 12 percent at 10,000, and 15 percent at 50,000.

a. What should the supplier's price be if his profits are to be 10 percent of the selling price—for 1,000, 5,000, and 50,000 units?

b. At what point will the $4 price allow the vendor

to earn $.40 on each unit? (Hint: Interpolate between unit costs at volumes of 1,000 and 5,000 units to obtain a volume which produces unit costs of $3.60.)

13. With fixed costs of $30,000 and variable costs averaging $4 per job, Gem Lawn Mowing has been mowing 6,000 lawns per year at an average of $10 each. What profit has it been earning? Would it be wise for it to spend $10,000 for advertising if advertising would raise the volume to 7,500 jobs? Assuming that the advertising has no carryover benefits into future periods, how much better or worse off will the company be if it spends the $10,000?

14. Continuing Problem 13, suppose that Gem believes that a $5,000 advertising expenditure would raise the volume to 7,500 jobs, but its managers don't feel very sure about this. They feel that a $5,000 expenditure for advertising will be likely to increase volume as follows:

Volume	Probability
6,300	.05
6,600	.10
6,900	.15
7,200	.18
7,500	.25
7,800	.17
8,100	.10

Should the company advertise? What is the probable payoff (or loss)?

15. Suppose that the company that owns the three kinds of machines described in Figure 2–2 received an order for 100 units. Referring to Figure 2–2, we conclude this work should be done on automatic screw machines, but the automatics are busy, so the work has to be done on turret lathes or regular lathes. How much more would it cost to do this work on either of the two less efficient kinds of machines?

16. Two kinds of paint are being considered. A gallon of brand A costs $6 and will cover 300 square feet of surface. It will last about three years and can be applied at 75 square feet an hour. A gallon of brand B costs $10 a gallon and will cover 400 square feet of surface. It goes on at a rate of 90 square feet an hour. Painters cost $10 an hour.

How long will brand B have to last to be competitive with A?

17. The Day Company is bringing out a new product, the parts for which may be bought or made. If

purchased, they will cost $2 per unit for the 10,000 units expected to be made.

a. Making these parts will cost $5,000 for tooling plus $1.30 per unit variable cost. Should Day buy or make these items?

b. Day can go more automatic and spend $15,000 for machines, which would reduce variable costs per unit to $.60. Should Day buy or make these items and, if it should make them, by this method or the other?

Chapter 3

Capital Investment Productivity Analysis

Productivity does not result from manual work alone but rather from the work of people using machines and facilities. They use simple hand tools or operate highly sophisticated machinery and equipment, and both people and the facilities they use are housed in appropriate buildings.

These facilities and machines always cost money, often a great deal of money, and capital must be invested in them before production (or service) can begin. In several industries in the United States, the steel industry for one, these investments are over $60,000 per employee, which is equal to an employee's wages for several years. Commitments of such large sums of money are made only after careful economic analyses of relevant costs and benefits which are translated into expected returns on these capital investments.

THE NEED FOR CAPITAL EXPENDITURES

The need for capital expenditures comes from several sources. First, fixed assets (other than land) are continually wearing out. Machines are always, figuratively, marching down the road to the junk heap, and some reach the end of the road every year. Sometimes the end of the road is reached because a machine is obsolete even though it may still be operable. Computers made only a few years ago are in this category.

The first priority, and usually the largest need for capital investment, is to keep production facilities operating efficiently. Existing machines and equipment can be overhauled or rebuilt, or they can be replaced. Of these, the replacement of existing facilities is the big item so far as capital requirements are concerned.

The second need for capital investment is for expansion. Most organizations grow year after year, so they have to keep buying more plants, office space, and equipment year after year. Growth needs may, however, be somewhat irregular and normally require smaller expenditures than those made for replacing assets.

A third need is for investment in socially desirable projects, such as equipment to reduce air and water pollution. Costly equipment sometimes has to be installed for worker safety and health.

A fourth need might be said to be sustaining projects, such as facility landscaping. These are projects which may not add directly to profitability or efficiency but are necessary to sustain operations or to maintain good community relations.

The money a company has (from its cash flow) and the money it needs do not always match. Often the total cost of requested projects exceeds the money or credit available. The chairman of U.S. Steel's finance committee once said that he had to make up his annual $500 million capital-expenditure program out of department heads' "Christmas lists," which usually asked for more than double what was available.

Top managers should not, however, regard the capital investment proposals of their subordinates as "Christmas lists." Nearly all of these proposals will be for projects which are expected to produce a net cash flow. Nor should top managers start with the idea that only a certain amount of money is available. Rather, they should consider how productive each proposal promises to be, and, if they are money-saving proposals, how much they can save.

Only after all of the promising proposals have been evaluated should a decision be made about what to do. Then managers must decide to approve only as many projects as can be paid for with the money at hand; or to approve more proposals if they look profitable enough to justify borrowing money or selling more stock; or to approve the leasing or installment purchase of new equipment.

Discovering Capital Investment Needs

When does a machine need replacing? When does an automobile need replacing? Neither machines nor automobiles wear out all at once, in which case we would know for certain when they need replacing. Actually, it is possible to keep old machines or old automobiles running for years by continuing to repair and rebuild them. Many Boeing 707s are still flying, but they are expensive to maintain and much less efficient than the newer Boeing 767s. But repair costs are usually high for old machines, just as they are for old automobiles or old airplanes. Obsolescence, too, occurs. Every new and more efficient model of a computer, for example, makes it less economical to continue to operate the old one.

The point is that uneconomical operations have to be discovered. Managers have to watch for uneconomical operations of old equipment. Single-spindle lathes that are over 50 years old can turn out considerable quantities of products which would cost less if they were made on newer automatic screw machines. The fact that an old machine still operates and can be fully utilized does not necessarily mean that it is economical to use it. It is also necessary for lower-level managers to search out places where money needs to be spent to reduce noise, smoke, or water or air pollution, as well as to make conditions safer for workers.

CHOICE OF PROJECTS

Since there are usually more economically worthwhile projects and more socially desirable projects than a company has money for, its managers have to choose from among them. Normally, the projects which promise the highest rate of return on the investment are approved. But this cannot be the only guide because sometimes no-rate-of-return socially desirable "must" projects as well as sustaining projects required to carry on the business also need a share of the money.

In addition, various projects with uncertain payoffs might be approved if they might some day pay off very well. An electric power company might, for example, build a nuclear power plant which is not expected to be very profitable but is expected to serve as a pilot project to pave the way for more efficient nuclear power plants in the future. The probability of future higher payoffs needs to be considered in the analyses of projects.

Nor are capital-expenditure decisions always clear and distinct from operating decisions. A company could, for example, spend money for research and for advertising. But it could also spend less on reseach and advertising and buy more machines. Top managers usually have to make hard choices between allocating working capital among operating costs and capital investments. Figure 3–1 shows information flows and

FIGURE 3-1
Typical Large-Company Capital Expenditure Decision-Making Model

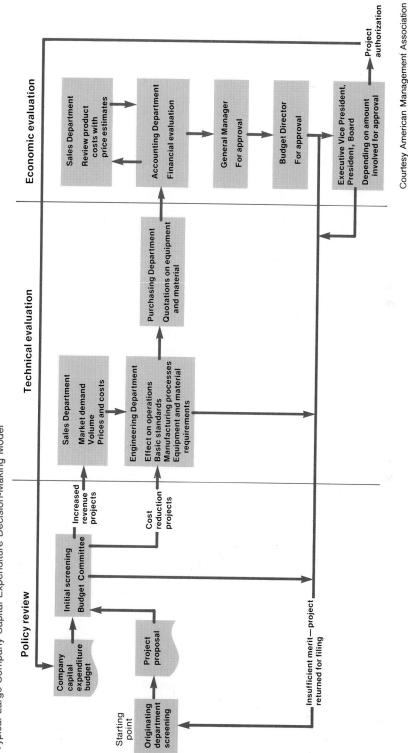

Courtesy American Management Association

capital-expenditure decisions made in a typical company.

CASH FLOW

Often, the money to pay for new machines, new equipment, and new buildings comes from the net cash flow resulting from an organization's operations. However, investment capital is also obtained by selling stock or borrowing money. Cash flow, however, is not the same as a company's profits or losses. Net cash flow is the difference between cash inflows from sales (taxes in government organzations), and other sources (such as the sale of old machinery) and the outflows for labor, materials, overhead, and taxes. Normally, most of every company's gross cash inflow flows right out again as it is used to pay today's bills for electricity, taxes, to buy replacement machines, to build buildings, and so on.

The gross cash inflow not only pays all of a company's day-to-day expenses but also includes money which recovers the decline in the value of machines and buildings because of their wearing out. This decline, called depreciation, is a *noncash outflow* expense which is included in the company's profit and loss statement, which reduces profits and thus reduces taxes, which is a cash outflow avoidance. Thus a company's net cash flow is equal to retained profits after taxes and dividends, *plus* depreciation on machines, equipment, and buildings, plus any income from the sale of fixed assets.

This does not mean that a company will have all of its net cash flow left over at the end of a year. Much of this cash, perhaps all of it, will be spent for new machines or other new capital investment projects as the year progresses. The point is that during the year, cash, free of immediate commitment to current bills, flows into the company and its managers must decide how to use it.

Since net cash flow provides much of the money used for capital projects, its size has much to do with capital investment decisions for products or services. Since prices hopefully are

set to cover depreciation in the value of assets as well as other expenses so that a profit results, the part of net cash flow which is created by accounting for this depreciation of assets should provide most of the money for machinery replacement purposes. But today's new machines always seem to cost more than the ones they replace, so companies often have to use part of their profits for replacement projects. And, of course, all of the money for *expansion* has to come out of cash flow, or else the company will have to sell more stock or borrow money.

DEPRECIATION

Depreciation Methods[1]

Managers and their accountants still have to calculate a money value for depreciation every year. There are several ways to do this and the differences are important because they effect the size of depreciation expenses and thus the amount of taxes paid.

The Internal Revenue Service (IRS) wants everyone to depreciate everything over its full life. But because no one really knows how long equipment or other assets will last, business practice is to write machinery investments off on a minimum—not a maximum—life expectancy. This means claiming that machines will not last very long and claiming full depreciation in just a few years. If a company does not do this, it may end up showing an asset on its books—as still being worth money—when in fact it is valueless. The government allows these fast write-offs as incentives to invest in new capital equipment to maintain a healthy economy.

Straight-line method. Historically, the straight-line method has been the most common method for calculating depreciation. This method starts with a machine's installed cost minus its expected scrap or salvage value at the end of

_____
[1] Depreciation rules are becoming more complex. Tax accountants should be consulted for specific situations.

its expected useful life. This number is divided by the number of years it will be used. A $10,000 machine, expected to last 10 years and to then be sold for $1,000, will have a $900 depreciation expense each year for 10 years.

Declining balance method. In the declining balance method, an item is depreciated by a certain *percentage* of the balance of the value each year. A $10,000 machine which is expected to last 10 years can be depreciated, on an accelerated basis, at a 20 percent depreciation rate. Twenty percent of $10,000, or $2,000, is the first year's depreciation. At the beginning of the second year, the machine is valued on the books at $8,000. Twenty percent of that, $1,600, is the second year's depreciation. The third year's depreciation is 20 percent of $6,400, and so on.

The declining balance method allows for larger depreciation expenses in the early years of an asset's life and then less and less as time goes on. This reduces profits and reduces taxes in the early years of the investment. This tax avoidance provides more cash for investment now and is frequently done because of the "time value of money." This method never depletes all the values, so users of this method, near the end of an item's life, switch over to straight-line depreciation.

Sum-of-the-years' digits. Another method is the sum-of-the-year's digits. If we take a 5-year-life item and add 5 + 4 + 3 + 2 + 1, we get 15. In the first year we depreciate the item $5/15$ of its cost, next year $4/15$, and so on. For a 10-year item the sum of the digits is 55, so the first year's depreciation would be $10/55$ of its cost. Although it is not particularly complicated, this method is not commonly used.

(See Figure 3–2 for a graphic comparison of the above three depreciation methods.)

Variable or unit depreciation. Variable or unit depreciation is becoming more popular. This method requires an estimate of the number of units a machine will produce during its lifetime (these units can also be expressed as hours of operation). Depreciation is then calculated on a unit basis and charged to accounting periods according to the number of units produced in the period. The amount charged to any period, therefore, depends on the asset's use in the period. Many accountants feel that this method

FIGURE 3–2

Comparison of Straight-Line, Declining Balance, and Sum-of-the-Years' Digits Depreciation Methods

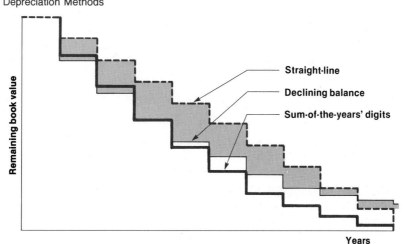

gives a better picture of the amount of depreciation expense which should be charged than do other methods.

Group depreciation. In practice, large companies usually do not depreciate each machine separately. Instead, except for assets where considerable money is involved, machinery investments are grouped into life groups. All machines with 10-year life expectancies are put into one class in the company's accounts. Every time a new 10-year-life machine is purchased, its cost is added to the total for all 10-year-life machines. Every year 10 percent of this total is charged off as depreciation, if the straight-line method is used.

This makes it necessary to have separate accounts for several life classes: 5 years, 10 years, 15 years, and so on. But there is no need for thousands of separate depreciation accounts—one for every machine. The effect of depreciating by groups is to put depreciation largely on a straight-line method of depreciation which neglects salvage value.

Other methods. There are still other methods of depreciation, but the five that have been described here are the ones commonly used by manufacturing companies. The sinking fund method, for example, sometimes used by utilities and railroads is not commonly used in manufacturing.

INCOME TAX CONSIDERATIONS

Federal income taxes are high for companies which make large profits. In 1978, General Mo-
tors earned $8.34 billion but paid out $3.09 billion of it to the government as income taxes. In recent years auto industry profits (and thus taxes) have been nearly nonexistent, but nonetheless, no one is required to carry on business in such a way as to pay the utmost in taxes, so when there are choices, as occurs with depreciation methods, the tax shields should be considered.

In the case of depreciation, all machines ultimately become fully depreciated (or sold) no matter what method is used. Yet, the depreciation method that is used affects when taxes are paid. Some methods allow a company to retain more cash earlier in an asset's life than other methods. If the company can put this money to work profitably right away, this is an advantage.

We will use a one-machine factory, the Northern Company, as an example to show how the straight-line, declining balance, and sum-of-the-year's digits depreciation methods operate. Straight-line depreciation is a slow depreciation method whereas both of the other two methods recover depreciation faster.

Northern has a new machine which costs $10,000 and has an expected life of 10 years and an expected resale value at the end of that time of $1,000. This machine reduces operating costs by $2,000 a year, in addition to recovering the $900 of depreciation claimed to have occurred in the straight-line depreciation method. The machine thus produces a pretax relative cash flow of $2,900.

Here is how taxes and cash retention would work out in the first year with these three methods of depreciation:

	Straight-Line	Declining Balance	Sum-of-the-Years' Digits
Claimed depreciation	$ 900	$2,000	$1,636
Savings (or pretax profits)	2,000	900	1,264
Income taxes (46% of profits)	920	414	581
Cash retention	1,980	2,486	2,319

By using declining balance rather than straight-line depreciation, the company gets to keep $506 more in the business for the time being. The sum-of-the-years' digits method lets it keep $333 more than with straight-line.

One could wonder why the government allows the use of fast depreciation when this deprives it of taxes for the time being. The government allows it because it wants to encourage, rather than discourage, new machinery purchases since this increases the nation's productive capacity and promotes economic growth. Also, later on, as the machine gets old, the remaining depreciation is small and taxes will be higher. The effect is to change the timing of paying the tax. Businesses gain because they can put the retained extra cash to work. In billion-dollar companies the extra retention amounts to millions of dollars. Fast depreciation also provides protection against unexpected obsolescence of equipment and facilities.

(2(2)85

Investment Tax Credit

The federal government has now made an "investment tax credit" a permanent part of an Internal Revenue Code. Under this tax shield a company can usually take a credit on their tax bill of up to 10 percent of the value of certain capital investments in the year they are put into service. As with fast depreciation, the purpose of this credit is to stimulate investment in new equipment and facilities in order to improve productivity and sustain economic growth.

INVESTMENT COST AND INCOME FLOW PATTERNS

Capital equipment projects require a cash outflow during their construction or implementation period. As construction continues, more and more money is paid out. Then, when a project comes online (which, for a steel mill, may be three years or more), it starts to generate a cash inflow from sales or from savings over the previ-

ous method of production. After a shakedown period, during which problems may keep costs high and which may last for several months, the flow of savings usually is high for several years. Thereafter, as the project "ages," its savings flow lessens.

Future cash flows often have different patterns. They do not all have a steady or regular pattern. This would occur, for example, if a company builds more capacity than it needs in the near future. When such a project becomes operational, its savings or income flow will be small initially but will grow in later years as the excess capacity begins to be used. A few years ago, for example, the John Deere Company built a farm equipment machinery factory in France even though the company expected to lose money for the first five years before sales would be enough to generate profits.

In any case, in considering capital investment proposals, the analyst must forecast the cash flow pattern the project is likely to generate because the timing and shape of these streams have much to do with a project's profitability or potential savings over the present method.

ANALYZING CAPITAL INVESTMENT PROPOSALS

Most organizations use one or all of the following methods in their evaluation of capital investment proposals.

1. Payback period (nondiscounted).
2. Average return on investment (nondiscounted).
3. Discounted payback period.
4. Net present value.
5. Discounted return on investment (internal rate of return).

These methods are not perfect. Return on investment and payback period are easy to calculate but are not very incisive. Discounted payback period, ROI, and cash flow (net present value) require more involved calculations but they more truly reflect the relative merits of alternative choices.

Before we consider these methods individually, two fundamental difficulties inherent in all methods should be pointed out. First, whether a new machine should or should not be purchased depends upon what its cost to operate will be compared to what it will save. And, as was said earlier, what it will save depends as much upon the company's present machine as it does on the costs of the proposed machine. Thus, in replacement problems, there can never be any absolute measure of the profitability of the investment. It depends as much on how inefficient the preset method of production is as on how efficient the proposed method will be.

The second difficulty is uncertainty. These methods of analysis are only as good as the estimates of costs, savings, useful life, salvage values, and other factors utilized in the evaluation. If they are under or overstated, poor and often costly decisions result.

Computer-Based Inventory Control System Example

We will demonstrate the use of the various capital investment analysis methods by showing how they could be applied to the analysis of a computer-based inventory control system which is under consideration.

The situation. The managers of Xenox Industries are considering investing in a small business computer which will be dedicated to managing such manufacturing functions as customer order control, inventory planning and control, and order preparation and control. The computer and the software they are considering is in the "minicomputer" class, which they feel is about the right size for their company, whose annual sales are about $25 million.

An evaluation team has been formed to evaluate this project. The team leader is the manager of production and inventory planning and control (PIPC). Other team members are a systems analyst from data processing, and representatives from the purchasing department, marketing department, and a financial analyst from the controller's office. This multifunctional team was formed to consider the proposal because its use would have a substantial impact upon the way each of these people do their job.

After much discussion, and after reviewing the costs associated with the way Xenox was currently performing these tasks, the team developed the following estimates of cash flows which they forecasted would result if the new system were installed. (See Figure 3–3.)

Developmental costs. The costs to acquire and install the system were estimated to take one year and would cost $75,000: The computer and the CRT terminals (cathode ray tubes for displaying information on a viewing scope) would cost $30,000 and purchased software would cost $15,000. Testing and modifications to this software to fit Xenox's procedures would cost $8,000. Incorporating customer, supplier, and inventory records into the new computer system would cost $12,000 while the training of users would cost $10,000.

The team considered leasing the computer and the software rather than buying it but decided to recommend buying rather than leasing the system, if it proved possible.

Future investment in the system. After the system is installed and tested, the team estimates that the newly installed capacity would be adequate for three years. Because of probable growth, operations beyond three years would need more disk storage capacity and two more CRT terminals. Because the prices of computer equipment usually decline with advances in technology, it is estimated that this additional equipment would cost only $5,000.

Operating costs and benefits. Xenox is currently handling customer orders, inventory planning and control, and purchase order preparation on a manual basis with several clerical workers. But as Xenox has continued to grow, it has become more and more difficult to keep

FIGURE 3–3
Summary of Cash Flows for Proposed Computer-Based Inventory Control System

Line		Year → 0 (Initial Investment)	1	2	3	4	5	6	7	8	9	10
1	CASH OUTFLOWS:											
2	Computer	30,000										
3	Software	15,000										
4	Software Modification & Test		8,000									
5	Loading Records		12,000									
6	Training		10,000									
7	Operating Costs			25,000	27,500	30,250	33,275	36,602	40,262	44,289	48,717	53,589
8	Total Out-Flows	45,000	30,000	25,000	27,500	30,250	33,275	36,602	40,262	44,289	48,717	53,589
9	Cumulative Outflows	45,000	75,000	100,000	127,500	157,750	196,025	232,627	272,889	317,178	365,895	419,484
10	Cash In-Flows or Out-Flow Avoidance											
11	Investment Tax Credit		4,500									
12	Holding Cost Savings			25,000	27,000	29,160	31,492	34,012	36,733	39,671	42,845	46,273
13	Purchasing Order Savings			15,000	15,000	15,000	15,000	15,000	15,000	15,000	15,000	15,000
14	Savings from Improved Service			10,000	10,500	11,025	11,576	12,155	12,763	13,401	14,071	14,775
15	Salvage Value of System											2,000
16	Tax Avoidance from Depreciation *		4,140	3,342	2,650	2,120	1,696	1,357	1,357	1,357	1,357	437
17	Total In-Flows		8,640	53,342	55,150	57,305	59,764	62,524	65,853	69,429	73,273	78,485
18	Cumulative In-Flows		8,640	61,982	117,132	174,437	234,171	296,695	362,548	431,977	505,250	583,735
19	Net Cash Flow	−45,000	−21,360	28,342	27,650	27,055	26,489	25,922	25,591	25,140	24,556	24,896
20	Cumulative Net Cash Flow	−45,000	−66,360	−38,018	−10,368	11,657	38,146	64,068	89,659	114,799	139,355	164,251
21	Discount Factors @15%	1.0	.870	.756	.657	.572	.497	.432	.376	.327	.284	.247
22	Net Present Value	−45,000	−18,583	21,424	18,171	15,435	13,165	11,198	9,622	8,221	6,974	6,149
23	Cumulative Net Present Value	−45,000	−63,583	−42,179	−24,298	−11,623	1,342	12,540	22,162	30,383	37,357	43,506

* See Figure 3–4.

this work up to date and accurate by manual methods.

Service to customers has been slipping. Orders are not all processed fast enough and particular styles and sizes of products are out of stock too often. Material suppliers are often late with their shipments and internal records of both raw materials and finished products are often inaccurate.

The proposed system would reduce these problems substantially and would allow Xenox to give better service while at the same time doing it with a smaller inventory.

The project team estimates that the operating costs of the new computer system would be $25,000 in the second year and would go up 10 percent a year thereafter.

The benefits from installing the system are estimated to be:

a. Savings from inventory reductions: No savings during the year of the computer's installation. Then a saving of $25,000 the next year. And because of inflation and business growth, inventories will expand and the savings for the years after the second year will increase by 8 percent a year. This savings estimate is based on the team's belief that the system would allow the company's current $1 million in inventory in the areas which the new computer would serve to be reduced by 10 percent, or $100,000. Xenox's managers believe that it costs 25 percent of the value of inventory to hold it for a year because of storage, opportunity costs of money tied up in idle inventory, insurance, taxes, and obsolescence. Thus, $100,000 × 25 percent = $25,000.

b. Savings due to simplifying purchase order processing, eliminating some clerical labor, and gaining more control over suppliers: $15,000 per year.

c. Profits from increasing customer service: $10,000 the first year of operations, and increasing 5 percent per year for the remaining eight years.

Other assumptions that the team made are that they would scrap or sell the system at the end of 10 years for $2,000; and that their opportunity cost of capital (called the "hurdle rate") is 15 percent; that the company's income tax rate will be 46 percent of profits; that the computer and the purchased software capital investment of $45,000 will be depreciated over a 10-year period; and that the double declining depreciation method will be used and that the rate used will be 20 percent. After the fifth year, the depreciation method used will switch over to straight line. (See Figure 3–4.) It is also assumed that this investment qualifies for the 10 percent investment tax credit allowed by the Internal Revenue Code.

All of this information has been summarized in Figure 3–3 to arrive at the figures needed so that a recommendation can be made when the various methods of analyzing capital investment projects are applied.

Payback Period

The payback-period method for analyzing the merits of alternative capital investment projects estimates, in a "rough cut" way, how much time it will take to recover the initial investment.

In our proposed computer-based inventory control system, the information in Figure 3–3, line 20, shows that cumulative net cash flow becomes a positive $11,657 in the fourth year. Thus, interpolating between the third and fourth years (to estimate where the cumulative net cash flow is approximately zero, or cash inflows equal the cash outflows), the payback period is 3 years plus $15,398/(15,398 + 11,657) × 1$ year, or $3 + .57$, or 3.57 years.

Average Return on Investment (Nondiscounted)

This method calculates an average return on investment, without considering the time value of money. Referring to Figure 3–3, lines 8 and 17,

Figure 3–4
Depreciation Schedule for Proposed Computer-Based Inventory
Control System *(data for line 16, Figure 3–3)*

Capital costs: Computer $30,000
           Software   15,000
                    $45,000

Assumptions: 10-year life with salvage value of $2,000. Use
double declining depreciation method (10 percent × 2 = 20
percent per year) with a switch over to straight-line when double declining amount of depreciation is less than or equal to
straight-line amount. This occurs in the 6th year in this case.

Year	Book Value	Depreciation	Tax Avoidance
1	$45,000 × 20%	$ 9,000 × 46%	$ 4,140
2	36,000 × 20	7,200 × 46	3,312
3	28,800 × 20	5,760 × 46	2,650
4	23,040 × 20	4,608 × 46	2,120
5	18,432 × 20	3,687 × 46	1,696
6	14,745/5 years	2,949 × 46	1,357
7	11,796/4 years	2,949 × 46	1,357
8	8,847/3 years	2,949 × 46	1,357
9	5,898/2 years	2,949 × 46	1,357
10	2,949–2,000*	949 × 46	437
		$43,000	$19,783

* Expected salvage value.

we calculate the average ROI as shown in Figure
3–5.

Thus, 5.348/10 years = .5348, or a 53.4
percent average return on investment per year,
without considering the time value of money. As
we shall see later, this ROI can be misleading.

FIGURE 3–5

Year	Cash Inflows	÷	Cash Outflows	ROI
1	$ 8,640		$75,000	−.884*
2	53,312		25,000	1.132
3	55,150		32,500	.696
4	57,305		30,250	.894
5	59,764		33,275	.632
6	62,524		36,602	.708
7	65,853		40,262	.635
8	69,429		44,289	.567
9	73,273		48,717	.504
10	78,485		53,589	.464
				5.348

* ($8,640 − $75,000)/$75,000 = − .884.

Discounted Payback Period

The simplified payback-period and ROI methods
calculated above do not take into account the
time value of money, as discussed in Chapter
2. Since Xenox has chosen a discount rate of
15 percent, we have developed the present
value of each year's net cash flow and the cumulative present values for each year. To do this,
we have utilized the values in Appendix B, which
are the present value of $1 to be received in
future years, at various assumed discount rates.
For example, with a discount rate of 15 percent,
the present value of $1 to be received or paid
out today is 1.0 or $1.00; of $1 to be received
or paid out in year 1 is $.87; and so on. We
have placed these discount factors in line 21
of Figure 3–3. So, in Figure 3–3, for example,
multiplying line 19 by line 21, the net present
value of the initial outlay of $45,000 for the com-
puter and the software is 1.0 × −$45,000, or
−$45,000. Likewise, in year 1, the present value

of the net cash flow is −$21,360 × .870, or −$18,583.

By considering the time value of money and calculating the cumulative net present value of cash flows, as shown in line 23, we can see that the payback period is extended from 3.57 years to 4.89 years—4 years + [11,823/(11,823 + 1,342)] = 4.89 years.

Net Present Value (with Specified Hurdle Rate)

Often organizations specify, as a policy, a minimum return they expect to get from investment opportunities. This is sometimes called a *hurdle* rate. The term means that the investment will be considered only if the expected cash inflows equal or exceed all cash outflows *plus* the hurdle rate of return on the investment during the expected life of the investment. Managers have to justify their proposals in terms of meeting or exceeding the hurdle rate of return.

Xenox's managers have set its hurdle rate at 15 percent. In our example, line 23 of Figure 3–3 shows the cumulative net present value of cash flows discounted at the hurdle rate of 15 percent. The test for "making the hurdle" is to see if the cumulative net present value of the cash flow turns from negative to positive at or before the 10 years are up.

In our example the cumulative net cash flow becomes positive between years 4 and 5 (actually, at 4.89 years as calculated earlier by the discounted payback method). At the end of the 10th year, the net present value is expected to be $43,506. So, not only is the project expected to return all costs plus the hurdle rate of 15 percent but it is expected to return $43,506 more in equivalent current dollars.

The net present value method is commonly used to evaluate two or more investment opportunities which can do the same job—say two different machines which do the same job, yet which have different initial costs, different incomes or cost savings, different expense patterns, and different useful lives and salvage values.

Xenox could, for example, also consider some other computer system which might be more costly yet not require much if any new programming. Or, it might compare the NPV of investing in a computer system versus staying with a manual system which might require more investment in office space, furniture, more manual calculating machines, and so on.

Discounted Return on Investment (Internal Rate of Return)

Earlier, in calculating the discounted payback period, we saw that it was 4.89 years. At this point in time (4.89 years into the future) we will have recovered our investment and will have earned 15 percent on it as well. The 4.10 years is our estimate of the point of time in the future when the discounted cash outflows and inflows cancel each other out. They "net to zero." If, for some reason, the computer system has to be discarded in less than 4.89 years, we will not get back all of our money and 15 percent return as well. If it lasts beyond 4.89 years, it will actually yield more than 15 percent.

The actual rate that a project does yield is sometimes called the "internal rate of return." Calculating the internal rate of return is a trial-and-error process. The procedure requires us to discount the net cash flow values at successively larger discount rates until we find a rate which, over the 10-year period, results in a present value of the net cash flows which is approximately zero. In our example, we found this to be at 4.89 years at a discount rate of 15 percent. In this calculation, we held the discount rate constant at 15 percent and let the number of years vary until the present value of net cash flows was zero.

To determine the expected internal rate of return for our example, we hold the years constant at 10 and let the discount rate vary until we find the zero point. We have not reproduced all of our trial-and-error calculations here. We already knew that the project yielded more than

FIGURE 3–6
Calculations for Internal Rate of Return

Year	Net Cash Flow (from line 19, Fig. 3–3)	25 Percent Factor	PV (25 percent)	30 Percent Factor	PV (30 percent)
0	$−45,000	1.000	$−45,000	1.000	$−45,000
1	−21,360	.800	−17,088	.769	−16,426
2	28,312	.640	18,120	.592	16,761
3	22,650	.512	11,597	.455	10,306
4	27,055	.410	11,093	.350	9,469
5	26,489	.328	8,688	.269	7,126
6	25,922	.262	6,792	.207	5,366
7	25,591	.210	5,374	.159	4,069
8	25,140	.168	4,224	.123	3,092
9	24,556	.134	3,291	.094	2,308
10	24,896	.107	2,664	.084	2,091
Net present values			$ +9,755		$ −838

15 percent. So, we tried 20 percent. The sum of the discounted cash flows was still positive, as it had been for 15 percent. This meant that the project was expected to yield more than 20 percent. Then we tried 25 and 30. The sum was still positive at 25 percent but it turned negative at 30 percent. This meant that the internal rate was between 25 and 30 percent. The calculations for 25 and 30 percent are shown in Figure 3–6.

At this point we know that the internal rate is between 25 and 30 percent but we don't know just exactly what it is. We know also that it is at the point where the discounted present value is zero. To calculate this point, we interpolate.

There is a difference of $9,755 + $838 = $10,593 between the two totals we have at 25 and 30 percent. This is a 5 percentage point spread. The zero point can be estimated to be at 25% + (9,755/10,593 × 5%). 25% + 4.6% = 29.6%. This is the internal rate of return in our example. Figure 3–7 shows this graphically.

Thus, if the expectations for savings, expenses, and the life of the system are believed to be accurate, the investment would bring an ROI of almost double that of Xenox's hurdle rate of 15 percent.

Which Method Is Best?

Of the five methods discussed, the nondiscounted payback period is the quickest and easiest to understand—and may be used to make a rough estimate of the potential profitability of an investment opportunity. But, unless it is a clear-cut case, the three methods which take account of the time value of money should be used for more accurate evaluation. The primary reason for this is that different capital outlays, revenue, expense, salvage values, and lives of the investments can be directly compared on an equivalent basis. For example, one investment may have a lower initial investment than

FIGURE 3–7
Graphic Depiction of Interpolation in Internal Rate of Return Calculation

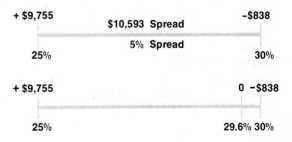

another, but have lower savings. The only way the analyst can compare varying cash flow patterns is to use the approaches which utilize discounting.

The nondiscounted average return-on-investment method should be used with caution because it can be extremely misleading, as was shown in our example, We have included it in our discussion so the reader may see how it is calculated and understand its limitations.

DEALING WITH UNCERTAINTY

As mentioned earlier, capital investment analyses are only as good as the estimates of the numbers that are assumed. There are, however, a number of ways to deal with this uncertainty.

Project Teams

One of the best approaches to managing uncertainty is to have an experienced multidisciplined project team involved in the analysis. Engineers, cost accountants, production people, consultants, and even outside technical sales representatives can be included in such a team. (Remember though—their objective is to sell you *their* machine! But, if they are experienced, forthright, and helpful they will eventually get their share of the business if their products are reasonably competitive.)

Sensitivity Analysis

As in our discussion of sensitivity, or "what-if?" analysis, in break-even analysis in Chapter 2, a similar approach can be useful in analyzing capital investments. *What if,* for example, the cash flow is different; the life is shorter or longer; the discount hurdle rate is higher or lower?

Many companies have computer software available to perform the calculations we have illustrated here. They are designed to allow the asking of these and other "what-if?" questions. Using a program like this, Xenox could have determined, for example, that with a 5-year life instead of a 10-year life, their hurdle rate of 15

percent would have been exceeded.

Analysts can use these systems to quickly see *how wrong* they could be in their cash flow estimates before an investment would no longer be attractive.

Review Questions

1. Who in an organization should normally see the need for a capital expenditure project and originate the request?
2. What is a company's "cash flow"? What is it made of? How is it related to capital expenditures? To profits?
3. Why is depreciation important in a company's capital investment program? To its profitability?
4. Explain the most commonly used depreciation methods Which recover the investment the quickest? Which the slowest?
5. How do the nondiscounted average return-on-investment and payback methods differ from each other? What are their advantages? Shortcomings?
6. Explain how the various discounted cash flow methods are calculated.

Questions for Discussion

1. What good does it do to have divisional and central office staff groups study capital investment proposals carefully? How can they, 1,000 miles away, tell if the proposals are sound or not?
2. Division heads know what new machine they need. Why not let them have the final decision on what they get?
3. The employees have been complaining about poor locker room facilities. Explain what you would need to calculate the nondiscounted rate of return on the prospective investment required to modernize these facilities.
4. Should the analyst always, sometimes, or never include overhead and sales and administrative costs in the calculation of break-even points for individual projects, such as one machine? Why? If sometimes, when and why?
5. Some people say that it is impossible for a company to increase its cash account in years when it loses money. Can it? Explain.
6. Will using the sum-of-the-years' digits deprecia-

tion method instead of straight-line depreciation give a company more or less protection against inflation? (This relates to the matter of normal depreciation providing inadequate funds to buy replacement machines.)

7. How can sum-of-the-years' digits depreciation be handled by a company using group depreciation?

8. The text says to mechanize if the analysis shows it to be a toss-up so far as saving money is concerned. What justification is given? Is this sound? Discuss.

9. Do income taxes encourage or discourage the making of capital investments? Why?

10. Calculating a rate of return by comparing a new method to an existing method makes the new method look good or bad, depending on how bad the current method is. How can the disadvantages of the current method have anything to do with the benefits of a new method? Why not do away with these comparisons and calculate the absolute rate of return on new proposals?

11. "The only thing you can say for sure about a forecast is that it will be wrong!" Try to forecast the number of miles you will drive your car next year and the amount you will spend on gasoline and repair bills. What is the use of trying to forecast a machine's productivity and operating costs?

12. Some people say that in cost-saving calculations made when comparing new machines with old machines, the prospective loss in book value of old machines to be discarded if a new machine is bought should be disregarded. Do you agree or disagree? Why?

Problems

1. Suppose Xenox Industries is considering the following alternative to the computer-based inventory control system used as an example in the text:

Hardware and software costs	$85,000
Testing and modifications	$ 3,000
Loading records cost	same
Training users	same
Extra capacity cost at 4th year	$ 1,000
Operating costs	$20,000/yr. plus 10%/yr.
Savings due to inventory reduction	same
Savings due to simplifying PO processing	same
Profits from increasing customer service	same
Salvage value at end of 10th year	$ 6,000

a. Calculate the nondiscounted payback period and average rate of return on investment for this alternative system.

b. Calculate the discounted payback period and the net present value.

c. Calculate the internal rate of return.

d. Which system would/should Xenox choose, the one proposed in the text example or this one, and why?

2. Suppose that $500,000 is available for investment in the following capital projects:

Project	Capital Requirement	Expected Internal Rate of Return
A	$300,000	18%
B	50,000	25
C	350,000	15
D	175,000	15
E	100,000	20
F	100,000	30
G	Invest excess in 5% bonds	5

a. Which projects should be chosen and what would be the average internal rate of return? (Hint: Consider combinations of projects which are ≤ $500,000.)

b. In the above solution, has any project been selected which has a lower return than any omitted project? If so, what would be the effective rate of the high-return project if it were put into the list of approvals at the expense of dropping a project to make room for it?

c. If the company could borrow $50,000 more at 15 percent, should this be done? What projects should be approved, and what would their average internal rate of return be? (Do not forget the interest charges as an offset to the income.)

3. McBurger Queen buys a hamburger patty-making machine for $6,000 and uses a 20 percent declining balance method of depreciation. Maintenance costs are expected to be $300 in each of the first two years and then to go up annually as follows: $500, $700, $1,000, $1,400, $1,900, $2,500. Their tax rate is 46 percent, and their discount rate is 15 percent. When should this machine be replaced? (Hint: When do maintenance costs equal or exceed tax savings?)

4. Some years ago, TRW bought a Warner & Swasey lathe for $18,000. It was straight-line depreciated on a 12-year basis. Last year, at the close of the 12th year, it was fully depreciated on TRW's books.

The lathe, although practically worn out, still had a resale value of $2,000.

A replacement lathe to do the same work is priced at $34,000, but since today's work is more exacting, the proper lathe to buy (attachments included) costs $48,000.

If, over the 12 years, the depreciation cash generated by tax avoidance had been put to work each year earning 15 percent and if income taxes were 50 percent of profits:

a. How much more money would TRW now need to replace the machine with the $48,000 machine?

b. How much more sales revenue would it have taken to generate this additional amount of money (TRW would get a pretax profit of 20 percent of the sales price on products made with this machine)?

c. Suggest a solution to the problem that TRW faces.

5. Compare the following two alternatives:

	Machine A	Machine B
Installed cost	$8,500	$14,000
Estimated life	10 years	10 years
Salvage value at end of estimated life	$2,500	$ 1,000
Annual savings over present method	$6,000	$ 7,000
Annual operating cost	$3,500	$ 2,000
Interest cost	15%	15%

a. Using first-year costs and savings only, and straight-line depreciation, which investment is better if the tax rate is 46 percent?

b. Is the answer to (a) influenced by the depreciation method used? Show the figures for straight-line, sum-of-the-years' digits, and declining balance methods for the first year.

c. Using the net present value method and straight-line depreciation, which alternative is best?

d. What is the discounted payback period for each alternative if double declining depreciation is used?

6. The question is whether to replace an existing mechanical money-counting machine in a bank with a new microprocessor-controlled counting machine. The new machine will cost $12,000 and will have an expected life of 12 years, with an expected salvage value of $1,500 at the end of 12 years. This machine will be depreciated on a straight-line basis each year and, when compared to using the old machine, will show a $2,500 pretax savings besides. The company is in the 46 percent tax bracket and can earn 15 percent (pretax) on alternative investments.

a. Should this machine be bought, and if it should, what is its nondiscounted payback period?

b. What additional information would you require to calculate a discounted payback period?

7. Because of the lack of sensitivity of the weigher, a company's automatic coffee can–filling machine is set to put 16¼ ounces of coffee into the cans so that no can will contain less than 16 ounces.

This weigher cost $3,000 five years ago and is expected to last for 10 more years. The machinery salesman offers a new, more sensitive solid-state weigher which could be set at 16⅛ ounces. He will allow a $400 trade-in on the old weigher against the new machine's purchase price of $8,000. The new machine is also expected to last 10 years. Neither it nor the present weigher will have any final salvage value. Coffee costs $3 a pound. Opportunity cost of capital is 10 percent.

How many one-pound cans of coffee must be sold per year to pay for the new weigher? (Hint: Equate coffee savings with machine costs.)

8. Assume the following data:

Cost of a new tool	$800
Expected life of new tool	5 years
Interest rate on invested funds	10 percent
Insurance and repairs per year	$80
Number of times used per year	10
Setup cost per time used	$10
Estimated labor cost savings per unit from using new tool	$.05
Increased material cost per unit	$.015
Tax rate	40 percent

Using only first-year costs and savings:

a. Compute the volume required to break even (include a savings in overhead at 100 percent of direct labor) if straight-line depreciation is assumed.

b. What would the break-even volume be if the overhead savings were omitted?

c. What would the true break-even point probably be?

9. There are two independent proposals for making a new product, an electronic mailbox. (A buzzer goes off in the house when the mail is delivered.)

Method A equipment costs $250,000, will last 10 years, and will have a salvage value of $25,000. Method B equipment costs $450,000, will last 15 years, and is expected to have a salvage value of $45,000. Each method should produce a $150,000 annual revenue.

Besides the original investment, method A's operating cost is $90,000 a year. Method B has annual operating costs of $60,000. The company has a hurdle rate of 15 percent on this kind of project.

a. What internal rate of return will method A yield?
b. What internal rate of return will method B yield?
c. Assuming that funds are available to do both A and B, what action should be taken?

Case 3–1

Fraser Razor has been considering several capital investment projects on which various rates of return appear to be in prospect. The accountant who has prepared the figures has been careful to point out that the anticipated returns have been reduced to almost half because of income taxes. (If projects save money, presumably they will show up as a profit and be taxed at 46 percent.)

There has been a question about how to evaluate the cost of borrowed capital. The bank will lend money at 12 percent. The accountant carried this cost in the calculations at the full 12 percent. This had the effect of reducing the effective rate to 6.5 percent, since if the company were to use its own money, the whole 12 percent would show up in profits and be taxed at 46 percent. Since this is the normal situation, it is therefore customary to regard the true cost of borrowed capital as just over half of the stated interest rate.

Fraser has earned no profits during the last two years and therefore has paid no income taxes. The question the president raised with the accountant is about this matter of considering the interest on borrowed money as costing only about half of its actual rate, considering the fact that Fraser is currently paying no income taxes.

The president saw even more to this problem, however. He asked: "If it is proper to say that costs associated with capital equipment investments should be thought of as costing only half because of income taxes, then why should we not say the same about labor and materials? These costs, too, are deductible for tax purposes, so let's consider them to have a net cost of only half of their actual cost."

There seems to be a problem here. What is it? Is there something wrong in considering interest to cost only half of its rate? What is the true interest rate?

Case 3–2

The Daisy Company has asked for a review of its practice of making its own gunstocks (the part of the gun which fits against the shoulder) out of wood or whether it should buy gunstocks made out of plastic. Historically, all were made from wood and all were made by Daisy. In recent years cheaper plastic gunstocks have become available and have been used in increasing number on low-price BB guns.

Daisy calculated that it made a $.30 profit on each wooden gunstock it made and $.10 on each plastic gunstock it bought. The volume of purchased plastic gunstocks have grown to 1 million a year. It is expected that this volume will grow steadily to 2 million in five years and hold at that level for the next five years. This analysis concerns only the next 10 years.

Daisy is considering several choices: (1) continuing the present practice and buying all plastic gunstocks, (2) continuing to buy for five years and then change to making, (3) buying enough plastic-making equipment to make 1 million gunstocks a year, (4) after five years expanding this plastics operation to an annual capacity of 2 million gunstocks.

Alternative 2 will require an investment at the end of five years of $3 million, which will have to be written off in the next five years. There is a 20 percent chance that operating costs will be $2 million in the first year and $600,000 per year for the last four years. There is an 80 percent chance that first-year operating costs will be $1.2 million, and $600,000 per year for the last four years.

Alternative 3 will require the immediate purchase of $2 million worth of equipment (which will be worthless at the end of 10 years). There is a 75 percent chance that the first year's operating costs will be $1.5 million, and $700,000 a year for the remaining nine years. There is a 25 percent chance that operating costs will be $1.2 million the first year, and $600,000 a year for the remaining nine years.

Alternative 4 will cost another $1 million at the start of the sixth year. Additional operating costs associated with operating the expanded operations have a 60 percent chance of being $700,000 a year for all five remaining years and a 40 percent chance of being $500,000 a year.

What should Daisy do? Why? What profits prospects do the various alternatives offer?

Section Two

Product Design and Quality Management

New products and new ways to serve people are being developed continually. Neither the managers of factories nor service organizations can safely rest on their present products or methods of serving for their organizations' future well-being.

It is necessary to commit resources to the search for new and better ways of doing things so that one's own company, rather than a competitor, will bring out the new product or introduce the new way of serving that may someday replace today's products and service methods.

Research and product development, the subject of Chapter 4, differs from most of the other subjects in this book in that the work being discussed is not production in the usual sense. Often the end product is more knowledge. And sometimes it is not obvious how this new knowledge can be incorporated into the organization's products or services. Chapter 4 considers research as the search for new knowledge. Then the discussion turns to development, the means by which this knowledge is incorporated into improved products.

Development shades off into designing products and services, the subject of Chapter 5. Designers, however, have to be more practical and earthier people than researchers. They have to work within two very important constraints. First, they have to consider what customers want and what they don't want. And second, there is always a cost limitation. Products must not cost too much in comparison to their value or else they will not sell.

In addition to these two constraints, which design engineers have always had to be concerned with, there is one more, and where it applies it is of overriding importance: this is the need to comply with all laws and obligations to protect consumers.

Besides these operating constraints, designers are concerned with such technical matters as explaining their designs and quality specifications to the factory through drawings, specifications, tolerance and quality assurance procedures.

Finally, Chapters 6 and 7 deal with the areas of quality management and statistical quality control. These are important topics these days, with the strong challenges from foreign competitors and consumers to improve the quality of products and services.

Chapter 4

Research and Product Development

All organizations have purposes. They make and sell products or render certain services. Business organizations have to be ever alert to see that the design of the products and the kind of service they render are what customers want and that prices charged provide enough revenue to cover costs and make a profit. Public organizations such as government agencies also try to carry out their missions so as best to serve the public. One of the most important of all managerial functions in all kinds of organizations is to see that the inputs of the organization's resources result in properly designed products and services, or "outputs," which suit customers' desires.

New products and services come into existence because someone believes there is a need for a product that no one makes or a service that no one offers or a product/service that costs too much.

Managerial imagination is usually needed because opportunities are often not readily apparent. Several years ago, Kentucky Fried Chicken uncovered an enormous market for fast foods that no one realized existed. And it took years of greater and greater sales in the United States of small foreign compact cars and an energy crisis to convince Detroit that many Americans wanted small cars.

So it is the responsibility of managers to be constantly on the lookout for new products and new services which they might provide. One need only walk through a department store, such as Sears, to imagine how much effort goes into the design of new products and the redesign of old products. Similarly, one has only to open the yellow pages of the telephone book to see the broad array of services which have been developed to meet our every need.

RESEARCH AND DEVELOPMENT

Everything in old movies looks out of date because it is out of date. Old products are continually being redesigned, and new products are continually being developed. Procter & Gamble, makers of a wide range of consumer products (Crest toothpaste, Duncan Hines cake mixes, Pampers disposable diapers), had as many as 22 major new products being tested in 1983.[1]

Research has produced the scientific knowledge that lies behind the development of television, jet aircraft, seawater desalting plants, wonder drugs, insecticides, nuclear power plants, lasers, microcomputers, kidney machines,

---

[1] Damon Darlin, "Faced with More Competition, P & G Sees New Products as Crucial to Earnings Growth," *The Wall Street Journal*, September 13, 1983, p. 29.

FIGURE 4–1
High-Technology Industry Is Giving U.S. Industry a Shot in the Arm

Source: *Business Week,* February 13, 1984.

space shuttles, and thousands of other things. And today a larger portion of research dollars is being directed toward solving air and water pollution problems, product- and worker-safety problems, and health services.

Research Activities

Usually organizations carry on research to try to:

1. Search for basic chemical or physical relationships, particularly those having to do with their own products or processes.
2. Improve their products and services.
3. Find new uses for their present products or services.
4. Develop new products and services.
5. Reduce the cost of present products and services by improving their operations and processes.
6. Develop tests and specifications for operations and purchased materials.
7. Analyze competitors' products and services.
8. Find profitable uses for by-products.

Of this list of eight objectives of research, probably number 4, developing new products, is the most important because the ultimate possibilities of new products are often so great. Once in a while such a new product can double or triple the organization's business, as computers did years ago for IBM, as copiers did for Xerox, and as instant-picture cameras did for Polaroid.

Rarely can ordinary product improvement or cost-cutting innovations have such an effect.

Cutting out research aimed at minor improvements in products and cost reduction, however, is not suggested. Nor is there any intent to discount the efforts that supervisors and methods analysts continually put into reducing costs. Design and tool engineers, too, are always making improvements. This work is usually not thought of as research, nor is its cost treated as a research expenditure, but it really is research and is extremely worthwhile.

R&D's Impact upon Our Economy

There is, however, some concern about the reduction in research activities by companies and by the federal government. For example, in the late 1970s Bethlehem Steel, Alcoa, Zenith, and Du Pont each closed down one of their major research laboratories. In Du Pont's case, this saved them over $50 million.

While the United States is still the world leader in research (we spend about $30 billion a year), West Germany and Japan are challenging us. This is because many of our research dollars are being diverted away from product/ service development toward research to satisfy federal safety and environmental regulations. General Motors says that about *half* of their research dollars are now spent to meet regulations.

Another drain on product research dollars is research money spent on finding new ways of producing and saving *energy*.

All of this is of great concern to some economists who have estimated that about half of the nation's growth between 1929 and 1969 was caused by technological innovation and that high-technology companies create jobs 88 percent faster than others and are more productive.[2] As a result of this concern, Congress is considering faster tax write-offs for R&D expenditures as an incentive to revitalize research efforts by private industry.

Research Payoffs

New discoveries and innovations are becoming harder to come by, even though occasionally there is a new major scientific breakthrough (such as microprocessors) which creates whole new products and has a substantial impact on existing products, possibly making them obsolete overnight.

But even in these cases, competition usually holds profits down to nominal amounts after the new industry beings to mature. Hand-held, pocket-sized calculators for under $20 drove older, desk-top mechanical calculators off the market in only two or three years. Then competition among the little-calculator makers themselves drove prices to less than $10 for some models and almost drove all of them out of business.

Acrylic-type fibers have taken away most of wool's former near monopoly in carpets. And today most of the clothes we wear are made from synthetic fibers and not from cotton or wool.

Apple, Radio Shack, and Commodore introduced home microcomputers in the late 1970s, and by the mid-1980s, everybody was making them. Competition has become so keen that some companies have gone bankrupt (Osborn) and others lost so much money, they stopped making them (Texas Instruments and Mattel Toy). Atari and Victor have lost millions on their home computers, and the shakeout will continue throughout this decade, with only a few manufacturers expected to survive.

All of these innovations have come out of research; yet, because of competition, the makers of these products have not earned excessive profits.

Product Design Improvements Growing Out of Research in Microprocessors

But even though bonanza payoffs from research are now rare, further improvements continue to

[2] "The Right Way to Spur R&D," *Business Week,* July 3, 1978, p. 112.

be made all the time. One of the most important in the 1970s was the development in microprocessor or microcomputer technology. Figure 4–2 shows a greatly magnified "chip" (sometimes called a "computer on a chip") which contains memory and logic units, transistors, diodes, and electrical circuitry, all so small that the whole chip could be covered by only four of the grains of salt which are shown, also greatly magnified in the figure, lying around the chip. Such a chip will perform work formerly done by equipment bigger than desk size. Yet these chips are being mass-produced and sell for only a few dollars apiece. Other chips, which are much, much larger (about the size of the fingernail on a person's little finger!) have the calculating capability equal to that of the room-size computers we had 15 years ago.

Microcomputer technology is being adapted to literally thousands of innovative uses. Some of these applications have been made by newly established small companies which saw new application possibilities.

Microcomputers have replaced electromechanical control systems in such home appliances as ovens, refrigerators, dishwashers, and washing machines. And they are used in all kinds of medical equipment, arcade games, and aircraft instrumentation. In automobiles their use is becoming widespread in ignition systems, pollution control, and monitoring engine (and automatically readjusting) performance. The car of the late 1980s will probably look like the one described in Figure 4–3.

And, although electronic controls of large complex machinery are not new, they are becoming more sophisticated and are replacing machine operators' judgments. In some cases this reduces the years of training formerly needed to develop skilled machine operators and allows less skilled people to operate the machines. This leads to more consistent production quality, less scrap, and less cost.

SOURCES OF IDEAS

Although research provides the base from which new innovative applications can be developed, innovative ideas come from many sources rather than just from researchers. Marketing people see the need for something their customers want. Production people see opportunities to improve methods and processes. Everyone in an organization is a potential source of ideas. In order to try to tap this source of ideas, many firms try to generate a creative environment for their people. They tell them about technical advances and ask for ideas about how they can be incorporated into products and services. And they tell them about areas where new products or services are needed. And they form quality circle programs to stimulate ideas from everybody. (Quality circles are discussed in Chapter 6.)

Sometimes new products and services are developed by individual people who are not associated with any company at all. Most of us never become aware of this source of ideas because most small-scale inventors have neither the capital nor the production nor the marketing know-how to bring their products to market. So they sell their ideas to companies, something

FIGURE 4–2
A Microcomputer Chip with Its Circuits Etched on Compared to Grains of Salt, Indicating the Extent of Miniaturization

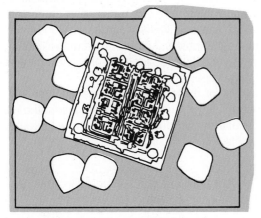

Source: International Business Machines.

FIGURE 4–3
A Look at the Car of the (not-far-off) Future

The sun is barely cresting the horizon as you finish your coffee, grab your briefcase and hurry out the door. You've a lunch meeting to make in another city, a good five hours away—*if* you beat the rush-hour traffic.

You head toward your car, pressing the button on a Laser Key as you approach it. The car begins to rise on its suspension, its driver's door swings open, and a dozen little motors whine softly as the seat, steering wheel, pedals, entertainment and climate-control systems adjust themselves to your preset preferences.

You slide into the seat and glance at the pop-up Systems Sentry as it runs a "preflight" check of all mechanical and electrical systems. After you close the door, the car settles down to driving height. A second touch of the Laser Key activates the rear-view TV and navigation screens; the Systems Sentry, its task done for the moment, drops out of sight.

Touch the Laser Key again to start the engine, and a small, "heads up" instrument screen rises from the base of the windshield in front of you. As in the latest jet-fighter aircraft, important instrument readings are reflected onto this screen from below so you don't have to take your eyes from the road to monitor them.

You load a map cassette into the navigation computer, touch a third screen, a multi-function "Command Center," to display the proper map and scale, then touch it again to link up with the NavStar satellite that will help keep you on course during the trip. When the satellite locks onto your present position, a blinking dot (cursor) appears on the navigation screen.

A touch-button on the steering-wheel hub shifts the transmission into gear and you're on your way, your progress mirrored on the video map and your heading displayed on an electromagnetic compass. Accelerating onto the freeway, you touch the Command Center screen to call up a larger-scale map. No accidents or tie-ups are indicated along the way.

The car's front suspension begins to settle and the rear rises slightly to a more aerodynamic "angle of attack." The front air dam and rear spoiler deploy to increase stability and lower wind drag even further as your speed increases.

Tiring of the radio, you touch the Command Center screen to call up an entertainment-system-control display, load a disc into the compact digital audio deck and settle back to enjoy your favorite road music. This Command Center screen also displays and activates controls for the car's Trip Computer, electronic climate control, calendar and a number of other functions on demand.

After an uneventful hour or so, a buzzer suddenly interrupts your thoughts. It's the Traction Monitor, sounding and flashing a warning that the road surface is dangerously slick for the speed at which you're traveling. You slow until the buzzer stops, thankful for the warning, and notice a couple of cars off in the median. The outside temperature reading flashes 29 degrees, explaining why the few remaining puddles of melted snow are beginning to turn to ice.

You check the Trip Computer for a new ETA (estimated time of arrival), and it indicates a few minutes after noon. Oh well, better late than never. It also reports an average fuel economy of 37 miles a gallon for the trip so far, and seven gallons of fuel remaining (280 miles to "empty" at the lower speed), with just over 100 miles to your destination.

You decide to call ahead to report you'll be a little late. A touch-button on the steering-wheel pad switches on the voice-actuated radio-telephone. You request the number orally, and, like a human operator, the computer acknowledges. In a few seconds you're talking with your party, with both hands still safely on the wheel.

Far out? Not as far as you might think. For the car already exists.

Called the Buick Questor, the futuristic concept sports car was introduced at the 1983 Detroit Auto Show to demonstrate some of the thinking and capabilities of the talented group of electronics engineers at General Motors' Buick Division. The Questor had no engine or drive-train, but its wondrous electronic systems are very real and achievable in the not-very-distant future. Some, in fact, are already available.

Source: Gary Witzenburg, "Shifting to Digitals," *Friendly Exchange,* Spring 1984, p. 20. Reprinted by permission of *Friendly Exchange,* the magazine of Farmers Insurance Group of Companies © 1984.

which is not hard to do, since most companies are always on the lookout to buy the rights to marketable innovations.

In addition, some firms buy and sell ideas among themselves, and some companies specialize in generating new ideas which they can sell or lease to other companies. Companies like Gulf and Western, GE, Continental Can, and consulting firms like Arthur D. Little "see such a demand for product ideas that they have been setting up whole departments, just to buy and sell them . . . and they become just another commodity that's bought and sold around the world."[3]

Developing a Climate Favorable to Innovation

In spite of what has just been said, however, a great deal of innovation comes from researchers. Other employees have their regular work to do and don't get to spend much time innovating. The desirable "creative environment" which can be so helpful can have the most far-reaching effects if it exists in the research area itself. *Business Week* describes the practice at 3M (formerly Minnesota Mining and Manufacturing) as follows:[4]

> At 3M, a researcher who prefers to get lost in a lab can spend his career there and be well rewarded for his work, but the ambitious inventor is free to move on. Managers are always promoted from within, and promotions are frequent. It is just as common for inventors as it is for marketing and production men to ride upstairs with their products, to become product managers, then heads of departments, and keep going from there. . . .
>
> One such inventor, A. G. Bush, the father of Scotch tape, went on to become chairman of 3M. When an engineer conceives a product, he is encouraged to make a prototype before discussing it with his superiors. Then, if he really does have something, he, the engineer-inventor becomes part, and often the leader, of a development team. (The team also usually includes a production man, and—at this early stage of a product's life—a marketing expert.) If the product continues to show promise, the division can authorize a pilot production run. Only in the next phase, where higher production and test market-

ing begins, do officers at the group and corporate levels become involved.

The research climate at 3M allows engineers and inventors to go out on a limb without being afraid of damaging their careers or losing their jobs. One idea, an attempt to farm oysters under controlled conditions, failed miserably, but no one was criticized for trying to develop the idea. It was not known to be a failure until it was tried out.

Polaroid, a company that has had its financial ups and downs, is changing its approach to new product development. Faced with steadily declining sales in the early 1980s, the camera and film maker has had to drastically change the way they approached R&D from the philosophy of E. H. Land, the company founder:

> Land believed that success depended on coming up with innovative products, then persuading people to buy them, and in his day Polaroid used little or no market research. The strategy worked as long as Land could dazzle the world with his ever-improving instant pictures. But it started to pale with the advent of easy-to-use 35-mm cameras, 24-hour film processing, and competing versions of his once-exclusive products.
>
> By contrast, Land's successors are looking outward to the market. They are taking their cues from potential customers—particularly in commercial and industrial markets.[5]

Polaroid designers have thus become much more "customer needs" oriented as opposed to their traditional technology orientation. Marketing and consumer behavior research plays a much larger role than before in product development activities.

For example, Autoprocess (a new $100 product that allows users of 35 mm cameras to develop color slides at home for about 46 cents each) uses the same basic technology behind Polavision, their instant home movie camera which flopped in the late 1970s, was taken off

---

[3] "Ideas for Sale: More Firms Buy, Sell the Fruits of Research to and from Outsiders," *The Wall Street Journal*, February 18, 1976, pp. 1, 18.

[4] "How Ideas Are Made into Products at 3M," *Business Week*, September 15, 1973, pp. 224–27.

[5] "Polaroid Sharpens Its Focus on the Marketplace," *Business Week*, February 13, 1984, p. 132.

the market in 1980, and lost them almost $270 million. Technologically, Polavision was a breakthrough, but the market rejected it.

Polaroid's approach to the development of Autoprocess focuses much more on the needs and desires of the marketplace.[6]

Some innovative products are of the "Why didn't I think of that?" kind. For example, years ago lacing up and later unlacing ski boots was a tiring and bothersome job. Then someone invented the buckle boot and changed the whole ski boot industry. Similarly, McDonald's and Kentucky Fried Chicken perceived that people wanted simple foods served quickly and at low prices. The result has been the multibillion-dollar fast-food industry with new fast-food chains emerging almost monthly.

Very few people ever had thought that they needed a Sony Walkman, or lightweight running shoes, or a telephone answering machine, or to join a Nautilus health club. But, when given a chance to buy them, millions of people bought. Imagination often pays off in product creation and service improvement.

RESEARCH RISKS

Only after the research on a project is done and money is spent on it can it begin to save money or produce income. RCA had $50 million invested in color TV before its color sets reached the American living room and had $125 million invested in it before it began to pay off.

RCA, Holland's Philips, MCA, and other electronic firms invested over $200 million in developmental costs for "videodiscs." (A videodisc is a victrola record-like disc on which a half-hour of a movie has been recorded. Played on a record player connected to a television set, the movie, sound, color, and all comes out through the TV set.)

While color TV has certainly paid off for RCA and the whole TV industry, enthusiasts for videodiscs thought that the profits here could reach half a billion dollars annually by the mid-1980s, while the sales of accompanying accessory items might amount to half as much more.

Unfortunately, research does not always pay off. Videodisc sales for RCA have been *half* of their expectations, and they lost almost $300 million on them from 1979 to 1982.[7]

Du Pont spent $25 million over 25 years developing Corfam (artificial leather) before putting it on the market in 1964. Six years later, after losing $100 million on Corfam, Du Pont stopped making it. Polaroid spent over $350 million in its SX–70 camera, but initial sales were much less than expected. Later on, after price cuts, SX–70 sales improved. Then after more heavy research and development expenditures, their new instant movie camera, Polarvision, emerged, and it was a dismal failure, as mentioned earlier. General Motors developed and successfully tested a new gas-turbine truck engine and had firm orders for a substantial number of these engines from Greyhound Bus Lines. Yet GM backed off from starting into mass production because of its expected $200 million start-up costs. Zenith dropped the Sony-made Beta-format VCR videorecorder from its line to concentrate on the VHS videocassette, because that's what more people wanted, and because substantially more of the recorded programs are available in VHS than VCR.[8]

Unfortunately, risks are not always limited to the research expenditures themselves. If a company does not do research, it risks losing out to its researching competitors.

The dilemma is even worse, however, because competition is interindustry. Plastics have taken over part of paper's position in wrappings.

[6] Ibid.

[7] Laura Landro, "RCA Reaches Crossroads on Future of Its Troubled Videodisk Player," *The Wall Street Journal,* September 13, 1983, p. 29.

[8] H. Klein, "Zenith Radio to Sell VHS VideoRecorder and Drop Beta Line Made by Sony Corporation," *The Wall Street Journal,* January 3, 1984, p. 4.

And paper has taken away part of wood's market for containers. Nuclear power plants are cutting in on coal in electric-power generating plants, and perhaps some day solar heaters may seriously cut into the sale of furnaces, heating oil, and natural gas.

The biggest risk in research, however, lies in the high mortality rate of research projects. RCA estimates that 90 percent of its research ideas are useless. Du Pont reports that one third of its chemical research projects prove unfeasible while still in the laboratory. And even after succeeding in the laboratory, most of the rest prove impractical in production and in the marketplace. Overall, it is estimated that 40 to 50 percent of new consumer products fail, and those that do succeed have much shorter lives than products used to have.

Even technical successes sometimes go sour. Plastic pipe, made from vinyl, styrene, and polyethylene, grew from nothing to a $100-million-a-year business some years ago. Plastic pipe was a great success, but everybody got into the act. Within a few years, none of the 80 manufacturers of plastic pipe was making much money out of it because of price competition. Similar experiences occurred in the mid-1970s in the hand-held calculator industry, and now we see it happening in the word processor and microcomputer industries. And with deregulation in transportation and banking services, we see the same thing happening to airlines, trucking companies, and financial institutions.

Yet, since everyone knows that research payoffs are hazardous and that few projects pay off, one might ask why do almost all companies of any size carry on research. Aside from having to research in order to compete, it is still true that some of the successes pay for themselves several times over. In general and in total, research usually pays off.

Furthermore, if a company does not do research, then income taxes will take nearly 50 percent of its profit dollars—so tax savings pay for almost 50 percent or more of research costs.

The question is not, "Is research worth its cost?" but, "Is research worth half of its cost?"

DESIGN BY IMITATION

The first firm to bring a new product to the marketplace almost always has an advantage from being first. But, at the same time, this company is exposed to a risk that a later entering company will imitate the product or, worse yet, improve upon it and capture a large share of the market.

In fact, the greatest "newness" in many companies' products comes not from innovation but from imitation, since a company cannot possibly be first with everything new in its industry. Part of most companies' product development programs is usually directed at developing imitative equivalents of someone else's successful products. Procter & Gamble brought out its Puff facial tissues only after Kimberly Clark's Kleenex and Scott Paper's Scotties proved to be successful.

Sometimes imitative design is done through "reverse engineering." A competitor simply buys a product, takes it apart to see how it works and how it is made, and then makes its own product. Russian automobiles and airplanes are often carbon copies of certain specific automobiles and airplanes made by Western nations.

When Procter & Gamble introduced its new Duncan Hines chocolate chip cookie mix in a Kansas City test market in 1983, their competitors bought the mix by the case to "taste the results of P & G's new patented baking process."[9]

The Japanese, of course, have been the biggest imitators over the years. They attend our trade shows, take pictures, and ask questions, and we see their similar products emerge months or years later to compete strongly against ours. The Japanese have an extensive information-gathering network in the United

---

[9] Darlin, "Faced with More Competition."

States and in Europe for this purpose, and it has paid off. Now we are beginning to do the same as the Japanese are more advanced than we are in many areas, including advanced ceramics, optical fibers, and large-scale microprocessors.[10]

Also, and unfortunately, there have been cases where designs have been stolen through "industrial espionage," or by employees who quit and then join a competing company or who start their own company, where they use product designs or processes developed by their former employing company. For example, Hitachi, Ltd. agreed in an out-of-court settlement to pay IBM $300 million for the use of computer software they claimed Hitachi had stolen from them.[11]

And, in another 1983 case Exxon faced charges of stealing trade secrets from Union Carbide. Exxon is accused of stealing "floor plans, chemical samples, and processing information" for Union's production of carbon fiber, a substance made from carbon pitch. (Carbon fiber is designed to have the strength of steel at only a fraction of the weight and is believed to have a promising future in the automotive and aviation industries.)[12]

Most imitative product development is, however, aboveboard. No refrigerator or TV set is remarkably different from another. Competing companies are largely just trying to do the same job a little better than their competitors.

Companies which adopt imitation as a policy can sometimes be the "second with the most." It is true that imitators start a step behind, but often they can move faster than the original innovator since they have his designs and market success to look at. In the 1950s Sperry Rand had the first computers, but IBM soon had most

of the market. Then came Apple and Radio Shack microcomputers. Again, IBM lagged behind but introduced their PCs in the early 1980s and are again moving toward domination of this market. In the 1960s, 3M's Thermofax method unearthed the big paper-copying market (which A. B. Dick's mimeograph had never revealed), but then Xerox moved in and took it away. Now IBM, Kodak, and several Japanese manufacturers are threatening Xerox with their new copiers just as Kodak is competing head-on with Polaroid with its instant camera.

The obvious gain from following instead of innovating is the saving of R&D money that the leaders spend on failures and on debugging their new products. Yet, this saving is made at the risk that an early start will pay off well and quickly and generate a permanent lead. None of the imitators of Procter & Gamble's Pampers have been able to dislodge P & G much from its leading position in disposable diapers.

PRODUCT LIFE CYCLES

Most new products that are offered to the public go through a life cycle. (See Figure 4–4.) First, when products are very new, they do not always work very well, and they are high-priced. Only the venturesome consumer buys at this stage. The market for the product has to be developed. Next comes the second stage: The product is improved and standardized, becomes dependable in use and lower in price, and consumers buy it with little urging. It sells in much larger quantities as it comes into common use.

In the third stage, the product is mature, dependable in performance, reasonably priced, and does not change much from year to year. Sales volume may even fall off because everybody now owns one, so sales are largely dependent on replacements or on population gains. Automobiles, radios, television sets, and kitchen appliances all have gone through these stages. Industries based on important innovations seem to take up to 30 years to reach maturity although

---

[10] "America Starts Looking Over Japan's Shoulder," *Business Week,* February 13, 1984, pp. 136, 140.

[11] J. B. Stewart, "IBM Settled Hitachi Ltd. Lawsuite after a Secret $300 Million Accord," *The Wall Street Journal,* November 9, 1983, p. 21.

[12] S. Mufson, "Exxon Employees Face Accusations of Stealing Ideas of Other Firms," *The Wall Street Journal,* November 9, 1983, pp. 1, 18.

FIGURE 4–4
Typical Product Life Cycle

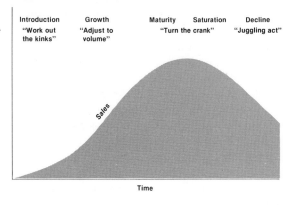

the pace is sometimes quicker, as has recently occurred in the cases of semiconductors and microcomputers.

Finally, most products come to a fourth stage, the decline in demand, when they are supplanted by new products. Admittedly, this does not happen to all products. Knives and forks have been around for a long time as have been scissors and paper clips. Newer products, electric carving knives and electric scissors, have not displaced them. Nonetheless, because so many products keep coming to the end of the line, companies have to work continually at developing new products to take their places.

Merck Company reports that, as a normal thing, 70 percent of its pharmaceutical sales come from products introduced within the last 10 years. And, year after year, RCA consistently gets 80 percent of its sales from products introduced in the preceding 10 years. It is little wonder that so many companies spend so much on research and development.

Sometimes products go on the market too soon. Often it takes from three to five years or more to perfect complicated products—to get all the bugs out—but venturesome customers don't want to wait. Customers hear about new things and how they will help them with their problems and want them right away—even before they are fully developed. Apple Computer's

and they are still feeling the repercussions. And IBM's PC jr's sales got off to a slow start because of problems with their keyboard design and its power. Some people found it cumbersome to use and, for its price, not as powerful as the Apple II.[13]

International Business Machines always has orders for new designs of computers before they are fully engineered and long before they go into production. (This has, in fact, caused problems for IBM. IBM's competitors have complained that IBM competes unfairly by "leaking" information about new products ahead of time so that the customers will wait for IBM's next model instead of buying the competitor's currently available computer.)

But is it too soon, after all, to go to market with an incompletely engineered product? Actually no product is ever fully engineered. It just is not possible to wait until a product is perfect before starting to sell it. Sewing machines have been with us for over 100 years, as have telephones, but they keep changing for the better. And the automobiles and airplanes of 50 years ago were, by today's standards, crude and not well engineered. But they were produced and sold, and they rendered good service to the buyers. Generally, firms should not wait for final permanent designs before they offer their products to the public, so long as they provide reasonable value, are safe to use, and the competition is not about to release a superior product.

The important question is, When is a product developed well enough to sell it? Somewhere along the line it should be offered for sale, and, at this point, its design has to be "frozen"—so far as manufacturing is concerned—long enough to allow production to proceed. Engineers rarely get to do as much design perfecting as they would like before their product goes to market. They do get their chance, however, to make fur-

---

[13] J. Marcom, "IBM's Hotly Touted PC jr Receives Cooler-than-Expected Reception," *The Wall Street Journal,* February 21, 1984, p. 29.

ther improvements as new models are introduced.

TRENDS IN PRODUCT DEVELOPMENT

Changing markets, new technologies, and other factors are always creating new trends in the design of products. Some of today's trends promise to have substantial impact upon the kinds and arrays of products we will see in the future.

Narrowing Product Lines

Raw materials scarcities, higher energy costs, and other economic conditions are causing many companies to reduce variety and to discontinue making items in their product lines which are only marginally profitable. For example, in the mid-1970s General Electric discontinued making food blenders, electric fans, heaters, humidifiers, and vacuum cleaners.

During the 1970s the number of American-made automobile models was reduced about 25 percent. Still fewer models are made today. In the case of automobiles, part of this reduction came from offering essentially the same car under different names. General Motors introduced its new "X" car in 1980. Chevrolet called it the Citation, and Buick called it the Skylark. At Oldsmobile it was the Omega, and at Pontiac it was the Sunbird; and Cadillac called theirs the Cimarron.

Product Simplification

In addition to reducing variety in end products and services, many firms are trying to simplify their products by redesigning parts and components so that fewer pieces will do the job. By making parts do double duty, Chrysler cut the number of parts in a car by 20 percent. Ford Motor has a formal program which it calls "complexity reduction," which is given credit for reducing the number of emission control compo-

nent parts by 56 percent. International Harvester also reports substantial reductions.

Other organizations are also streamlining their products. AM International has reduced the number of cylinders in its duplicating machines by over 75 percent. NCR has simplified its products by making them out of "families" of components which may be used interchangeably in such diverse products as computers for the medical profession and for automatic bank tellers.

Automobile companies work continually at simplifying and reducing the weight of their cars. Aluminum bumper-reinforcing bars are now used, for example, instead of steel, because they weight 47 pounds less. And plastics have replaced much of the steel used in auto interiors because lighter-weight cars get better gasoline mileage.

Standardization

Auto companies also simplify their products by having more "optional" items become "standards." The Japanese have led in this area. They found that people like to buy cars with more luxury items built into them and also found that it was cheaper to include these options in their standard product than to carry a worldwide inventory of these components to satisfy customers' specific orders.

Review Questions

1. What's happening to R&D expenditures around the world, and how is this likely to affect U.S. economic health?
2. What impact is the microcomputer industry having on product design?
3. Where do new ideas for new products and services come from?
4. What are the stages in the life cycle of most products? Of what significance are these phenomena in research and development?
5. Since the costs and risks of research are so great, why would it not be a good idea for a company to cut out research and let other companies do it

and then either develop something similar very quickly or pay the other company a royalty for using its idea?

6. What role do materials play in product design?

7. Why do organizations carry on R&D?

8. Why is "reverse engineering" so widespread?

9. What trends are taking place in product design?

Questions for Discussion

1. Since a high proportion of research projects are failures, can most companies really justify spending 2 percent of their gross income on research? Discuss.

2. Should research departments be set up according to fields of science (such as chemistry, metallurgy, and the like), or by product lines (such as automobiles, refrigerators, and the like), or some other basis? What might be the advantages and disadvantages of each choice?

3. A scientist develops an improvement for a carburetor. This improvement has value for cars and for the company. How might a top manager go about judging the value of this contribution from research?

4. Is "reverse engineering" ethical?

5. What can be done to spur more R&D investment?

Problems

1. It is anticipated that Reed Feed and Seed will make 800,000 sacks of chicken feed in a year and will have a factory cost of $2.50, of which $.95 will be spent for materials. The rest of the factory cost is for processing. Reformulating the chicken feed should save 2 percent of processing costs and 5 percent of materials costs. There is a question, however, about how much the reformulation will cost. The designers think that a $25,000 budget will do the job.

   a. If it is required that the $25,000 be recovered out of savings in one year, should this expenditure be approved?

   b. Suppose that the $25,000 is approved and has been spent but that the reformulation is still far from finished. If it is cut off now, no gain at all would be realized, and the $25,000 would

all be lost. The design engineer and chemist, however, are very enthusiastic and feel sure that for an additional $50,000 budget they can be certain of getting the savings originally expected. Should the top manager approve this additional $50,000? Assume that he agrees with the designers' expectation of success. (Hint: Think about "sunk costs.")

2. From what we hear, many television viewers resent loud and blatant commercials: The Urp Company, a television manufacturer with national distribution, has had an occasional request from a dealer for a remote control cutoff box that would turn off the speaker (or the picture also, as the viewer chooses) for one minute. Then the program would turn on again automatically.

   Urp's analysts estimate that it will cost $25,000 to develop such a "Hush Button" and $40,000 more to get it into production. Besides this, it will take a $50,000 advertising campaign to introduce the product to the market.

   It is proposed, in the future, to supply Hush Buttons without added charge on all sets retailing for $250 and up. For lower priced sets, it is to be available as an "extra" for $25. Owners of any make TV can buy a Hush Button and have their sets modified for its use for $40.

   It is estimated that Hush Buttons will cost $3 each in variable costs to produce. Besides this, there will be an additional fixed cost of $30,000 in the first year. It is proposed to sell Hush Button units to dealers for $20. It is expected that the Hush Button will boost the sales of sets priced at over $250 (where its cost will be included in the set's price at no extra charge) enough to offset the cost of providing it on all such sets.

   With this cost-price structure, how many Hush Buttons will Urp need to sell in order to recover all its initial expenses out of profits during the first year?

3. Sales of Exertech's computerized fitness evaluators are $10 million a year. Fixed costs are $5 million (which includes $300,000 now being spent annually for research). Variable costs are $4 million a year. Greg Todd, the research director, wants to double the research expenditures, claiming that this will boost sales. After talking it over with the sales department, the following estimate was arrived at concerning the sales probabilities if the research expenditures are doubled:

Sales ($ millions)	Probability
10	.50
11	.30
12	.10
13	.05
14	.03
15	.02

Should the research expenditures be doubled?

4. The New Screw Company finds that because a competitor has brought out a new product it is lagging behind, but it can probably catch up if it starts immediately on a crash design program. Doing this will probably get New's new screw product line out in six months. Less expenditure will still produce results, but more slowly. A crash program will cost $1.5 million instead of the $800,000 a slower program would cost. The hurry-up job also opens the door to a 0.1 probability that the design will be faulty, in which case another $300,000 will have to be spent, and it will take six more months to correct the trouble.

If the crash program succeeds, New will not only catch up, but its managers think that New will have a six-month lead on its competitors with its new screws. This will mean profits of $400,000 during that period. Besides this, there will very likely be a continuing advantage to New for the five remaining years of the product's life. The payoff prospects for the next five years in total are:

With Crash Program

Profits	Probability
$2,000,000	.50
1,500,000	.30
1,000,000	.15
500,000	.05

Without Crash Program

Profits	Probability
$2,000,000	.20
1,500,000	.30
1,000,000	.35
500,000	.15

What action should be taken if you knew New's new screws would produce the above expected results?

Chapter 5

Designing Products and Services

Research and development activities discussed in Chapter 4 provide the necessary backdrop for the design of new products and services, and the specification of their quality. However, while R&D may develop such things as a microcomputer or a new synthetic fiber, it is up to others to translate these technological advances into practical products and services which work and will sell at a profit. Many decisions must be made which continually trade off "form" against "function." Automobiles do not have to look so sleek and attractive (form) to perform the people-moving job (function).

The job of analyzing these trade-offs is termed *value engineering and value analysis* and is one of the key functions in successful output design.

VALUE ENGINEERING AND VALUE ANALYSIS

Value engineering (usually done by design engineers) or value analysis (usually done by the purchasing department) means that everything that is made or purchased is thought of as being made or bought to serve a particular purpose. Before deciding to make or buy parts, if substantial amounts of money are involved, engineers and buyers should consider what purpose these parts serve. Would another lower-cost design work as well? Could another less costly item fill the need? Would less expensive material do the job? And, on purchased items, are the vendors' prices as low as they could be for the level of quality and delivery dates required?

In many cases there are different ways of making things. If two parts have to be fastened together, the design engineer should not first think of how to design a low-cost bolt. Rather, he should think about making the two pieces as one. If this cannot be done economically, he might consider riveting the pieces together, welding or gluing them, or making the parts interlock like pieces of a jigsaw puzzle. If he still thinks that a screw or bolt is the best solution, then—and only then—should he consider the bolt's size and shape and whether the factory should make it or purchase it from a vendor. Figure 5–1 shows how one company reduces costs of components by substituting wire parts for castings, plastic, and stampings.

Design engineers need to be conscious of trade-offs. Silver wire, for example, conducts electricity better than copper, but it is rarely used in place of copper because it costs several times as much per pound. Silver's extra conductivity is not sufficient to offset copper's lower price, unless the weight saved from being able to use

FIGURE 5–1
Examples of Part Redesign to Reduce Costs by Using Substitute Materials

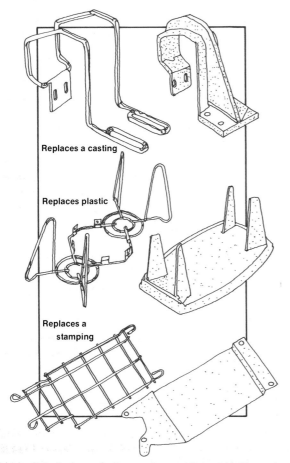

Replaces a casting

Replaces plastic

Replaces a stamping

Substituting wire parts for castings, plastic, and stamped parts can help lower unit costs by eliminating unnecessary material and streamlining component assembly and can provide a component that is stronger, light in weight, and often functionally superior.

Courtesy E. H. Titchener & Co, Binghamton, N.Y.

thinner wires, as well as extra reliability, is extremely important as, for example, in a spacecraft's electrical system. Aluminum is also a good conductor of electricity, and it is cheaper than copper. Many builders turned to aluminum wire until they found it caused fires in homes due to corrosion, so they resumed their use of copper.

Value analysis, particularly in purchasing, sometimes saves substantial amounts of money. At General Electric, a screw of special design had cost 15 cents, but value analysis found a way to make it for 1.5 cents. A hand-made gasket, costing $4.15 each at GE, was found to cost 15 cents when purchased from an outside gasket maker. White Consolidated's Frigidaire division reported this savings: For aluminum doors bought for an evaporator, three vendor quotations ranged from $2.40 to $2.70. Frigidaire's estimate of what it should pay was $2.05. The final price was $2.10.

Both engineers and purchasing people should try to avoid setting unnecessarily high specifications. In one plant the purchasing agent found that its engineers had specified that certain parts be made to very exact measurements—although the parts were later enameled before they were used. After enameling, the measurements were much less exact, but the parts were still quite suitable for the purpose. Loosening the part's dimension tolerances cut the purchase price. Some firms, taking the lead from the Japanese, give very loose descriptions of the part to reliable suppliers and let them be creative as to which material to use and how it is designed.[1]

In spite of what has just been said, there are times when value analysis should *not* be used. A man can use a paper clip to hold his necktie instead of a $5 tie clip, and it would do the job satisfactorily. Where aesthetics and price economy clash, designers and buyers need to decide which should rule. Value analysis generally focuses on function, not on form.

MATERIALS DECISIONS

In many cases designers can choose from among different materials to use. Just as a carpet can be made of wool, cotton, flax, rayon, nylon, or other synthetics, so can industrial products

---

[1] R. J. Schonberger, *Japanese Manufacturing Techniques* (New York: Free Press, 1982), p. 165.

be made from different materials. A gear can be made from steel, iron, brass, aluminum, nylon, or other plastics. Wrapping and covering materials can be made of cloth, leather, paper, or hard or soft plastics.

In making the choice from among the possibilities, the designer needs always to keep in mind (1) the performance requirements of the product or part, (2) the relative material costs, (3) the relative processing costs, and (4) the visual appeal of the material.

Often, since each of the alternative materials will perform well, the real choice depends on the relative costs of the materials and on their processing costs. And by no means is the low-cost material always chosen. Many small metal parts, for example, are made out of copper or brass instead of steel—even though steel costs less than one tenth as much per pound—because copper and brass can be machined so easily that their processing costs are far less. Similarly, in spite of its costing at least five times as much as steel per pound, zinc is often used for small, intricately molded parts because it works so well in die casting, which is a low-cost way of making high-volume items. (Today, however, zinc is being replaced by molded plastics because plastic materials now cost less and can be die-cast even more readily than zinc.)

When materials contribute to a product's final appearance (form), the designer can sometimes have the better of two worlds. A walnut cabinet makes an attractive television set, but walnut is very costly and is not as durable as steel. Today, however, very lost-cost and reasonably realistic simulated vinyl coatings can be put on metal surfaces. The television set can be made of durable steel yet have an attractive simulated walnut finish.

The question of what material to use is usually an enduring one. If the price of one metal goes up and that of the alternative drops, it may become economical to reverse the choice. In its early days, plastics cost too much for general use, but now they compete successfully with various metals. Similarly, in the late 1970s, when

Third World countries producing raw materials raised the price of copper, many users turned to aluminum. But aluminum requires vast amounts of electricity to manufacture, so when energy costs rose, so did the cost of aluminum. Then the bottom fell out of the mining industry in the early 1980s, and copper became competitive again.

The choice is often related to the prospective volume. For low volume, costly but easily worked raw materials are often the best because small low-cost general-purpose machines can handle easily worked material such as brass or bronze. But these machines are not very economical for working hard materials such as steel. For high volumes, on the other hand, expensive machines can handle hard-to-work materials economically. Thus, purchasing departments and designers should always be alert to price and volume changes which might justify changing materials.

The food industry is especially watchful of material costs of ingredients used in their recipes. For example, the list of ingredients on the label for Coffee-mate (a nondairy creamer) says it contains "partially hydrogenated vegetable oil (may contain one or more of the following oils— coconut, cottonseed, palm, palm kernel, safflower, or soybean)." Carnation, the manufacturer, is of the opinion that these oils are substitutes for each other and so uses oil bought on the commodity market at the lowest cost, given their quality specifications.

STANDARDIZATION

When you buy a light bulb, you know it will screw into the socket because light bulb bases are standardized (only a few kinds of bases are made). But an American light bulb will not fit into a socket in Europe, or vice versa, because their bases are different. Or, if you buy a new hose to sprinkle your lawn, you don't have to wonder if it will screw onto the water faucet because the size of the pipes and screw threads are standard.

Also, most people probably never think

about a light bulb's voltage because, in the United States, 110 volts is standard in homes. But again, Europe is different; several voltages are used there. An American traveler in Europe using an electric shaver has to buy an adapter.

We have used the word *standard* as meaning that only certain specific sizes are made and sold. Some people prefer to call this process of limiting the number of sizes "simplification." "Standardization," these people would say, is something else; it is the process of *specifying* the size, shape, performance, and other characteristics of the items being made. These two concepts are so closely related, however, that we will use them here as being nearly the same.

Standardization (including simplification) usually means that nonstandard items will not be made—except when a customer orders them specifically (and pays more for them).

Sometimes standards have been enacted into law for safety or health reasons. Automobile windshields, for example, must be made of safety glass (which does not shatter and make jagged edges on impact). Although standardization has largely been voluntary in the past, today's product safety laws are making it mandatory in many areas. The glass now used in eyeglasses, for example, must now be very resistant to breakage. It is standardized at a high-quality level.

Most industries, even those producing consumer products where there are no legal regulations, can and do standardize extensively on a voluntary basis. This holds true in the setting of shoe sizes, photographic film, automobile tire sizes, nails, pipe, and even razor blades. In the service sector, there are standard insurance policies, college credits, airline ticket forms, computer languages, and medical tests.

Advantages of Standardization

Standardization reduces the kinds, types, and sizes of raw materials which have to be purchased and the variety of items to be manufactured internally. Since the total quantities to be bought or made are distributed over fewer varieties, economies of scale for suppliers can result, which means lower costs per unit and fewer patterns, tools, jigs, fixtures, and setups, all of which contribute to lower costs.

Disadvantages of Standardization and Simplification

Some manufacturers, especially those making assembled products, do not accept industrywide standardization because they find that using "the perfect part" is better for them than using a standard part that is not well suited to their particular use. A company making power lawn mowers may not want the same engine which is used for chain saws, or motorcycles, or outboard motors on boats. Instead, it may be better for this company to use an engine designed especially for their machines.

Manufacturers using large volumes of nuts, bolts, wire, valves, bearings, electric motors, switches, and other such items also frequently find that making "the perfect part" for a particular purpose is cheaper in use, even if it costs a little more to make, than buying a standard part.

There are other reasons why industrywide standardization programs often are only partially successful. Standardization tends to favor large, well-known companies, because small (or new) companies can rarely get much business by making and selling the same things and at the same prices as larger companies. They often survive by offering something different at the same, or close to the same, price as large companies charge for standard products.

Manufacturers of "style goods" such as clothing do not standardize very much because people want "something different." They do, however, usually abide by industrywide size standards, which need to be consistent. But even this can vary. That's why waist size 34 pants from different manufacturers can be tight, loose, or just right!

From the social point of view, there is a potential danger in standardization. If new products are standardized too soon, before their design is fairly mature, standardization may become an obstacle to progress. Color television, for example, appeared in Europe later than in the United States. This permitted European television to incorporate more advanced technology and to use 160 lines to the inch instead of the American standard of 120 lines to the inch; consequently, their pictures are sharper.

Typewriter keyboards, too, were frozen too soon (many years ago), and this has stood in the way of improvement. They have a poor arrangement of letters (60 percent of the workload falls on the left hand, whereas most people are right-handed). We know how to arrange them better but have had substantial barriers to change because millions of typists are trained to use the present keyboard—to say nothing of our already having millions of typewriters with the poor keyboard.

However, some hope exists for changing from a "Qwerty" keyboard (the letters on the top row of letters below the number row) to a more efficient Dvorak layout (developed by August Dvorak in the 1930s) because of the electronic rather than mechanical construction of today's typewriters. Some electronic typewriters can be "re-programmed" to accept the more efficient keystrokes.[2]

Improvements which call for different nonstandard products must always be made if progress is to continue. A standard should, therefore, be in a sense more a prevailing style than it is a permanent standard. Standards should not be permitted to be frozen or be kept only for their own sake.

THE METRIC SYSTEM AND PRODUCT DESIGN

The United States is well on the way to adopting the metric system of measurement. This system is almost universally used throughout the world.

---

[2] S. McDonald, "Dvorak Typewriter Keyboard May At Last Have Chance to Challenge Qwerty Design," *The Wall Street Journal*, June 21, 1984, p. 35.

It is not that very many of us, the population in general, want the metric system but it is a more logical system than our English-type system with ounces and pounds, inches and feet, pints and gallons, and other units of measure. Large measures are not multiples of 10 of smaller measurements.

Because the metric system is more logical and more economical to use, Congress, in President Ford's administration, passed an act which embodied a statement of purpose, to try to get the people of the United States to use the metric system. But since the system is new to us, progress has been slow.

The metric system takes some getting used to. The milkman will leave a one-liter bottle of milk (1.05 quarts), and a husband may be asked to buy 450 grams (1 pound) of hamburger on his way home where his wife, size 91–72–91 centimeters (36–28–36 inches), will greet him. When the customer at the gas station says, "Fill 'er up," he may end up buying 60 liters of gasoline (15.8 gallons). And the air pressure in his tires will be 12.7 kilograms (28 pounds).

When a man steps on a scale he will find that he weighs 68 kilograms instead of 150 pounds. Instead of being 6 feet tall, he will be 1.83 meters tall. Pike's Peak in Colorado will be 4,301 meters high instead of 14,110 feet. And an 8½ x 11-inch sheet of paper will be 21.6 x 27.9 centimeters.

A city lot 60 x 150 feet will become 18.29 x 54.86 meters. A farmer who used to own 200 acres of land will have 81 hectares. Whereas it used to be 10 miles to town, it will become 16.1 kilometers. The speed limit will be 88.5 kilometers per hour instead of 55 miles per hour. And the distance from New York to Chicago will change from 840 miles to 1,351 kilometers.

Summers may seem cooler, though, when the thermometer gets up to only 35 degrees (centigrade) instead of 95 degrees (Fahrenheit). Winters may, however, seem colder. Instead of 14 degrees above zero, the thermometer will show 10 degrees below.

It all sounds confusing to an American's ear,

but the changeover is already well under way. It may be comforting, however, to look at the clock and calendar. Three P.M. will still be 3 P.M. and Monday, March 20, will still be the same, since there is no metric time system.

Why Should We Change?

The metric system for measurements is a more rational system than the English system which the United States has always used. An inch was first defined in England to be the length of four dried barley corns (grains of barley) laid end to end. Other measurements in this system, such as quarts and pounds, similarly grew out of traditional measurements, none of which have any orderly relationships to each other as does our decimal monetary system where 10 cents equal a dime, 10 dimes equal a dollar, and so on.

The metric system is also a decimal system with relationships between various units being based on powers of the number 10. A meter is formally defined as one ten-millionth of the distance from the equator to the North Pole and is slightly longer than our yard (39.4 inches). For units smaller than a meter, the prefixes are deci (tenths), centi (hundredths), and milli (thousandths). So, a tenth of a meter is a decimeter; a hundredth of a meter is a centimeter; and a thousandth of a meter is a millimeter. On the other side of a meter, 10 meters is a dekameter, 100 meters is a hectometer, and 1,000 meters is a kilometer.

The other basic measurements in the metric system are the liter (which is about 5 percent more than a quart) which is used to measure volume, and the gram which is the basic unit for measuring weight. A kilogram (1,000 grams) is about 2.2 pounds. The same prefixes (deci, centi, and so forth) apply to these units as well.

The metric system, which is also known as "SI" or "System International," is used by every large country in the world except the English-speaking countries, and even these, except for the United States, have been changing to metric. Our being out of step has occasional disadvantages in international trade.

Hard versus Soft Conversion

We can convert to metric in either of two ways. First, the so-called soft conversion is just changing all existing measurements which are in inches, pounds, and so on, into their metric equivalents. The other, more costly approach is the so-called hard conversion. Hard conversion gives up our characteristic sizes and substitutes metric sizes. Such changes would be more costly because they would, in some cases, require extensive changes in equipment.

In soft conversion, a 12-ounce glass of Coco Cola would merely be restated as .34 liters. In hard conversion, the 12-ounce bottle would disappear and be replaced and become a ¼ of a liter bottle or a ½ liter bottle. This change has, in fact, already been made. Soft drinks now come in half liter bottles. These changes have required new bottle-making equipment—which has been costly. Many believe these kinds of changes are wasteful and have little advantage.

There are difficulties in other areas also. Workers have to be educated to use the system. And during the changeover period there would be need for dual dimensioning (showing inches and centimeters) on drawings and machine dials. There would be additional costs from keeping track of two separate inventories of the items which were being changed in size. And there would be problems of reconciling past and present cost accounting and statistical information which would have to be collected by both methods during the changeover. Miles per gallon will, for example, become kilometers per liter.

Going metric may also put a severe burden on smaller firms. They are usually short of cash, and the costs of changing would weigh heavily on them. There would be problems, too, for a small company which provides parts for one customer who wants them to be in metric units whereas other customers want their products in inches.[3]

---

[3] See Martin F. Schmidt and Kenneth A. Reed, "Small Business and the Metric System," *Colorado Business Review*, October 10, 1976, pp. 2–4.

Advantages to Going Metric

We would not be going metric, however, unless there were consequential advantages. Its greater convenience has already been mentioned, and this is itself important, but there are other advantages. Many American manufacturers are already providing items based on the metric system. Often this requires them to have two production facilities, one for the American market and the other for the rest of the world. The saving from consolidating these facilities would be substantial.

Design engineers would also welcome the change. Most engineers are already well versed in the metric system and find it much easier to use. Boeing estimates that savings in drafting time in the aerospace industry alone will exceed $1 billion a year!

Also, educators believe that they could save an estimated $1 billion in teachers' salaries because the metric system requires about 25 percent less time to learn than the English system.

One of the biggest advantages, however, lies in the simplicity of the interrelationships between the basic measurement elements in the metric system. The seven elements, listed in Figure 5–2, are: length, volume, weight, temperature, power, pressure, and energy. Engineers work with all of these measures, but most people would be concerned with only the first four.

In all cases, the metric system shows differences in measurements between very small and very large by using powers of 10. There is only one basic unit. But in our English-based system this is not so. It takes 12 inches to make a foot, 3 feet to make a yard, and 5,280 feet or 1,760 yards to make a mile. All the way up and down the line, greater or lesser measurements are not multiples of 10 nor are they sequenced logically.

And, although it is of no importance to most people, the basic metric units are interrelated in a coherent way that helps engineers and scientists. For example, one kilogram accelerated one meter per second, produces a force of one newton. (Measures of force were omitted from our list above because they are not significant to most of us.)

Some American companies started to go metric in the 1970s and so have already made some of the necessary changes. Ford Motor began manufacturing automobiles to metric specifications in one factory in 1973. Other auto manufacturers are making similar changes, as are Caterpillar Tractor, International Harvester, IBM, and many others.

Ford Motor Co. estimates that in the fastener area alone (nuts, bolts, screws, and rivets), the conversion to a single international measurement system for these items would save American manufacturers half a billion dollars a year. Unfortunately, going metric in fasteners is not enough because it is not only a matter of the number of threads per inch or per centimeter and the diameters and lengths of bolts and screws, but also a matter of angles and pitches of threads. The American and European standards are different on all of these. Restating mea-

FIGURE 5–2

Element Being Measured	American Units	Metric Units
Length	Inch, foot, yard, mile	Meter
Volume	Pint, quart, gallon	Liter
Weight	Ounce, pound, ton	Gram
Temperature	Fahrenheit degree	Centigrade degree
Power	Horsepower, watt	Watt
Pressure	Pounds per square inch	Pascal
Energy	Foot pound, British thermal unit, calorie	Joule

surements in metric units is not enough. So far, little progress has been made in reconciling the two sets of standards.

Resistance to Change

In the late 1970s, the resistance to metrication grew in the United States. Consumer groups such as WAM (We Ain't Metric) succeeded in slowing down the conversion process. There has been some progress, however. In many states, it is legal to sell gasoline by the liter; the wine and liquor industry started using metric-sized bottles in 1980; and U.S. companies selling goods to Common Market countries are marking their products metrically—which has been required since 1978.

MODULAR DESIGN

With repair labor being just about as costly in a factory as it is in a home and with breakdowns being costly in both cases, designers are turning to modular construction with products being made of easily detachable subassemblies or sections. When a single item fails, the whole module (of which the item is a part) is removed and a new module is put in. Later the removed module can be repaired and put into replacement stock or it can be thrown away.

Electrical printed circuit boards (or "cards") and integrated circuits are usually components of this sort. Plug-in bases are made as integral parts of such boards, thus allowing for their easy removal. If a transistor or diode fails, the whole card on which it is mounted, along with other diodes, condensers, and the like, is removed and replaced by a new card.

Modular design is used extensively in computers, both in the microminiature and circuit board way, and also in another way. Standardized major components are made with their physical dimensions and electrical systems compatible so they can be hooked up in different combinations to make what are essentially different computers. In computers, for example, the units which store information, the units which

"read in" information to the calculating section, and the units which print out results are available in several sizes and with varied capabilities. They can be connected in several combinations to fit the customer's needs. In fact, the first Apple computers were made in the garage of one of the founders almost entirely from purchased modular parts.

RELIABILITY

As a person sits in a comfortable chair in the evening reading the newspaper, the light bulb in the reading lamp suddenly burns out. Designers can rarely design, nor can manufacturers make, products which will not eventually fail. Nor can they design or make products which will last for an exact length of time—no more, no less.

A product's length of life is dependent upon its design, upon the degree of manufacturing perfection, upon the conditions under which it is used, and upon chance. Usually the longer a product is supposed to last, the more costly it is to make.

Reliability is the probability that a part or a product will last a given length of time under normal conditions of use. Thus, the *first* aspect of reliability is expected length of life. In the case of a light bulb, the goal could be 1,000 hours or it could even be 2,000 hours. (Ordinary light bulbs have a "rated" or "expected" life of 1,350 hours.) Obviously even ordinary light bulbs are very reliable up to 1,000 hours, perhaps with a reliability of 0.98, meaning that only 2 bulbs in 100 will probably fail before 1,000 hours. But very few bulbs will last 2,000 hours; possibly here the probability might be 0.05. If someone wants bulbs which will usually last for 2,000 hours, he or she will need to order special bulbs.

A *second* aspect of reliability is the condition of use. A light bulb of the usual design is unlikely to last even 1,000 hours if it is continually bumped around. But flashlights get bumped around, and so their bulbs need to be sturdier than reading lamp bulbs.

Sometimes the conditions of expected use

are most extreme. Many of the parts that go into space vehicles often must operate at temperatures of more than 200 degrees above zero and at other times at temperatures of more than 200 degrees below zero.

Parts, therefore, need to be designed to have the desired reliability under their expected conditions of use. For most consumer products, conditions of use are not extreme, although everyone recognizes that some products, such as automobiles or motorcycles, are sometimes misused and not well maintained. And, while the reliability of most consumer products is satisfactory to most users, we have all had "lemons" of one product or another.

Third, reliability has to do both with individual parts and entire products. Products fail when *any* critical part fails, so the reliability of entire products is much less than the reliability of individual parts. The more critical parts there are, the less the reliability of the whole product. Sewing machines, power lawn mowers, and automobiles all have many parts whose failure individually would cause the product to fail. And

computers, space vehicles, and other exotic products have thousands of parts whose operating is critical to the operation of the whole product. Back in the 1960s it took the United States 13 tries to get a space vehicle to take the first close-up pictures of the moon; the first 12 tries were failures. Several years ago, the United States submarine *Thresher* sank, and 129 men lost their lives because one pipe joint—out of 8,000— failed.

A system of 100 interacting parts, each of which has .9999 (or 99.99 percent) reliability, has an overall reliability of 0.9900 (or 99 percent). This is simply $.9999^{100}$. A system with 1,000 interacting parts has 90 percent reliability; 3,000 parts have 75 percent; and 10,000 parts have 37 percent. (See Figure 5–3). The Telstar communications satellite has more than 10,000 electronic parts, and even though these parts do not all interact, and not all are of critical importance, extremely high reliability had to be built into Telstar's parts to get it to operate in the first place and to keep it operating in the years since it was put into orbit in 1963.

FIGURE 5–3

Overall System Reliability as a Function of Each Component's Reliability and the Number of Components

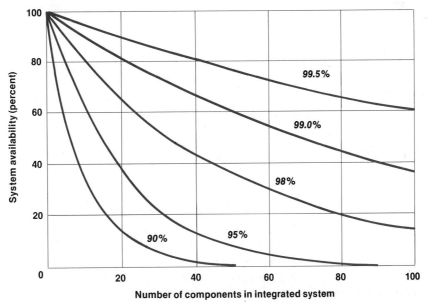

A *fourth* matter is how serious is failure? If an automobile steering mechanism fails, it can cause a wreck, but sometimes the failure of a part is not critical. If a lamp bulb in a reading lamp fails, little harm is done. Or, if a person drops a telephone and the plastic casing cracks, the casing has "failed" but the telephone still works. But if rocket engines fail on the Space Shuttle it could be a disaster.

Point *five* is a corollary of point *four:* How quickly can a part failure be fixed, and how big a job is it to fix it? Indeed, the seriousness of a failure often depends upon how quickly and how cheaply it can be fixed. Quick maintenance returns the system back into operation right away so that little harm is done. When a storm knocks out the electric power for part of a city, the potential harm is great, but usually the actual harm is much less because the power company gets the power restored so quickly. And, of course, when the light bulb in a lamp burns out, we can unscrew it and put in another. When replacement is simple and fast, product reliability is less important.

Unfortunately, points four and five sometimes do not apply because there is no chance to fix or replace a critical part that has failed. The United States missed taking pictures of the moon the first 12 tries because the parts that failed were critical and there was no way to fix them in outer space. And, in 1984 Western Union and Indonesia each lost multimillion dollar communication satellites launched from the space shuttle Columbia because of faulty components. These are now "space junk" and irretrievable. Further, broken steering mechanisms in automobiles can cause accidents before there is any chance to fix them. Faulty electronic components in computers can cause wrong answers, and possibly no one will know that they are wrong (although several checks for accuracy are built into today's computers). In such cases, a high degree of reliability is very important even if it costs more money.

A *sixth* point is that the reliability of systems can usually be improved by making products out of more perfect parts, parts which are made to fit more exactly or which are made out of special long-wearing materials. But, as almost always, the greater the reliability, the higher the cost.

An example from Texas Instruments illustrates how greater reliability requirements caused costs to skyrocket. TI sold one kind of transistor for consumer and industrial use for $.25 each with no guarantee of its reliability. But for its use in military systems, it had to give reliability guarantees, so the price was $.85 for the same (but more carefully processed and tested) transistor. But when it came to spacecraft use, its very careful manufacture and testing, which were required to insure its high reliability, increased the costs of this same transistor up to $10. Figure 5–4 illustrates this relationship between component cost and component reliability.

Fortunately, greater quality does not always cost very much more money. Parts which might fail can often be "overdesigned" at nominal cost. A handle or a hinge on a suitcase can easily be made far stronger than it needs to be at very little extra cost. So can a door hinge on an automobile. Added strength in these cases cost very little.

The discussion so far might lead one to think that reliability is a black-or-white matter: A product works or it doesn't. Often, however, failure is not like that. This leads to point *seven,* the degree of failure. If a television tube sometimes goes zigzag or gives snowy or fuzzy pictures, has it failed? Has there been a failure in an automobile if the brake pedal has to be pushed farther down than formerly? Poor performance is often a matter of degree, with absolute failure as the final stage. In a practical sense, failure occurs when performance is so poor that there is a decision to repair or replace the part.

There is also the question of performance expectations. When a television picture tube fails, the customer regards it as a failure, whereas if it lasted 10 years before failing, it is not—in the eyes of the manufacturer—a failure at all.

Point *eight* is that reliability is closely tied

FIGURE 5–4
Relationship between Component Cost and Component
Reliability: Costs Rise Disproportionately to Increased
Reliability Requirements

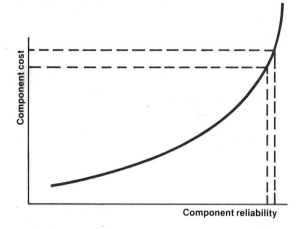

to maintenance, particularly preventive maintenance. A reading lamp will probably never burn
out while someone is reading if the old bulb is
taken out and a new one is put in every 800
hours. Normally, preventive maintenance can result in high reliability for a product even where
long term reliability is not engineered into the
parts of the product, It is only necessary to replace parts before they have been used enough
to become unreliable. If a person buys a new
storage battery for a car every two years, the
car will usually start in the winter. Unfortunately,
however, preventive maintenance costs money,
so it is only a different (and usually somewhat
costly) way to increase the reliability of products.
In cases like this, most people simply follow a
"replace-when-failure-occurs policy."

Many of today's products are designed,
however, to simplify their "maintainability."
Volkswagons and other automobiles, for example, have a "plug" which, when connected to
an engine diagnostic machine, can pinpoint
problems.

We have said that the failure of a noncritical
part often does not affect the whole product's
operating performance. This may be misleading
because the failure of one part may hasten the
failure of others. A broken telephone case lets

dust and dampness creep inside, and in time
this may cause it to fail. Or an automobile will
run when one cylinder is not firing, but if it is
continued in operation it will cause the car's
bearings to fail sooner.

"Bathtub" Curves

Unless final inspectors do a good job of testing,
the actual length of life of an item may have a
shape like that of a bathtub silhoutte. It is high
on the left, then has a long, relatively flat and
low, middle section, and then increases at the
right. (See Figure 5–5.)

Some items will fail quickly. One of the authors purchased an Apple II+ in 1979, and when
he plugged it in one of the floppy disk drives
"failed" after the first few hours of use. But it
was repaired easily and the system has performed perfectly, with heavy use, for over four
years. These are truly faulty items which inspection and testing should catch. Thereafter, failures
should be rare until normal use raises the failure
rate again, as the items wear out. In cases where
the manufacturing process cannot be improved
enough to eliminate the bathtub effect, the company may have to "age" the components by
operating them on a test basis through the "in-
fant mortality" period, thus screening out those
that are initially defective. Items that survive this

FIGURE 5–5
The "Bathtub" Curve Length-of-Life Pattern of Many Items

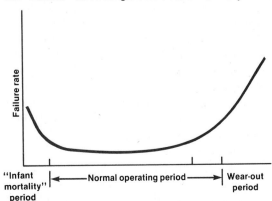

early period will then have a low mortality until old age is reached.

Bathtub curves sometimes do not have a chance to appear because items which fail are replaced one by one, as they fail, with new items. Ultimately, the failure rate levels off since some of the items in use are new and some are older, while some are near the end of their normal life. The actual failures include the composite effects of many age curves, each in a different stage of its life cycle. The failure statistics are summations of failures from different age groups. Because of this there may be no visible evidence of the operation of bathtub life-curves.

REDUNDANCY

Where the failure of a part or subsystem is critically important, engineers often add a redundant part or subsystem as insurance. It is like wearing a belt and suspenders at the same time or having a backup quarterback. The spare is not used at all unless the regular part fails. Should the regular component fail, then the total system may automatically switch over to the standby component.

The need for redundancy depends primarily on the seriousness of a failure, and secondarily on its cost, The specter of a nuclear disaster resulting from an accident in a nuclear electric power generating plant frightens us all. Because of this nuclear power plants are designed to withstand the worst earthquakes, floods, or other "acts of God" ever recorded in their areas. Every piece of equipment has to meet the stiffest quality controls anywhere in civilian industry. If any component fails, layer after layer of "redundant" safety features are ready to be activated. MIT scientists estimate that the way today's nuclear plants are built, even 100 such plants, considered together, would have a probability of an accident involving 1,000 or more deaths only once in a million years.[4]

---

[4] "The Great Nuclear Debate," *Time,* December 8, 1975, p. 36.

Redundancy for safety's sake is actually quite common. Every automobile, for instance, has a mechanical handbrake as well as its regular hydraulic brake system, which itself has a redundant system built into it. If the foot brake fails, the driver is not without a brake. Aircraft have independent ignition systems and can continue to fly if one of the ignition systems fails.

Today's large-scale electronic computers have two sets of every subsystem whose failure would be critical to their operation. And, with minicomputers being so inexpensive, some organizations are actually using two computers where one could do the work. The second is merely backup if the first one goes out. Cities and state police are also doing this where critical information needs to be kept "online" and right up to date, as is the case with information about fugitives and stolen cars.

In industry, we hear most about redundancy in exotic products such as space vehicles where every critical subsystem is backed up by a second emergency system. In smaller ways, however, the redundancy idea is used in everyday products. Men's shirts are usually sewn with double seams where one is usually enough. Or, in a factory, if two pieces of steel have to be welded together with four spot welds and there has been trouble with the welded spots not holding, it is easy to specify six spot welds instead of four.

Even nature believes in redundancy. We all start with two eyes, ears, lungs, and kidneys, but we can get along with one. Nature's redundancy, however, usually calls for the regular use of both components, whereas industry's redundancy is usually a first-unit-use, second-unit-standby arrangement.

Redundancy Economics

Redundancy economics can be quite complex, but a simple problem will illustrate the principles. Suppose that a system has two components, A and B, which operate as in Figure 5–6. The probability of A's being operative for as long

FIGURE 5–6

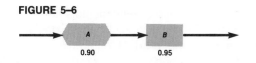

as the normal life of the system is 0.90 and B's is 0.95. Since both have to operate, and either can fail, the system reliability is 0.90 × 0.95 = 0.855.

Suppose that a failure costs $1,000. The probability of failure during the system's normal life expectancy is therefore 1 − 0.885 = 0.145 and the long-run expected cost of failure is 0.145 × $1,000 = $145.

To make the system more reliable, it is proposed to put in a second A unit, together with a switch, so that if the first A unit is inoperative, the second (A') will switch on automatically—a system like that shown in Figure 5–7. Should such a redundant system be put in at a cost of $300 if the switch has a reliability of 0.98 and the reliability of unit A' is 0.90?

If called into use, the redundant system will be operative 0.98 × 0.90 = 0.88 of the time. the redundant system will then take care of 88 percent of the expected 10 percent failures of part A. So the reliability of the A–A' part of the system becomes 0.90 + (0.10 × 0.88) = 0.988. B, however, has not been improved; so the whole system's reliability has now become 0.988 × 0.95 = 0.939. The probability of failure is 1 − 0.939 = 0.061. Now the expected failure cost will be 0.61 × $1,000 = $61.

Expected failure costs are now reduced by $84 (from $145 to $61), but the protection cost $300, so the total expected cost is $361. Without the redundant system, the expected cost of fail-

ure was $145; so the redundant system will not pay for itself. It would be better to take the 14.5 percent chance of having a $1,000 failure than to spend $300 to reduce the risk to a 6.1-percent chance of having such a failure. It would pay in the long run only if the cost of the redundant system was reduced from $300 to less than $84.

COMPUTER-ASSISTED DESIGN (CAD)

Computers are being used more and more in product design activities. The movement has gained momentum in the early 1980s because of the growing availability of systems such as those developed by Computervision Corporation and General Electric.

In addition, these systems can substantially increase the productivity of design engineers and drafting personnel by about three to one over conventional methods.

General Electric uses CAD systems to design electric motors. I-T-E Circuit Breaker uses them to design custom-built transformers. Allis Chalmers uses them to decide the best shapes for drying kilns. General Motors uses them in automobile design. Aircraft companies use them to compute the contours of wings, to design integrated circuits, and to design parts. Even De Puy, Inc., a small Indiana firm that makes prosthetic devices (artificial limbs and joints), uses a Computervision system for the design of their specialized products.

When there are several ways to do anything, a computer can quickly make all the comparisons and pick the best way, whereas, without a computer, an engineer cannot make all the comparisons and would have to rely on judgment. Once the computer has made its calculations, it can have the automatic drafting machine make the drawings while the computer itself proceeds to produce all the manufacturing instructions needed for making the product, including instruction tapes for direction "numerically controlled" machines (discussed in Chapter 19). Alternatively, before the final design decision is

FIGURE 5–7

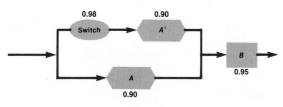

made, the designer can consider several different designs.

A computer can also project, on a CRT, a drawing which it has made from the design instructions, put into its memory by the designer. Then, after looking at it, if it is necessary to eliminate a line or draw in a new one, it can be done on the CRT with an electronic pen connected to the computer. The computer will change its memory instructions so that it will thereafter project the revised drawing. The computer will change its memory instructions so that it will thereafter project the revised drawing. The computer can also enlarge a picture or turn it so that it can be seen from another angle, such as left front, rather than from front. And it can also pair up mating parts to see how they fit.

As if this were not enough, this process is now well enough developed so an engineer can even draw a preliminary rough design on the CRT with his electronic pen and the computer will reproduce it on call. It will even straighten out lines, smooth out curved lines, and reproduce the improved sketch on call.

Some newer CAD systems can do even more. Boeing, for example, is using a new $150,000 system called Syntha Vision which can "generate a three dimensional model of a nonexistent part and display it on a video screen with the realism of a photograph" . . . and the picture "can be sliced through at any point from any angle, rotated in space, 'exploded,' and used to create line or shaded drawings" . . . and "because the model is a 'solid' representation, it can be used to calculate the part's weight, volume"[5] and other properties.

DESIGN CONFLICTS

Production, engineering, marketing, and finance people in organizations often have different objectives, all or any of which may affect the final design of products and which may be in conflict with each other.

[5] "The Faster 3-D Way to Computerized Design," *Business Week,* November 21, 1977, p. 66.

Figure 5–8 humorously depicts some of the possible differing viewpoints about design. Everyone sees the product differently. In actual practice, at the one extreme, production people want to make only a few kinds of products and with few variations so that they can have long production runs. And if any changes have to be made, they want them to be simple so that they can be made easily.

On the other hand, design engineers usually

FIGURE 5–8
Miscommunication Can Cause Design Conflicts

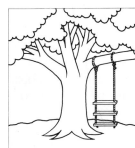
As proposed by the marketing department

As specified in the product request

As designed by the senior designer

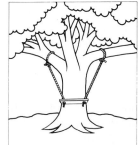
As produced by manufacturing

As used by the customer

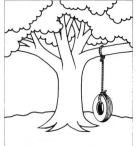
What the customer wanted

want to build durability into products so that they will serve well for a long time, even if this means using more costly materials or processes. Marketing people almost always want a wide variety in the product line so they can attract the customer's eye and have something different for every customer. And, in order to follow what the market wants all the time, marketing people want frequent redesigns of existing products.

Finance people have still other objectives, such as high profitability, fast cash flow, rapid inventory turnover, and a quick return on the investments in plant and equipment.

QUALITY DIMENSIONS OF PRODUCT DESIGN

"Quality," to most people, seems to mean "high quality." It is a little like mother, God, Queen, and country—everyone is for it, and the more quality the better. Yet, one can ask, do people really want the highest possible quality of everything? The answer has to be no, because costs are always a part of customer decisions.

Supermarkets sell millions of pounds of candy, millions of water glasses and dishes, generic items, and millions of other things—practically all of which are admittedly of medium or low quality. Not all people buy their candy and glasware and dishes from supermarkets, but obviously many do.

Most people do not want the very best of very many things—at least not to the extent of being willing to pay the cost of high quality. What we want is the best quality we can get for the money we are willing to spend. Our quality-cost calculus is sometimes more cost-sensitive than it is quality-sensitive. All we want is for the product or service to be good enough.

This is why Sears and Kmart are the world's largest merchandisers, even though they rarely carry the best of anything. And this is what quality means to a manufacturer. He tries to make the best product he can for the price that most of his targeted potential customers are willing to pay. Campbell Soup doesn't put prime beef in

their soups because beef noodle soup buyers wouldn't pay the price.

The price that a prospective customer is willing to pay is related both to what he wants and what he can afford to spend for an item. Marketing experts tell us that what people want, their desired "bundle of utilities," includes durability, dependability, workmanship, exclusivity (few other people have one), eye appeal (shape, color, and so on), and price. Curiously, sometimes consumers are impressed by a high price and seem to think that a higher-priced product must be better and that a very high-priced product must be very much better. Mercedes and BMWs get part of their reputation from being expensive.

Figure 5–9 shows relationships between quality, costs, and what people might be willing to pay. Note that the cost usually rises at an increasing rate as the level of quality increases. Also, note that the "value" or worth of higher quality increases at a decreasing rate. People usually want something better than the very cheapest and are willing to pay more for higher-quality items or services. But, of most items, not very much more. Before long the worth to them of further extra quality diminishes. An economist would say that this is an illustration of the concept of "diminishing marginal utility."

Conceptually, the optimal level of quality for an organization to build into its products or services is where the gap between the "cost to provide" line and the "value of the bundle of utilities" line is the widest (point A.)

While Figure 5–9 is nice to look at as depicting relationships, in reality it is hard to draw as reflecting actual relationships because of the difficulty in estimating the shapes of the two curves. The cost curve, for example, depends, among other things, on the volume of demand. Similarly, the utility value curve is influenced by the availability of substitute products or services, the general health of the economy, and such unpredictable things as "fashion."

Because this is so, product designers need to work closely with marketing people so that

FIGURE 5–9
Relationship between Quality, Cost, and Value

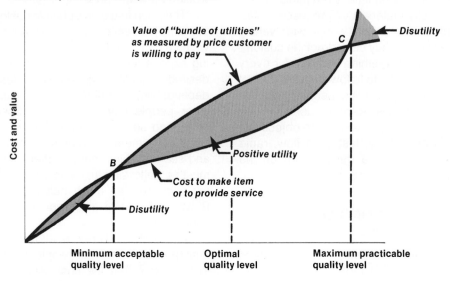

the level of quality chosen is within the range between points *B* and *C* in Figure 5–9. The quality level which satisfies this requirement is usually determined by market surveys and by test marketing a product in one or two small geographical areas before offering products on a nationwide basis.

Year by year the quality of most products improves. An automobile or a television set which was a best seller in 1965 was no longer acceptable in 1985. It wasn't good enough. And 1985 cars and TV sets will not be acceptable in 1990. *They* won't be good enough. Quality improves because of technological advances and because both customers and competitors force almost everyone to incorporate these advances into their products.

Sometimes, however, customers do not see quality improvements directly because they take their gain in lower prices rather than in more quality for the old prices. Today's color television sets, for example, are both better and cheaper than they were at first. But they could be even better yet today is customers were willing to pay more. TV manufacturers have found from experience, however, that most customers will not pay much more for still higher quality.

Quality control people usually wince at the idea that most manufacturers try only to make the best for the money instead of simply the best. Many production managers also disagree with this view because they like to think that they are making the best. *Yet neither quality control people nor production managers can afford to forget costs.* People making Ford Fiestas are not making Mercedes, nor are they going to sell them for Mercedes prices.

Quality control people are likely, too, to wince at the notion that dimension and performance standards for parts and components are sometimes too tight. They like to feel that the standards they so zealously enforce rest on solid ground and not on an engineer's overly tight specification. It is also true, of course, that no one can ever really know that an item 3/1,000 of an inch away from an exact dimension is acceptable whereas 4/1,000 of an inch is not acceptable.

Designers of military products are said sometimes to put in a "military fear factor" (they make parts three times as strong and as exact-fitting as seems necessary). Designers of consumer products also sometimes over-design products. When they do this, the quality standards really ask for too much, and this usually causes unnecessarily higher costs. The parts of a pair of pliers or of a crescent wrench do not have to be made to dimension tolerances (allowable deviations) of thousandths of an inch.

The factory is often accused of being quantity—not quality—minded. Supervisors cannot see why the engineers ask for such exact measurements. Their objections may be a lack of understanding of the need for exactly fitting parts. But they may also be based on the knowledge (knowledge that engineers share) that every specification is of necessity a little arbitrary, just as every speed limit on the highway is a little arbitrary.

Most products with slight imperfections are acceptable for most purposes. A Lenox china dish with a speck of ingrained dirt on the underside is not up to standard, but the dinner guest will probably never know. And if the electric cord on an electric typewriter is six inches short, its performance will in no way be impaired. Neither of these products meets specifications, and both would probably be rejected by the inspectors. But these items are perfectly all right for practically every use. (This is behind the strong growth in generic products offered by supermarkets. These items may not be up to brand name quality levels, but as their labels say, "they are suitable for every day use.") Admittedly, however, it is necessary to draw the line somewhere and to say *this* is acceptable but *that* isn't. It is impossible to escape some arbitrariness when setting standards.

Even more important, products differ and have different advantages and disadvantages. Is, for example, appearance quality? Or is performance quality? Furthermore, competing products are frequently all very good products, but they embody slightly different features. One automobile saves gasoline, another starts more easily in cold weather, another costs more. Is a Ford, Plymouth, Chevrolet, Toyota, or Audi the best car? Is a Black & Decker drill better than a Craftsman (Sears, Roebuck) drill? Also, which is the better buy when price is considered?

Quality is a hard concept to pin down or even detect. Consumers often cannot even tell if there is a quality difference—as, for example, in the case of gasoline, bread, milk, roofing material, and many other items. The customer cannot tell which is best. Mixing in product characteristic differences as well as price differences complicates these comparisons even more.

In the service area, customers don't have quite as much trouble defining good service, but the managers of service organizations do. A Holiday Inn manager wants customers to get good service, but good service is made up of quick service; attentive and sympathetic clerks; clean rooms and bed sheets; plumbing, lighting, television, and air conditioning and heating that work; and quiet atmosphere, as well as good meals and easy check-in and -out—and all at a reasonable price.

Very few of these services are rendered under the direct supervisory eye of managers, to they have to define quality standards for all of these things for their staffs and train them in what good quality is and try to see that the staffs give good quality service.

Service at a Hilton hotel or a Ritz hotel is different, however, from service at a Howard Johnson motel. At the Hilton or Ritz, customers want more personal attention and pay more to get it. Usually, at such hotels, one expects to pay more, to wait longer for a meal, and to take longer eating, but to get a better meal. At the other end of the eating spectrum, McDonald's tries to provide a meal of the customer's choosing but from a limited list of offerings and with no frills—no tablecloths (not even paper), no waitresses or waiters serving meals, no silver (in fact, no knives or forks, other than plastic), and no plates, only a plastic dish.

Perhaps more than in the case of products, people's "bundles of utilities" (what they want) in the way of services differ a great deal. "Good service" is a matter of matching up the quality of the services offered with what certain segments of the market want.

IMPLEMENTING PRODUCT DESIGN POLICIES

We have said that today's managers try to comply with the wishes of society so far as safety and consumer protection are concerned. In order to do this, they may have to set up implementation programs which are in addition to their quality management systems.

The additions are largely in designing products with safety and user protection in mind. Some companies are enlarging the job of the "product engineer" and assigning him this general responsibility. In the past, a product engineer usually had the responsibility for putting a product into production. He determined the equipment needs, saw that it was ordered and installed, and supervised the initial production runs. He did not, however, design the product nor control its quality.

His added responsibility today concerning product safety is one of coordination, communication, and education throughout the entire organization.[6] The product engineer often gets this part of his authority and general directions from the company's "product safety audit program."

As part of this program, each major product periodically undergoes a formal review by an audit group. This group is led by someone from the engineering laboratory. Its meetings are also attended by the director of engineering for the product being audited and by the director of engineering for a totally unrelated product. Other areas represented are design, test, manufacturing, and quality control. All audits for major products are also attended by the director of product safety for all products. In addition, repre-

sentatives of the reliability group and customer assurance and service are present.

At Whirlpool Corporation, the typical product safety audit covers such subjects as:

1. Performance characteristics during normal use, during misuse, and during foreseeable abuse.
2. Nonperformance aspects: construction, clearances, edges, burrs, and so on; electrical, chemical, certifications, codes, standard tests and procedures.
3. Human engineering: man/machine considerations, instructions, cautions, labels, customer exposure to product.
4. Producibility, reliability, life.
5. Serviceability, removal and replacement of components, accessibility.
6. Product identification on packing cartons.
7. Provisions for handling packed products, shipping containers and shipping performance, unpacking procedures and instructions.

If a product is judged by the review group as being not acceptable in any way, suggested improvements are made and a timetable is prepared for corrective action. There is a follow-up on this action to determine compliance.

Whirlpool reports that this approach allows everyone in the company to know their products better and to know what they will do, what they will not do, and how the company will respond to situations involving use, misuse, and even abuse by the users. They find out if their products will tolerate operator errors without causing damage or causing injuries. With this knowledge, the company can lay out programs for improvement.

DESIGNING SERVICES

For some time, the service sector of our economy has been growing at a faster rate than other sectors. Today well over half of the employed

---

[6] The practice of Whirlpool Corporation on this matter is described in H. E. Brehm, "How to Establish a Product Safety Program," *Quality Progress,* February 1975, pp. 28. 29.

people in the United States are engaged in rendering services rather than in producing products. Employment in government work, education, transportation, health care, finance, and other service-type organizations exceeds that of the production-type industries of manufacturing, construction, mining, and farming.

What are the basic differences between designing products and designing services? In a service organization, the service it renders is really its "product." Actually, in many ways, producing services and producing products are not altogether different, although the design of services is a much "fuzzier" activity than the design of products.

When a *product* is designed and manufacturing commences, "What you see is what you get." But *services* are usually less subject to exact definition, and the emphasis is placed upon the people needed to perform the services and their training and on the facilities they will need in order to render the service.

Service organizations are usually more flexible and can change their activities more readily than can manufacturers because they usually do not have heavy investments in plant and equipment. If they change their activities, their office space can be changed to the new uses rather easily. And, if changes in personnel are needed in order to change the nature of the activities, this would be the same for both manufacturing and service organizations. Admittedly, service companies sometimes have heavy investments in equipment, as in the case of airlines and hospitals. But, in most cases, it is easier for service companies to change the nature of the services they offer than it is for manufacturing companies to change to quite different products.

Lines of Services Offered

As we have said, the concept of designing, or developing, services is much more elusive than that of designing products. Services are not something one can hold in one's hand, and they are perishable and cannot be stockpiled. A service not rendered today cannot be inventoried and added to the services to be rendered tomorrow.

Service organizations must decide how wide their lines of service shall be. Should an insurance company, for example, offer both life insurance and property and casualty insurance? Should it have its own claims adjusters, or should the company use independent claims adjusters? Colleges and universities have to decide whether to offer a broad range of courses or to confine their efforts to fewer areas and to do them in greater depth.

Cities also have to make decisions about what services to offer their citizens. Should they provide free trash pick-up or should they let private companies provide this service at a charge to its citizens? Should a city provide day-care centers, job training programs, and extensive public health services? Or should these services be provided by private or nonprofit organizations? Do cities have an obligation to provide bus transportation for people who need it since it is not profitable enough to be done by private companies?

In many organizations these decisions are not open choice decisions. Few organizations have enough money to do everything that they deem worthwhile. In the face of costs rising faster than tax revenue many cities have had to curtail the services formerly offered. Day-care centers, rehabilitation programs, and similar activities are reduced when money is short.

We could go on but these examples illustrate some of the problems faced by service organizations. Nor are there easy answers to most of these questions because they depend on how widespread the demand is, how willing people are to pay for the service, what skills and capabilities the organization's people have, and what its physical equipment is suited to do. Essentially, the providing of a service or the addition of a service to an existing organization's programs needs to be analyzed just as carefully as a manufacturer analyzes the matter of adding a new product to the product line.

Service Availability

When designing services, managers need to consider when the service is to be available. (Eight hours a day? Twenty-four hours a day? Five days a week? Seven days?)

There is also the question of where to locate facilities in order to provide good service and of whether to have only one centrally located facility or to decentralize and have several satellite facilities spread around the market area. The current trend is to provide decentralized service facilities, such as neighborhood health clinics, state unemployment offices, and branch banks. In a factory there are usually several decentralized production control and quality control offices. Maintenance crews, too, are often partially decentralized. These are all responses to the general goal of putting services closer to where the need is so that, on the one hand, people do not have to travel long distances to receive the services and, on the other hand, service people do not have to go far to render these services.

"Servicing What We Sell"

An important part of many manufacturing firms' "total product" concept is servicing the products that they make and sell. For these firms this is one of the strongest competitive advantages they may have. In the computer industry, where products are extremely technical and complex, one of the major competitive advantages that large firms like IBM, Burroughs, and Control Data have is their extensive network of service engineers who are *always* available to respond to a call of a customer whose computer has "gone down." Of course, the service engineers actually spend most of their time doing preventive maintenance so that stoppages in service rarely occur.

Not all firms service what they sell. Rather, they rely on local dealers to handle all "after-sale" matters. Companies making typewriters, refrigerators, washing machines, and any number of other items find it more satisfactory to rely on local repair firms who may also service competing lines, because the volume of repair work is not enough to justify a company-owned chain of service outlets.

Level of Service

The level of service which an organization provides for its customers has to do with balancing its ability to supply the services wanted by customers against the need to operate economically at the same time. The problem that the managers of service organizations face is how to operate economically and yet give customers good service when service calls are irregular. Sometimes the demands for service are heavy in a short time, and sometimes few service demands are made over a long time. In order to give good service there must be enough service people to meet these calls, yet during slack periods they don't have enough to do. The manager has to trade off the cost of waiting customers and waiting employees.

Sometimes the need for quick service is so critical that sufficient capability to meet unusual demands should be available almost on a standby basis. A city should have enough fire-fighting equipment, and it should be located where it can respond to fire calls in minutes. Similarly, a police department's squad cars should be able to respond to a robbery call quickly. In contrast, half a day is not too long to wait until a trash collection truck comes along and picks up the trash.

Chapter 18 will discuss the use of waiting-line analysis and Monte Carlo simulation. These are techniques that aid in analyzing the consequences of various service levels.

Review Questions

1. Describe the objectives of value engineering and value analysis.

2. What is the logic of the metric system that allows measurements to be simplified?

3. What is hard versus soft conversion to the metric system?

4. What are the advantages and disadvantages of our switching to the metric system?

5. Should a manufacturer standardize products? Why?

6. What are the dangers to society from standardizing too soon in the development of a new product?

7. Reliability is a trade-off between product life and cost. Discuss.

8. How does the reliability of a product's individual component parts affect its overall reliability?

9. Summarize the text discussion of reliability but from the point of view of the consumer.

10. How does redundancy relate to reliability?

11. What does the probability of failure have to do with redundancy economics?

12. How does the design of services differ from the design of products?

Questions for Discussion

1. Should a product designer pay more attention to form design (what the product looks like) or to functional design (how it operates)? Why?

2. How can a value analysis analyst do a very good job when he really does not know what it costs to do things in other companies? Besides, he doesn't know how "hungry" other companies are for business and what prices they might, under pressure, quote. Without such knowledge, isn't the analyst limited in what can be accomplished?

3. The designer for a nut and bolt manufacturer has been selected by his company to be a member of an industrywide committee on standardization. What should he want to know and how will he be able to decide what is good for the industry, his company, and the consumer?

4. An administrator says, "Why can't technical people think less about abstractions and more about end products with real market potential?" What can an administrator do to develop a realistic attitude in the minds of his company's scientists?

5. Some companies "expense" their research costs, meaning that they regard them as part of the costs of doing business today. This is in contrast with some other companies which "capitalize" part or all of today's research costs, in which case they regard the capitalized portion of these expenses as an increase in a new capital asset (the partly developed hoped-for new product). Which is the better way to handle such costs? Why?

6. Would you pay more for a hand-made product? Why? If you would, how has mass production failed?

7. Oscar Mayer is famous for weiners. How should a specification writer for this company go about writing specifications for a weiner? What problems would be involved? Is a specification worthwhile here?

8. Who is in the best position to decide whether certain parts and components should be made inside or bought outside? Would a committee help? Who should be on it?

9. How are tolerances usually set? Is there a better way? What should a company do to try to have its tolerances set as reasonably as possible?

10. In automobiles, "soft" springs make for a smooth ride at low speeds. But at high speeds, soft springs cause more swaying. And, when heavily loaded, cars with soft springs ride very low. What kinds of springs should be put into cars?

11. Design is always a compromise, a trade-off of quality versus cost. How can a designer know where to set the performance level? If a company makes carpets, should it make them to wear for 40 years of heavy traffic? Or to wear out in 5 years of light traffic? Should the company go for the $15- or the $30-a-yard business?

12. Make a freehand sketch of the parts of the chair you are sitting on, and show dimensions and tolerances. Discuss the problems involved.

13. An airplane crashes because its altimeter (a purchased part for measuring how high up the airplane is) gave a wrong reading. Who is responsible? The altimeter manufacturer? The airplane maker? Suppose that the altimeter had been in use for a long time; does this affect the answer? Discuss.

14. How do companies manage product safety design?

Problems

1. Modular components are designed so that although each module contains several parts, a module can be put in or taken out as easily as if it were just one part. Almost always the modules are small, and their component parts are quite small—so much so that if one of the small parts fails it does not pay to repair the module. Instead it is removed, like a burned-out light bulb, and thrown away. This means that when one component fails, several good components are thrown out. It costs too much to disassemble the module in order to save the good parts.

   We are dealing with a module whose parts have the following probability of failure rates in 2,000 hours of operation. A: .003; B: .012; C: .004; D: .009; E: .020; F: .011; G: .006; and H: .012. Assume that these parts, separately, cost as follows: A: $.19; B: $.72; C: $.04; D: $.22; E: $.11; F: $.19; G: $.38; and H: $.30.

   These parts have to operate sequentially, but they can be split into two modules between any two components; for example, between A and B, B and C, C and D, and so on. Assembly work costs $.10 more if the parts are split into two modules. Should they be made as one or as two modules? And if the choice is two modules, which parts will go into each module?

2. The Amrine Company offers to deliver five small machines for $1,700 each and guarantees a mean time between failures (MTBF) of 1,000 hours and a useful life of about 5,000 hours. The Phillips Company bid is $2,500 per machine with a guaranteed MTBF of 1,500 hours and a useful life of about 7,500 hours. Breakdowns cost $50 each for repair time and lost production. Replacement parts of the kind needed for the Amrine machines will normally cost $25 per repair. Parts for Phillips machines cost $50.

   a. Which machines should be bought?
   b. How many machines of each kind would operate a year without a breakdown? To answer this question, divide 2,000, the operating hours in a year, by the MTBF. Use the answer as an exponent and raise the fraction 1/2.72 to the power indicated. If, for example, the exponent is 1, then 1/2.72 is simply 0.37. This is the probability that one machine will operate for a year without failure. Multiply this probability by the number of machines to answer this question.

3. Orange Microcomputers, Inc., pays a royalty of $.60 a unit on a component part it manufactures. Royalties are paid at the end of the year and will have to be paid for five years before the patent runs out. Production for this year and the next five years is expected to be 7,000; 8,000; 10,000; 12,000; 12,000; and 11,000, respectively.

   The patent holder has offered Orange the opportunity to pay $25,000 in lieu of all future royalty payments.

   Assuming that money is worth 15 percent to Orange in other uses, what should it do? Show the calculations.

4. In the case of the redundancy example in the text, what would the answer be if part A had a reliability of .94 and part B .92, with all other figures remaining the same?

5. Visit a manufacturing firm which is changing to the metric system. Report on the problems they are experiencing and what advantages they have found.

6. Visit a service organization, and report on the process they went through (or go through) to design their service activity.

Case 5–1

Lifeworks Fitness Center has an excellent reputation for teaching their members how to effectively use their exercise equipment. They insist upon spending three separate one-hour sessions with new members on the machines so they get into a good exercise routine, won't hurt themselves, and use the machines properly.

Currently, they have an experienced instructor take only two members through each of the three different training sessions. This is done by advance appointment, and because the new membership is large, some cannot make appointments for up to two weeks into the future. This has concerned Lifeworks' management, and they are considering starting training sessions for larger groups (15–20 new members at a time) and holding these sessions during off-peak times so the equipment won't be unavailable to the other experienced members. It is anticipated that two or three instructors could service the larger group. However, each of the three sessions might take longer than an hour each. In addition, some of the "personalized" service might diminish with the group workouts. Adding more instructors is not something management will consider.

You have been asked to evaluate the group-training-session proposal. What information would you collect, and how would you analyze it to help you make your recommendation? What trade-offs are involved?

Chapter 6

Quality Management Systems

QUALITY—AN ISSUE OF NATIONAL PRIDE

In 1981, the American Society for Quality Control conducted a comprehensive survey of U.S. consumers to measure their satisfaction or dissatisfaction with the quality of American-made products. The results were disturbing: Almost 50 percent of the people in the poll felt the quality of U.S.-manufactured goods had dropped in the previous five years; further, a little more than half thought that this quality would stay at the same low level or fall even lower in the next five years; 28 percent thought foreign products were better; while 72 percent thought U.S.-made products were no better or worse than foreign-made. Curiously, they simultaneously polled a sample of U.S. chief executive officers and, in this sample, the results were nearly the opposite in some instances. (See Figure 6–1.) In addition, when these same executives were asked to rank the "factors most critical to their firms' success, product quality was ranked fourth behind productivity, rising costs of materials and labor, and government regulation."[1] It seems that U.S. manufacturing has, in the past, not been very responsive to consumers' desire for quality products.

Thus, in recent years, the quality of U.S.-made products seems to not only have slipped but, when compared to many foreign-made products from Japan and Western Europe, the disparity seems even wider in some areas. However, a general statement like this is not entirely fair. U.S. industry does produce a wide array of high-quality products that are the standard for the world. But, nonetheless, there have been severe problems, and this attack on our national pride seems to be creating a strengthening movement to correct it. U.S.-built automobiles are better engineered and of higher quality in 1984 than they were a few years ago. So are our electronic products such as computers, home appliances, and industrial equipment.

Interestingly, much of Japan's emphasis on quality came from the teachings of two statisticians, W. E. Deming and Joseph M. Juran, who in the 1950s went to Japan to extoll the virtues of statistical quality control. At this point in time, a "Made in Japan" label on an item was synonymous with "cheap" and "poorly made." Deming, as a result of his teachings, "has been elevated in Japan to the status of industrial folk hero. The Deming quality control award is now

---

[1] "Quality and Productivity: America's Revitalization," *Quality Progress,* May 1981, p. 24. © 1981, American Society for Quality Control. Reprinted by permission.

FIGURE 6–1
Survey Results of Quality Perceptions of U.S. Products by U.S. Consumers
and Chief Executive Officers

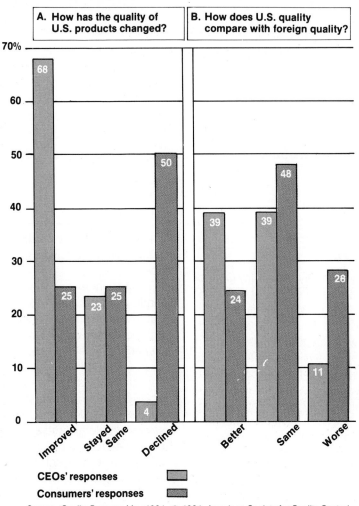

Source: *Quality Progress* May 1981. © 1981, American Society for Quality Control.
Reprinted by permission.

one of the most sought-after prizes among Japanese firms."[2] As a result of this and other characteristics of the Japanese culture and their production methods, "Made in Japan" now means quality.

The reason the United States has been gaining in the "quality war" has been due to a refocused emphasis on product design, where *quality is being designed into the product* from the beginning so that fewer defects occur during manufacture or during use. However, this only solves part of the problem. There is still a need

[2] "How Japan Does It," *Time,* March 30, 1981, p. 57.

for a strong emphasis on formal quality management systems and statistical quality control to ensure that products (and services) meet these tougher design standards. This chapter talks in general about the quality management process and Chapter 7 covers statistical quality control.

SPECIFYING QUALITY

A product's or a service's quality is embodied in its characteristics. The organization's managers decide these characteristics and then they have their designers try to develop products and services which incorporate these characteristics.

The end product of managerial decisions on quality may take the form of quality policy statements. In this form, these statements cannot be used by the factory because they do not contain instructions telling it what to do. They are goal statements. Some samples are:

1. We wish to provide dry cell batteries of such a quality that no more than 2 percent are defective (defective being defined as batteries whose average life in a typical transistor radio is less than 20 hours of playing time or those which leak). Manufacturing cost should be less than 12 cents per unit.
2. The failure rate of our computers should average 130 percent per year (meaning that they will fail on the average of once every nine months). But we will develop a service repair organization and carry spare parts inventories which can provide "same day service" to 95 percent of our customers.
3. In our city we wish to provide a level of fire protection such that the average waiting time of a fire (once the alarm has been turned in) for the first arriving fire engine will be two minutes, with a maximum waiting time of six minutes under normal traffic and weather conditions.
4. We wish to produce a machine part whose diameter is one centimeter $\pm$ 1 millimeter.
5. We wish to produce soap that is 99.44 percent pure.

6. We will make our bread from ingredients which are organically grown and without artificial preservatives.

Most of these quality goals as stated above are not "operationized." The factory cannot make products using only these instructions. Rather these policy statements are in the nature of the delegation or "mission charges" to designers. After receiving such a delegation, the designers, in conjunction with process engineers and industrial engineers, develop the specific instructions which the factory will have to have when it performs the operations which, taken together, implement these policies.

The instructions to the factory take the form of specifications and drawings showing dimensions and tolerances, or they are formulas, processing instructions, and the like. They also cover inspection and testing methods and specify acceptable levels. Again, this aspect of quality management will be discussed in Chapter 7.

All of these instructions are really, however, statements of goals, of desired quality. The factory then tries to accomplish them. But sometimes the factory falls short and fails to turn out products of the desired quality or turns out too many products which fail to pass inspection.

Quality problems are sometimes beyond the control of the production supervisor. For example, perhaps rejects could be reduced by using better materials. If so, top managers will have to decide whether to buy better (and more costly) materials. Or, perhaps the machines are too old and worn to do the precision work required. Managers would then have to choose between high scrap ratios, or rebuilding the present machines, or buying new machines, or relaxing the standards. The responsibility for quality does not rest wholly on factory operators and their supervisors.

Similarly, the quality of the service rendered by service people is not wholly dependent on the attitudes of the service people. Plumbing systems in old hotels are likely to get out of order now and then. And, in the case of an airline, the quality of the service rendered may be almost as much a result of how well the maintenance work is done as it is dependent on the quality of service provided by ticket clerks and flight attendants.

QUALITY MANAGERS

The job of managing the quality function in U.S. organizations usually falls under the quality assurance department and is staffed by professionals, usually engineers, who are versed in testing, inspection, and statistical quality control techniques. Professionals have been trained in these areas in colleges of engineering and/or have been certified through testing by the American Society for Quality Control. Certification is in three areas: Certified Quality Engineer; Certified Quality Technician; or Certified Reliability Engineer.[3]

INSPECTION

The primary quality control implementation activity on a day-to-day basis is inspection. Obviously, products and services should be inspected in order to weed out inferior units. Inspecting products while they are being made also avoids further work on already defective units. But, if these savings are all that the inspector[4] accomplishes, then larger gains are being overlooked.

The primary objective of inspection should be prevention—not remedy. The object is to stop making defective items (or stop inferior service). This requires that inspectors (or production workers) tell management not only that a product is being rejected but also why, so managers can concentrate on improving the situation. Statistical quality control is helpful here because it

is performed right at the operation and helps to prevent the continued production of defective units.

TESTING AND INSPECTION

Testing is a specific kind of inspection. *Inspection,* a broader term than *testing,* includes all activities, among them testing, to see if the products are up to standard. If, to inspect an item, a person has to do more than just look at it or measure it, it is usually called testing rather than inspecting.

Tests may be performance or operating tests, as is depicted in Figure 6–2, or they may be "destructive" tests which end up ruining the particular product being tested. Automobiles that are driven into brick walls for crash testing are an example. The question may be: How much will products stand before breaking? Or, how long will it be before they wear out? In tensile strength testing, for example, the products are broken in the test. A test may also be a chemical analysis of a sample of the product. It too destroys the sample. Not all tests, however, destroy the product. X-ray methods, for example, are nondestructive. Hardness tests, too, are usually nondestructive since they only make a slight dent on the surface of the product. Performance and operating tests (such as driving automobiles on a test track) of finished products are also typically—it is hoped—nondestructive.

INSPECTING PURCHASED ITEMS

As a rule, all purchased items should be inspected to see that they are of the right kind and quantity and so that damaged or unsatisfactory items can be returned to the supplier and new ones obtained quickly.

Most materials and purchased parts create few problems so far as inspection is concerned; yet, this is not true for all purchased *components*. Such things as a specially designed instrument, a hydraulic pump, or an electrical control item are difficult to inspect or test. Receiving inspectors usually cannot tell whether they are good

---

[3] For information regarding this program, contact ASQC, 230 W. Wells St., Milwaukee, WI. 53203

[4] The term *inspector* may apply to a person whose primary job is to inspect. However, in most cases, production workers themselves are also inspectors and are required or encouraged in many firms to make this a part of their job.

FIGURE 6–2
Performance Testing of Two Meshing Gears. The Inspection Job Duplicates Operating Conditions and Shows Whether the Gears Actually Mesh.

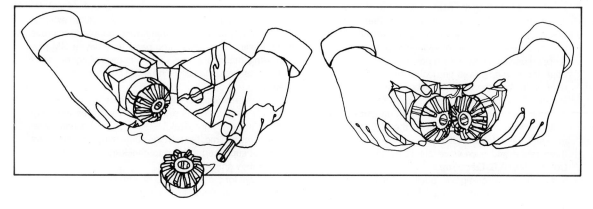

or not, so they need special checking instructions from engineering. Engineers themselves may need to inspect highly technical items.

The receiving department is usually under the direction of the stores department, although it may be administered by the purchasing department. Historically, the receiving inspection department has had little or no direct connection with the factory inspection department but, today, receiving departments often use statistical sampling inspection techniques in its inspection of incoming materials. Thus, it may be necessary for the quality control department to develop the proper methods.

Above we have just said that "as a rule" everything purchased should be inspected, but this rule can be relaxed for materials coming from vendors whose final inspection has proved to be reliable. A company can usually bypass incoming inspection where materials have already passed a rigid inspection in the vendor's plant. Automobile's "big three" have been able to eliminate receiving inspection on many incoming items because they put one of their own inspectors in the vendor's plant to oversee the vendor's inspection of these items before they are shipped. IBM even provides special inspection equipment to its vendors. These "source inspection" or "surveillance at the source" or "certified vendor" programs improve the certainty that only good lots are shipped. And it saves double inspection and the wasted transportation costs of faulty lots being shipped out and then returned. (See Figure 6–3 for a story on how companies put pressure on their suppliers to improve quality.)

FIGURE 6–3

CONCERNS' PUSH TO IMPROVE QUALITY OF PRODUCTS PUTS HEAT ON SUPPLIERS

MIDDLETOWN, Ohio—The executives at Armco Inc., a steelmaker here, decided early last year that they had to change. General Motors Corp. had just passed word that if its suppliers didn't improve quality, they wouldn't be GM suppliers much longer.

Armco's quality record was generally good, but GM made it clear that it wasn't good enough. So Armco adopted a complicated quality control system and a new attitude that Armco executives call "a sort of spiritual reawakening."

"We are changing the culture of this company," says Peter J. Trepanier, Armco's vice president for productivity and quality. "Religion is the only word that describes the response from the people involved in the program."

FIGURE 6–3 *(continued)*

Like GM, a lot of manufacturers these days are determined to improve product quality, and suppliers such as Armco are feeling the heat. In most cases, manufacturers and suppliers are working together, trying to change employee attitudes and improve design, production, and inspection. But sometimes, suppliers are being dropped because they don't measure up. Manufacturers hope the new emphasis on quality will help them compete better with the Japanese. And it should give consumers more for their money.

"We are in direct competition with Japanese manufacturers who have about half of the U.S. microwave market," says John Gildee, director of purchases for three range and microwave plants owned by Tappan Co., a unit of A.B. Electrolux of Sweden. "That provides a real incentive to improve quality, and higher quality parts are essential to accomplish it."

Quality Rises during Slump

Some companies aren't as involved in new quality programs as others, of course. And manufacturers and suppliers admit they still have a long way to go. But some people are encouraged because attention to quality doesn't seem to be slipping as the economy picks up. Quality typically is emphasized during a slump, to give companies an edge on competitors. GM, for example, started some of its quality programs after sales were hurt by the recession and competition from imports. But when the economy picks up and suppliers hustle to meet demand, quality typically falls.

This time, that won't happen as much as usual because "top management throughout industry has gotten a lot more involved in demanding a higher-quality product," says Kenneth J. Semelsberger, executive vice president of Scott & Fetzer Co., a manufacturer. And many suppliers are still producing below full capacity, giving manufacturers the leverage to demand higher-quality parts.

"Suppliers and subcontractors are highly sensitive to our needs because they've seen thousand of other companies in the building industry go out of business," says Victor E. Steinfels, vice president of operations for Cardinal Industries Inc., a producer of manufactured housing.

Changing production methods are also forcing manufacturers to pay more attention to the quality of parts and materials. "As you automate some of the assembly, you tighten tolerances on parts," says Mr. Gildee of Tappan. For example, a person using a screwdriver can adjust the pressure if the screw isn't exactly the right size, "but a machine will twist it off, strip off the thread or fail to tighten it completely."

Manufacturers are prodding suppliers several ways. Above all, they are encouraging an attitude that emphasizes quality, starting with top management. At GM, for example, the interest of top managers puts "an extreme amount of pressure" on purchasing people to improve the quality of materials and parts they buy, a GM purchasing managers says. The purchasing agents pass that pressure on to suppliers. A GM purchasing manager says:

"I tell my suppliers that if my secretary puts a letter on my desk and tells me I better read it before I sign it, I'll throw it right back . . . . It better be right when she gives it to me. I expect the same thing from suppliers. I'm not supposed to have to check the quality of everything they ship."

Then, for the pressure to be effective, suppliers must try to change the attitudes of their factory workers.

"Japanese companies build quality into their products," says James E. Harbour, a Detroit consultant who studies foreign competition in the auto industry and other areas. "Americans aren't building quality in, they're trying to inspect it in" by throwing out defective products after they are made.

Like many other companies trying to change employee attitudes, Armco seeks employee suggestions and has involved workers in what it calls corrective action teams. Armco figures it can save millions of employee hours by building products right the first time; inspecting, scrapping, and reworking products accounted for 10 to 20 percent of manufacturing costs under the old system, the company says.

Manufacturers are also trying to improve quality by reducing the number of companies they buy supplies from, and by working more closely with the ones that remain.

"We want to be important enough to each supplier so he'll give us his best," says Steven C. Mason, president of Mead Corp., a forest products and computer services concern. "We're better off with 3 or 4 suppliers than with 20, none of whom cares that much about us."

At Cardinal Industries, the producer of manufactured housing, close ties with suppliers helped it solve a costly problem. Some of the lumber Cardinal used had been arriving warped because planks got damp during shipment. Cardinal and the supplier worked out a way to wrap the lumber in plastic to keep it dry.

"Our suppliers are becoming an extension of our business," says Mr. Steinfels, Cardinal's vice president of operations. "We expect our suppliers to watch our operation so they know how important quality materials are to our end product. And we expect to participate on their turf, showing them how they can do things differently to ensure that quality."

FIGURE 6–3 *(concluded)*

Pushing Responsibility

Such close ties are part of the reason for the high quality of Japanese products, some say. David C. Clark, vice president and treasurer for Jervis B. Webb Co., a conveyer maker in Farmington Hills, Michigan, says the company's Japanese licensee spends "more time with each supplier so he understands the application for his part in the conveyer system. Then they push the responsibility for quality down to his production workers."

A few purchasers, such as Sears, Roebuck & Co., are so closely involved with their suppliers that they even help design the product and set up the production system. Sears engineers and buyers often visit a supplier's plant, assessing the production process. The visits are a better way to monitor quality than inspecting only the product, says Frank Hartley, Sears staff administrator for buying.

Some manufacturers have persuaded their suppliers to install a management tool called statistical process control. Managers and engineers set standards for the quality of parts or materials, such as the minimum and maximum width of steel sheet. Then products are tested as they are being made; when the quality varies too much, the process is corrected. That sounds like common sense, but engineers say the mix of computers, statistics, and immediate information lets companies catch problems as they occur.

"Previously, it was a judgment call" on when to adjust the manufacturing process, an Armco engineer says. "But when you analyze a process and know what normal variation in the process is acceptable, it eliminates subjective judgment."

Armco says that in the short time it has been using the process, its steel products have had a better finish, more uniform paint coating, and more predictable forming properties.

Many manufacturers are also more rigorously inspecting products after they arrive at their plants. Stanley Interiors Corp., a furniture and draperies concern in Stanleytown, Virginia, samples a portion of each shipment and has a computerized rating system for supplier performance. Daniel Wagner, purchasing manager for Halsey W. Taylor Co., a Freeport, Illinois, company that uses a similar system, says such monitoring quickly exposes "outfits that have poor workmanship in the shop and an attitude of shipping everything they produce."

Mr. Wagner says he recently dropped several suppliers of small metal parts because only 50 percent to 60 percent of their shipments met standards. He requires that 98 percent meet standards.

The changes seem to be working for some companies. White Consolidated Industries Inc., a major appliance maker, made Leon Reid the director of product quality two years ago. In the past 18 months, Mr. Reid says, the number of defective products White makes has declined by 30 percent to 35 percent.

Source: Ralph E. Winter, *The Wall Street Journal,* September 20, 1983, pp. 29 and 56. Reprinted by permission of *The Wall Street Journal,* © Dow Jones & Company, Inc., 1983. All rights reserved.

INSPECTING WORK IN PROCESS

Inspectors actually do very little of all the inspecting that goes on. Each worker inspects his own work enough to see if he is doing the job correctly. (At Hewlett-Packard's Loveland, Colorado, plant, for example, only three inspectors are required to monitor the work of its 900 highly trained electronics workers.) If things go wrong, the supervisor will try to correct the situation. Workers also catch bad work that comes their way from earlier jobs and put it aside for the inspector to look over. Easily seen defects are usually caught this way.

Regular inspection is usually not directed by the supervisors of manufacturing departments. The inspectors in a production department usually report to a chief inspector, who reports to the plant manager or a director of quality assurance. This separate chain of command exists because many manufacturing companies believe it is a good idea to separate inspection from production. They believe managers should not let anyone pass final judgment on the quality of his own work lest this person begin to put quantity above quality. In a sense, a supervisor would be passing judgment on his own work if both operators and inspectors worked for him.

However, more and more companies (IBM is one) believe that it is possible to make both workers and supervisors responsible for both quantity and quality. Also, in many companies, the inspectors who are located along assembly lines report to the supervisors of the lines. And in many Japanese factories, each worker on an assembly line inspects each part they have just produced before passing it on.

Regardless of the method used to inspect work in process, the *final inspection* of the product should probably be done by an independent inspection department which does *not* report to production supervisors. Final inspection, unlike most in process inspection, often includes a performance test. (Performance testing can rarely be used to test partly fabricated products.)

The engineering department sometimes eliminates large amounts of inspection of products during their manufacture by building automatic inspection devices into the machines. Automatic scanning devices and automatic measuring devices are now built into many machines. The machine (or its tool) may even be automatically reset to correct any deviation from standard. The engineering department also designs special devices to allow workers on the job and inspectors to inspect effectively and quickly.

WHEN AND HOW OFTEN TO INSPECT

Because of its cost, it is best to inspect as little as possible while still ensuring that the product's desired quality level will be maintained.

But since some inspection is usually wise, the question is: When and how often should we inspect? Like most issues, it is a matter of cost trade-offs. What does it cost to inspect? However, this is a philosophical question rather than a practical question because in many cases one can never know the opportunity costs resulting from not inspecting. The cost of not inspecting may be the loss of a new customer or a repeat customer. In actual practice, companies usually spend 5 percent (or a little more) of their labor cost for inspection. Here are several general rules about when to inspect:

1. Inspect *after* operations which are likely to produce faulty items so that on more work will be done on bad items.
2. Inspect *before* costly operations so that these operations will not be performed on items which are already defective.
3. Inspect before operations where faulty products might break or jam the machines.
4. Inspect before operations which cover up defects (such as electroplating, painting, or assembly).
5. Inspect before assembly operations which can't be undone (such as welding parts or mixing paint).
6. On automatic and semiautomatic machines, inspect first and last pieces, but only occasional in-between pieces.
7. Inspect finished parts.
8. Inspect before storage (including purchased items).
9. Inspect and test finished products. Be sure that nothing is shipped out without inspection of at least a sample of everything. From here on customers are the "inspectors." If the product fails, they go elsewhere. Worse yet, they tell everybody that this company's products are no good.

Product safety can also determine the "depth" of inspection. Gates Rubber, for example, inspects automobile power steering belts more thoroughly than water pump fan belts. If a steering belt fails, an accident can occur. If a fan belt fails, the car just gets hot. And aircraft components and finished aircraft are subjected to substantial 100 percent flight testing before being released to the buyer. Proper inspection and testing can aid in reducing costly product liability claims made on faulty products.

HOW MANY TO INSPECT

Should some, most, or all of the products be inspected? Ideally, the products should be made so well as not to need inspection at all. Practically, however, it is necessary to inspect some. One of General Electric's plants inspects 5 percent of production during runs of machined parts but goes up to 10 percent for hand-produced items. For extrusions and stampings, it cuts inspection down to 2 percent.

How many to inspect is again a matter of trading off the cost of inspecting against the costs of not inspecting. But here the element of probability is more important than it is in deciding *when* to inspect.

Probability analysis is important because in most cases inspection can and should be done only by sampling. One hundred percent inspection—looking at every item—is often too costly, unless the testing is automated and part of the manufacturing process—which is not uncommon. And, in many situations, 100 percent inspection can't be used in tests which destroy the items tested.

Bulk materials must also be inspected by sampling. It isn't possible to test a coal pile or burn up a tank car of gasoline to find out their heat content or to look at every grain of wheat in a freight car to see if it is moldy. Because of inspection costs, samples are usually used for many items which otherwise could be 100 percent inspected. The determination of sample sizes using probability will be discussed in Chapter 7.

WHERE TO INSPECT

Inspection can take place either at the job or in a central inspection crib. If it is done at the job, it is called "floor" inspection. Both floor inspection and central inspection have advantages and disadvantages.

Floor inspectors, sometimes called "patrolling," "roving," or "first piece" inspectors, move from machine to machine to approve setups before production starts and to catch defective work before a large quantity has been produced. They also check the products of semiautomatic machines from time to time and record the measurements on quality control charts. Defective

operations are caught and remedied before serious loss has occurred.

As a rule, floor inspectors have authority to stop an operation if it is out of adjustment. On the other hand, if the item is badly needed by assembly or the customer, or if the defect can be remedied by rework, engineering may let the operation continue temporarily, even though unusual numbers of defective items are being produced. In some companies, though, only the supervisor can stop an operation. The inspector can require 100 percent inspection, but he is not allowed to order the operation stopped.

Floor inspection saves extra handling of materials and allows materials to move faster through the plant by eliminating their need to be hauled to and from central inspection. Nor do they lie around waiting their turn to be inspected, thus reducing lead time. And, of course, floor inspection is the only possible way to inspect large, unwieldy items such as a 50-ton casting or an aircraft.

One disadvantage of floor inspection is that workers and machines sometimes have to wait for the inspector before they can continue. He may be busy elsewhere when a machine operator finishes setting up a machine, but the operator cannot begin to run the job until the inspector approves the setup.

Another disadvantage of floor inspection is that the inspector has to carry around the inspection tools. Yet it may be impossible to carry around delicate testing or measuring equipment, so inspection that requires this had to be central—if not in a central department at least at the inspector's workbench. Most roving inspectors have a "home" inspection workbench somewhere in the area where they check things that take special gauges or are too difficult to check right at the job.

Central Inspection

With central inspection, materials to be inspected are trucked to a central inspection crib, where they are left to be inspected. Central inspection has several advantages. First, it saves inspector's time because they never have to wait for jobs to inspect. Second, the work can be done by less costly inspectors, who work under close supervision and are away from the pressure of the people whose work they inspect. (Actually, however, central inspectors often do highly skilled inspecting and testing work, using sophisticated equipment, and they are highly paid workers.) Third, special equipment can be used to good advantage at a central inspection location.

But there are some bad features to central inspection. Materials handling and transportation costs are higher because of all the trips that materials make to and from central inspection cribs. And there are more delays, so materials move more slowly through the plant which increases work in progress (WIP) and its associated holding costs. Scrap and rework losses are higher because of the time lag between production and inspection. If anything is found to be defective, a large number of defective units have probably already been turned out before the discovery.

Assembly Line Inspection

Assembly line inspection of mass-produced products is really another type of floor inspection in which inspection becomes just another operation along the line. The inspector, instead of going from job to job, inspects each unit as it comes along. Occasionally, inspection on a sample basis is done. This method is a form of central inspection and is used, for example, for inspecting automobile body tops made of single sheets of steel stamped into the proper form. The contour of the stamped sheet of metal can usually only be checked by taking a body top from the line occasionally and inspecting it at a center, where it can be carefully checked against a master.

The final inspection of a product is usually done centrally. If the product is an operating mechanism, such as an electronic product, it is usually put through a performance test, often by attaching it to a computer-based testing system which simulates the working environment of the item to see if it will operate correctly or fail.

INSPECTION SHORTCOMINGS

Judgment is involved in almost all inspections, even when mechanical devices such as micrometers, gauges, or comparators are used, because there are always borderline cases. Often an inspector has to judge whether a product passes or not. In the case of micrometers, for example, a tight fit—as against a loose fit—probably changes the measurement indicated by at least .0005 of an inch. Plug gauges and thread gauges can fit snugly or loosely. An inspector discovering a slight blemish on a surface must decide whether it is bad enough to justify rejection.

The inspector must decide whether the item passes or not, and the decision is important because they are the ones that enforce standards. If they pass products which should be rejected or reject products which should pass, they are really making a new and unofficial set of quality specification standards for the company. Care should be taken to be sure that inspectors do not substitute their own standards for those set by engineering.

Inspectors are human beings; all of them make errors once in a while. In central inspection, the work is often repetitious and monotonous. Fatigue may cause the inspector to miss some of the bad products. And, even if he or she is not tired, at best surely *some* of the bad ones will be missed.

In one study of the amount of defects missed by inspectors, 100 defective items were mixed in with a large lot of good ones. The inspectors were not told about the experiment. Then the entire lot was 100 percent inspected by regular inspectors, who found only 68 of the defectives. Still without telling the inspectors, the lot (with the remaining 32 defective items still mixed in) was sent through inspection again as if it were another lot. This time the inspectors found most, but not all, of the defective items. The process was repeated a third and a fourth time, after which 98 bad ones had been found; but 2 of them were still in with the good products.

The results of this little experiment may be surprising. What kind of inspectors do such poor work? Well, they *are* just human; they *do* miss things now and then. Also, they do have to pass judgment. Maybe they saw the two defectives but decided that they were not bad enough to reject. Suppose a person has to look at 100 pieces of toast in a restaurant and decide which are too burned to serve to customers. Or a professor has to "inspect" the examinations of 100 students and decide who passes and who fails and must repeat the course. Factory inspectors don't pass judgment on toast or students, but some of their deciding is just as difficult. We must recognize that inspection is partly subjective.

Managers should be careful about letting inspectors think they are using their own judgment. The inspection procedure should eliminate as much of the judging as possible. Still, inspectors like to judge and to think that they have superior judgment. They prefer the kind of judging which allows them to pass things not in accord with the drawings. If the specifications say "Cadmium plate .003 inch thick" and the plating is .0025 inch, the inspector would like to judge that it should pass. (After all, the engineers have sometimes accepted such items before.) Again, managers should be careful that inspectors do not set and follow their own standards.

REDUCING INSPECTION ACTIVITY

Most inspection requires handling the product being inspected; the piece is picked up, turned over, and put down. This is repeated every time a product is inspected during its manufacture. It all adds up to quite a few inspectors doing a great deal of manual work. Repetitive manual jobs, including inspection, can often be mecha-

nized. Even the visual part of inspection can sometimes be transferred to the machine. In the automobile industry, for example, mechanical selectors sort oversize valves from undersize valves and put each in with other valves of the same size. In the bearing industry, ball bearings are sorted mechanically to size.

Sometimes it is unnecessary to know a part's exact size but only that it is between two limits and not beyond. This lets inspection time be reduced by using go/no-go gauges which incorporate the two dimensions but show no measurements. They have two slots, one for the product's smallest and one for its largest acceptable dimension. A part which can slide into the small slot is too small; a part which will not slide into the large slot is too large. If an item does not fit the first slot but does fit the second, it is within limits. Go/no-go gauges are so simple that inspection can be done by unskilled people.

Still another approach to the problem of cutting inspection costs is to improve the machine so that it does not get out of adjustment. Such machines (for example, the presses and dies that make automobile fenders) can turn out only good pieces when they are set properly. All that is necessary is to inspect the first few pieces, and then another piece occasionally to assure that the machine is still in adjustment.

Finally, probably the best way to reduce the need for inspection by inspectors is to install a sense of pride of workmanship in each worker and, within reason, let them be responsible for checking their own work and reporting problems as they occur.

PROCESS CONTROL

A different approach to the problem of mechanizing inspection is to build machines which check their own work. This is called *process control*. Some of today's machines will stop if out of adjustment. Others will even correct their settings so they are put back into adjustment. For example, thickness gauges on calenders in the paper, rubber, plastic film, and linoleum industries give continuous readings of the thickness of the material being produced, although usually they don't automatically reset the machine if it gets out of adjustment. Martin Marietta, for example, runs test tapes on their numerically controlled machines to check tolerances before they begin working on parts. The inspection of the work turned out by these machines now is usually done by microcomputers which analyze hundreds of performance checks every minute and then adjust the machine if it needs it.

In fact, with the movement toward more automation through computer-aided manufacturing (CAM, see Chapter 19) and robotry, more and more process control exists, and it usually is built into these machine systems.

SELECTIVE INSPECTION

Selective inspection is sorting inspected parts by size so that over- and undersize parts can be matched. This is important where parts have to fit together and work as mating parts. Selective inspection cuts the losses which would otherwise be suffered where close fits of mating parts are necessary. Instead of rejecting or reworking parts just over or just under the tolerance limits, they are put into piles by size for use with mating parts having offsetting discrepancies in size.

Automobile motor blocks are an example—they have holes for the pistons. If inspection shows that one or more of the holes is either too large or too small, the block does not need to be reworked or thrown away. Instead, each hole is matched with a piston that fits. This is not hard to do because some of the pistons come out a little too large and some a little too small. Similar matching up of slightly varied parts is done in many situations, even in ski manufacture, for example. Since each ski is a little different, they are sorted and matched into pairs so they will perform equally on the slopes.

Obviously, this process should not be carried too far. Products which vary too much from the standard should be reworked or scrapped.

Also, assembly work is a little more complicated with selective inspection because the parts are not completely interchangeable. But, properly operated, selective inspection is not only economical but actually makes a good product since, in spite of the fact that the parts are imperfect individually, they are matched to compensate so that the assembled product operates with well-fitting parts. This will not matter for future repairs because, after the product has been used long enough to need repairs, the repair parts are not going to fit perfectly—no matter whether the original block and pistons fitted perfectly or not.

INSPECTION AND TESTING EQUIPMENT

Quality standards are often so high that the inspector cannot, by looking at a product, tell whether or not it is acceptable. Here, special gauges and instruments are required. These special gauges and instruments, themselves, need periodic checking and resetting; otherwise they too get out of adjustment. IBM's Boulder, Colorado, plant, for example, does this kind of work in a "metrology laboratory" which checks delicate instruments and resets and recalibrates them. In order to ensure extreme accuracy, the work is done in humidity- and temperature-controlled rooms.

The computers in this lab can "talk" to the computers at the National Bureau of Standards. They use a special machine, a Ziess Precision Measuring System, which costs $600,000. Using a part or unit which is the "standard," the machine probes its precise measurements in up to five dimensions. These measurements are translated into computer language and are then used to both make and recalibrate gauges and instruments.

A factory inspector may have to check many characteristics, such as dimensions, smoothness of surface, contours, hardness, strength, ductility, resistance to abrasion, ability to withstand flexing, resistance to rust or wear, internal strain, shrinkage, chemical analysis, plasticity, viscosity, color, fastness of color, solubility, life of the product in use, efficiency and speed of operation, electrical connections, and other things.

Sometimes the test simulates the product's use (or even abuse) to see how long it lasts before failure. In other cases the item is used in its normal way until it wears out. Light bulbs are burned until they burn out. Auto tires are put on cars and driven day and night till they wear out. Paints are put on trial pieces and put out on the roof to see if they will fade in the sunlight and how they weather. Most tests give answers about a product's acceptability right away; but with "wearout" tests it is necessary to wait for answers.

For close measuring (such as detecting variations of less than 1/1,000 of an inch), inspectors need some kind of magnifier or electronic inspection gauge. There are also magnifiers which throw an enlarged shadow of the product's outline on a screen, where its proper contour or size can be compared with the specified contour already marked on the screen. And today there are surface smoothness gauges which are accurate to a millionth of an inch. There are even devices to gauge the thickness of a coat of paint. Automatic electronic sorters, which sort items by size, have already been mentioned in connection with selective inspection.

In inspection, infrared rays can detect minute separations in bonded or laminated materials. X rays (beta rays) are used to take pictures through opaque materials, just as a dentist takes pictures of teeth. Internal flaws show up as dark spots or as being different from the surrounding material. X rays are not very powerful, however. To take a picture of a casting, or forging, or a welded joint by directing rays through it, it is necessary to go to gamma rays, which are many times more powerful.

Both beta and gamma rays are also useful for measuring the thickness of paper, steel, plastic sheet, and the like, or even an electroplated coating. The accuracy of the measurements can range down to millionths of an inch. Radioactive materials are also sometimes mixed in in minute quantities with other materials (perhaps metal for making into castings) or into fluids. Later, by detecting the strength of the emissions in various spots, it is possible to study the flow of the metal or fluid.

In another application of science to inspection, the steel industry uses pictures of the spectrum of light to show the chemical makeup of steel in the making. A photograph is taken of the spectrum of light coming from a "heat" of molten steel. The lines that appear in the spectrum show the chemical elements present, and their width shows the amount of each element. The pictures can be taken and developed quickly, thus permitting corrections to be made in the chemical composition of the heat before it is poured. TV cameras also are used to show operations which are otherwise impossible to watch—as inside a furnace or vat or machine. TV tapes are sometimes used, so the scene can be played over again and studied if anything went wrong.

Robots, too, are being used in testing and inspection. At Lunkenheimer Valve, robots test the quality of gas and fluid regulation valves. Valves are fed to the robot, which tests them on a test console for a leaky seat or shell. It then deposits good valves on one conveyor and rejects on another.[5]

Bendix Automation and Measurement Division also has produced a new robot-based, high-speed, automated inspection system which is five times faster than conventional inspection equipment. Called the Quadrax, it can be programmed to measure hole and shaft sizes, distances between parts parallel or at angles to each other, and other relationships. The robot is controlled with a microcomputer and can work in such unfriendly environments as auto assembly, but it can measure nearly as accurately as ultra-accurate laboratory machines.

Laser-based automatic inspection systems

---

[5] See John Mihalasky, "Robots: Their Impact on the Quality Function," *Quality Progress*, October 1978, pp. 12–15.

FIGURE 6–4
A Sketch of a Laser-Based Inspection System

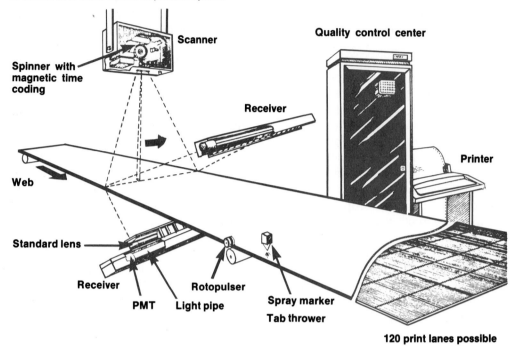

Source: *Quality Progress,* December, 1981, © 1981 American Society for Quality Control. Reprinted by permission.

are also now available and are used primarily for the inspection of the manufacture of continuous sheets of material such as paper, plastic sheeting, or film. This is called *continuous web* production. Laser inspection devices (see Figure 6–4) not only improve the automatic detection of defects but allow it to be done faster. In one application inspecting cross-laminated film used as backing for packaging materials, the company was able to increase the speed of their manufacturing line by 600 feet per minute because of the accuracy of the laser equipment.[6]

ONLINE AND ONLINE–REAL-TIME QUALITY MANAGEMENT

More than ever before, quality management today is being directed toward the *prevention* of

faulty work, so that its cause can be eliminated. Often computers are used, and often they are "online," and "online–real-time."

Being "online–real-time" means that that operation is connected at all times to a central computer or has "satellite" or "distributed" mini or microcomputers located at several key operations which are tied to the central controlling computer. The machine's or the process's output is constantly monitored and defects are reported in "real-time," or *now.* The computer keeps track of the defects as well as of the good units turned out. Should the *ratio* of defectives go up, the computer reports this to the person whose job it is to control the process, or, in some applications, the computer automatically adjusts the process.

Some companies have online systems which are not real-time because operations are

---

[6] "Laser-Based Automatic Inspection Systems," *Quality Progress,* December 1981, pp. 26–27.

not directly connected to the computer. Instead, there are a number of remote terminals in operating departments into which inspectors enter frequent reports. Each reporting station serves as a report center for several operations. They are often at "buy-off" points, where the products go from one department to another, such as weld, paint, electrical, and final assembly line.

It might seem that such a system would not be of much help since the only new thing about it seems to be the quick reporting. But in large factories quick reporting and the quick recognition by the computer that the ratio of defects is going up can be very helpful.

Picture, for example, how helpful it must be in Chrysler's Mound Road plant in Detroit, where they use the method we have just described. This automobile assembly line is two miles long and has 1,200 people spread along it. Some 1,500 cars are in the system at any time. Each car has 6,400 parts and 4,500 welds. There are some 4,000 points where defects can occur. Even when things go well, there will be some 30 defects per car, or 15,000 defects in an eight-hour day. Most of these details are minor, and almost all of them are discovered and remedied.

The point to online reporting is, however, that the computer watches *trends.* Inspectors are busy watching for defects as such, and they are not likely to notice *trends* in defects. The computer keeps track of every kind of defect reported and calls immediate attention whenever the ratio of defects is going up. Chrysler reports that its online quality control has paid big dividends.

At Ford Motor, computer systems are used to enable quality control technicians to read, process, analyze, and plot up to 200 separate measurements on their cars undergoing performance tests on their test track proving grounds.

At Martin Marietta Cement online–real-time computers monitor the chemical characteristics of the raw materials in six different storage "silos" as they feed material into the central mixer. Every 10 minutes a sample of materials from each silo is drawn and tested in a "specto-graphic analyzer," which measures the composition of the minerals in the sample. The computer then uses these measurements and solves a linear programming model which determines the proportional blend of materials from the six silos to be used so that the least amount of the most costly ingredient, limestone, is used. Then the computer adjusts the feed screws from the six silos to put this "least-limestone-use" solution in effect. Nine minutes later, the process is repeated.

Online–real-time feedback can also be given directly to operators working on a line. This feedback, however, need not always be computer-based. For example, at Lamb Weston's huge french-fried potato processing plant near American Falls, Idaho, a simple yet effective quality feedback system is used.

This plant processes about 250,000 tons of potatoes a year into french fries (primarily for McDonald's) and potato flakes (for Pringle's). One specific job that many of their 1,200 employees do along a conveyor system (which carries thousands of potatoes per hour) is to cut out the "eyes" and bad spots in potatoes which have been previously peeled in a chemical solution. This has to be one of the duller jobs industry has to offer, and, as a result, minds tend to wander, "eyes" slip by, and quality slips. To keep the peelers alert, Lamb installed a series of multi-colored "traffic light" devices along the line. Quality controllers simply turn the lights to green when quality is acceptable, yellow when it begins to slip, and red when it becomes unacceptable.

In the semiconductor industry (microprocessors, computers on a "chip," and so on) tiny chips are 100 percent tested by special computer systems which have probes which successively "hook up" to each of the hundreds of chips at a time which are printed on small pieces of silicone. These systems test the circuitry of each chip in an instant, and, if one is faulty, it automatically marks it with a felt-tip-like pen so it can be discarded when the silicone disk is cut into the hundreds of chips which are on each one.

DISPOSITION OF REJECTED MATERIAL

Rejected parts and material are rarely thrown out. Often they can be salvaged by rework operations and cycled back through the manufacturing process.

If this can't be done, or if it is too expensive to do to a rejected item, they can often be made into other items, perhaps smaller-sized ones. Or often the rejected material can be sold as "seconds," as is done with dishes, tires, day-old bread, "generic" items in supermarkets, and the thousands of other things sold through "damaged merchandise" discount stores.

Illogical though it may seem to be, there is still another way to eliminate rejected parts and material: to treat them as if they had passed to start with! And do it with the engineering department's approval! Some companies have material review boards to pass on rejected material. These boards include everyone who will be affected by the fact that the items may be rejected: the superintendent, the chief engineer, and, in the case of aircraft, the customer (often the government). This often happens where parts are not quite as perfect as they should be, but where the product's operation will be affected little if at all.

This sounds as if standards are set up and then disregarded. But, actually, the standards are not disregarded. The point is that sometimes no harm is done if a borderline lot is passed. Yet passing borderline products should not be a regular practice. If an automobile tire tread is supposed to be a centimeter thick and it comes out nearer to 1.1 centimeters, this does not hurt the tire if it is still in balance; customers just get more rubber than they are paying for. Or if the gasoline gauge in an automobile dashboard is supposed to be 6 centimeters from the speedometer but the hole for it in the dashboard is 5¾ centimeters away, it can be passed. Or if electroplating is supposed to be a certain thickness and it is more, this does no harm. There are cases where the specification can be relaxed

without harm being done. Yet such "relaxations" should be individual decisions, not the general practice.

Another important reason for relaxing standards temporarily comes from the practice of carrying practically no inventory of parts when a firm is practicing "just-in-time" purchasing methods. This gets a company into a jam every time there is any delay in parts supply. If many parts are held up, the assembly department will soon have to close down (and then all other parts departments). This is a case where one of top management's policies (to hold inventories down) has an effect (loosening up on quality) that they probably do not want and in fact is rarely recognized as a consequence of their just-in-time inventory policy.

If a lot of internally manufactured parts are rejected which would close down the final assembly department, engineering—rather than close down the plant—may give in and approve passing the lot "just this once, but don't let it happen again." The same thing can happen with purchased parts. If an assembly department is almost out of the parts which the inspector wants to reject (and for purchased items it may take weeks to get a new supply), the question becomes: Are the defectives bad enough to justify closing down operations, or can they be passed? Again, there is a strong temptation to say OK—pass them this time, but don't let it happen again. But of course it *does* happen again. Actually, these temporary relaxations rarely seem to cause many problems—the products still work and work well. It makes one wonder if the standards were not too high in the first place.

Of course, vendors were not born yesterday, and they know all about hand-to-mouth JIT inventories. So when a customer rejects a lot and returns it, the returned goods inspector in the vendor's plant may just put the lot to one side. Sooner or later the customer will be very anxious for an extra shipment, which he can get only if he accepts the previously rejected lot. They are the only ones available. The vendor gets rid of the substandard lot and helps the customer out of the tight spot. Customers will eat burned toast when they are hungry and there is nothing else to eat. This policy by vendors might work once or twice, but sooner or later the buyer will catch on and look for a new supplier.

Quality standards are, therefore, somewhat flexible. If a factory is to operate effectively, quality standards must yield at times to pressures which conflict with their strict enforcement.

Reworking Rejects

Generally, rejects are either clearly scrap or reworkable. To rework them, additional—and often different—operations are needed, depending on the nature of the defects. Defective items are sorted according to the kind of defect, and the rework operations for each group are decided upon.

All rework is an extra cost which should be charged to the department responsible for it. But this is not always easy to determine. Suppose that a coat of paint tends to flake off. Is it the purchasing department's fault for buying the wrong kind of paint for the job? Or did engineering fail to specify the right kind of paint? Or is the material under the paint the right kind? Or did the shop fail to get the right surface finish on the piece? Or did the clearning department fail to get every bit of oil off the surface?

Some products, because of difficulty in making them to quality standards the first time, have extensive rework required as a matter of course. Graphite tennis racquets made by Head is an example. Their graphite molding process produces "raw racquets" with slight imperfections which must be filled with graphite putty, sanded, and otherwise reworked to meet their high standards.

"Work Away"

In some industries it is possible to "work away" unacceptable materials by mixing them, a little at a time, into future mixtures. Off-color material,

for example, can be put into mixtures of dark materials in the rubber, glass, and paint industries, thus saving the full value of the raw materials. If chemical mixtures contain too much of certain chemicals, they can be mixed into new batches that are intentionally made up with too little of these chemicals. This is what Martin Marietta Cement does. By law, they cannot ship defective cement, but they can "recycle" it into future mixtures. And Samsonite grinds up the plastic in rejected suitcases and simply uses it over again.

Work away, as a way of salvaging rejects, is sometimes used by vendors in a somewhat questionable manner. A customer rejects a certain lot of materials—say, nuts and bolts—because they find it contains 3 percent defectives whereas the contract said no more than 2 percent. The customer sends the lot back, and the vendor merely mixes it with the next lot, and back they all come as part of the next shipment. This is not always as bad as it sounds. If the next lot started with only 1 percent bad, the new mixture will be 2 percent bad, which is the quality specified.

QUALITY CIRCLES

Involvement of production workers in job improvement and quality improvement and control has always been around to some extent, but only in the last few years has this process become more formalized. Again, we have taken our lead from Japan where their extensive quality circle programs abound and account for part of their success:

> In Japanese plants and factories, workers are not only encouraged, but actually expected, to make quality control their top priority. At Matsushita Electric, the country's second largest electrical company (1980 sales: $13.7 billion), workers are instilled with the notion that each one of them is a quality control inspector. If they spot a faulty item in the production process, they are encouraged to shut down the whole assembly line to fix it. Pressure to improve quality reaches beyond

the shop floor and often pits entire plants of competing companies like Hitachi and Sony in furious statistical battles to produce the lowest defect rates for products.

The Japanese today look down on what they regard as the poor quality of American products. Kenichi Odawara, professor of economics at Sophia University in Tokyo, recently published a book on the problems of the U.S. economy and workmanship entitled *The Great American Disease*. One example of that disease is familiar to any Japanese car dealer attempting to sell an American-built automobile in Japan: the cars have to be given an additional coat of paint before they can satisfy the demanding Japanese.[7]

Quality circle programs are now spreading throughout U.S. industry and government in both manufacturing and service. Many of them have been successful; however, some programs which are poorly managed have produced poor results or have been scrapped.

What Is a Quality Circle?

A quality circle consists of a small group of production workers (or engineers, or office clerks, or salespeople, or quality inspectors, or welfare counselors, and so on), who meet regularly to identify a broad array of problems related to their task and work toward developing ways to solve them. The problems may relate to minute production activities; to the cause of product or service defects; to the way they communicate with their supervisor; to the way their workplace is arranged; and anything else that *they* deem to be a problem with meeting output quantity and quality goals set by management.

After an initial training period on how to identify the priority problems and how to do creative problem solving, the circles (with the aid of a "facilitator" who usually is not their boss) are "turned loose" to work on problems. After a reasonable time, they present their recommendations to management. (See Figure 6–3).

---

[7] "How Japan Does It," p. 57.

Quality Circles Must Be Taken Seriously to Be Successful

Quality circles have been effective in improving overall quality as well as improving job methods and other workplace-related activities if they are taken seriously by management and by the circles themselves. If management gives them "lip service," that's what they'll get in return. Well-run programs often have a staff of professionals assigned to support the circles by providing them with information and other services needed to make progress.

The Quality Circle Program in a Commercial Bank—An Example

As mentioned earlier, quality circle programs exist widely in service organizations as well as in manufacturing. As an example, the following describes one bank's program:

There are 135 quality circles in operation at the bank with an average of eight members per circle. These circles have been implemented in such diverse areas as systems, check processing, operations, and accounting.

Each operating unit involved with the circle process determines what individual policies, procedures, and guidelines should be set for its quality circle operation. This is achieved through individual steering committees that review implementation plans and the progress of individual circles.

Allowing all employees the opportunity for circle membership required a network of part-time facilitators who could train supervisors to be group leaders and assist with member training. Representatives from each unit's facilitator group meet on a monthly basis to share experiences, concerns, and insights regarding the circle process.

Supervisors are trained in three-day sessions for circle leadership responsibilities. This training includes the subjects of motivation, group dynamics, communications, as well as eight audiovisual modules which introduce topics such as Pareto analysis, cause-and-effect diagrams, and problem prevention. Role-playing, case study exercises, and discussion periods round out the seminars. Four of the audiovisual modules are used to train all employees in a given work unit. After completing this training, the employees are given the opportunity to volunteer for quality circle involvement. Those individuals who volunteer are trained in the remaining four modules for which the circle meets once a week. We have found this method to be effective in orienting employees in circle operation, concepts, and responsibilities.

The projects which are worked on by our circles are selected by the members, although any interested employee, staff person, or manager can suggest topics. Examples of project themes include new procedures for handling claims, balancing with the Federal Reserve, a glossary of bank terms, reduction of paper costs, and improved handling of customer inquiries.

Management support of circle activities has been overwhelming. Unit managers have given immediate and positive attention to circle recommendations. They have committed people and other resources to the process. And most importantly, they are actively involved themselves with individual circles in their area.

While the jury is still out on the success of our quality circle program, we are happy with the results of our first nine months of operation. Our overall participation rate is 65 percent of potential circle members.[8]

Review Questions

1. The text says that "quality" is a hard concept to pin down. Yet a factory has to make products of specified quality. Why not always try to make the best?

2. Students were visiting a factory which makes ready-made dresses for sale by Sears, Kmart, and other chain stores. A student asked how they determined the quality of the cloth, belts, zippers, and so on. The answer was: "We start with the price, subtract a profit and cost for making, and use the best materials that we can afford to buy with what is left." Comment on this practice. Is this a good way to set selling prices?

3. Has the perception of the quality of U.S.-made goods changed in the past few years?

4. "Quality control starts when the product is still on the drawing boards." Discuss this statement. Shouldn't it both start and finish there?

5. How can product designers resolve the cost/valve problem when customers want different things? How can a designer ever settle on a design?

6. Why do supervisors often think that engineering sets tolerances too tightly? Is there any merit to their position?

7. Discuss the matter of supervisors being responsible both for turning out work and for supervising the inspectors.

8. "You can be sure if it's Westinghouse." So why should a company buying parts from Westinghouse spend money to inspect incoming products which are almost always perfect? After all, Westinghouse gave them a thorough check before shipping them.

9. How should a company go about deciding how often and how many items to inspect? What kinds of rules or guidelines should be issued to the factory?

10. If maintaining quality is so important, why not always use 100 percent inspection?

11. Compare floor inspection and central inspection, giving the advantages and disadvantages of each.

12. How reliable are inspectors? If they carry out 100 percent inspection, how certain is it that the outgoing quality is all that it should be? Discuss.

13. What happens to rejected materials? Is this bad? Discuss.

14. "Selective inspection represents a compromise and weakens the enforcement of quality standards." Comment on this statement.

15. What is the purpose of a quality circle, and how does it work?

Questions for Discussion

1. There is always someone who can make it cheaper—but weaker or poorer. And there is always a customer who wants it that way. What should be done about this?

---

[8] C. A. Aubrey and L. A. Eldridge, "Banking on High Quality," *Quality Progress,* December 1981, pp. 18–19. © 1981, American Society for Quality Control. Reprinted by permission.

2. Do you think the overall quality of U.S.-made goods and services has improved in the 1980s? Support your answer with examples.

3. Which is the better buy, a deck of Bicycle playing cards bought at a variety store for $1.50 or a deck of Congress playing cards bought at a gift shop for $2.50? What makes your choice the better buy?

4. The Firstline Company makes the "best electric iron you can buy." But one of its competitors makes the cheapest. Which is the right policy? Why?

5. Pick some commonplace minor item, such as a pair of scissors, a paper stapler, or a ballpoint pen. Decide on and define its quality. What are the critical characteristics which you think should be inspected for?

6. Customers might have trouble deciding whether a Ford, Chrysler, or Chevrolet is the best car. What is actually the best? What makes it so?

7. Assume that you have been appointed general manager of the division making the car you put at the bottom of the list in Question 6. You are told to make it the best of the three, but you must still operate at a profit. What will you do?

8. A college student got a summer job in an automobile factory loading seat cushions onto the supply conveyor which took them to the workers on the final assembly line. He came to a cushion with a badly frayed spot, which obviously made it defective, so he reported it to his supervisor and asked what to do. "Load it on," he said. "Maybe no one will complain." Discuss.

9. The text says that "how often to inspect" depends on the cost of inspecting versus the cost of not inspecting. How can a company find out what it costs *not* to inspect?

10. In an aircraft factor, it is necessary to test the fuel lines and develop a test which will ensure that the lines which pass will operate 150,000 hours without a failure.
    a. How can 75 years of use be simulated?
    b. Suppose that after a simulation of 60,000 hours, the line being tested fails. What has the company learned? What should be done?
    c. Suppose that the sample unit does not fail. What does this tell the company? (The question is how much a sample of one can reveal about the other items not tested.)

11. Free service during guarantee periods on new cars costs over $200 a car. Why not spend more on inspection at the factory and cut down on this expense? Discuss.

12. A company has decided to use incentive pay for its inspectors who look for defects in instrument "clusters" that go on the dashboard of the automobiles it makes. What should be done about defects? Should an inspector be paid less for clusters found with defects? Or should he be paid more? And if the decision is to pay more, may it not cause the inspector to pull a wire loose once in a while in order to raise his pay? Discuss.

13. Are American workers too detached from the products they make to care much about quality? Discuss.

14. What conditions must exist for a quality circle to be successful?

Problems

1. A machine is starting on a run of 500 parts. This will keep the machine busy for four hours at a cost of $15 per hour. The machine has been set up by its operator, a relatively unskilled worker, at a $6 cost, so it may not be set up just right. Rejects may therefore be 5 percent—decidedly more than the probable 1 percent rejects if a regular setup mechanic had prepared the machine.

   The concern here is not with making up the lost quantities but with whether or not a regular setup mechanic should check the setup before the operator starts the job. If he does check, the total cost of added machine dead time, plus the idle operator, plus the setup mechanic's own cost comes to $9.

   Forty percent of all rejected products have to be scrapped, at a loss of $.58 each. The other 60 percent of rejects can be repaired at $.30 each.
   a. Should the setup mechanic check the setup?
   b. Will it pay to check the setup if defects would otherwise be 4 percent? What is the break-even ratio, where it doesn't matter whether the setup is checked or not?

2. If a part A is not inspected carefully, the 3 percent defectives which are produced will all go through.

If they are inspected carefully, one third of the rejects would be caught, thus raising the quality of the parts passed along to the customer to only 2 percent bad. Should careful inspection be done if the cost of inspecting is $.01 per unit and the cost of each defective is $4? What would the answer be if inspection cost $.05 per unit? At what point would it be a toss-up?

3. Supplier A charges $15 per 100 and sends products of which 3 percent are defective. It costs $2 to inspect 100 units and to catch 90 percent of the defectives, which are scrapped. Defectives which get through and into assembled products have a 50-percent chance of causing a $25 damage. Supplier B charges $14.50 per 100 and sends 5 percent defectives. From which vendor should these items be bought?

4. In Problem 3, supplier A suggests a sliding price scale, depending on how high a quality is desired. He proposes this scale:

Price per 100	Percent Defective
$14.00	10.0
14.25	7.5
14.50	4.0
14.75	3.0
15.00	2.5

Using the other figures from Problem 3, which price-quality offer should be accepted?

5. A machine has been developed to produce a special product. It costs $9,000 and will probably have a five-year life and no salvage value. Interest is at 15 percent. This machine produces five units an hour and can easily produce the 8,000 units needed in a year. The total cost of operating this machine (excluding depreciation but including the operator's wage) is $8.80 per hour.

The machine produces 6 percent scrap. Scrap products lose all of the $7.30 per unit cost of the materials used.

a. What is the cost of each nondefective unit?
b. How much could the company afford to spend

to rebuild the machine so that it would produce only 2 percent defectives?

6. The normal scrap loss for four successive operations is 2, 6, 10, and 20 percent, respectively. How many units should be started through in order to finish with 1,000 pieces? How much machine time will be needed if the operation times are 4, 2, 7, and 4 minutes, respectively?

7. If the normal scrap loss on the milling operation is 5 percent, on the following slotting operation it is 6 percent, and on the following drilling operation it is 4 percent, how many pieces should be started into production in order to get 180 finished pieces? Suppose that the operator actually spoils 11 percent on the milling operation; how many pieces short is the order likely to be after the last operation? If the order needs 180 pieces, and it is held up until a replacement lot can be brought up through milling, how many pieces should the replacement lot contain?

8. A product can be made from grade B material, which costs $1 a pound (each unit requires one pound of material) and takes $2 in labor to make one unit. The supplier suggests to the customer company that it buy grade A material, which costs $1.25 a pound but probably would save 5 percent of the labor.

Products made from grade B material are 4 percent defective, but half of them can be repaired at a cost of $.75 each. The other half are scrapped, resulting in the loss of both the original material cost and the labor cost. Grade A material is claimed to reduce rejects from 4 percent to 2.5 percent, half of which can be repaired, also at $.75 each.

The customer company thinks there is perhaps a 50–50 chance if it changes to material A that the supplier will be proved correct in his claims. But there is a 50–50 chance that there will be no improvement at all, even if the material is changed. Since certain processing adjustments will have to be made if material A is used, the company wants to feel fairly sure that changing is the better thing to do. Should the company change to material A?

Case 6–1

Consider that in the following paragraph, all letter *f*s are defects. Inspect the whole paragraph once and count the defects. Mark down your count. (You can check the count later for accuracy.)

"Effective quality control in manufacturing enterprises, in office operations, in service functions, and in job shops has undergone many innovations of late. From early times it has been presumed that if you had few inspectors and they were on the ball, your quality of product would be OK. If your firm still adheres to this outmoded concept, you may be missing an immense potential for quality improvement and defect elimination for your operation. If this test demonstrates anything, it should show the difficulty of finding all defects, even if you have 100 percent inspection. Far better to never build defects into the product in the first place. How can this be done? Many firms have found the total approach to quality control called *zero defects* is the only systematic way to achieve perfection in quality, but it does mean that from first to last you'll have covered most of the possible loopholes in purchasing, receiving, material control, process design, and shipping and packing, at which key points in final product quality are checked out. Above all, ZD is a team effort, which should energize the entire organization toward a common goal. If you'd like to discover how this method has worked and test its possible application to your quality problems, why not enroll one or more of your supervisory management teams in the seminar offered by the University of Michigan's Bureau of Industrial Relations. The time will be well spent."

How many *f*s did you find? Have three other people count the *f*s. What do the results of this experiment tell you about the reliability of 100 percent inspection?

Chapter 7

Statistical Quality Control Systems

While good product and service design and a highly motivated and caring work force are necessary for maintaining proper quality output, it is still necessary to have formal quality planning and control systems in place to assure that quality objectives are being met.

Statistical quality control (SQC) applies the theory of probability to sample testing or inspection. A great deal of inspection work has always been done by sampling; a small part of a certain lot of products is inspected and its quality is assumed to be the quality of the lot. This is called *statistical inference*. The characteristics of the entire lot or "population" are inferred to be like the sample. Sampling, however, has some risk because it is always possible that a sample will not have exactly the same characteristics as the lot.

Years ago, before statistical quality control methods were developed, no one knew how much risk was involved. Often larger samples than necessary were inspected. These entailed wasted inspection costs. For other items, higher risks than realized were taken, resulting in, at times, more defects than desired being passed by inspectors. This allowed costs for defects to be too high. With the development of statistical quality control, inspection is more reliable, and

it allows for balancing off of these costs as their least costly combination.

Statistical quality control deals with *samples* and their reliability as indicators of lot characteristics. Sampling inspection, where it can be used satisfactorily, eliminates most of the cost of 100 percent inspection, and it is the only possible method for products which must be tested until they fail or break (as in tests of length of life or tensile strength). Sampling is also the only way to test the chemical or physical characteristics of liquids and powdered or granulated material, or the thickness gauge of sheet metal, paper, and cloth. Sampling is therefore desirable in many cases because it saves money. And in other cases there is no other way to inspect.

Statistical quality control does not create risks, nor does it eliminate risks. With or without statistical quality control, there is always some chance that any sample from a lot will not be exactly like the rest of a lot. The objectives of statistical quality control are to *show how reliable the sample is and how to control the risks.* It lets managers decide the risks they are willing to take (that bad products will slip by or that good products will be rejected). they can then decide whether it will cost more to catch the possible bad products or to let them go and save inspection costs. They can make a conscious decision about how much risk they want to assume. SQC also helps control processing by warning managers if machines are getting out of adjustment so that they can be reset before many defective products are made. Figure 7–1 shows the interaction between quality control and production. (Again, it should be noted that much inspection and some testing goes on *within*

production operations and is not entirely performed as a separate function.)

SQC procedures which check products already completed are called *acceptance* sampling. This is where most of the "risk controlling" applies. But SQC (still using samples and still dealing in risks) can also be used to *control processes while things are being made*. Not only does SQC indicate when a process is out of adjustment and turning out bad work, but it warns the operator if the machine is getting out of adjustment. It monitors operations and indicates drifts toward defectives. This *preventive* quality control can reduce defectives and cut losses due to scrap.

AREAS OF USE

Statistical quality control has three general uses: (1) to control the quality of work done as individual operations while the work is being done; (2) to decide whether to accept or reject lots of products already produced (whether purchased or made within the company); and (3) to furnish management with a quality audit of the company's products. A fourth result—checking the reasonableness of the quality standards and setup specifications—is generally accomplished, more or less, as a by-product of SQC in operations.

When statistical quality control is used to control operations, samples of products are checked from time to time, and their *measurements* are plotted on "control charts." Since it is impossible to make two absolutely identical products, some minor variations in measurement always occur, even when the machines are in adjustment. A machine will occasionally produce an unacceptable item, even when it is in adjustment, because the material being worked on may vary or a cutting tool may be dull. Control charts show when operations are producing too many unacceptable products and indicate to operators when they need to reset their machines.

Statistical quality control for accepting or rejecting entire lots of products ("acceptance" sampling) usually deals with the *proportion* of

FIGURE 7–1
The Quality-Production Interaction System

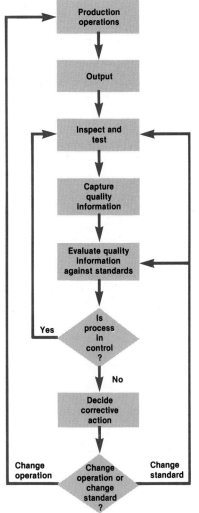

rejects found in a sample. When a lot contains considerably more or considerably less than the allowable proportion of rejects, this will usually be revealed by even a small sample. Additional samples need be taken only when the small initial sample provides borderline (or near borderline) results.

Statistical quality control for quality auditing also operates on a sample basis. Faults in sam-

ples of completed products are classified according to their seriousness, and demerits are assigned (see figure 7–2). Major defects—those which will interfere with the product's salability or its operation or which might be dangerous— may be assigned, say, 25 to 50 demerits, depending on the seriousness of the defects. Minor defects, which might shorten the life of the product or increase its maintenance costs, may be

FIGURE 7–2
Portion of a Demerit List for Quality Defects

Item	Dem.	Defect Description	Item	Dem.	Defect Description
		DEMERIT LIST—STEP-BY-STEP SWITCH MECHANISMS			
		1. ELECTRICAL			Rotary pawl springs:
101B	50	Breakdown between *(parts)* on *(specified)* voltage	2010C	10	Opening in loop exceeds specified limit
		Cross or ground between *(parts):*			Rotary pawl play:
102A	100	Affecting circuit, not readily corrected	2011C	10	Rotary pawl binds
					Vertical position of rotary armature:
102B	50	Affecting circuit, readily corrected	2012B	50	No overlap
			2012C	10	Overlap not as specified
102C	10	May affect circuit	2013C	10	Rotary pawl position not as specified
103C	10	Clearance between insulated parts insufficient			Rotary magnet position:
		Open circuit:	2014C	10	Rotary dog and ratchet tooth clearance not as specified
104A	100	Not readily corrected			
104B	50	Readily corrected			
		Current flow; release magnet coil:	2015C	10	Armature does not strike both magnet cores
105B	50	More than 10% outside of specified value			Rotary pawl front stop position:
105C	10	10% or less outside of specified value	2016C	10	Clearance between rotary pawl and front stop not as specified
106C	10	Armature does not release after operation on specified current			Rotary pawl guide position:
			2017C	10	Rotary pawl tip does not strike tooth as specified
107B	50	Contacts dirty; breaking continuity	2018C	10	Normal pin position:
		2. MECHANICAL			Rotary pawl does not strike first tooth in same relative position as other teeth
2001C	10	Bank or wiper contacts not cleaned or treated			

Source: Western Electric Company.

assigned 10 demerits. Incidental defects, such as appearance blemishes, may be given 5 (or even only 1) demerits, depending on their seriousness. Ratios of the numbers of demerits found, per unit of product inspected, can be compared for products made at different periods of time. Ratios can also be combined to get department—or even plant-wide—averages to use in further comparisons.

Quality audits are not just limited to defects detected *before* they are sold. Hewlett-Packard, for example, maintains a worldwide product defect surveillance system which classifies product failures in the field. This information is fed back so SQC, engineering design, and manufacturing can take corrective action, as shown in Figure 7–1.

An SQC by-product is the evaluation of the reasonableness of tolerances and specifications. SQC may reveal that the standards cannot be met satisfactorily with the company's existing labor skill levels and machines. If so, the labor force need to be trained or upgraded, or the company may have to invest in better machines. Or, finally, if the rejects are still high, the managers may have to relax the standards or simply "live with" high reject rates.

SQC may also show that the design itself is faulty. If individual parts meet all the quality standards but the finished product still does not perform well, then the fault is in the design and not in the manufacturing processes.

ATTRIBUTES AND VARIABLES

When inspectors look at a product and say "It passes" or "It is a reject," they are dealing with *attributes*. But if they measure "how much," "how thick," "how round," and so on, they are dealing with *variables*.

A distinction needs to be made between attributes and variables because they require different statistical procedures. Attributes deal with *percentages* (or proportions) of products rejected. Variables deal with *averages* of measurements and the *extent of the deviations*. Attri-

bute inspection is most important in acceptance sampling—inspecting products away from the operation and after considerable quantities have been made—as in the case of purchased items. Variable inspection is more important in controlling operations as they are being performed because most of it is done at the job.

Attribute inspection is used (1) when items are obviously good or bad (an alarm clock rings or it doesn't); or (2) when the characteristics cannot be easily measured, thus forcing an inspector to judge them (as in the degree of shine on a polished surface or deciding whether a soldered connection is good enough); or (3) when a characteristic can be measured but the exact amount is not needed (as when go/no-go gauges are used to inspect for size). Most inspection of metal, glass, cloth, or painted surfaces for cracks, scratches, or surface irregularities, and most inspection of color finish are attribute inspections.

Most measurements of dimensions, however, as well as types of length-of-life tests, are inspection of variables. The tested items always differ somewhat, and it is necessary to tabulate and analyze the frequency of each measurement.

REPRESENTATIVE SAMPLES

As mentioned earlier, the entire lot from which a sample is taken is called the "inspection lot," the "total population," the "parent population," or the "universe."

If statistical quality control is to operate successfully, samples *must* be "representative," meaning they *must* have about the same characteristics as the lots from which they are taken. In SQC, the word *sample* always refers to a representative sample. It does *not* mean a nonrepresentative, nontypical, or poor sample. When samples are referred to as "random" samples, the intent has been to obtain a *representative* sample. A random sample from a barrel of material would include materials taken from the top, middle, and bottom of the barrel. A random sample of automatically machined products should include items taken at the start of the run, a few periodically during the run, and a few at the end.

Products being sampled should be, and usually are, homogeneous (the same throughout). If they are not—if some tote boxes of parts have more bad items in them than other boxes—the inspector must be very careful to see that he gets a representative sample. He should, for example, draw part of the sample from every tote box or at least allow each box to have an equal chance of being included in the sample. In fact, the inspector should always do this, whether he suspects that the various boxfuls are of unequal quality or not.

In factory inspection, ordinarily only one universe, such as a shipment of products received from one vendor or one run of products from an automatic machine, needs to be considered at a time. It is desirable, however, to consider each day's output from automatic machines as a separate lot. A random sample of each day's, or each hour's, output should be inspected separately in order to catch gradual changes in the products which might be caused by tool wear or by the machine's gradually getting out of adjustment.

SIZE OF SAMPLE

It seems logical that large samples should be more reliable than small samples. One might even suspect that if one sample is twice as large as another it would be twice as reliable. Large samples are more representative of the population but not at all proportionally better. We can't say exactly *how much* better a large sample is because, whereas a sample of 20 is considerably more reliable than 10, there is almost no gain in reliability if a sample of 1,000 is increased to 2,000—yet, in each case the sample size is doubled. In fact, in the inspection of variables, the gain in reliability from inspecting a sample of 300 instead of 200 is rarely worth the added inspection costs. Sample sizes in the hundreds

are usually quite reliable, depending, of course, on how *much* variability there is in the population being sampled and how tightly the item is to be controlled. From there on, little reliability is added by inspecting more pieces. For attribute inspection, typical sample sizes need to be a little larger, but they, too, become quite reliable at the 300 or 400 level.

Even small samples are almost completely reliable for lots whose items are quite good or quite bad. When inspecting variables, a sample size of 25 will produce virtually conclusive results if it is found to be *much better* or *much worse* than the limit of acceptability because it is very unlikely that a sample will be very good or very bad when the entire lot is not correspondingly good or bad. A sample of 100 pieces, in such a case, would add little to the reliability of the results found in the smaller sample. But, if a 25-piece sample turns out to be of borderline quality, it is not so certain whether the whole lot should pass. Inspecting a 100-piece sample adds a great deal of certainty that the lot is either good or bad.

Another matter is the size of the sample as it relates to the total population. The reliability of a sample *does not depend* on its *proportion* of the total population; its reliability is almost entirely dependent on its own *numerical* size. The size of the whole *lot* has little effect on the *sample's* reliability. A sample of 200 taken from a lot of 5,000 is almost as reliable an indicator of the whole 5,000 as a sample of 200 taken from a lot of 1,000.[1] Yet, in the first case it is a 4 percent sample as against 20 percent in the second case. This fact, used in sampling inspection, permits considerable inspection cost savings by confining the sample to the smallest practicable quantity. Only very small samples, proportionately, need to be inspected from large lots.

Eastman Kodak sets the sample size for much of its inspection by using the following for-

---

[1] This slight improvement in reliability can be estimated with a finite population correction factor, which is explained in most statistics texts.

mula (in which *n* is the sample size and *N* is the whole lot):

$$n = \sqrt{2N}$$

Using this formula, a sample of 200 would suffice for a lot of 20,000. Eastman inspects larger samples for products it thinks might be of uneven quality. But the largest samples, even if Eastman suspects that a lot is of uneven quality, are limited to 2.5 times the usual sample size, or 500 in the case of a 20,000 lot.

Sometimes, no matter how large a sample is taken and how sophisticated the quality control system is, enough "bad" items slip through which can be disastrous. For example, *The Wall Street Journal* reported that H. J. Heinz had to shut down its production process for instant dry baby cereal because of the *fourth* complaint over metal particles found in the food. Heinz "recalled" about 600,000 boxes from the market. The total cost of the recall was $250,000.

THE NORMAL CURVE AND THE STANDARD DEVIATION

Statistical quality control is based on the concept that no two things are exactly alike. And that when either people or nature try to make identical products, their actual sizes will vary from small to large with most items being close to the middle size. The most frequent size will be the middle size with less frequent items being at the larger and smaller extremes.

The count of items by size, when plotted on a chart, usually approximates a "normal" or "bell-shaped" curve. See Figure 7–3. Occasionally the curve is pulled off to one side ("skewed"), showing that there are more extreme deviations above the norm or more extreme deviations smaller than the norm. However, even if there is a pronounced variation from the normal distribution, and the sample is large enough (generally more than 30), with a simple adjustment in the calculations, misshapen distributions can be made the equivalent of a normal distribution. This can be done because of the *central limit theorem,* a basic concept which lies

FIGURE 7–3
The Normal Curve Distribution Pattern Which Lies behind Statistical Quality Control

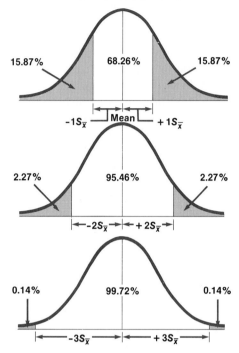

behind statistical inference and is discussed in basic statistics texts.

In a normal distribution there is a progressive tapering off of the number of items above and below the point of greatest frequency, which itself is the highest point on the curve and is in the middle of the curve. This highest point is the average measurement (the "arithmetic mean") of the series. Expected variations in measurements of individual items from the mean can be determined on the basis of the way the data vary when the overall pattern follows the normal curve.

SQC deals with samples, not entire lots. Each item of a sample is measured. Then a tabulation of the frequency of each measurement can be tabulated and plotted on a chart. Usually this chart will turn out to be a bell-shaped curve but based on perhaps 50 to 100 measurements rather than 10,000 measurements for an entire lot. The distribution of measurements between large and small in the sample will be about the same as in the parent population. If the sample is of reasonable size and is random, it will be representative of the whole population but with some *error*.

Thus, with statistical quality control it is also necessary to calculate this error which is called the *standard deviation*. The standard deviation for a population is indicated by the Greek letter sigma, "σ." The letter *sigma* refers to the standard deviation for the whole population, which is actually never known when samples are used. When a sample is used, the standard deviation of the measurements of the items in the sample is denoted "*S*." This *S* is then adjusted for possible non-normality of the population to obtain $S_{\bar{x}}$. $S_{\bar{x}}$ is called the "standard error of the mean of the sampling distribution." Its formula is:

$$S_{\bar{x}} = \frac{S}{\sqrt{n}}$$

where *n* is the sample size.

In a normal distribution, as shown in Figure 7–3, the mean $\pm 1\ S_{\bar{x}}$ sets limits between which 68.3 percent of the measures of the products in the population are expected to lie. The mean $\pm 2\ S_{\bar{x}}$ sets limits which include 95.5 percent of the measurements while $\pm 3\ S_{\bar{x}}$ sets limits which include 99.7 percent of the measurements.

An example will show how this works. If a part 4 inches long is being manufactured, close measurement will show that the parts vary in size, most of them being close to but not *exactly* 4 inches long. The arithmetic mean of the pieces in our sample, however, should be almost exactly 4 inches. We will say that the mean length of the parts in our sample is exactly 4 inches and $S_{\bar{x}}$ as calculated from our sample is .002 inches.[2] Therefore 4 inches + and $-1 S_{\bar{x}}$ is 4.002 and 3.998 inches respectively; so 68.3 percent of the population measurements (or very close to it) are expected to lie within these limits. Calculating $2 S_{\bar{x}}$s produces measurements of 4.004 and 3.996 inches. These measurement limits

include 95.5 percent of the cases. Three $S_{\bar{x}}$s out each way, or 4.006 and 3.994 inches, include 99.7 percent of the cases.

Statisticians have developed short-cut methods for doing the calculations. An example demonstrating a short-cut for setting control limits for control charts is shown in Figure 7–5.

SQC is also helpful in the cases where *extremes* are important as, for example, with the weakest link in a chain. It is all very good for the average strength of each link in a chain to be well above the minimum, but, even if *one* link is too weak, the chain breaks. Charts can be set up so that attention is focused on such extremes.

In other cases *consistency* is more important. Suppose a company buys two lots of ⅛-inch (.1250 inches) diameter ball bearings. And suppose lot A's mean is .1248 inches but lot B's mean is exactly .1250 inches. But *within* lot A the individual balls range between .1247 and .1251 inches, while in lot B, with the perfect mean, the individual size range from .1240 to .1260 inches. Which lot would probably work out to be the best? Probably lot A, because no ball bearing varies more than 3/10,000 of an inch from the specified ⅛-inch size, while in lot B some vary as much as 10/10,000 of an inch. Many SQC applications deal with this matter of consistency.

Whether the interest is in means, extremes, standard errors, or percentages, statistical quality control is directed (1) toward obtaining measurements, test scores, or percent defectives of items in the sample; (2) to computing the combined measures for the sample; (3) to comparing the combined sample measures to preset scales showing the limits of acceptability; and (4) if the measures exceed the limits of acceptability, some action must be taken to remedy the situation.

CONTROL CHARTS FOR OPERATIONS

Books on statistical quality control do not furnish precomputed control charts for general use. In-

---

[2] We will show how to calculate $S_{\bar{x}}$ later in this chapter.

FIGURE 7–4
Steps in Setting up a Control Chart

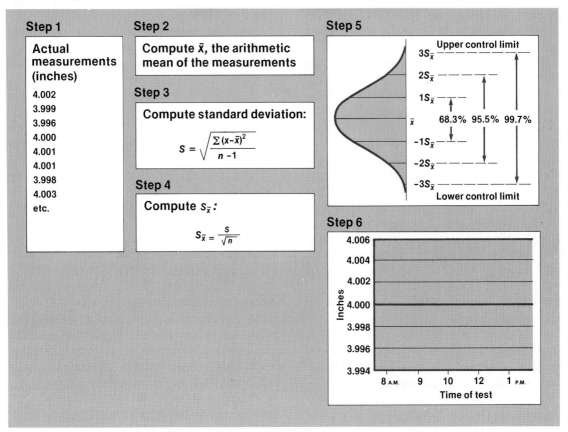

stead, they explain how to develop and use control charts. This is because every control chart has to be unique for the operation it serves.

Figure 7–4 shows the steps to go through for setting up control charts—the end product of a process that starts with collecting and analyzing certain figures about an operation. This has to be done separately for *every* job where control charts are to be used.

To develop a control chart, it is first necessary to measure each item of a random sample of items produced by an operation. Suppose that 40 such measurements are made of parts intended to be 4 inches long. The mean of the 40 proves to be 4 inches exactly and $S_{\bar{x}}$ is .002 inches, as in our earlier example.

$S_{\bar{x}}$ is computed by the formula shown in steps 2, 3, and 4 in Figure 7–4. First, determine the sum (Σ) of the squared differences between each measurement (x) and the arithmetic mean of the measurements $(\bar{x})$; divide this numerator by the number of measurements in the sample, minus one; take the square root of the above calculation to obtain S. $S_{\bar{x}}$ then is obtained as shown in step 4.

The 3 $S_{\bar{x}}$ control limits (3.994 and 4.006 inches, respectively) are then plotted in along a vertical measurement scale, as is done in Figure 7–4.[3] Horizontal lines are drawn across to

---

[3] Traditionally, control charts are set up with ±3 $S_{\bar{x}}$s. However, for tighter controls, something less than ±3 can be used.

the right to "fence in" the area of acceptable measurements. The horizontal scale is a time scale for plotting the measurement taken periodically throughout the day.

Before using a control chart on a regular basis, however, it should be checked against the job's specified tolerance limits. The 3 $S_{\bar{x}}$ limits are 4.006 and 3.994 inches, respectively. If the specification says 4 inches ±0.10, then the operation can proceed because all of the current production is well within the 4.010 and 3.990 limits. But if the specification says 4 inches ±.004, then only 95 percent of the products will pass. The operation will probably have to be improved or the specification relaxed.

Now that the control chart is set up, it is used by having the inspector in the factory measure a very small sample of products (as few as three to five every half hour or so) and plot the mean of those measurements on the chart, as is done in Figure 7–6. If one of these means falls outside the control limits, something is almost certainly wrong with the production process. This is called *assignable* or *cause variation* because almost always the variation can be said to be caused by the machine being out of adjustment, bad material, or operator error. If the mean fluctuates *within* the control limits, these fluctuations are called *chance variations* and are regarded just as normal variability representing the best that the machine, materials, and operator can do.

The point is that when the plotted data fall outside the control limits, this serves as a signal, and the inspector and the operator are warned to stop the machine and get it back into adjustment. Some companies also show lines on the chart for ±2 standard errors. When the means being plotted get beyond these limits, this serves as a warning that the machine is getting out of adjustment, and although it is not yet off far enough as to be producing rejects, it is moving that way.

As we said, however, statisticians have developed short-cut methods for determining control limits for control charts. Suppose we plan to inspect a sample of four every half hour after the chart is set up. First it is necessary to take a random sample of items, say as many as 40. These measurements should *not* be sorted into any order (as from large to small). They should be used just as they come.

For *each* set of four, its mean measurement is calculated, as is its range (the difference between the largest and smallest item in the set of four). This produces 10 means and 10 ranges. Next, the *grand* mean should be calculated (by adding the 10 subsample means together and dividing by 10). The grand mean range is calculated the same way (by adding the 10 subsample ranges together and dividing by 10).

Reference can now be made again to Figure 7–5. Reading down to four, the number in our subsample, we find the factor: .73.

The upper control limit is obtained by multiplying the mean range by .73 and adding the result to the grand mean. The same amount is subtracted from the grand mean to get the lower control limit. Let us assume that the pieces are supposed to be 4 inches long and we find that the grand mean is exactly 4 inches and the mean range of the 10 samples is .009 inches. Multiplying .009 by .73 gives .006. Adding this to—and subtracting it from—4 inches establishes control limits of 4.006 and 3.994 inches. We can now plot these lines as the control limits on the control chart.

FIGURE 7–5

Number in Each Small Sample	Factor
2	1.88
3	1.02
4	.73
5	.58
6	.48
7	.42
8	.37
9	.34
10	.31

CONTROL CHARTS FOR VARIABLES

We have been talking about controlling the means of subsamples, but there is usually a need to control variability as well. Two pieces, one 3 inches long and one 5 inches long, average 4 inches long. But this is not much comfort to an assembler who wants two pieces each 4 inches long.

Variability is controlled by paying attention to the *range* (the difference between the largest and smallest items in the samples). Control charts to monitor the range are developed in almost exactly the same way as charts to control means. Short-cut methods are also available to allow these charts to be set up in a matter of minutes.

The example we just used to illustrate the development of a control chart dealt with a dimension. It required *measuring* the subsample items, so it dealt with a *variable.* It also dealt with the average size and variations from the average.

Control charts of this type are called *"x̄-charts"* (x̄-bar charts). And, as we said above, sometimes the interest is in the *range* between the largest and the smallest. Sometimes there is more concern about the product's *consistency*—the usual variations between sizes. Charts can be developed to control any or all of these. These are called *"R charts"* (for range).

Often there is also a need to watch two or more variables at once. If so, it helps to combine their charts and put one directly below the other, as in Figure 7–6. Here we have combined an x̄ and R chart. This makes charting simpler, and it ties together the results from each sample because they are all charted on the same vertical line. In Figure 7–6, for example, the 10:30 A.M. sample of five items averaged 0.877 inch in diameter, and the largest item in that lot was 0.004 inch larger than the smallest, as shown on the R chart.

Control charts are usually kept near the machine they are controlling. A worker or an inspec-

tor checks a small sample of the product periodically and plots its average size on the chart. Or, with an automated process control system, the measurements are plotted on a lie detector-type printer which, if any of these averages are beyond the permissible control limit, indicates the products are unacceptable and the operation should be stopped and corrective action undertaken. Some of these automated systems have alarms that go off when a control limit is exceeded.

CONTROL CHARTS FOR ATTRIBUTES

Attributes are "yes or no" characteristics; products pass or they don't pass. These items may or may not be measured, and, if they are measured, it is not to determine their exact size, but only to determine if they are acceptable or not. Sometimes it is either impossible or very difficult to measure the quality characteristic (as the shininess of a polished surface or the excess solder on an electrical connection), so the inspector just decides. Sometimes there is no need to measure anything (a glass tumbler has a crack in it or it doesn't), so there is little problem deciding. Instead of measuring every item in a sample, the inspector (or an automated measuring device) just looks at each one and decides whether its attributes are acceptable or not.

P-Charts

Control charts for attribute inspection (sometimes called P-charts) are based on the *proportions* (or percentages) of products rejected by the inspector. Constructing control charts for attributes is usually less time-consuming than charts for variables because the inspection itself is generally less expensive (the items usually don't have to be measured).

To construct a control chart for attributes a random sample of items is first drawn (the sample size for attributes is usually much larger than for variables). The sample is 100 percent in-

FIGURE 7–6

A combined $\bar{X}$ and R chart in use. Samples are taken periodically during the day and the sample means and ranges plotted.

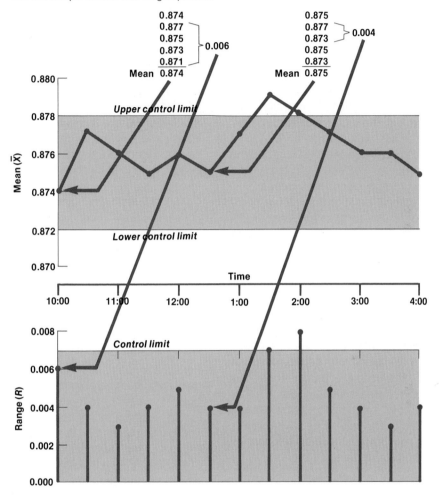

spected, and the proportion of rejects in the sample is determined. For example, if a sample of 200 items yields 10 rejects, the rejects would amount to 5 percent. The next step is to calculate the "standard error of a sample reject proportion" (this is similar to $S_{\bar{x}}$, except it is for reject *proportions* instead of arithmetic means of measures). This is calculated by the formula:

$$S_{P_s} = \sqrt{\frac{P(1-P)}{n}}$$

In our example:

$$S_{P_s} = \sqrt{\frac{.05(1-.05)}{200}} = .0154$$

Next, control limits similar to those for variables control charts are set up. In this case, the control limits of $\pm 3\ S_{P_s}$ would be .05 + (3 × .0154) = .0962; and .05 − (3 × .0154) = .0038. Rounded off, the control limits would be 9.6 percent and 0.4 percent. If the process normally produces 5 percent rejects and this is considered acceptable, then future individual samples with rejects between 9.6 percent and 0.4 percent would be acceptable as being within normal process variablity.

Attribute charts show both upper and lower control limits. If 5 percent rejects are normal for an operation and the control limits are 0.4 percent and 9.6 percent, why have a lower limit? It would seem to be a good performance to get rejects down to as near zero as possible. This is of course true, but, if rejects actually go below the lower limit as set from past data, the job is not being run the way it used to be. Going below the lower limit reveals that there probably has been some kind of change in the process.

If managers could be sure that such a good performance (on the record) resulted from improved and cost-effective practices, they would look no further into the matter and would set up new control limits to cover the new performance. But, if the record is going below the lower control limit, this justifies investigation because the "improvement" may be coming from wrong reasons. Possibly inspectors are passing too many items which should be rejected. Or possibly the workers are producing better but fewer products. If the workers are working more slowly and carefully, this increases unit costs. If either of these things is happening, management should weigh the cost trade-off of having fewer rejects. It may prove to be less costly to continue the higher proportion of defects.

C-Charts

Not all attribute control charts deal with proportions. Some deal with *ratios*—often the number of defects per 100 feet of the surface or length of a product. These are called *C*-charts. Defect ratio charts are set up the same way as other attribute control charts. Defect ratio control charts are helpful in controlling surface defects in metal, wood, or paper, insulation defects on wire, air bubbles in glass, and imperfections in a bolt of cloth, in rolls of film, and on painted surfaces. In most of these cases the defects are

not repaired; they are just accepted as facts. But, as before, the control chart sets limits which are considered acceptable.

Ratio charts are constructed much as are charts for variables and proportions. The only difference is in the way the standard error is calculated. Suppose, for example, that we wish to develop a ratio chart for controlling the number of blemishes on the surface of steel coming out of a continuous steel-rolling mill. Here we have a situation where the number of possible blemishes is extremely large—virtually all over the steel's surface. Suppose that our inspection procedure here is to count the number of blemishes in each 10 feet of steel and, if there are "too many," the rolling process is adjusted or possibly shut down. (This counting is usually done automatically by computer-connected scanning devices such as the laser-based system discussed in the previous chapter (see Figure 6–4), but analysts must set the control limits which signal problems.)

Using the Poisson Distribution for Constructing *C*-Charts

For situations like this, the calculation of the standard error is usually based on a probability distribution different from the normal distribution. This is the Poisson distribution. Suppose we randomly sample 100 10-foot sections of steel coming out of the rolling mill and count the number of blemishes. The result is a total of 2,000 blemishes, so the arithmetic mean per 10 feet is $2,000/100 = 20$ blemishes. The standard error for a Poisson distribution is simply calculated as $\sqrt{20}$, which equals 4.47. The upper control limit would be $20 + (3 \times 4.47) = 33$ blemishes. The inspector (or the monitoring computer) would count the blemishes in 10-foot sections, and, if they exceeded 33, corrective action would be undertaken.

Use of Control Charts in Service Organizations

The control charts mentioned above can be used to monitor the behavior in many other areas besides parts or materials production.[4] They can be used to monitor costs, sales, absenteeism, errors in keypunching, typing, and many other clerical "production" activities. Thus, they are useful for service organizations as well as in manufacturing. In law enforcement, they can monitor the *ratio* of convictions as compared to arrests; traffic violations to accidents per day; and so on. In health care, online computers are given control limits to monitor a patient's critical functions such as heart beat, temperature, and respiration rates. And fleets of trucks, taxis, or repair vehicles' use of tires, gas, and costs of repairs can also be monitored with control chart procedures.

Banks, too, can apply statistical quality control to their operations. One bank controls clerical errors with control limits on proportions of defects, as shown in Figure 7–7. Notice that their standards (shown in column 6) range from .004 percent to .3 percent, and that their upper and lower control limits (UCL/LCL) are shown in column 7. The bank uses this system to calculate a quality control index (QCI) each month. Since they had problems in two areas of "missing items" which were out of control, the month only received an overall quality performance of 80 percent.

Even so-called chartists in the stock market and pension fund and mutual fund portfolio managers use control chart-type procedures to monitor prices of the often hundreds of stocks and bonds they buy and sell.

ACCEPTANCE SAMPLING

Acceptance sampling means accepting or rejecting entire lots of completed products on the basis of the number of defects in the sample. Inspectors are told how many pieces to inspect and how many bad items to allow: so many, or less, and the lot passes; more than that, and the lot is rejected.

Most often acceptance sampling is found in the receiving inspection department, where receiving inspectors check in the things that the company buys. Acceptance sampling is used less in fabrication or assembly operations because control charts or online computer systems are usually used to monitor these ongoing operations. Large lots of end products are rarely completed and *then* inspected.

Acceptance sampling is usually attribute inspection rather than variable inspection. And even more than the case of operations control charts, acceptance sampling is a matter of calculated risks because it deals with large quantities of already finished component parts. There is always a chance that bad lots will be passed or that good lots will be rejected.

When there are large quantities of products, there are usually going to be at least a few defective pieces in every lot. Both buyer and seller understand this and contracts are drawn accordingly.[5] In fact, the allowable number of defects will be reflected in the price. If buyers want items to have a very low percentage of defectives, they may pay more than if they are less demanding.

When the products arrive at a buyer's plant, they are inspected and either accepted or rejected, depending on whether the proportion of bad items in the sample is above or below the proportion allowed. Both buyer and seller (SQC calls them the "consumer" and the "producer") take some risks. The *consumer's risk* is that now and then the accepted lot will have too many defectives (the sample might have a smaller proportion of rejects than the whole lot has). The *producer's risk* is that now and then a good lot will not pass inspection (if the sample happens to contain proportionally more defectives than are actually in the lot). In both of these cases the sample is, in fact, not representative, although this is not known.

Acceptance sampling does not eliminate

---

[4] See Joseph R. Troxell, "Standards for Quality Control in Service Industries," *Quality Progress,* January 1979, pp. 32–34.

[5] Actually, the buyer and seller relationship is unimportant. The problem of accepting or rejecting complete products exists regardless of whether a company buys or makes the items.

FIGURE 7-7
Quality Control Feedback System for a Commercial Bank *(bookkeeping services)*

Defect/Control Subject	This Period's Defect Ratio	This Period's Defect %	Last Month's Defect %	Previous Month's Defect %	Standard	Process Capability UCL/LCL	QCI Unweighted	Weight	QCI Weighted
Wrong account number/total deposits	76/37,936	.2	.3	.1	.1	.4/.08	50		
Nonendorsed deposits/total deposits	113/37,936	.3	.2	.1	.3	.4/.1	100		
Input quality:									
Missing items/total statements	60/49,538	.12*	.08	.09	.08	.1/.05	67	6	402
Stop payment incorrect/total stop payments	6/2,376	.25	.23	.21	.26	.28/.02	104	5	520
Misfiled items/total checks and debits	24/236,799	.01	.03	.04	.01	.04/.007	100	4	400
								(15)	1,322
Internal quality performance:									88%
Wrong statement sent/total statements	14/49,538	.03	.03	.04	.02	.06/.01	67	4	268
Missing items/total statements	4/49,538	.008*	.005	.002	.004	.006/.001	50	3	150
Incorrect adjustment/total statements	33/49,538	.07	.08	.07	.06	.09/.05	86	5	430
								(12)	848
External quality performance									71%
								(27)	2,170
Overall quality performance									80%

* Out of control

Source: *Quality Progress*, December, 1981. © 1981, American Society for Quality Control. Reprinted by permission.

these risks, but it does let managers decide how much risk they are willing to accept and to inspect accordingly. The more certain they want to be, the larger the samples must be (with higher inspection costs), or the fewer the number of defects are allowed in the sample before the lot is accepted.

With acceptance sampling—and unlike with control charts—users of statistical quality control do not have to make up their own tables of sample sizes and rejection numbers for their inspectors. Statisticians have developed and published sets of inspection tables which are readily available.[6] Also, most of the calculations could be done anyway, using computer packages which a company can buy or can use through a computer time-sharing service.

The published inspection tables also provide figures for several "levels" of inspection. A company's receiving inspectors inspect normally until a vendor has sent several satisfactory lots. Then the customer company reduces its inspecting and inspects only occasionally and may even stop entirely if the supplier becomes a "certified vendor." But, if a subsequent lot is rejected or if large numbers of defects begin showing up from certified vendors, the procedure reverts. The vendor is decertified and the receiving inspectors go to more frequent inspecting.

OPERATING CHARACTERISTIC CURVES

Every acceptance sampling plan has an "operating characteristic" (OC) curve which shows how well it is expected to work in rejecting bad lots and accepting good lots. The OC curve, however, does not determine the plan; the plan is developed, and the curve depicts its "power" to accept good lots and reject bad lots.

The starting point of determining an acceptance plan is to determine an "objective" defective percent (or proportion).

---

[6] See *Military Standard 105D, Sampling Procedures and Tables for Inspection by Attribute,* which is a widely used set of tables for SQC.

The objective percent is the particular desired percent of bad items in the lot which the buyer will accept. The buyer does not want to accept lots with more defectives, nor does he expect lots to be much better without paying more for them.

Both buyers and sellers appreciate these points. They also know that a "plan" is one which will average out over the long run. The seller is going to deliver many lots of parts over a period of time. Some will surely be very good and contain no defects or fewer than the allowable fraction of defectives. Others will be poorer and will contain more defects than the allowable proportion.

An acceptance sampling plan is one which, based on inspecting a small sample, accepts nearly all lots which are as good as or better than the objective percent and rejects most lots which are worse. If the lots submitted are of quite varied quality, some good, some bad, the average proportion of defectives contained in all accepted lots will be close to the objective percent. In the example which follows, this objective percent is set at 2 percent, or .02, defective.

Having first decided the objective percent, the next step is to choose four other numbers. The first is called the "acceptable quality level" (AQL). In our example we set this at 1 percent defectives, or .01. The AQL is always a better quality level than the objective percent. In fact, "acceptable quality level" is a misnomer in the sense that the term refers to a considerably better quality level than the objective percent. It is so *much better* that the inspection plan is set so as to accept the AQL percent defectives in almost every case where lots this good are submitted.

Usually the plan is designed to incorporate a 5 percent risk at the stated AQL. This is called the producer's risk, or the α (alpha) risk. It means that lots which contain as few or fewer defectives than the AQL will be accepted about 95 percent of the time and rejected 5 percent of the time.

The third figure to be determined is the "lot tolerance percent defective" (LTPD). This is sometimes also called the "lot tolerance fraction defective" (LTFD). In our example, this was set at 3 percent defectives, or .03.

The customer (the consumer) wants the inspection plan to detect and reject almost all lots with, in this case, 3 percent defectives or more. The consumer's risk, also called the β (beta) risk, is usually set at 10 percent. This 10 percent is the fourth of the four numbers required to develop an acceptance sampling plan. This means that lots with as many as 3 percent defectives will be rejected 90 percent of the time. Lots with higher percent defectives will have even less chance of passing inspection.

These four decisions, the AQL (1 percent), the alpha risk (5 percent), the LTPD (3 percent),

and the beta risk (10 percent), are the constraints to the inspection plan. The objective percent is not directly used in the calculation; it is, however, behind the setting of AQL and LTPD.

From this point on, setting up the inspection plan is mathematical and is based on rather involved formulas. The end product is a set of instructions to inspectors or computerized inspection systems. These instructions tell inspectors, for all possible sizes of lots, the size of the sample they should draw and how many bad items found in the sample are acceptable and how many constitute too many bad ones.

In our example, it turns out that for a lot of 10,000 or more the inspector should inspect a sample of 400 and reject all lots whose samples

FIGURE 7–8
An Operating Characteristic Curve

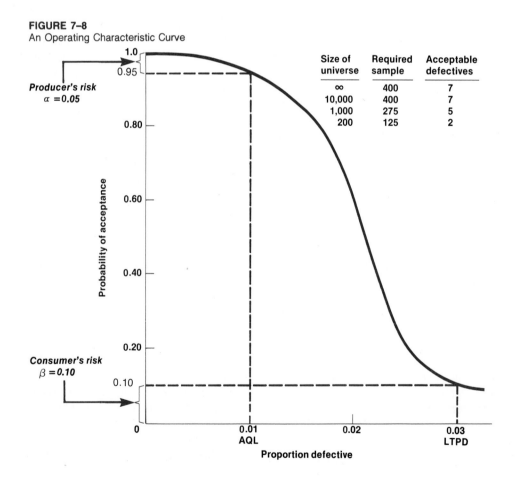

Size of universe	Required sample	Acceptable defectives
∞	400	7
10,000	400	7
1,000	275	5
200	125	2

Producer's risk
$\alpha = 0.05$

Consumer's risk
$\beta = 0.10$

contain 8 or more rejects. (The plan would be expressed as $N = 10,000$, $n = 400$, $c = 7$). The $c = 7$ means that with 7 or fewer defectives the inspector accepts the lot. The c is the "cutoff" number. But if the lot is only 1,000, we get the same quality assurance by having the inspector inspect a sample of 275 and accepting the lot if he finds no more than 5 defects. If the whole lot is 200, he should inspect 125 and accept it if he finds 2 or fewer rejects. The plan, therefore, tells the inspector, for each size lot, how big a sample to take and the number of defects that is acceptable.

Reading an OC Curve

Figure 7–8 is this particular plan's operating characteristic curve. On this chart, the horizontal line at the bottom is an "if" line. *If* a lot submitted *actually* has 1, 2, 3, 4, and so on, percent defectives, then we can read up to the curve and across to the left to see what the chances are that such a lot will be accepted. Lots which *actually* contain 1 percent defectives will pass about 95 percent of the time. Lots with actually 2 percent bad items will pass about 60 percent of the time. Lots actually containing 3 percent defectives will get by only about 10 percent of the time. And lots with higher percentages of defectives will have even less chance of being accepted.

The real meaning of OC curves is more apparent when there are many successive lots of products. OC curves relate to average results covering many lots. If, over a period of time, in our example, several hundred lots of a product were submitted, and, if some lots were very good, some very bad, and some in-between, then the OC curve indicates what would happen on the average.

This plan will accept lots wiht 1 percent bad items 95 percent of the time, but, although there is no intention to do so, it will accidentally reject 5 percent of the lots submitted which are this good. (This is called a Type I error in statistics.) It will also reject lots with up to 3 percent defects

90 percent of the time. And again, although it is unintentional, the plan will accept lots this bad 10 percent of the time. (This is called a Type II error.)

Lots of in-between quality have the probability of acceptance as the curve shows. If the lots vary uniformly from very good to very bad, the average quality of those accepted will be a little more than 2 percent bad, which is shown as a .5 probability of acceptance.

Every acceptance inspection plan has its own operating characteristic curve, as shown in Figure 7–9. The shape of the line depends on the quality desired and the degree of certainty that this quality will be assured. The slope of the curve reflects the plan. If managers want more or less assurance, they can change any of the four original decisions. If they want more certainty, for example, they could increase the sample size and hold the acceptable number constant, or vice versa. Doing this, however, changes the whole plan, including the AQL and the LTPD. This new plan would have its own OC curve.

SINGLE, DOUBLE, SEQUENTIAL, AND CONTINUOUS SAMPLING PLANS

For very good lots or very poor lots, relatively small samples are all that are needed because the samples will contain high proportions of good or bad items; there is little doubt whether the entire lots are good enough to pass or bad enough to reject. This property can be used to advantage in SQC by first inspecting only a very small sample to see whether it is cleary good or bad. This may result, however, in many borderline cases where it is not clear whether the lot is good or bad. When this happens, it is necessary to inspect another sample and add it to the first. Having a larger sample allows the inspector to decide more certainly whether a borderline lot is good enough to pass or should be rejected.

Some SQC people, though, prefer to use

FIGURE 7–9
Family of Operating Characteristic Curves

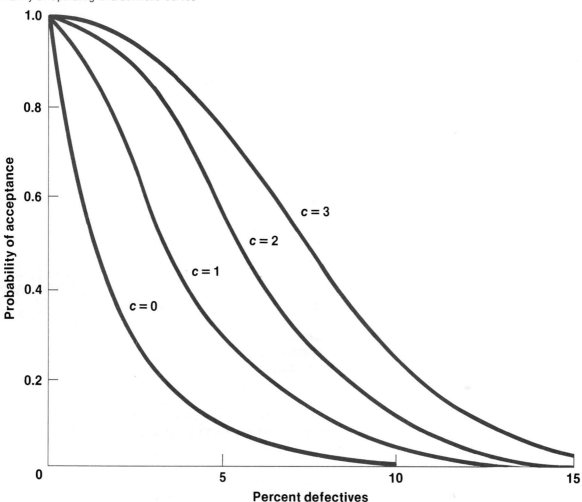

These curves are for four different inspection plans and show how much the change in the acceptable number of defects *(c)* changes the plans.

just one sample and no more. This is "single sampling." Here one and only one fairly large sample is used. After inspection, the lot is accepted or rejected. There are no more samples.

"Double sampling" begins by first drawing a smaller sample. Using this small sample, the inspector accepts or rejects all but borderline lots. With borderline lots, a second sample is drawn, inspected, and added to the first, and the accept-reject decision is again made. Figure 7–10 depicts this procedure.

"Sequential sampling" begins by drawing still smaller samples. As before, these very small samples are conclusive for very good or very bad lots, so they can be accepted or rejected right away. But there will be more doubtful cases because the very small first sample is conclusive for only very good or very bad lots. If the first

FIGURE 7–10
Single, Double, and Sequential Sampling Alternatives

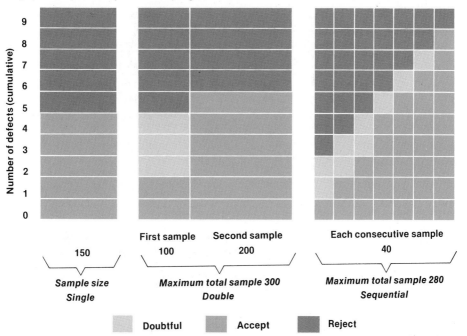

These three diagrams are for essentially the same inspection objective. If numerous lots are submitted and some are inspected one way and the others a different way, the same number of acceptances and rejections would result.

sample is inconclusive, another small sample is inspected and added to the first. Putting the two samples together makes a larger-size sample, and this provides more certainty, so more of the borderline lots can be passed or rejected. But a few will still be very close to borderline lots—not yet passed or rejected. So a third sample is inspected and added to the first two. This provides more certainty and disposes of more cases. If there are still close-to-borderline lots where the sample is inconclusive, the inspector goes on to a fourth sample (or more). Figure 7–10 also shows how the successive samples work.

Another acceptance sampling procedure is "continuous" sampling. This is appropriate for assembled items which pass inspection stations or are otherwise being continuously produced by a process.

Hewlett-Packard uses such a continuous sampling plan to control the quality of their electronic products (see Figure 7–11). They inspect every fourth item. If they find even one defective unit, they inspect each of the next 30 units. If they find no defects among the 30, they go back to every fourth unit again until they find another defect, then to 30 again, and so on. Hewlett-Packard estimates that this gives them an average outgoing quality level (explained in the next section) of about 98 percent acceptable products.

AVERAGE OUTGOING QUALITY LEVEL (AOQL)

If rejected lots were always scrapped, the average quality of products would probably be about halfway between the AQL and the LTPD, al-

FIGURE 7–11
Hewlett-Packard's Sampling Inspection Plan

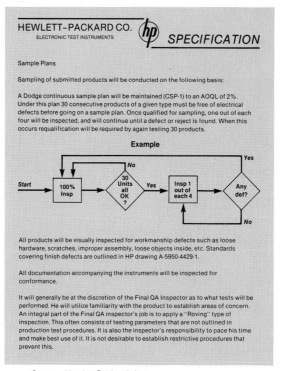

HEWLETT–PACKARD CO.
ELECTRONIC TEST INSTRUMENTS
hp SPECIFICATION

Sample Plans

Sampling of submitted products will be conducted on the following basis:

A Dodge continuous sample plan will be maintained (CSP-1) to an AOQL of 2%. Under this plan 30 consecutive products of a given type must be free of electrical defects before going on a sample plan. Once qualified for sampling, one out of each four will be inspected, and will continue until a defect or reject is found. When this occurs requalification will be required by again testing 30 products.

All products will be visually inspected for workmanship defects such as loose hardware, scratches, improper assembly, loose objects inside, etc. Standards covering finish defects are outlined in HP drawing A-5950-4429-1.

All documentation accompanying the instruments will be inspected for conformance.

It will generally be at the discretion of the Final QA Inspector as to what tests will be performed. He will utilize familiarity with the product to establish areas of concern. An integral part of the Final QA inspector's job is to apply a "Roving" type of inspection. This often consists of testing parameters that are not outlined in production test procedures. It is also the inspector's responsibility to pace his time and make best use of it. It is not desirable to establish restrictive procedures that prevent this.

Source: Hewlett-Packard, Inc.

though this would also depend upon the average quality of the lots submitted. But, when bad lots of *parts* are rejected, they can be 100 percent inspected, and the lot's quality can be improved just by removing the bad items. This means that the quality of the lots which pass end up being quite good—and the *worse* the quality of lots first submitted, the *better* the ending quality. Figure 7–12 shows how the average outgoing quality level, the AOQL, relates to the quality of the lots submitted for inspection. If most lots are rather bad, SQC will catch nearly all of them, and after 100 percent inspection, they will be nearly perfect. Averaging these in with other lots which passed, including the few bad lots that got through, produces an average outgoing quality level which will be better than if most lots were just good enough to pass.

Figure 7–12 probably claims a little too much, however. The true AOQL will probably not be quite this good because even 100 percent inspection is not 100 percent perfect. It rarely catches all of the defects. The true AOQL will contain a few more defectives than it should theoretically.

DEGREES OF DEFECTS IN ACCEPTANCE SAMPLING

Many products can have major or minor defects, or both, and at the same time. If so, the receiving inspectors may need to use two or three inspection plans at the same time and on the same sample. It may be necessary, for example, to allow no defects at all in the sample for critical or major defects. The curvature of a spring for

FIGURE 7–12
An AOQL Curve

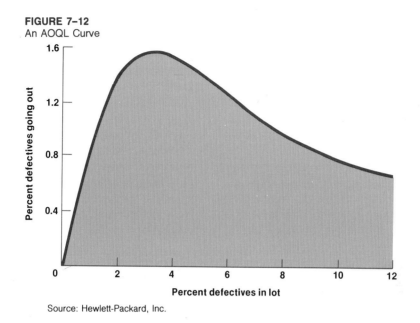

Source: Hewlett-Packard, Inc.

an automobile door latch might be critical. If it curves too much, it might exert too much pressure and break and let the door swing open. If a sample contains even one major defective, the lot should probably be rejected.

Sometimes it may be desirable to watch for defects because they will jam machinery. The diameter of the head of a rivet installed by an automatic assembly machine must not be too large or it will jam the machine. The defect is unimportant functionally; yet, it is important in keeping production moving. Again, it might be necessary to use an inspection plan which allows for virtually *no* defects in the sample.

But, where minor defects will not affect the product's operation, higher defective rates can be allowed. Perhaps a plan should be used which would accept the lot even if the sample had 10 percent minor defectives if the cost trade-offs warrant it.

Thus, inspectors often are applying two or three inspection plans when they inspect a sample. The rejection number would be low for serious defects and high for minor or trivial defects. However, with the recent re-emphasized trend

toward "zero defects" (as emphasized by the Japanese) parts need not be critical to require that no defects be in a lot.

SQC IN OPERATION

SQC may not work in practice quite the way it is supposed to. On the positive side is the extra degree of reliability from samples' being inspected thoroughly. Because they are only samples, they are usually checked more carefully, whereas inspectors on 100 percent inspection jobs often get careless. Western Electric says that sampling provides more reliable information about how many bad electrical connections there are on a switchboard with 10,000 soldered connections than does 100 percent inspection. And the United States Bureau of the Census feels that its mid-decade samples of population size are characteristically more accurate than their actual census of the entire population (required by law) which occurs at the end of every decade.

Also, some 100 percent inspectors may think that they have to throw out a few products now and then, or the boss won't think that they are doing a good job.

On the negative side, particularly with acceptance sampling, SQC may end up *not* being as reliable as it is supposed to be. Acceptance sampling procedures are designed to provide average qualities—but with knowledge that an occasional good lot is rejected and an occasional bad lot gets through.

This should produce an acceptable average result. But what really happens when a lot which is actually good enough to pass is rejected? It goes back to the vendor, who checks it and finds it good enough to pass; so back the lot comes as the next regular shipment, and it probably passes this time. The result is that *a good lot rarely stays rejected*. Vendors cannot be criticized for doing this because they are sending lots that are of acceptable quality.

However, lots with a poor quality level cause problems. A few of these slip through the first time; the others go back to the vendor. Some vendors are not above sending them back for a second try. Perhaps there is only one chance in four that they will pass. But one fourth of these lots got by the first time. Another one fourth of the remaining bad lots might get by if the vendor tries again. By trying two or three times, the vendor may get quite a bit of bad work accepted. Of course, good vendors don't do this.

Another thing (and this may happen with control charts, too, but it is more common in acceptance sampling) is the tendency for inspectors not to follow the rules. An inspector dips into a lot and finds just enough rejects in the sample to reject the lot. But he or she may not *reject* the lot, but throw the sample back and take another sample, hoping this time to get a sample that passes. Inspectors sometimes do things like this, so the result is likely to be a poorer quality than SQC should ensure.

In fairness to inspectors, it might be pointed out that it is often hard to get a representative random sample. Suppose, for example, a shipment of 100,000 bolts comes in on a pallet holding 48 boxes arranged four boxes wide, four boxes deep, and three boxes high. It is hard

for the inspector to get a random sample. To make this worse, vendors know all about this problem, and some unscrupulous ones put their substandard boxes inside and low down in the load.

Sometimes, too, parts come in metal containers and the inspector can't burrow in sideways to try to get a random sample. Vendors know about this too and a few may put the items of dubious quality out of easy reach.

These practical difficulties interfere with inspectors' getting representative random samples and, in some cases, reduce the validity of the findings of the SQC sampling plan.

Review Questions

1. If statistical quality control neither creates risks nor eliminates risks, what *does* it do? Discuss.
2. If SQC is to be used as a quality audit system, does this mean that a certain amount of faulty work is expected to pass? Explain.
3. Compare random and representative samples.
4. How are the normal curve and the standard deviation made use of in statistical quality control?
5. Distinguish between attribute and variable inspection. Show why the distinction is important.
6. Should there be a lower control limit on a control chart for percent defectives? Why? Could such a limit ever be a minus number? Explain.
7. What is meant by "consumer's risk" and "producer's risk"?
8. A quality control plan in operation has an AQL of 5 percent. Just what does this mean to the supplier? To the purchaser?
9. When should sequential sampling be favored over single sampling? Why?
10. How can it be that the AOQL gets better as the quality produced gets worse? Explain.
11. SQC sometimes doesn't work out in practice quite the way it is supposed to. How does it work? Is what happens good? Explain.

Questions for Discussion

1. How could statistical quality control be used to help control the quality of roof repairing jobs?

2. How can a person tell, in statistical quality control, if there has been a change in "population"? What difference would it make if there has been?

3. A specification says 4 inches ±.002 inch. The control chart shows .398 inch as the average with a standard error of .009 inch. Do these figures call for any action by anyone? Who? What action?

4. A specification calls for the dimension to be 5 inches ±.005. The control chart shows a mean of 4.998 inches and a standard error of .001 inch. What should be done about this? Suppose that the control chart showed a mean of 5 inches and a standard error of .002 inch. Should anything different be done? Why?

5. What should be done about the individual pieces outside the control limits in question 4?

6. A company had promised to ship 1,000 pieces to an important customer on the very day when something went wrong, and most of the pieces had a defect which the supervisor felt sure would not pass the customer's inspection. The boss "blew his top" and then ordered: "Ship them anyway! I promised to deliver today, and we'll do it even if the whole shipment comes back." Discuss.

Problems

1. The quality control analyst is setting up a control chart for part A, which is to be one inch in length. The plan is to inspect a sample of four every half hour. Here are the actual measurements obtained from ten sets of four parts that were made to provide the data for the control chart:

Group	(1)	(2)	(3)	(4)
		Measurement in Inches		
1	1.011	1.008	.995	.991
2	.991	.988	.986	.989
3	.987	.996	1.007	1.013
4	.999	.990	1.002	.991
5	1.001	1.008	.991	.998
6	1.009	.990	1.008	.993
7	1.013	.988	.996	.993
8	.987	.994	.999	.990
9	.995	1.001	.988	1.012
10	1.001	.999	1.010	1.007

a. Set up control limits for this operation.
b. Suppose that we already had set up this control chart with the limits just obtained and that the above measurements were obtained by mea-

suring a sample of four every half hour during the day. Was the operation ever out of control? When?

2. In order to set up a control chart, the following ten samples of four items were measured. These measurements are:

Sample	(1)	(2)	(3)	(4)
		Measurement		
1	6	15	13	6
2	11	12	7	12
3	9	14	7	8
4	5	9	10	10
5	14	13	16	14
6	6	13	12	16
7	9	18	8	12
8	11	8	13	9
9	13	15	9	5
10	8	10	10	9

a. Set up a control chart for this operation.
b. After this chart was constructed, measurements of production were made every half hour. Here are the first four sets:

Time	(1)	(2)	(3)	(4)
		Measurements		
8:30	7	10	10	7
9:00	10	11	10	8
9:30	10	8	9	11
10:00	16	12	15	8

Is the operation in control? Is there any tendency toward bad work? Show the figures.

3. According to the control plan, eight bolts will be measured every half hour, and the machine will be stopped if it is out of adjustment. Ninety-five percent of the bolts should be within 4 inches ±.004 inches. The last set of eight showed these measurements:

4.001	3.990
3.998	4.002
4.009	3.998
3.997	4.000

Should the machine be stopped and reset? About what percentage of the bolts is likely to be beyond the limits the way the machine is now running?

4. The Tab Typewriter Company tests the strength of the metal stampings on which key faces are mounted. Below are the test results for samples

from two different suppliers. These samples were pulled apart and their tensile strength recorded.

If Tab wants greater strength, which source should it buy from? If it wants consistency, which one? Is either difference very certain from these samples?

Source A*	Source B*
171.2	134.9
139.3	155.2
152.7	170.4
154.1	160.7
156.7	151.0
145.0	155.2
133.4	184.6
163.1	148.2
148.3	131.6
159.4	166.1

* Tensile strength in thousands of pounds per square inch.

5. Construct a control chart for percent defectives based on these data (percent defectives found in samples of 400):

Sample Number	Number of Defects	Sample Number	Number of Defects
1	2	11	3
2	0	12	0
3	8	13	5
4	5	14	6
5	8	15	7
6	4	16	1
7	4	17	5
8	2	18	8
9	9	19	2
10	2	20	1

6. What will be the average percent defectives which will be received and passed if the quality of 20 lots is the same as those listed in Problem 5? In this case, use the OC curve in Figure 7–8.

Section Three

Production and Inventory Planning and Control

The production process adds value to materials by changing their form into individual items designed for particular uses. In this new individualized form, the products have far greater value than they had as raw materials.

This section considers the process of integrating demand forecasting, production, inventories, purchasing, and capacity into total systems to achieve timely and economical outputs of goods and services.

The first chapter in the section, Chapter 8, presents an overview of integrated production-inventory systems as well as a description of basic inventory control methods. Chapter 9 presents issues and methods relating to forecasting demand for products and services. This is followed by a discussion in Chapter 10 of capacity requirements planning and its interactive role with the development of master pro-duction schedules—the key planning document for many organizations.

Next, we introduce the important topics of material requirements; planning (MRP I) and manufacturing resource planning (MRP II) in Chapter 11 and the important role that computers play in this activity.

This is followed by Chapter 12, which is a discussion of reorder point and reorder quantity methods in both MRP and more classical production control activities.

Then we move to the execution and control of planned production by discussing order scheduling in job shops and in high-volume (repetitive) production (Chapters 13 and 14).

Finally, the topic of purchasing management—the execution and control of orders to vendors—completes this section with Chapter 15.

Chapter 8

Basic Production and Inventory Planning and Control Concepts

The area of production (or operations) and inventory planning and control in manufacturing and service organizations provides an interesting and challenging career opportunity for people who study business and engineering. PIPC specialists are at the core of the nervous system of the *supply* side of organizations. They participate in demand forecasting; planning the overall capacity of the organization; determining *how much* inventory of parts and material to carry and *when* to acquire them; and if parts are manufactured internally, they are responsible for when they are made and on what machines so that master production schedules or final assembly schedules are met to satisfy the *demand* for the output of the organization.

This is a challenging task which requires PIPC people to coordinate their efforts with marketing, finance, engineering, and personnel management. Sometimes conflicts arise among these functional areas, as shown (perhaps in their extreme!) in Figure 8–1.

But these conflicting objectives usually get resolved, production happens, and products and services emerge. However, in a very real sense, little of a manufacturing organization's work is making *products* because most products are made of *parts* and most of a factory's activities have to do with making *parts*. Until the parts are assembled there is no product, just parts. PIPC tells the factory what kinds of parts to make, how many to make, and when to make them. And it tells the factory what assembled products to make, and when, and out of what parts.

But parts are usually not completed in a single manufacturing operation. To make a chair leg, for example, it is necessary to saw, plane, sandpaper, drill holes, and do other things to a piece of wood. It ends up the right size, shape, and finish to be a chair leg, but these changes are not accomplished all at once. They are accomplished little by little, operation by operation. PIPC does not just tell the factory to make chair legs. It gives the factory detailed directions telling the workers to do certain operations to certain kinds of materials. Making parts is a directed process with the PIPC department in control.

Manufacturing is just as varied as the products we buy—only more so because many products are made and used that we consumers never see. (They are component parts which are hidden away, like the inside of a television set.

FIGURE 8–1

Conflicting Objectives in a Manufacturing Organization: Or the Sometimes Painful Birth of a Master Production Schedule

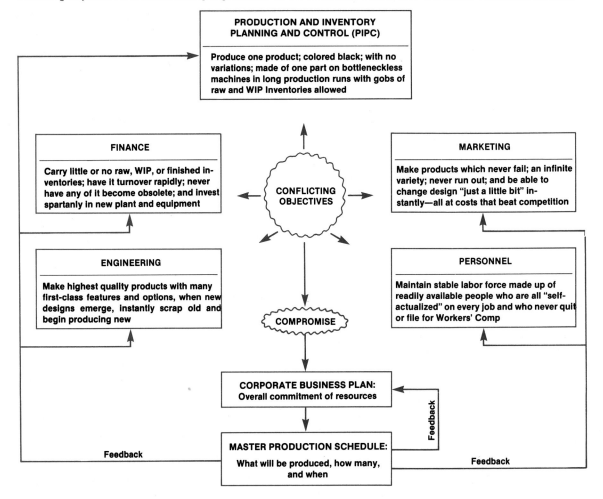

Or else they are equipment or supply items consumed in manufacturing processes.)

PIPC is also varied among different companies and different industries. It takes different kinds of directions to tell people what to make (or do) in a shoe, nut and bolt, or aircraft factory, or in a service industry, such as a hotel, insurance company, police department, or the post office.

One of the most difficult PIPC jobs is in factories making assembled products out of metal parts, and perhaps the most difficult of all is in the aerospace industry. In no other industry is

it necessary to make a quarter of a million parts, all on schedule, so that they can be assembled into one product, an aircraft or a spacecraft.

PIPC is difficult, though, even with products simpler than an aircraft. An automobile has 16,000 parts. Even a typewriter has 2,000 parts. A metal part which can be made in as few as 10 operations is a simple part. When making assembled products from metal parts, production control may have to direct thousands and thousands of operations.

In talking about PIPC we will spend most of our time, because of their complexity, discussing finished products assembled from component parts which are either fabricated in the factory or purchased from outside suppliers. While other "production" activities in manufacturing and service organizations can be complex, their production is usually simpler to control than this widespread class of manufacturing activities.

TERMS

If industries would settle on words and definitions, it would be easier to talk about PIPC. But industry is not very consistent in its use of terms, so it is difficult to set exact definitions.

For example, the name of the main department doing most of the PIPC activity may be the *production department, production control department, plant operations, production planning department, production planning and control department,* or *production and inventory planning and control (PIPC),* the one we have used here. (We use this one because of the extreme importance of *integrating* production and inventories in the planning and control of production activities.) In manufacturing industries, more companies probably use *production department* than any other term. This means that the production department is *not* the factory department working on the product, but it is the department which develops and issues directives to the factory and controls production and inventories of parts and finished products.

Various parts of PIPC activities also have different names in different companies. For example, a list of parts for an assembled product may be called a *bill of materials,* a *materials list,* a *parts list,* or a *requirement list.* A sequenced list of operations for making a part may be a *route sheet,* a *process sheet,* a *layout,* or an *operations list. Scheduling* may mean: (1) setting dates for the completion of *orders,* (2) setting dates for the completion of individual *operations,* (3) setting specific starting and stopping times for operation performances on machines, or (4) developing lists of jobs needing certain machines. There are few areas in PIPC where terms have standard definitions; however,

this is being improved by APICS (American Production and Inventory Control Society), the professional organization for people who work in this field. We will try to use their terms and definitions as much as possible in our discussion.

PRODUCTION AND INVENTORY PLANNING AND CONTROL

Although PIPC activities are different in every situation, there are nevertheless certain functions that are common.

APICS defines the terms *production control* and *inventory control*—or PIPC in our combined terminology—as "the function of directing or regulating the orderly movement of goods through the entire manufacturing cycle from the requisitioning of raw materials to the delivery of the finished product to meet the objectives of customer service, minimum inventory investment, and maximum manufacturing efficiency . . . and includes inventory control . . . [which is] the technique of maintaining stockkeeping items at desired levels whether they be raw materials, work-in-process, or finished goods."[1]

More specifically, PIPC specialists perform the following activities:

1. Participate in developing master production schedules which are *realistic* as compared to available capacity. Report to the marketing department what promise dates are feasible for prospective customers' orders.
2. Participate in planning labor requirements needed to meet master production schedules.
3. Receive orders to manufacture products.
4. "Explode" the orders (usually with the aid of a computer) for assembled products from bills of material, thus determining the quantity requirements of parts and operations needed. Issue requisitions to the purchasing department for parts to be bought.
5. Determine raw materials requirements for manufactured parts.

---

[1] *APICS Dictionary,* 3d ed., ed. Richard C. Sherrill, (Falls Church, Va.: American Production and Inventory Control Society, 1970), pp. 18, 32.

6. Determine the tools necessary for production. Issue requisitions for tools to be purchased or made internally.
7. Operate the raw materials stockroom and maintain stocks and accurate records of receipts and disbursements. Issue purchase requisitions for the necessary materials.
8. Work with manufacturing engineering to do original routing (determine, the first time a product is made, the operations and machines required to make products and parts).
9. Prepare production orders directing the performance of the operations necessary to make parts and products.
10. Develop schedules for the performance of operations on particular machines.
11. Ensure that everything needed for production will be available in the right quantities at the right time when production orders are "released" to the factory.
12. Determine how many orders to release to the factory for manufacture to balance the order backlog against available capacity.
13. Release orders to the factory to particular people and machines, and determine the priorities in which jobs are worked on.
14. Direct the transportation of work-in-process (or work-in-progress, as it is sometimes called) (WIP), from work center to work center and control its buildup, location, and ensure record accuracy on the factory floor or in WIP inventory stores.
15. Receive reports of work completed and compare them with that scheduled. Keep up-to-date records of the progress of jobs moving through the plant, and revise priorities.
16. Help solve problems which cause delays in production, such as machine breakdowns, high scrap rates of parts; or lack of materials or tools.
17. Revise plans when original plans are not carried out and where there are changes in the size of an order or its required completion date.

18. Operate the finished component parts stockroom and control the stock of parts and their record accuracy.
19. Operate the finished products stockroom and control the stock of finished products and their record accuracy.
20. Answer inquiries concerning the progress of orders in process.
21. Aid in developing cost estimates for prospective new orders.

These basic functions are usually assigned to the PIPC department in most companies, but sometimes a few of them are assigned to other departments. Also, one or more non-PIPC duties, such as operating the plant's mail service or the tool storeroom or setting time standards for incentive purposes, are often assigned to PIPC.

There might appear to be one important omission in this list: only items 2 and 13 mention people. PIPC has very little to do with staffing the factory. In some companies, however, PIPC determines how many people the factory will need. They may be assigned the responsibility for translating future work schedules into future labor needs so that the personnel department can develop staffing plans for certain specialists. But it is usually the supervisors' and the personnel department's job to provide the necessary workers. Except during extremely high levels of production, PIPC assumes that the necessary workers will be there.

Also, PIPC usually has little to do with providing the facilities required for production. In some companies, everything having to do with getting production started the first time a new product is manufactured is turned over to a product or manufacturing engineer who has final authority over how things are made. He may choose the machines, order their purchase, decide the layout, supervise machine installation, and monitor operations until production is going smoothly. The engineer may also decide on all of the tools needed and order them and decide on which materials to use, but PIPC usually places the orders for materials. After the product has been fully integrated into the production process, the engineer usually fades away, and PIPC takes over. However, if the product is complex and requires many changes the engineer may be involved for a longer period of time.

Coordinating PIPC Functions

Manufacturing firms of the 1980s are turning more and more to the use of computer-based PIPC systems to aid them in planning, coordinating, and controlling their production and inventory management activities.

This does not mean that most, or even the majority, of manufacturers have installed these systems—or, of those that have; have solved all of their coordinating problems with them. On the contrary, many successful, well-organized manual (clerical-based) PIPC systems are used and work extremely well. And, many computer-based systems are so poorly designed and managed that they actually make PIPC functions more difficult.

But, well-designed and well-managed computerized systems which operate in a *formal* company environment rather than in an *informal* one literally revolutionize the way large, medium-sized, and small manufacturers manage their production activities. Small companies are not precluded from using computerized systems because of the minicomputer/microprocessor revolution which is also taking place.

Systems appropriate for a small company's PIPC functions which can be completely installed for $50–100,000 are available from most computer manufacturers. This is in contrast to the cost of medium and large systems, which can range from several hundred thousand to several million dollars. In addition, over 200 "software" firms exist which develop both standard and tailor-made computer programs which can often be implemented on a variety of small computers. (Recall our capital investment analysis example in Chapter 3. While this is only an example, it is a realistic one.)

Formal versus Informal PIPC Systems

Before describing in more detail how PIPC systems work, an important point must be made. We mentioned earlier that successful PIPC systems require a high degree of *formality* or *discipline* to enable them to operate efficiently. Formal PIPC systems are those in which the users of the system are expected to use the system as designed and not exercise a great amount of discretionary freedom (informality) to do their "own thing."

But formal systems do *not* mean that everybody says "yes sir" and wears coats and ties or dresses. Nor do we mean that these systems do not allow for creativity or responsiveness to changing situations. On the contrary, formal PIPC systems should be designed to react to change and to show PIPC people the possible impact of proposed changes in schedules, new product designs, new ways for machine processing, and so on, upon production inputs and outputs. And if actual problems do arise, these systems can aid them in assessing their impact on delivery due dates, idle capacity or overtime, and inventory levels.

However, in order to get PIPC people to use the system, they need to be able to rely on it containing accurate and timely data. They also need to be able to rely on reports being calculated from logic which is realistic for *their* manufacturing environment. Formal systems are *credible* systems because the people who enter data into the system care that it is accurate, and people who use the reports provided by the system do not ignore them and continue to operate off the "back of an envelope," or informally.

For example, if people are careless in recording quantities which are produced or drawn from stockrooms, then the computerized system becomes confused. It may report we have 100 parts but the stockpicker only finds 3 because someone failed to fill out the paperwork when they picked this item, or entered the wrong amount into the computer's files, or made some other mistake. Before long, if informality continues to prevail, total inventory record accuracy may fall to 60 percent or so, and users of the system lose confidence in the schedules and other information the computer produces. Similar problems develop when a computerized bill of material calls for a 3-centimeter bearing when the shop has found they need one which is 2.5 centimeters. Whose fault is it? Engineering design? The shop's supervisor? When this happens, people are often forced to revert to their informal systems to get the product out the door on time. This causes further deterioration in the system's believability; and it is doomed to failure.

In this respect, PIPC *is* concerned with people, their motivation, their responsibility, and their ability and willingness to maintain the system's integrity.

Integrated PIPC Systems (MRP I and MRP II)

Today's PIPC systems—which have evolved in the 1970s and continue to be refined in the 1980s—are "closed loop" systems. Their component parts fit together in an orderly way. They plan, implement plans, control activities according to plans, and then feed back information to PIPC people so new or revised plans can be implemented and controlled, and so on, as time unfolds.

These systems were called *material requirements planning* (MRP) systems *by tradition,* although they plan (and control) much more than just materials. They aid in managing capacities, inventory and work force levels, machine loading, and the movement of orders through the manufacturing facility. In addition, they monitor orders released to vendors for purchased parts and materials.

In the early 1980s the concept of MRP was expanded to include the planning and control of all *resources* required to perform production. The result is MRP II, which means *manufacturing resource planning.*

MRP II encompasses the planning and control of all the things mentioned above, plus a more formal integration of PIPC with marketing, finance and accounting, personnel, and engineering. Figure 8–2 shows an overview of a closed loop MRP II system. This chapter and the chapters which follow in this section will discuss the topics of Figure 8–2.

Here, however, we will briefly introduce the concepts and terms.

Corporate business plan and master production schedule. As shown earlier in Figure 8–1 the functional areas of PIPC—marketing, finance/accounting, personnel, and engineering—take an active role in the development of the overall corporate business plan. This results in an updated master production schedule, the key plan that determines production decisions and activities. Each of their inputs (as shown in Figure 8–1) must be considered and balanced, and commitments to the quantity and mix of outputs need to be made. Marketing commits to sell the output; PIPC commits to produce it; finance commits to finance it; personnel commits to staff for it; and engineering commits to support it.

Closed loop. The *closed loop* nature of this activity means that it is a repetitive or ongoing process which is updated continuously at some lower levels, and periodically at the master production schedule and corporate business plan level.

Inventory levels. Current overall levels of raw, work-in-process, and finished goods, and problems with critical vendors.

Capacity loads. Current loads on the manufacturing capacity, and problem areas.

Order backlog and lead times. Backlog defines the orders for products that have been accepted but have not entered the production system; lead times are an estimate as to how long a customer must wait before the order is completed. Lead times are discussed further in Chapter 11.

Customer orders. Customers place orders for products. When they do, they are placed in

FIGURE 8–2
Closed-Loop Manufacturing Resource Planning (MRP II) System

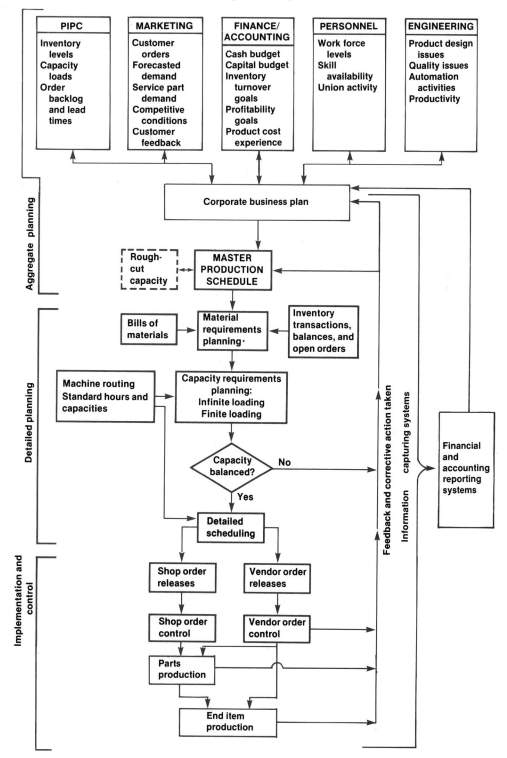

the master production schedule as orders for specific customers. This is called *producing to order.*

Forecast demand. Companies usually produce in anticipation of demand, not only for fulfilling specific customer orders. This is called *producing to stock.*

Service parts demand. Often manufacturers must produce replacement parts for their products. For example, auto manufacturers not only need to manufacture water pumps to put in their cars but must produce extra pumps to replace those which fail. Also, they may make pumps for other auto divisions or for other auto manufacturers. This "service" parts production must also be scheduled.

Competitive conditions. Simply, what is the competition up to in terms of products, pricing, lead times, quality, and so on.

Customer feedback. Feedback regarding the product, prices, quality, and new orders now or in the future.

Cash budget. Cash available to support the proposed master production schedule.

Capital budget. Capital available to add plant and equipment (if necessary) to support the MPS.

Inventory turnover goals. Finance's goals as to the investment they wish to carry in inventories—usually expressed as the number of "turns" per year. A common measure of turns is annual dollar sales divided by average inventory value.

Profitability goals. Return on investment and cash flow goals as determined by top management and/or investors.

Product cost experience. Cost accounting information or production costs of labor, materials, and overhead.

Work force level. Current work force levels by skill area.

Skill availability. Labor market conditions and availability of skilled people needed to support the MPS.

Union activity. Current and forecast labor union activities as they relate to cost, work rules, and other production-related issues.

Product design issues. Changes in design, materials used, cost, and manufacturing difficulty.

Quality issues. Current quality levels and problems and their effects on design, cost, and manufacturing activities.

Automation activities. Plans for automation of production activities and the effect on cost, quality, and jobs.

Productivity. Current labor and machine productivity and causes for changes up or down.

Master production schedule (MPS). Customer orders, forecasts of demand, and service parts demand result in an *initial* master production schedule. The MPS is a detailed plan of *what* and *how many* the company plans to *make* of each of their end products (not sell) in each time period (usually weeks) for the next several months. The MPS is the company's master plan, and once agreed upon, is said to "drive" the rest of the PIPC system. However, it can be changed frequently to reflect new orders and forecasts as time unfolds.

Rough cut capacity. Before a final master schedule is agreed upon, however, the resources required to produce these amounts in the scheduled time periods are compared, in a "rough cut" way with available capacity of machines, labor, and other long-lead-time resources. If in past experience a company's current capacity has allowed them to produce about $10 million of products per month, and next year's master schedule calls for $12 million in production per month they may have to see about adding a large amount of capacity or reducing the quantities in their master schedule—

or at least spreading production out over a longer time period.

On the other hand, if the MPS calls for only $8 million, the company may have to reduce capacity with layoffs, bring subcontracted work back into their factory, have a sale to increase demand, or do something to balance capacity with the MPS.

When this balancing is done, then more *detailed planning* can begin, to see if the proposed MPS can actually be met. This is done by considering more specific availability of materials, machine capacities, and labor.

Bills of materials. The way a product is actually made is defined by its bill of materials. But a BOM is not simply a parts list. It also defines the sequence in which component parts must be built. A wagon needs four wheels, but before they are put on the axles, the axles must be made, and the rubber and steel of the wheels must be subassembled into finished wheels. BOMs define in explicit detail both the parts and materials which are required for *each* end product and each *part,* and the assembly buildup sequence required to manufacture each.

Inventory transactions, balances, and open orders. Suppose we need 400 wheels to satisfy our MPS's plan for, say, 100 wagons. We currently have a *balance* of 50 wagon wheels in stock and have another 100 wheels currently being made in the factory (an *open order*). But since we have just sent 25 wheels out to replace faulty wheels for wagons previously sold, we really only need to produce $400 - 50 - 100 + 25 = 275$ wheels. The inventory transactions part of the system keeps track of the arrival and withdrawal of all parts and of orders already placed but not yet received, so we will order or manufacture the correct number—not too many not too few.

Material requirements planning. All of the above feeds into the MRP I part of the system where it calculates the material and part requirements plan needed to satisfy the master production schedule. It takes time to make things and to buy things from suppliers. MRP I also determines when orders for parts and materials need to be "released" to the shop for internal manufacture or to vendors. MRP I also determines how many items are required, based upon current balances, open orders, and bills of materials.

The outputs from MRP I are "planned order releases," for each part and material. These are for the future and form the basis for *detailed scheduling* of machines and labor as well as for telling the purchasing department what to buy and when to buy it.

Capacity requirements planning. Before *detailed scheduling* of shop orders and orders to vendors for purchased parts can be done, a much closer check of machine and assembly capacity is made. Here machine loads are planned first as though there were no capacity restrictions (infinite loading). Later, loads are balanced to meet the realism of capacity (finite loading) at machines. This requires the knowledge of specific *machine routings, standard hours,* and *machine capacities* to be able to make these calculations. Where severe capacity problems occur which cannot be solved with overtime, an extra shift, or subcontracting, the master production schedule may have to be revised to match this lower capacity.

Detailed scheduling. After capacity is balanced with the MPS, the detailed scheduling of parts, assemblies, and purchased parts can be determined. This scheduling takes into account specific machine routings, order due dates, and other priorities.

Shop and vendor order releases. When all is ready (all of this is actually a continuous process) the planned order releases produced by MRP I become "authorized" orders. Authorized shop orders are released to the factory floor, materials are pulled from stock, and production begins. Likewise, authorized purchased material and parts orders are sent (released) to vendors with enough lead time so materials arrive at the right time and in the right quantities to be integrated into the production process.

Shop order and vendor order control. Once orders are actually released to the factory, the system monitors their progress as they move from process to process to see if they are behind, on time, or ahead of schedule—in terms of meeting the master production schedule. For *parts* and *end item production,* purchasing specialists monitor the progress of orders they have placed with vendors (called *follow-up*) to determine their status—on time, late, quality problems, threatened strike, etc.

Feedback, corrective action and information capturing systems. As time unfolds, this information is captured and fed back to the proper place in the system either directly to PIPC or to accounting and finance. Corporate plans and master schedules are revised; the system recalculates needs; and the process repeats itself from day to day and week to week, continuously going through an updating process. In addition, the system is updated with *changes* to the bills of materials (as product designs are revised), machine routings (as new machines are purchased), assembly sequences, standard hours, and hundreds or thousands of other things which are constantly changing in a dynamic manufacturing environment.

BASIC INVENTORY CONCEPTS

During the early 1980s General Electric sold over $25 billion of products per year and at the end of a year owned over $4 billion of inventories—stocks of materials and products. General Foods sold over $6 billion per year of products and ended owning over $1 billion of inventories. RCA sold over $7 billion of products and services and carried an inventory of over $600 million. In these three companies (and they are typical) inventories accounted for more than one fourth of all the companies' invested capital.

Some inventories are in the form of *raw materials* and *purchased items* to be used in making products; some inventories are *supplies* to be used up in the manufacturing process; some are *partially manufactured* items (work-in-process) in production departments; some are *finished parts* ready to be put into assembled products; and some are *finished products* in shipping rooms and warehouses. Overall, about 37 percent of manufacturers' inventories are in materials and supplies, while work-in-process and finished inventories share the 63 percent balance about equally.

Holding Costs

Inventory is *money* that is temporarily in the form of a bar of brass, a sheet of steel, an iron casting, a bag of chemicals, a bolt of cloth, or a spare grinding wheel. But it isn't at all like money in the bank. It is money on which the company *pays* interest rather then earns interest. After a year, $100 in the bank may be worth $110. After a year on the shelf, $100 of inventory is worth nearer $75, because it may have cost $25 in expenses to carry it.

Most companies estimate that it costs about 25 to 40 percent of the value of inventories to carry them for a year. This is because inventories cost money in several ways. They take up space, and space costs money; they have to be put into and taken out of storage; they tie up money and cause an "opportunity cost." Usually inventories are insured, resulting in insurance premiums; and there are property taxes on inventories. They need to be managed (they have to be counted frequently), so it is necessary to keep records. They need to be protected from the weather and from pilferage. Even so, some things will deteriorate or disappear. Some items (rubber products and food products, for example) have only a limited shelf life, and some obsolescence occurs all the time. All of these costs, added together, may easily exceed 25 percent of the value of the inventory.

Inventory Conflicts

Inventory control people monitor inventories, but there is more to the job than mere record-keeping. They attempt to reach several objectives which are actually in conflict with each other. They try: (1) rarely to run out of anything, while (2) keeping as little as possible on hand, and (3) avoiding the payment of high prices because of buying in small quantities. Inventory managers try to determine what the proper inventory level should be to give good service to manufacturing departments and to outside customers, yet holding down costs.

It is difficult to produce and sell large volumes of products while having very little in transit and at the same time never run out of anything— or pay high prices because of hand-to-mouth buying to support production schedules. As a result, huge inventory investments are involved. If GE, through poor control, let its inventories increase 10 percent, it would have to invest over $400 million more into the inventories it owns. But if proper control were able to cut 10 percent off its present investment, it would have $400 million it could invest elsewhere. In addition, GE would save more millions from not having to store all the extra inventory.

An uncontrolled inventory is usually *too much* inventory. It is particularly pernicious because it is painless—even pleasant. No harm is done if new supplies do not arrive on time. The production department never runs out of anything. Nor does a customer ever have to wait for a finished product. Everyone is happy; but the money tied up in inventory can be enormous, as are all the other costs that large inventories entail.

Obsolete Inventories

It would not be so expensive if everything finally was used or sold. But uncontrolled inventories always seem to contain a substantial number of "buggy whip" items which eventually have to be thrown away. (Think of the once "useful" things in your garage which are now "junk.") Their value is gone, as are the expenses of carrying them for several years before they are thrown away.

Low Inventories May Be Suboptimal

Inventory planning and control, however, which considers *only* holding down the level of inventory could easily be suboptimal and be poor planning and control. Managers need to consider the impact of inventory policy on the entire organization. For example, it is sometimes desirable to build up inventories during low-demand periods in order to allow the factory to operate at a steady rate. While our attention here may seem to be directed wholly toward holding down inventory costs, this should *not* be done when it runs counter to the interest of effective overall operations.

KINDS OF PHYSICAL INVENTORIES

As mentioned earlier, there are several kinds of inventories. Each has its own peculiar characteristics and the way it is managed.

Raw Materials

Heavily used raw materials such as steel, wood, chemicals, and purchased parts are usually purchased on blanket contracts with deliveries scheduled to match the organization's needs. Almost no reserve supply is carried—incoming shipments are scheduled to arrive daily or even at specific times during the day. This usually works well if the items are made locally. But for shipped-in items it is usually necessary to allow more delivery lead time. Rarely is it safe to carry less than two or three days' supply as a safety stock. Release orders to suppliers, telling them exactly how much and when to ship, are usually given directly to the vendors by the PIPC department.

Less heavily used raw materials are usually

controlled by dollar limits, time limits, or other methods to be discussed later.

One problem in raw materials control is material shrinkage. Shrinkage comes from buying in one unit and issuing in another. For example, sheet steel is purchased by the ton and issued by the sheet. If the sheets are a little thicker than usual, there are not as many sheets in a ton as would be expected, and the sheet inventory will run out sooner than if they were thinner.

Also, some things are measured out as they are issued: wire (purchased by the pound, issued by length), liquids, pipe, lumber, and so on. Issuers often give liberal measure, so the supply ends up short. Or, as in sheet metal, pipe, lumber, or glass, the lengths or sizes purchased are standard, but scrap is created when they are cut to size. Experience will reveal what shrinkage or scrap to expect, and inventory controllers or design engineers can factor this into the bills of materials for use in their material requirements planning.

Work-in Process Inventories

Materials moving through production account for a large portion of total inventories in all companies which have manufacturing cycles (the time it takes to make products) in weeks or months. (At Westinghouse they account for 80 percent of the investment in inventories.) Controlling work-in-process is largely a matter of moving products through production as fast as possible, but it is also concerned with getting orders out in their proper priority order.

This is a scheduling problem and is PIPC's responsibility. But even companies which count their manufacturing cycle in days instead of weeks can have substantial amounts of money invested in work-in-process inventories.

Supplies

Supplies are supporting materials that are consumed in running the plant or in making the company's products but which do not themselves go into the product. (Sometimes these are called MRO items—for maintenance, repair, and operating supplies.) While the cost of MRO items over a year is usually low compared to that of materials going into products, their control should not be neglected. In many companies, both large and small, supplies are often handled carelessly and wastefully. Often they are handed out without requisitions, and no check is made for their use. Further, duplicate inventories tend to build up in various locations in the plant, and obsolete items tend to accumulate because "We may need one of those some day." Finally, since most supplies are expendable, except perhaps complicated tooling, it is difficult to check on their proper issuance and use.

To control supplies, it is often necessary to have several separate supplies stockrooms: one for maintenance department supplies and materials, another for tools and tooling, another for cutting oils and lubricants, another for stationery supplies, and so on. Materials (except for very little things) should be issued only upon presentation of written requisitions, properly authorized and showing the account to be charged, unless, of course, the cost of this paperwork is high compared to the value of the supplies. Budgets can be established limiting departments in their use of supplies in order to discourage numerous little "private inventories" besides those of the stockrooms.

Centralizing these stores should also be considered instead of having them throughout the factory. Often, less stockroom labor and total MRO inventories will be required, but, walking time to the centralized MRO store should be analyzed as a trade-off against the advantages of centralization.

Finished Goods Inventories

Final products and spare parts for previously sold products are usually stored in separate locations from other kinds of inventories—some at the manufacturing facility, and some at various locations in the distribution pipeline, such as regional warehouses and retailers. Some are also "stored" in trucks, ships, and boxcars as they move through the distribution system.

Some companies carry very little finished goods inventory if they build only to specific customer orders because they immediately ship the completed product. Others who build for no specific customers also carry little or no finished inventory if there is a strong demand for their products and there is not a very wide variety of products in their line. Coors beer, for example, immediately transfers their beer to waiting trucks and boxcars as it is produced, ships it to their wholesale beer distributors, and lets *them* carry the finished inventory.

FUNCTIONAL PURPOSES OF INVENTORIES

Inventories are used in a number of ways and perform several functions in organizations. First, it should be remembered that inventories are batches of physical products at various stages in their transformation from raw materials to work-in-process to finished goods. These inventories may be sitting still in stockrooms, warehouses, or retailers' stores. Or, they may be on the move—around the factory floor, in a truck moving across the nation, or in a ship crossing the Atlantic.

Decouple Function

An important function of inventories is to provide some degree of *independence* between successive component parts of the total manufacturing-distribution process. A retailer, for example, carries an inventory of racquetball racquets because it takes time to order and receive another shipment of them from the manufacturer. This inventory *decouples* him from the supplier and allows him to meet customers' demand with-

out being dependent on the supplier to provide *instant* replenishment of racquets.

The same decoupling function applies to batches of work-in-process sitting between work centers on the factory floor. If there is sufficient WIP waiting to be worked on at a machine, that machine is decoupled from the previous machine operation. Thus, if the previous machine breaks down, the downstream machine can continue to operate—until its bank of WIP is depleted. This decoupling function of inventories exists at many places in a manufacturing-distribution organization—and in many service organizations as well that require materials to support their delivery of services.

Pipeline Inventories

Pipeline stocks are minimum quantities of the various kinds of inventories mentioned above which are needed within and between the various stages of the total manufacturing-distribution system.

For example, when we manufacture a *new* product and begin to move it around the plant and then begin to ship it throughout our market, it takes *time* to first *fill* this production-transportation-warehouse-retailer pipeline. These are real inventories, and they must be managed, and holding costs must be incurred until units are actually paid for.

Cycle Inventories

While pipeline inventories represent a minimum amount of stock required to keep things flowing through the production-distribution system, this flow is rarely as continuous as water flowing out of a hose. But, if we let the water from a hose flow into a watering trough for our horse, we are accumulating a *cycle* inventory in the trough. Why? Because we don't want to constantly monitor the water level and spend all of our time holding the hose waiting for the horse to take a drink before we put another drink's worth into the trough.

Inventories are similar to this analogy. For convenience, we usually *batch* them or buy them in multiple quantities so we don't have to be continually placing separate orders for single items. In addition, these orders we do place take time to prepare, to mail to the vendor or release to the shop, and to receive. Thus cycle inventories are those quantities required in addition to pipeline stocks to keep things operating during these time delays, and to use between the times we place and receive orders for new batches of materials, parts, or supplies.

Seasonal Inventories

Often our production output rate of products is not sufficient to meet seasonal peaks in demand. But, on the other hand, if the rate is higher than the seasonal dips in demand, we can build *seasonal* inventories during the dips so we can meet demand during the peaks. Here, the stocks we accumulate in anticipation of future higher demand are *seasonal* inventories.

Safety Inventories

Because there are always uncertainties in lead time and demand for items during the reorder lead time can vary, extra quantities of stock are often carried as *safety* against these uncertainties. Actually, these safety stocks aid in the decoupling function mentioned earlier.

MANAGING INVENTORIES

Managing all of these physical inventories (raw, WIP, supplies, and finished) and functional inventories (decoupling, pipeline, cycle, seasonal, and safety) requires PIPC specialists to balance several factors, which will be discussed in detail in the next few chapters. But, in general, they want to manage inventories so that excessive holding and ordering costs will not occur. Yet they need to have enough so that production

and distribution proceeds in a smooth and orderly fashion without undue interruptions caused by out-of-stock conditions.

Enclosed Stockrooms

Most materials are kept in enclosed and secured stockrooms, from which they are issued only when a person presents a requisition. Materials in enclosed stockrooms are generally better cared for than things left out in the open. Also, enclosed stockrooms are essential for accurate records of the stock that comes in and goes out (see Figure 8–3). This is especially important for computerized inventory control systems.

Separate stockrooms are often needed for raw materials, semifinished items, finished parts (including finished subassemblies), finished products, and supplies. Often, more than one stockroom is needed for each kind of material so each will be near its point of use.

Having small substockrooms is, however, a mixed blessing. Even if one-day replenishment service is given from central stores, substores tend to accumulate supplies as if they were the sole source. Each substockroom manager remembers that "Central stores was out of stock last time"; or he says, "It's too much trouble to reorder so often."

Timken Roller Bearing found that three substores were each using 20 U belts a month, and each one averaged 50 on hand. In addition, central stores used 40 a month and carried 200. In total, a stock of 350 belts was carried to support a usage of 100 a month. Timken then changed its procedure and saved over half of the inventory by not allowing the substores to reorder until they ran out and then confining their reorders to only one month's requirements.

Individual stockrooms often stock several thousand items. This can cause some real problems with receiving materials, identifying them, knowing where they are kept, and putting them away. Besides this, there are record-keeping problems as well as problems of stockroom arrangements and indexes to where things are

FIGURE 8–3
Characteristics of a Good Stockroom Operation

1. The inventory is stored inside a stockroom that has preassigned bins [or a good random locator system] and an overflow area that is clearly identified.
2. The stockroom has a fence.
3. The fence has a door.
4. The door has a lock on it, and there are very few keys, which are distributed only to authorized people.
5. No unauthorized people ever wander in and out of the stockroom.
6. Service is prompt, and the stockroom hours are known in advance.
7. Every receipt is accompanied by a proper document.
8. Every issue has a corresponding document identified with it.
9. The stockroom people are well trained, a job description is available, and there is a break-in period for new people.
10. The objective of zero defects [in terms of record accuracy] is clearly well understood.
11. Time is allowed every day to reconcile transactions with inventories.
12. Audits are taken periodically, and discrepancies are totally unacceptable.
13. The users have complete confidence in the stockroom's integrity, and that is most important.

The inventory in a company is cash, and the stockroom is the local bank, a company from which we can learn a lot. Is it not remarkable that the average manufacturing company with several million dollars' worth of parts in inventory—more than your local bank would ever have in cash—does not insist on similarly stringent procedures? Even though it is our money in the bank, we do not walk in and help ourselves but follow definite procedures. A stockroom storing parts must be operated in the same way.

Source: George W. Plossl, *Materials Requirements Planning and Inventory Records Accuracy,* International Business Machines, 1973, p. 3.

stored. Computer-controlled systems, however, are solving these problems.

Fixed versus Random Locations

There are two main schemes for putting parts away in stockrooms (and warehouses). First, is to have specific or *fixed* locations for each part. These locations might be designated by aisle, shelf, and location on the shelf. This, of course, requires a spot for each item and enough room for the maximum quantity order size.

The other approach, which is becoming more widely used, is random location. Under this method, parts are put away in any available place, and this place (or places) are then recorded—usually by entering the location into the inventory control computer. This approach requires less total storage space than the fixed location method.

One more thing should also be done in stockroom location methods: items which are frequently put into or picked from stock should be put in more accessible locations in relation to the entrance/exit from the stockroom to reduce travel time. Items may be designated as being high-, medium-, or low-traffic items and placed close, in the middle, or at the back of the storage area. For fixed location systems, this designation must be done when the location system is set up; for random systems, zone designations are sometimes used, and stock handlers can put parts away anywhere within a zone, which is determined by a predetermined traffic volume code.

Open Stockrooms

A great deal of paperwork and handling of materials can be saved by point-of-use storage (storing materials right next to the operation where they are needed). This can be done where the same kinds of material are used day after day and where the materials are not likely to be stolen or otherwise misappropriated for use in some other manufacturing process. It can also be done with parts along assembly lines. As parts are made, or as purchased parts arrive (particularly if they arrive in small quantities in frequent repeat shipments), they are checked in and taken directly to their point of use and left there rather than in stockrooms. The operators just help themselves to whatever they need.

Even when open stores are used, however, the supply (or "bank") of materials stored at the operation is usually relatively small because there is very little storage space next to operations. Rarely (for large items) is the open supply sufficient to decouple one operation from the previous operation for more than an hour. New supplies must be continually added from larger "back-up" storerooms, where the conditions described in Figure 8–3 should prevail.

Cycle Counting and Record Accuracy

Inventory records can never stay wholly accurate, so an actual count needs to be made (a "physical inventory") of what there is on hand from time to time. Companies used to close down for a week at the end of the year to count everything. This is still done sometimes, but now it is more common to count all the time. The stores clerk counts what is on hand in the bins in one section this week, another section next week, and so on. This periodic checking, called *cycle counting,* is usually scheduled into the regular duties of stockroom clerks so they can check the entire inventory two or three times a year, depending upon the value of an item. Very high-valued items may be counted as frequently as once a week or month, and, at the other extreme, nuts and bolts need to be only weighed once a year and never actually counted.

Counting at least once a year is usually desirable. The government insists that a company's inventory records be accurate because income taxes depend on profits. And profits are the difference between sales income and the cost of sales. And the cost of sales equals the January 1 inventory value plus the cost of things bought and made in the year, minus the December 31 inventory. It is kind of a long way around, but

the amount a company claims its inventory is worth affects its profits and that affects the government's taxes, and the income tax collector says: Be sure it's right—count.

Besides federal taxes, local property taxes on inventories have to be paid. So local authorities, too, are interested in the counts of inventories being accurate so that the value put on inventories will be right.

Actually, it is not legally required to count everything at the end of the fiscal year or even during the year. A company's auditors are allowed to certify the accuracy of the counts shown on the records if their (the auditors') own small sample counts verify the card records or the computer records for the items they sample. Samsonite (luggage maker) reports that its computerized inventory control system keeps its inventory records accurate to within less than 3 percent of their physical inventory. This accuracy level is maintained by a full-time cycle counting team of over a dozen people who do most of their counting at night when the plant is not in operation. Samsonite believes the cost of this team is more than justified because of the importance of record accuracy to their computerized MRP system.

At Hewlett-Packard, a "zone defense" system is used for counting and maintaining record accuracy integrity. Each stock clerk is assigned a zone of responsibility where only they can go to place or pick parts. They are responsible for the housekeeping, cycle counting, and record accuracy for their zone and are expected to reach and maintain a high level of accuracy in a reasonable period of time. (This is not unlike bank tellers who are responsible for their own cash drawer—and who must, on a daily basis, reconcile receipts and disbursements of cash with beginning and ending cash balances.) Charts of accuracy objectives versus accuracy performance are kept and displayed on the wall to encourage a healthy competition and "ownership" of responsibility for each person's zone.[2]

---

[2] See William Z. Sandras, Jr., and Steven F. Bolander, "Zone Defense Improves Stockroom Record Accuracy," *Production and Inventory Management,* 2d quarter 1978, pp. 1–11.

Item Identification Systems

It is hard to imagine a supermarket where the cans are without labels. No one would ever know what they were getting. Materials, parts, supplies, and finished products are more varied in looks than tin cans, but without identification they are just about as hard to identify. Figure 8–4 is a picture of gears, but they are all different. A person cannot tell what they are for just by looking at them. An assembler asking a stock clerk for a certain kind of gear might have difficulty describing it correctly. Further, a computerized PIPC system needs a way to transfer items from bills of material into material and part needs. And, customers need a way to identify what they are buying without a long verbal description.

An identification system is mandatory. First, word descriptions of each item are needed—descriptions which tell what every item is and descriptions which set every item apart from other items. But word descriptions which clearly set every item apart from every other item are too long and cumbersome for most uses, so, second, a number system is needed. Numbers are shorter and they are unique. Coded number systems (or number-and-letter systems) are often used to give similar numbers to similar items.

FIGURE 8–4
Gears Need Seperate Identification Numbers

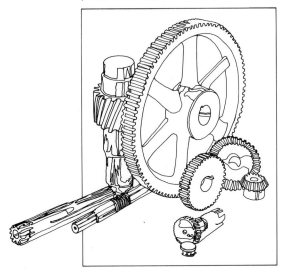

This helps people who have to work with the records to recognize the items more readily.

Significant numbering systems. There are two types of numbering systems—*significant* and *nonsignificant.* Significant numbering systems are those which can be understood by a person looking at the number who knows how to read the code. Nonsignificant systems, discussed later, are purely sequential numbers assigned to items, and mean nothing to a person looking at them, unless he or she has memorized what they stand for.

For raw materials, the significant numbering code usually shows the kind of material. Groups of numbers are reserved for sheet steel, steel bars, tool steel, steel wire, steel castings, malleable iron castings, and so on. Other groups of numbers stand for brass items. Paints and varnishes have a totally different number set.

The coded part of significant numbers is usually on the left. If an item's entire identification number has six or eight digits, the first two or three show its general class. The next one or two show its subclass. Only the last three digits are probably uncoded. An index is then used to find out exactly what the item is. The index would also provide the full word description. Many computer systems keep a dictionary of verbal descriptions of each item which may be called out by keying in the number. If the number isn't known, the user can enter key words describing the item until the computer finds the exact item.

The base used for coding raw materials (the *kind* of material) cannot be used with finished parts and components because finished items are often whole assembled products. They might be pumps, electric motors, compressors, or other such items. None of these can be classified according to what they are made of. Besides, trying to classify finished parts by what they are made of doesn't help people tie the product and its number together in their minds.

Using kinds of materials would give different numbers to steel, brass, nylon, and fiber gears. But since all are gears and serve the same purposes, it would seem better to have groups of similar numbers for the kinds of items. Then gears of all kinds would have similar numbers. Some companies do this. But this is not a perfect arrangement, either, because it can give the parts of a finished product unlike numbers.

For finished parts, it seems best to class things on a basis of use. Separate groups of numbers are set aside for parts for each finished product or each kind of finished product. This is the way most significant number codes for finished parts are set up, although there will always be many exceptions.

Using a related-use approach, electric motors, pumps, roller bearings, and oil cups would be numbered in the number system of the product they go in. But that would cause unlike numbers for electric motors. Pumps, bearings, and oil cups, too, would bear unlike numbers.

Common parts also upset all orderly numbering schemes. These parts are used in several products, and so their number is always out of series in all lists for a product's parts except one. Some companies give common parts a separate series of numbers; but then, of course, the number tells nothing about the item except that it has several uses.

Nonsignificant item numbering systems. Many companies which have computerized PIPC systems are moving away from significant numbering systems to simple sequential or serial numbering systems that are not broken into subparts. The primary reasons for this is that they often "run out" of significant numbers. And, since a longer item identification number is usually needed to build "significance" into it, more mistakes are made when it is written down or entered into a computer. Nonsignificant numbering systems can be shorter (often 7 digits as compared to up to 20 for some companies!), which requires less computer space, and results in fewer errors because there are no letters to worry about—only numbers

For example, a seven-digit significant system which is:

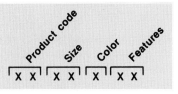

will only be able to describe (if 0, and 00 are not used) 99 + 99 + 9 + 99 = 306 different items, while a nonsignificant set of seven can describe 9,999,999 different items! Our social security numbers are nonsignificant—the dashes only make it easier to read, and only nine digits are required for the entire country.

The reason nonsignificant systems can work is that the computer is able to instantly tie each number to an abbreviated description of the item (which is usually in the computer "item master file" anyway, whether a significant or nonsignificant system is used) so that people can check to see what it is, if they need to. And, the computer file can also be organized to show which nonsignificant numbers belong to each product group, size group, and so on.

Nonsignificant item numbers are also more efficient when it comes to computerized data processing. It is easier to manipulate 30,000 seven-digit numbers in a massive bill of materials MRP explosion (explained in Chapter 11) than 30,000 significant numbers which contain nine digits, a few letters, and a dash or two.

Error control with check digits. As we continue to stress, record accuracy is extremely important in developing and maintaining formal PIPC systems. Major problems can result from errors in writing down item identification numbers or entering them into computers. For computerized systems, a "check digit" is often made a permanent part of an item's identification to aid in maintaining record accuracy. Only six digits may be actually used for identification, with the seventh being a check digit. Figure 8–5 shows an example. Suppose the second and third digits (93) were mistakenly transposed (39) when recorded. If undetected, the wrong part

FIGURE 8–5
Check Digit Example

```
Correct I.D. number              7 9 3 4 6 2 2*
        7 × 1 =  7                          ↑
        9 × 2 = 18
        3 × 3 =  9
        4 × 4 = 16
        6 × 5 = 30
        2 × 6 = 12
               ────
                92*              compare
Way entered into computer        7 3 9 4 6 2 2*
        7 × 1 =  7                          ↑
        3 × 2 =  6
        9 × 3 = 27
        4 × 4 = 16
        6 × 5 = 30
        2 × 6 = 12
               ────
                98*              compare
```

   * Check digit.

gets ordered, made, shipped, or whatever—which could be minor or could be disasterous.

In Figure 8–5 we simply multiplied each digit by 1, 2, 3, 4, 5, and 6 and summed the products. The predetermined check digit for the correct number would thus be 2. But, when we follow the same procedure with the incorrectly entered number, the check digit is calculated as 8. Of course, the computer does all of this, and, when check digits "don't check," an error list is printed and the numbers are checked and reentered.

With our simple check digit system, the chance of having an error yet calculating the correct check digit is 10 percent—which doesn't make it perfect, but is better than not having one. If errors are made 10 percent of the time, and the check digit fails to detect them 10 percent of the time, the expected undetected error rate is only 1 percent, with an accuracy rate of 99 percent. Other more sophisticated check digit systems exist which reduce this probability even further.

Of course, a combination of significant and nonsignificant systems can be and are used in many companies. A nine-digit number may have significance in its first three digits, and use the next five in a nonsignificant way, with the last

as a check digit. For some companies, this incorporates the advantages of both, yet the numbers do not become too unwieldy.

There are also other problems in both kinds of numbering systems because design changes cancel some old parts and their numbers and add others. Old part numbers should not be reassigned to new parts (at least not for years), or there will be confusion.

Many companies use a double numbering system. Every part on an airplane has a regular number, but, in addition, it has an "indent" number. For an aircraft manufacturer, the indent number tells at what point each part enters the plant. This information is needed to schedule its manufacture at the right time. A part may, for example, go into the left wing flap, which goes into the left wing, which goes into the airplane. Some items go into one subassembly, which goes into another subassembly, which goes into another, and so on for seven or eight "levels." These relationships result in an "indented" bill of materials and is sometimes referred to as a *product tree*. (These are discussed in Chapter 11.)

The indent number system can be quite complex, but there is no other way to get the quarter of a million parts of a big aircraft together at the right time and in the right order. Indented bill-of-material numbering systems help get the parts and subassemblies ready at the right time.

The government may also upset a company's numbering system. Companies selling products to the government may be required to use the government's parts numbers. Sometimes the government furnishes some parts which are identical to parts the contracting company uses regularly in other products but with the government numbers attached. Thus, two numbering systems must be maintained.

Engineering drawings both help and confuse identification problems. Most parts for assembled products have drawings showing their size, dimensions, and other information. In the engineering department, the drawings must be numbered. So many companies just use the drawing number as all or part of a part's identification number. But some parts, such as pieces of wire in a radio set, and such materials as welding rods and paint need identification numbers but have no drawing numbers. Their numbers are usually part of the raw material series in significant systems.

Identifying Materials

In addition to numerical and computerized identification systems, it is also necessary to physically identify the items themselves. There are two easy ways to do this so far as items in stock are concerned. For packaged items, the items' descriptions can go on the package. And for all items, packaged and unpackaged, a tag on the storage bin can identify its contents. For materials in process, the material or its container can be tagged. This is important because the material is changed in form a little after every operation, often making it difficult to tell what an item is by looking at it.

Tags and labels take care of most of the problem. These tags may be manually marked, or they may be computer-generated punched cards on special labels which can be read by computer-based electronic scanning devices which automatically keep track of items as they move throughout the production process and into and out of inventories. But tags get lost and separated from materials. Tags can't be run through heat-treating furnaces or degreasing tanks. They have to be removed from the containers and later be reattached. Or five tote boxes of an item go through an operation, but the operator puts them into six boxes; yet, he has only five tags. Errors can easily occur.

Also, some items—steel sheets, castings, and others—are not suitable for tagging, nor are they kept in bins. In these cases it is better to stamp, mold, paint, or etch some kind of identification on every item. Castings nearly always have their numbers molded into them. Bars and sheets of metal are stacked and are usually painted with coded colors on the end.

PRICING THE MATERIALS ISSUED

When materials are made into products, their money value is deducted from the raw materials account and added into the account showing the value of work-in-process. Later, their investment is taken out of the work-in-process account and added into the finished product account.

This sounds simple, but there is a problem—one that keeps cost accountants busy. Suppose there is a bin full of an item—say 125 in all. Suppose that they were acquired (whether they were purchased or were manufactured internally is immaterial) as follows: 25 units at $5 each, 50 units at $6 each, and 50 units at $7 each. These differences are extreme, but they will illustrate the point. The actual investment is $775 (although buying them all at today's price would cost $875). Now suppose that 100 pieces are issued. What price should be put on the requisition—$5, $6, $7, or some combination thereof?

There are four choices or methods for answering this question: FIFO, LIFO, weighted average cost, and standard cost.

FIFO

FIFO means "first in, first out." Using FIFO, the first 25 items issued would be priced at $5, then 50 items at $6, and the last 25 items at $7, giving a total of 100 items issued and reported as costing $600. The 25 items left in stock would be shown to be worth $175. In our example, FIFO understates the cost of materials, and this in turn decreases the calculated costs of goods sold, increases apparent profits, and increases taxes.

LIFO

LIFO means "last in, first out." Using LIFO, the first 50 items issued would be priced at $7, the next 50 items at $6 for a total of 100 items costing $650. The 25 items left would be shown to be worth $125. LIFO has the opposite effect on profits and taxes from FIFO. During times of increasing raw material prices, profits are held down as are taxes.

Weighted Average Cost

The 125 items cost $775, or an average of $6.20 each. So, using this method, the 100 items issued would be priced at $6.20 each, or a total of $620. The 25 items left would be shown to be worth $155.

Standard Cost

Here, some standard figure that items *should* cost is determined. This method is commonly used for items a company makes itself because no two lots ever cost exactly the same. Suppose the standard cost in our example is $5.75. All items going into inventory would be priced in a $5.75 each, with all actual cost differences being carried to a variance account. If 100 items were issued, they would all be charged out at $5.75—a total of $575. The remaining 25 items left in the bin would also be valued at $5.75 each, or a total of $143.75.

Discussing these various methods of pricing may seem to be just a play on numbers because the actual costs are the same and so are the selling prices, no matter how the matter is handled. Actually, the valuation method used is important because the problem goes on forever (prices and manufacturing costs are always changing), and it affects nearly every item used in making products.

Each method produces somewhat different product cost figures. This means the calculated profits are different, and this affects the company's income taxes. Also, if prices of finished products are set based on manufacturing costs, the method of charging for material used affects selling prices and probably the sales volume too.

FIFO gives lower cost values during periods of raw material price increases. In such a case, FIFO would show more apparent profit and would result in higher income taxes. Also, remaining inventories will be valued at a higher amount, which can increase inventory taxes.

LIFO is the reverse. As raw material prices go up, the calculations presume the last purchased, and most costly materials, are used first.

LIFO boosts apparent costs and holds down profits and taxes, but it values remaining inventories lower, resulting in lower inventory taxes. (In the late 1970s when raw materials and purchased component prices went up substantially, many companies changed their accounting procedures to LIFO?)

ABC INVENTORY ANALYSIS

Many large organizations have to stock and keep track of 25,000 or more different items. They may be end products, parts or components of end products, service parts for products no longer made, supplies, raw materials for general use, maintenance items, and items for other purposes. The investment in these items is substantial.

One purpose of inventory control is to control inventories at the least cost. Some items, such as paper clips and rubber bands, are not worth monitoring very closely. It is better just to keep a supply on hand and let people help themselves. It does not matter if these things are used somewhat wastefully because it usually costs less to absorb the waste than to control it.

Obviously, loose controls should be limited to unimportant items. This means that a decision has to be made as to which items are little things and which need more careful control. Pareto's *vital few* and *trivial many* concept, the "20–80 principle," applies here. The inventory controller should review the stock records, item by item, and classify them into A, B, and C groups.

A Pareto curve would show clearly which items are A, B, and C. In Figure 8–6 the numbers are for the usage of materials and parts. The conclusion is: A few of the items are responsible for most of the value of all materials and parts used.

"A" items are the large investment items: the vital few. Ten percent of the items commonly account for 70 percent of the money spent on materials. These items should be carefully controlled. Their specific quantity needed to support the master schedule needs should be calculated

FIGURE 8–6
Typical ABC Inventory Distribution

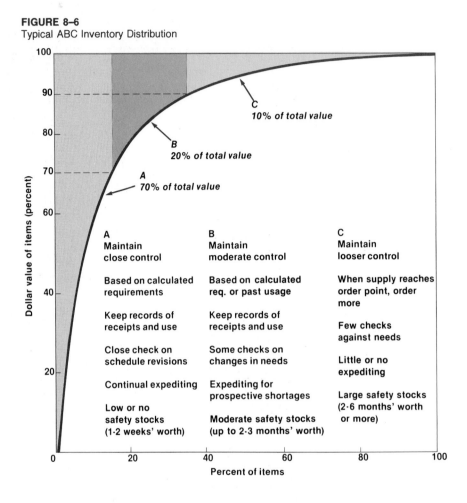

A	B	C
Maintain close control	Maintain moderate control	Maintain looser control
Based on calculated requirements	Based on calculated req. or past usage	When supply reaches order point, order more
Keep records of receipts and use	Keep records of receipts and use	Few checks against needs
Close check on schedule revisions	Some checks on changes in needs	Little or no expediting
Continual expediting	Expediting for prospective shortages	Large safety stocks (2·6 months' worth or more)
Low or no safety stocks (1·2 weeks' worth)	Moderate safety stocks (up to 2·3 months' worth)	

in advance according to the period of use. And their manufacture or purchase should usually be scheduled so that they arrive just before they are needed. These are the items most suitable for ordering by the computerized MRP methods which are described in detail in Chapter 20. In most cases these items should be ordered a few at a time, and frequently, in order to hold down inventories.

"B" items are the 15 to 20 percent of the items which account for about 15 percent of the investment. While they are less important than A items, they are costly enough to make it desirable to keep careful records of their use.

If the company doesn't have a computerized MRP system, minimum stock limits and standard reorder quantities can be set and used for B items. Replenishment reorders can be made out automatically whenever the stock of an item gets down to its reorder point. "Economic order quantities" (see Chapter 12) might be used to advantage here.

"C" items are the "trivial many." It is not uncommon for 75 percent of the items to account for only 10 percent of the value of materials. Large safety stocks of C items can be carried, and they should receive minimal attention. Often they are on a reorder point system and not carried in the computerized MRP system. (Some, however, are carried in MRP systems, and their needs *are calculated* as are A and B items, to support the master schedule.) C items can be put at the operatives' workplaces, where they can help themselves without using requisitions. And they are usually not priced to products individually; rather, they are charged to an overhead account.

Looser controls of C items coupled with large safety stocks will increase investment and their costs from shelf wear, obsolescence, and wasteful use but usually not as much as the cost to control them more tightly. PIPC people should be sure, however, *not to run out of a low-cost but critical item.* For example, an inexpensive washer used in the manufacture of lawn mowers might be classified as a C item. But, if the lack of this washer stops final assembly of lawn mowers, the downtime costs could be substantial. So, while C items need not be watched too closely, they should not be allowed to run out unless replacement lead time is virtually instantaneous or unless an allowable substitute can be used. In the final analysis, C items, too, are essential.

INVESTMENT LIMITATION CONTROL METHODS

Inventory Turnover

Inventory turnover is the cycle of using and replacing materials. It is a ratio—the number of "turns" to the investment in a year. If a company sells $100,000 worth of products a year and has an average inventory valued at $50,000, it has two turnovers a year. But, if this company could produce sales of $100,000 with an average inventory worth $25,000, it would have four turns a year. More turns reduces the investment and saves carrying costs as well.

Some companies use an inventory turnover ratio as an inventory control method. They insist on a certain number of turns a year. This control should not be carried very far, however. A high turnover rate means very low inventories, but very low inventories may mean being out of stock more often. High turnover and low inventories at the same time also force frequent and often uneconomical small reorders which can result in higher unit costs.

Sales volume and reasonable inventory turnover ratios are also related. It is not difficult to obtain more turns when sales volume is high. But, if sales volume decreases to half and if inventories are also cut in half in order to keep the turnover ratio constant, there will probably be more stock outs. This could lead to costly, frequent, and small-quantity reorders, as well as idle production—which, of course, if sales fell this much, might be justified.

Dollar Limits

Most companies set dollar limits or budgets on the amount which they will allow to be invested in each class of materials. Each class has an account in the accounting department showing its investments and the inventory planning and control manager is responsible for seeing that the amounts stay within the allowed budgets.

This approach is usually applied only to broad classes of materials and not to individual items except perhaps A items; it is just too costly to set dollar limits for each item separately. Dollar limits do not tell inventory managers when or how much to reorder; all they do is to tell them not to exceed an upper investment limit. They have to determine how much of each individual item to provide, while keeping the investment for the item class within the limit.

Dollar limits should be used with discretion when prices or business levels change; otherwise they automatically tighten or loosen the amount allowed to be carried. If, for example, prices rise and the dollar limits are not changed, the inventory manager has to reduce the quantities carried. Similarly, if business improves, dollar limits, if unchanged, hold down the inventories when some increase is really needed to support the larger master production schedule.

Time Limits

Time limits are a common way to put dollar limits into effect. To translate dollar limits into time limits, it is only necessary to divide the dollar limit by the dollar usage per month. A $20,000 limit is a two-month limit for an item used at a rate of $10,000 per month.

While dollar limits can best be used directly to control broad classes of items (or perhaps only A items), time limits can easily be applied to every item. In fact, one single time limit can apply to any number of items at the same time.

Time limits do not directly determine when or how much to order. They merely say, for example, do not have more than 30 days' supply on hand. Indirectly this sets upper limits on how much can be ordered at one time. To hold the average investment for a class of items down to a month's usage, the inventory controller can never order more than a month's supply of any item on a single order.

For long-lead-time items, time limits control when reorders are released as well as how much is ordered. If it takes three months lead time to receive an item and inventories are limited to one month's supply at one time, it will be necessary to place a new order every month for one month's needs, but each order will always be for the third month ahead. Thus, there will always be several orders out at the same time. (Items on order do not count in the inventory so far as investment is concerned.)

The inventory "coverage" (the quantity on hand plus the amount on order) is the true available inventory. Assuming reliable lead times, the coverage, in our example, is adequate even though much of it is, for the moment, in the form of open orders rather than stock on hand. So, the short time limit permitted for stock on hand does not mean that we have to stock out of long-lead-time items.

Time limits are easy to set, easy to change,

and easy to operate. And they can be different for different items. If an item's use changes, the time limit can remain unchanged because the reordering quantity can change to reflect the new requirements.

A disadvantage of time limits is that they are not often the very best for entire groups of products, although they are usually applied to entire groups. A 30-day limit is probably too much for some items in a group and too little for others. For this reason, both dollar limits and time limits, while commonly used, are not always appropriate.

Review Questions

1. What conflicting objectives are likely to exist between departments in a manufacturing organization? Are these conflicts different in a service organization?

2. What are "formal" PIPC systems, and why are they necessary?

3. What are the main components of an integrated PIPC system?

4. The text says that holding inventories down may be unwise suboptimization. How is it that this might be unwise?

5. What are the different kinds of physical inventories?

6. Differentiate between MRP I and MRP II.

7. What are the various functional purposes of inventories?

8. Compare enclosed and open stockrooms, and fixed versus random locations. When should each be used?

9. How often should actual physical counts of inventories be made? Why?

10. Differentiate between significant and nonsignificant item numbering systems. What are their advantages and disadvantages?

11. What kind of an identification system seems best for raw materials? Why? What kind is best for finished parts? Why?

12. Should actual purchase costs or actual production costs be used for pricing requisitions? Why or why not? What problems are involved? If nei-

ther of these cost figures should be used, what price should be used?

13. What methods for pricing materials out of stock are available? Which is best? Why?

14. How do inventory ABCs work? How does a company which recognizes this concept benefit as compared to one which does not? Discuss.

15. Describe the differences in inventory control techniques which should be used for A, B, and C items in inventory.

16. Inventory turnover is commonly used as part of the method for controlling inventories. What dangers might appear if this idea is pursued too far?

17. If a company uses dollar-limit control and the limits stay fixed, what happens to the inventories when business volume increases? When prices decrease?

Questions for Discussion

1. Whom should the inventory controller listen to as he tries to do his job? The purchasing agent does not want to have to expedite orders. The treasurer wants him to hold down the average inventory investment. The sales manager wants him never to run out of anything. The plant manager doesn't want to have production held up by not having materials, and he also wants long runs on production jobs. Try to reconcile these conflicting desires.

2. Does MRP II allow a company to become more centralized or decentralized? Discuss.

3. A question from the inventory controller: "How can I get the information I need to analyze and to prove that I am doing a good job?" How can this question be answered?

4. If a company is to end up with a certain number of obsolete items in stock, where is it worst for this to occur? In raw materials? In in-process materials? In finished parts? Or in finished products? Why?

5. Do inventories contribute to reducing overall company costs, or do they increase total costs? Discuss.

6. Do large inventories have any effect on worker productivity? If so, what effect?

7. Is it more or less fruitless to try to hold inventories to the barest minimums when railroad companies sometimes hold freight cars for several days in order to make up long trains? Discuss.

8. How hard should a company try to keep inventories down on parts it makes itself when the machine setup costs in some departments run as high as 25 percent of all labor costs? Is this bad? Discuss.

9. How can a company count heavy material, such as bins partly full of 100-pound castings?

10. In the late 1970s, many companies changed from FIFO to LIFO inventory valuation practices. Why?

Problems

1. Item 294's record shows the following:

Received January 24	300 @ $.42 each
Received February 15	200 @ .46 each
Received March 27	400 @ .51 each
Received April 15	200 @ .47 each
Received May 25	350 @ .54 each

Issues were as follows:

From January 24 to February 14	176
From February 15 to March 26	145
From March 27 to April 14	502
From April 15 to May 25	120
From May 25 to June 1	47

If the company uses FIFO, what price was put on the withdrawal requisitions for the stock withdrawn in each period? What would the prices have been if the company had used LIFO? What would be the calculated remaining inventory value each time a new stock came in?

2. Suppose that the following 15 items are representative of the 40,000 items kept in stock. Construct a maldistribution curve and find out what proportion of the items are A, B, and C items. What fraction of all items are probably responsible for 70 percent of the total value of all items used? 20 percent? 10 percent?

Item	Value of Use in One Year ($000)	Item	Value of Use in One Year ($000)
1	6	9	40
2	45	10	9
3	17	11	12
4	4	12	5
5	13	13	60
6	32	14	3
7	2	15	26
8	1		

3. *a.* How many items can be identified uniquely with the following significant part numbering system?

		Character
XXX	(product code)	Numeric
XX	(size)	Numeric
X	(color)	Alphabetic
XX	(features)	Numeric

b. Using a nonsignificant numbering system and the above number of characters, how many parts could be uniquely identified?

c. What condition would be required to use a nonsignificant numbering system?

Case 8–1

The Elk Company analyzed its stockroom investment turnover and found it to be considerably below what the management thought it should be. A quick review of the stock records showed that a six-months' supply of many items was on hand. Very few items had less than two months' supply on hand. The purchasing agent of the company bought the major materials used in the company's products. They were bought on the basis of price forecasts, and it was felt that that practice should be continued. The stocks of items ordered from the records by the stock clerk were regarded as excessive. The record clerk ordered replenishment supplies of these items as he saw fit, although he was supposed to order no more than three months' supply on any one reorder. He could, however, use his own judgment as to when to reorder; and, if he thought that the demand might increase, he ordered a new supply sooner than he normally would, even when the current stock was ample for the time being. Before he took the job, shop work had been held up frequently for lack of stock. He was quite proud of having solved that difficulty.

Is there a problem here? Since it will all be used in due time, is there any harm in having plenty of stock on hand? Set up a procedure to reduce the inventory without running out of stock.

Case 8–2

Rhinegold Refractors was having a severe problem with inventory record accuracy. The accounting department, after completing an annual inventory audit, found a $200,000 discrepancy in what was on hand compared to what the books showed inventory value to be. (There was $200,000 *less* in inventory than the books showed!)

As a result, management immediately instituted a cycle-counting program, locked up all the inventory behind cyclone fences, and thought they had the problem solved. However, the bean-counters (accountants) insisted on another complete physical inventory six months later. This time there was $300,000 *more* in inventory than the books showed.

You have been asked to investigate this situation by conducting a series of interviews. Who would you interview, and what questions would you ask of each person? Also, you have access to the shop floor and to the inventory stores area. What would you look for as you walked around the facility?

Chapter 9

Forecasting Demand for Finished Products and Services

The forecasting of future demand for *finished products* is very important in production planning and control, as is forecasting demand for services. Good forecasting is essential to efficient manufacturing and service operations. (Forecasting demand for *component parts* with MRP is a quite different process, and will be discussed in Chapter 11.)

METHODS OF FORECASTING

Forecasting is sometimes done by a "top-down" method. In other cases, the reverse, a "bottom-up" method, is used. And in still other cases, past experience is extrapolated into the future by using mathematical and statistical procedures.

Top-Down Forecasting

The top-down method often starts by using forecasts of general business conditions made by economists in the government and in large companies and universities. Such forecasts appear frequently in government and private publications. Other more detailed and customized forecasts are purchased from organizations which specialize in "econometric" forecasting (forecasting economic trends, using statistical and mathematical procedures). The experts may say, for example, that next year's gross national product will be $1.25 trillion. In a company making kitchen stoves, refrigerators, disposals, dishwashers, and the like, the question then becomes: How will this affect us? The forecaster in the company must first translate general forecasts into terms of his industry's future business. Then he has to estimate his company's share, and, finally, how many of each product the company will be able to sell each month.

Often, as they try to develop specific forecasts for major individual products or for important groups or classes of products, the forecasters use "extrinsic" forecasting methods. Extrinsic forecasting methods are usually used for forecasting groups of products, such as lawnmowers, men's shoes, or electric motors. These forecasts are usually developed by the marketing staff of the organization.

Extrinsic forecasting assumes that, in the past, there has been some relationship between the sales of an item or group of items and one

THE WALL STREET JOURNAL

A·1 Trampolines

Nick

Source: *The Wall Street Journal,* March 7, 1984, p. 31. From *The Wall Street Journal,* with permission of Cartoon Features Syndicate.

or more external factors, such as population growth, personal incomes, Dow Jones Stock Index, money supply, number of people employed, or the number of new houses being built. It also assumes that since changes in these external factors have had a strong relationship with the product's sales in the past, this relationship will continue in the future.

The most common statistical method used to find these relationships is regression analysis, which calculates an equation that, for example, might be:

Steel demand (thousands of tons per quarter)[1] =

$\quad$ 452.127 ×$\quad$ Domestic retail sales of
$\quad\quad\quad\quad\quad\quad\quad\quad$ autos (millions of $)

---

[1] This equation is an approximation of one actually used by Union Carbide to forecast steel demand. They use this forecast in turn to forecast the demand for their products that are used in steel making after considering their market share and other factors.

$+191.141 \times$$\quad$ Investment in capital equipment (billions of $)

$+\ 69.465 \times$$\quad$ Investment in residential construction (billions of $)

$+129.084 \times$$\quad$ Change in nonfarm business inventories (billions of $)

$+202.642\ +$$\quad$ Investment in nonresidential and government construction (billions of $)

and so on.

If the estimate for each of these five predictor or extrinsic variables for the next quarter year in a particular state are 100, 10, 20, −1, and 15, respectively, then the predicted demand for steel for the next quarter would be:

$$\text{Steel demand} = 452.127(100) + 191.141(10)$$
$$+ 69.465(20) + 129.084(-1)$$
$$+ 202.642(15)$$
$$= 51.42 \text{ thousands of tons}$$

In order to use this method, analysts need historical data from which to develop the equations, and they also need to be able to develop estimates of the predictor factors (as we did above) in order to make a forecast. Obviously, if the estimates of the predictor factors prove to be wrong, as sometimes happens, then the estimate of future demand will also be wrong.

Fortunately, sometimes one or more of the predictor series "leads" other series. It moves first and then is followed by other series. If employment and personal income go up, then a little later the sales of automobiles and other durable consumer products will go up. When one or more such leading factors can be found, then their performance today reveals what will happen to the following series tomorrow. Carpet manufacturers' demand follows new housing starts, for example.

The methods for determining regression equations which can be used in forecasting will not be explored here since they are covered in detail in statistics textbooks.[2] However, a word of caution is in order. These methods, which can be calculated easily on computers, require skill and judgment in determining the proper predicting factors and their importance in predicting demand.

Bottom-Up Forecasting

The bottom-up method begins with individual end product demand expectations. How many of each end product does it appear that the company can sell next year? Or, how many hours of service will be demanded? In this method the forecaster receives estimates from sales people and from dealers and customers. He also looks at past sales patterns. Finally, he adds up the different product forecasts and gets a total, which is the aggregate forecast.

Actually, most companies use both a top-down and a bottom-up method at the same time and combine the resulting projections into a single forecast. But before settling on a final forecast, they may also use the "jury of executive opinion" (sometimes called the *Delphi* method) approach to adjust judgmentally the more technically determined forecasts. The forecasts are adjusted up or down according to what the organization's top people think about the future.

Neither top-down or bottom-up methods are, however, very useful for forecasting how many of each of the thousands of individual products to make. Here the most common method is simply to extrapolate past demands for each item into the future by mathematical and statistical procedures. At first this does not sound very practical because these mechanistic forecasts do not consider outside factors and thus may

not always be very good forecasts. At the same time, however, the other methods of forecasting described above are much too complex to be used for each individual item of the thousands of items in normal inventories. Extrapolations and calculations of future needs by computers, using mechanistic methods, are perhaps the best that one can do for individual items or demands for service.

Demand Interpretation

Unfortunately, forecasting is done in a dynamic economy and therefore can rarely be perfectly done. As weeks and months pass and actual demand becomes known, it is often found that forecasts did not anticipate demand perfectly. In fact, some forecasters say that the only "true" statement one can make about a forecast is that *it will be wrong!* This introduces a new complication: How should the departures of demand from forecasts be interpreted? The first thing that happens when sales differ from forecasts is that inventories become different from those planned. This immediately raises the question: Should these differences be continued? Or should production levels be changed instead? And if so, how much and how soon? A new forecast is needed, and this new forecast may require the development of new inventory plans and new production schedules.

To illustrate the problem, suppose that the forecast and sales of product A for the first four months of the year are as shown in Figure 9–1. It is now May 1. The figures are in thousands.

The sales forecasters now have the problem of determining what to do next. How should they interpret the April sales exceeding the forecast? Was there a strike at a competitor's plant? Did customers just buy earlier this year? If there is no evidence that extraneous factors such as these caused the sales upsurge, then customers have either bought ahead (in which case lower sales probably lie ahead), or else the forecaster has underestimated the market. If the latter is the case, perhaps production schedules should

[2] See Donald R. Plane and Edward B. Oppermann, *Statistics for Management Decisions* (Dallas: Business Publications, 1977).

FIGURE 9–1

Month	Sales (000 items)		Inventory (end of month) (100 items)	
	Forecast	Actual	Forecast	Actual
January	30	10	30	50
February	30	25	60	85
March	40	55	100	110
April	120	160	60	30
Total	220	250		

immediately be revised upward as the inventory level is already down 30,000 below the planned level of 60,000 units.

This is a capacity problem, a scheduling problem, and an inventory control problem. Up to now (through April) the schedulers have not changed the master production schedule and instead have let the inventory level vary. Now, though, with sales catching fire, and if the best months are still ahead, the production rate should probably be increased immediately and substantially. Otherwise we may soon be out of stock of product A.

We won't decide here what to do in this case, but this is one of the problems of coordinating capacities, schedules, and inventories. To appreciate the importance of the problem, it should be remembered that it exists with almost every one of a company's many finished products. Also, its effects ripple all the way back to raw materials stores. If production schedules are increased or decreased, this may upset raw materials inventory plans, purchase order delivery schedules, and even supplier plant production schedules. It is important to emphasize the point that, because completely accurate forecasting is rarely possible, production planning and control systems should be designed to *react* to errors in forecasts so that schedules can be changed and at low cost when necessary. The speed of this reaction, however, should not become an overreaction—but should reflect true changes in demand, and a policy of "standing

pat" should be followed when it is believed the difference is short-lived or random.

SPECIFIC ITEM FORECASTING

As we said, neither top-down nor bottom-up forecasting helps much in forecasting the demand for the thousands of finished items that some companies make. Consider, for example, the sales prospects at Singer for 6-inch scissors, or at Black & Decker for ¼-inch portable electric drills, or at Eli Lilly for aspirin sold in 5-grain pills in 100-pill bottles. Neither top-down nor bottom-up forecasting tells forecasters how many of these individual items are likely to be sold during the next several months. And, because there can be thousands of these items, it is not practicable to spend much time or money having specialists make forecasts for each item. Yet, these companies manufacture these items and have to decide how many of each to make and when to make them.

This is an area where computer analysis has taken over a large part of the work. It is an important function in many companies because it may cover tens of thousands of items which constitute a substantial part of the company's sales.

The simplest forecast of next month's demand is this month's usage, but rarely is this very reliable because the usage of most items varies too much. Furthermore, the planner does not even know this month's usage of an item until after the end of the month. By this time the order for next month's supply has already been placed. Yet, in practice, these two objections are not of overriding importance.

Using an item's record of demand in the past to forecast future demand is called *intrinsic* forecasting. *Demand* is defined as actual sales plus back orders. Back orders are demands that could not be met because of out-of-stock conditions. The record of past demand or past usage is a "time series" which shows the items' historical demand by week, month, or year. A historical time series may contain several subpatterns. These subpatterns may be caused by *trend, seasonal, cyclic,* and *random* forces at work. Figure 9–2 shows an example of these components of a time series for a hypothetical item or service.

In Figure 9–2, the broad dip, which bottoms out in Year 2 and has risen in the years since, appears to be part of a five- or six-year *cycle*. Yet this may not be so, and it might be an economic recession and recovery which will not recur. Second, in Years 2 to 4, there is an upward *trend* which may not last. This upward trend may

be caused just by the recovery of the economy, or it may reflect new markets opening up, less competition, or obtaining a larger share of an existing market. Third, demand seems, in Figure 9–2, to vary *seasonally.* Sales are greatest each year around January and July with low points in February and September. Such seasonal patterns are quite common in the demand for products and services, and they can usually be isolated and taken into account in planning production and service levels. As examples, the sales of soft drinks are usually highest in the summer and lowest in the winter; college textbooks have sales peaks at the beginning of each school term; and ski lifts are busy only in the winter, and then only on weekends.

Finally, there may be "blips" in any time series. These may be caused by a known abnormal condition, such as the summer Olympic games, a baseball World Series, a sales campaign, a severe snowstorm, or some other explainable and nonrepetitive reason. In other cases the blips are "random effects" whose

FIGURE 9–2
Time Series Showing Effects of Seasonal, Cyclical, Trend, and Random Factors Operating Together

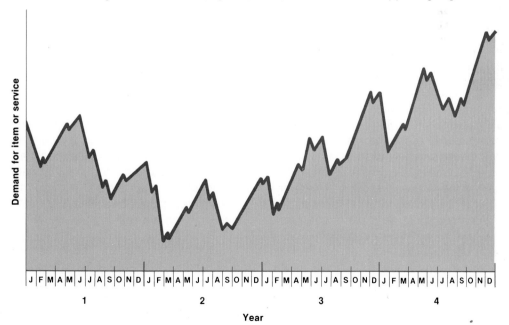

FIGURE 9–3

	Month	Period Number	Demand		Month	Period Number	Demand
Year 1	January	1	100	Year 3	January	25	146
	February	2	128		February	26	175
	March	3	138		March	27	173
	April	4	127		April	28	161
	May	5	112		May	29	150
	June	6	115		June	30	162
	July	7	128		July	31	171
	August	8	134		August	32	173
	September	9	130		September	33	168
	October	10	116		October	34	157
	November	11	100		November	35	130
	December	12	95		December	36	125
Year 2	January	13	125	Year 4	January	37	161
	February	14	148		February	38	178
	March	15	155		March	39	183
	April	16	138		April	40	178
	May	17	128		May	41	158
	June	18	142		June	42	178
	July	19	152		July	43	190
	August	20	156		August	44	188
	September	21	140		September	45	176
	October	22	122		October	46	165
	November	23	108		November	47	158
	December	24	100		December	48	135

causes are either unknown or cannot be easily explained by cyclical, trend, or seasonal effects.

INTRINSIC FORECASTING METHODS

There are many different methods used for forecasting mathematically and using statistical methods. We will present a few of the methods which are the most widely used.

Figure 9–3 shows a four-year demand record for a finished item we will call a "Needem." These figures are plotted later in Figure 9–5. (It is usually a good idea, as a first step in time series analysis, to plot historical demand so that the analyst can visualize[3] what effects seem to be at work.) In Figure 9–5 it is apparent that there are trend, seasonal, and some random ef-

fects in operation. The overall trend is upward; seasonal peaks usually occur in March and August, with valleys usually occurring in May and December; and there seems to be some randomness in the series.

To illustrate statistical forecasting methods, we are going to use only the first three years (36 months) of Needem demand figures in our analysis. Then we will forecast the monthly demand for the 12 months of the fourth year. Actually we already know the monthly demand for the fourth year so this will allow us to review the accuracy of our forecasts to see if the methods we used are satisfactory.

Trend Calculation

A common method for calculating the trend is to draw or "fit" a straight line through the plot of demand figures so that the points above and

---
[3] Some call this "interocular analysis," or "eye-balling" the data!

below the line are more or less equal in number and distance from the line. Such a line can be calculated mathematically, using the least squares method, or it can be drawn freehand with a ruler. When calculated mathematically, this line is called a *regression* line and is expressed by the following equation:

$$Y_c = a + bx$$

Where:

Y_c = Trend value at time period x
a = Trend value when $x = 0$
b = Slope of trend line
x = Time period where $x = 1, 2, 3, \ldots,$
$\quad n$ time periods

For our Needem example, we used a computer to calculate the regression line (or trend line) for the first three years of our Needem data. Appendix G details these calculations. The computer found that the equation for the trend was:

$$Y_c = 114.35 + 1.22\,x$$

Regression analysis of this sort produces a Y_c (or Y computed) value for every month. When these are extrapolated into the future, they become (before adjustments for seasonal variations) the forecasts for the months ahead. These extrapolations for Year 4 are shown in Figure 9–4.

FIGURE 9–4

Forecast for Future Months	Y Computed	Seasonal Index	Y Forecast
37 January	159.4 ×	0.94 =	149.9
38 February	160.7	1.14	183.2
39 March	161.9	1.17	189.6
40 April	163.1	1.06	172.9
41 May	164.3	0.96	157.7
42 June	165.5	1.02	168.9
43 July	166.7	1.09	181.8
44 August	168.0	1.11	186.6
45 September	169.2	1.04	176.2
46 October	170.4	0.93	158.4
47 November	171.6	0.79	135.5
48 December	172.8	0.74	128.1

Seasonal Calculation

In our analysis of the demand figures for Needems, the computer program we used calculated both the trend and the seasonal variations. Seasonal indexes were calculated by averaging ratios of actual monthly sales to the trend line value (the Y_cs) for each month. The calculation of the seasonal index for March, for example, was as follows:

	Actual Sales	Trend Line Value (Y_c)	Ratio of Actual to Trend
March, Year 1	138	118*	1.16
March, Year 2	155	133	1.16
March, Year 3	173	147	1.18
			3.50

Average $= 3.50 \div 3 = 1.17$

* March, Year 1, is where $X = 3$, so $Y_3 = 114.35 + (1.22 \times 3) = 118$; March, Year 2, is where $X = 15$, so $Y_{15} = 114.35 + (1.22 \times 15) = 133$, etc.

This index of 1.17 means that March demand is typically 17 percent above the trend value in any year. If, instead, the index were .85, this would mean that March is typically a below-average month and normally is 15 percent below the month's trend calculation.

Forecast for Year 4. Our computer program, after computing the trend line and the seasonal indices, then extrapolated the trend ahead for Year 4 (months 37 to 48). It also applied the seasonal indices to each month's Y_c to obtain the forecast for Year 4 after adjusting for expected seasonal variations. These are shown in Figure 9–4.

In Figure 9–4, the calculation for January's Y_c value is:

$$Y_c = 114.35 + 1.22(37) = 114.35$$
$$+ 45.09 = 159.4$$

Then the January seasonal index is applied:

$$159.4 \times .94 = 149.9$$

FIGURE 9–5

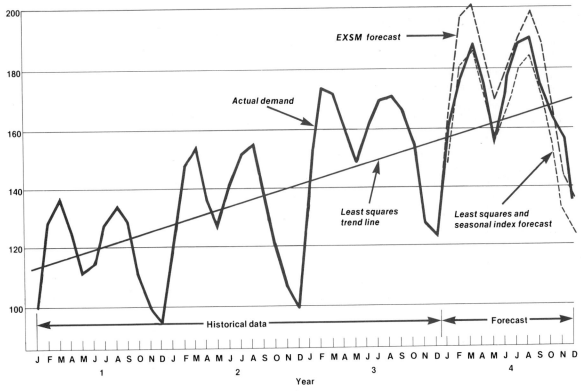

The least squares trend line and the monthly forecasts for Year 4 are plotted in Figure 9–5 as are the actual monthly demand figures for Year 4 (which we kept out of our calculations for comparative purposes). The "EXSM" forecast, also shown in Figure 9–5 will be explained in the next few pages.

As can be seen, this method, using regression analysis plus a seasonal adjustment, forecasts Year 4 quite well for this particular time series. It should be strongly emphasized, however, that this approach may provide poor forecasts for other time series if, for example, there are cycles or changes in trends. If this is the case other forecasting methods may need to be used.[4]

_____

[4] Statistical measures of forecast error and "confidence intervals" of the forecast can be calculated for regression-derived estimates. See any standard statistics textbook for an explanation of these calculations.

EXPONENTIAL SMOOTHING (EXSM)

The extrapolated trend with adjustments for seasonality method of forecasting which we have just discussed weights all of the historical data the same—both the oldest and the most recent—in developing the forecast. But, it stands to reason that we may want to give *more* weight to more recent historical data (and less weight to older data) because it might better reflect our current demand situation.

Another forecasting method, "exponential smoothing," allows us to do this. The EXSM method "washes out" random fluctuations; it accounts for trends, and it takes seasonal influences into account in determining a forecast. And, as time unfolds and new actual demand experience is known, it updates the influence which each of these time series components has on forecast values. While the EXSM method does not directly calculate long-term cyclic patterns, it does, by its very nature, help reveal major turning points in the cycle by showing a lessening or increasing of trends. We will continue to use our Needem time series to illustrate how this method works.

EXSM is an efficient way to calculate a moving average of a time series. What is a moving average? If we wish to develop a forecast which smooths out random effects in a time series, we might compute the average actual demand for January through May. This average might then be used as our forecast for June's demand. When June's actual demand becomes known, we then would drop January's actual demand out of our calculation and compute a new average demand for February through June and perhaps use this average as our forecast for July, and so on. This would be called a five-month moving average.

If we wished to have an even "smoother" forecast (one which does not respond or "react" up or down so much to the most recent actual demand) we might increase the number of months in our moving average. Conversely, if we wanted to give more weight in our forecast to the more recent actual demands, we could decrease the number of months in our moving average. At an extreme, we might only use last month's actual demand as our forecast for next month, which puts *all* the weight on the most recent demand, and none on previous data, which is usually not practical.

EXSM is a moving average, but it is a more efficient way of calculating one than the way described above because, in its simplest form, it requires only two numbers to produce a forecast—the current period's *actual demand,* and the *forecast* made earlier for this same period. A new moving average is calculated every period by simply adding together some fraction (say 90 percent) of the last moving average forecast and the complement (100 percent—90 percent, or 10 percent) of the current period's actual usage. The 10 percent weight given to the current period's usage (called the *smoothing constant*) is represented by α, the Greek letter alpha. Al-

though many users of this method use an α of 10 percent, this is not a requirement of the method. A higher or lower percent could be used if it gives better forecasts.[5]

We will present examples of three different EXSM models. *Model 1* is the simplest model, and does about the same thing that a moving average does; it smooths out the random effects in a time series, but does so by giving more weight to newer data, and less and less to older data.[6] *Model 2* is designed to be used where both random effects and trend effects are apparent in the time series, but no seasonal pattern is evident. Finally, *Model 3* is designed to account for all three: random, trend, and seasonal effects. In addition, we will also discuss a measure of the errors in forecasts, called the *mean absolute deviation,* or MAD.

Again we ran our Needem 36-month time series on a computer, this time using a program designed to do all the calculations for Models 1, 2, and 3. Then we had the computer forecast the monthly sales for the 12 months of Year 4. The computer outputs are presented in Figure 9–6. This forecast is then compared, in Figure 9–7, with the actual usage in all four years.

Model 1. The equation for Model 1 is:

$$F_t = \alpha \ (D_t) + (1 - \alpha) \ F_{t-1}$$

Where:

$F_t =$ The forecast average for the present period, t, and the best estimate for the next period, $t + 1$

$\alpha =$ The smoothing constant

$D_t =$ Current actual demand

$F_{t-1} =$ Last period's forecast average

---

[5] There is a direct relationship between the α value used and the number of equivalent periods included in a moving average. This relationship is $N = (2 - \alpha)/\alpha$ where N is the equivalent number of periods. Thus if $\alpha = .1$, $N = 19$. Or, if we wish to use EXSM to calculate a 12-month moving average, $\alpha = \dfrac{2}{N+1} = \dfrac{2}{12+1} = .153$. Thus, we should use an α of .153.

[6] The weight given to older data decreases at a decreasing rate, which is the shape of a curve which declines exponentially—hence, the name for this forecasting method.

FIGURE 9-6

EXPONENTIAL SMOOTHING

INITIAL CONDITIONS:

NUMBER OF PERIODS SMOOTHED	36
AVERAGE EXPONENTIAL SMOOTHING CONSTANT	0.10
INITIAL AVERAGE USAGE	100
TREND EXPONENTIAL SMOOTHING CONSTANT	0.10
INITIAL AVERAGE TREND	1.22
SEASONAL EXPONENTIAL SMOOTHING CONSTANT	0.40
NUMBER OF PERIODS IN A YEAR	12
NUMBER OF PERIODS OF CALCULATED PROJECTED FORECAST	12
INITIAL FORECAST AVERAGE FOR MODEL 2	100.00
INITIAL FORECAST AVERAGE FOR MODEL 3	100.00

INITIAL AVERAGE SEASONAL INDEXES
0.94 1.14 1.17 1.06 0.96 1.02 1.09 1.11 1.04 0.93
0.79 0.74

		MODEL 1		MODEL 2		MODEL 3	
PERIOD	USAGE	F(t)	MAD	E(t+1)	MAD	E(t+1)	MAD
1	100	100.0	0.0	111.0	0.0	117.4	0.0
2	128	102.8	11.2	115.5	6.8	123.2	4.2
3	138	106.3	20.8	121.3	13.1	114.5	8.5
4	127	108.4	20.8	123.9	10.2	106.4	10.1
5	112	108.7	13.9	123.1	10.9	115.4	8.3
6	115	109.4	10.8	122.9	9.7	125.0	5.1
7	128	111.2	14.0	125.3	7.9	129.5	4.2
8	134	113.5	17.5	128.4	8.2	123.6	4.3
9	130	115.2	17.1	130.2	5.6	112.7	5.2
10	116	115.2	10.6	128.9	9.0	97.5	4.4
11	100	113.7	12.4	124.5	17.0	92.9	3.7
12	95	111.8	15.0	119.6	22.0	122.3	3.0
13	125	113.2	14.2	121.5	15.3	152.9	2.9
14	148	116.6	22.5	127.6	19.8	160.3	3.7
15	155	120.5	28.8	134.2	22.8	146.2	4.3
16	138	122.2	24.3	136.3	15.2	130.9	5.9
17	128	122.8	16.9	136.1	12.5	137.8	4.7
18	142	124.7	17.8	138.6	9.8	151.1	4.5
19	152	127.5	21.6	142.7	11.3	156.5	3.1
20	156	130.3	24.4	146.8	12.1	149.4	2.1
21	140	131.3	18.5	147.1	10.0	133.2	5.0
22	122	130.4	14.8	143.7	16.1	113.4	7.5
23	108	128.1	17.8	137.9	23.9	106.7	6.6
24	100	125.3	21.9	131.3	29.5	138.5	6.6
25	146	127.4	21.4	134.8	23.6	169.5	7.0
26	175	132.1	31.9	143.6	30.2	178.1	6.4
27	173	136.2	35.5	150.6	29.9	160.5	5.9
28	161	138.7	31.2	154.1	22.1	145.9	3.7
29	150	139.8	23.2	154.9	14.9	156.9	3.9
30	162	142.0	22.8	157.8	11.8	170.1	4.4
31	171	144.9	25.3	162.0	12.4	175.2	3.0
32	173	147.7	26.4	165.9	11.8	163.0	2.7
33	168	149.8	23.9	168.1	7.9	145.3	3.6
34	157	150.5	17.2	167.8	9.2	127.4	6.8
35	130	148.4	18.5	161.9	20.6	120.1	5.1
36	125	146.1	20.5	155.9	27.1	164.5	5.0
37		146.1		155.9		164.5	
38		146.1		156.9		198.9	
39		146.1		157.8		203.9	
40		146.1		158.8		186.6	
41		146.1		159.8		171.2	
42		146.1		160.8		183.9	
43		146.1		161.8		196.8	
44		146.1		162.7		201.3	
45		146.1		163.7		190.5	
46		146.1		164.7		172.3	
47		146.1		165.7		146.6	
48		146.1		166.7		138.8	

ENDING AVERAGE SEASONAL INDEXES
0.98 1.18 1.19 1.08 0.98 1.04 1.10 1.12 1.05 0.94
0.79 0.74

Note: Sample calculations are given for shaded numbers.

As we said, F_t is actually a moving forecast average which is calculated in our example by adding 10 percent of the current month's actual demand of an item to 90 percent of its last forecast average. The new forecast average becomes the forecast for the next month coming up or, if commitments have to be made farther ahead, as the forecast for the several months whose demand must be forecast.

In order to begin the EXSM process, there has to be an assumed beginning forecast average, or F_{t-1}. We will start by assuming a previous period's forecast average (F_{t-1}) of 100. If an analyst is starting today and has no previous demand data—which is rare—he will simply have to just use today's actual demand to start with. If he has historical demand data he might use the first month's data values or an average of the first two or three months. It usually doesn't matter very much how he begins because the

effects of the initial F_{t-1} will soon wash out if the smoothing process is carried on for several periods.

Using our 36-month time series of Needem demand, calculations for F_t for the first four periods are:

Period		
1	$F_t = .1(100) - .9(100)$	$= 100.00$
2	$F_t = .1(128) + .9(100)$	$= 102.80$
3	$F_t = .1(138) + .9(102.8)$	$= 106.32$
4	$F_t = .1(127) + .9(106.32)$	$= 108.39$

Similar calculations were made for all 36 months of the first three years, and extrapolated for the 12 months of Year 4, plotted in Figure 9–7. (Note that the forecast values for all 12

FIGURE 9–7

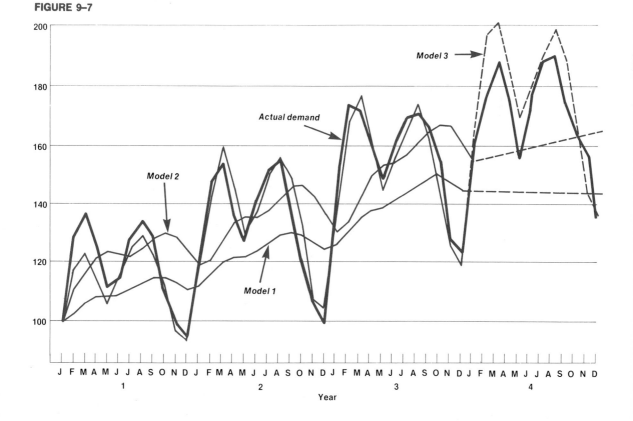

months of the fourth year are 146.10, which is the last F_t calculated in Figure 9–6 for Model 1.) As can be seen in Figure 9–7, this method smooths out the irregularities in our time series, but it consistently underestimates the actual demand. This is because this particular series contains an upward trend, and a simple forecast average always lags behind whenever there is a trend. If there were a downward trend, the lagging effect would cause the EXSM forecast to be too high. Finally, Model 1 doesn't "track" the seasonal effects in our historical data and include them in the forecast.

Model 2. The equations for Model 2, which account for trend effects in addition to random effects, are:

(1) $\quad F_t = \alpha(D_t) + (1 - \alpha) F_{t-1}$

(2) $\quad T_t = \alpha(F_t - F_{t-1}) + (1 - \alpha) T_{t-1}$

(3) $\quad E_{t+1} = F_t + \dfrac{1 - \alpha}{\alpha} (T_t) + T_t$

Where: Equation (1) is the same as Model 1, and

T_t = Average trend in the present period
T_{t-1} = Average trend in previous period
E_{t+1} = Forecast average for the next period, considering random and trend effects.

As in Model 1, we can also smooth out the random effects in the series' trend behavior, and have arbitrarily chosen $\alpha = .10$ for α, the smoothing constant. And, we have determined an "initial" average trend for the previous period (T_{t-1}) to be 1.22 which is the b coefficient (the slope or average increase in demand per month) from our earlier least squares analysis. Alternatively, we could have estimated our initial T_{t-1} from a freehand plot or simply set it at zero, or by some other thoughtful process. Calculations using this model are also shown in Figure 9–6. The first two period's calculations are:

Period

1 $\quad F_t = .1(100) + .9(100) = 100$
$\quad T_t = .1(100 - 100) + .9(1.22) = 1.10$

$\quad E_{t+1} = 100 + \dfrac{1 - .1}{.1} (1.10) + 1.10 = 110.97$

2 $\quad F_t = .1(128) + .9(100) = 102.80$
$\quad T_t = .1(102.80 - 100) + .9(1.10) = 1.27$

$\quad E_{t+1} = 102.8 + \dfrac{1 - .1}{.1} (1.27) + 1.27 = 115.47$

Similarly, each E_{t+1} for Model 2 has been plotted in Figure 9–7, as have been the monthly forecasts for Year 4. Model 2 forecasts are relatively smooth as compared to actual demand but follow the general upward trend of the actual demand. Model 2 does not, however, effectively track seasonal fluctuatins. The forecast for Year 4 simply increases .98 each month, which is the final smoothed PitT$_t$ for month 36, as shown in Figure 9–6.

Model 3. Model 3's equations, which are designed to account for random, trend, and seasonal components in a time series, are more complex. In addition to choosing a smoothing constant for smoothing the seasonal indexes (we chose .40), we must also develop initial seasonal indices for each month. We used the indices from our previous least squares seasonal analysis procedure here. They are shown in Figure 9–6, and the final smoothed indices which are used in the forecast for Year 4 are also shown in Figure 9–6. The equations are:

$$F_t = \alpha \left(\frac{D_t}{I_{t-L}} \right) + (1 - \alpha) (F_{t-1} + T_{t-1})$$

$$T_t = \alpha (F_t - F_{t-1}) + (1 - \alpha) T_{t-1}$$

$$I_t = \alpha \left(\frac{D_t}{F_t} \right) + (1 - \alpha) (I_{t-L})$$

$$E_{t+k} = [F_t + (k \times T_t)] \times I_{t-L+k}$$

Where:

L = Number of periods in a year
k = Number of periods to project the forecast

l_t = Current average seasonal index for period t

l_{t-L} = Old average seasonal index for period $t - L$

E_{t+k} = Forecast for the $t + k^{\text{th}}$ period

The Model 3 calculations are also shown in Figure 9–6 and plotted in Figure 9–7. The computation for the first two periods are:

Period

1   $F_t = .1\left(\dfrac{100}{.94}\right) + .9(100 + 1.22) = 101.73$

    $T_t = .1(101.73 - 100) + .9(1.22) = 1.27$

    $l_t = .4\left(\dfrac{100}{101.73}\right) + .6(.94) = .96$

    $E_{t+k} = (101.73 + 1 \times 1.27) \times 1.14 = 117.43$

2   $F_t = .1\left(\dfrac{128}{1.14}\right) + .9(101.73 + 1.27) = 103.93$

    $T_t = .1(103.93 - 101.73) + .9(1.27) = 1.36$

    $l_t = .4\left(\dfrac{128}{103.93}\right) + .6(1.14) = 1.18$

    $E_{t+k} = [103.93 + (1 \times 1.36)] \times 1.17 = 123.2$

Finally, we have plotted the forecast values for all three models on Figure 9–7 and back on Figure 9–5 for comparative purposes. Model 3 tracks actual demand reasonably well; however, the monthly forecast for Year 4 overshoots actual demand for all but November and December.

At this point in the process the analyst might experiment with some other smoothing constants and rerun the program to see if improvements can be made in the forecast. While the constants we used (.10, .10, and .40 for F, T, and l) are often used in practice, others may be more appropriate for other time series. But, before the analyst begins to experiment, he should evaluate the forecast error to see how well each model performs.

MEASURING FORECAST ERRORS

Forecast error has two components which should be reviewed carefully by the analyst— the size or *magnitude* of the difference between actual and forecasted demand; and the *direction* of the error—whether actual is above or below the forecast.

The easiest way to measure forecast errors is simply to compare the forecast against the demand which actually occurs. However, when thousands of items are being forecasted each month, it is usually more practical to use some calculated measure of forecast error which can be monitored by the same computer system which is generating the forecasts. It is common to program the computer to notice when actual demand seems to be varying substantially from forecasted demand and to bring this to the attention of managers. These reports of "exceptions" allow managers to review these situations and revise the forecasts if conditions seem to warrant it.

A common measure of forecast error is the mean absolute deviation (MAD). This is simply the difference between the forecast and the actual demand. In formula form the forecast error for a single period is:

$$\text{Forecast error} = |D_t - \text{Forecast}|$$

In this formula, the vertical bars mean absolute value—or disregard whether differences are positive or negative.

We can calculate a simple moving average of errors in forecasts or we can use exponential smoothing just as we did for the forecasts themselves to estimate the average forecast error. The equation for this model is:

$$\text{MAD}_t = \alpha|D_t - \text{Forecast}| + (1 - \alpha)\,\text{MAD}_{t-1}$$

As before, we must choose an initial value for MAD_{t-1}. In our example $\alpha = .40$ and $\text{MAD}_{t-1} = 0$, which are commonly used. MAD calculations for the first three months for Model 1 are:

Period

1   $\text{MAD}_t = .4|100 - 100| + .6(0)$ $= 0$

2   $\text{MAD}_t = .4|128 - 100| + .6(0)$ $= 11.2$

3   $\text{MAD}_t = .4|138 - 102.8| + .6(11.2) = 20.8$

The mean absolute deviation can be used two ways. First, the analyst can evaluate the MADs calculated to determine which model and which smoothing constants seem to produce the best forecasts. For example, the MADs for Model 3 are generally smaller (the forecasts are, therefore, better) than those in Models 1 and 2 which can readily be seen in the plots in Figure 9–7.

Tracking Signals

The second use of MADs is for automatic forecast monitoring—to check the performance of the forecasting model being used as actual demand unfolds over time. Here another error measure, called a *tracking signal,* can be used. Tracking signals are used to call attention to management when forecasts differ substantially from actual demand experience.

A tracking signal is simply a warning given by the computer that the forecast errors have become unduly large. But, in order to give this warning, the computer has to be given rules telling it how to tell if the error is unduly large. The method used here is first to calculate a running total of the net forecast errors, with minuses offsetting pluses. Thus, unless the forecasts are very poor and are also consistently too high or too low, the cumulative total should not stray very far above or below zero.

The next step is to evaluate the magnitude of the cumulative forecast error so that the computer will report if this number gets too large. The tracking signal is obtained by dividing the cumulative error by the exponentially smoothed MAD figure. If the signal is ±3 or more, for example, the forecasts would be reviewed.

We will use an example to illustrate the method. The hypothetical numbers used in Figure 9–8 are no longer the Needem figures but are chosen to illustrate the tracking signal procedure. They are also obviously quite extreme. No good forecasting system would continue to forecast demand going up in the face of sales going down month after month as occurs in Figure 9–8.

In Figure 9–8, column 1 shows the forecast, column 2 the actual demand, and column 3 the error in each month's forecast. Column 4 is the cumulative net error, considering pluses and minuses. Column 5 is the exponentially smoothed MAD, and column 6 is column 4 divided by column 5, or the cumulative error expressed as the number of MADs. This column provides the tracking signals. Note that the predominance of negative tracking signals tells us the *direction* of the error—that the later forecasts are consistently higher than actual demand.

Figure 9–8 is presented here only to illustrate how the tracking signal is calculated. The use

FIGURE 9–8

Period	Forecast of Demand (1)	Actual Demand (2)	Difference (3)	Running Sum of Forecast Errors (4)	Exponentially Smoothed MAD* (5)	Tracking Signal (6)
1	100	102	+2	2	0.8	2.50
2	105	104	−1	1	0.88	1.13
3	110	112	+2	3	1.33	2.25
4	115	108	−7	−4	3.6	−1.11
5	120	105	−15	−19	8.16	−2.32
6	125	100	−25	−44	15.16	−2.90
7	130	95	−35	−79	23.1	−3.42
8	135	100	−35	−114	27.86	−4.09
9	140	90	−50	−164	36.71	−4.46
10	145	85	−60	−224	46.02	−4.87

* $\alpha = .4$; $MAD_{t-1} = 0$.

FIGURE 9–9
Approaches to Forecasting

Legend: ■ Extensive ▨ Medium use □ Limited use

Approaches			Short description	Time horizons of forecasting			
				A	B	C	D
Informal forecasting			Ad hoc, judgmental, or intuitive methods	Medium	Medium	Medium	Medium
FORMAL FORECASTING METHODOLOGIES — Qualitative methods — Causal or regressive		Single and multiple regression	Variations in dependent variables explained by variations in independent one(s)		Medium	Medium	
		Econometric models	Simultaneous systems of multiple regression equations			Medium	
Quantitative methods — Time series		Naive	Simple rules, such as: Forecast equals most recent actual value or equals last year's same month + 5%	Extensive	Medium		
		Trend extrapolation	Linear, exponential, S-curve, or other types of projections			Medium	Extensive
		Exponential smoothing	Forecasts obtained by smoothing, averaging, past actual values in linear or exponential manner	Extensive			
		Decomposition	Time series broken down into trend, seasonality, cyclicality, and randomness				
		Filters	Forecasts expressed as linear combination of past actual values; parameters or model can adapt to changes in data				
		Autoregressive/moving averages (ARMA), (Box-Jenkins methodology)	Forecasts expressed as linear combination of past actual values and/or past errors			Medium	
Subjective assessment		Decision trees	Subjective probabilities assigned to each event and Bayesian statistics approach used			Medium	
		Sales force estimates	Bottom-up approach aggregating sales force's forecasts			Medium	
		Juries of executive opinion	Marketing, production, and finance executives jointly prepare forecasts			Medium	
		Surveys anticipatory research	Learns intentions of potential customers or plans of businesses				Medium
Technological		Exploration	Uses today's assured basis of knowledge to broadly assess future conditions				Medium
		Normative	Starts by assessing future goals, needs, desires, objectives, etc., and works backward to determine necessary developments to achieve goals, etc.				Extensive

A Immediate (less than one month). **B** Short (one to three months). **C** Medium (three months to less than 2 years). **D** Long (two years or more).

Source: Adapted from Spyros Makridakis and Steven C. Wheelwright, "Forecasting: Issues and Challenges for Marketing Management," *Journal of Marketing,* October 1977, pp. 26–27.

of this signal rests on statistical relationships which are explained in statistical inventory control books.[7] These relationships tell us that the numbers in column 6 should, by chance, exceed ± 3 only about 2 percent of the time and ± 2 only about 11 percent of the time.

Obviously, our example given in Figure 9–8, where the tracking signal is almost -5, is far above these limits, so the forecasting method being used needs to be reviewed. The computer can be programmed to watch these tracking signals for thousands of items, and it can be programmed to print out exception lists of all cases where the signal is ± 2 or more (or whatever ratio is regarded as signaling danger), thus bringing these items to management's attention.

Adaptive Response Systems

Calling managers' attention to the need to adjust the forecasting procedure does not in itself make any improvement. Usually if the forecasting procedure has become unreliable it will be because of abrupt changes in levels of demand or in seasonal patterns. To take care of these, managers might temporarily increase the value of α as used in the calculations to put more weight on recent data. Later, when the system has adjusted to the new conditions, it can be changed back.

Even this part of the work, too, can be computerized. IBM has an adaptive forecasting feature in their communication-oriented production information and control system (COPICS) which adapts to new demand conditions it senses by evaluating a tracking signal.

OTHER FORECASTING METHODS

The methods we have described here are some of the most commonly used for forecasting. There are, however, a number of others which are summarized in Figure 9–9. Notice that the methods are categorized first as *formal* versus

informal; then *quantitative* versus *qualitative;* and next as *casual* or regressive, time series, subjective assessment, or technological. Also note that each is categorized as to the length of time horizon into the future it is designed for, and, finally its frequency of use by organizations in forecasting.

Review Questions

1. Compare top-down and bottom-up methods of forecasting. Which should a manager use and why?
2. Should sales forecasts be expressed in terms of money or of physical units? Why? If money, who translates them into units, and when? Is this more important in high-volume production or in job lot activities? Why?
3. Differentiate between "extrinsic" and "intrinsic" forecasting.
4. What are the subpatterns in a typical time series? What causes each?
5. How can regression analysis be used to forecast demand?
6. What is a seasonal index? How is it calculated?
7. What is a moving average? What component of a time series is it designed to "wash out"?
8. How is the length of a moving average related to the "smoothness" of a forecast?
9. Why use EXSM instead of a moving average?
10. Whar are the three EXSM models designed to account for in a time series?
11. Generally how does the size of the smoothing constant relate to the weight given to the most recent actual demand?
12. How does the analyst know which smoothing constants are best for a particular time series?
13. What is a "mean absolute deviation"? How is it used?
14. What is a tracking signal, and how do managers use them?

Problems

1. The marketing department expects the demand for electronic duck decoys to go up this year (from

---

[7] See, for example, Oliver W. Wight, *Production and Inventory Management in the Computer Age* (Boston: Cahners Books, 1974), p. 154.

last year's total of 10,000) to 15,000. Past experience shows the following probable seasonal sales pattern, and next year's calendar shows the number of workdays:

Month	Percent of Average Month's Demand	Number of Possible Regular Workdays
January	60	23
February	50	20
March	60	23
April	120	20
May	200	22
June	180	22
July	90	11*
August	70	23
September	90	20
October	120	22
November	100	21
December	60	19

* Plant closed first half of July.

Develop a forecast of expected demand, month by month, for electronic duck decoys for the year. Be sure to pay attention to the fact that demand has an upward trend. This means that the trend is upward within each month and not just between the years.

To solve this problem, first calculate the monthly average for each year. Then find the difference between the two averages, and divide this difference by 12 to get the increment by which the trend increases each month.

The average for the first year is regarded as the trend figure for the middle 30 days of the year, or June 15 to July 15. Adding one monthly increment gives the trend value for the next 30 days, July 15 to August 15. Next, these two months' trend figures are averaged together to get the trend for the calendar month of July, the 30-day period centered on July 15. (The different number of days in months is neglected in calculations of trend values.)

After the figure for July is determined, trend values for other months can be obtained by adding the appropriate number of monthly increments until the trend is extrapolated for each month in the year ahead.

Finally, each month's sales estimate is obtained by multiplying each month's trend value by the month's seasonal percent. The January trend

would be multiplied by .60, February's by .50, and so on. Once the sales estimates are calculated for each month, production and inventory planning can proceed.

If these products are all made in the month of sale, what will be the daily average rate of production each month? If production is leveled out, what will be the daily rate each month? Show, month by month, what the month-end inventory will be. If it costs $2 a month to carry a finished record player in stock, what will the inventory carrying cost be?

2. The forecast of sales during the first four months of the year for talking microwave ovens was 22,000, 18,000, 35,000, and 50,000. Actual sales have been 16,000, 19,000, 41,000, and 61,000. This leaves the April month-end inventory 12,000 under the expected figure, although there are still 30,000 units in inventory.

Production has been at the rate of 40,000 per month for several months and can go as high as 60,000. The earlier sales forecasts anticipated sales of 70,000 per month for May through September.

What schedule changes should be made right now, if any? Why? Make a forecast of sales, production, and inventories at each month-end for the next five months.

3. The following demand data for edible tennis balls represents a trend situation without seasonal effects. The initial value for T_{t-1} should be 10.

Quarter	Demand (1000s)
0	90
1	100
2	110
3	120
4	130
5	140
6	150
7	160
8	170
9	180
10	190
11	200
12	210

a. Compute the trend line using the least squares as shown in Appendix G.
b. Examine the behavior of EXSM forecasting

models 1 and 2, using the following smoothing constants.*

	Smoothing Constants		
Case	Average	Trend	Seasonal*
1	.10	.1	.4
2	.30	.3	.3
3	.01	.3	.3

* Not used in problem 3.

(Note: Examining the response of the forecasting systems can be accomplished by plotting the actual demand versus the forecast and by examining smoothed or unsmoothed MAD values for each model over time.)

c. Compare the different forecasting approaches.

4. The following time series represents an extreme random observation. Examine the behavior of the EXSM forecasting Model 1 to this situation. Again, use the smoothing constants specified in Problem 3.*

Quarter	Demand
0	100
1	100
2	100
3	100
4	200
5	100
6	100
7	100
8	100
9	100
10	100
11	100
12	100

5. The following time series represents demand with a strong seasonal component. In Year 3 there is also a trend component. Using initial seasonal indexes of 1.0, calculate E_{t+k}, using Model 3. Next, recalculate, using as the initial seasonal indices the final seasonal indices from the first set of calculations. Use the smoothing constants of case 1 in Problem 3.*

	Demand		
Month	Year 1	Year 2	Year 3
1	259	259	269
2	500	500	500
3	707	707	737
4	866	866	906
5	966	966	1016
6	1000	1000	1000
7	1000	1000	1070
8	966	966	1046
9	866	866	956
10	707	707	807
11	500	500	610
12	259	259	379

6. The following figures are the record of the demand for a finished product of the Scientific Products Company.*

a. Experiment with the data, using EXSM and different smoothing constants until you find a good model.

b. Develop a forecast using least squares analysis (see Appendix G), and compare your results with part a.

Quarter	Demand
0	100
1	102
2	98
3	110
4	114
5	99
6	105
7	101
8	92
9	109
10	99
11	105
12	88

7. The Rex Company produces air conditioners. Three years of past demand data are given below. Experiment with the data to find a good forecasting model and smoothing constants.*

---

* This problem is suitable for solution with provided computer software. However, it may also be hand-calculated. See Preface for an explanation of the computer software.

* This problem is suitable for solution with provided computer software. However, it may also be hand-calculated. See Preface for an explanation of the computer software.

	Demand		
Month	Year 1	Year 2	Year 3
1	274	283	263
2	510	431	462
3	656	680	695
4	915	909	931
5	1221	1081	1121
6	943	941	895
7	1097	918	1070
8	909	971	1036
9	866	880	1050
10	661	748	830
11	531	506	621
12	275	275	425

8. The actual demand for an item is not behaving as was forecasted as can be seen below. Using an $\alpha = .4$ and an initial MAD value of 0, when would the tracking signal exceed limits of ± 3?

Actual Demand	Forecast
80	100
100	100
110	100
100	110
90	110
80	120
70	120
60	130
50	130

Chapter 10

Capacity Requirements Planning and Master Production Scheduling

When Florsheim builds a plant to produce shoes, its managers have some idea of the number of pairs of shoes the plant will be capable of turning out. When General Motors builds an automobile assembly plant, its managers have certain expectations concerning the number of cars the plant will be able to produce. A hospital is built to house a specified number of beds, and a school's enrollment is limited by the number and size of classrooms and the size of the faculty. These facilities are all built to a size that has certain "capacities." The task of determining and updating these capacity needs is called *capacity requirements planning.*

THE CONCEPT OF CAPACITY

The capacity of a facility is an ambiguous concept. It is not like the capacity of a wine bottle which will hold one liter of wine and no more under any circumstances.

Capacity is a *rate* of output, which translates into a quantity of output in a given *time,* and is the highest quantity of output that is possible during that time. Yet, an organization's capacity is at the same time a dynamic concept which can be changed and managed. To some extent, it can be adjusted to meet fluctuating sales levels which are reflected in master production schedules.

The relationship between *capacity* and *master production schedules* is extremely important. Since a master production schedule reflects what the organization will produce (not necessarily what it will sell), the ability to meet this plan depends upon its current or near future capacity, or upon its ability to expand or reduce this capacity in the longer run. And, as we have seen briefly in Chapter 8 and will see later in more detail, a *realistic* master production schedule—realistic in terms of capacity—becomes for the organization the key blueprint which causes a number of different resources to be committed to satisfy its quantity requirements and delivery date commitments. Because of this important relationship, we combine their discussion in this chapter.

The Unit of Output

One problem with the concept of capacity is the unit of output. An automobile tire factory turns out tires, but tires come in many varieties. A tire factory can turn out more of some kinds and sizes of tires than of other kinds and sizes. So its capacity when expressed in the number of tires is ambiguous.

In a one-product factory there would not be this kind of ambiguity, but single-product factories are almost unknown. Even a Kellogg's corn flake factory turns out several kinds of breakfast cereals. Oil refineries turn out different kinds of gasolines and oils. Book-printing companies turn out large books and small books and in various quantities. Fire departments put out large fires and little fires. It is possible to express a refinery's capacity as so many barrels or gallons of oil or gasoline, and it is possible to express a book printer's capacity as so many books, but neither would be accurate because the number would differ according to the mix of the kinds of products being made. The units of production are not homogeneous.

The matter of product mix is important when planning for the future. Sometimes, when a company's top administrators approve plans to spend money for added capacity, they express the new capacity only in terms of dollars' worth of sales. They leave it to marketing, production, and engineering to develop a prospective product-mix breakdown which eventually becomes the master production schedule. Then, production and engineering have to calculate the kind and number of machines needed to produce the expected dollar volume for the mix they anticipate.

Time

Time poses another problem. A person talking about capacity is talking about a quantity of output in a given amount of time, but how much time? Some kinds of manufacturing processes require continuous operation. A steel mill must operate continuously, 24 hours a day, or not at all. When it is not operating, the furnaces cool down (unless money is spent to keep them hot though idle), and they must be relined with new fire bricks at a high cost. The only way a steel mill can change its scale of operation is to open up or close down furnaces. So, when talking about the capacity of a steel mill, a manager probably would be thinking about the total amount of steel it can turn out while operating all of its furnaces 24 hours a day, 7 days a week. On the other hand, the capacity of a golf course would probably include only daylight hours.

Most operations do not operate around the clock; instead, they operate from 8 to 5 daily, Monday through Friday. Their capacity is re-

FIGURE 10–1
Generally Accepted Definitions of Capacity

Design capacity	That output per unit of time for which the plant was designed.
Rated capacity	That output per unit of time that the facility is theoretically capable of producing. (Usually larger than the design capacity due to periodic improvements made to machines or processes.)
Standard capacity	The output per unit of time set as an operating "goal" for management, supervision, and machine operators; can form the basis for budgets. It is equal to rated capacity less the standard scrap rate, standard personal allowance, standard maintenance downtime, standard quality control allowance, etc.
Actual and/or operating capacity	The average output per unit of time over the immediate past periods of time. This is standard capacity ± actual scrap, allowances, downtime, etc.
Peak capacity	Some output per unit of time (probably something less than rated, but more than standard) that can be obtained by maximizing output, which would probably be done by increasing labor, eliminating shutdowns for breaks, lunch, etc.

Source: Charles F. Bimmerle.

garded as being their normal output in a 40-hour workweek. But a 40-hour week is not their maximum capacity. It is usually possible to work more hours a day through overtime or by adding a second or third shifts or more days a week. In most cases, the maximum possible capacity is considerably more than the 40-hour output.

Figure 10–1 presents the general accepted definitions of capacity.

CAPACITY, INVENTORIES, AND STABLE PRODUCTION RATES

Capacity should never be considered by itself but rather as part of an organization's total strategy. Often, because of sales volume variations, a company has to choose between increasing or decreasing its production levels or carrying inventories, both of which are costly. Christmas is a time of seasonal sales in department stores, spring is a busy period for automobiles, and bathing suits sell well in the summer. But sales dip for many items in off seasons. Such variations make it difficult to operate efficiently.

If a facility's managers were to expand and contract production to follow seasonal demand, their plant's capacity would have to be large enough to take care of peak sales, but the plant would not work at top capacity very much of the time. Operating this way is usually impractical because it is impossible to keep an efficient work force with off-and-on employment. A factory's normal production capacity probably should be set at a point well below its peak needs.

While operating steadily is preferred from the production point of view, if sales are irregular, other costs must be considered. Management could continue to produce at low volumes and pass up the increased sales during high-demand periods. This might be a costly solution to the problem because of the sales which would be lost. Another alternative would be to produce at a higher level, but this would cause inventories to build up during slack periods, and carrying inventories is also costly.

In the case of automobiles, for example, the late fall and winter months are low demand months, followed by heavier demand in the spring. It would be very expensive for Chevrolet to make 50,000 extra cars in October, November, and December just to keep producing steadily. By the end of December it would have 150,000 extra cars on hand. Even at $5,000 each, $750 million would be needed to carry the inventory. By the first of April the inventory might be up to 200,000 cars, worth $1 billion! Farms and fairgrounds would be needed as parking lots for all of these cars.

Besides the staggering investments, there is a danger of a poor sales year. If car sales in the spring do not come up to what was expected (as happened in the early 1980s), production would have to be cut back. Such miscalculations can bankrupt companies, as Chrysler was predicting for itself in 1979. Stockpiling finished products may be dangerous because no company knows for sure just what volume it will sell in the future.

There are, however, some things a company can do to smooth production. It can change its capacity by increasing or decreasing work hours. And, although it is not a happy solution, the organization can change its capacity by hiring additional employees or laying off people as demand changes. And it can change its capacity by subcontracting more work during peak periods and doing all the work itself in slack periods. (IBM uses this approach to maintain its "no-layoff" policy.) It can also do some stockpiling and try to stimulate sales in off seasons. Possibly, too, it can try to hold back some peak-season business, promising later delivery and hoping that business will not be lost. And, as a long-run policy, a company can try to diversify into related product lines whose seasonal demands are opposite to those of existing products.

No one of these measures can, by itself, eliminate all changes in production rates. A little of each, however, carried on at the same time, will allow a reasonable leveling of production rates.

Finally, it is well to note that idle plant capacity is a tremendous incentive to try to increase demand. It might stimulate sufficient extra sales effort to generate enough added demand to alleviate much of the problem.

Capacity as a Lower-Limit Constraint

The discussion so far has emphasized how a facility's lack of capacity sets upper limits to production schedules. But capacity also serves as a lower-level constraint. During slow sales periods it is usually desirable to produce more products than are currently being sold because it is so uneconomical to reduce capacity drastically when it is highly probable that demand will soon again pick up.

Capacity as a limiting constraint to master production schedules at the low side is different from the way it works at the upper end. At high levels it becomes a very real limiting factor. No more can be produced. However, at the low end capacity is a managerial decision constraint. Physically, it is possible to stop production altogether, but this would usually be so uneconomical that managers impose a constraint requiring a certain amount of production even when some of the production is not needed and has to go into inventories.

USING OVERTIME TO EXPAND CAPACITY

Although workers in the automobile industry almost always work partial shifts in the winter, in the spring they are usually on overtime. Management plans it this way. Yet, when we say that management plans it this way, we do not mean that management wants the short hours or to pay for overtime. We mean that companies plan for overtime in the spring rather than planning to hire large numbers of additional employees who would soon have to be laid off. Similar decisions are also common in other industries with large seasonal variations in sales.

Planned overtime to meet seasonal peaks has many advantages. It increases the employee's pay and usually more than offsets the lowered earnings during seasonal lulls, so most of the employees like it. It minimizes the need for hiring more people and laying them off later. Changing employment up and down usually results in low productivity. Besides, this would increase unemployment taxes when the new workers were laid off. And sometimes a company cannot find enough people with the right skills to hire anyway.

Furthermore, in autos, steel, and many other industries, full work crews are needed for many of the operations. It is often not possible to get, say, 10 percent more output by increasing labor 10 percent. Longer hours for a regular crew is often the only way to increase output.

Overtime is not, however, without its problems. One is that workers' incomes fluctuate because the overtime is not regular and continued. Another problem is the lowered productivity when work is not machine-paced or paced by fixed-speed conveyors. Obviously, if production drops off drastically during overtime hours, labor costs during these hours become prohibitive.

Important, too, is the drop in a worker's pay when overtime stops. A cut from a 50-hour week to a 40-hour week pares a person's pay by 28 percent (from 55 to 40 hours' pay). Most workers do not like 28 percent pay cuts. So, if they have any notion that operations are going down to 40 hours and if they are not machine-paced, they may slow down. It may be necessary to continue the overtime just to get a normal 40 hours of work done.

We are saying that workers like to work overtime because of the high pay. Sometimes this is so. When only a few people are asked to come in on Saturday and work overtime, workers frequently use their seniority to be among those chosen.

Yet, in some cases, the reverse happens. Some workers do not want to work overtime. In particular, they often object to surprise decisions, such as a supervisor asking them at 3:30 in the afternoon to work until 8:00 or 10:00 P.M.

Normally, workers can be disciplined for refusal to do the work assigned, so it is not surprising that the question of being allowed to refuse to work overtime is covered in the labor contract, meaning that managers are not entirely free to make overtime decisions. Today's labor contracts often give workers a right to refuse to work overtime unless they are told ahead of time and unless the whole department works extra hours. (This became an issue in auto workers' labor negotiations in the late 1970s.)

This has a curious effect on assembly lines. If it is decided on short notice to work a line overtime, some of the workers will surely say no. Then the foreman has to recruit people from other jobs for the overtime on the line. He ends up with a mixed crew of workers, some of whom are inexperienced. Yet, production continues because of the fixed pace of the line. If these jobs are difficult to learn quickly, quality may suffer. On the other hand, if the tasks are relatively simple, quality is usually not affected.

INCREASING CAPACITY WITH EXTRA SHIFTS

A small plant, operating day and night, can turn out just about as much as a plant twice its size operating only one shift. So, when a company plans its operations, it can choose whether to build a small plant and use it intensively or a larger plant and use it less intensively.

Most manufacturing companies can operate 8, 16, or 24 hours a day. A plant operating 8 hours a day needs to be nearly three times as large as one in 24-hour operation in order to produce the same daily output. Similarly, operations can be carried on for 4, 5, 6, or 7 days a week. The fewer hours worked, the more physical plant capacity is needed for a given output.

At first, operating a small plant long hours looks like the best arrangement because the overhead costs per unit of product are reduced. It gains economies of scale. However, it often costs less to operate a larger plant fewer hours.

In the past it has been common practice to have a plant large enough to take care of normal needs when it operates 8 hours a day and 5 days a week. However, this is changing somewhat. More companies are adding additional shifts to save on capital expenditures and overhead costs.

However, there are trade-offs, and this may backfire. Although single-shift production requires a larger plant and more machines than 24-hours-a-day production, equipment depreciation costs per unit of product may, in the long run, be about the same either way. Three-shift operations permit one machine to produce almost as much as three machines would produce in one shift, but a machine that is used 24 hours a day last only about one third as long as a machine that is used 8 hours a day. Over the years, a company may have to buy about the same number of machines in either case.

Many overhead expenses, such as building depreciation, insurance, taxes, interest on investment, and obsolescence of machinery, are reduced when a small plant is used intensively. But a three-shift operation has certain costly disadvantages which may offset the gains. Second- and third-shift employees get higher hourly pay rates (commonly a 5 percent premium on the second shift and 10 percent on the third shift). And unless they are paced by production lines, night-shift workers may be less productive than first-shift workers. Night shifts often have more new employees than day shifts because most people like the day shift, and, as soon as they can, they use their seniority to transfer to first-shift work. There is also usually a little more turnover and more absenteeism among night-shift workers. Also, night-shift people often do too many things during the day and may come to work tired and, as a result, are less productive.

In any case, and as a consequence of all these factors, night-shift workers may be no more than 90 percent as efficient as their day-shift counterparts. Thus, products made on the night shift are likely to cost 10 percent more than products made on the day shift, depending, of course, on how important labor costs are in total manufacturing costs.

Maintenance is also easier with a one-shift, five-day operation than with a three-shift, seven-day operation. In the former case, most repairs can be done in off hours with no interference to production. Less intensive use of the plant also permits production to be expanded during peak periods with little increase in overhead costs because adequate plant capacity is already available.

Many companies use parts of their plants intensively (16 or 24 hours a day) and other parts only 8 hours a day at the same time. They buy the smallest possible number of very expensive machines and operate them two or three shifts, while other machines work only the normal first shift.

Detroit's auto companies, GM, Ford, and Chrysler, usually size their automobile assembly factories to operate, during their busy periods, 53 hours a week (five 9-hour days plus one 8-hour day). They do not plan to use second shifts even during seasonal peaks because there are just too many problems and costs involved in hiring large numbers of people for short periods of time. And the auto companies have found that work weeks of more than 53 hours cause too much absenteeism and quality problems. People just don't show up for work.

Automobile companies do not, however, have enough capacity to handle their peak sales volumes in 53-hour weeks. Rather, they set the 53-hour capacity at 75 to 80 percent of their peak needs. This means that they are not able to fill all orders from current production during sales peaks. So during peak seasons, some customers have to wait. To avoid losing too many sales, the companies stockpile in advance of the peaks and persuade their dealers to do the same. By setting capacity production below their peak needs, they can operate at capacity for most of the year unless, of course, they experience a severe drop in demand.

Yet automobile plants operate at night, performing some second-shift operation. This, however, is usually confined to parts-making departments, where machines are costly. In these cases, normal parts-making capacity is the output of two shifts. The capacity of two-shift parts-making plants is required to meet the one-shift needs of the assembly plants.

BREAK-EVEN CHARTS AND CAPACITY

When a factory is operating at or below capacity, the relationships among costs, sales, and profits are as they are shown in the break-even chart in Figure 2–1 (Chapter 2).

But there are times when demand exceeds capacity. If this excess demand appears to be temporary, capacity should probably be expanded by working overtime in spite of the extra costs. In this case, the company's break-even chart would change from that shown in Figure 2–1 to that shown in Figure 10–2. So long as the new profit spread, A in Figure 10–2, exceeds the old B profits in Figure 10–2, this would be a profitable action.

Should, however, the larger sales volume appear to be permanent, then perhaps the ca-

FIGURE 10–2
Break-Even and Capacity Planning

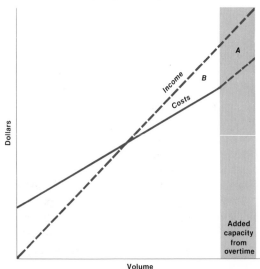

FIGURE 10–3
Break-Even with Added Capacity

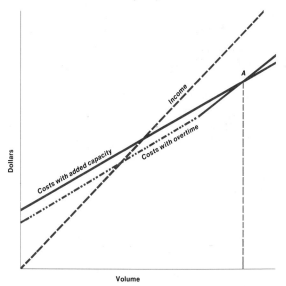

pacity should be expanded by adding more machines rather than using overtime. Such a change would result in a new break-even chart: Figure 10–3. The new higher level of fixed costs would move the break-even point a little to the right (a higher volume would now be required). But since considerably higher volume is expected, the profit spread should be greater than before.

Even if above-normal-capacity demand is only seasonal, it may still be profitable to make the permanent additions to the capacity indicated in Figure 10–3. This would be true, for example, if the additional profits, even though available for only part of a year, were greater than the reduction in profits during the rest of the year when operations return to the old capacity level.

WORK FORCE CAPACITY

We have emphasized that it is usually uneconomical to increase and decrease the work force with every sales increase and decrease. This might sound as if we were saying that a given number of employees is a fixed capacity resource.

But this is far from true. Substantial adjustments can be made without having to resort to hiring more people and then laying them off.

For example, suppose that the labor requirements needed to make a company's products while working a normal five-day, 40-hour week produces the following expectation of employee needs:

June	300
July	400
August	600
September	450
October	400

The labor load in August is double that of June. However, the number of people needed are for "equivalent employees" who work 40 hours a week. But, as we have suggested earlier, the hours per week can be changed, and so can the amount of work sent to outside contractors. And, by stockpiling, some output from peak months can be transferred to earlier months, as shown earlier.

Here is a feasible plan for factory work hours to take care of the sales needs while holding the work force constant:

Month	Number of People	Hours a Week	Equivalent People Contracted Outside
June	350	34	—
July	350	46	—
August	350	58	92
September	350	51	—
October	350	46	—

Using overtime, varying the work force more, subcontracting out more work, or building inventories are largely managerial decisions (except where the labor contract provides otherwise) and depend, as before, on the relative costs of the alternatives.

Labor planning requires other considerations. We did not, in our example, allow for any loss in production from fatigue during long work weeks, which would probably be substantial during the 58-hour work weeks planned for August. Nor have we allowed, in our example, for any stockpiling of inventories.

Nor are all months alike. Some have as few as 20 and some as many as 23 workdays. So a given workload *per month* is not the same employee load in different months. Absences also need to be accounted for. It takes at least 105 people on the payroll to keep 100 people on the job. And it takes even more in the summer when everyone takes vacations (presumably, because of its peak summer sales, employees in this company would take their vacations at other times during the year). Labor turnover may also need to be considered. There is always a loss in production when an employee leaves and is replaced, so if there is a significant turnover this needs to be allowed for.

Indirect labor to support the work of direct workers needs to be planned just as much and perhaps more than direct labor. This is partly because "indirect" people may be technical employees and hard to find and partly because it is difficult to estimate how many indirect workers are needed. Most companies use some kind of ratio of indirect workers to direct workers or to the factory's workload to make these estimates. They rarely, however, continually increase and decrease indirect employment in proportion to factory workload changes.

MACHINE CAPACITY BALANCE

For companies that make varied products, the mix of products shifts all the time, and this places unequal loads on different machines and work centers. Also, some machines are slower than others; consequently, some equipment will often be working full time while other equipment is idle. Some work centers will be working overtime while others are on short hours.

Bottleneck Limitations

When machine capacities are out of balance with needs, it is the bottleneck machines which limit what can be done. Often a bottleneck can be loosened by improvisations which expand the capacity of bottleneck machines temporarily. They can be operated through lunch periods and they can be worked overtime. Normal overhauls can be postponed by running the machines until they break down. Or they can be speeded up, even if this is hard on the machines and tools. Two or three people, instead of one, can be assigned to do setups and repairs.

The supervisor can also ask people who operate bottleneck machines to temporarily skip their coffee breaks. Also, it is not unknown for supervisors to "roll up their sleeves" and pitch in and help—if union rules allow it, that is (usually they don't). Finally, it may be possible to supplement the bottleneck machine's capacity by doing some of the work on older, less efficient machines. Or perhaps part of the work can be sent out to other companies.

Most of these improvisations are only expediencies, however, and they do not solve imbalances between operations permanently. And because individual machines' capacities differ and the workloads generated by sales keep shifting, there will always be a few bottleneck spots.

A plant's capacity is therefore limited by the capacity of its bottleneck operation. If this operation can be changed, this single change affects the capacity of the whole plant or department. It may even be economical to redesign the bottleneck machine so that it will run faster, or maybe a second machine of this kind should be installed.

The gain in total capacity, however, will not be equivalent to the improvement in the bottleneck operation. If the latter's capacity is increased by 25 percent, the increase in a department's capacity might increase only 5 percent, because now *some other* operation becomes a bottleneck. Capacity expansion becomes a matter of handling a succession of bottlenecks which emerge as the output rate rises.

Later, in Chapter 13, we will discuss a new technique called OPT (Optimized Production Technology) which focuses on the scheduling of bottlenecks to increase capacity and output.

LEARNING CURVES AND CAPACITY

An organization's capacity for doing work is usually a changing characteristic. As time passes, equipment is added where it is needed or taken out of service where it is not needed, thus creating new levels of capacity.

The capacity of the human side of organizations changes, too, and not only because of additions to or subtractions from the work force. People learn and acquire competence, thus increasing the capacity of the organization. It is possible, when operations are new, to anticipate the degree of improvement which learning will produce and thus to calculate with some degree of accuracy the size of the work force as well as the cost of doing work both early in a new work experience and later on after learning has occurred.

This is the essence of the "learning curve" concept. This concept assumes that practice leads to improvement: People need fewer labor-hours for producing a given quantity of work. Learning, with its reduced labor-hour input implications is always at work in organizations. Most experience at making anything can always lead to more economical methods.

Aerospace and electronics manufacturers have found that the learning curve concept operates when they make products in large numbers. Knowing about the curve and the expected rates of improvement allows their managers to project the need, later on, for fewer labor-hours per unit of product as well as lower costs per unit. Many airplane and electronics makers therefore use the learning curve (on all government contracts for such products, in fact, the government requires them to expect lower costs per unit as quantities mount) in estimating the cost of direct labor and in scheduling, planning labor needs, and for budgeting, purchasing, and pricing.

Frequently, these companies use an 80 percent learning curve or something very close to it. An 80 percent curve means that every time the production quantity doubles, the average amount of *direct labor* for all units produced up to that point goes down to 80 percent of its former level. This is an average for *all units* and not just the direct labor-hours put into the last unit. Thus, if the first 10 units require an average of 600 direct labor-hours per product, the first 20 units (including the first 10) will average 480 labor-hours per unit of product. Aerospace companies plot this relationship on double-logarithmic paper (see Figure 10–4) which makes the learning curve become a straight line.[1]

Learning Curves in Decision Making

An example will illustrate how the learning curve can help in managerial decision making. The Strand Company has a government contract for 1,000 infrared bazookas. Labor is $8 an hour, and the contract is taken with the idea that the labor cost should eventually average out at 10 hours or $80 per unit.

---

[1] The formula for the line is:

$$\log Y = S \log X + \log C$$

where S is the slope, X is the number of units of product, and C is the direct labor-hours required by the first product. Y is the average number of labor-hours. The formula for the slope of the line is

$$\text{Slope} = \frac{\log \% - 2}{\log 2}$$

For an 80 percent curve the formula becomes:

$$\frac{\log 80 - 2}{\log 2}$$
$$= \frac{1.90309 - 2}{.30103}$$
$$= -.322$$

The slope of the line is always negative since the method assumes that hours per unit decrease as volume increases.

FIGURE 10–4
Typical Learning Curve for Airplanes

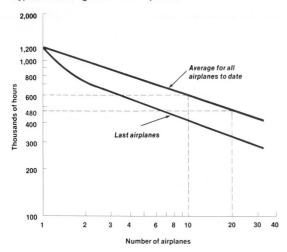

Here are the production records:

Month	Bazookas Produced	Direct Labor-Hours
March	14	410
April	9	191
May	14	244
June	18	284
July	20	238
August	38	401

Strand has now been producing for six months on this contract and the president asks for a report. He wants to know (1) what is the average labor cost per unit for all of the bazookas to date; (2) what did the last unit produced cost; (3) at what volume will the average labor cost be down to $80 per unit; (4) will the company make or lose money on the labor part of the contract, and by how much; (5) what learning curve percentage is operating, and what is its slope.

First, it is necessary to compute cumulative production, the cumulative labor-hours, and the average labor-hours per product:

Month	Cumulative Production to Date	Cumulative Labor-Hours to Date	Average Labor-Hours per Unit
March	14	410	29.3
April	23	601	26.1
May	37	845	22.8
June	55	1,129	20.5
July	75	1,367	18.2
August	113	1,768	15.6

The easiest way to approach the president's questions is to start by plotting the average labor-hours per unit on a double-log chart, as is done in Figure 10–5. The horizontal scale is cumulative production and the vertical scale is the average labor-hours per unit. After plotting the points, the

FIGURE 10–5

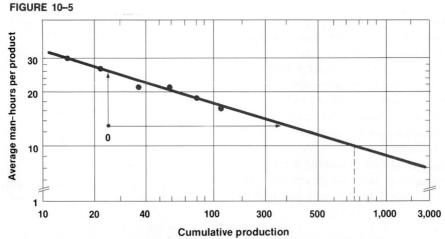

next thing is to draw in a straight line that best fits the location of the dots. (Usually this line can be drawn by hand, but the line could also be calculated by the least squares method.) The slope of this line defines the learning curve that is operating.

Most of the president's questions can be answered by looking at this line of best fit. What is the average labor cost for all of the production to date? To answer this, it is not necessary to use the chart at all since the actual data are available and were used in calculating the average labor-hour figures. As of the end of August the bazookas have averaged 15.6 hours; so, up to now, the direct labor cost has averaged $124.80 per unit.

At what volume will the average labor cost go down to $80, or 10 hours? To answer this question, it is necessary to extend the line in Figure 10–5 downward to the right and read the quantity below the point where the curve intersects the 10-hours line. Although this is too fine a measure to be read off such a small chart as Figure 10–5, the answer is actually 604 units. Will Strand make or lose money on the labor content part of the contract? At 1,000 units and at the rate labor utilization is improving, average labor will be down to 8.65 hours, or $69.20 per bazooka. So Strand stands to earn $10.80 per unit, or $10,800 in total, on the labor part of the contract. This is in addition to the profit originally expected and included in the price for each bazooka.

Strand's analysts were also asked for the slope of the line. To find this they should insert (in Figure 10–5) a point 0 anywhere below the curve. Then they should measure from point 0 horizontally to the right to where it intersects the learning curve line. (In Figure 10–5 this measures 1.75 inches.) Next they should measure vertically up to the curve (.49 inches on Figure 10–5). The next step is to divide the vertical measurement by the horizontal measurement to get the slope of the line. In our example this slope proves to be −.28. (We will show what this slope is used for in a moment.)

Strand's president also asked the percent at which the improvement curve is operating. The analysts can get this by doubling any production quantity and reading off the gain. For example, at 20 units the curve shows 26.6 labor-hours; at 40 it is 21.8 labor-hours. Dividing 21.6 by 26.6 shows that doubling the quantity reduced the labor-hours to 82 percent of their former level. So this is an 82 percent curve. (Both the slope of the line and the curve's percent can also be calculated more accurately by least squares procedures.)

Still one other relationship can be established: the relationship between the incremental cost of the last individual bazooka and the average cost up to that point. This relationship is always the average cost multiplied by 1 minus the slope of the line. In this case it is $1 − .28$, or .72. Since the average time of all units produced to this point is 15.6 hours, the last bazooka uses $.72 \times 15.6$ hours, or 11.23 hours of labor, which cost $89.84.

Limitations in the Use of Learning Curves

Outside the aerospace, electronics, and other "high-tech" industries, learning curves are rarely used because of certain limitations. One difficulty pertains to carryover knowledge of the work force, because new products usually are not entirely new. Even new aircraft are not wholly unlike earlier models. And each year's new automobiles are much like last year's. Even a new industry, such as television was in 1950, depended on electronic tubes and circuitry which were familiar to radio makers. When manufacturers turned to making TVs they already knew much about making them. This carryover knowledge makes it difficult to set a starting point for learning curve calculations.

Another limitation is that the curves are concerned only with labor. Where machines (or robots) are heavily used, an 80 percent curve calls for more improvement than can probably be realized, and it may be necessary to use an 85 or 90 percent curve. The problem is deciding, for the case at hand, what curve to expect—80, 85, 90, or whatever?

Still another problem is that curves may exaggerate labor savings. In order to achieve reductions in direct labor costs, it is necessary to put industrial engineers, tool engineers, supervisors, and others to work trying to make improvements. But these specialists are indirect labor, and their costs are usually not shown as offsets against the gains in direct labor costs, but rather they go into overhead. Many firms, however, do try to account for this by charging specialists' time to particular jobs. This is not only good cost accounting procedure, but often government contracts require this to be done.

Still one more difficulty is that companies that are not used to using learning curves are likely to misinterpret the expected savings unless they change the way they keep their cost accounting records. To use a curve correctly, setup and preparatory costs incurred before the contract starts should be kept apart and excluded from the calculation. If these are charged to the contract and later incorporated into a cost calculation for the first units produced, the first units will appear to cost a great deal.

Similarly, all work hours should be charged to the products which receive the benefit of the work. If some of the hours worked in March are for units of products to be finished in April or May, these hours should be charged to April's or May's products and not to March's products. Proper charging is easy for large complex products such as airplanes but is less feasible for stoves and refrigerators. If a company's regular cost accounting records are not separated this way (so that direct labor costs throughout production are charged to the specific products that received the benefit of the work done), it will have to change its record-keeping procedures so that the charges are made properly.

MASTER PRODUCTION SCHEDULES: MANUFACTURE TO ORDER

A master schedule is a written plan showing how many of each finished item to make in each period of time in the future. Ideally, once made

up, it remains fixed for the immediate future so that production can progress. In fact, however, master schedules are usually changed as time moves along in response to changed conditions.

When products are made to customers' orders, the job of master schedule development is largely one of reviewing the future workload of orders already on hand (the backlog), seeing when the customers want these orders and when new order deliveries can be promised. This means that the schedulers must know approximately how many labor-hours, or tons, or some other overall measure of workloads the orders already accepted will amount to in each major department. This reveals the quantity and timing of open (uncommitted) capacity in each department. In addition, for the orders that the sales department is bidding on, estimates need to be made concerning how much capacity they will require, department by department, so that they can include delivery dates in their proposals to customers.

It is necessary also to pay attention to the sequence or routing of workloads in different departments. If an item needs to be designed, the engineering workload will have to be committed first. Capacity will be needed in the foundry or forge or sheet-metal shop later on, and still later in the machine shop, and final assembly. Unless the workloads needed in the early-stage departments can be done on time, work in later-stage departments will be delayed. Finally, when all of this has been considered and an order accepted, its workload is added to the loads of the appropriate departments and their uncommitted capacities are reduced accordingly.

The master schedule is—when production is geared to actual sales orders—an updated summation of the booked but unfinished jobs for future periods—usually accumulated by weeks or months. It extends as far ahead as the last delivery date on the last order already on the schedule. And it shows, period by period, the orders which are planned to be finished and shipped. Figure 10–6 shows a typical master schedule for make-to-order products.

In this kind of master production schedule

FIGURE 10–6
A Typical Master Production Schedule

Arista MANUFACTURING SYSTEM	MASTER PRODUCTION SCHEDULE	EXOTIC BICYCLE ASSEMBLERS, INC						MASTER SCHEDULER C			PAGE 6

ITEM NUMBER		ITEM DESCRIPTION	M/S TYPE	ASSEMBLY LEAD TIME	ON HAND	LOT SIZE	SAFETY STOCK	TIME FENCES DEMAND	PLAN	CONSUMPTION METHOD	PRODUCTION PROPAGATION QUANTITY	INTERVAL	SERVICE PROPAGATION QUANTITY	INTERVAL
0010000		COMMON PARTS	M	15	0	100	0	10/06	11/24	PAST PERD	100	1	0	0

SPECIAL INSTRUCTIONS

	OVERDUE	09/01/5	09/08/5	09/15/5	09/22/5	09/29/5	10/06/5	10/13/5	10/20/5	10/27/5	11/03/5	11/10/5	11/17/5	11/24/5	12/01/5	12/08/5	
SERVICE FORECAST																	SERVICE FORECAST
PRODUCTION FORECAST		95	95	100	100	100	100	100	100	100	100	100	100	100	100	100	PRODUCTION FORECAST
ACTUAL DEMAND			190	50	140		180				200						ACTUAL DEMAND
AVAILABLE		0	-10	40	40	40	60	60	60	60	60	60	60	-40	-140	-240	AVAILABLE
AVAILABLE TO PROM			-10	50			20	100	100	100	100	100	100		200	100	AVAILABLE TO PROM
MPS			180	100	140		200	100	100	100	300	100	100		200	100	MPS

	12/15/5	01/12/6	02/09/6	03/08/6	04/05/6	05/03/6	05/31/6	06/28/6	07/26/6	08/23/6	09/20/6	10/18/6	11/15/6	12/13/6	01/10/7	02/07/7	
SERVICE FORECAST																	SERVICE FORECAST
PRODUCTION FORECAST	400	400	400	400	400	400	400	400	400	400	400	400	400	400	400	400	PRODUCTION FORECAST
ACTUAL DEMAND																	ACTUAL DEMAND
AVAILABLE	-640	-1040	-1440	-1840	-2240	-2640	-3040	-3440	-3840	-4240	-4640	-5040	-5440	-5840	-6240	-6640	AVAILABLE
AVAILABLE TO PROM	400	400	400	400	400	400	400	400	400	400	400	400	400	400	400	400	AVAILABLE TO PROM
MPS	400	400	400	400	400	400	400	400	400	400	400	400	400	400	400	400	MPS

	03/07/7	04/04/7	05/02/7	05/30/7	06/27/7	07/25/7	08/22/7	09/19/7	10/17/7	11/14/7	12/12/7	01/09/8	02/06/8	03/06/8	05/29/8	TOTAL	
SERVICE FORECAST																	SERVICE FORECAST
PRODUCTION FORECAST	400	400	400	400	400	400	400	400	400	400	400	400	400	1200	1200	15490	PRODUCTION FORECAST
ACTUAL DEMAND																760	ACTUAL DEMAND
AVAILABLE	-7040	-7440	-7840	-8240	-8640	-9040	-9440	-9840	-10240	-10640	-11040	-11440	-11840	-13040	-14240		AVAILABLE
AVAILABLE TO PROM	400	400	400	400	400	400	400	400	400	400	400	400	400	1200	1200	14960	AVAILABLE TO PROM
MPS	400	400	400	400	400	400	400	400	400	400	400	400	400	1200	1200	15720	MPS

MASTER SCHEDULE DETAIL						ACTUAL DEMAND REFERENCE											
DUE DATE	ORDER NUMBER	LOT NO.	QUANTITY DUE	CODES	REQUIRED ACTION	REQUIRED DATE	REQUIRED QUANTITY	REFERENCE NUMBER	ORDER NUMBER	LOT NO.	CODES P R T	REQUIRED DATE	REQUIRED QUANTITY	REFERENCE NUMBER	ORDER NUMBER	LOT NO.	CODES P R T
09/08			180			09/08	76	SALEM BIKE	A1341		NA						
09/15			100		R/I 01	09/08	114	KMART	A1910		NA						
09/22			140			09/15	50	JC PENNY	A4524	001	NA						
10/06			200			09/22	80	JC PENNY	A4524	002	NA						
10/13			100			09/24	60	INDY BIKE	A4595		NA						
10/20			100			10/09	120	SAM'S BICYCLES	A7510		NA						
10/27			100			10/10	60	WESTERN AUTO	A7650		NA						
11/03			300			11/04	200	JC PENNY	A7690		NAY						
11/10			100														
11/17			100														
11/24			100		SCHED												
12/01			100		SCHED												

Source: Arista Manufacturing Systems.

development and maintenance, the PIPC department takes an active part because they know how large the existing backlogs of work are in terms of capacity commitments. They, of course, *must* coordinate master schedule development with marketing, finance, and personnel.

Manufacturing items to order is not without its problems so far as schedules are concerned. Sometimes, when bidding for jobs, tentative promise dates are made on several possible contracts, although only one or two contract proposals are expected to be accepted. All of these promise dates are predicted on using the same open capacity, but this causes problems if more of the orders are obtained and if capacity cannot be expanded easily. Another problem arises when a promise date is offered and the customer places the order but wants earlier delivery. In addition, there are order cancellations, or the factory may not get things done on time, or customers may delay signing the contract. In the meantime the open capacity is assigned to other orders and then the factory is still expected to meet the originally promised delivery date. This often occurs on large government contracts.

WORKLOADS AND PRODUCTION CAPACITIES

Master production schedules often are an attempt to try to level out sales peaks and valleys; yet, in practice this is not carried very far because it costs so much to carry inventories. As a result, PIPC ends up having to do a great deal of schedule changing as they go along. Many of these changes are put into effect by increasing or decreasing work hours in response to sales changes. Yet steady operations are important, so the first response to sales changes is probably not a change in work hours.

Rather, if order backlogs begin to build up a little, the sales department gives new customers more distant promise dates. But, if backlogs build up very much, most companies first try to expand capacity by increasing work hours to avoid losing sales. And, conversely, if the backlog shrinks, capacity is not cut as the first move. Instead, new customers get earlier promise dates on their orders. If orders continue to shrink, operations may be curtailed or else a new sales promotion campaign is undertaken to stimulate new orders.

MASTER SCHEDULES: MANUFACTURING TO STOCK

Manufacturers of almost all consumers' products—the things we all buy—manufacture ''to stock.'' Products are made and assigned to specific sales orders as they are finished, or they are put into finished goods inventory in anticipation of their sale. Many such products are assigned to large continuing contracts with large retail companies such as Sears and K mart. Many of the to-stock items, however, have not been sold at the time they are being made and no one knows exactly who will buy them. Companies manufacturing to stock forecast what and how many of everything that they think their customers will buy and then try to make these items in those quantities. This kind of forecasting was discussed in Chapter 9.

The development of a master production schedule for manufacture-to-stock items begins with a sales forecast. As a rule, this forecast may have too many extreme ups and downs to allow its direct use as a master production schedule. The peaks and valleys usually need some leveling out which can be done by building up inventories during low periods. Again, the amount of leveling which can be done depends on the relative costs of carrying inventories versus the costs of changing production levels up and down.

Changing production levels may involve overtime or layoffs, the purchase of new machines or letting certain machines set idle, and other similar costs. There is also need, as in

the case of automobile tires, to forecast the product mix because some of the factory's equipment is specially designed for certain tire sizes.

PIPC participates in the adjustments made as the tentative schedule congeals into the approved master schedule because it has to determine whether the factory's capacity can handle the tentative schedule. Will there be enough machines? Will more employees be needed, or will some have to be laid off? These and other questions have to be answered by PIPC.

As mentioned, one of the major functions of master schedules when manufacturing to stock is to resolve conflicts between irregular sales and steady production, largely by using inventories to cushion the differences. This has the effect of ''decoupling'' production and sales.

As a typical example of this in operation, we might consider a toy manufacturer. Toys is a highly seasonal business, with Christmas being the big selling peak. For the company, this means an August and September production peak, since retail stores do most of their Christmas buying at this time.

The company's objective is to not lose sales in its peak period yet to level out production as much as it can without carrying large inventories. Also, it doesn't want to get caught with toys that are out of style.

The company first makes a sales forecast for an item month by month for 12 months—for example, a microprocessor-based LaCrosse game. Figure 10–7 shows its expected monthly sales and cumulative sales for a year.

In working out a production schedule, the schedulers have to contend with the cost of changing production levels—$100 per 1,000 units of change each time the production level is changed up or down. These change costs are overtime, hiring and layoff costs, changes in supervision, and other overhead required to increase production—or reduce it if output decreases. It also costs $60 per 1,000 units carried over each month's end. And, if the LaCrosse games run out of stock at any time, it is estimated that although little of the unfilled demand will be

FIGURE 10–7
Expected Sales of LaCrosse Games *(in thousands)*

Month	Unit Sales Forecast	Accumulated Sales
January	30	30
February	30	60
March	40	100
April	120	220
May	80	300
June	60	360
July	140	500
August	300	800
September	250	1,050
October	80	1,130
November	40	1,170
December	30	1,200

lost, there is nonetheless a loss of goodwill of $10 per 1,000 units of orders that have to be backordered. Customers who are dissatisfied by a stockout may not buy from the company again.

The schedulers' problem is to develop a schedule which will minimize the combined cost of production-level changes, inventory carrying costs, and losses from stockouts and backorders.

If the schedulers opt for no carrying costs, they would have to produce to "chase" sales demands and would have to change production levels almost every month, with consequent high change costs. If they choose to avoid changes, they can do this by producing steadily and building up inventories. With this choice, inventory carrying charges would be high.

The schedulers might, as we did, try first to see how steady production throughout the year would work out. We tried 100,000 a month and found that this did not work out very well. The buildup of inventory in the first half of the year was insufficient to prevent production from being behind orders all through the fall. Although this program incurred no production-level change charges, the inventory carrying costs and the costs of backorders came to $77,210.

Next, at the other extreme, we tested a schedule of producing exactly to sales expecta-

tions. This program eliminated both inventory carrying charges and backorder costs but entailed costs from changing production levels of $66,000.

One might suspect that a compromise strategy somewhere between these two extremes might product a lower total cost. Figure 10–8 (depicted graphically in Figure 10–9) shows a first attempt to develop such a compromise strategy.[2]

This proposed schedule (the heavy line in Figure 10–9) is much flatter than the sales forecast line. The peak production of 160,000 games per month from June through September is down almost to half of the August sales peak. From the factory's point of view, this is a great improvement over the extremely fluctuating sales rate shown by the thin line in Figure 10–9. This schedule is also less costly at $60,500 than either of the first two extreme alternatives.

This schedule is not perfect, however, from the production point of view because peak production is still more than double the normal off-season production. And even this much production leveling can be accomplished only by building up inventories during the slack season. The scheduler could test other proposed schedules and might find that some other strategy may produce even lower total costs.

Figure 10–10 shows the toy company's inventories of games. It is a plot of the figures in Figure 10–8 where it was found that the inventory will reach a peak of 180,000 at the end of July. Yet the average inventory for the whole year is only 50,000 or about two weeks' average monthly sales.

Figure 10–10 shows a negative inventory at the end of September—although there can't really be a negative inventory. The minus figure just means that for a week or so at the end of

---

[2] While this compromise strategy was developed by trial and error, more advanced methods are available to find least-cost solutions, using such mathematical models as linear programming and linear decision rules. For a discussion of these methods, see E. Buffa and J. Miller in "Aggregate Planning and Master Scheduling: Technique," *Production-Inventory Systems: Planning and Control* (Homewood, Ill.: Richard D. Irwin, 1979), pp. 253–310.

FIGURE 10–8
Compromise Strategy

Month	Sales Forecast (000)	Production Schedule (000)	Change in Production Rate (000)	Capacity Change Cost	Inventory at End of Month (000)	Inventory Holding Costs	Stockout Costs
January	30	50	0	$ 0	20	$ 1,200	
February	30	50	0	0	40	2,400	
March	40	60	10	1,000	60	3,600	
April	120	100	40	4,000	40	2,400	
May	80	100	0	0	60	3,600	
June	60	160	60	6,000	160	9,600	
July	140	160	0	0	180	10,800	
August	300	160	0	0	40	2,400	
September	250	160	0	0	−50	0	$500
October	80	130	30	3,000	0	0	
November	40	40	90	9,000	0	0	
December	30	30	10	1,000	0	0	
				$24,000		$36,000	$500

Total costs:
Capacity change costs	$24,000
Inventory holding costs	36,000
Stockout costs	500
Total costs	$60,500

September the company will not be able to fill all of the expected orders out of stock or out of current production. Their managers hope they won't lose any sales if they fill these orders early in October, when they will have the inventory.

Our example uses only one item: electronic LaCrosse games. But the company has to do the same thing for all its major products. For lesser items, they will probably forecast for groups at a time—perhaps using only sales dol-

FIGURE 10–9
Compromise Production Schedule Which Allows Sales Needs to Be Met Economically

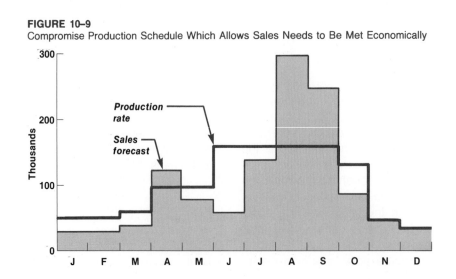

FIGURE 10–10
Planned Inventory Levels Needed to Meet Sales Demand while Allowing Manufacturing to Produce Somewhat Evenly

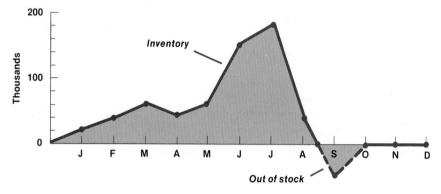

lars figures. After making forecasts, production schedules, and inventory projections for the items separately, they will combine them into overall figures. Here we are concerned with the factory's overall or "aggregate" capacity and how this capacity can be adjusted to respond to total sales needs, taking capacity change costs, inventory holding costs, and stockout costs into account. Figure 10–11 shows how various products would be aggregated and

FIGURE 10–11
Tentative Allocation of Factory Labor Capacity to Varying Quantities of Several Main Products

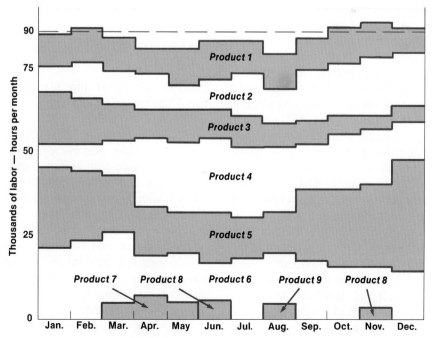

"loaded" into a factory's overall labor capacity of 90,000 hours per month. Note that some overtime will probably be required in February and later during the last quarter of the year.

PRODUCTION PROGRAMS

Many companies make end products which can be completed in a very short time (hours or days), but these are usually made out of materials or parts which require longer lead times to buy or manufacture. These companies often work from production "programs," or lists of general classes of products to make. And because of the high volume (as in automobile upholstery fabrics and automobile tires), they use so much raw material that they have to plan for and to order materials months ahead of time.

Production programs differ from other master schedules in that an approved program does *not* give production control authority to produce anything. Rather, these programs authorize the materials control department to procure raw materials with long lead times, and they give suppliers with blanket contracts a preview of expected near future delivery needs.

The PIPC department gets its authority to go ahead and schedule products to be made in the form of weekly "releases" against the program. The releases are determined by the finished products inventory control group, which is closely associated with the sales department.

These releases may arrive in PIPC only two or three weeks before the products are required. This method, therefore, can work only where the manufacturing cycle is short. Nonetheless, it gives the factory considerable flexibility to shift from one product to another (as from one automobile tire size to another or, in a shoe factory, from one size or style of shoe to another) and to follow market trends. It requires only that the total volume forecast be flexible enough to handle normal variations in the product mix. The total volume forecast has, however, to be reasonably accurate because raw materials arrive on a schedule to meet this volume.

MASTER SCHEDULES: CLASSES OF PRODUCTS

Some companies make thousands of products, very few of which, considered individually, amount to much in dollars. Companies making plumbing fittings, pipe connections, tees, ells, and so on, or nuts and bolts, or even medicines of hundreds of kinds and in many sizes of packages are like this.

Some companies that make thousands of items use aggregate master schedules for only whole classes or groups of products. Their quantities are shown in dollars, tons, pounds, gallons, or some other unit common to all items in the class. Their planned inventories are also shown only for classes of products.

It is up to PIPC to develop a specific master schedule by deciding how many to make of each individual item and when to make them. PIPC has to meet the planned overall inventory size and keep the factory working as planned and yet try not to stock out of any item very often. In cases like this, PIPC usually sets its own specific finished product inventory levels, and it keeps records of past production and sales.

MASTER SCHEDULES: THE TIME PERIOD

Master schedules may plan production for as much as two years or more in companies where it takes a long time to make products as, for example, aircraft or oil drilling rigs to drill for oil in the ocean. Not many things, though, need this much lead time in manufacturing.

Many companies, however, and especially those with computerized MRP systems, have master schedules that extend a full 52 weeks or more into the future. This is necessary so that decisions can be made about how much mechanization (the "depth" of tooling) is necessary and to plan for other required capacities such as labor and plant size. Large volumes usually allow high payoffs from heavy mechanization because they spread the investment over so many items that production costs per unit are very low. But these new machine and facility requirements have to be determined, and they have to be ordered or built so they can be available when the master schedule requires their capacities. Figure 10–12 shows an example of a resource plan for machines and labor. Note that where the total percent utilization exceeds capacity, machines need to be purchased, jobs shifted to other machines, or work shifts added to meet the master schedule's requirements.

Time Fences

Although many companies master schedule for an entire year or two ahead in order to help them decide on the degree of mechanization, they usually do not make these master production schedules an unchangeable plan for more than a few weeks or months into the future. Rather, they allow the future schedule to be updated by changes in orders, demand forecasts, or material availability. But, in the near future— a few days to a few months—the master schedule is usually "frozen," and it takes a top management decision to change it. This period where the master schedule is frozen is called a *time fence* and provides for stability in the manufacturing process, and it reduces the large costs associated with changing due dates for orders already started, canceling material purchase orders, and so on. In addition, if the time fence is well known to all concerned and very few exceptions made, it sets a tone for better planning by PIPC, marketing, and others in the organization.

Some companies (makers of machinery, locomotives, and so on) make long-lead-time products which require months to complete, so they need to have master schedules that actually authorize production several months ahead and, accordingly, have time fences of several months into the future. They need to be far ahead, not only because the products take a long time to make, but because raw materials control is likely, in these cases, to be PIPC's job too. They have

to know what end products are going to be made at least six months ahead in order to determine what materials or parts to make or buy.

There are several kinds of longer-term master schedules. One kind covers the next five or six months, often broken down into weekly requirements. When one month ends, the sixth month ahead is added. This is how General Motors' electro-motive division (which makes diesel electric locomotives) plans.

In another pattern, six months at a time are added. For example, in February a schedule is set up through the following December, but it is not extended any farther in March or April. Then, in August, a schedule is issued for another six months, January to June, of the next year. Then nothing more until February, and so on. The Cincinnati Milicron Company plans this way, and so do many other machinery makers. Another common pattern, especially for companies like Hewlett-Packard with MRP systems, is a rolling 52 weeks, with updating each week, two weeks, or month. And, many other patterns are used, depending on the product. Samsonite, the luggage manufacturer, master schedules *daily* for two weeks into the future, then shifts to weekly, for the next two months. And, they virtually have *no* time fence, which means they can reschedule tomorrow's production if need be. Samsonite can do this because of the relative simplicity of luggage, and its short manufacturing cycle.

Many other patterns are in use. The reason for the difference is largely a matter of volume, the degree of product standardization, lead times, and the length of the manufacturing cycle.

MASTER SCHEDULES: BASIC AND OPTIONAL COMPONENT PARTS

PIPC's authority to commit resources to make end products usually is specified by master schedules for *finished products*. This authority and responsibility includes seeing that all parts manufactured internally are made in the required quantities and on time. Authority to make parts

Source: L. James Burlingame.

FIGURE 10–12
A Machine and Labor Resource Plan Based on Master Schedule Capacity Requirements

RESOURCE PLAN 1985

Center 03–08	Type	Quantity	No. of Shifts	Capacity	A	B	C	D	E	F	G	H	I	Total	Required Capacity Adjustments
BD	2AC CHUCKER	4	3	1561	15	18	26		12	10	13	2		96	−564 hrs. = 1½ machines
BR	3AC WARNER & SWASEY	8	3	2966	4	20	56	11	18	2	1	2		114	
CA	REISHAUER GEAR GRINDER	2	3	900			74		6	4	16			96	−713 hrs. = 1½ machines
CAB	REISHAUER GEAR GRINDER	2	3	950		22	76	46	17	4			5	170	
CD	P. & W. GEAR GRINDER	1	3	544			78		18					96	
CEA	MAAG GEAR GRINDER	4	3	3044		14	71		21	3			17	126	−944 hrs. = 3⅓ machines
CG	P. & W. GEAR GRINDER	4	3	1190			137		39					176	−964 hrs. = 3⅓ machines
CI	PFAUTER HOBBER	5	3	2374	2	26	49	10	13	1	5		3	109	−332 hrs. } = 2 machines
CJ	BARBER COLMAN HOBBER	1	3	620	25	64	73		45	20		13	2	242	−911 hrs. }
CN	GEAR SHAVER	3	2.5	700	7	41	12	15	10	6	4			95	
CQ	GEAR POINTER	1	1	22	15	60	1		12	5				93	
CS	FELLOWS SHAPER	1	3	549		30			10					40	+302 hrs. relieve CX, CY
CW	BARBER COLMAN HOBBER	3	3	1530	7	25	34	17	9	5				97	−437 hrs. } off load to CS
CX	BARBER COLMAN SHAPER	1	3	546	1	35	52	47	9	2	29			175	−776 hrs. } + 2 machines
CY	FELLOWS SHAPER	1	3	514	13	158	22		22	27			4	246	
FD	INTERNAL GRINDER	1	3	285	5	27	25	10	15	5	7			94	
FI	INTERNAL GRINDER	1	3	275	24	50	40	23	29	6	12			184	−245 hrs. = 1 machine
FJ	SURFACE GRINDER	1	1	328	7	60	31	3	16	12	5		4	138	−141 hrs. = add 1 shift
FM	VERTICAL INTERNAL GRIND.	1	2	368		30	31	14	11				6	92	
FY	GEAR HONE	2	2	528	9	40	19	21	9	7	6			111	−84 hrs. = add 1 shift
H	ENGINE LATHE	1	3	427	21	59	43	9	19	8	7		2	168	−312 hrs. } = 1 machine
HES	W. & S. LATHE-SPECIAL	2	2	234	2	49	41	21	13	11				137	−101 hrs. } & 1 shift HES
JA	HORIZONTAL BROACH	1	1	90	4	20	50	17	2					93	
NH	GEAR CHAMFER	1	3	307	11	45	12	6	12	7	5			98	
PC	MAGNAFLUX	1	1	240	5	47	62	11	15	1	2		1	144	−118 hrs. = add 1 shift

Work Center Description (Center 03–08, Type, Quantity, No. of Shifts); *Percent Utilization of Capacity for Each Customer Order* (A–I).

derives from the approved master schedule authorization to make finished products. PIPC has to determine what parts have to be made, how many, and when. This is being done more and more with computerized MRP systems, which are described in more detail in the next chapter.

Complex products, however, often are made in considerable variety with many options. For example, factory machines such as lathes, grinders, and drill presses are built in different sizes and different designs. But many of their component parts, such as roller bearings and electric motors, are the same for several kinds of finished products.

Common Parts and Modular Bills of Material

These standardized components are sometimes called *basics,* or *commons,* and since they have a demand from several sources, they can be made on a schedule of their own which is not directly tied in with the final assembly schedule of any single kind of finished product. Storage batteries and automobile headlights are examples of basics. Also, eight-cylinder engines for automobiles can be made without regard for the product mix between station wagons and two- or four-door cars. As basics are finished, they can be assigned to specific finished products, or they can go into finished parts stock temporarily. Using the basics approach uncouples the strict timing of their manufacture from assembly schedules and allows for more economical production.

A pump manufacturer, for example, may offer a standard pump but also allow the customer to have different-sized motors, pumping capacity, and be waterproof, to name a few. In cases like this, there can be many basic or common parts and many optional components that need to be manufactured.

But, rather than completely assembling and carrying an inventory of every conceivable kind of finished pump, the company's master schedule is for these basics and optional components—not finished pumps. They must, of course, forecast the probable mix of component options which will be demanded, so they can proceed to purchase materials and parts and manufacture these components. Then, when an order arrives, they assemble it rather quickly from their finished inventories of basic and optional component inventories which were master-scheduled. This method of master scheduling is becoming more popular with computerized PIPC systems and uses a very special kind of bill of materials called a *modular bill of materials.*[3]

FINAL ASSEMBLY SCHEDULES

As mentioned above, most master schedules are for final products, not component parts. But, often, companies prepare separate final assembly schedules which are specific directives to the assembly department telling them the specific assembly configuration of component parts. This allows more flexibility by allowing the manufacture of parts in economical lot sizes and yet gives final assembly the flexibility to respond more quickly to marketplace demands.

MAINTAINING MASTER PRODUCTION SCHEDULES

Master production schedules are dynamically changing plans which must be continuously updated as time unfolds, and as changes occur in demand, capacities, and so on. Because of the critical importance of the master schedule and the key role it plays in a manufacturing organization, some PIPC specialists' entire responsibility is that of building and maintaining the master schedule. Usually called *master schedulers,* they work closely with marketing, finance, and engineering, as well as materials and purchasing specialists and production planners. They are responsible for keeping the master schedule *realistic* in terms of what manufacturing can pro-

---

[3] See Joseph A. Orlicky, George W. Plossl, and Oliver W. Wight, "Structuring the Bill of Material for MRP," *Production and Inventory Management* 13, no. 4, pp. 29–38.

duce, as well as keeping it accurate and up to date.

Review Questions

1. Why is it so difficult to know the capacity of a production facility?
2. What are the different definitions of capacity?
3. What helpful adjustments can production schedule planners make in order to bring the capacity available to meet sales demands into reasonable balance?
4. Overtime is commonly used as a way of temporarily expanding capacity. How costly is it?
5. How might variations in work loads be handled without changing the size of the work force? Discuss these possibilities.
6. How are hours of work related to output? What changes in quantities ought a manager expect from longer or shorter hours? Discuss.
7. Is it better to have a small plant and work second and third shifts, or to have a larger plant and to work one shift only?
8. How is a learning curve used to estimate capacity?
9. What differences are there in master production scheduling for make-to-stock versus make-to-order production?
10. What trade-offs must be considered in master scheduling make-to-stock items?
11. What is a time fence?
12. How are master schedules related to resource plans?
13. Why are some master schedules extended another month ahead continually as months go by, whereas in other companies future schedules are pushed ahead six months at a time?
14. When should master schedules be stated in terms of classes of products instead of specific products?
15. How do assembly orders differ from master production schedules?

Questions for Discussion

1. The president of a company asks an analyst to make up an "index of capacity" for the plant. He wants the analyst to reduce the company's various products to some kind of common denominator so that he can compare the capacity requirements of schedules to the plant's capacity to produce. How should the analyst go about making some kind of a measure of "standard units" output which would serve this purpose?
2. The analyst has just reported to the general manager that the figures show that the company should not expand its capacity right now, because this would mean idle capacity during future low periods. The president decides to expand anyway. He says that an idle plant is a tremendous spur to the sales department to get out and sell. Discuss.
3. If shorter work weeks boost hourly production and cut unit costs, why not work only 30 hours instead of 40? Discuss.
4. A master schedule is a key document which reconciles conflicts between marketing, production, finance, personnel, and engineering. Discuss.

Problems

1. A company with a capacity of 1,000 units a month has fixed costs of $2,000 a month and labor costs of $6 a unit. Materials costs are $2 per unit. The company has been producing at 80 pecent of capacity and selling its product for $12. What is its net income? What would it be at 100 percent of capacity?

   What would its net income be at 120 percent of capacity if it is assumed that 20 percent more products could be produced on overtime at an extra $3 labor cost per unit for all production above 100 percent? What would the net income be if production declines by 2 percent per hour because of the long hours? Should the company accept a contract which will call for 120 percent capacity for an extended period of time if the price is $12 and if the company could not otherwise operate at 100 percent of capacity?

2. There are five products which are made on each of six types of equipment. The table below shows the operating times (in decimal hours) and the job setup times for each operation. In each block there are two times: The upper number is the job setup time and the lower number is the operating time per unit.

How many of each kind of machine will be needed if the plant works at 170-hour month?

Equipment	Products				
	1	2	3	4	5
Mult-Au-Matic	.670		.761		.073
	.036		.078		0.97
Vertical mill		.543	.790		.870
		.097	.102		.105
Turret lathe		.732			.839
		.019			.021
Forging machine	.521	.434			.768
	.017	.049			.057
Centerless			.087	.161	
grinder			.036	.016	
Simplex mill	.617	.614	.911	.658	
	.053	.073	.081	.077	
Quantity needed per month	700	2,300	1,400	100	300
Manufacturing lot size for each production run	300	200	500	200	400

3. The production schedule for a certain part calls for manufacturing 1,500 units per week. While there is some fluctuation in this requirement, the fluctuation is very small. Production of the part calls for five operations performed on five different machines. The time requirements for each of these operations are as follows:

Machine	Time per Unit (hours)	Maximum Machine Utilization Ratio	Operator Efficiency*
1	.045	84%	110
2	.101	77	130
3	.089	91	90
4	.049	69	105
5	.050	81	130

* 110 means the operator can work 10% faster than the average operator.

Calculate the number of machines required for these operations if the plant works 40 hours a week. If you feel that more information is needed before it is possible to decide how many machines will be needed, what information is lacking?

4. Machines A, B, and C characteristically lose .3, .7, and .2 hours each day for maintenance. Besides, frequent rush orders have in the past taken up .5 hours each on these machines. In planning work, it is necessary to allow for such orders. The department works 8 hours a day. Operators on these machines are usually 110, 135, and 120 percent efficient respectively.

How many hours will it take for an order to be produced which calls for 20, 15, and 25 standard hours of work on each machine, respectively?

5. In the following example, should one machine be purchased and operated 24 hours a day, or should three machines be bought and operated 8 hours? The machines cost $100,000 each and have a normal life of 10 years with no salvage value. The discount rate is 20 percent on investments of this kind.

Twenty-four-hour operation is really only 21 hours because of lunch periods and the loss of production at shift changes. But it is necessary to pay for 24 hours of operator time. First-shift operators get $10, second-shift operators $11, and third-shift operators $12 per hour. Production efficiency on the second and third shifts is only 98 percent of the first shift.

With regular one-shift production the company does not pay for lunch periods, and it gets eight hours' work for eight hours' pay. Since the plan is to work only five days a week, there is plenty of time in either arrangement for major repairs, so this matter need not be considered.

6. It is required to make 3,000 pump housings a month which requires grinding-machine time. The standard time for this operation is .17 hours per unit.

a. How many machines will be needed if they work eight hours a day for 20 days a month at 100 percent efficiency and there were no scrap losses or lost machine time?

b. What is the answer if the company gets only 80-percent machine utilization from the machines and the operators are 105-percent efficient?

c. How many housings should be started into production if the scrap rate is .07? And how many machines (using the production expectations arrived at in b) will be needed?

7. The Home Appliance Company has been developing a new line of washing machines and expects to have them on the market by November. The company has installed enough capacity to make

4,500 units per month. First-year sales are expected to be:

	Sales		Sales
January	4,000	July	5,500
February	3,500	August	7,500
March	2,500	September	6,000
April	2,000	October	4,500
May	3,500	November	5,000
June	4,500	December	5,500
			54,000

a. The production director wants a level and stable master production schedule throughout the year. If the plant were to produce steadily, what would the inventory level be at the end of each month? And what would inventory carrying charges be at $3 per washing machine per month on the quantity in inventory at the end of each month?

b. The treasurer is worried about inventory carrying costs and suggests considering an increase of capacity at a cost of $60 per unit of added capacity. If the production manager's viewpoint can be neglected, and if production can be raised or lowered, should any new capacity be added? How much capacity? Show the new master production schedule and the resulting inventories at the end of each month. (For purposes of this problem, any costs incurred beyond the $60 per unit of added capacity because of changing production levels can be ignored.)

8. The up-to-date figures on the Aeromatics Company's contract for making 500 small airplanes show the following:

Number of Airplanes	Direct Labor-Hours per Pound
10	21.0
15	19.5
25	18.9
35	16.2
50	15.8
100	15.3
150	14.3
200	13.9
250	13.2
350	12.3
450	11.9

The contract price anticipates that the average direct labor-hours per pound will be down to 10.5 by the time the contract ends.

a. Suppose the contract includes an expected $10 per labor-hour cost (the airplanes weigh 3 tons each), $300,000 for materials and purchased components, $400,000 overhead, and 8 percent on all costs for profit. What is the average price per airplane?

b. Will the average be down to 10.5 at the end of the contract?

c. What is the *incremental* cost of the 450th airplane?

d. At the rate things are going, how much profit will the company make or lose on this contract?

e. Negotiations are being started for a second contract for 100 *more* of these airplanes. What should the new contract price be if all arrangements are carried over from the first contract, but the achievements to date of the learning curve (for the first 500 airplanes) are recognized?

9. The toy company's new forecast for LaCrosse games for the next 12 months follows. Suggest a master production schedule if the cost of changing production levels is $150 per 1,000 units of change, and $50 per 1,000 units carried in inventory per month.

	Games (000s)		Games (000s)
January	165	July	197
February	199	August	201
March	204	September	191
April	187	October	172
May	171	November	147
June	184	December	139

Note: This is the same forecast developed for Year 4 of Needems in Chapter 9 on forecasting.

Case 10–1

The production manager of the Xenonetics was considering the unusually large backlog of orders with early promise dates. Quite a few of the company's best customers were wanting quick delivery.

Just then he got a call from the sales manager about one of these orders. The sales department had promised delivery last Friday, but because of the factory's heavy load it had not been shipped—and was, in fact, not finished on Tuesday, when the sales manager made his call.

"I thought that order went out days ago. I promised that we would get it to them by last Friday. What is happening? What can I tell them now? Tomorrow for sure?"

"Wait until I check on today's reports. According to my reports, that order won't get shipped until Friday of this week. We've got a rush tag on it, but everything that has to go through the gear hobbing machines is rush, so many orders are going to get behind. And you want all of those other orders, too, don't you?"

"Yes, we do; it has taken us a long time to land two or three of those new orders, and it is very important for us to give good service if we are to get any more orders from them. And we can't let our regular customers down either; they depend on us. I think you ought to be working overtime."

"Well, I asked about that for last Saturday and the supervisor turned me down. He said no—that you had to bid pretty low to get most of those jobs, and the price just won't stand the added cost of overtime work. I'll ask him again, and maybe you ought to call him, too. If he still says no, then maybe we can send a few jobs out to other shops. That would help the schedule, but we don't make much money sending work out."

"OK, but how about giving me a call tomorrow morning so I can tell the customer something? And something he can rely on, too."

Almost immediately, another call came through to the production manager—from the general manager. He, too, wanted to know about one of the late orders, because he had had a call about it from the customer company's president.

Discuss this case.

Chapter 11

Material Requirements Planning (MRP I) and Manufacturing Resource Planning (MRP II)

As mentioned in Chapter 8, materials requirements planning (MRP I) plays a key role in answering the questions of *what* raw materials and parts should be made or purchased, *how many* are needed, and *when* they are needed—all to satisfy an ever-changing master production schedule. This is no small task and requires a considerable amount of human power and/or computer power to do effectively. As review from Chapter 8, Figure 11–1 shows the basic elements of a MRP I system.

Manufacturing resource planning (MRP II) has expanded the concept to tie in marketing, finance/accounting, personnel, and engineering. This topic will be discussed in more detail later in this chapter.

ORDER POINT VERSUS MRP I

There are *two* very distinct ways of answering the what, how many, and when questions with regard to material requirements. These two methods are "order-point-order quantity," and MRP I. The first of these, order-point-order quantity, will be discussed in more detail in Chapter 12. This method has been used for many years, and it is an excellent way to manage certain kinds of inventories—but not others. Essentially, using an order-point method, PIPC (or computers) monitors the on-hand balances of each item in inventory, and, when it seems time to place an order for more (taking the rate at which it is being used and the replenishment lead time into account), the order point is reached, and a new order is placed for some appropriate order quantity. If things go as planned, the new shipment arrives from the supplier (vendor or internal manufacturing) about the time the stock of the item is depleted. As will be seen in Chapter 12, statistics and other mathematical methods are used to determine the order-point stock level and the size of the order for each item.

ELEMENTS OF MRP I SYSTEMS

Independent versus Dependent Demand

A weakness of the order-point method from managing *all* materials and components is based

FIGURE 11–1
Elements of a Materials Requirements Planning (MRP I) System

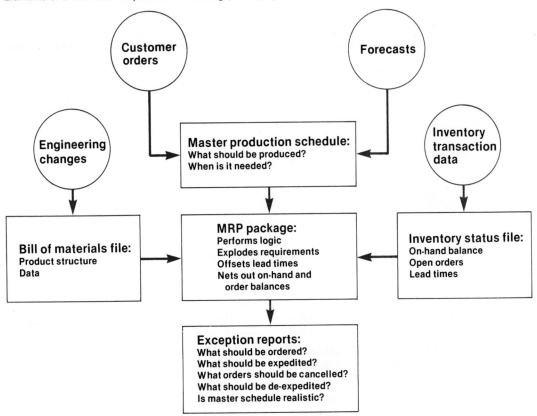

in the concept of "independent" demand versus "dependent" demand items.

Independent demand is the demand from customers for finished products or for spare or *service parts* for the repair of finished products that have already been sold. Items specified in the master production schedule are independent demand items. Dependent demand items are the required materials and components which are fabricated and assembled into the final product—as specified by bills of materials.

For example, Figure 11–2 shows how a simple file cabinet is constructed from materials (sheet metal, paint, and packaging materials), subassemblies (drawers and cabinet shell), and purchased parts (handles).

The finished and packaged file cabinet is the independent demand item, as may be replacement handles that customers order to repair those that have broken. All of the other 11 items are dependent demand items. Their quantity requirements *depend* upon the independent demand quantities from customers for finished cabinets and replacement handles. (Note that the handle is *both* an independent and dependent demand item.)

Now, back to the order-point method. The order-point method presumes that items are independent of each other. This is a correct presumption for finished goods and spare parts, but *not for dependent demand materials and component parts.* If PIPC exclusively used an order-point approach, they would have separate order points and order quantities for each of the 13 items involved in the file cabinet. This could easily lead to poor coordination of the quantities received and their timing, and could cause stockouts of certain materials and parts, while others build up in inventory or WIP waiting for their arrival.

On the other hand, if we recognize the independent-dependent demand relationships between the finished products and components,

then we can *calculate how many* of these dependent items we need if we know how many finished file cabinets and spare handles are called for from the master production schedule. For example, if our master schedule calls for 500 finished and packed cabinets, then we can *calculate* that we need 1,000 painted drawers— or perhaps 1,050, if the scrap rate on this part is 5 percent. Likewise, 1,000 drawers creates a dependent demand for, say, 500 pints of paint, if .5 pints are required per drawer, as specified by the bill of materials, and so on.

The point to distinguishing between independent and dependent demand is that independent demand is not wholly calculable. In planning,

FIGURE 11–2
Material, Part, and Assembly Requirements for a Simple File Cabinet

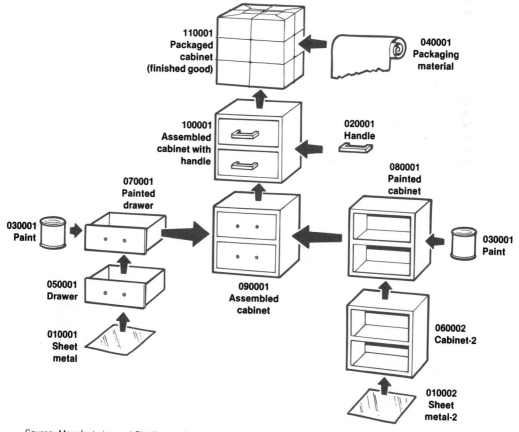

Source: Manufacturing and Distribution Control Systems, McDonnell Douglas Automation Company.

the quantities of independent demand items needed come from orders, if there are such orders. Or, if manufacture is to stock, the independent demand comes from forecasts even though these are recognized to have some error. For planning purposes, once a quantity of an independent demand item has been accepted as part of the master schedule, the quantities of dependent demand items (materials and parts) generated are determinable, and it is possible to *calculate* their demand with considerable accuracy.

And, since some components are sold for repair purposes as well as their being used in newly assembled end products, their total demand is therefore a sum of the dependent demand generated by the end products into which they go, plus their own independent demand. This is the MRP I approach to answering the *what* and *how many* questions. The *when* question revolves around *lead times*.

Lead Times

Lead times are the times it takes to get things done. For items we make, lead times are the times it takes to prepare the necessary order release papers, plus the time to perform operations, plus the waiting, or "queue" time between operations. For purchased items and raw materials, lead time is the time it takes to prepare orders and release them to vendors. In addition, it includes the vendor's lead time to receive materials from *their* suppliers, make the parts, and ship them to us. When they arrive, we must inspect them, and check them into inventory before these items are actually available for use in manufacturing.

Since lead times for internal manufacture and for purchased items can differ widely, the timing, or *when* questions, require methods to coordinate and manage lead times in an efficient way so that the right materials and parts are available at the right times—not too late, and not too early. For if they are too late, production is held up, capacity is idle, and orders are late. If materials arrive too early, unnecessary inventory carrying costs are incurred. Again, order-point methods do not handle this very well, whereas MRP I is designed to solve this problem.

Common Use Items

In most manufacturing situations, some component parts and many kinds of raw materials are used in two or more subassemblies and end products. Thus, their total requirements are sums of requirements being generated from two or more sources. These several requirements for common use items often are combined into single orders to vendors or manufacturing lots in order to save on ordering and setup costs. In our file cabinet, paint and sheet metal are common use items. MRP I procedures combine these needs as they determine each item's requirements.

Data Base Requirements for Material Requirements Planning I

The requirements from independent demands and those generated by dependent demand for each of the thousands of components and parts which can exist in a typical fabrication-subassembly-final assembly operation are stored in several computer files which "talk" to each other as MRP I-based PIPC functions progress.

Bills of materials and product structure trees. Among the most important of these data bases for MRP I are the bill of materials and product structure files which define both what and how many materials and parts are required to make each item, and the sequence in which materials, parts, and subassemblies are combined into final products. Figure 11–3 shows the bill of materials and *indented* product structure for our file cabinet.

Figure 11–3 shows the unit of measure (each, feet, and pint) and the quantity of each item required for *one* finished and packaged cabinet. The indented item numbers show the product structure or sequence of manufacture

FIGURE 11–7
Flowchart of MRP Calculation Process

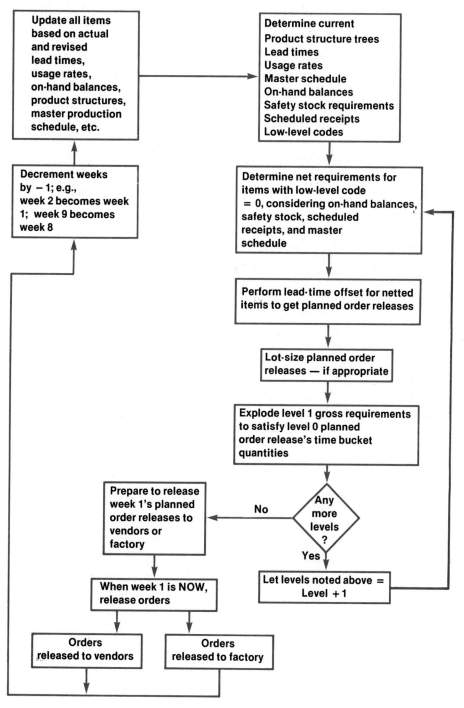

FIGURE 11–8
MRP Computational Worksheet 2

Item number	On hand	Safety stock		Week 1	Week 2	Week 3	Week 4	Week 5	Week 6	Week 7	Week 8
A	0	0	Gross requirements					⑩			⑮
			Scheduled receipts								
			Available								
			Net requirements					10			15
			Planned order receipts					10			15
			Planned order releases			10			15		
B	⑮	⑩	Gross requirements			23			27		
			Scheduled receipts		⑬						
			Available	5	18	18					
			Net requirements			5			27		
			Planned order receipts			5			27		
			Planned order releases		5			27			
C	②	㉚	Gross requirements	①	10+1	21	①	54+1	31	①	①
			Scheduled receipts	100							
			Available								
			Net requirements								
			Planned order receipts								
			Planned order releases								
D	㉕	5	Gross requirements			33			42		
			Scheduled receipts								
			Available								
			Net requirements								
			Planned order receipts								
			Planned order releases								
E	⑤	0	Gross requirements		15	13		81	12		
			Scheduled receipts								
			Available								
			Net requirements								
			Planned order receipts								
			Planned order releases								
F	0	0	Gross requirements				⑬			⑫	
			Scheduled receipts								
			Available								
			Net requirements				13			12	
			Planned order receipts				13			12	
			Planned order releases			13			12		

FIGURE 11–9
MRP Computational Worksheet 3

Item number	On hand	Safety stock		Week 1	Week 2	Week 3	Week 4	Week 5	Week 6	Week 7	Week 8
A	0	0	Gross requirements					(10)			(15)
			Scheduled receipts								
			Available								
			Net requirements					10			15
			Planned order receipts					10			15
			Planned order releases			10			15		
B	(15)	(10)	Gross requirements			23			27		
			Scheduled receipts		(13)						
			Available	5	18	18					
			Net requirements			5			27		
			Planned order receipts			5			27		
			Planned order releases		5			27			
C	(2)	(30)	Gross requirements	(1)	11	21	(1)	55	31	(1)	(1)
			Scheduled receipts	(100)							
			Available	72	71	60	39	38			
			Net requirements					17	31	1	1
			Planned order receipts					17	31	1	1
			Planned order releases			17	31	1	1		
D	(25)	(5)	Gross requirements			51 + 33	93	3	3 + 42		
			Scheduled receipts								
			Available	20	20	20					
			Net requirements			64	93	3	45		
			Planned order receipts			64	93	3	45		
			Planned order releases		64	93	3	45			
E	(5)	0	Gross requirements		15	13 + 17	31	81 + 1	12 + 1		
			Scheduled receipts								
			Available		5						
			Net requirements		10	30	31	82	13		
			Planned order receipts		10	30	31	82	13		
			Planned order releases	10	30	31	82	13			
F	0	0	Gross requirements				(13)		(12)		
			Scheduled receipts								
			Available								
			Net requirements				13		12		
			Planned order receipts				13		12		
			Planned order releases			13		12			

C of 17, 31, 1, and 1 units in weeks 3, 4, 5, and 6.

Lot-Sizing

At this point, we pause in our process to briefly discuss lot-sizing in MRP. It will be discussed in more detail in Chapter 12.

We have seen that we have four planned order releases for item C in weeks 3, 4, 5, and 6 for 17, 31, 1, and 1 units. If we let these four orders be released this way, we will have to prepare four separate orders and track each one of them through the factory if C is a manufactured part or monitor their arrival if they are purchased from a vendor.

Obviously, this may be inefficient because two of the orders are for only one unit each. Thus, we may wish to lot size these four orders into fewer orders of more units. We might, for example, add weeks 5 and 6 orders to week 4, and order 33 units at once in week 4. Or, we might combine all of these four orders into week 3 and order 50 units at once. By doing this we would cut our order preparation costs substantially, but on the other hand we may get a quantity discount for the larger order size. Also, since we would then carry 31 units for an extra week, 1 unit for an extra two weeks, and 1 unit for an extra three weeks (we don't need them until these weeks), we would increase our inventory carrying costs.

There are several lot-sizing methods designed especially for MRP systems which analyze these trade-offs, and they will be covered in Chapter 12. We will not lot-size C in our example here, but if, for example, it were economical to combine all four planned orders into one order for 50, we would have only one planned order release for C of 50 units in week 3. Once this was done, we would continue in our normal net–lead-time offset–explode procedure, stopping at each level to consider whether or not the lot-sizing of a string of planned order releases is appropriate.

Returning to our example, we next explode out level 3's requirements of Ds and Es which are used to make Cs. This is also shown in Figure 11–9, as are the final net requirements and planned order releases of D and E, since we have reached level 3, which is their low-level code.

This completes our example showing the essentials of how MRP I works. We now know *how many of what* to order and *when* for the next eight weeks as defined by the quantities of planned order releases in each time bucket. Had there been more levels, it would have been necessary to carry through more iterations of the kind we have just been through.

It is hard to believe that our simple example could have produced such a complicated calculation just to determine the right quantities of parts and subassemblies to order at the right time. It is obvious that real-life complicated products would require a computerized MRP I system to handle all of the necessary calculations and updating as time unfolds.

And, *updating* is an important part of the MRP I process, as shown in the left side of the flowchart presented in Figure 11–7.

REPLANNING AND RESCHEDULING WITH MRP 1

Updating and recalculating planned order releases is often done weekly or every two weeks as a normal part of the process.

Master schedules are extended another week or two and are often changed, thus upsetting all of the MRP I calculations. These changes are caused by customers wanting to change the quantities on their orders or to change the delivery schedules; or there may be changes caused by delays in the arrival of raw materials or changes in the bills of materials; or changes due to machine breakdown, and so on.

One of the important advantages of a computerized MRP I system is that the computer will recalculate everything quickly and usually at a reasonable cost.

Priority Planning

This ability to update planned orders is especially helpful when the changes mentioned above require changes in the priorities among orders that are scheduled for the factory. This is called *priority planning* and aids PIPC people in determining which orders should receive priority in the various work centers in the factory. If an order is delayed because a key purchased part is late in arriving from a vendor, they can reschedule it, or if a good customer wants an order earlier or later, it too can be rescheduled. This aids in keeping priorities "valid," which reduces "hurry up and then wait" complaints, as well as complaints caused by late orders.

The same is true for planned or already-released purchased item orders. Keeping priorities valid for purchased items allows the purchasing department, within reason, to ask vendors for earlier or later due dates if some other changes require it.

Regenerative versus Net Change Replanning and Scheduling

There are two major ways that MRP plans are updated. The first is called *regeneration* and is the process described in our computational example and in the flowchart in Figure 11–7. With regeneration, each week or two, the *entire* calculation process is repeated for every item—both those which have had changes or revisions, and those whose status has not changed at all from the previous MRP I explosion. Regeneration systems were the first kind to be developed, and many are still being used successfully today.

The other way to update is with more modern *net change* MRP I explosion systems. Net change systems recognize that not every item's status changes from week to week, and so it only explodes through those product trees (or orders for a given product) where changes have occurred since the previous run, and ignores the others. Net change systems usually require less computer time since perhaps 80 percent or more of the items in the systems may not

be affected in any given week or two. As a result, complete regeneration of MRP I output may be required only periodically (perhaps once each six months), and then only to "purge" out the errors which may have crept in over time by not completely regenerating each week or two.

Batch versus Online Computerized MRP Systems

As mentioned earlier, computerized MRP I systems of all sizes are now readily available for both small and large companies. Computerized MRP I is no longer just available and practical for General Motors, but can often be extremely cost-effective for manufacturers with as few as 25–100 employees, depending upon the company's complexity.

The two major kinds of computer systems available for MRP I (and other things as well) are *batch* and *online* systems. With batch systems, all information is accumulated for a week or two and then run through the computer, say, on a Saturday so that the following Monday, PIPC can release orders and reschedule others based on the update. For changes or questions that occur during the week (or two weeks), PIPC must handle them without the updated data being in the computer. In practice, this is usually not too difficult to do. In fact this may actually improve efficiency and on-time orders because PIPC cannot change things *too* frequently and quickly, which can cause "nervousness" in the output from the system. (Nervousness means that too many changes are being made and there is too much starting and stopping of orders, changing due dates, etc.)

Of course, being able to have up-to-the-minute information about the status of orders and the impact of changes on them is also useful. For this reason, online systems are available which allow PIPC (and others who are authorized) to quickly inquire through CRTs as to the *current* status of customer orders, planned or open vendor and factory orders, bills of materials, lead times, and so on. In some advanced net change systems, changes which occur are immediately reflected, through the net change logic, in revised planned order releases, again, with some limitations, to reduce the negative aspects of a too-nervous system.

COMPUTER-GENERATED MRP REPORTS

Several reports are generated from MRP systems, but space does not permit us to show examples of all of them. The main output, of course, is the MRP I Schedule Report for each item. We return now to our file cabinet example to show a sample output of this report for levels 0 and 1 items. Referring back to Figure 11–4, this includes the packaged cabinet, which is made up of the assembled cabinet with handles, and the packaging materials. The MRP I schedule report for these three items is shown in Figure 11–10. The master schedule (Total Requirements) calls for two packaged cabinets each in weeks 4, 5, 6, and 7. With none on hand, no safety stock required, and no scheduled receipts (open orders), this, with a *one-week* lead-time offset, generates planned order releases (planned orders) in weeks 3, 4, 5, and 6. This in turn explodes the total requirements for assembled cabinets with handles and packaging materials in the appropriate time buckets and gross quantities. After considering on-hand, safety stock, and open orders, their planned orders are then determined.

This MRP I report format uses "net available" rather than "net requirements," as we did in our numerical example. This is why the numbers are negative. In addition, this report format accumulates net available from bucket to bucket. Otherwise, the approaches are essentially identical. Again, space will not permit showing the entire report for all 13 items used in manufacturing the file cabinet.

Use of MRP I Reports

How does a production planner use a report as shown in Figure 11–10? First, the planner knows today (presume it is period zero) that orders for the finished file cabinet must be released in periods 3, 4, 5, and 6; and that orders for the two dependent demand items must be released in their appropriate weeks. So, when these weeks become the present, the planner knows what needs to be done. The planner may have several hundred items under his control, so this report tells him what action should be taken each week. This, of course, may change if there are problems, but the information is there to know specifically what action should be taken.

MRP I IN SERVICE ORGANIZATIONS

While the vast majority of MRP I applications are used in piece-part fabrication manufacturing, some progress is being made in its application to service organizations.

The general concept of independent-dependent demand is the key as to whether MRP is practically useful in nonmanufacturing activities. If some final service output has some reasonably fixed "bill of resources" which are required to complete or deliver the service, then MRP is a possibility.

MRP I in a College Food Service[1]

One application which is being developed is in the food service industry. Here, at a university, the menu plan for the semester is the master production schedule, and the recipes for individual food items are the bills of materials. In fact, there are even subassemblies which can be planned; such as making large batches of spiced tomato sauce which is used in such end items as spaghetti, lasagna, sloppy joes, and pizza. And since there is a substantial overlap in common "materials" such as salt, sugar, flour, and hamburger, the problem of accumulating requirements and their timing can be handled nicely by MRP I.

It is expected that additional applications,

---

[1] See Jeffery Jones, "The Use of Material Requirements Planning (MRP) in a Food Service Installation," *Production and Inventory Management*, 2d quarter, 1979, pp. 1–15.

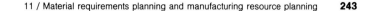

FIGURE 11–10
Computer-Generated MRP Output for Levels 0 and 1 of File Cabinet

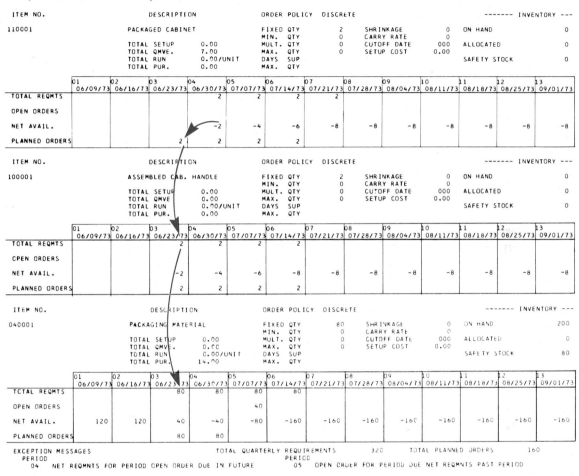

Source: McDonnell Douglas Automation Company.

like this one, will be forthcoming in other situations, such as nurse and hospital-bed planning, educational planning, and other service organizations where a reasonably well-defined bill of resources can be developed, and master scheduling grows in its use in the service sector.

MANUFACTURING RESOURCE PLANNING (MRP II)

As we said in Chapter 8, the generic concept of MRP has proved to be much broader than simply for planning *material* requirements. This broader concept, MRP II, or *manufacturing resource planning,* attempts to integrate other functional areas as shown earlier in Figure 8–2.

By the mid-1980s, MRP II has gone well beyond the conceptual stage and is being implemented rather widely by companies who have had earlier success with MRP I. Currently, over 50 different companies offer MRP II-oriented software systems.

Capital Requirements Planning and Budgeting Control with MRP II

Financial managers have found that MRP II is an extremely important tool for them to use in forecasting capital and cash flow requirements. Inherent in an approved master production schedule is a commitment by management to *finance* the resources needed to make it work. And since planned order releases can easily be "dollarized" and translated into capital and cash flow requirements, financial managers, too, can obtain (although in summarized form) the *quantity* and *timing* of money requirements for months and often years ahead. This planning information comes from specially designed financial requirements planning reports which are produced by the computer from essentially the same data base used to plan materials, orders, and capacities. In this sense, money is being treated as if it were just another raw material or component part. Part of it might be obtained from vendors (banks, financial institutions, and investors) and the rest of it comes from the organization's internally "produced" cash flow. And, as the master schedule is implemented, reports of system performance also are provided to financial managers for monitoring budgets and controlling costs.[2]

IMPLEMENTING MRP (I AND II)

By now the benefits received from a formal MRP I or II system may be apparent; however, the experiences of a firm which has successfully implemented them may add to our understanding of these powerful systems and the problems which need to be overcome. The following article from *Industry Week* tells how Corning is going through this sometimes painful but rewarding process.[3]

---

[2] See Robert J. Campbell and Thomas M. Porcano, "The Contributions of Material Requirements Planning (MRP) to Budgeting and Cost Control," *Production and Inventory Management* 20, no. 2 (1979), pp. 63–71.

[3] For a good discussion of research findings on MRP benefits and costs and the factors needed for successful MRP implementation, see R. A. Schroeder, et al., "A Study of MRP Benefits and Costs," *Journal of Operation Management* 2, no. 1 (October 1981), pp. 1–9; and E. M. White, et al., "A Study of the MRP Implementation Process," *Journal of Operations Management* 2, no. 3 (May 1982), pp. 145–53.

WHY CORNING IS STICKING WITH MRP
By Bruce Horovitz

Take an inventory of the typical American household and these items are almost certain to show up: one refrigerator, two television sets, and three pieces of Corning Ware.

Surprised about the Corning Ware? Executives at Corning Glass Works, Corning, N.Y., aren't. They're well aware of America's appetite for cookware. But they were surprised at times in the mid-1970s to discover that incoming orders couldn't be filled—at least not within a satisfactory period—because, for example, a Pennsylvania plant of theirs wasn't producing enough lids to cover all the bowls rolling off a Corning assembly plant in West Virginia.

So the brass at Corning went hunting for a better way to manage production. Their search took them right back to the shop floor. It was time, they decided, to begin balancing the items on hand with the demands of the production schedule. And it was time that Fred in finance made connections with Mark in marketing, Mike in manufacturing, and Peter in purchasing.

The solution: MRP.

Commonly recognized as an acronym for "material requirements planning," MRP has evolved into more than a computerized inventory control method—although that is still a key element. (*Industry Week*, Oct. 13, 1980, page 86.) In some companies, like Corning, MRP has been expanded to a centralized scheduling system encompassing all company divisions. An executive in finance, for example, can now press a few buttons on a computer terminal and find out what his counterpart in purchasing is up to. Even the translation of the acronym has been altered—to "manufacturing resource planning."

Corning, a company with an estimated $1.6 billion in sales in 1981, is undergoing a sometimes-agonizing process—bringing MRP systems up to top status at a dozen of its 39 domestic plants. Three have already

(continued)

made it: plants in Greencastle, Pa., Martinsburg, W. Va., and Harrodsburg, Ky. By the end of this year, another six facilities are expected to duplicate that success.

Corning's MRP program has required an investment of more than $1 million a year for the last four years.

Slightly more than half of the expense is for salaries for project leaders and inventory-accuracy clerks. The software—an "Arista" package purchased from Xerox Corp.—and the data-processing support staff consume about 35% of the MRP budget. And about 10% is spent on staff training. Very little computer hardware was needed, since Corning was able to use equipment (primarily IBM) already in place.

The payoff didn't come overnight, but the company now boasts savings of some $2 million a year directly related to MRP. Since its system went on-line in 1978, Corning has shaved $17 million from its inventories. The ultimate goal is to reduce overall company inventory by $30 million.

Look Again

At first blush, Corning may not seem like the sort of company that needs MRP. It churns out a hefty volume of baking dishes and coffee pots, but just how much product variety could such a homey manufacturer have?

Plenty. And much of it has nothing to do with anybody's kitchen. While the 130-year-old firm is best known for its consumer products, nearly two-thirds of its business is now in technical, scientific, medical, and industrial products. Its electronic components can be found in computers. Corning produces lens blanks for millions of pieces of eyewear. Corning glass can be found in automobile headlamps and television tubes. The company has been in the forefront of science since the 19th century. When Thomas Edison began tinkering with the electric light, Corning helped him develop the glass bulb. And a rugged version of Corning glass is used in the nose cones of sophisticated spacecraft.

In all, Corning manufactures about 60,000 different kinds of products. It employs 29,000 workers, operates 63 plants worldwide, and exports products to more than 90 nations.

The switchover to MRP wasn't easy. Some employees left the company rather than accept the new system. On several occasions the entire project was nearly scratched by an impatient board of directors. And to prevent panic in the ranks—bred by "horror stories" about MRP failures elsewhere—management decided to disguise the project. They knew the term MRP might send managers and workers heading for the exits, so

they christened their program EPIC (for "efficient production inventory control").

The epic of EPIC won't end until all of Corning's plants have mastered MRP. That may take a decade or longer. In the meantime, Corning is attempting to convince all of its plant managers of the value of MRP—by dangling statistics from its three successful MRP operations, like corporate carrots, before their eyes. The highly touted plants are a distribution center, a cookware-making facility, and a plant that produces lens blanks for eyeglasses.

Enthusiastic apostles. Conversion to MRP isn't presented as an ultimatum at Corning. Nonetheless, the message is quite clear. Managers of successful MRP operations get royal treatment. When a plant's system makes the grade, a senior corporate executive flies to the site and presents the plant manager with a Steuben glass bowl. These plant managers have been recruited as MRP apostles to spread the word to their counterparts in the company.

Last fall, at a semiannual get-together of plant managers—this one at a resort in Wilmington, N.C., on a 72-degree day with the golf links beckoning—attendance was splendid at a session in which three plant managers explained why MRP is a must.

"It is so simple, straightforward, and logical that even I understand it," declared Jim Siner, who oversees the giant Corning distribution center in Greencastle. His down-home comments had a positive impact. And he supported his logic with statistics demonstrating remarkable improvement in plant performance since MRP took hold in 1979. Most noteworthy: Inventory accuracy has leaped from 69% to 86%, and schedule compliance—meeting internal deadlines—has improved from 71% to 90%.

Richard Sphon, plant manager at Harrodsburg, emphasized another dividend. The MRP system, he said, "allowed us to increase the complexity of our business without adding people." And the technology isn't all that intimidating, he added. "It's more like a fast calculator than a big computer," he said. Robert Sanders, who runs the Martinsburg plant, cited a significant reduction in last-minute schedule changes due to inventory error.

Skeptics. Nonetheless, MRP has presented a tough selling job. "Not every plant in our company has embraced this with open arms," admits Daniel E. Hull, corporate manager of inventory control and Corning's chief MRP cheerleader. "If the plant doesn't want it," he insists, "we don't dictate that they have to do it." But he does offer incentives—like "front-end" corporate funding and technical support.

MRP can create ego problems. Though it promises

(continued)

to make their jobs easier, many plant managers view it as a threat to their personal power. The nature of the computerized scheduling system enables headquarters officials to make some of the decisions the plant manager once made.

Maybe the guy feels he is no longer king of his fiefdom," explains Robert W. Matthews, manager of manufacturing for Corning's Consumer Products Div. "As a former plant manager, I suppose I would view it as a threat." But it can also be a power booster, he adds. Since MRP eliminates many minor headaches, the plant manager should find he has more time to spend on key decisions.

Where to begin? MRP didn't exactly take Corning by storm. "We didn't all of a sudden wake up two years ago and decide this was the way to go," explains R. Lee Bailey, master production planner for the Consumer Products Div. Inventory practices have improved, considerably at Corning since 1960, when at least one plant manager was known to keep inventory records on the backs of envelopes.

The three plants that became Corning's MRP pioneers were selected with great care. Even before adopting MRP, each was well on its way to achieving some mastery over inventory. Corporate planners were determined to choose "can't-miss" plants that would present a good picture to the rest of the company.

Still, there were glitches. "We made all the classic errors," recalls Mr. Bailey. At one plant the new system was put on-line before inventory accuracy had been brought even close to an acceptable level (most analysts recommend 90% or better before making the switch). The result was a bigger mess than before. And, at one consumer products plant, inventory levels actually began to grow after MRP took hold, "because they started making more of the right things before they got rid of the wrong things." The planners had promised management a spiffy, new system in one year. Instead, it took four. The initial results nearly persuaded top management to cut the MRP cord.

Big Push

Any successful MRP system requires a commitment at the top. A driving force at Corning has been Thomas C. MacAvoy, president and chief operating officer. He was instrumental in persuading top management to budget $4 million to implement the program. But the executive who keeps the closest tabs on MRP is Van C. Campbell, senior vice president for finance. "The real problem," he points out, "is that you can maintain people's interest in a program for only a short time. If you haven't

made it in a few years, you can fall back to ground zero."

One key to the success of the three Corning plants has been careful monitoring. The MRP system is reviewed quarterly at each plant. Under an annual self-rating system, each plant manager must spell out his MRP progress—and provide documentation.

Customers, after all, are the driving force. Two of Corning's biggest accounts are the K Mart and Sears retail chains. A few years ago, Corning executives were aware that these major customers were unhappy. Only 50% of their orders were being delivered on time. "If we had continued at 50% customer service, we wouldn't have been doing business with them much longer," acknowledges Corning's Mr. Bailey. But, thanks to MRP, customer service in the consumer division now exceeds 90%.

ABCs of MRP. Oliver Wight, president of Oliver Wight Inc., Newbury, N.H., hopes that the Corning experience will prove enlightening to other firms. In seminar after seminar, Mr. Wight and Walt Goddard, his executive vice president, have labored to teach executives the ABCs of MRP. The two men offer 21 top-management courses annually. Three years ago, Corning placed a standing order for ten seats in every one of their classes.

"Corning had enough insight to realize that MRP applied to them, even though they're quite different from the typical manufacturing company that's attracted to MRP," says Mr. Goddard, who has worked step-by-step with Corning.

Mr. Wight sees MRP as common sense. But, as common as he'd like it to be, Corning is an exception to the rule. Mr. Wight remains befuddled as to why some of America's largest corporations continue to operate on blind guesswork, hunches, and rush catch-ups. "People assume that most manufacturing companies run the way they should. The fact of the matter is, they don't," he insists.

But MRP is ushering in a new era of reality at Corning. "In the past we had meetings filled with opinions," says Corning's Mr. Matthews. "Now we're having meetings filled with facts."

HARRODSBERG
Cutting Back on Busy Work

Two winners were bred in Harrodsburg, Ky. (Pop. 12,000). Genuine Risk, the 1980 Kentucky Derby winner, was foaled in a Harrodsburg barn. And Corning's first top-flight MRP operation blossomed at the company's prescription glass manufacturing plant.

(continued)

This is horse country. It is also an area of galloping growth. Lexington, one of the nation's ten fastest-growing cities, is just 20 miles away. Corning is one of the area's major employers. More than half of the 380 workers at its Harrodsburg plant have been on the payroll for 20 years or longer.

Plant manager Dick Sphon points out that since MRP went on-line there three years ago, it has been a real labor-saver. "In our mind," he says, "MRP has eliminated the need for [taking] physical inventory." Because its computerized system is so accurate, the plant was exempted from that chore in 1981, saving an estimated 800 manhours.

The plant melts 65 different types of glass, and job changes can exceed 4,000 annually, making Harrodsburg a good candidate for MRP. The plant, which runs 24 hours a day, seven days a week, houses a variety of operations—from mixing, melting, and forming processes to inspection and shipping. But despite a proliferating product line, it hasn't been necessary to add staff—thanks to MRP.

Harrodsburg's MRP hardware and software costs totaled roughly $400,000 over three years, but it has more than paid for itself. In 1981 alone, Mr. Sphon says, the system saved over $500,000.

He isn't the only one who's pleased with the results. "I don't have to dig through stacks of reports anymore to find numbers," says Al Webber, production supervisor. "The computer does the busy work. We manage the plant instead of firefighting.

Overall plant inventory accuracy exceeds 90%, but some individual operations do even better. In the maintenance department, for example, where more than 8,000 different types of items—tools and materials—are stored, the accuracy level is 99%.

"Ask me for something," challenges Gene Curtsinger, maintenance manager, "and 99% of the time I've got it." The only time problems arise, he adds, is when there is confusion over the precise description of an item. In the past, maintenance workers often referred to certain tools by nicknames—"I need the green gizmo." That doesn't work now. If an item isn't properly identified, the computer can't find it.

Charles Haven, warehouse and shipping supervisor, calls MRP a lifesaver. "If that machine tells me something is there," he says, pointing to a desk-size computer terminal, "I can go out there and find it."

GREENCASTLE
1 Million Square Feet of MRP

Corning's biggest facility doesn't manufacture a thing. It packages and warehouses some 1,250 finished-goods items shipped in from eight different manufacturing plants.

About the size of a large shopping mall, the 1 million-sq-ft facility is in Greencastle, Pa. (Pop. 3,500), 3 miles down the road from the Gibbles potato chip factory, the area's other large employer. In the Corning cafeteria, employees can do more than nibble on Gibbles or bite into a burger. They can also keep tabs on the plant's performance by glancing at a chart on the rear wall. The chart shows how well their MRP system is working.

MRP is breaking new ground at Greencastle. For years, critics have argued that the computerized technique can succeed only in a manufacturing setting. But at Greencastle it has improved performance in packaging, storage, and distribution. Over a three-year period, from 1979 through 1981, inventory accuracy climbed from a disappointing 69% to a respectable 86%; inventory turns increased from 5.4 to 6.6 per year; schedule compliance improved from 71% to 90%; and the percentage of on-time customer deliveries leaped from a pathetic 64% to an enviable 91%.

We were the world's worst at jerking suppliers around," recalls Jim Siner, plant manager. But MRP has changed all that. "In the old days," recalls Donald E. Eshleman, the divisional supervisor who spearheaded the Greencastle MRP program, "we'd get up to a few days before a crisis and then all hell would break loose."

A key to success has been MRP education, right down to the forklift driver. "He can relate to the frustration of looking for something and not finding it," says Mr. Siner. To ensure that accurate data are entered into the computer, precise recordkeeping is a must—not only of what's on hand, but where it's located.

Line workers weren't inundated with details, but they were shown how MRP would make their jobs easier. In the beginning, resistance to MRP prevailed, but "now we have people showing up at [MRP] meetings who weren't even invited," says Mr. Eshleman.

Because it is easier to maintain and adjust inventory levels, MRP has eliminated a good many last-minute surprises. Mr. Siner says he can now give employees a clearer picture of long-term shceduling—he can notify workers six months in advance when the plant will shut down.

The cost to adapt an existing computer system at Greencastle to MRP was $250,000, but that outlay resulted in a $2 million decrease in inventory.

Crisis management has all but disappeared. The plant floor no longer is thrown into a state of panic when unexpected orders arrive; that makes for happier employees.

---

continued)

MARTINGSBURG

No More Crying "Wolf"

It's hard to imagine that many folks in Martinsburg, W. Va. (pop. 14,626), home of the state's 1974 Little League champs, would give two hoots about MRP.

The truth is, most of them don't. But the 750 employees at the Corning Ware plant there certainly do. Daily, the plant melts 300,000 pounds of glass to produce thousands of saucepans, baking dishes, skillets, teapots and coffeepots, and platters. Using a patented process, the glass products are transformed into rugged ceramic glass. It is the only factory in the world that makes Corning Ware.

Generally, MRP is regarded as practical only when a product's bill of materials is lengthy. And a product as uncomplicated as a coffeepot might not seem to warrant the complexity and expense involved in an MRP system. But even a cofeepot is the sum of its parts—including the plastic handle, the stainless steel band around the handle, and the all-important "floral bouquet" decal that gives the pot its personality. Then there is the special cardboard box that gives the product its "sellability." Each of these items must be on hand before production can begin.

No one realizes this better than Robert Sanders, manager of the 456,000 sq. ft. Martinsburg plant which is equipped with state-of-the-art glassmaking machinery. In 1979, when MRP was introduced at the plant, inventory accuracy was about 81%. By the end of 1981 it had reached 95%. What that meant, says Mr. Sanders, was "a lot fewer late-night calls."

And a lot less inventory. Since 1979, inventories have been pared from $18 million to $14 million. The $4 million reduction yields a direct annual savings of $400,000 in carrying costs.

"The key to success," explains Mr. Sanders, "is accuracy in forecasting. MRP forces us to be accurate." Indeed, forecasts are vital to an operation that depends on seasonal sales—for Christmas, Easter, and Mother's Day. Few people buy Corning Ware on impulse; an estimated 67% of the purchases are as gifts.

Martinsburg's employees regard MRP as a gift. "I don't think we could compete without it," suggests one department head.

W. Hollis Leith, a purchasing supervisor, was among those who raised objections at first. He thought management was toying with another "computer game," he says. But his opinion has changed dramatically. "It gives us credibility with suppliers," he asserts. "We don't cry 'wolf' so often."

Winnie Glenny, a production planner, was another early doubter. She admits that it took careful—almost painstaking—explanation by top management to lure her onto the MRP bandwagon. "There is a grand scheme, and it makes sense," she says, "but I needed someone to convince me of that."

Source: Bruce Horovitz, "Why Corning Is Sticking with MRP," *Industry Week*, January 25, 1982, pp. 44–47.

Reprinted with permission of *Industry Week*.

Review Questions

1. Distinguish between order point and MRP I methods for inventory planning and control.

2. Distinguish between MRP I and MRP II systems.

3. Why not use order point methods for dependent demand items?

4. What is a time bucket?

5. How are lead times used in materials requirements planning?

6. How does a "product structure tree" relate to a bill of materials?

7. Why are level codes important in MRP I systems?

8. Define gross and net requirements in MRP I.

9. Trace the steps involved in the "explosion" process, from the list of finished products needed back to the parts and raw materials required.

10. What questions do "planned order releases" answer for an item?

11. Differentiate between net change and regenerative replanning and scheduling.

12. How do MRP II concepts relate to capital requirements planning?

13. What are the essentials required to apply MRP I and II concepts to service areas?

14. What did Corning do to aid in implementing their MRP systems?

Questions for Discussion

1. Discuss the logic of MRP I netting, exploding, and offsetting for lead times to determine planned order releases.

2. How can allowances for scrap, tools, and spare parts be incorporated into an MRP I system?

3. Why is so much record accuracy and formal adherence to MRP I-produced plans essential to make a system work correctly?

4. MRP, being such a formal system, stifles individual creativity. Discuss.

5. Do you think that someday many companies' MRP systems will communicate directly with many other companies' MRP systems over a nationwide telecommunications network? What are the implications of this if it happens?

6. "Since forecasts are always wrong, we should attempt to build PIPC systems that are able to react quickly to forecast error." Discuss.

7. Well-run MRP systems are credited with reducing inventory holding costs, improving customer service, and keeping priorities "straight" on the factory floor. What does this mean?

8. What do you think Corning's strategy was for implementing MRP?

Problems

1. Fishburn Fabricators has a backlog of orders for product A (which is made up of 2 units of part B and 1 unit of part C). B is a purchased item and has a lead time of two weeks. C is manufactured internally and has a lead time of one week. Once parts B and C are available, end item A has a one-week lead time for final assembly. There are 100 Bs and 200 Cs now on hand, and an order for 100 Bs is due in the third week. Given the following requirements for product A by weeks, what size orders for Bs and Cs should be released for purchase and production, and when should these orders be released? (Do not combine orders, but release them as their needs indicate.)

Week Number	Number of As Needed
1	0
2	0
3	0
4	400
5	300
6	200
7	400
8	200

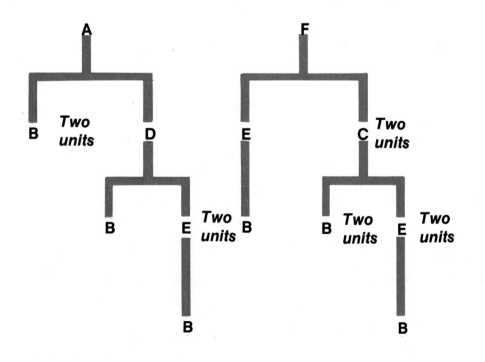

2. Given the following product structure trees and master production schedule for items A and F, determine the size and timing of planned order releases for items A, B, C, D, E, and F. All lead times are one week, and unless otherwise indicated, one unit is required for the parent item.*

Independent Demand (week)	Item					
	A	B	C	D	E	F
1					10	
2					10	
3					10	
4					10	
5	30				10	50
6	100				10	100
7			20		10	
8	50				10	75
Currently on hand	0	50	0	10	10	0
Scheduled Receipts (week)						
1		10				
2			200			
3						200
4	20					
5						
6						20
7						
8						

* May be calculated with provided software, or done manually. See Preface for explanation of this software.

3. Repeat the calculations of the MRP numerical example given in the chapter, with the following changes:*

a. The inventory records were corrected after a cycle count as follows:

Item	On Hand
A	5
D	0

b. An additional scheduled receipt of 20 Es is due to arrive in the fourth week.
c. Design engineering redesigned the product structure of C, and manufacturing engineering reduced its lead time to one week as follows:

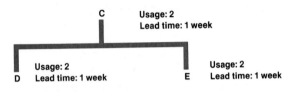

4. Product A, an electronic product, has the following product structure tree, master schedule, and other information:*

_____

* This problem can be solved with the aid of provided MRP software, or it can be done by manual calculation. Warning: Manual calculation of parts a through f of problem 4 will take half of a day or more out of your life!

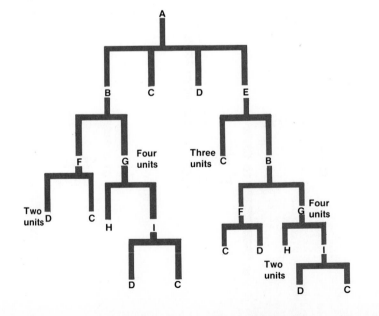

Master production schedule and other information:

Master Schedule (week)	A	B	C*	D*	E	F	G	H	I
1									
2			3	10					
3			3	12					
4			4	14					
5			4	16					
6	250		5	18					
7	100		5	20					
8	400		6	22					
On hand now	50	100	10	50	150	0	0	0	50

* Items C and D are service parts as well as dependent demand items.

All lead times are one week; all usage rates are one unit for each percent, unless otherwise indicated. There are planned order receipts as follows: 100 Bs in week 3; 200 Ds in week 6; 400 Gs in week 2.

It is now the week prior to week 1.

a. Explode the product structure tree, and determine the planned order releases for items A–I.

b. A cycle count of item E revealed that the on-hand balance of 150 was actually 50. How does this affect planned order releases?

c. A major customer for product A called and asked to have their order moved up a week. As a result, the master schedule for item A in weeks 7 and 8 are now 150 and 350. What effect does this change have upon planned order releases?

d. Engineering has found a mistake in the product structure tree for subassembly I. It is being assembled on the shop floor with *two units* of C, along with one unit of D. How does this effect our plans?

e. Item D is a purchased part. The vendor has just called and reported that the scheduled receipt for 200 Ds in week 6 has been delayed two weeks (to week 8) due to a fire at their factory. What happens to our plan? What would you suggest be done?

f. Mechanical engineering has just reported that subassembly G is now experiencing a 25 percent scrap rate. One out of four Gs made is faulty. In addition, since G is a "black box," the components that make up Gs are not salvageable. How does this affect our plan?

Chapter 12

Reorder Point and Reorder Quantity Methods

REORDERING POINTS (ROP)

When and how many items to reorder are the perennial inventory control questions. Reordering points are the *when*. The ROP operates as a "trigger" point which triggers the reorder. When the supply of an item diminishes to the reorder point quantity, a new order is placed for more of the item.

In Chapter 11, in the discussion of MRP I, we found that the assembled products' need for subassemblies, parts, and raw materials have to be calculated both as to how many and when they will be needed. We also saw that by working backward from end product master production schedules we could determine when subassemblies, parts, and raw materials needed to be ready.

By working backward and allowing for procurement or manufacturing lead time, we also found the time period when subassemblies and parts themselves had to be started or purchased-part orders placed with vendors. And we noted that essentially this becomes the reordering point. In this instance the reordering point is a point in *time,* not a *quantity*. The ordering quantity is the quantity needed for the end products on the schedule, and the time for reordering is set by the cumulative lead-time offsets.

In many large companies today, the needs for parts and components are calculated by the MRP I process, using computers. In smaller companies they are calculated manually.

Furthermore, in almost all companies, the items needed to repair and maintain the companies' facilities number in the thousands and they are usually not included in the MRP I system.[1] Neither are supplies consumed in operations that do not become part of end products (these are "MRO" inventories, discussed in Chapter 8). The annual cost of these items is, however, much less than the cost of parts and materials going into a company's end products.

But, no matter how a company calculates its expected needs, whether it generates them by a computerized MRP I explosion process or manually, it arrives at a list of parts and components that will be needed and it knows when they will be needed. This applies not only to A items but to B and C items as well. When these needs are compared to supplies on hand plus any others already ordered, the additional quantities needed to take care of the demand are established.

For the expensive and most heavily used items, these needs become the basis for order "releases" to the factory and to suppliers. Often,

---

[1] Coors Breweries, however, uses MRP extensively for scheduling the components required for the preventive maintenance and maintenance repair of their high-speed can-manufacturing machinery.

there is no "ordering" in the usual sense, since the vendor may have a contract to supply the company's entire year's needs. The vendor receives releases specifying exactly the quantity required in each period. These quantities are based primarily on the needs of the end products called for by the master schedule.

For parts internally manufactured, the process is much the same. Parts and components are being made either all the time or in frequent large lots whose exact quantities reflect the assembly needs.

But, by no means are all items made in this continuous or near-continuous fashion. Many items, B items in particular and even C items, are made in larger, less frequent lots. Even though their dependent demand is generated through an MRP I process, they may not be reordered in quantities defined by the size of planned order releases.

And, it is often more economical, at this point especially for dependent demand C items or items that are used at an *extremely steady* rate, to use reorder points as the basis for reordering, and to use economic lot sizes (discussed later in this chapter) to determine the reorder quantities.

Whenever the reorder point is used in this fashion, it is a number and not a time period. The reorder point is the sum of the quantity of an item expected to be used during the reorder lead time plus an additional "safety" quantity which serves as protection against variations in use or in replenishment lead times. Each item has to have its own reorder quantity. The inventory level fluctuates as is shown in Figure 12–1.

When reorder points are used in this fashion, there is really no need to calculate the future need for each item if they are used at a fairly steady rate, as shown by the somewhat irregular, but steady drop in inventory in Figure 12–1. Everyone knows that items used in end products will continue to be used regularly, but the exact quantities do not have to be known. They can be replaced on a usual-use basis. As we have said, many companies, particularly small ones, in fact, do not *calculate* the needs of all B and C items. Instead, and particularly in the case of multiple-use items, these companies just estimate future needs, largely by looking at the recent past. If, for a certain item, the recent use has been 50 per month, then 50 per month will be the estimate for the near future (unless there is some good reason to think that it will be different).

FIGURE 12–1
Relationships between Reorder Points and Usage When Usage Is Regular and Procurement Lead Times Are Constant

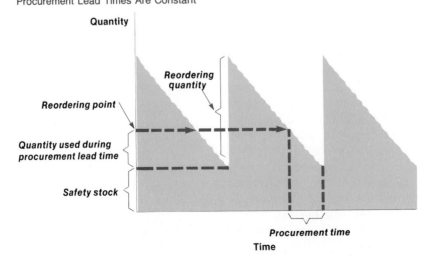

FIGURE 12–2

Inventory of an Item Whose Usage and Procurement Lead Times Are Both Variable

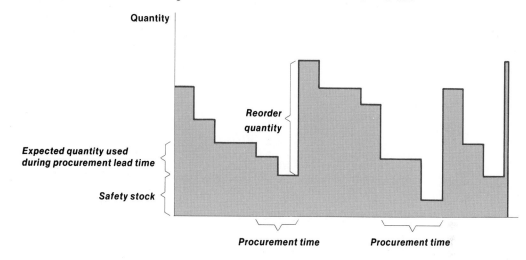

The same judgment is used to determine lead times. How long did it take in the past? Usually six weeks? Then this is the lead time to use. And how much variation has there been in usage and in lead times? After looking over recent experience the inventory controller can decide upon a safety stock quantity. Actually looking at the past, however, will often show a picture of usage and procurement times like that in Figure 12–2 rather than that in Figure 12–1.

In real life it is not possible for the inventory controller to spend the necessary time to give each item much consideration. There are just too many items—thousands or even tens of thousands of items. It is necessary, therefore, to develop policies, rules, and computational procedures for computers so that they can do a reasonable job in this matter.

CALCULATING REORDER POINTS

We will use an example to show how the job of determining reorder points can be performed by a computer. In Figure 12–3, column 2 is the actual history of the use of a C-type item whose demand has not been calculated by MRP 1 methods. In addition this item is not important enough to justify its future demand being forecasted us-

ing careful economic analysis done by analysts, so we rely on an exponentially smoothed projection of expected demand which can be made by a computer using historical demand for this item.

It should be pointed out that the table in Figure 12–3 is unreal in that it is a static picture of a dynamic situation. It depicts the generation of data as time passes. In real life, this table would never exist as a working tool because, month by month, a new line is added at the bottom and all preceding figures are carried in the exponentially smoothed forecasts.

The purpose of Figure 12–3 is to establish the reorder point for one item whose use during lead time is somewhat variable. We will calculate a reorder point, which is really made up of two parts: first, the expected usage in the normal replenishment lead time; and, second, a safety stock whose size will be set to provide us with a 95 percent chance of not running out of stock before the new shipment arrives. This is called a 95 percent *service level,* which will be discussed shortly.

We have said that a new horizontal line of figures is generated every month in Figure 12–3 and that it should be regarded as an ongoing data set. Consequently, we are not much inter-

FIGURE 12-3

Date 1	D_t Actual Demand 2	F_t 3	T_t 4	F_t Fore-cast 5	Fore-cast of Use in Lead Time 6	Actual Use in Lead Time 7	Error in Pre-dicted Use in Lead Time 8	Aver-age of Devia-tions Squared 9	Stan-dard Devia-tion in Units 10
Start		201.0	0				31	901	30.0
January	194	200.3	−0.07	199.7	399	373	26	879	29.7
February	211	201.4	−0.05	201.9	404	393	11	803	28.3
March	162	197.5	−0.34	194.4	389	428	39	875	29.6
April	231	200.9	+0.03	201.2	402	371	31	884	29.7
May	197	200.5	−0.02	200.3	401	393	8	802	28.3
June	174	197.9	−0.28	195.4	391	466	75	1285	35.9
July	219	200.0	−0.04	199.6	399	492	93	2021	45.0
August	247	204.7	+0.43	208.6	417	468	51	2079	45.6
September	245	208.7	+0.79	215.8	432	432	0	1871	43.2
October	223	210.1	+0.85	217.8	436	398	38	1828	42.7
November	209	210.0	+0.76	216.8	434				
December	187	207.7	+0.45	211.8	424				

ested in old starting data (the exponential smoothing method soon washes out the effects of initial data). To explain Figure 12–3: Column 2 represents actual monthly demand. Column 3 is the exponentially smoothed demand determined with the first equation in Model 2, as explained in Chapter 9, with $\alpha = .1$ (Last month's exponentially smoothed demand $\times$ .9 + The current month's actual demand $\times$ .1.)

Column 4 is the adjustment for trend (using equation 2 in Model 2) which results in column 5, the forecast, with trend effects (Equation 3, Model 2). The January forecast in column 5 is 199.7, which we use as our best estimate of the demand for near future months. If we could receive replenishment stocks in one month, then this 199.7 would be our estimate of February's usage. In our example, however, we will use a replenishment lead time of *two months* so we will use 2 $\times$ 199.7 as the estimate of usage for February and March. This produces the 399 in column 6.

As another example of this calculation procedure, let us move down toward the bottom of Figure 12–3. At the end of October, our best

estimate of the use of our item for November and December is 217.8 units each month or 436, in column 6, for the two-month lead time. By the end of November, and incorporating the actual usage for November, we recalculated December's expected usage and arrived at 216.8, resulting in the expected usage of 434 units during December and January. Since the demand for this item continued to fall off in December, the revised expectation for January became 211.8, and the projection for January–February made at the end of December became 424.

Errors in Expectations of Use during Lead Times

Column 7 shows the actual use in the lead time and is, of course, determined after the lead time has gone by. Our item's actual use in February and March was 373 units. This contrasts with the forecast (made at the end of January) of 399 units, so the forecast had an error of 26 units. March and April's actual use totaled 393 units as compared to the 404 expected in the forecast made at the end of February, so here the forecast error was 11 units.

Thus, column 8 compares the forecasted use with actual demand. It shows the amount of the forecast error (disregarding whether the estimate was too high or too low) during the procurement lead times.

Column 9 values are further steps on the way to column 10, the one we will use. They are based on column 8 and are exponentially smoothed values of column 9's forecast errors squared.

To start the smoothing of squared forecast errors, we assumed that the column 8 values for the three months before our table began were 29, 30, 31. Thus, the sum of the squared forecast errors for these previous three months is $29^2 + 30^2 + 31^2 = 2,702$ and the average for these three months is $2702 \div 3 = 901$, the first figure in column 9. We then calculate the next values in column 9 by exponential smoothing, using Model 1, and $\alpha = 0.1$. For example, January's value is: $.1(26^2) + .9(901) = 879$; February's is $.1(11^2) + .9(879) = 803$, and so on.

The column 10 numbers are the square roots of the column 9 numbers and are actually smoothed standard deviations. This is the measure of forecast error we have been working toward for use in setting safety stock levels for specified service levels.

The advantage to this method is that a computer can apply these simple calculations to several thousand items; yet, if need be, it can individualize the procedure and use different smoothing models and/or weighting factors if certain items need individual treatment.

Service Levels

Service levels in inventory control refers to the probability of not running out of anything. It is important in inventory control because, if inventories are large enough never to run out of anything, then they are probably too large. It takes very large safety stocks to have enough *never* to run out of anything before new supplies arrive unless, of course, they are *very* steadily used— which is the exception, not the rule. It is usually less costly to have smaller inventories on hand even though this will cause occasional stockouts.

For example, managers may wish to set a service level objective to have enough stock on hand so that in 95 percent of the cases new replenishment stocks will arrive before the old stock runs out. If usage were entirely predictable and if lead times were entirely reliable, there would be no need for considering the service level concept. Reorders would be placed at the proper time so that new supplies would arrive just as the last of the old supply is depleted.

But usage and lead times both vary so it is necessary to estimate how many of an item will be used or demanded during the typical lead time. The reorder point then becomes the sum of two numbers: first, the expected usage during the lead time and, second, a safety stock for protection if usage is heavier than anticipated or if the lead time is longer, or both. A service level of 95 percent sets a reorder point so that in spite of the variability in usage and lead times new stocks will arrive in time to prevent stockouts about 95 percent of the time or, conversely, allow stockouts to occur no more than 5 percent of the time.

Calculating Reorder Points with Safety Stock Considerations

This service level objective can be translated into a reorder point quantity by using the appropriate column 10 number in Figure 12–3. This number is the standard deviation of the smoothed forecast errors for the two-month lead time required to replenish the supply of our item. It is always two months behind the current period since it is calculated only after the two months have passed. Meanwhile two more months have passed, and estimates have already been made of the item's use during those months.

Thus, at the end of December, the expected use during the January–February, 60-day, procurement lead time is 424 units. Also, at the end of December, the latest standard deviation of forecast errors is for October, which is 42.7

FIGURE 12–4.

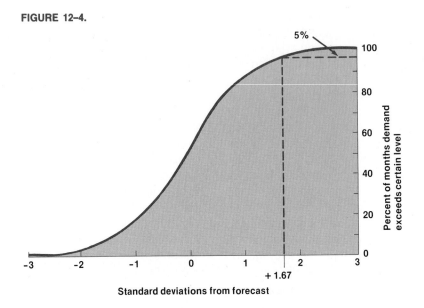

Standard deviations from forecast

units. This 42.7 is the standard deviation we will use to calculate the number of units to carry to provide a 95 percent service level for this item.

Figure 12–4 shows a cumulative normal curve with the horizontal scale marked off in standard deviations from the mean or, in our case, from the expected use of our item. We draw a horizontal line across from the 95 percent level to where it intercepts the curve and then go down vertically to the bottom scale and find that the intercept is at +1.67 standard deviations. (We don't have to do this graphically; instead, we can refer to the figures for the area under the cumulative normal curve as given in Appendix C, Section A. It shows us that 95 percent of the cases (interpolating between 94.3 percent and 95.3 percent) are included in the expected usage during lead time +1.67 standard deviations.)

The required stock to give 95 percent protection is then 42.7 × 1.67 = 71 units. When this is added to the expected usage of 424, it results in a reorder point of 495 units. Thus, inventory controllers, or computers, monitor the inventory level for this item, and when the quantity reaches 495, another order is released.

LIMITATIONS TO REORDER POINTS BASED ON SERVICE LEVELS

As we have said earlier, reorder points based on service levels ("statistically determined" reorder points) are most useful where the future demand for an item is *forecast* and *cannot be calculated,* or when the usage rates are fairly stable. In other words, reorder points based on service levels are best for independent demand items, not dependent demand items which *can* be calculated.

As can be seen, order-point systems usually require that safety stocks be carried. Safety stocks can add substantially to the investment in inventories. In our example, adding 71 units to the expected use increased inventory by over 16 percent. If this item were a dependent demand item, we could have more closely calculated our expected use and reduced, or eliminated, our need for safety stock. In fact, some companies, when they install MRP systems, find that by *calculating* when new supplies will have to arrive and hence when to place orders, they are able to eliminate a large portion of their safety stock and have substantial holding-cost savings.

Lumpy Dependent Demand

Often parts and materials are withdrawn from stockrooms infrequently, yet in substantial quantities when they are withdrawn. While this is convenient for the assembly department and for parts manufacturing departments, it creates a record of "lumpy" demand on the storeroom. This is shown graphically in Figure 12–5. Because the withdrawals are for large quantities, lumpy demand situations have the effect of in-

FIGURE 12–5
Lumpy Demand

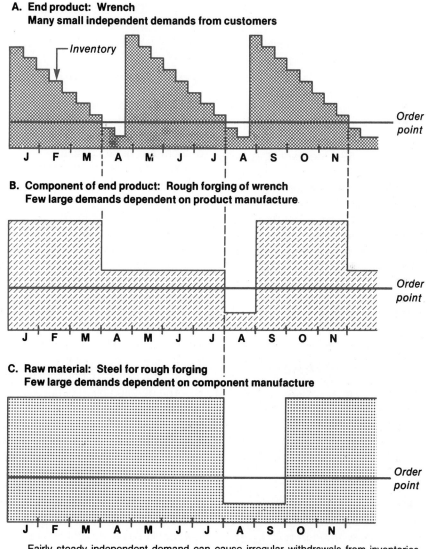

A. **End product: Wrench**
   Many small independent demands from customers

B. **Component of end product: Rough forging of wrench**
   Few large demands dependent on product manufacture

C. **Raw material: Steel for rough forging**
   Few large demands dependent on component manufacture

Fairly steady independent demand can cause irregular withdrawals from inventories of dependent demand items when a reorder point is reached.

Source: Joseph Orlicky, *Materials Requirements Planning* (New York: McGraw-Hill, 1975), p. 26.
Copyright © 1975 by McGraw-Hill, Inc. Used with the permission of McGraw-Hill Book Company.

creasing the variability of use during lead time, thus increasing the size of the safety stocks and consequently increasing average inventory levels. In the case of dependent demand items, MRP methods eliminate the need for large safety stocks in spite of the lumpy nature of the withdrawals from stock and at the same time reduce idle inventories substantially.

Joint Probability of Simultaneous Availability of Items

Another argument against the use of statistically determined order point methods for dependent demand items is demonstrated in Figure 12–6. If, for example, the service level on *each* of 10 dependent demand component parts used in an end item or subassembly is 95 percent, the joint probability that all 10 items will be simultaneously available is only .599 or 59.9 percent (this is simply 0.95^{10}). For 25 items, it is only 26 percent! For 100 components (not too uncommon for complex products) it is only 0.6 percent!

These are rather bad odds. These poor chances of having all components available to complete end items is what causes some firms which use statistical reorder points for dependent demand items to be continually in a *reactive* state of having to expedite a large share of their component parts. Excessive expediting is costly. It upsets schedules, sometimes requries machine setups to be torn down and set up for behind-time jobs, and generally results in more expediting and longer lead times. This is why the MRP 1 approach is generally more appropriate than ROP methods for dependent demand items.

OTHER ROP CONSIDERATIONS

Space does not permit us to pursue the matter of statistically determined reorder points further, but there are many more facets to it, and some of them are quite complex.

We have not, for example, pursued the joint possibility of lead times varying along with usage. If lead times vary by much, then the safety stock will need to be increased to allow for variable lead times, as well as variable usage. This involves more complicated calculations.

Nor have we considered the overall service level, considering that 95 percent protection against reorders' not arriving on time is only part of the story. Sometimes, for example, the stockroom is out of stock but the factory is not. The 50 items the factory just withdrew depleted the stockroom's stock, but they will keep the factory going for a week. The factory is not out of stock.

The duration of an out-of-stock situation also is often very important, as is the question of how many items is the stock short. And, how costly it is to run out? Sometimes, money spent on expediting would bring the new supply in quickly, thus holding down the out-of-stock costs.

In addition, there may be substitute items available. If there is need for a 75-watt light bulb and it is out of stock, a 100-watt bulb will probably substitute nicely. But this upsets the use statistics for both items. Sometimes, too, people wait for the arrival of an out-of-stock item, and

FIGURE 12–6
Probabilities of Simultaneous Availability of Component Items at Various Service Levels

Number of Dependent Demand Component Items in an End Item	Service Level (percent)		
	90	95	99
1	0.90	0.95	0.99
2	0.81	0.90	0.98
3	0.73	0.86	0.97
4	0.66	0.81	0.96
5	0.59	0.77	0.95
6	0.53	0.74	0.94
8	0.43	0.66	0.92
10	0.35	0.60	0.90
15	0.21	0.46	0.86
20	0.12	0.36	0.81
25	0.07	0.26	0.77
50	0.005	0.07	0.60
100	0.00002	0.006	0.36

when it comes in its use is unnaturally high because of the backlog of demand. This distorts the usage figures for the month when the new supply arrives. We also mentioned seasonal patterns in demand but have not considered them here. And, it is often better to forgo low inventories and build up stocks in order to give the factory reasonable operating schedules. Or, if money is short, it may pay to cut not only reorder quantities but safety stocks as well.

Some of these complicating conditions can be handled well by computers, but some of them remain problems that baffle even computers. Monte Carlo simulation (see Chapter 18) can help in such cases. In general, however, computers can do most of the things we have discussed here and do it economically.

DETERMINING REORDER POINTS WITH STOCKOUT COSTS AND VARIABLE LEAD TIMES

If the cost of stocking out and of carrying inventory can be estimated and the demand during lead times is known, we can evaluate alternative reorder points and determine the one which promises the least expected cost even though procurement lead times are variable.

An example will show how this can be done:

Use			50 per week		
Cost of running out			$200		
Cost to carry 1 unit in stock for 1 week			$.75		
Past reorder experience:					
Weeks elapsing between ordering and receiving new supply	3	4	5	6	7
Number of instances in last 25 reorders	2	6	10	4	3
Percent of instances	8	24	40	16	12
Cumulative percent	8	32	72	88	100
100 − Cumulative percent	92	68	28	12	0

The objective is to find the reorder point with the least expected cost. If orders are placed three weeks in advance, the reorder point will have to be for at least 150 units. At the end of three weeks the inventory will be down to zero: then it will return to 150 and begin to work down again. The average inventory will be half of 150 or 75. The cost to carry 75 units for one week is $75 \times \$.75 = \$56.25$.

But, because of the variability in lead time, most orders will not be received in three weeks, and this item will usually be out of stock (in 92 percent of the cases) before the new lot arrives (100 percent − 8 percent = 92 percent). Thus, the expected out-of-stock cost will be $.92 \times \$200 = \$184$ every three weeks, or $61.33 per week. The total cost per week of this alternative is $117.58.

Next, the same calculation can be made using a reorder point of 200 units, the normal four-week usage. Other calculations can be made for the other possibilities with the results being those shown in Figure 12–7. In this example the reorder point which minimizes total expected weekly costs is about five weeks usage, or about 250 units.

Calculating reorder points this way does not indicate what fraction of the inventory is regarded as the safety stock. The safety stock quantity, however, is implicit in the calculation. If 250 units are ordered each time, they will be received in three weeks 8 percent of the time. One hundred units would still be on hand after the 150 were issued during the three-week lead time.

The new 250 units will arrive in four weeks 24 percent of the time, so 50 units would still be on hand. The new order of 250 will arrive in five weeks, just as the old stock is used up 40 percent of the time. The rest of the time the stock will have run out before the new supply comes in, so there would be no stock on hand. One hundred units 8 percent of the time and 50 units 24 percent of the time translates into an expected average on-hand balance of 20 units $(100 \times .08 + 50 \times .24 = 20)$. In this instance a safety stock of 20 units is implicit in the reorder calculation.

FIGURE 12–7

Lead Time (weeks)	Number of Instances	Percent of Instances	Usage during Lead Time	Weekly Average Inventory during Lead Time	Weekly Cost of Carrying Average Inventory	Percent of Time Out of Stock	Cost per Order of Outage	Cost per Week of Outage	Total Cost per Week
3	2	8	150	75	$ 56.25	92%	$184	$61.33	$117.58
4	6	24	200	100	75.00	68	136	34.00	109.00
5	10	40	250	125	93.75	28	56	11.20	104.95
6	4	16	300	150	112.50	12	24	4.00	116.50
7	3	12	350	175	131.25	0	0	0	131.25

REORDER POINTS, USING MRP

When MRP I methods are used, reorder points are not quantity triggers but time period triggers. This is one reason why MRP I is sometimes called *time-phased requirements planning*. As we have said, MRP I systems can probably reduce the size of the safety stocks for most dependent demand items in the MRP I system because there is less need to provide for variations in demand and lead times are assumed to include some additional time for lead time variability.

Where safety stocks still seem to be appropriate, it helps to express them in terms of added lead times instead of quantities. Safety stocks in MRP would be expressed as "so many days' or weeks' worth of stock." Safety stocks would become components of the total lead time.

Figure 12–8 shows how reorder points can be calculated when safety stocks are expressed in terms of time. We have purposely made the requirements quite irregular (or lumpy) throughout the 13-week planning horizon. Our problem assumes that normal lead time is one week, *safety time* is two weeks, and the order quantity is 500 units. (Admittedly, it would be unusual to need a two-week safety stock when new supplies can be obtained in one week, but doing this in our example will illustrate how the system works.)

This means that every week when we consider reorders, we will look ahead three weeks beyond the current time period and add up the requirements for the various items. These requirements are then compared to the amount on hand and any new supplies due to be re-

FIGURE 12–8

Lead time: 1 week
Order quantity: 500 units
Safety time: 2 weeks' unit requirements

					Weeks					
	0	1	2	3	4	5	6	7	8	9	10–13
Requirements		100	110	90	80	0	150	175	100	35	200
Scheduled receipts		—	—	—	500	—	—		500		500
On-hand	400	300	190	100	520	520	370	195	595	560	860
DDNLT + DDST		280	170	230	325	425	310	335	435	600	—
Order releases		—	—	500	—	—	—	500	—	500	—

FIGURE 12–9

Lead time: 1 week
Order quantity: 500 units
Safety time: 0

						Weeks					
	0	1	2	3	4	5	6	7	8	9	10–13
Requirements		100	110	90	80	0	150	175	100	35	200
Scheduled receipts		—	—	—	—	—	500	—	—	—	500
On-hand	400	300	190	100	20	20	370	195	95	60	360
DDNLT		110	90	80	0	150	175	100	35	200	300
Order releases						500				500	

ceived during the three weeks. If these requirements—demand during normal lead time (DDNLT)—plus the demand during safety time (DDST) exceed the amount that will be available, then there will be a prospective negative balance so a replenishment order is placed. A negative number serves as a reorder point.

In Figure 12–8 we begin with 400 units "on hand." This amount is reduced to 300 after deducting week 1's requirements of 100 units. The sum of the requirements for weeks 2, 3, and 4 is 280, but there are 300 available so a new order is not needed yet. After week 2 has passed, the available stock is down to 190 units, but this time only 170 units are needed for weeks 3, 4 and 5 so there is still ample stock.

After week 3, the supply is down to 100 units which will not take care of the 230 needed for weeks 4, 5 and 6. This triggers an order for 500 (this is our standard reorder quantity in this example), placed in week 3 and expected to be received in week 4.

In Figure 12–8 it is easy to see how safety time (and the resulting safety stocks) can be reduced or even eliminated by using the calculated order-point method if requirements and lead times are reasonably accurate. Note that the "on-hand" quantities are always well above the requirements for the next week, the normal lead time. The average inventory proves to be 392 units.

The program illustrated in Figure 12–8 is not nearly as economical as it could be. As we said earlier, a two-week safety stock for a one-week lead time item must of necessity be most uneconomical. We have changed this in Figure 12–9 by eliminating the two-week safety stock altogether. As one would expect, the new calculation reduces the average inventory substantially (to 192 units).

The feasibility of eliminating the safety stock, or course, depends on the accuracy of the requirements figures and of the one-week lead times. However, as mentioned in Chapter 11, the ability of computerized MRP I systems to update requirements weekly, daily, or even in real time, allows safety time and safety stocks to be reduced materially by highlighting those items which need attention and possibly expediting them.

LOT-SIZING

Lot-sizing answers the question of *how many* to order at one time. The problem is one of minimizing the sum of the "costs of acquisition" and the "costs of owning" stock. It costs money (whether the item is made internally or purchased outside) to do the paperwork associated with ordering, and it costs more yet to set up equipment to produce the item. These are acquisition costs and are one-time relatively fixed costs for every order whose total is generally unaffected by the quantity ordered. Obviously, the acquisition costs *per unit* go down as the quantity ordered in a single order goes up.

But the larger the order quantities, the greater the inventory when the new supply arrives, and the longer it takes to use it up. And, as we have seen before, it costs money to carry inventories. The larger the quantity ordered, the greater the cost of carrying the ensuing inventory.

There are several methods for determining how large individual orders should be. Some are designed to be used with MRP I systems, and others are more appropriately used with reorder point methods. Orlicky lists nine of them, but none of these nine is clearly superior in all situations, and all of them have weaknesses.[2]

Lot-Sizing with MRP

Lot-sizing methods designed to be used with MRP I are called "discrete" methods because they answer the question: How many future individual (or discrete) planned order release time-bucket quantities (if any) should be combined with earlier planned order releases quantities. Again, the trade-off costs are usually ordering costs and inventory carrying costs, but some lot-sizing rules do not explicitly consider this trade-off.

Fixed order quantity. One method, called "fixed order quantity," is to always order in fixed amounts, say, 100. This method considers such things as machine batch capacity, die life, and standard packages.

Lot for lot. A second method is "lot-for-lot" ordering. This means ordering just the quantity in each planned order release in each time bucket. This is sometimes done with MRP I if

the calculated planned order releases are more or less regular in size.

Period order quantity. A third method, called "period order quantity," is to order the sum of whatever quantities are needed, say, in the next three time buckets. The "three" is based on an estimate of the average time between orders after considering order costs, holding costs, and annual demand.

Least unit cost. The other methods used do consider the order cost–carrying cost trade-off, but each in slightly different ways. One method, the "least-unit-cost method," is somewhat similar to the calculation we worked out in Figure 12–7. The least-unit-cost method calculates the combined ordering and carrying cost per unit when ordering for each time-bucket period separately, for two periods combined, for three periods, and so on, and selects whichever method produces the lowest unit costs.

For example, look back at Chapter 11, Figure 11–9, where we generated planned order releases for item C of 17, 31, 1 and 1 for a four-week period. Intuitively, lot-for-lot reordering would be uneconomical here. Ordering 17, then 31, then 1, and 1 again would be wasteful, as would two weeks' ordering if we used POQ = 2. This method would order 48 and then one week later, none, and then in the third week, would order 2. Obviously, the standard practice of ordering no more than two weeks' needs is probably not appropriate, and the original order should probably be 50 units. But, while our intuitive lot-sizing decision for item C may hold, it is not so obvious what to do for item E's planned order releases of 10, 30, 31, 82, and 13, in Figure 11–9. Thus, we will demonstrate the calculation of two of the more popular MRP-oriented lot-sizing rules—"least total cost," and "part-period balancing" for item E.

Least total cost. This method trades off ordering costs and carrying costs by calculating the point where the *two costs are approximately*

---

[2] See Joseph Orlicky, *Material Requirements Planning* (New York: McGraw-Hill, 1975), chap. 6.

equal. At this point, total costs are considered to be approximately minimized.

Figure 12–10 develops these costs for item E. First, we need some additional information: Assume it costs $45 to prepare an order; that item E is valued at $100 each; and the cost to carry idle inventory is 25 percent of the item's value, or .48 percent per week. Thus carrying cost is $.48 per item per week.

In Figure 12–10, column 1, we have entered item E's planned order releases from Figure 12–9. Column 2 shows the time bucket when they were to be released—before considering lot-sizing. Column 3 is the total lot size if all of the planned orders up to this point in time are accumulated and released as a single order *in week 1.* Columns 4 and 5 show the inventory that would be carried and the number of weeks it would be carried if it were ordered in week 1. For example, if the lot size were for 71 to be released in week 1 (and to arrive in week 2, because lead time is 1 week), 30 units would

be carried for one extra week, and 31 units would be carried for two extra weeks. Column 6 shows the carrying-cost calculations. For example, the $29.76 cost is $.48 × 31 × 2 weeks. Column 6 also shows cumulative carrying cost for each successively larger lot size. Finally, column 7 is the order cost that we wish to approximately equalize with cumulative carrying cost. This occurs where the lot size is 71 units, as $44.16 is about equal to $45. Thus, we should combine the first three orders into a single order for 71 units and plan to release it in week 1.

Our process would then continue beginning with week 4 to determine the next lot size by considering combining orders for 82 and 13 into one order for 95 to be released in week 4. But, suppose instead week 1 has gone by, we have released the order for 71 units, and we now have four more *new* weeks of planned order releases which have resulted from an *MRP I update rerun.* Week 2 in our previous example now becomes week 1, and so on.

FIGURE 12–10
Calculating Lot Sizes for Item E with Least-Total-Cost Method

```
LEAST TOTAL COST LOT SIZING

INITIAL CONDITIONS:

NUMBER OF PERIODS CALCULATED          5
ORDERING COST                      $45.00
INVENTORY CARRYING COST             $0.48
```

PLANNED ORDER RELEASE	CUMULATIVE LOT SIZE	INVENTORY NOT REQUIRED	EXTRA PERIODS CARRIED	INDIVIDUAL CARRYING COST	CUMULATIVE CARRYING COST
10	10	0	0	$0.00	$0.00
30	40	30	1	$14.40	$14.40
31	71	31	2	$29.76	$44.16
82	153	82	3	$118.08	$162.24
13	166	13	4	$24.96	$187.20

```
THE LEAST TOTAL COST WOULD BE TO COMBINE THE FIRST
 3 PERIODS INTO A SINGLE ORDER FOR 71 UNITS
```

FIGURE 12–11
Lot-Sizing Item E after an MRP Update Rerun

	Planned Order Release	Week	Cumulative Lot Size	Inventory Not Required	Extra Weeks Carried	Carrying Cost Individual	Carrying Cost Cumulative	Ordering Cost
From previous MRP run	82	3*	82	0	0	0	0	$45
	13	4	95	13	1	6.24	6.24	45
From new MRP run	10	5	105	10	2	9.60	15.84	45
	0	6	105	0	3	0	15.84	45
	15	7	120	15	4	28.80	44.64⟵——⟶	45
	30	8	150	30	5	72.00	116.64	45

* Formerly week 4.

Figure 12–11 shows the results of this analysis. It says that we should plan to release an order for 120 units three weeks from now, because this is where cumulative carrying costs ($44.64) are about equal to $45, the ordering cost.

Part-period balancing. This method also determines lot sizes by trading off ordering and carrying costs, but in a different way. This method defines a *part-period* as follows:

Part-period = Number of items in inventory × Number of periods carried before being used

The objective of this method is to find an order size which equates the cost to carry a part-period in inventory with the cost to prepare an order. This number is called the *economic part-periods* (EPP) and is:

$$EPP = \frac{Order\ cost}{Cost\ to\ carry\ 1\ part\ for\ 1\ period}$$

Returning to our original example as shown in Figure 12–10, the economic part-periods for item E is:

$$EPP = \frac{\$45}{\$.48} = 93.75,\ or\ 94$$

The lot size is then determined by accumulating planned orders until their cumulative part-periods is *approximately equal to* 94. This is shown in Figure 12–12. This method *also* tells us to order 71 units because 92 part-periods is approximately 94, the economic part-periods. As with our previous example using the least-total-cost method, a similar analysis after updating results in a lot size of 120.

Other methods. There are still other methods for discrete lot-sizing methods for MRP, but they will not be pursued here.[3] Some are extremely complex (the Wagner-Whitin method, for example) and are not as widely used as the ones discussed above. Others which consider quantity discounts for larger lot sizes are quite practical.[4]

Which Method Is Best?

The most commonly used MRP lot-size methods seem to be the simpler ones such as lot-for-lot, fixed order quantity, and period order quantity. Of those companies which have implemented

[3] For a good discussion of lot-sizing methods for MRP systems, see E. C. Theisen, Jr., "New Game in Town—The MRP Lot Size," *Production and Inventory Management,* 2d quarter, 1974, pp. 1–13.

[4] See W. C. Benton and D. C. Whybark, "Material Requirements Planning (MRP) and Purchase Discounts," *Journal of Operations Management,* February 1982, pp. 137–43.

FIGURE 12–12
Calculating Lot Sizes for Item E with the Part-Period
Balancing Method

```
PART PERIOD BALANCING LOT SIZING

INITIAL CONDITIONS:

NUMBER OF PERIODS CALCULATED          9
ORDERING COST                     $45.00
INVENTORY CARRYING COST            $0.48
```

PLANNED ORDER RELEASE	CUMULATIVE LOT SIZE	INVENTORY NOT REQUIRED	EXTRA PERIODS CARRIED	PART-PERIODS	CUMULATIVE PART-PERIODS
10	10	0	0	0	0
30	40	30	1	30	30
31	71	31	2	62	92
82	82	0	0	0	0
13	95	13	1	13	13
10	105	10	2	20	33
0	105	0	3	0	33
15	120	15	4	60	93
30	30	0	0	0	0

```
THE LOT SIZE WOULD BE 71 SINCE THE
CLOSEST CUMULATIVE PART PERIOD TO THE
ECONOMIC PART PERIOD, 94 IS 92


THE LOT SIZE WOULD BE 120 SINCE THE
CLOSEST CUMULATIVE PART PERIOD TO THE
ECONOMIC PART PERIOD, 94 IS 93
```

the more complex methods, part-period balancing seems to be the most popular. The reason is that it is simple to understand, and simple for a computer system to calculate—and it does trade-off ordering and holding costs in a fairly noncomplex way.

ECONOMIC ORDER QUANTITIES (EOQ) OR ECONOMIC LOT SIZES (ELS)

The best-known lot-sizing methods are the family of "continuous" *economic order quantity* or *economic lot-size* models. By "continuous" we

mean that it is assumed that inventory is used from stock at a steady, or continuous, rate. This is in contrast to the "discrete" lot-sizing methods discussed in the previous section, where the planned orders were discrete, or "lumpy."

The methods also can be used for lot-sizing both purchased and manufactured items if their use is reasonably steady. EOQ is the common name for purchased items, while ELS is the name for items manufactured internally. The main difference is that, for ELS, the ordering cost includes both the cost to prepare the order to release to the factory *and* the setup costs on the machine(s) required to do the work. But, this approach to lot-sizing is usually not appropriate for dependent demand items because of the lumpy nature of their demand. In our discussion, we will use the term *EOQ* to mean both EOQ and ELS. In theory, the concept of EOQ/ELS is simple: The best lot size is the quantity which yields the lowest total cost per unit, as in discrete lot-sizing, where total cost consists of acquisition costs and costs of possession. The optimum quantity, where the total cost will be the least, is the quantity where the total cost of preparing orders plus the cost of carrying inventories is at a minimum. Larger lots increase the costs of possession more than the decline in the cost of acquisition. Smaller lots require more orders to be prepared which increases acquisition costs.

Figure 12–13 shows these relationships in graphic form. It is interesting to see that the total cost curve is relatively flat over a range of lot-size quantities. This means that it is not necessary to specify the economic lot exactly in order to get reasonably low costs. In fact, total costs are almost as low for reorders up to 25 percent more (or less) than they are for the precise EOQ.

Since it is unnecessary to use an exact EOQ in order to obtain low costs, most companies that calculate EOQ/ELS use simple formulas

FIGURE 12–13

Although the economic lot can be computed as a specific quantity, total cost is relatively flat over a range of 25 percent above and below the EOQ.

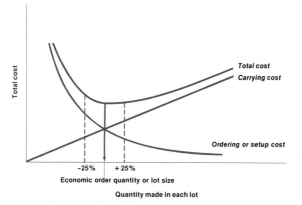

Computer Solution to Our Example

```
ECONOMIC ORDER QUANTITY

INITIAL CONDITIONS:

SET UP OR ORDERING COST IN DOLLARS      $10.00
PERIOD USAGE                             2000
PERIOD CARRYING COST PERCENTAGE          25.00%
PRICE OR COST PER PIECE                  $2.00




ECONOMIC ORDER QUANTITY                   283
NUMBER OF ORDERS PER PERIOD                 7.07
```

which leave out such minor factors as the likelihood of obsolescence. Here is the most commonly used formula:[5]

$$EOQ = \sqrt{\frac{2 \times D \times C_p}{V \times C_h}}$$

Where

2 = A constant in the formula
D = Expected usage per time period
C_p = Cost to place an order (order preparation and/or machine setup)
V = Value of the item
C_h = Holding-cost percent per time period

Working this out for an expected annual usage of (D) 2,000 units (used more or less steadily throughout the year), an ordering cost (Cp) of $10 per order, a $2 per unit value (V), and an annual inventory carrying cost of 25 percent of value (Ch), we get: (Also see Figure 12–13.)

$$EOQ = \sqrt{\frac{2 \times 2,000 \times \$10}{\$2 \times .25}}$$
$$= \sqrt{\frac{40,000}{.5}} = 283 \text{ units}$$

Note that if we changed the time period from *annual* usage to *monthly* usage of 167 units, the results would be the same, after we adjust the 25 percent annual percentage to a monthly rate of 2.08 percent:

$$EOQ = \sqrt{\frac{2 \times 167 \times \$10}{\$2 \times .0208}} = \sqrt{\frac{3340}{.0416}} = 283$$

---

[5] The formula for EOQ is derived with calculus by taking the first derivative of the following total-cost equation with respect to Q, setting it to zero, and solving for Q to obtain EOQ:

$$\text{Total cost} = \frac{Q}{2}V\,C_h + \frac{D}{Q}C_p$$

The first term defines holding costs and the second, ordering costs. In the first term, $Q/2$ is average inventory. This is why it is called a *continuous* lot-sizing model: the average inventory is assumed to be one half the order quantity, Q, which implies a continuously steady (not discrete, or lumpy) depletion of inventory. In the second term, D/Q defines the number of orders which are placed of size Q.

Economic order quantities can also be expressed in terms of months' or weeks' supply. The formula is just expressed differently:

$$EOQ, \text{ in months' supply} = \sqrt{\frac{24 \times C_p}{(D \times V/12) \times C_h}}$$

For our example,
EOQ, in months' supply

$$= \sqrt{\frac{24 \times \$10}{(2,000 \times \$2/12) \times .25}}$$
$$= \sqrt{\frac{240}{83.33}} = 1.7$$

Thus, if our monthly demand averages 167 units, our EOQ would be 167 × 1.7 = 283, as before.

EOQs with Delivery over a Period of Time

Sometimes ordered items do not all arrive at once. This is particularly true with high-volume steadily used items which flow rather regularly and continuously into inventory as well as flowing out at a fairly constant rate. When this condition exists, the formulas previously given will understate the EOQ. They assume that the maximum inventory on hand will be the order quantity amount. But actually, since some of the items are being used as they are delivered, the maximum inventory will never be that high. Thus the carrying charges are overstated because average inventory on hand will be smaller.

When a new supply comes in over several days and part of it is used up before the last of the order comes in, the saw-tooth diagram in Figure 12–1 becomes slanted, as in Figure 12–14.

To correct for this in the calculation of the EOQ, it is necessary to adjust the denominator under the square root size in the EOQ formula by multiplying it by:

$$1 - \frac{\text{The use rate } (R)}{\text{The production rate } (P)}$$

FIGURE 12–14

Delivery of an order over a period of time allows it to be used to hold down maximum inventories. Computer solution to our example is shown below.

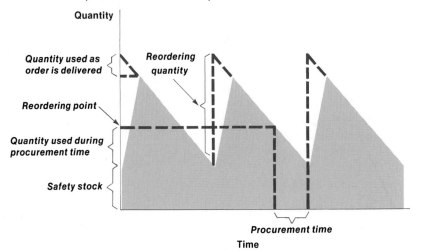

```
ECONOMIC ORDER QUANTITY

INITIAL CONDITIONS:

SET UP OR ORDERING COST IN DOLLARS          $30.00
PERIOD USAGE                               100000
PERIOD CARRYING COST PERCENTAGE              20.00%
PRICE OR COST PER PIECE                     $15.00
USAGE RATE                                    400
PRODUCTION RATE                              1200



ECONOMIC ORDER QUANTITY                      1414
NUMBER OF ORDERS PER PERIOD                 70.72

EOQ OVER A PERIOD OF TIME                    1732
NUMBER OF ORDERS PER PERIOD                 57.74
```

For example, assume the following:

Use per year *(D)*	100,000 ($R = 400$ per 250 workdays)
Ordering and setup cost per order *(C_p)*	$30
Labor, material, and overhead cost per piece *(V)*	$15
Holding cost *(C_h)*	20%
Maximum production rate per year	300,000 ($P = 1,200$ per 250 workdays)

First we will solve this problem with the entire lot arriving at one time:

$$EOQ = \sqrt{\frac{2 \times 100,000 \times \$30}{\$15 \times .20}}$$

$$= \sqrt{\frac{6,000,000}{3}}$$

$$= \sqrt{2,000,000}$$

$$= 1,414, \text{ which is about } 3\frac{1}{2} \text{ days'}$$
usage (See Figure 12–14.)

Now, allowing for usage during the delivery of each order, the formula becomes:

$$EOQ = \sqrt{\frac{2 \times D \times C_p}{(V \times C_h)\left(1 - \dfrac{R}{P}\right)}}$$

$$= \sqrt{\frac{2 \times 100,000 \times \$30}{(\$15 \times .2)\left(1 - \dfrac{400}{1200}\right)}}$$

$$= \sqrt{\frac{6,000,000}{2}}$$

$$= \sqrt{3,000,000}$$

$$= 1,732, \text{ or about } 4\frac{1}{3} \text{ days' usage}$$

Thus, the EOQ can be larger because the holding costs were overstated using the standard formula.

EOQs IN MANAGERIAL DECISION MAKING

So far we have discussed EOQs only with respect to setting the size of manufactured or purchased lots. They can, however, be used to help managers choose the best course of action when there are alternatives.

Purchasing Decisions When Quantity Price Discounts Are Offered

Whenever the purchasing department can receive quantity price discounts from suppliers, this creates a different EOQ for each price offered. But sometimes the EOQ cannot be purchased at the discount price quoted because the vendor does not offer the lower price unless *more* than the EOQ quantity is bought. Yet the price cut for larger quantities may save enough to justify buying more than an EOQ amount.

Suppose, for example, that it costs $10 to place a purchase order, 25 percent a year for carrying costs, and that 2,000 units a year are needed. The vendor quotes a price of $2 per unit for all orders under 500 units and $1.95 for 500 or more. How many should be ordered?

Before we begin, we need to introduce a new total-cost equation to use in our analysis. Total cost is:[6]

$$TC = \left(\frac{Q}{2} \times V \times C_h\right) + \left(\frac{D}{Q} \times C_p\right) + (D \times V)$$

The first term defines inventory holding cost; the second ordering or setup cost; the third is the annual cost to buy the item. We will use this equation later to aid us in evaluating this problem.

To answer this question, it is first necessary to calculate the EOQ for each offer. First,

$$EOQ_{\$2} = \frac{2 \times 2000 \times \$10}{\$2 \times .25} = 283$$

$$EOQ_{\$1.95} = \frac{2 \times 2000 \times \$10}{\$1.95 \times .25} = 286$$

So far as the buyer's needs are concerned, at $2 the EOQ is 283 units and at $1.95 it is 286 units. The price difference is so small that it doesn't change the EOQ much. But, actually, the buyer does not get to choose between these two EOQ quantities because she cannot get the $1.95 price unless she buys 500. Will it pay to increase the order size to 500 to get the benefit of the $1.95 price? Here, we calculate TC for the EOQ amount of 283 at $2 each, the price allowed for this quantity, and the TC for ordering *just enough* to get the price discount of 5 cents per unit, or 500 units:

---

[6] See footnote 5 for a partial explanation of this formula.

$$TC_{283} = \left(\frac{283}{2} \times \$2 \times .25\right) + \left(\frac{2,000}{283} \times \$10\right)$$

$$+ (2,000 \times \$2)$$

$$= 71 + 71 + 4,000$$

$$= \$4,142$$

$$TC_{500} = \left(\frac{500}{2} \times \$1.95 \times .25\right) + \left(\frac{2,000}{500} \times \$10\right)$$

$$+ (2,000 \times \$1.95)$$

$$= 122 + 40 + 3,900$$

$$= \$4,062.$$

If the customer buys 283 units at a time, she will spend, in a year, $71 for 7.1 orders (2,000/283 × $10) and another $71 to carry an average inventory of 142 pieces valued at $2 each (283/2 × $2 × .25). The items themselves will cost $4,000 (2,000 × $2). The total annual cost of this practice will be $4,142.

The alternative is to buy 500 units at a time for $1.95. With this policy the costs will be $122 to carry the average inventory of 250 units valued at $1.95 each (500/2 × $1.95 × .25) and $40 for 4 orders (2,000/500 × $10). The items will cost $3,900 (2,000 × $1.95). This policy will cost $4,062 a year, or $80 more than ordering the EOQ of 283. The manager's decision should therefore be to buy 500 at a time. If more than one price break is offered, the same procedure as outlined above can be used. Figure 12–15 graphically shows the costs involved in quantity discount situations like this and a computer generated solution to our example. This approach can also be used with discrete lot-sizing methods, mentioned earlier.

Releasing Working Capital

The EOQ can also be helpful if, for example, money is tight and management would like to reduce inventories in order to release working capital. This could be done if order quantities

were reduced and reorders placed more frequently. The managers know that placing additional orders for smaller quantities is somewhat uneconomical, but this is the price they will have to pay in order to reduce the inventory investment.

The question is: How much will it cost to release the capital? We will use our earlier problem as an example. It costs $10 to place an order, 25 percent a year for carrying costs, and $2 per unit for the 2,000 units needed in a year. The EOQ was 283 units. If we omit the safety stock, the average inventory would be 283 ÷ 2 = 141.5 units, which would have a value of $283.

Management asks: How much will it cost to cut the inventory investment by one fourth, thus releasing $71 in capital? The new order quantity would be 212 units (75 percent of 283). The average inventory would be 106 units with a holding cost of $53 (106 × $2 × .25) as compared to the EOQ holding cost of $70.75 (141.5 × $2 × .25). This results in a *reduction in holding cost of $17.75.* But, ordering in quantities of 212 will require 9.4 orders per year instead of 7.06 orders of 283 each. This results in an *additional ordering cost of $23.40.* Thus, the net cost of releasing $71 in inventories is $5.65, which is the equivalent of a 7.9 percent cost of capital. This rate seems reasonable, so management should probably reduce their investment in inventory by 25 percent.

Actually, order quantities perhaps should be set at something less, possibly as much as 25 percent less, than the EOQ anyway. This is because the total-cost curve is relatively flat in the area near the EOQ. Quantities below the EOQ do cost slightly more but they release idle capital tied up in inventories.

A manager should be careful, however, when using this kind of analysis. The approach we have just used may be incorrect if the unit price varies for different order quantities. Suppose, for example, that the vendor charges $2.05 per unit for orders as small as 212 units (versus $2 when ordering in lots of 283). This additional unit cost would increase total costs

FIGURE 12–15

Quantity discounts for purchased items complicate reorder problems because the price reduction often makes it economical to reorder considerably more than the EOQ amount. Computer solution to our example is shown below.

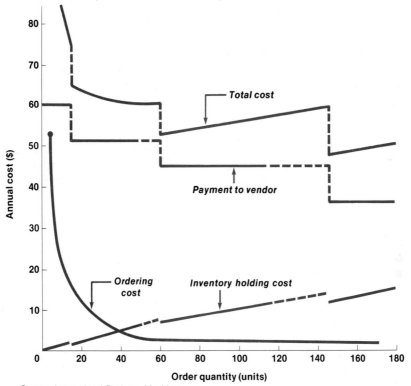

Source: International Business Machines.

```
  ECONOMIC ORDER QUANTITY

  INITIAL CONDITIONS:

  SET UP OR ORDERING COST IN DOLLARS        $10.00
  PERIOD USAGE                               2000
  PERIOD CARRYING COST PERCENTAGE           25.00%
  PRICE OR COST PER PIECE                    $2.00
  NUMBER OF RANGES                             2

  LOWEST VALUE FOR EACH RANGE
        1     500
  UNIT COST PER ITEM WITHIN EACH RANGE
        $2.00       $1.95



  ECONOMIC ORDER QUANTITY                     283
  NUMBER OF ORDERS PER PERIOD                7.07

  EOQ WITH PRICE BREAKS                       500
  TOTAL COST FOR EOQ                      $4061.88
  RANGE EOQ FALLS IN                          500
  UNIT COST PER ITEM WITHIN RANGE           $1.95
  NUMBER OF ORDERS PER PERIOD                4.00
```

by $100 and require a total cost of $105.30 to release $71 of capital from inventory investment, a 148 percent cost of capital! *All* of the ramifications of changing an order quantity policy should be considered in this type of analysis.

Enlarging Reorder Quantities during Slack Periods

Another instance where EOQ analysis can be used may arise during slack periods. The question in this case is whether to make more parts or products than are needed in the immediate future in order to keep the work force busy. We will continue to use the same example, except that the $10 ordering cost is the cost of placing a factory shop order and setting up machinery, and the $2 is the cost for direct labor and materials.

Again the EOQ is 283 units and the average inventory is 141.5 units. But, in order to keep the work force busy, management wants to know what it will cost to double the order quantity. This means making lots of 566, or 3.5 orders, a year, costing $35. The average inventory would be $566, which would cost $141.50 to carry. Total costs would be $176.50, or $34.50 more than the total cost using EOQs. Actually, management would not, of course, plan to do this all year long but perhaps only over a short period of one to three months. The actual cost, therefore, for the part year involved would probably be less than one quarter of $34.50, or $8 more or less. Knowing this cost, managers can decide what to do more intelligently than without this analysis.

EOQs as Tests of Rule-of-Thumb Practices

Managers can also use EOQs to test rule-of-thumb practices. One company, for example, which does not use EOQs, uses the following practices in determining reorder quantities for the parts it makes. If setup costs are less than $10, it orders four months' supply. For setup costs up to $25, it orders six months' supply. Above $25 it orders eight months' supply.

This policy may be more costly than using EOQs. To test it, examples can be calculated. One example might assume a usage of 7,500 units a year, setup costs of $20, and inventory carrying charges of 25 percent, with the item's value being $3 per unit.

In line with company policy, the inventory controller orders six months' supply of this item each time. Thus, he reorders 3,750 units twice a year. The average inventory is 1,875 units, with a value of $5,625. Inventory carrying costs are $5,625 × .25, or $1,406.25. Ordering costs are 2 × $20 = $40. So the total annual cost for this inventory policy is $1,446.25. Next, the EOQ is calculated:

$$EOQ = \sqrt{\frac{2 \times 7{,}500 \times \$20}{\$3 \times .25}}$$
$$= \sqrt{\frac{300{,}000}{.75}}$$
$$= \sqrt{400{,}000}$$
$$= 632$$

If 632 units are ordered each time, the ordering cost per year is 7,500 ÷ 632 = 11.9 orders per year × $20 = $238. Carrying costs would be 632 ÷ 2 = 316 units average inventory × $3 = $948 average investment × .25 percent = $237. The total cost would be $475.

The company's rule-of-thumb policy is, therefore, in this example, costing an extra $971 to handle the inventory of this one item in a year ($1,446 − $475 = $971). Similar tests could be made for other examples. If other items are anywhere near comparable to this example, the failure of the company to use EOQs may be costing them a great deal of money.

Imputed Carrying Cost Rates

The EOQ approach can be reversed to calculate the imputed carrying cost percentage for a given inventory order size policy. In the example above, the calculation would be:

Imputed carrying cost %

$$= \frac{2 \times \text{Annual usage} \times \text{Cost to prepare 1 order}}{\text{Value per unit} \times (\text{Order quantity})^2} \times 100$$

$$= \frac{2 \times 7{,}500 \times \$20}{\$3 \times 3{,}750^2} \times 100$$

$$= \frac{300{,}000}{3 \times 14{,}062{,}500} \times 100$$

$$= \frac{300{,}000}{42{,}187{,}500} \times 100$$

$$= .0071 \times 100 = .71\%$$

The company's reorder policy would produce an EOQ of 3,750 units only if the annual carrying charge percent were as small as .71%. But for any higher carrying cost rate, the EOQ is less than 3,750.

Sensitivity Analysis

Managers can also use EOQ calculations to see how sensitive the solution is to changes in any of the factors that go into its calculation. They can change the carrying charges, for example, to see how sensitive the answer is to the size of this factor. (It will usually be found that the formula is not very sensitive to minor changes in any single factor but is quite sensitive to large changes because the change in the EOQ varies according to the square root of changes in individual factors.)

Curiously, using EOQs to aid in decision making seems to be rare. All of the several possible applications given here seem to have greater merit than is recognized.

REASONS FOR NOT USING EOQs

Many companies do not use EOQs for both practical and technical reasons.

Among the practical reasons is the need to use data that are often not available unless money is spent to collect it. These figures include the cost of reordering and factory setup costs. Besides, both rates of use and material costs change and this may require the recalculation of the EOQs.

Among the technical reasons is the fact that EOQs are best suited for independent demand items, but rarely for A and B dependent demand items. Technicians also object to the implicit assumption in the formula of steady withdrawal from stock. The formula considers an item's average inventory to be half of the reordering quantity plus the safety stock. But the patterns of use of some items are not like that. Instead, withdrawals from stock are "lumpy"—infrequent but large, thus probably invalidating this basic assumption. Obviously, EOQs should not be used for such items if their investment is of consequential proportions.

EOQ assumption of steady use also invalidates the method when there are strong seasonal variations in demand. EOQ formulas, however, can be adapted to handle seasonal variations but the mathematics are more complicated.

Another reason for not using EOQs is that they suboptimize, which is not always advantageous to the entire company's operations. This is particularly true in their overuse of capital. Ordering a little less than the EOQ will usually release a certain amount of capital at the equivalent of a very low cost of capital.

And, as we have mentioned, EOQ methods (and statistical reorder point methods) are generally not applicable to the largest A items and to most C items. The A items usually need more careful attention than EOQs and the usual associated ROPs can provide, while C items (probably) need less attention than EOQs provide.

Rather, the increasing practice of planning orders for materials and parts against master production schedules using MRP I methods and *discrete* lot-sizing methods is expected to reduce their use in the years to come for items where they should not be used. However, their use in determining order quantities for *steadily used* independent demand items is expected to remain about the same where setup and ordering costs are a factor. However, if Japanese methods of manufacture are adopted more, and setup and ordering costs are minimized (or disregarded), then lot sizes can be very small, and the use of EOQ/ELS becomes less important. This aspect will be discussed in more detail in Chapter 14.

Review Questions

1. Why shouldn't order points methods be used for most dependent demand items?

2. Explain how to calculate the size of the safety stock by the method explained in the text.

3. How are order points defined in MRP I systems?

4. What is the difference between "discrete" and "continuous" lot-sizing models?

5. How does "lumpy" demand affect the way inventories are managed?

6. Are not the least-total-cost and part-period-balancing methods for discrete lot-sizing designed to accomplish the same thing?

7. Is it true that in all EOQ diagrams, such as that shown in Figure 12–13, the EOQ is the point where the declining and sloping curved line crosses the rising straight line? Explain.

8. Would it ever be true that the EOQ curve is not relatively flat for volumes of, say, 25 percent above and below the EOQ? If yes, explain how it could be.

9. Is the economic order quantity ever a part of the safety stock? When?

10. Explain the procedure which could be used to find out how much it would cost to release capital from investment in inventory by ordering less than economic lot quantities.

11. The company is considering using mathematical decision rules to set the size of safety stocks. The analyst is told to gather the necessary data. What data does he or she need, and why?

12. In computerized inventory control, why does the computer calculate the expected error in a product's usage during the reorder lead time?

13. On Figure 12–7, the calculation table, the following figures appear on the first line: 8, 150, 75, $56.25, 92, and $184. How were these calculated?

14. If a company aims for a 95 percent service level in reordering, does this mean that 95 percent of the time when stock is needed it will be on hand but that it will be out of stock 5 percent of the time? Explain.

15. How does the constant usage rate assumption of EOQ sometimes make EOQ inappropriate for dependent demand items?

16. What effect do Japanese inventory methods have on EOQs and ELSs?

Questions for Discussion

1. "Order point is dead," a prominent consultant in PIPC once said. If this is true, why do so many companies still use it? Discuss.

2. It has been said that the reason order point systems (with safety stocks) are used for dependent demand items is that "we thought we had a *statistical* problem, when in fact, we really had a *calculation* problem." Discuss in terms of computer-based MRP systems.

3. In a company using direct costing, will its calculations of economic order quantities be like everyone else's? Why? If not, whose kind of calculations give the right answer?

4. If the new labor contract gives everyone a pay raise, is it necessary to recalculate all EOQs? Discuss.

5. The company's stock of storage batteries has a loss of life of 3 percent a month from shelf wear. How can this be handled in EOQ calculations?

6. In EOQ formulas, a carrying charge of 25 percent or more is common. Yet the calculations in the text claimed that by ordering less than the EOQ, capital could be released at an implicit interest charge of a much lower rate, perhaps 7 percent. If this is so, isn't there something wrong in the calculation which bases the EOQ on a claimed cost of 25 percent? Discuss.

7. ROP has been called a "reactive" inventory control system, while MRP I (with master production schedules) has been called a "proactive" system. Discuss.

8. Japanese inventory planning methods affect which variable the most in EOQs and ELSs?

Problems

1. Suppose the demand forecasts (F_t, in column 5, Figure 12–3 in the text) are now as follows:

January	205	July	197
February	200	August	207
March	195	September	217
April	203	October	218
May	198	November	217
June	201	December	215

Everything else is the same as the example in the text.
a. Calculate the reorder point for a 95 percent service level.
b. Of the reorder point quantity, how much is safety stock?

2. The planned order releases for item D in Figure 11–9 in Chapter 11 are as follows:

Week	Planned Order Releases
1	0
2	64
3	93
4	3
5	45
6	0
7	0
8	0

Also, Ds are valued at $50.00, annual inventory holding costs are 25 percent of value, and the setup cost on machines that make D is $50.00.

*a. Determine the economic lot size(s) for these planned order releases, using the part–period balancing method.
*b. Do the same, using the least–total–cost method. Are the results the same? Why or why not?

3. The inventory record microfiche for item G-2357 (an MRO item) reads as follows:

Date	Quantity Ordered	Received	Used	On Hand
1-15	—	300		300
1-16	—	—	75	225
2-16	—	—	75	150
3-16	—	—	75	75
3-17	300	—		75
4-16	—	—	75	0
7-19	—	300		300
8-25	—	—	75	225

These items are worth $7.00 each and cost $.10 a month to carry in stock. Assuming that standard package limitations can be neglected, set up a reordering policy. When should they be reordered and how many?

4. Calculate the reorder point for the following item:

Use	2,000 per week
Cost of running out	$1,200
Value of one unit	$20.80
Carrying cost	25%

The past record of time elapsed between ordering and getting new supplies is:

Weeks	Number of Instances
3	1
4	2
5	6
6	6
7	7
8	3

5. Vendor A is located 500 miles away from the Davis Company. Shipments of part M-62, an item bought in quantity by Davis, is by rail. From one half to one week must be allowed for shipment. Vendor A's plant needs another two weeks to process orders.

The smallest quantity of M-62s which can be produced economically is 5,000 or one half a week's usage by the Davis Company. Davis' usage, however, fluctuates between 8,000 and 12,000 per week.

How far ahead should Davis release orders? How big an inventory of item M-62 should Davis carry? If more data are necessary in order to answer, what data? With such data, how should one go about calculating the answers to these questions?

---

* May be calculated with provided software or by manual calculation. See Preface for explanation of software.

6. Given: an item whose value is $3.00 per unit, reordering cost $25.00, and an inventory carrying cost of 20 percent. This item's stock record shows the following:

Withdrawal Quantity	Days until Next Withdrawal	Reorder Lead Times (days)
69	12	20
58	19	30
93	8	15
76	12	20
81	17	20
59	10	10
64	7	30
51	7	20
49	19	25
60	14	30
Total 660	Total 125	Average 22

Find:
a. The reorder quantity.
b. The reorder point.
c. What kind of an item should this be if your answers in parts a and b are to be implemented?

7. Given the following:
A safety level of 75 units.
Replenishment lead time of 15 days.
Maximum inventory of 810 units.
Usage of EOQ in 35 days.
Calculate the reorder point in units and days.

*8. a. Calculate the economic lot size for the following end products:

Product	Cost per Unit (excluding setup)	Cost to Change Assembly Line	Carrying Charge	Annual Usage
A	$ .50	$ 100	20%	10,000
B	.20	60	15	25,000
C	2.00	300	25	100,000
D	.75	1,000	25	500,000
E	5.00	1,000	20	40,000

b. Assume item D is used at a rate of 2,000 units a day and can be produced at a maximum rate of 6,000 units per day. What is the economic lot size?

---

*May be calculated with provided software or manually. See Preface for explanation of software.

*9. In Problem 8, what change occurs in the EOQ if product A's carrying costs are 10 percent instead of 20 percent? 30 percent? From these answers, what should be concluded about the sensitivity of EOQs to variations in the carrying charge percentage rate?

*10. In Problem 8, what change occurs in the EOQ if usage of product A is cut in half? If it doubles? From these answers, what should be concluded about the sensitivity of EOQ to variations in the usage rate?

11. In Problem 8, how much capital will be released from inventory by an edict to cut the overall investment by 25 percent? What will be the cost effects of such an edict? What will be the effective interest cost rate to the company for the released capital?

12. After the cut required in Problem 11, what will be the implicit interest rate if the new ordering quantities are regarded as the EOQs but at a higher rate?

13. The Equipment Manufacturing Company has decided to purchase a certain type of rheostat required in the operation of a machine which it manufactures. The company fairly steadily uses 2,000 rheostats per year; the average use is eight per working day; the minimum use is five per working day, and the maximum is ten per working day. It takes 30 working days to receive delivery on the rheostats after the ordering point is reached. The cost of preparing each order is $10. The inventory carrying charges are 20 percent of the average inventory investment. The purchase prices are as follows:

Price (each)	Size of Order
$4.60	200 or less
4.50	201 to 400
4.40	401 to 600
4.35	601 to 800
4.30	801 to 2,000

Determine the safety stock, the ordering point, the ordering quantity,* and the normal maximum inventory.

14. In the past, a company has followed this general rule and has not calculated economic order quantities:

Setup Cost	Order
Under $10	4 months' supply
$10–25	6 months' supply
Over $25	8 months' supply

Following this policy, item 319 (a replacement part for machines already sold to its customers), with a setup cost of $20 and an annual usage

of 6,800 units, was ordered in lots of 3,400. Labor and material for item 319 cost $.75.

If it costs 25 percent to carry inventory, how good is the company's general rule? How much does following the rule on item 319 cost the company in a year? If item 319 constitutes 2 percent of all replacement part inventories, and if this finding applies to all other items proportionally, what is the approximate cost to the company of following these general rules?

15. A company uses 500 grinding wheels in a year and pays $3.10 each for them. They have been ordered 100 at a time, and ordering costs are $25.

   a. What is the implicit interest rate?

   b. Could this item be added to the bill of materials for the products ground on it, and MRP'd? Why? Why not?

16. An item's use record has been, month by month, 57, 43, 62, 51, 63, 72, 77, 69, 62, 43, 67, and 70. Using the method described in the text, what is this item's expected use in the reorder period of three months following the last month of those given here in this example? Also, what is the standard deviation of the errors in reorder quantities?

If the policy is to reorder so that new supplies arrive before present stocks run out in at least 90 percent of the cases, what is the reordering point?

17. Hanson Industries has an MRP I system and utilizes safety time in their reorder points. Given the following requirements for an item, when will orders be released?

							Weeks				
	0	1	2	3	4	5	6	7	8	9	10
Requirements		200	0	100	200	200	100	0	0	400	100
On hand	200										

Lead time: 1 week
Order quantity: 300
Safety time: 1 week's units requirements

*18. Plastic beads used in the plastic injection molding machines at Delila Suitcase Company are used at a rate of 5,000 tons per year. Their supplier, Bead City, is located several hundred miles from Delila's factory, so freight costs are a factor in their inventory ordering decisions. (Delila pays the freight costs.) Bead City also offers a price discount for larger orders, and the freight company also gives discounts on the rate per ton. When these two discounts are combined, the following information is available:

Order Size (tons)	Price/Ton (delivered)
1–10	$100
11–50	95
51–100	90
101–200	80
201 or more	75

If the ordering cost is $100, and holding costs are 30 percent of the beads' value, what is the EOQ?

---

* May be calculated with provided software or manually. See Preface for explanation of software.

Chapter 13

Low-Volume Job Shop Scheduling and Control

Planned order releases which have been determined with MRP, reorder points, or other methods eventually get released to the factory or to vendors. In this chapter, we shall discuss the processes required to schedule small- and medium-sized "job orders" for internal manufacture in work centers, and to control their progress toward completion target dates, as specified by the master production schedule. While the overall volume of production may be high, each order is relatively small because of the diversity of parts being made. Thus the term *low volume*. The next chapter will be devoted to a similar discussion of order planning and control for *high-volume* repetitive manufacturing operations such as auto assembly and chemical processing. Chapter 15, Purchasing and Vendor Management, will cover the management of orders for purchases from vendors.

CAPACITY LOADING

A factory's load is the amount of total capacity that has been allocated to orders from customers or to the production of items for stock. It can be expressed in tons, dollar value, time, or in other ways. For PIPC's use, it is usually expressed in time. A plant, department, or machine is said to have so many hours', days', weeks',

or months' worth of capacity. The capacity which has been committed to orders already released to the factory is called *backlog*.

As we said in Chapter 10, master schedules should not be approved until their load requirements are compared to the factory's uncommitted capacity. Generally this is done in aggregate, or "rough cut," capacity planning terms—as we discussed in Chapter 8—if the company makes only a few kinds of products. If, however, the organization has a sophisticated computer-based MRP system, rather detailed comparisons can be made between master schedule requirements and specific machine-center open capacities.

If a company manufactures to order, the load is the summation of the capacity needs of the orders already in hand for as far into the future as the master schedule is projected. New Orders, as they come in, are added to the present load, not as increases to today's load but as extensions of the assigned capacity in future months. These orders get more distant promise dates according to when there is open capacity.

A plant with a load which matches its overall capacity usually has all departments loaded about equally. Product-mix variations, however, sometimes create unequal loads onto departments as is shown in Figure 13–1, which is a

FIGURE 13–1
Work Center Infinite Load Planning Report

07/15/—

WORK CENTER: 20516

PER-IOD	TIME UNIT FROM-TO	AVAIL. CAP.	REQ'D. CAP.	REQUIRED CAPACITY IN PERCENT	AVAIL. CAP. (SUM)	REQ'D. CAP. (SUM)	REQUIRED CAPACITY IN PERCENT (SUM)
06	026–030	36.0	40.0	111.1	36.0	40.0	111.1 ....
07	031–035	40.0	30.0	100.0	76.0	90.0	105.2 ....
08	036–040	40.0	56.0	140.0	116.0	136.0	117.0 ....
09	041–045	45.0	60.0	133.3	161.0	196.0	121.8 ....
10	046–050	45.0	72.0	160.0	206.0	268.0	130.1 ....
11	051–055	45.0	34.0	75.5	251.0	302.0	119.9 ....
12	056–060	40.0	16.0	40.0	291.0	318.0	109.3 ....
13	061–065	40.0	20.0	50.0	331.0	338.0	102.1 ....
14	066–070	40.0	12.0	30.0	371.0	350.0	94.3 ....
15	071–075	32.0	8.0	25.0 ...	403.0	358.0	68.8 ....
16	076–080	64.0	80.0	125.0	467.0	447.0	95.7 ....
17	081–085	80.0	96.0	120.0	547.0	543.0	99.2 ....
18	086–090	80.0	115.0	133.7	627.0	658.0	105.0 ....

FUTURE CAPACITY: 139.5

WORK CENTER: 23363

PER-IOD	TIME UNIT FROM-TO	AVAIL. CAP.	REQ'D. CAP.	REQUIRED CAPACITY IN PERCENT	AVAIL. CAP. (SUM)	REQ'D. CAP. (SUM)	REQUIRED CAPACITY IN PERCENT (SUM)
06	026–030	40.0	60.0	150.0	30.0	60.0	150.0 ....
07	031–035	0.0	60.0		30.0	120.0	300.0 ....
08	036–040	24.0	60.0	250.0	63.0	180.0	281.0 ....
09	041–045	80.0	60.0	75.0	133.0	290.0	186.0 ....
10	046–050	80.0	48.0	60.0	223.0	288.0	128.6 ....
11	051–055	90.0	42.5	53.1	303.0	330.0	108.8 ....
12	056–060	90.0	42.5	53.1	363.0	373.0	97.1 ....
13	061–065	80.0	40.0	50.0	464.0	413.0	89.0 ....
14	066–070	80.0	45.0	56.3	533.0	368.0	86.2 ....
15	071–075	32.0	48.0	150.0	576.0	516.0	89.6 ....
16	076–080	32.0	48.0	150.0	608.0	564.0	92.7 ....
17	081–085	40.0	48.0	120.0	648.0	612.0	94.4 ....
18		40.0	54.0	135.0	688.0	676.0	98.3 ......

FUTURE CAPACITY: 56.3

Source: Univac, Sperry-Rand Corporation.

computer-generated work center load-planning report. Similarly, within departments, individual machine loads vary. Thus, when it appears that the approved rough-cut master schedule will provide for a smooth, balanced operation, it does not always work out quite so smoothly for individual work centers or machines. The point is that orders can be scheduled which will apparently not overload the plant, and then it is found that some machines are overscheduled while others are underscheduled. MRP I methods often include checking the workloads that planned order releases generate at different work centers against the loads the centers already have.

Infinite Loading

For planning purposes, most companies check loads being generated by new orders without regard for the amount of uncommitted capacity of work centers. This is called *infinite* loading.

Infinite loading shows how much work we would like to load in each work center in each work period as defined by the planned order releases from MRP I, if MRP I is used. If an overload results, then work centers may have to go on overtime, some orders may have to be shifted around to balance needs with capacities, or the master schedule will have to be changed.

An infinite load planning report is shown in Figure 13–1. For Work Center 20516, note that loads exceed 100 percent in several periods as shown by the horizontal bar chart; other periods have less than a 100 percent load. But, in the bar chart to the right, which shows cumulative load, capacity exceeds 100 percent less often. This shows that, overall, the total load can be shifted around into a more balanced load, with a little overtime required only in periods 6, 8, 9, 10, and 11.

However, for Work Center 23363, the cumulative load exceeds capacity most periods and is especially overleaded in the early time periods. This problem can only be solved by changing the schedule, subcontracting out part of the work, or perhaps assigning the work to another work center, if possible. Using infinite loading, these adjustments are made by production planners and schedulers, *not* computers. The computer simply reports how level or lumpy the load is, and they adjust and readjust the load by trial and error until a solution is found.

Finite Loading

In contrast to infinite loading, *finite* loading computer systems try to automatically fit planned order releases into future uncommitted work center capacities, recognizing the prior allocations of capacity to other orders. Finite loading systems often fall short of their promise and do not do a very satsifactory job of loading because of the complexity of the problem and the dynamic nature of most master production schedules. Later, however, we will discuss Optimized Production Technology (OPT), a new method that shows great promise as a useful finite loading system.

Actually, infinite loading is not such a haphazard matter as it might seem. Normally the overall capacity requirements, stated in terms of new orders, are considered before these orders are accepted and promise dates set. The company's managers know just about how much load the present schedules are calling for. Rarely would they accept new orders and make promise dates beyond what can be handled. Top managers would accept a known overcommitment only if they were willing to approve overtime or the delaying of other orders. Generally, a load that is feasible for the entire factory is also feasible for its individual internal departments.

Input-Output Control

The overall rate at which orders should be released to the factory is an extremely important function of PIPC and depends upon several factors.

The first factor, of course, is the quantity of orders ready to be released. The second is the current load in the factory.

The two major trade-offs are, first, that orders which are released almost *instantly create WIP inventories* and the carrying costs associated with them. If there is currently too much of a WIP Load, lines get longer at work centers and the factory gets saturated. On the other hand, if not enough orders are released, backlogs may disappear at some work centers, and they become *idle or underutilized*—with their fixed costs continuing.

The job of *input-output control* by PIPC is to monitor the rate of orders entering the production system and their rate of completion so that there is "enough" of a backlog of work in process to prevent idle capacity—yet not so much that WIP builds up to excessive levels and the factory becomes congested.[1] A good example of this is a bathtub where the faucet is on and

---

[1] Some PIPC specialists (and the Japanese) believe that preventing idle capacity is a false economy. If machines and people *should be* idle because of the mix of customer order due dates, let them be idle, rather than building unneeded parts—just to keep them busy. This concept has merit.

the water flowing in while the plug is out, and the water is draining. The inflow relates to the order-release rate and the draining to the completion rate of orders from the shop floor. The water level is the WIP in the shop. Stop for a moment to visualize what would happen to the water level with changes in the inflow and outflow rates.

Research studies have shown that, if orders are sufficient, WIP should be allowed to increase in the factory until workers are utilized about 92 percent of the time, on the average, and idle about 8 percent of the time, *if customer demand justifies it.* (In our example the bathtub is 92 percent full of water.) This is shown in Figure 13–2.

The rate at which orders are released depends in part, as we said earlier, upon the rate at which they are received from customers, or upon the rate of demand if building to stock. The way PIPC keeps WIP at the proper level is to release orders earlier or later, and, when possible, give earlier or later corresponding promise dates to customers. Essentially, they manipulate the number of weeks of backlog (or lead time to fill customers' orders) up and down, in an attempt to achieve their target WIP, which meets their target utilization.

Some MRP systems produce input-output reports which are designed to aid in these backlog manipulations.

FIGURE 13–2
Level of WIP versus Worker Utilization

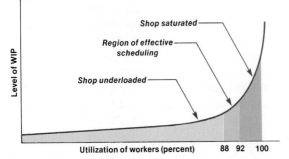

Source: John L. Colley, Jr., Robert D. Landel, and Robert R. Fair, *Production Operations Planning and Control* (San Francisco: Holden-Day, 1977), p. 609.

If a company finds that its WIP is too high or too low (with underutilization of the work force), a good approach to bringing it back in line is gradually—not all of a sudden. PIPC may, for example, increase the order release rate at 1 to 2 percent per month, if WIP needs to be increased. This allows the factory to adjust to the new rate in an orderly way.

AUTHORITY TO RELEASE ORDERS

Among the objectives of PIPC is to rarely have the factory make anything which can't be sold in the near future, yet to make as many of everything as can be sold soon. This means that production orders need to be planned and specifically authorized so that just the right number of products will be made and so that the proper materials can be procured.

As we have seen, PIPC receives this essential information and authority from master schedules and MRP output covering the demand for each product for the next several weeks or months.

Producing Authority

The factory receives its authority to make products from the PIPC department. PIPC usually tells the factory four things: (1) what to make, (2) how many, (3) when, and (4) how. The first three give the factory "producing" authority to proceed and make products. The fourth gives the factory "processing" authority.

Producing authority instructs the factory (1) to assemble parts into finished products, (2) to make single-piece finished products (such as a casting sold to customers), (3) to make individual component parts, or (4) to process bulk materials (liquids and powders) and pack them into various-sized packages.

Assembly orders instruct the factory's assembly department what and how many finished products to make and provides bills of materials of the subassemblies and parts needed for each assembly order. The manufacture of parts and individual-piece finished products, however, often requires more detailed producing directives. In most companies *every operation* done on parts and integral products must be separately planned for and *individually authorized.*

Producing authority is one-time authority. When the factory finishes what it has been authorized to do, it requires more directives. New producing authorizations must be issued continuously. And, although we call it *authority,* the factory has little discretion. PIPC's directions are also *instructions.* This "authority," then, tells the factory to make the quantity of products the master production schedule calls for, and it must try to get things done on schedule.

Processing Authority

Processing authority deals with the specifications for making products, which smaller companies leave to experienced supervisors. They let the engineers determine the product's shape, size, and material requirements but let the supervisor determine how to make it.

But, in larger companies, leaving it up to the supervisor leaves too many things to chance. Engineers design parts and products; then other engineers decide how to make them. Some of these people are called manufacturing or product engineers, and sometimes they work in the PIPC department. Industrial engineers and methods people also help decide how workers are to perform operations—not only in parts manufacturing but also in assembly.

Master Bills of Materials (BOMs)

We have already discussed bills of materials and their use in planning. But, they are also used in production. Master bills of materials for each kind of assembled product are used to give the factory specific material requirements. They are primarily a listing of the subassemblies and parts needed to assemble one unit of the end product. They also show how many of each component

and part will be needed and, usually, the sequence of assembly if the product structure is indented as shown earlier in Fig 11–3. The master BOM lists all parts names, identification numbers, drawing numbers, and the source of the item—whether it is made inside or purchased outside.

A master bill for an end product may list subassemblies as if they were individual parts. Each subassembly in turn may have its own master bill of materials. If the subassembly is composed in part of lesser subassemblies, each of them may have its own master bill. And, each component for these lesser subassemblies may have its own "mini" bill. This bill-of-materials format is called a *single-level* BOM structure.

The list of parts is arranged in such a way as to indicate the order in which the parts are to be assembled so, in effect, the master BOM is also a form of processing instruction. For some purposes, the list is sorted and reprinted in the order of part numbers, or in the order of the arrangement of the finished parts stockroom.

The master bill shows the sequence in which items go together into subassemblies rather than directly into the product as piece parts. Engineering usually decides this, but in some companies PIPC can switch things around, based on practical considerations. It is not always possible to tell, on an engineer's drawing board, which sequence is best. Should, for example, an automobile door lock be assembled first and then put into the car door, after which the door goes on the body, and finally the body be put on the chassis? Or should the door be put on the body and then the lock assembled to the door? Sometimes these questions can be decided in the factory after people see what is involved.

Master bills are usually confined to listing the items that make up the end product. But some companies have extended them to include expendable tools. If, for example, a tool is likely to last for the production of 1,000 units before it will wear out, the bill of materials will list a requirement of 1/1,000 of a tool per unit of product. When the quantity of output nears 1,000, a second tool is provided just as if it were any other raw material or part.

Master bills of material, which are of course updated continually to keep up with design changes, confer continuing processing authority on PIPC, and PIPC may use this authority over and over again for repeat orders for the same product.

Master Route Sheets

Engineering also develops a "master route sheet" for each part, showing the operations and the sequence needed to make the part. Master route sheets list the operations necessary to make a part, the machines needed for each operation, the special tooling required, the machine time needed to set up for the operation, the machine time needed to perform the operation on one part, the normal between-operation dead time, and the kind and amount of raw materials needed to make one unit. In some companies, the route sheet also shows the classification of the worker who will perform each operation or the piece rate if the company uses incentives. Sometimes, this information is computer-generated from a computer-aided design (CAD) system, which is discussed in Chapter 19.

As in the case of master bills of materials, master route sheets confer continuing processing authority to PIPC. Repeat orders can be made out without new processing instructions from engineering.

In some companies, usually small ones, engineering does not develop master route sheets. Instead, the shop supervisor decides how to make things. In this case, the record of how it is done the first time serves as a master route sheet for future reorders.

In many large companies, too, the manufacturing department's production engineers may redesign parts in minor ways to suit manufacturing needs. In these cases, the route sheet, as first issued by engineering, is really only a preliminary draft which becomes final after any such minor adjustments.

Processing instructions. The master route sheet lists the required operations; yet these descriptions of operations are so brief (the words *clean, paint, broach,* and so on in Figure 13–3 are operations) that machine operators sometimes need more specific instructions covering what is to be done. Usually both an engineering drawing and a "specification" go along with orders to the shop to provide these more complete instructions.

Manufacturing instructions usually do not include instructions concerning the inspection tests that items need to pass to be acceptable. Quality assurance engineering must develop instructions about how tests are to be carried out and how inspectors can tell acceptable from unacceptable parts. Often special testing equipment has to be purchased or developed for particular tests, and inspectors need to be trained in their use. Also, procedures need to be determined for reporting test results back to engineering so that it can keep informed about the quality of work done by manufacturing in case a product or part needs redesigning to overcome some problem.

Most factory workers do about the same thing every day. So once they are trained to do their job, there are few problems with shop instructions, and drawings usually provide sufficient directions. Sometimes, though, particularly on difficult assembly jobs and jobs with many wires to fasten, more instructions are needed. Sometimes a person's assignment covers a half

FIGURE 13–3

A Shop Order *(all the information, except the order number, quantity, processing times, and start dates, comes from the master route sheet)*

OPER.	OPERATION DESCRIPTION	MACH. CENTER	TOOL NUMBER	NO. REQD	PROCESSING TIME	START DATE	DEPT.
PART NAME			PART NO. 8 6 3 8 D		NO. OF SHEETS 1		
DATE 10/20		DATE DUE 1/20	ORDER NO. 1 6 2 4		ORDER QUANTITY 2 0 0		
	CR STEEL SAFE 1020						
10	CLEAN	1		1	320	572	25
20	PAINT	2		3	100	581	25
30	FACE SHORT HUB SWEEP 1 IN DIA FORM HAND GRIP	30	3687	2	334	584	34
40	FACE FIN TURN AND RAD HUB FORM RAD ON GRIP CTR DR AND REAM	30	6211	7	306	594	34
50	DR AND REAM	21		5	86	587	31
80	BROACH	53	6329	8	180	603	33
90	BURR	3		9	160	608	33
110	POLISH	47		4	60	610	33
120	INSPECT	4					44

hour or more of work per item and includes a hundred or more little things that need to be done.

Here, very careful instructions on the whole set of things to be done are required. And the worker may need occasional instruction later, too, if he or she forgets or if something goes wrong. Tape recordings, televised instructions, and colored slides (at the work station) help in such cases. Hughes Aircraft has used these materials for some time. Hughes reports production gains of more than 50 percent, and inspection and supervision costs were reduced 75 percent when this kind of instruction was first installed.

Assemblers can also be supplied with tape recordings explaining what to do step by step. They can turn it on any time they forget details of the operation. Collins Radio has developed a soundtrack moving picture projector with a six-inch screen to serve this same purpose. The operator can turn it on and see and hear how to do the job. General Electric uses closed-circuit TV to flash pictures or drawings on the drafting, assembly planning, and assembly areas. Users can even control a zoom lens from their viewing station if they want a close-up.

All of these methods for providing processing instructions are improvements over less thorough methods used in the past, but they are costly.

ORDER BILLS AND SHOP ORDERS

When the time comes for planned orders to be released to the factory to make a certain number of products, PIPC (or the computer) makes out individual assembly orders and, for the parts, individual shop orders. Both tell the factory what to make and so constitute producing authority. We call the orders to assemble *order bills* and the orders to make parts *shop orders*. When these documents are completed and a check has been made to see if enough materials are available, these orders are ready to be released to the shop.

Order bills differ from master bills in that they

show how many to make *this time.* If the order is for 50 units, the quantities of all the items on the master bill are exploded, as shown in Chapter 11. Also, an identification number is assigned to the order, as is a schedule (dates by which the products are to be made). Copies of order bills go to the assembly department, the finished parts stockroom, and wherever else they are needed. Often this communication takes place electronically through CRTs and printers at various locations.

Shop orders to cover the making of parts provide specific processing authority. Figure 13–3, a shop order, lists the required operations, and how much standard time each operation should take in order to turn out the full order of 200 items. Cleaning should take 32 hours, painting 10 hours, and so on.

Shop Calendars

The *start date* column may be confusing because this company is using a "1,000-day shop calendar," and cleaning is to start on day 581. With 1,000-day shop calendars, every scheduled workday for four years ahead is given a consecutive number. These numbers are used on all work schedules instead of regular dates. Everyone in the company also has a regular calendar with the equivalent day-number printed in. Outside purchase orders, however, use regular calendar dates. The advantages of using a shop calendar is to avoid ambiguity on items with very long lead times, and to facilitate computation of the timing of orders in computerized systems.

ORDER SCHEDULING

Assembled product schedules show certain quantities to be made (assembled) in a week or month. Some are actually assembled early in the week or month, others later. In job-lot manufacturing, normally *all* the parts and subassemblies are finished and complete *before* the first finished product in the lot is assembled. This can create some large WIP inventories on the first day of a week or month. To keep WIP within reason, parts lots are sometimes cut up into several smaller lots which are scheduled to be finished one after the other during the week or month as they are needed.

Backward Scheduling

But whether a week or month's needs of a part is processed as one lot or not, schedule setting for subassemblies and parts begins with the end product's master production assembly schedule. The scheduling process can begin by working back in time from the final-assembly completion dates to final-assembly start dates, then to subassembly completion dates and to subassembly start dates. As we have seen, this is essentially what MRP I does.

This provides the dates when parts need to be finished. This scheduling allows for a between-operations time allowance back to the end of the preceding operation, and so on, until times are determined for starting each operation. This is shown graphically in Figure 13–4. All of this, of course, has to be done separately for each different part and is often done on a computer. Figure 13–5 is a typical computer-generated order schedule report. But in manual PIPC systems, and even those with computerized MRP I systems, this detailed scheduling of job orders

is done by production planners without the help of computers.

This process produces a desired date for releasing the order to the factory for each parts order and is the date that goes on the shop order. Sometimes the desired completion date for every operation is put on the order. This serves as a priority system and tells supervisors which jobs to do first and whether jobs are on time or are behind schedule.

What we have just described is *backward scheduling.* It starts with the master schedule's completion dates and works back to necessary start dates. If backward scheduling results in start dates which *are in the past* then PIPC knows it will have to take some action to speed things up, or slip the final completion date. The point is they have an "early warning" system. On the other hand, if the start date is *in the future* (they usually are), PIPC has the flexibility to move the order start date to level the load on the factory, if needed.

Forward Scheduling

Sometimes, however, the scheduling process starts with a specified order starting date and lets the processing cycle and capacity limitations determine the completion date in the future. This approach is common in process industries such as chemicals, food processing, and other indus-

FIGURE 13–4
Processing Cycle of a Shop Order

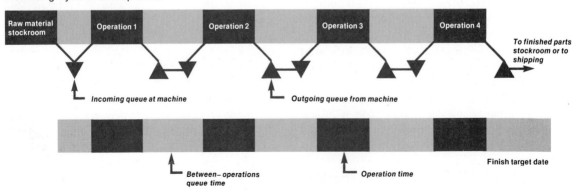

FIGURE 13–5
Order Schedule Report

07/15— —   Page 1

ORD. NO.	PART NO.	ORDER QTY.	LEAD TIME	EARL. START DATE	LATEST START DATE	GIVEN END DATE	CALC. END DATE	RED. % MAX.	RED. % USED	OPRTN NUMBER	WORK CENTER NUMBER	CALC. SPLIT NUMBER	START DATE	END DATE
32470	204-162	23	12	019	023	065	065	20		150	20262		026	028
										160	30272	2	029	031
										200	30274		031	036
										250	30401		037	040
										300	30405		040	045
										310	30409	2	046	048
										320	25880		049	054
										350	25890		055	056
										400	22402	2	057	059
										450	30401		060	062
										500	30405		063	065
37460	304-206	120	27	026	026	053	053	15	15	50	20264		026	030
										100	25880		031	033
										150	25890		034	040
										180	30273		041	045
										200	30276	4	046	053
31620	134-908	6	47	026	026	071	073	40	40	50	20265		026	029
										60	22665		030	030
										70	22675		031	033
										100	22685		034	043
										120	28120		044	045
										150	30401		045	047
										200	30405	3	048	057
										250	25880		058	060
										300	25890		061	065
										310	26120		066	068
										350	26220		069	073
32380	919-734	14	90	026	026		106	30		200	20260		026	030
										250	30272		031	040
										300	30274		041	053
										320	30276	1	054	059
										350	30402		060	065
										400	30408	2		
										450	25880			
										500				

Source: Univac, Sperry-Rand Corp.

tries where their output is severely limited in the short run by capacities which take a long time to change.

But, if the projected completion date is not acceptable, then appropriate corrective action can be considered.

Safety Lead Times

If an order falls behind schedule, it is usually not too difficult to get it back on schedule if the cause for its delay can be taken care of quickly. This can usually be done because the normal lead time allowed to complete the order usually has some "safety lead time" built into it. More lead time is actually allowed between operations than is really needed.

Much of this safety lead time factor is not apparent but is inherent in the way computerized methods operate. Back in Chapter 11, in our example explaining the MRP procedure, we used a lead time of two weeks for final end-product assembly and another two weeks for making one of the main subassemblies. Thus, end products due by the end of period 5 were said to need to have their main subassemblies ready at the end of week 3. And the subassemblies themselves were to be made from parts which were to be ready at the end of week 1.

But these lead times may be somewhat arbitrary. Note that they were not set with any particular quantity in mind (an order for 10 and an order for 100 would have the same lead time), and they do not give specific consideration to the true processing time needed—witness there being no lead times stated as fractions of a week. If there is a true "make span" of the three days,

it would be stated as one week; if it were six days, it would be given as two weeks.

Our discussion here has used the word *date* as if it meant a specific calendar day. And it is true that computers can calculate lead times down to exact days, and this is done in some companies who use so-called bucketless MRP I. But, MRP I time buckets are usually weeks and not days, and scheduling to the nearest week is the most common practice. This allows actual lead times to have some safety time, and a few behind-schedule orders or a few high priority orders—if they are only a few—can easily

FIGURE 13–6

Time Compression Possibilities for Shortening Processing Time by Overlapping Operations and "Squeezing out" Queue Time

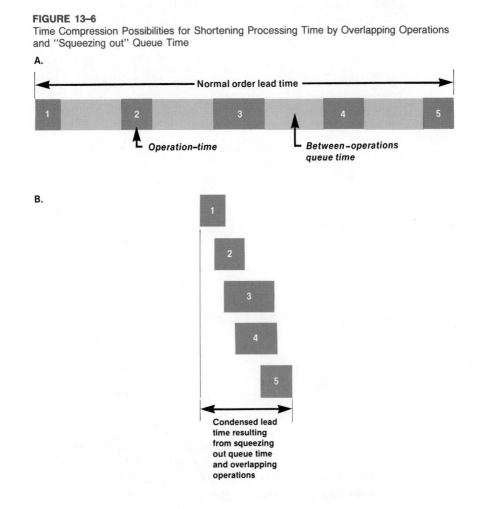

be expedited successfully without causing much disruption to the rest of the schedule.

Overlapping Operations and Split Orders

Another way of condensing lead times in job shop operations is to "overlap" operations or "split" orders. This means that operation 2 starts on part of the order which has completed operation 1 *before* the whole order has gone through operation 1. In job shops, however, operations rarely overlap or split orders because this would increase materials handling costs and would put work on such a tight schedule that any delay becomes serious.

Although operations are not often overlapped, or jobs split, jobs behind schedule often are pushed along (often by expediters) by "squeezing out" some of the between-operation time allowed for in the normal scheduling procedure. This between-operation time, which is called *queue* time or *waiting* time, often accounts for most of the total time it takes a job to be completed. Figure 13–6 illustrates lead-time compression possibilities which can be achieved by overlapping and order splitting.

Setup Time and Order Scheduling

As mentioned in Chapter 12, the ELS (economic lot size) is a trade-off of machine setup costs and inventory holding costs. High setup cost results in larger economic lot sizes because the cost of making many small lots to meet demand becomes expensive. Machines are being torn down and reset up too frequently. But, larger production runs can result in higher inventory holding costs. However, if setup time (and cost) can be reduced substantially, then smaller lots can be run and both setup and holding costs are reduced. This is an area where the Japanese are well ahead of the United States. One of their goals is to reduce lot sizes substantially, and they do this by redesigning machines for quick setup, and thus easy change-over from part to

part. This lower setup cost makes smaller lot sizes more economical.

OPTIMIZED PRODUCTION TECHNOLOGY (OPT)

OPT is a fairly recently developed technique for job shop scheduling, which essentially is a finite work center loading system. OPT was originally developed in Israel by Eli Goldratt and has been successfully used by a few large firms in the United States, including Ford, General Motors,[2] General Electric, Westinghouse, and RCA. Others, including Black & Decker and Deere & Company, have not found it to work well for them.

OPT is both a "philosophy" as well as a technique.[3] As a philosophy, it focuses attention on bottleneck work center capacities and attempts to schedule them tightly and efficiently so throughput is maximized. The philosophy is straightforward: If you concentrate on scheduling the bottlenecks, the nonbottleneck work centers generally will not inhibit production flow. As a technique, OPT utilizes an advanced mathematical programming algorithm (see Chapter 17 for a general discussion of this topic), which optimizes throughput while simultaneously considering multiple constraints such as customer due dates, routing sequences, economic lot sizes, setup time and cost, WIP value, and work center capacities.

Goldratt's OPT algorithm is secret, and his firm, Creative Output, Inc., provides their clients with a "black box." The box (which self-destructs, if it is tampered with!) has circuitry that allows access to the users but does not allow them to see how it works.

OPT uses much of the same data base as is required for MRP II; however, it requires a much more rigorously developed model of rout-

---

[2] G. Bylinsky, "An Efficiency Guru," *Fortune*, September 5, 1983, pp. 120–32.

[3] For a good overview of OPT, see R. E. Fox, "OPT *vs.* MRP: Thoughtware *vs.* Software," Part I, *Inventories and Production*, November–December 1983, pp. 9–19; and Part II, *Inventories and Production*, January–February 1984, pp. 13–18.

FIGURE 13–7
Conventional versus OPT Scheduling Rules

Conventional	**OPT**
1. Balance capacity, then try to maintain flow.	1. Balance flow not capacity.
2. Level of utilization of any worker is determined by his own potential.	2. Level of utilization of a nonbottleneck is not determined by its own potential but by some other constraint in the system.
3. Utilization and activation of workers are the same.	3. Activation and utilization of a resource are not synonymous.
4. An hour lost at a bottleneck is just an hour lost at that resource.	4. An hour lost at a bottleneck is an hour lost for the total system.
5. An hour saved at a nonbottleneck is an hour saved at that resource.	5. An hour saved at a nonbottleneck is just a mirage.
6. Bottlenecks temporarily limit throughput but have little impact on inventories.	6. Bottlenecks govern both throughput and inventories.
7. Splitting and overlapping of batches should be discouraged.	7. The transfer batch may not and many times should not be equal to the process batch.
8. The process batch should be constant in time and along its route.	8. The process batch should be variable not fixed.
9. Schedules should be determined by sequentially: • Predetermining the batch size. • Calculating lead time. • Assigning priorities, setting schedules according to lead time. • Adjusting the schedules according to apparent capacity constraints by repeating the above three steps.	9. Schedules should be established by looking at all of the constraints simultaneously. Lead times are the result of a schedule and can't be predetermined.
Motto	**Motto**
The only way to reach a global optimum is by ensuring local optimums.	The sum of the local optimums is not equal to the global optimum.

Source: R. E. Fox, "OPT *vs.* MRP: Thoughtware *vs.* Software, Part I," *Inventories and Production*, January–February 1984. Reprinted by permission of the author.

ing flows of each part through work centers, capacity data, and setup and unit cycle times for both machines and labor.

In addition, it utilizes split or overlapping "send ahead" lots to keep production flowing through the bottleneck centers. For example, a lot size may be 1,000 units at a beginning work center but later may be split into smaller lots and sent to the next work center before the 1,000 units are completed at the current center. This split lot size, OPT has calculated, is the optimal

size to keep the downstream bottleneck work center working at full capacity. Figure 13–7 summarizes the basic differences between conventional and OPT scheduling rules and philosophies.

It is too early to tell if OPT will become a major new method for scheduling for smaller firms, because the cost to install OPT can run to several hundred thousand dollars. However, if a company can afford it, it can be cost effective. One of GE's aircraft-engine plants cut inventories

$30 million in a year by using OPT. And Bendix *doubled* their inventory turnover rate at two of their brake lining plants.[4]

In general, "OPT seems to work best in industries with relatively long production cycles and high material content—large job-shop operations, for instance, such as the ones that build expensive components for aircraft engines or machine tools."[5]

And while the developers of OPT say that it is clearly superior to MRP II, that remains to be seen. It may not be a replacement for MRP but simply an enhancement to the capacity planning and shop loading components of an integrated MRP II system.

ELECTRONIC PRODUCTION REPORTING

Electronic reporting of the progress of orders is now common and is replacing older methods. Large, costly operating machines can be linked directly to the central computer so that their output is reported as it occurs. Closed-circuit TV is also commonly used where there is need for production control to monitor operations closely. More often, however, electronic reporting is less directly online. When a worker finishes a job, he or she puts the job ticket (a prepunched card) into a nearby "transactor" reporting station box, which transmits a report of the job's completion to the computer.

Sometimes, though, it is too expensive to have a computer online. Many companies do the electronic *reporting* as work is done, but the computer updates its records only once a day or even once a week. It accumulates reports until the end of the day or week and then it updates all records and produces a report of how things stand for managers' use the first thing the next morning or the following week.

In other systems, the worker places a personal plastic identification card into the terminal.

The computer then allows this worker to get from the computer whatever information he or she needs, either printed out or shown on the CRT. Figure 13–8 shows the variety of files that are updated by a "job completion" entry in a sophisticated computer system.

EXPEDITING

Expediters ("stock chasers") move troublesome or rush jobs through the plant, find lost orders, circumvent reasons for holdups, and push orders through in a hurry. They work from a "hot list" or a "short list" of orders behind schedule. They are necessary because things go wrong, and they help to get them straightened out. They are a necessary evil because often the only way they can rush things through is to get supervisors to disregard regular schedules and even to tear down machine setups to do the rush job. This is unfortunate because it wastes machine production time, reduces total output, and may cause *more expediting* because it upsets the rest of the production schedule.

Only a small fraction of jobs should ever need expediting. If this is not the case, then the job order planning and control system is not working as it should. There is less expediting today than there used to be since the formal computerized production control systems allow managers to keep better track of things.

"De-Expediting"

There is a common tendency to forget to "de-expedite" an order if the need to hurry disappears. It is frustrating as well as costly to expedite something through several operations and to get it back on schedule only to find that there is no longer any hurry because the end product schedule has been changed. (The same holds for purchased parts which are often expedited and then sit around for weeks until they are finally used.)

One job shop, which fell into this "expedite

[4] Bylinski, "An Efficiency Guru."
[5] Ibid.

FIGURE 13–8
Activities Occurring at the End of the Job Completion

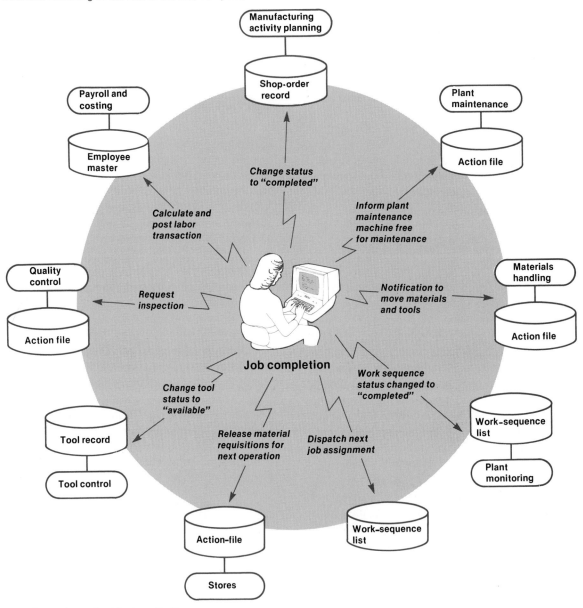

Source: International Business Machines.

but don't de-expedite" trap, had so many *red* expedite tags on the orders in their shop that they outnumbered the other orders. Their solution was to place *green* tags on the items that "really" needed expediting and, when this didn't work, to place *orange* tags on the ones that "really-really" needed expediting. They had serious problems, and of course all of this was very costly until they did a thorough job of de-expediting orders. Again, computer-based systems reduce these problems by keeping track of those items which should be de-expedited as well as those which should be expedited.

DISPATCHING

Dispatching means actually releasing work orders to employees (see Figure 13–9). Normally, dispatching creates few problems, but sometimes there are more orders than the work center can handle; then problems arise.

Earlier in this chapter we said that the work center workloads sometimes exceed their capacity. When this is so, some kind of order priority system for choosing the orders to work on next has to be developed. Generally, the due dates on the orders won't answer this question because the department is overloaded. Too many jobs are supposed to be done too soon. So it becomes necessary to neglect order due dates, at least to some extent, and set up some other rule for deciding which orders should be worked on next and which are to be delayed. Such a rule or rules should be quite mechanistic so that a computer or supervisor or machine operator can make the choices. It is just not possible to use rules which depend entirely on human judgment when the choices have to be made from among hundreds and thousands of orders. We will discuss these *priority dispatch rules* in the next few pages.

We have noted earlier that, theoretically, departments should not be overloaded severely—except, of course, for the planned backlog. But we have also noted that product mix variations sometimes throw unequal workloads on particular work centers when the total plant load contains no overload.

FIGURE 13–9
Daily Dispatch List

07/15/—			WORK CENTER: 224				PAGE 1
SHOP DATE: 172			MACHINE CENTER: 224-50				

ORDER NUMBER	PART NUMBER	OPERATION NUMBER	OPERATION DESCRIPTION	SETUP HOURS	RUN HOURS	LOT SIZE	REMARKS
30824	8024X	030	GRIND	.2	2.5	100	
48299	1937A	070	ROUGH GRIND	.1	1.2	50	SPECIAL FEED
87541	2888B	040	ROUGH GRIND	.1	1.5	75	SPECIAL FEED
52204	4155A	070	GRIND	.2	.7	25	
63714	7629X	050	FINISH GRIND	.4	1.1	30	COMMERCIAL TOLERANCE

Source: Univac, Sperry-Rand Corporation.

Overloads, at least in spots, are common. They come from accepting too many orders for a time period, from changes in master schedules, from product mix variations, from too much unexpected demand from minor independent demand items, from the factory having difficulties and not getting as much work done as usual.

Rescheduling

Rescheduling also creates problems (especially in manual systems) because when priorities among jobs are changed the traveling copy of the job order that goes along with the products is unchanged until someone comes out in the shop and changes it or replaces it. Changes occur frequently in master schedules because customers change the quantities they want, or they change their desired delivery date, or they cancel their order. Changes also occur in schedules of items made to stock as sales prove to be greater than or less than anticipated. In computerized systems, the whole MRP I process is redone every week or so to reflect new quantities, new time schedules, and other things which have changed during the period. When done properly, this can result in a more orderly rescheduling of jobs, and priorites can be kept straight.

Rescheduling, however, may still cause priority conflicts among orders because if one order moves up another may have to move back. If these orders are on tight schedules then some sort of priority system will have to be developed so that rescheduling causes as few disruptions as possible of the more important orders.

By no means is all rescheduling caused by changes in end product demand. Many internal slippages also occur which affect individual orders. Individual orders should always be planned and scheduled as if nothing ever goes wrong, because things do not go wrong on most orders in a well-managed company. Everyone knows the kinds of things that happen that delay production here and there—but no one knows where they will strike next. Tools sometimes will not be on hand, and workers will be absent.

Sometimes an inspector throws out more (or fewer) than the usual number of rejects. Consequently, there are not enough pieces in the lot (or there are more than was expected). Or some pieces just disappear. Or a whole order is lost. Or engineering (or the customer or the Consumer Product Safety Commission) requires a change in the product design so that some operations have to be done over or new operations must be added, others deleted. Or the customer wants to raise the quantity—or cut it—or decides that the order is needed now instead of next month. Or OSHA orders a machine to be shut down and requires that it be safety-shielded.

Occasionally there are even mistakes in the order. It may not list every operation, or it may list a wrong operation, or ask for the wrong quantity. Not all master bills of materials or master route sheets or standard times are always perfect. And occasionally there are errors in the calculations of quantities needed.

All of these changes upset PIPC's plans and schedules. But none of them can be anticipated as probably delaying *specific orders.* Because of this, individual orders must all be planned and scheduled *as if no delay would occur* to them. Then, when delays occur, the orders have to be replanned. People doing PIPC work probably spend more of their time remaking plans and schedules than they spend making them the first time. Fortunately, computers can update everything and reschedule orders so fast that they have made a big problem into a manageable one.

PRIORITY DISPATCH RULES

We have said that scheduled completion dates for orders are often inadequate as priority dispatch rules—the rule which *determines which job to work on next at a work center.* While many companies, perhaps most, choose to work next on the order with the earliest completion due date, this is usually not the best rule to follow. Thus, it is necessary to have other rules to go by to tell each work center what *operation* to work on next.[6] Large departments doing machining work often have hundreds of jobs in the department at the same time. This makes it impractical to have *people* investigate the needs of different orders and make priority decisions. Rules need to be used for choosing, and if a computerized system is in use, these must be in a form which a computer can follow.

Operations researchers have studied the problem of how to decide priorities and have used simulation to see which priority dispatching rules are best. Among the rules they have tested are:

Choose the next job:

1. Based on first come, first worked on.
2. Which has the highest dollar value to minimize WIP holding costs.
3. Which can be completed the quickest at this operation.
4. Which will take the longest time at this operation.
5. With the earliest overall due date.
6. Randomly.
7. Which is due out of *this* work center the soonest.
8. With the most remaining operations.

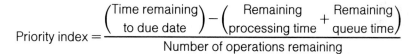

$$\text{Priority index} = \frac{\left(\begin{array}{c}\text{Time remaining}\\\text{to due date}\end{array}\right) - \left(\begin{array}{c}\text{Remaining}\\\text{processing time}\end{array} + \begin{array}{c}\text{Remaining}\\\text{queue time}\end{array}\right)}{\text{Number of operations remaining}}$$

9. With the fewest remaining operations.
10. Which has to pass later through an overloaded work center.
11. Which has to pass later through presently idle work centers.
12. Based on the priority importance of the customer.
13. Which has the highest expected profitability.
14. Which has the least slack time in all remaining operations.

Unfortunately, computer simulation has shown that no one rule will solve all the problems. None will always get all of the most needed jobs out first. Doing short jobs first (rule 3) causes the fewest holdups, but delaying a few large jobs can be more serious. Hughes Tool Company dispatches "hot jobs first." The decision as to which are hot jobs is made by managers and not by the computer. Then, after the hot jobs, priority goes to jobs with the least average slack time between remaining operations (rule 14). Hughes reports that by following these rules it has been able to let computers set schedules for factory departments. At the same time it has reduced the number and seriousness of behind-time orders and has reduced expediting costs. New priorities for jobs for each department are updated in "real time."

Some of the most logical-sounding rules relate priority to the order completion due date. One such rule, that used by Hughes, establishes a priority index based on the average slack time (between-operations queue time) per remaining operation. Orders with the smallest average slack time get a high priority rating.[7] This priority index is calculated as follows:

If, for example, a job is due in 30 days, it has total process time remaining of 10 days, remaining *scheduled* slack or queue time of 15 days, and 6 operations yet to be completed, its priority index would be:

$$\text{Priority index} = \frac{30 - (10 + 15)}{6}$$
$$= .833$$

The lower the index, the higher the priority. In this case, this job would have a lower priority

[6] For a discussion of recent research which documents this, see J. J. Kanet and J. C. Hayya, "Priority Dispatching with Operations Due Dates in a Job Shop," *Journal of Operations Management* 2, no. 3 (May 1982), pp. 167–75.

[7] For a simulation of this rule and certain other rules, see William L. Berry, *Priority Scheduling and Inventory Control in Job-Lot Manufacturing Systems,* Institute for Research in the Behavioral, Economic, and Management Sciences, reprint series no. 471 (Lafayette, Ind.: Purdue University, 1972).

than one with a smaller index. If an index is less than zero (negative), that means the job probably will not meet the due date unless some of the queue time is compressed, as shown earlier in Figure 13–6. If an index is extremely negative (days until due plus scheduled queue time are much less than the remaining operation time), then the order will likely be late even if the queue time is eliminated.

A priority index such as this is very helpful for MRP I-generated orders where desired completion dates are specified. But they would not take care of item replenishment orders which are triggered by reordered points and which do not automatically have due dates. This is not, however, a serious weakness. At the time of the order release, the normal lead time could be projected forward to establish a desired completion date.

Each company should probably do a little internal research and try to develop priority dispatch rules which best suit its needs. The object is to develop rules a computer can follow so that it can handle in a logical way all of the time-consuming work related to setting priorities originally and to updating them all when changes occur. The alternative is to have experienced dispatchers handle priorities—but, often, experience will not be enough because of the complexity of the problems.

OPT and Priority Dispatch Rules

Is OPT, as discussed earlier, a replacement for priority dispatch rules? Probably not. OPT seems to simply develop scheduling priorities in a more sophisticated way, taking bottlenecks' open capacities into account and scheduling work orders at these critical machine centers to optimize throughput.

SCRAP, SHORTAGES, AND LOST ORDERS

In order to maintain control, PIPC needs up-to-date physical counts of items as individual operations are finished because they need to know the "attrition" rate (how many items are spoiled or rejected and thrown out after each operation). The remaining number of items in a lot diminishes a little after most operations. A report only of jobs on time or behind schedule does not show what the attrition rate is. If an order ends up with too few pieces, it may be necessary to send through a rush order for enough pieces to bring the lot up to size—and these orders are very expensive. A materials shortage list is shown in Figure 13–10.

False counts and "disappearing" orders also cause problems. Piece workers sometimes report that they turned out more than they did. Or sometimes workers scrap items and, in order to avoid criticism, throw them away without reporting them. If PIPC believes the job card reports, sometimes they will not know about a shortage until several operations later. It helps here to have inspectors count production output when they inspect the products, if not always, perhaps on a random basis. Woodward Governor handles this problem by making their materials handlers (who move WIP around the factory) responsible for counting parts after each operation.

Orders are lost, too. There are so many trays, racks, or tote pans of materials for future jobs, jobs completed, or jobs held up and lying around that they just are lost now and then. Sometimes traveler copies of the shop order are lost, so no one can easily identify the half-made parts. Or a lot is held up until some of its rejects are reworked, because the lot is rejected, or because the next operation's tools aren't ready.

Every company and department has its nooks and corners where things pile up with no one interested in them until the day when a wild-eyed expediter comes desperately looking for them, or an auditor questions why so much WIP with dust on it is sitting around. Meanwhile top management wonders why in-process inventory values are so high.

REDUCING PAPERFLOW

One of the gains years ago from letting supervisors pass out work orders and control the prog-

FIGURE 13–10
Materials Shortage List

07/15/—											PAGE 1
	ITEM NO. 40000100		LIGHTING MECHANISM			START 277		DUE 292		QTY. 200	
						OPEN		ORDERS			
COMPONENT NO.	REQ. DATE	QTY. REQ.	ON HAND	RSRV. QTY.	DUE DATE	QTY.	DUE DATE	QTY.	DUE DATE	QTY.	NOTE
40200000	277	1200	200	1200	267	400	277	400	289	400	200, SHORT
30200100	277	200	0	200	277	1000					
40300000	277	400	400	400							
10101000	277	400	200	400	277	100	282	100	287	100	100, SHORT
40300002	277	200	50	200	272	400					
30410000	277	200	400	200							

Source: Univac, Sperry-Rand Corp.

ress of orders through their department was the savings in paperwork. It reduced the need for written move orders for truckers and written reports of completed work that central office people used to hand-post to records of job progress. Today, with computers and remote terminal reporting on a real-time basis of work done, the paperwork has been substantially reduced.

Actually, even before computers, there was not necessarily much loss in control if some of this paperwork was eliminated. Unless a factory is swamped with work, most jobs will go through production on time. They *have* to go through because the factory is working and turning out jobs hour by hour and day by day. Workers and machines need jobs to do, and this need "pulls" work through the plant. So long as the factory is not overloaded and so long as the supervisors keep priorities straight, most orders will be completed on time. It is not necessary to "push" jobs through.

The problem is—and computer systems cannot altogether handle this either—that bottlenecks, large and small, interfere with normal pro-

duction. Workers are absent, a machine is out of order for a day or two, more materials are scrapped halfway through than was expected, an order is lost, and so on.

If a good reporting system did not exist, the PIPC department would not find out about delays until the finished item was due. By then the item would be needed badly. Online computer systems have made a double contribution here. They have eliminated most of the paperwork; yet, by being online, they keep the status of jobs up to date.

GRAPHIC LOADING AND SCHEDULING

Almost all of our discussion relating to production and inventory planning and control assumes the use of computers, but there are many smaller companies where the problems are relatively simple and where computers are not needed for effective shop loading and scheduling purposes.

Graphic planning boards, once used widely,

are still often used to show plans and the progress of production against the plans. Productrol boards, Schedugraphs, and Boardmasters have been used for years. All of these use a time scale across the top. Along the left side are lists of machines, orders, or inventories—whichever are being pictured. Bars extend from the left to the right according to the activity being depicted. Control boards are most often kept in the central PIPC office and not out in the shop.

There are other commercial devices, such as magnetic boards and roll charts. With magnetic boards it is only necessary to place metal bars on the board, and they will stay wherever they are put. With roll charts, the chart is rolled from right to left, one day's space each day, and the bars are extended on the chart to the right.

Production control charts are helpful in that they are relatively simple, and they highlight possible trouble spots usually before trouble occurs. A certain amount of work is required to keep them up to date, and they replace no other records. Unless they are posted right up to the minute, they may actually be misleading because here and there they show wrong information. Also, as days pass, they run off the right side of the board, and it is necessary to keep redoing them and moving them back to the left. But they are useful in many operations.

Review Questions

1. Is a shop order for a certain lot of parts an example of producing authority or processing authority? Where does it come from? Explain.

2. What is processing authority? Where does it come from?

3. If master schedules are in line with the factory's overall capacity, how does it happen that individual machine centers sometimes end up with more work than they can take care of?

4. Are machine loads and schedules the same thing? If they are different, where should each be used?

5. How is MRP I related to "backward scheduling?" How is it different from "forward scheduling?"

6. Generally, which takes most of the scheduled time for an order's completion—being worked on or waiting in line to be worked on?

7. How can operations overlapping and order splitting speed up order completion dates?

8. When manufacturing to order, and when business is good, the master schedule allocates the plant's capacity to existing orders for some time ahead. Under what circumstances would still more orders be added to current loads rather than as further extensions of capacity allocations into the more distant future?

9. Differentiate between infinite and finite loading.

10. What is input-output control, and what two costs does it trade off?

11. What are the main objectives of OPT?

12. Why is de-expediting as important as expediting?

13. What is the purpose of priority dispatch rules, and how is rule 14 calculated and used?

14. Manual loading and scheduling has been replaced by computers. Discuss.

Questions for Discussion

1. The factory needs to keep operating in order to keep costs down. Is it therefore bad for it sometimes to go ahead and produce unauthorized production? Presumably this excess production would be for products known to be reordered frequently. Discuss.

2. In the women's clothing industry, dress manufacturers cut cloth for exactly the number of dresses ordered. Then any faulty dresses which can't be repaired become shortages on the order to the customer (and are not replaced).

   Is this a good practice for all companies to use? What problems would it cause in the dress industry? In other industries?

3. The lead times for special orders are one month. Yet under pressure, the factory has from time to time gotten "hot" jobs out in a week. Why not let the sales department really treat its customers well by using one-week lead times for all jobs?

4. "Engineers design products, but they should let the factory decide how to make them." Discuss.

5. A member of the American Production and Inventory Control Society asked for ideas about how to set up a short-cut method for estimating labor for the machine shop, mechanical assembly, and

electric assembly work. His company is seeking "ball park" figures and a nomograph, chart, or slide-rule type method. What suggestions might be given him?

6. What might the production control department do to help solve the "contractor's dilemma"? (When the workers see the end of a contract or job approaching with no other job in sight, they slow down to perpetuate their jobs, or even create overtime possibilities in order to get the contract out on time.)

7. It is usually possible to push one more order of parts through the plant quickly if the individual operations are "lap phased." Lap phasing means to overlap operations and to start operation 2 on the first units finished by operation 1 before operation 1 is finished with all items in a lot. Lap phasing is not used very often in job-lot production. Why not?

8. Why not simplify the matter of dispatching and just adopt a priority dispatch rule of "do the job with the earliest due date"? Would this result in the fewest number of delayed orders? What would happen to long-production-time orders? Is this a good policy to adopt?

9. Discuss the pros and cons of permitting changes to be made after production has been started in a schedule period.

10. An air rifle company, after its Christmas sales peak, has to repair thousands of misused and out-of-order rifles in the early months of each new year. What problems does this create for production planning and control?

11. The customer has just sent a design change notice. The company is already halfway through making the parts affected, so it doesn't want to change. The manager of production control calls the customer and then hands you the telephone so that you, the production scheduler, can explain your problems to him. What do you tell him?

12. Record accuracy of WIP and scrap on the production floor is not too important, because actual production output eventually gets counted when it reaches inventory stores. Discuss.

Problems

1. The customer has, in the last six months, ordered a total of 30,000 closure covers at $10 per unit and has just now sent in an order for 10,000 more. He has always ordered 10,000 at a time, each time saying that he does not know whether he will want any more of this design.

It costs $4,000 to set up for a run of these covers and $4 per unit for labor and materials. The PIPC manager points out that the company could save money by making 20,000 or 30,000 and storing the excess until the next order. It costs $.10 a month to store these covers. And, if it should turn out that the customer no longer wants this design, and the inventory has to be scrapped, they have a salvage value of $1 each.

How many, if any, should the company make if there is a 90 percent chance that the customer will take them? 75 percent? 50 percent?

*2. In Chapter 11, Figure 11–9 shows the final planned order releases for items A through F, which are summarized below:

Planned Order Releases (by week)

Item	1	2	3	4	5	6	7	8
A			10			15		
B		5			27			
C			17	31	1	1		
D		64	93	3	45			
E	10	30	31	82	13			
F			13			12		

In addition, the following information shows the work centers required to make A–F, their operation sequence at these work centers, and setup and machine time required per unit:

Item	Work Center	Operation Sequence Number	Machine Setup Times (hours)	Machine Cycle Time per Item
A	X	1	.5	.1
A	Z	2	1.1	.2
B	Y	1	2.2	.3
C	Z	1	0.0	.2
D	X	1	3.2	.4
D	Y	2	.5	.1
D	X	3	.2	.3
E	Z	1	0.0	.1
E	X	2	0.0	.2
F	X	1	.3	.5

---

* May be calculated with provided software or manually. See Preface for description of the software.

a. Develop an infinite-load bar chart which shows the load in each of the eight weeks for work centers X, Y, and Z. For example, the load in work center Z for item E for week 1 is calculated as follows:

Item	Operation	Setup		Order Size		Cycle Time		
E	1	0	+	10	×	.1	=	1

b. If the factory is operating at a 40-hour-per-week capacity (but with 10 hours of overtime per week authorized), how can the work load in centers X, Y, and Z be rescheduled to more evenly utilize available capacity?

c. If this rescheduling is done, in general terms, what impact will it have on the master production schedule (shown as gross requirements for items A and F in Figure 11–9)?

*3. This problem is to be worked in conjunction with problem 4, Chapter 11. First, answer 4 a to obtain planned order releases for items A–I.

a. Determine an infinite load on work centers 1, 2 and 3, given the following work center setup times, run times per piece, and routing sequences:

Item	Work Center	Operation Routing Sequence	Work Center Setup Time (hours)	Run Time per Piece (hours)
A	2	1	1.0	.05
A	1	2	.5	.09
B	3	1	.25	.10
B	1	2	.3	.04
C	2	1	.7	.03
C	3	2	.5	.01
C	1	3	.2	.009
D	1	1	1.2	.06
D	2	2	2.0	.04
E	3	1	.35	.03
F	1	1	.6	.15
F	2	2	.4	.02
F	3	3	.5	.007
G	3	1	.75	.03
G	2	2	.1	.04
H	3	1	.2	.01
H	1	2	.5	.05
I	3	1	.3	.08
I	1	2	.2	.01
I	2	3	1.0	.03

---

* May be calculated with software provided or manually.

b. Evaluate underloads and overloads (over 40 hours per week) for each week of the eight week planning horizon. Show your results with bar histograms for each work center by week. Suggest ways to level loads: offload to outside subcontractors; add new capacity to the work centers; use overtime or second or third shifts; or revise the master production schedule.

4. The new scheduler has found that the production operators, being on piecework, turn out work in less than standard time. Here are last month's records of five workers:

Worker	Hours Spent on Jobs without Standards	Hours Spent on Jobs with Standards	Standard Hours of Work Turned Out
A	23	145	172
B	5	163	203
C	16	152	169
D	8	120	152
E	11	149	167

a. How much work should the scheduler expect week by week from these operators in the future?

b. What problems will he have to contend with?

5. Part number 127B requires the following operations and has, from past experience, produced the following information:

Operation	Setup Time (hours)	Standard Operation Time per Piece (minutes)	Piecework Operator Efficiency	Scrap Percentage
1	.5	4	133	25
2	1.3	9	120	none
3	.6	2	100	30
4	.3	4	115	10

For an order of 200:

a. How many pieces should be started in each operation?

b. Using overlapped scheduling (where the following operation starts on the first units before the whole order is finished in the preceding operation), how many hours after you start to set up operation 1 should you start to set up operations 2, 3, and 4? (Do not start faster operations until a large enough bank of WIP has been built up to let them

complete the order in one uninterrupted run.)
c. When will the order be finished?

6. An order for an item which requires three operations is to be scheduled. The setup times for the three operations are 25, 45, and 15 minutes, respectively. Machine operation times are 10, 12, and 6 minutes, respectively. Scrap losses on each operation are 1, 4, and 2 percent, respectively. For a lot of 200 pieces:
   a. How many items should be started into production?
   b. What is the least time (using non-overlapping, or "gapped," scheduling) to finish the order? (Allow one hour between operations for moving materials to the next operation.)
   c. In order to start operations 2 and 3 as soon as the order arrives, how many minutes after the setup on operation 1 is started will it be necessary to start setting up for operations 2 and 3?
   d. Using overlapped scheduling, what is the an-

e. At $.50 per trip for carrying products from machine to machine, how much more will transportation cost for overlapping as opposed to gapped operations (where only two trips are required)?

7. The Kip Company has an order to make 50 units of a large part. Its costs are $100 per unit plus $1,000 setup costs. Units in excess of 50 are all scrap, yet shortages under 50 have to be made up. The rejects which cannot be repaired normally average 10 percent. (In this calculation, for simplicity's sake, it is possible to neglect the possibility that a replacement unit would itself be a reject.) Losses follow a Poisson distribution and not a normal curve. (The fewest possible number of rejects, if 55 were started through production, would be zero, or 5 less than the average. Yet, in the other direction, the number of rejects could be more than 5.) Here are the Poisson probabilities of defectives if the starting quantity were 55, 56, 57, 58, 59, or 60:

Number of Rejects	Number Started 55	56	57	58	59	60
	Probability					
0	.0041	.0037	.0033	.0030	.0027	.0025
1	.0225	.0207	.0191	.0176	.0161	.0149
2	.0618	.0580	.0543	.0509	.0477	.0446
3	.1133	.1082	.1033	.0985	.0938	.0892
4	.1558	.1515	.1472	.1428	.1383	.1339
5	.1714	.1697	.1678	.1656	.1632	.1606
6	.1571	.1584	.1594	.1601	.1605	.1606
7	.1234	.1267	.1298	.1326	.1353	.1377
8	.0849	.0887	.0925	.0962	.0998	.1033
9	.0519	.0552	.0586	.0620	.0654	.0688
10	.0285	.0309	.0334	.0359	.0386	.0413
11	.0143	.0157	.0173	.0190	.0207	.0225
12	.0065	.0073	.0082	.0092	.0102	.0113
13	.0028	.0032	.0036	.0041	.0046	.0052
14	.0011	.0013	.0015	.0017	.0019	.0022
15	.0004	.0005	.0006	.0007	.0008	.0009

swer to question b? (Do not, however, start operation 3 until it can operate steadily; do not have it wait six minutes each for items from operation 2.) The transportation delay can also be cut by 20 minutes when overlapped scheduling is used.

How many products should be started into production? What will be the expected cost of starting this quantity? Show the figures.

8. The order is for 100 aerial rotaters, a product requiring several parts which are different from anything the company has ever made before. The

customer makes it clear that he wants 100, no more and no less.

a. How many of part A, which go into the rotaters, should be started into production? The bill of materials for the finished product requires four units of part A for each rotater, and extras are scrap.

Operation	Machine Service Time Daily (minutes)	Percent Scrap after Operation	Operation Time/ Unit (minutes)	Operator Lost Time/8-Hour Day (hours)
1	40	1	2.41	.5
2	28	2.5	6.20	.5
3	17	1.5	0.76	.6
4	44	3	1.37	.4

* Time to adjust machine, oil it, and other dead time.

On somewhat similar items made in the past, the scrap rate of part A has been:

Spoilage Percent	Number of Jobs
0	0
1	0
2	1
3	1
4	4
5	7
6	12
7	4
8	1
9 and over	0

The setup cost is $100, and the material and processing cost per unit is $30. Rejected parts have zero value. Keeping in mind that if there is a shortage it is always possible to set the machines up again and produce enough items to

meet the requirements, how many parts should be started into production?

b. Based on your answer above, should the bill of materials be revised? How?

9. There is an order for 2,000 units of product X which requires the following sequence of four operations. Their operating data are:

How many clock-hours will it take to process this order if four hours are allowed between operations? How many parts will have to be started into production to produce 2,000 good units?

10. Here are figures for a new part used in a wind-powered generator which will take five operations:

Operation Number	Setup Time (minutes)	Standard Operation Time per Unit (minutes)	Operator Efficiency	Time Operator Works on Standard Work	Scrap (%)
1	10	6	110	100%	10
2	20	12	140	90	none
3	50	20	130	100	15
4	40	15	115	80	5
5	20	10	105	90	none

The time between operations is 40 minutes after an operation is completed until the next one starts, but setup can start before the lot arrives. How many hours will it take to produce a lot of 1,000 pieces?

Case 13–1

The Dee Company has had trouble with parts not arriving at the assembly floor. The difficulty has not often been serious but has caused minor delays. Parts intended for particular assembly orders have been made up and put into the finished parts stock instead of being taken to an accumulation bin in the assembly department. When assembly starts, their absence causes delays, because they must be brought from finished stores.

Parts are manufactured on individually released manufacturing orders and show the part identification and the identification number of the product they go into. The fact that some or all of the parts on the order are to be used for a particular assembly order is not shown on the parts order.

Should the assembly order number be put on all manufacturing orders for parts to be used for that assembly order? What if more parts are called for on the order than this particular assembly order requires? Would it be a good idea to deliver all parts directly to an accumulation bin at the assembly floor? How will the accounting department find out about parts orders finished and delivered to the assembly floor instead of to finished stock first? Will it matter if the parts are for two or more different assembly orders? Or will it matter if some of the parts being made are for stock whereas the others are for a particular assembly order?

Case 13–2

In a situation similar to that of the Dee Company, the Elk Company delivers parts directly to accumulation stalls in the assembly area. The assemblers help themselves to parts from these accumulation stalls as they need them. Parts which don't fit are tossed aside or back into the supply bin, and other parts are used. By the time the assemblers near the end of an order, they are short of parts or have only parts which don't fit. How can production control handle this situation?

This problem has also extended into the finished parts stockroom. The assemblers, needing more of a part, go to the stockroom and help themselves. How should this be handled?

Case 13–3

In order not to run out of stock, the Headington Engine Company tries to have all parts in stock one month before starting final assembly. Headington makes large diesel engines whose bills of materials contain several thousand parts, some of which are first subassembled into components which later go into engines as units. Assembly goes on more or less steadily from month to month, but there is some change in the product mix between sizes and types, and most engines sold are special in minor ways.

Assembly orders are released to the production control department five months before assembly is to start (assembly usually takes two months). The PIPC department calculates the parts required and orders them all four months before the month assembly is to start. The parts are all expected to arrive in finished parts stock during the next 90 days. This gives the PIPC department 30 days for expediting any items not on hand a month before assembly starts.

As a consultant, you are asked for suggestions. What do you say?

Case 13–4

Every order for special items is assigned to an expediter who sees it through production. The expediters are somewhat demanding at times. If orders ahead of a special order would tie up all the available machines for several days, they insist on their specials being put ahead of the other orders—even rush orders for regular items temporarily out of stock. They also insist, at times, that machine setups be torn down and production halted on other orders to get the specials out faster. The plant superintendent has finally told the supervisors never to tear down a setup to put a special order on the machines and to let the specials wait their turn after regular stock rush orders.

What lines of authority should be set up to cover production situations like the above? Who should decide priority among orders? What authority should expediters have? Or should there be any expediters? Who should do "de-expediting?" What kind of procedure would take care of the company's problem?

Chapter 14

Repetitive and Just-in-Time Production Scheduling and Control

Almost all companies use order control systems for their job shop operations, but very few companies use *only* order control in all of their operations. Whenever a company begins to receive repeat orders for items or when demand is or becomes larger and longer production runs are required, management should begin to think of using PIPC procedures designed for high-volume *product-oriented* manufacturing. Product-oriented manufacturing control systems have no one universal name; however, one common name for these systems is *flow control.* Later in this chapter, we will see how the newer concept of *just in time* also relates to high-volume production scheduling and control.

LINE-ASSEMBLED PRODUCTS

Standardized products which are made *repetitively* in large volumes—stoves, washing machines, automobiles, farm tractors, television sets, calculators, and many more—are made on production lines, using "flow control" PIPC methods.

A product is put together one or two parts at a time as it moves down a line. People perform their work at separate work stations which are, perhaps, only five or six feet from each other. As soon as a worker puts on a part, the product moves on and another product arrives for its part.

Products *flow* down the line past work stations and off the end of the line minute by minute. *Parts and subassemblies* have to *flow* into work stations along the line at a rate equal to their use. Thus, a main objective of flow PIPC is to match the rates of flow of parts, subassemblies, and final assemblies.

Yet within this flow there is need to control a certain amount of variety in both parts and finished products. Autos, for example, come in different models, colors, number of cylinders, with (or without) power brakes and power steering, and with all kinds of different trims and accessories. Ford and Chevrolet each have so many possible combinations of different things that they could probably run all year and never make two cars exactly alike. "The 1984 Ford Thunderbird, for example, comes in more than 69,000 variations, a Chevrolet Citation in more than 32,000 versions."[1] Yet cars continue to flow

---

[1] John Koten, "Giving Buyers Wide Choices May Be Hurting Auto Makers," *The Wall Street Journal,* December 15, 1983, p. 31.

off the assembly lines. Within this flow there is a need to be sure that red cars get red wheels and that four-door cars end up with four doors, not two. Also, if 50 cars are to have 8-cylinder engines, not only are 50 8-cylinder engines needed, but 50 6-cylinder engines are *not* needed. Not every manufacturer has as much variety as auto makers, but most line production companies have some variety.

Balancing the flow of parts to match their use is not an easy task. Automobile wheels may be used at the rate of five per car, and each assembly line makes one car about every minute. Forgetting for the moment that there may be several lines, wheels are needed at the rate of about one every 12 seconds. However, producing one wheel every 12 seconds may not be the most economical rate for making wheels. Perhaps the wheel production line works most effectively when it produces 1 wheel every four seconds, or 15 a minute, instead of the 5 a minute that the final assembly line needs. This creates a problem. One solution would be to slow down the wheel line by removing workers or wheel machines so the rate matches the requirements of the final assembly.

Or, as an alternative, we could continue to produce 15 wheels a minute and let wheel inventories accumulate hour by hour. Before noon each day there would be enough extra wheels to keep the final assembly line busy for the rest of the day. If there were only one final assembly line, the wheel line could be closed down and the people could be assigned other work. But this would cause wheel inventories to build up and would require space to store them. This would be costly. Often, however, there are two or more assembly lines in the company's several factories, so the extra wheels can be shipped to them.

Sometimes, however, it is the other way around. The wheel assembly line can produce only two wheels a minute, whereas five are needed. Then it would be necessary to work two or three shifts on the wheel line for each final assembly shift. Or, as alternatives, a second wheel assembly line could be set up or some wheels could be purchased from outside vendors.

Lack of perfect balance between production rates of parts and subassemblies and final assembly use is the rule, not the exception; *yet, production per day or per week must balance* and without carrying large inventories. Flow PIPC must cope with this.

The problem of matching parts production and use rates without carrying costly inventories and without running out of anything (if anything runs out, this stops the assembly line, which in turn stops everything else) is even greater for most individual-piece parts than it is for lines producing subassemblies.

Many parts are made in lots (if they were made continuously, a year's supply might pile up in a week or two). These parts are usually made in an unending series of successive lots produced perhaps a day, week, or month or more apart, depending on how their own production rate matches up with the master production schedule's requirements. Fortunately, it is usually unnecessary to use complex order control systems for such repetitive lots because new lots are made so often that everyone knows what the items are and what operations to perform. This saves money because there is no need to make new operation routing lists each time, nor to collect the costs of making each lot, nor to tell truckers where to haul materials, and so on.

Items purchased outside also come in as successive lots. Kelsey-Hayes makes auto wheels, but Kelsey-Hayes can't deliver one wheel every 12 seconds to General Motors or Ford. The best it can do is to send truckloads or freight carloads at the rate of so many an hour, day, or week.

To sum up: Flow control has to keep products flowing off the assembly line; it has to keep subassemblies and parts flowing to the assembly line; it has to control variety; it has to cope with lack of balance in production rates of parts and their use; and it has to deal with parts arriving in lots instead of in a steady stream. Later, we will explore how the Japanese developed "just-in-time" production control methods to tackle these problems.

Finished Assembly Line Control

Controlling finished assembly is usually a matter of controlling the *variety*—seeing that each separate product gets the combination of parts and accessories which is specified by each item's individual bill of materials. Once line production gets under way, the workers soon learn their tasks, and this eliminates the need to tell them what to do thereafter. Similarly, except at first, line assembly eliminates much of the need for instructing truckers about where to move materials.

Instructions do need to be given, however, to cover variations in the product and in attachments, trim, and so on. In the case of automobiles these instructions are quite detailed. For auto assembly, an "order of run" or a "build sequence" list is needed for the assembly line. It lists every car to be made in a day, its sequence in the line, and all other details. Boeing, the jet aircraft manufacturer, calls this sequence of aircraft they are building their "firing order."

For auto assembly, this information is distributed to several points along the line to tell assemblers what items to put on and to tell parts suppliers what parts to "stage" (line up components in the proper sequence for cars that will be coming down the line) at each work station. Some companies use online computers to perform this task. They simply print out parts requirements at terminals located at key points just before the cars come along the line. Also, as a cross-check, every car carries a tag listing the parts and accessories it is to have. This is not very helpful, however, in controlling the parts because people along the line don't get to see the list until the car arrives. Sometimes this is too late for them to get the required parts from stock.

Most line-assembled products are easier to schedule than automobiles. Much of the work in making clothing, shoes, radios, television sets, typewriters, cash registers, and telephones is bench work. Except in the cases of clothing and shoes, all that is needed are simple tools—bolt tighteners, soldering irons, and so on. Most of the people along the line do almost the same kind of work (see Figure 14–1). They put parts in place, or sew them together, or screw them down, or bolt, rivet, or solder them.

This often gives PIPC more freedom to raise or lower schedule quantities without changing shift hours, provided there are extra people available. This applies when it is possible to assign people at extra work spaces along the line. Normally PIPC does not have to concern itself with the effects of minor changes in production rate on labor capacity. The burden of getting more people (or removing some) falls on the supervisor and, often, so does the job of rebalancing the line so everyone will be equally busy.

PIPC in Multiplant Companies

Most companies which are large enough to use flow control are also multiplant companies. Some production control is done in the company's central PIPC department, and some is decentralized. The company's central PIPC department begins with sales forecasts and customer orders for specific products. Next, it determines weekly and daily final assembly schedules for each factory. It also determines the part and subassembly requirements for each factory perhaps with their MRP system. And, it also sets up schedules for subassemblies and parts production or purchase.

However, it would seem unwise to try to formulate production schedules in Chicago for Atlanta, Dallas, Seattle, and elsewhere. It would seem more reasonable to let each factory's PIPC department determine its own requirements for subassemblies and parts. And, of course, it might be better to let each plant develop its own schedules wherever there is little interdependency for parts among them. But it is different where components come in from outside,

FIGURE 14–1
Assembly of Electrical Products along a Horseshoe-Shaped Line

Operators push the units by hand between work stations. Each assembly is mounted on a carriage which can be rotated. Parts are brought in next to operators on mobile carts.

whether from other plants of the company or outside suppliers.

Since supplier plants often have to ship to a large number of customers, the suppliers have to know the customers' *total* requirements so they can plan their production. A producer of fabric for automobile seats, for example, has to plan runs of each fabric. The master production and shipping schedule can be determined more easily if they get one list from a centralized PIPC department rather than separate releases from a dozen of a customer's factories. One of the nice features of an integrated MRP system is, of course, that it automatically consolidates dependent demands for parts. So this centralized coordination of requirement is becoming easier.

Central PIPC departments usually make all of these schedules every week or month. And

there are thousands of them. For example, every month the Ford division of Ford Motor Co. sends out schedules to 800 suppliers, giving them quantity and timing requirements for sending 10,000 different parts to 16 plants. Again, most of these requirements schedules are generated by computers using MRP systems.

These "order releases" from the central PIPC department always show delivery schedules hour by hour, day by day, or week by week, and they also show cumulative figures—how many in total have been released (ordered) since the start of the year (see Figure 14–2). That lets everyone see how the order stands. If *total deliveries* are below *total releases,* the supplier has to catch up. Underruns in any period have to be made up in the next (see Figure 14–3). When deliveries have not kept up with releases, this

FIGURE 14–2
Release against Purchase Order, Economy Motor Division, Standard Motors Corporation

				Release No.: 16	
				Date: 3-14	
Source:			Purchase Order No.: 112579		
XASCO PRODUCTS CO.			Description: Cigar Lighter		
1500 Roag Road			Part No.: 1318534		
Detroit, Mich. 48140					

Date to Ship	Flint	South Gate	Linden	Kansas City	All-Plant Total
Prev. Cum.	109137	34878	38805	39923	222743
Week 3-4	5321	2631	2600	2573	13125
Cum.	114458	37509	41405	42496	235868
Week 3-21	5322	2631	2600	2573	13126
Cum.	119780	40140	44005	45069	248994
Week 3-28	5321	2630	2600	2573	13124
Cum.	125101	42770	46605	47642	262118
Week 4-4	5321	2567	2599	2572	13059
Cum.	130422	45337	49204	50214	275177

means that the customer's supply banks are running low. Or, still worse, it means that they are running completely out of an item now and then so they lose production in final assembly. Again, Japanese just-in-time methods aim at eliminating this problem and will be explained later.

Also, all of these schedules are redone periodically when there are changes. The company's forecasters can never guess the future market perfectly, so there are often changes in the quantities required and the delivery schedule. Sometimes it becomes necessary to make an urgent design change, and again schedules have to be changed. Such changes mean that all of the released orders already out in various plants and supplier companies have to be adjusted and new lists given to them. Suppliers need to know about changes as quickly as possible so they can rebalance their own master production schedules. Everyone's schedules have to be made and remade all the time. Computerized MRP systems are essential to keep track of all these changes when increases or decreases in demand change the master production schedule. In fact, some companies are experimenting with a process where their MRP system is able to communicate directly with their supplier's MRP system.

PIPC in Individual Plants

Each plant usually has its own PIPC department. It takes the hourly, daily, or weekly schedules sent from central PIPC and develops build-sequence lists for final assembly. It also makes specific "loading sheets" to tell material handlers what to put on the supply conveyors which bring subassemblies and parts to the assemblers along the line. A loading-sequence sheet might instruct a supply person to load a blue dashboard onto the supply conveyor for car number 20, a red one for car 21, and so on.

Back in the supply area, the plant's PIPC staff monitors parts inventories continuously. Materials suppliers tell PIPC when these banks of parts begin to build up or shrink. To PIPC, either one indicates there is trouble somewhere. If a bank of parts increases, final assembly is probably behind schedule. If it goes down, something is probably wrong in subassembly production. PIPC usually gets hourly reports, or even com-

FIGURE 14–3
Status of Deliveries versus Releases

Economy Motor Division
Status of Assembly Plant Parts Shipped

Part Number	Part Name	Assembly Plant	Shortage 2d Prev. Week	Shortage Prev. Week	Required to Ship Current Week	Shipped	Schedule through Current Week
1167494	Pointer	FL	1286	3692	6981	39758	46739
1167494	Pointer	SG	1126	3720	6795	45787	52582
1167494	Pointer	LI	704	3129	6144	47042	53186
1167494	Pointer	KC	402	1888	4515	29540	34055
1167497	Pad	FL				52496	52148
1167497	Pad	SG				51437	51052
1167497	Pad	LI				52221	51844
1167497	Pad	KC				35996	35743
1167516	Ring horn	FL			5499	42322	47821
1167516	Ring horn	SG				48525	48091
1167516	Ring horn	LI			4691	29317	34008
1167516	Ring horn	KC			4027	19503	21598

puter-monitored online, up-to-the-minute reports of final assembly's production so it knows the final line's use. But with the thousands of things it must watch, simply *watching* the parts banks (instead of relying wholly on production reports) is a quick way to detect problems. In fact, Japanese production methods prefer *visual* control over using computer information for control.

Subassemblies

Final products should be assembled from subassemblies rather than directly from piece parts. For example, it would be hard to imagine putting the separate pieces of an automobile turbocharger one by one onto a car going down the assembly line. The assembly line is no place to handle small parts. The turbocharger should be put together as a unit and be fastened onto the assembly as a unit. In fact, and better yet, the turbocharger should be put into the engine assembly first, and then the whole engine should be assembled onto the body of the car.

Most subassemblies are made continuously along assembly lines of their own at rates which are paced to match the final assembly line's needs. Problems caused by poor planning are shown in Figure 14–4. PIPC's work with subassembly lines is like controlling final assembly. There is often some variety, and it is still necessary to match the rates of parts production and their use. But controlling any one subassembly line is usually simpler than controlling the final assembly line because there are fewer parts and less variety.

Three things about subassemblies are different. First, the quantities made are usually greater than the final line uses because allowances have to be made for a few rejects as well as for spare or service parts for repairs. Second, the main user is final assembly. If the subassembly production rate per hour does not match final assembly's needs (as well as take care of the service parts requirements), the subassembly line will have to operate longer hours if its rate is slower or shorter hours if its rate is faster. Third,

FIGURE 14–4

"Who needs computerized production controls? When we run out of parts, we just improvise."

Courtesy of General Electric Information Services Company

the main factory usually makes some subassemblies for all of the company's other plants. In these cases the subassembly quantities are related to the company's total needs and not at all to the main factory's assembly needs.

Because of different production rates between final assembly and subassemblies and the extra requirements for service parts, as well as because of the needs of other plants, managers have to reconcile themselves to having some inventories. Once again, Japanese systems refuse to accept this fate, as we will explain later. Subassembly production and final assembly needs usually cannot be matched perfectly. Subassembly lines usually feed their output into temporary storage areas, from which final assembly is supplied. The proper size of these supply banks depends, of course, on the value of the items, how bulky they are, and how critical they are to keeping the final assembly line running. At the same time, should final assembly stop, subassembling will also have to stop from lack of space to store its output.

Purchased items or items shipped in from other plants are a little different. If they come from nearby, perhaps the assembling plant can get by with only a few hours' supply in the bank. But, if they come from farther away, it becomes necessary to try to schedule the arrival of freight cars or trucks on the days when the new supplies will be needed. However, rail service from distant points is not too dependable. The using plant cannot count on getting its items exactly when it wants them, so it will have to carry a safety stock to be sure of not running out if shipment is delayed. On the other hand, large companies' traffic departments watch their freight car schedules very closely. General Motors receives more than 2,000 freight cars and truckloads of materials every day. It is necessary to try to schedule these arrivals to suit the plant's needs so they arrive just in time for feeding the factory's lines.

Parts Control

Assembly lines are the "showy" parts of manufacturing, where the product takes form. All of the parts are ready—they are the right shape, size, and color—and they are ready on time and, hopefully, just in time. But behind all the smooth flow of final assembly lines lies the still bigger job: making subassemblies and making parts for subassemblies. All of their production schedules must mesh with assembly line use. This, as shown in Chapter 11, is one of the purposes of MRP I systems.

Most parts differ from subassemblies in that they are made in lots and not continuously. This is caused by setup costs that make it more economical to have larger lot sizes as discussed in Chapter 12. Yet, as was said earlier, making parts in lots does not necessarily mean using the same order control systems as those used for job shops. These lots are repetitive lots, and the process is sometimes called *cycling*. With cycled lots, the lot quantities are usually set to suit the lines' immediate needs and sent through, say, a new lot every three or four hours, days, or weeks depending on the economic lot size.

Repetitive lots may not have lot numbers and may not use move orders, route sheets, or drawings. Individual job tickets and job-lot costing may also be eliminated since standard costs are used.

If it takes a week to process a "lot" of a part, a lot perhaps large enough to sustain final assembly's needs for three weeks, it may be started into production on, say, Monday. By some time Tuesday the entire lot will be past operation 1 and some of the items will be past operation 2. Some may be even past operation 3 if overlapping and lot splitting is done. By the second Monday the first of the lot will be coming off the last operation, and the whole lot of that part will be finished by, say, the second Tuesday evening.

After finishing this lot, no more of this item is made until a new lot is started through production on the fourth Monday. Then every operation will be repeated. By the fifth Tuesday there will be a new supply on hand. PIPC decides how large the lots are to be (two hours', two days', or two weeks' supply, or whatever). And it determines *in advance* when it will be necessary to have new lots finished and when they must start into production. They also visually watch the banks of parts being used up as new supplies near completion to make sure that the supply does not run out. Japanese systems work differently than this, as we will discuss soon.

PIPC has to watch, too, to see that machines are not overloaded. The machines are used all the time but for successive lots of different parts. If a lot of one part is planned to start on a machine on Monday morning, that machine needs to be free on Monday morning. It cannot still be working, at least not for very long, on some other part that should have been finished last Friday. If the new lot is delayed very long, it may not be finished in time to prevent the item from running out.

Cycling allows most of the shop papers that go with order control to be eliminated. Directions are unnecessary because everyone knows what operations to perform, what tools to use, where to move products, and so on.

Cycling, however, causes many machine setups, and these will be costly unless the engineers design tooling so that it can be put on and taken off machines quickly. This, again, is what the Japanese attempt to do more of than we have seen in the United States. Cycling allows machines to be used for several parts and so keeps the machines busy.

Some companies still use shop documents in cycle orders, however. Identification tags may still be needed, for example, when different parts look a great deal alike.

GM's Electro-Motive Division (maker of diesel-electric railroad engines) assigns a sequence number to each repetitive cycled lot. First, a raw materials requisition for enough materials for the lot is produced. This requisition goes to the supervisor whose department will do the first operation. The supervisor then withdraws the necessary material from the stockroom. Sequence numbers are similar to job order numbers in job shop order control in that they identify the job. But they are also job priority numbers. Supervisors must process low numbers first.

There is no regular shop order, however, so the supervisor has to be otherwise told what operations to perform. This is usually unnecessary because he has made many lots of the same item before. Further, he has an operation routing list covering the operations to be done in his department, and can turn to his book of operation lists if he is in doubt. If an item is not a regular item, he will get a regular shop order, as in job lot order control, which will tell him what to do.

Electro-motive's method also tells the factory's central PIPC office how the lot is moving through production—but only as it moves from one department to the next, not as it moves within a department. Products going out of a department pass a final inspector who not only inspects what goes out, but reports to PIPC which lots and how many units have gone on to the next department. Supervisors always tell PIPC, though, when any lots are held up in their departments. In some companies, completions of each operation are reported to the computer on an online basis.

Service Conveyors

Except for small parts, only a few items can be stored at work stations along the assembly line because of lack of space. Usually it is necessary to use conveyors to supply a steady stream of parts from stock supply areas to the assembly line. These service conveyors are usually closed-circuit loops which move continuously. People in the supply areas load parts in the pans or trays or on hooks from which the assemblers help themselves. (Japanese factories do not favor the use of conveyors for a number of reasons which we will explain in Chapter 21.)

Loop-service conveyors should have many pans, and they should all (or nearly all) be filled as they leave the stock supply area so assemblers ready for parts will not have to wait. Whenever they need a part, they should be able to reach out and get it from the pan moving by. When there are several assemblers doing the same work, say, assembling electric motors, they all use the same parts. But, even if the pans are all full to start with, the last person served by the conveyor may have to wait while several empties go by before a part arrives.

To keep this from happening often, there should be more pans per minute going past the assemblers than they will ever empty at one pass. Whatever they do not use just stays on the conveyor and goes around again. Since service conveyors often come from distant points and move slowly for ease of unloading and loading, it may take an hour for them to move from the supply point to the assemblers. And since many parts may go around more than once, there may be several hours' supply of parts in the pipeline of the service conveyor all the time. Some conveyor systems travel a rather serpen-

tine path several feet above the factory floor and utilize this space for WIP storage.

In the automobile industry, all of the inventories on service conveyors and also on assembly lines are called *float*. But the parts brought to the assembly line by conveyors in the automobile industry never go around twice. Instead they come, one after the other, in the exact sequence and at exactly the right place and the right quantity just in time to take care of the line's needs.

Lead Time

As we said in earlier chapters, lead time is the time between ordering an item and receiving it. PIPC has to know the usual lead times on all items and particularly on all items made in lots or items shipped in. Irregular lead times can cause problems, especially for the shipped-in items. As we have seen in Chapter 11, PIPC determines "planned order releases" for making parts and assemblies and for purchased items with the usual lead times in mind.

It is so easy to say "allow for the usual lead times" that it makes it sound simple. General Motors Assembly Division's PIPC department has to make up several thousand schedules every month just for assembly work alone. GMAD has never counted the huge number of schedules its separate factory PIPC departments make for piece parts!

For a typical GMAD plant, lead times vary from a few hours to 10 days. This variability depends on where items come from, but part of the time allowed is to take care of irregularities in shipping time. It takes from a few hours to 30 days to make parts and subassemblies. It takes five to eight days to ship home-plant-supplied parts to the other plants. Then it takes from a few hours to 10 days to produce subassemblies in the other plants. And, as we have discussed earlier, these lead times accumulate in a chain-like fashion. First, it is necessary to allow lead time to receive purchased materials or parts; then, time is required to make parts and subassemblies, to ship to other plants, and for final assembly. This results in total lead time which adds up to anywhere from 5 to 58 days. PIPC must continually update lead times for every item.

In addition to these logistical complexities, there are such matters as scheduling things to arrive at different hours of the day or different days of the week so entire freight trains or semi-trailers will not be waiting to be unloaded on Monday morning, and then have nothing coming in on Thursday. Furthermore, every time the forecasters misread the market demand, all of these schedules have to be changed hurriedly in order to try to bring production back into line with sales. There are also strikes in supplier plants or a snowstorm or a flood along a railroad. These also upset production schedules and make it necessary to do them all over again.

Again, computer-based MRP systems can, however, allow much flexibility in responding to these changes by quickly updating lead times, calculating new requirements, and recalculating priorities among orders. Small changes are sometimes accumulated and then made once per week. But larger changes might better be made daily or even on a real-time basis.

JAPANESE PIPC METHODS

Our productivity problems and increased competition from foreign manufacturers have created an unprecedented interest in how foreign countries are able to produce such high-quality products at competitive prices—or prices that are lower than U.S.-produced goods. Automobiles and electronics-oriented products such as television sets, cameras, watches, stereos, copiers, and computers and their components are the items we generally think of in this case. But our steel, chemicals, and machine tool industries are also suffering from foreign competition. And when we think of foreign competition, Japan immediately comes to mind even though Korea,

Tiawan, and Western Europe are also fierce competitors.

Our discussion here will not, however, look at the productivity issues of the United States (that will be done in Chapter 24) nor the cultural differences and managerial styles of foreign competitors, but at the interesting and innovative ways the Japanese are approaching PIPC.

The Japanese seem to compete best with us in the consumer products areas. There are exceptions, but automobiles, motorcycles, electronic-based products, and other mass-produced or "repetitively" produced products are where the Japanese have been most innovative in their production and inventory control, purchasing, and quality management methods.

Just in Time

PIPC for the Japanese is best characterized by their just-in-time philosophy toward the flow of both manufactured parts and purchased parts. This philosophy means to them that idle inventories (raw, WIP, and finished) are wasteful, and their methods are designed to eliminate as much of it as possible. This is accomplished by managing the *timing* of the movement of manufactured parts within the factory and the receipt of purchased parts so they arrive in very small lots very frequently—sometimes every few minutes or hours, even from vendors who are located close to the factory.

These methods require a much higher level of cooperation from vendors, including their willingness and ability to design their own manufacturing operations to handle small lot sizes and frequent delivery to their customers. For manufactured parts, setup times must be reduced substantially to make the small lot sizes and quick changeovers from product to product economical. The Japanese spend much energy designing machine fixtures and jigs (part holders) with this in mind. For example, the engineers at Kawasaki, U.S.A., located in Lincoln, Nebraska, the motorcycle makers who have utilized many of the Kawasaki, Japan, methods, were able to reduce the final assembly model changeover time from "hours to five minutes."[2] They simply added a few gravity feed racks to the assembly line where the parts were loaded in the sequence matching the model changeovers.

In another example, the engineers redesigned the feeding mechanism for the dies for a 200-ton Bliss press used to bend a variety of motorcycle frame parts. They devised a roller carrousel track which circles the press for the various dies to sit on. The dies are sequenced on the roller track in the order the various parts are to be made. The mechanism allows the operator to set up the press alone, and it only takes from 2 to 10 minutes to do a die changeover.[3] (See Figure 14–5.) Finally, Toyota engineers reduced the setup time of an 800-ton press for hoods and fenders to just three minutes.[4]

Kanban

The Japanese use an interesting and simple manual system for parts order control which does not use computers. The system, which was originated at Toyota Motor Company, is called the *Kanban System*. While there are several variations of this system, the basic principles are the same. Kanban, in Japanese, means "sign post," and a Kanban essentially is a small card—about four by eight inches—on which information about a particular part is noted. Figure 14–6 shows a typical Kanban card.

There are several kinds of Kanban cards, but the three basic kinds we will discuss are (1) a *production authorization* card (we will call this a PA card); (2) a *vendor authorization* card (VA); and (3) a *move authorization* card (MA). The number of each of these cards that are is-

[2] Robert W. Hall, *Kawasaki, U.S.A.: Transferring Japanese Production Methods to the United States* (American Production and Inventory Control Society, 1982), p. 3.

[3] Ibid., p. 3.

[4] Yasuhiro Monden, "How Toyota Shortened Supply Lot Production Time, Waiting Time, and Conveyance Time," *Industrial Engineering*, September 1981, p. 22.

sued to the various fabrication and assembly departments is tightly controlled, because nothing can be *produced, purchased* from a vendor, or *moved* from department to department (or from the receiving dock if it's from a vendor) without one of these cards being attached or posted in the proper place. It is important to note this at this point, because the number of cards that are allowed on the production floor determines how loose or tight the production control of parts movement is, and thus the level of work-in-process—which controllers try to keep at a minimum. In fact, Kanban cards are removed from the system when WIP builds up or added when shortages occur too frequently.

A Kanban Example

A simple example will help illustrate the Kanban System: suppose we have a "mixed-model" final assembly line making a variety of end items made up of component parts made internally and purchased from vendors. For simplicity, let's look at one final product (A) which is made of two parts of B (an internally manufactured part) and three units of C, a purchased part.

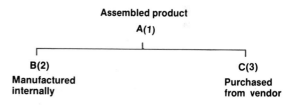

Assembled product

A(1)

B(2)
Manufactured internally

C(3)
Purchased from vendor

Suppose the final assembly schedule (not a Kanban) authorizes the production of three units of A which is a small but economic lot size to assemble because of changeovers required on the assembly line. When it's time to assemble the As, the assembler (or assembly team) goes to their nearby parts-staging area for Bs and Cs (and other parts) and empties six As and nine Bs from their respective tote boxes. (See Figure 14–7.) These boxes are sized to *hold only* six Bs and nine Cs because these are *their* eco-

FIGURE 14–5
Quick Change of Dies on Bliss Press *(sketch of carrousel method)*

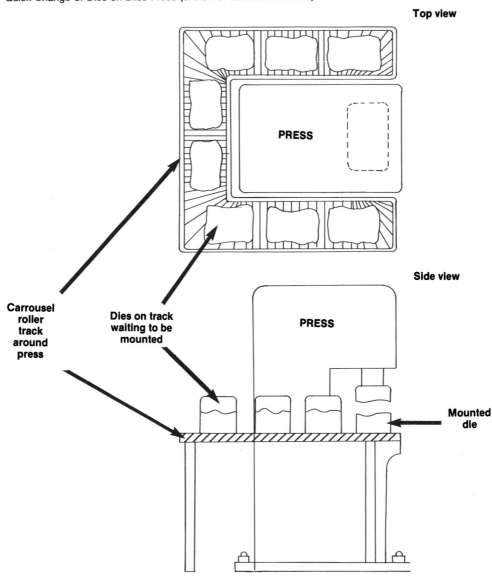

Top view

PRESS

Side view

Carrousel roller track around press

Dies on track waiting to be mounted

PRESS

Mounted die

Source: Robert W. Hall, *Kawasaki U.S.A.: Transferring Japanese Production Methods to the United States* (American Production and Inventory Control Society, 1982), p. 16.

nomic lot sizes. Also, assume there are *no other* tote boxes of As or Bs in the assembly staging area. When the assembler removes the Bs and Cs he simultaneously detaches an MA Kanban from each box and hangs the two of them on

a post which is visible for some distance. These Kanbans *authorize the movement* of new tote boxes of Bs and Cs from their sources, which we will explain later. After this posting is done, the Bs and Cs are taken to the assembly line

Figure 14–6
Layout of a Kanban Control Ticket

A. From	B. Part number		
	C. Name of part	D. Kind of part	E. Kanban number
To	F. Quantity per parent	G. Box number	H. Work station

Source: James W. Rice and Takeo Yoshikawa, "A Comparison of Kanban and MRP Concepts for the Control of Repetitive Manufacturing Systems," *Production and Inventory Management,* first quarter 1982, p. 3.

and assembled into finished As. Since other products are being assembled on the line—X, Y, Z, and so on, according to the final assembly schedule—similar MA Kanban posting activities take place for their component parts in the assembly staging area when they are to be made.

The whirligig beetle. The Japanese call a material mover (not the assemblers, but workers assigned to move parts from work center to work center) a "whirligig beetle" (mizusumashi in Japanese) because this insect whirls on the water's surface very swiftly.[5] This depicts the movement of material handlers in the Kanban-oriented just-in-time system. That is, they make frequent trips between producing, vendor receiving, and using centers, picking up and delivering tote boxes containing small lot sizes of parts.

The flow of Kanbans and materials. Returning to our example, the whirligig material movers travel throughout the factory (usually driving a forklift truck with a small trailer and usually in a fixed path) looking for posted MA Kanbans. When one is spotted they pick them from the post, pick up the empty tote box, and, in our example, on their next stop at the producing cen-

---

[5] Yasuhiro Monden, "Adaptable Kanban System Helps Toyota Maintain Just-in-Time Production," *Industrial Engineering,* May 1981, p. 38.

ter for Bs they do the following: (1) Unload the empty tote box; (2) Remove the PA from a loaded tote box of Bs (located in this department's finished material storage area), compare its information for accuracy with the MA Kanban picked up at the assembly center, and—if it is correct—hang the PA on a post which is clearly visible to the workers in the work center which makes Bs, as well as other parts similar to B. This posting is a signal *authorizing* this center to start *producing* six Bs—its economic lot size; (3) the whirligig attaches the MA Kanban (which he brought with him) to the tote box of Bs, loads them on the carrier, and continues on the route, this time stopping at the receiving dock assigned to the vendor supplying part C. Here, the whirligig performs similar activities done at the previous stop: Finds the tote box of Cs, checks the MA against the VA Kanban for accuracy, posts the VA Kanban on a post visible to the vendor's truck driver, puts the MA brought with him on Cs tote box, and returns to the assembly area where the replacement boxes of Bs and Cs are placed in the parts-staging area. In the meantime, the vendor's truck driver visits the loading dock, sees a VA for Cs, unloads a tote box of Cs, puts the MA on it, picks up an empty tote box, and takes the VA back to his facility which allows him to pick up another box of Cs.

Controlling the number of Kanban cards to achieve just-in-time objectives. Recall that we said that there were *no other* tote boxes of Bs and Cs remaining in assembly's staging areas when the first boxes of parts were emptied. What does this mean? First, if assembly wanted more Bs and Cs and none were there, they might like to post MA Kanbans for them. But they cannot, because the MA Kanbans are either posted, in the possession of the whirligig, or attached to the full tote box. So, if the cycle travel time for the whirligig (to get a full box of Bs and Cs) is greater than the elapsed time until As are next scheduled to be assembled, then one or two additional tote boxes (WIP) may have to be allowed to exist in the staging area. But this can

FIGURE 14–7
Generalized Movement of Kanban Cards and Whirligig Material Mover

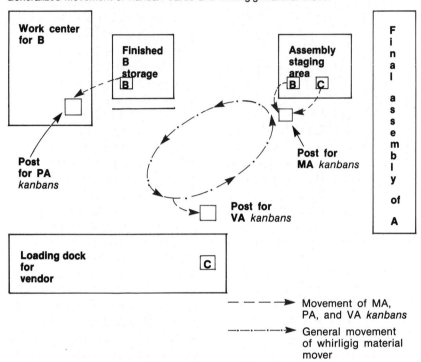

only happen if PIPC people give out one or two more MA cards which authorize moves of Bs and Cs and they are posted. And if the whirligig picks these up, takes them to the B department and C dock, and finds not enough tote boxes to match the number of MA Kanbans, then he cannot post the additional PA and VA Kanbans. Thus, PIPC must also add these PA and VA Kanbans to the system. Likewise, if PIPC finds too many tote boxes sitting any place, they may remove MA, PA, or VA Kanbans, thus tightening up on idle inventories, so the right part arrives in the right place, in the right quantities, "just in time."

Pull System

The Kanban approach is a *pull system* as opposed to a *push* system. That is, downstream (using) work centers authorize upstream (or feeding) work centers (or vendors) to provide them with parts or materials. A setup and a production run of a part is "triggered" only when they see a posted PA Kanban card. This means they only make what is required, not some higher quantity or some other part just to keep the work center from being idle. (The Japanese would rather see a work center idle than have it making parts that consume materials, increase inventories, and need to be stored.)

A *push* system, on the other hand, is what some say happens in a MRP system. Schonberger says, "A [MRP] push system is simply a schedule-based system. That is, a multiperiod master production schedule of future demands for the company's products is prepared, and the computer explodes that schedule into detailed schedules for making or buying the component parts. It is a push system[6] in that the schedule pushes the production people [by releasing planned order releases to work centers] and pushing the parts out and onward."[7]

Kanban Philosophies and Rules

The Kanban System is extremely formal in that specific rules must be followed in a disciplined way. (Some say the Japanese cultural attitude toward discipline is what makes the system work so well.) But, it also requires a high degree of cooperation and teamwork among workers in each work center and among vendors.

Zero WIP and lot size = 1. Philosophically, the Japanese strive for the ultimate: *zero* work in process and a lot size equal to one. Ultimately, they would have each worker produce one part, inspect its quality, and, if acceptable, pass it to the next user, and so on.

In reality, however, this objective is seldom achieved, except perhaps in final assembly operations for simple products where workers are well trained and the "bugs" have been worked out of the system. More realistically, they strive for very small lot sizes and minimal buildup of WIP between work centers or assembly stations.

Cross-training and worker teamwork. One of the reasons Kanban/JIT works so well for the Japanese is that they work as a team to manufacture and assemble products. This teamwork is enhanced by cross-training—that is, training workers to handle several jobs rather than specializing, as is often the case in American manufacturing, especially in assembly operations. In fact, in Japan, pay raises are often given based upon the number of different jobs a worker can perform efficiently.

The andon signal system. To aid in this cooperative teamwork, manufacturers such as Toyota have installed light signal boards (called an *andon*) on their assembly lines. These lights are red, yellow, and green, like traffic signals. If a worker is in real trouble, he or she can turn on the red light. In some andon systems (the Yoi-don system) the red light goes on automatically (after a predetermined time period) if the worker doesn't finish the operation and hits an "OK" button. When the red light goes on, other workers respond to help catch up.[8] This stops the line! Workers from other parts of the line then rush to help overcome the problem. Since workers are also usually trained to maintain their own equipment, they may have to help fix a machine, or simply help the signaling worker catch up so the line can be restarted.

A yellow light signals "Caution, I am falling a little behind." Again, cross-trained workers aid in catching up. Interestingly, PIPC people like to see a few yellow lights on. This says the line is working at near its maximum productivity. On the other hand, if they only see green lights (everything is fine) then they may pull an assembler off the line. Too many yellow lights or red lights would result in the opposite action—adding more people to the line.

Kanban/JIT versus MRP

Schonberger says that a weakness of MRP systems compared to Kanban is that MRP requires some guesswork. "You need to guess what customer demand will be in order to prepare the schedule, and you need to guess how long it will take your production department to make the needed parts."[9] But, as we learned earlier, MRP does allow for periodic updates in lead times and master production schedules, so these guesses can be fine-tuned with experience. Further, Kanban/JIT systems may have advantages for repetitive production where cycle times are

---

[6] Others argue that MRP is also a "pull" system, and that Kanban may be only an MRP-type system with very short time buckets. MRP explosions "pull" components into production "just in time." See Rice and Yoshikawa, "A Comparison of Kanban and MRP," p. 9.

[7] R. J. Schonberger, "Applications of Single-Card and Dual-Card Kanban," *Interfaces,* August 1983, p. 7.

[8] See Yasuhiro Monden, "What Makes the Toyota Production System Really Tick?", *Industrial Engineering,* January 1981, pp. 41–42.

[9] Schonberger, "Applications," p. 57.

short, there isn't as much variety, and set up times *can* be reduced substantially. But in a job shop environment where variety is high, MRP systems are superior.

Vendor Relationships in Kanban

As we have said earlier, vendors play an important role in JIT and Kanban systems. In a sense, the Japanese treat their suppliers as though they were an integrated department of their own. In general, substantially fewer vendors are used than in the typical U.S. manufacturing firm, and this promotes more dependency on both the buyer and the seller. They need to work closely together to achieve their mutual goals. We will discuss this further in Chapter 15.

Transferring Kanban to U.S. Manufacturers

Kanban and JIT methods are not being easily transferred into the United State's manufacturing community. However, something as different as this does not happen quickly, and it is likely that some of the general concepts will catch on as more is known about the advantages and simple logic behind it. The article which follows discusses the difficulties that our auto industry has been having in implementing JIT/Kanban as well as the prospects for future success.

AUTO MAKERS HAVE TROUBLE WITH "KANBAN"

DETROIT—Sushi may be sweeping the West Coast, but here in Motor City the latest craze is *Kanban*.

Kanban is the word for Japanese auto manufacturers' precise methods of controlling inventories so that suppliers deliver needed parts to the assembly line "just in time." Holding inventories of engines, axles, and other parts to an absolute minimum saves Japanese auto makers hundreds of dollars per car in storage and carrying costs.

American car makers would dearly love such savings, but, like raw fish, Kanban may be difficult to swallow. As they get deeper into it, the domestic auto companies are finding that their system of manufacturing cars favors large stockpiles of parts. Changing that system is going to be a difficult and expensive process.

Over the long haul, altering the inventory system probably will be worth the effort. Robert Burrows, a specialist in inventory management at Booz, Allen & Hamilton Inc., estimates that it costs General Motors well over $3 billion a year to carry its approximately $9 billion in worldwide inventories. The costs include storage, handling, staffing, freight charges, and losses due to obsolescence, defects, and tying up of inventory funds that otherwise could be earning a profitable return. GM, Mr. Burrows says, could cut those expenses by more than two thirds.

Some Success

Progress comes easy at first. Anthony E. Ewert, director of materials management at GM's Buick Motor division, found he could reduce stocks of metal body stampings at Buick's Flint assembly plant merely by switching to truck delivery from rail delivery. Trucks now make three deliveries of stampings a day, usually keeping the plant's inventory under 700. For years, stampings had been delivered every two days on rail cars, and the plant's inventory often totaled more than 4,000.

Other auto makers have had some success, too. Ford Motor Co. says it has reduced its stock by $750 million in the past two years, slashing its carrying costs by more than $250 million. Chrysler claims a $200 million reduction in inventories in the past six months.

But as they solve the easy problems, auto executives in charge of installing the new system are encountering other obstacles, including the different geographic distribution of U.S. factories and widespread resistance to change within their companies.

In Japan, most suppliers are clustered around auto makers' assembly plants, making timely delivery cheaper and more reliable. U.S. assembly plants and suppliers are scattered around the country. Some parts take weeks to be shipped, which increases both the amount of inventory in transit and the supplies needed to guard against interrupted deliveries. A GM executive estimates that at any time more than half of the company's inventory is on trucks and trains.

Demand and Supplies

Another difficulty for domestic auto makers has been to set accurate production forecasts. Faced with sputtering demand, the car companies have had trouble judging how many parts to order. "You need about 20 days of orders in hand to set a smooth schedule," says William J. Harahan, Ford's manager of manufacturing planning. "But lately we've been lucky to get 10 days."

The Japanese, on the other hand, have been able to run their plants at near full capacity, allowing them to schedule production weeks in advance and to send exact instructions to their suppliers. "They've got it down to where they can tell a vendor they want a certain number fo parts delivered next week at a specified hour," says GM's Mr. Ewert. "We can't do that."

The Japanese system also is simpler to manage because the companies rely on fewer suppliers. Toyota Motor Co. has less than 250. By comparison GM has more than 3,500 suppliers just for its assembly operations, an amount it hopes to reduce.

Stocking for Options

The drive to trim inventories at U.S. plants goes against long-standing practices. For years, marketing departments in auto companies have demanded numerous options and different trim packages so that customers can practically design their own cars. Manufacturing executives usually agreed to the idea of options because it didn't add much to the amount of labor that went into a car.

But the effect on inventories has been enormous. A buyer of one of Chrysler's Omni subcompacts can choose among several different chrome strips to go on the car doors. Because the strips require different mountings, the assembly plant has to stock several kinds of chrome strips as well as several kinds of doors.

Incentive systems in manufacturing also don't support inventory control. Robert Stone, a GM vice president, says a program to reduce stock at one plant ran into trouble because the production superintendent refused to turn off his equipment when the factory was building too many parts. The reason: His salary was based on the efficiency of his output.

Even the layout of their plants is an obstacle for U.S. auto makers. The Buick assembly plant in Flint, for example, was built in 1946 to accommodate mostly rail deliveries. Now that Mr. Ewert is trying to switch more deliveries to trucks, one of his biggest headaches is moving trucks in and out of the plant's small loading docks. If sales pick up, the loading docks could be swamped.

So far, most of the steps U.S. auto makers have taken involve their costliest parts: engines, transmissions, and axles. "That's the area to begin," says Buick's Mr. Ewert. "You can affect about 90 percent of the dollars you have tied up by tightening down on 10 percent of the parts."

GM claims success at some of its Midwestern assembly plants with a new procedure to control the supply of major components by ordering each morning only the parts needed that day. Previously, the parts were shipped based on an average daily requirement, which often varied significantly from the actual production.

Ford, however, recently had to abandon a similar system for shipping engines from a factory in Dearborn, Michigan, to a nearby assembly plant. A Ford official says sporadic production at the car plant was hurting the engine factory's ability to produce at a smooth, efficient rate.

Auto makers are confident that the new procedures will work better when car sales pick up. But they still see a long fight in the battle against inventories. "It took Toyota 10 years to implement their system," says Ford's Mr. Harahan. "We've really just begun."

Source: John Koten, *The Wall Street Journal,* April 7, 1982, pp. 29–45. Reprinted by permission of *The Wall Street Journal,* © Dow Jones & Company, Inc., 1982. All rights reserved.

PROCESS MANUFACTURING

Processing industries change the physical or chemical form of large quantities of materials. Included are companies producing gasoline, chemicals, paint, flour, glass, rayon, nylon, cement, asphalt tile, plaster, and paper. "Production" takes place inside tanks, retorts, vessels, and furnaces as materials are mixed or heated to produce the required changes. Equipment is connected by pipes, ducts, and conveyors which move the material from stage to stage.

Normally this equipment runs at full capacity or not at all. Changing quantities means changing work hours. Usually, however, large companies have several processing lines, so they can vary production by changing either work hours or the number of lines in operation.

Production is usually to stock or to large sales orders. However, if it is to stock, not much inventory is carried. Volume is so great that a few days' production would fill all the storage tanks or warehouses.

Process companies use flow PIPC, but it varies somewhat from that used in parts-fabrication-assembly industries. The factory receives weekly schedules or lists specifying products, quantities, and production sequences. These requirements lists are sent to operators in charge at key points in the operation where the equipment has to be reset to make different products.

PIPC usually gives few, if any, processing instructions to the factory on *how* to make products because processing instructions are in the supervisor's specification books. Nor are there usually any move orders or cost collection reports since standard costs are used. PIPC, however, does receive reports, perhaps hourly, of production, and at the end of each day they receive reports of the exact production quantities. And they receive reports instantly if anything goes wrong during the day. Online monitoring and reporting by computers is common.

As in automobile flow control, PIPC in processing companies releases orders to vendors. And the tremendous volume (one or more whole freight trains a day) of materials coming in daily necessitates careful scheduling and monitoring of the flow of incoming materials.

This is also true of the outgoing shipping schedules. It takes just as many freight cars to haul products away as it does to get raw materials in. PIPC, however, is usually not responsible for outgoing shipments. This is the responsibility of the traffic manager or the manager of physical distribution. PIPC is responsible, however, for having the materials ready to go out.

There are two PIPC problems in process industries that differ from other flow control operations. One occurs early in production, the other late in production.

Processing industries usually start with natural resource materials which are never quite consistent. Sulphur, iron, sand for glass, wood for pulp, and crude oil from different sources are not homogeneous. The laboratory continually has to inspect incoming materials for chemical and physical variations. Usually there is some variation which must be compensated for. Sometimes all that is necessary is to mix and blend together materials from different shipments. This eliminates much of the variation in the material which goes into processing. Or it may be possible to adjust mixing formulas, processing temperatures, processing times, or other factors to compensate for nature's variations.[10] The PIPC department is concerned here because changes in mixing formulas consume materials in unplanned ways and changes in processing times affect rates of output.

PIPC in processing industries also often has additional work to do in the last stages of production, particularly with packaging and labeling. They have to issue specific directions for the packaging operations so that the right number of each size or package or brand name or the right cuts to size are made.

Batching in Process Manufacturing

In early stages of manufacture it is often necessary to mix and process batches of materials. Batch processing occurs in many branches of the food processing and canning industry where materials are mixed and then cooked. In the paint industry, paints and coloring materials are also made in batches, as are rubber, and pharmaceuticals. Glass is often made by periodically melting fixed quantities of sand. Iron, steel, and other metals are usually made in "heats."

The size of the batch is usually dependent on the size of the equipment. Several hundred or thousands of pounds of ingredients are brought together into batches and put into masticators or mixers. Sometimes, as in extracting metal from ore, the process is heating rather than mixing. Frequently, chemical reactions are involved.

---

[10] Linear programming methods are sometimes used to determine the "recipe" which will compensate for nature's variations. This topic is discussed in Chapter 17.

In batch manufacturing the PIPC department has to load the mixing or heating equipment to match the time cycle for each batch as specified by the laboratory. They also must set finished product quantities so that entire batches are used up. Since batch sizes are usually fixed and only full batches are made, the entire batch usually is made into finished products. Often, as in the case of foods and rubber, this must be done because mixed but unfinished material is perishable. If it is mixed, it has to be made into finished products immediately. Thus, the exact lot size of finished products made at a given time is more dependent on batch-size capacities than it is on the demand for finished products. This results in a minimum of in-process inventory, but at times it results in larger inventories of finished products.

The control system most often used in batch manufacturing is load control. Order numbers, operation job tickets, and move orders are usually not needed.

BLOCK CONTROL

Block control, another variation of order control, is used in the clothing industry. For example, in the ski parka industry, before parkas are manufactured, styles and cloth patterns are decided upon, and pictures and samples of the year's "line" are sent out to the retailers. Retailers make their selections and order the parkas they want, distributed as they see fit among sizes, styles, and patterns.

Since the factory's capacity to produce parkas is relatively fixed at so many per day, PIPC groups the orders by cloth pattern and by style and adds groups together into "blocks." A block is the number of parkas the factory can produce in, say, half a day.

All orders in the block will be released to the plant at once. A new block is released each half day. Within a block, every parka has its own individual number so that the sleeves, pockets, and so on will be "assembled" together into the right coat. All parkas belonging to the same

order also carry the order number, and all parkas in the block carry the block number.

Each parka is inspected several times during its manufacture, and individual parka numbers are checked off as they pass the inspection station. Any parka in process can be located readily from the records at the inspection stations. Departments are required to finish a whole block before "clearing" the block. If any parka's production progress is delayed, PIPC knows it right away, and corrective action is taken, or that parka is replaced in the block by one from the next block.

Block control is both a method of releasing identical amounts of work to the factory at some interval (such as twice a day) and a method of input/output control. It does not cause any more items to be produced, but it assures that no item gets pushed aside and forgotten.

The women's shoe industry uses a method quite similar to block control except that no block numbers are used and individual pairs of shoes are not given individual numbers.

Women's shoes are not as standard as ski parkas, so it is not as reasonable to assume that the plant can produce the same number of pairs of shoes every day or half day. Instead, production control determines the piecework cost of cutting the leather upper part of the shoes on each order. Records show how much money the cutters in the cutting department earn every day, and this is a relatively fixed amount. So, in order to release orders to the factory in an even flow, it is simply a matter of accumulating order by order the cutting cost for each pair of shoes until the total equals what the cutters earn in a day. This many orders, and no more, are then released to the factory for the day.

After production begins, the shoes go through check points where the progress of each order is recorded. Reports are available to the production control department showing the progress of all orders. Often these control systems are computerized, and order progress is captured "online."

In both the clothing and the women's shoe

industries, shop orders are made out showing the number and kind of products to make. Operations are so standard, however, that printed operation lists are used. The list is printed on lightweight cardboard, on which each operation is represented by a detachable stub. When an operation is performed, the pieceworker (nearly all work in both of these industries is done on piecework) detaches the stub for the operation just completed, puts it with the others which he has accumulated, and turns them in as a report of the work done. These stubs are usually readable by a computer system through preprinted characters or from a magnetic strip with information encoded on it.

Block control uses no *schedules* in the usual sense of the term. What begins at one end of the factory has to come out the other end and in about the usual time. If it slows down, this will show up when it fails to pass the checking stations.

Bottlenecks are rare because the size of successive departments is in balance. The sewing department is just the right size to handle all that the cutting department turns out, and so on with other departments. Fortunately, normal differences in product mix have little effect on the workloads of different departments.

SCHEDULING AND CONTROL OF SERVICES

The scheduling and control of the "production" of services can be as complex and, in some cases, more complex than manufacturing activities. Scheduling the repair and maintenance of airplanes in order to keep them flying is extremely complex. Certain components, engines, for example, need periodic overhaul at certain mileage totals, and, when overhaul time comes, they need to be close to the repair base and not 10,000 miles away. Similarly, spare parts may need to be stocked in Tokyo and Paris as well as in San Francisco.

Airlines also have difficult scheduling problems with crews who might have to change going

west in San Francisco and then to wait over for a return assignment east on a later flight. Railroads have the same problems with train crews.

One major difference between production planning and control in manufacturing and services is that service capacities cannot be stockpiled. Empty seats on yesterday's airplane flight are not usable today. And yesterday's empty motel rooms don't help with today's crowd. Nor can a city inventory the idle time of firefighters who had no fire yesterday but several today.

If a service facility is waiting to serve and there is no demand, the product is instantly perishable. Thus, for service industries, the productive capacity must either be large enough to handle peak demand, or service capacity must be increased or decreased in line with service demands (summer resorts put on many extra people in the summer), or else peak demands are just not met and customers have to wait or go somewhere else. Having customers wait or be turned away has a cost to it, just as a factory has when it runs out of stock.

We have discussed several approaches to solving service problems in our discussion of waiting-line models and simulation earlier in Chapter 6.

Order and Inventory Control in Wholesale Service Organizations

Production and inventory control systems requirements of wholesalers are much different than those for manufacturing organizations. Davis Brothers, Inc., a large Denver drug wholesaler with annual sales of about $60 million, manages their $4 million inventory with an IBM IMPACT inventory control system which has been modified by Davis to include special online capabilities.

Their customers consist of thousands of hospitals, chain and independent drugstores, and professional pharmacies. Since many of their orders are taken by telephone, they need quick access to the status of thousands of items they have in inventory, as well as to information about the calling customer—such as their credit rating, current address, whether they are authorized to purchase narcotic drugs, and so on.

Order processing. Their online system allows their customer-order-processing people to sit at a terminal and, as they talk with the customer, "talk" to the computer which contains all of this information. The inquiries through the terminal are made from a "menu" of things the operator can choose from to perform the necessary tasks in processing the order.

While many orders come in via telephone, some customers use portable recording devices whose output the computer can also read. An order clerk at a large drug store, for example, simply walks around the store and "keys" in item identification numbers and the quantity desired. The magnetic tape is then mailed to Davis for direct processing by the computer, or is transmitted over telephone lines directly into the computer for processing.

Inventory management. The items that Davis buys from manufacturers are also ordered by the system. It tracks demand, monitors reorder points, and when they are tripped, automatically generates purchase orders. The system also handles returned merchandise, and when these shipments are received from manufacturers, this information is also put into the computer through the receiving department's terminal.

Order picking. After an order has been placed, the items have to be "picked" from inventory for shipment to the customer. The system prints out a "picking list" and sequences the items on it based on where they are in the warehouse so the picker can make one continuous "walk" with a minimum of backtracking as the order is picked. The system even keeps track of the volume of demand for each item so that heavily demanded items are in the close-in sections of the warehouse to minimize walking time—which can be substantial.

Review Questions

1. What problems are there in scheduling work along an assembly line? Explain.
2. What problems differ in controlling subassembly and parts production lines and final assembly lines? How does this affect production control?
3. In a multiplant company, what activities should the company's central PIPC staff do, and which work should be left to be done by each plant's own PIPC staff?
4. How does cycling operate in the manufacture of parts for assembly lines? How is cycling like, and how is it different from, order control?
5. What is the difference between load control and the subject of machine loads as discussed in Chapter 21?
6. What are the basic elements of JIT?
7. Explain the uses of PA, VA, and MA Kanban cards.
8. What role do setups play in "just-in-time"?
9. What is the function of the whirligig?
10. What do the rules WIP = 0, lot size = 1 mean?
11. What is the purpose of an andon signal system?
12. What role does the parts vendor play in Kanban systems?
13. How are block and load control alike? How are they different? Under what conditions would each be best to use?
14. How do the variations in raw materials as nature provides them affect the work of controlling production in mass production industries?
15. In companies using block control, little attention is paid to the capacities of departments other than the key department whose load is used as the control. How do such companies keep from sometimes ending up with substantially unequal work loads in other departments?
16. How does manufacture by batches affect production control? Explain.
17. How does the scheduling and control of services differ from manufacturing?

Questions for Discussion

1. Suppose that a product has several generations fo subassemblies (a part goes into a minor subassembly, which goes into a bigger assembly, which

goes into a major assembly, which goes into the final product). And suppose that final assembly is continuous. What are the pros and cons of making the earlier generations of subassemblies continuously as against making them in lots? What happens to inventories? To production costs?

2. Are lead times more important in flow control than in job order control? Explain

3. When changing models, is it better to close down the plant during the changeover or to phase new models in gradually? Discuss the problems involved.

4. How does parts manufacture for volume production differ from final assembly so far as production is concerned? What problems are peculiar to parts production? What should be done about them?

5. Assembled product manufacturers using assembly lines often go ahead and assemble a product discovered early along the line to be defective in some way. At first this does not sound very smart. Under what conditions might it be smart? What should be done at the end of the line with the faulty product? What should be done with the parts if they are not attached?

6. At the close of its model year, one of Detroit's Big Three car companies had 160,000 door han-

dles left over. How can high-volume production "balance out" and finish with just the right number of parts to complete the final products coming off the line, yet not have, say 160,000 door handles left over? In discussing this problem one should keep in mind the lead times listed in the text for GMAD.

7. In batch or semicontinuous processing operations, how do the materials handling operations differ from those where under control is used? Would one be more likely to find centralized or decentralized materials handling control procedures? Would highly automated handling systems likely be found in these operations?

8. In terms of the required information flow, how do block and load control compare with job order control? For operations of comparable size, would the work load on the production control staff be less or greater with block or load control as opposed to order control?

9. Is MRP a push or pull system? Discuss.

10. How successful have U.S. firms been in adopting JIT and Kanban methods?

11. Do American workers have the same "team spirit" as Japanese workers? How does this spirit affect the functioning of a Kanban system?

Case 14–1

The Reo Company wanted to make the most effective possible use of its machines used in making parts. Accordingly, it adopted a "cycling" arrangement whereby certain equipment was used on several jobs during the course of each two days. A set sequence of jobs and regular quantities of parts were turned out each two days. In all, the machines in the cycled group were each used for seven operations.

The objectives of the management (getting a steady flow of parts and full machine utilization) were realized. The management's satisfaction in this accomplishment was somewhat deflated, however, when the records showed that one quarter of the pay of the operators on the cycled machines was paid to them for changing machine setups and that the machines were idle one quarter of the time while being set up.

What are the values of short cycles? Are the benefits great enough to justify higher setup costs and machine idle time? Is there any way to work on short cycles and not lose considerable money and capacity because of setups?

Case 14-2

The S-P Spark Plug Company was somewhat chagrined to learn that its spark plugs were being marketed in the city where the factory was located, at a retail price below its factory selling price. A check of dealer records disclosed that Auto Parts-Cheap, Inc., where the spark plugs were being sold, was not listed as a purchaser. The spark plugs were genuine S-P plugs and were of first quality. It appeared certain that they were being stolen by workers in the factory. A careful watch was kept of all finished stock, but the leak was not discovered.

Production records disclosed no disappearance of materials in process, yet APC, Inc., continued to sell S-P plugs at prices under factory costs. All the checking was done without fanfare and was carried on for a whole year. One day, an unannounced inspection of empty lunch boxes of workers leaving at the end of the first shift was made. One lunch box was found to contain a substantial number of porcelain parts for spark plugs. Upon being confronted with this evidence, the employee explained the leak. Three employees were involved. Each took home an occasional handful of the completed parts made in his department. The spark plugs were assembled at their homes and sold to APC, Inc. Spark plug parts were made in very large numbers, and no exact counts were made during processing. Production records were all kept in terms of pounds instead of pieces, and tote boxes of parts were filled reasonably full and then sent on to the next operation. The few scrap pieces produced were thrown into scrap cans at the site of the operation. Generally no check was made on the volume of scrap except for an occasional check to see that it remained within the limits permitted. It was easy for workers to remove a few pieces at a time at any point in the operations without detection.

How might a system be devised to control such a situation? Is petty thievery a problem in very many companies? Should a company institute a regular lunch box inspection program?

Case 14-3

Richard Hamer, newly appointed head of the production control department of the Rigney Foundry and Machine Company, was 28 years old. He came to the company after two years of college and had been with the Rigney company ever since. In a factory management magazine, he read an article describing the operation of "block" control in the textile industry. It pointed out how scheduling was greatly simplified by assigning orders to "blocks" which moved through successive departments more or less as units. The idea seemed good, and Hamer decided to try it out.

He decided that the logical way of grouping orders was to use the molding department as the basis. A block was set as an amount of work which would keep the molding department busy for a half day. Various jobs were to be assigned to each block. Their total molding time requirements would equal that available in a half day. Individual orders would show the block number in addition to the order number. The supervisors of all departments were to be required to complete all orders in a block before another block would be cleared out of their departments.

What difficulties would probably arise in using this system in the foundry? What would happen in the machine shop (still assuming that block numbers were set to equate molding requirements of orders)? Can any part of the block approach be used in the case above? A requirement of block control is that the production capacities of successive departments be equal. How can that be accomplished in the above case?

Chapter 15

Purchasing and Vendor Management

Most manufacturing companies spend more than half of their revenues for materials and component parts that are already made and for services provided by others. International Harvester spends over $4.0 billion a year for materials (59 percent of its sales dollars). General Mills spends about $3 billion (64 percent of its sales dollars) for purchased materials. General Motors spends over $30 billion (49 percent). Service and public organizations such as banks, insurance companies, restaurants, schools, cities, and hospitals also purchase goods and services from each other. Purchasing might at first seem to be a simple task since it is easier to pay out money than to earn it. And it may be easier to buy cleverly than to make things economically. When buying, an organization can get the benefit of effective management just by placing orders with the lowest cost yet reliable suppliers. But, when a company makes its own components, its costs depend on its own operating effectiveness. It is easier to *choose* an effective source than to *be* an effective source.

Purchasing activities are more, though, than just spending money. A person who spends wisely pays less for what he or she buys. If a company sells $1 billion worth of products, it is selling products which probably contain purchased materials that cost over $500 million. The difference between a good and a poor job of buying could well be 5 percent or more. At 5 percent, the possible savings might be over $25 million for such a company. So, even though purchasing might be easier than selling, purchasing is still very important to an organization's productivity and profitability.

In some cases the earnings which can be made (or lost) through purchasing decisions can outweigh the earnings—or loss—possibilities from regular operations. The price of cotton and wool varies so much that textile companies can lose heavily through poor buying. Meat packers and flour millers have the same problem, as do retailers, whose lifeblood requires them to be experienced and smart buyers.

Purchasing's main job is to acquire the things the organization needs when it needs them and to pay as little as possible, considering quality and delivery schedule requirements. But this is too narrow a description of purchasing management. Today, many organizations say that purchasing professionals view their jobs as more than just placing orders. They become interested in the supplier's costs and quality control procedures, and if they are purchasing a service, the supplier's performance record, quality of personnel, and creativeness. Should the vendor need it, buyers even arrange to send their own organizations' specialists to the vendor to help them become a more effective source of supply.

MATERIALS MANAGERS

Some companies which buy large quantities of materials have created a materials manager job in order to coordinate everything having to do with materials. Purchasing is among these activities. So are the operation of storage and warehouse facilities and the control of inventory. While these activities are closely associated with purchasing, they are usually not under the direction of the purchasing agent. They would, however, become part of the assignment of a materials manager, as would the traffic department.

On the other hand, a PIPC department often remains outside the manager's jurisdiction even though it has much to do with materials used and with controlling inventories-in-process. PIPC's closest ties are with manufacturing's producing departments, not with purchasing.

However, this is changing for most companies that have installed MRP systems. They find there is much more of a need to coordinate materials management functions with production planning and control.

PURCHASING DEPARTMENT ORGANIZATION

The purchasing department is headed by a purchasing agent or director of purchasing, who may be a vice president but more often is not, in which case he or she usually reports to the executive vice president, or even to the director of manufacturing.

No two purchasing departments are alike, but most of them buy thousands of different things and usually from thousands of suppliers. U.S. Steel buys 40,000 items from 50,000 vendors. General Electric buys from 40,000 suppliers. Buying so much material and from so many sources means that buyers usually specialize in purchasing specific lines of items.

If, for example, a computerized MRP system is in place, each buyer might receive each Monday morning a computer-generated list of "planned order releases" (see Chapter 11) to work on that week. At Hewlett-Packard, for example, these lists come on microfiche and specify the item, quantity, vendors, due date, and other information to aid the buyer in releasing the order to a vendor. At H-P, buyers specialize in parts and materials groups, and each is responsible for the purchase of several hundred items or more. In addition, their buyers are thought of as "investment portfolio managers" of the items they are responsible for buying— and are believed to be as important in this respect as someone in finance who manages the company's investments of idle cash or their portfolio of stocks and bonds.

Besides buying materials and manufactured parts for the company's products, the purchasing department also buys supplies, containers for products, energy (or coal), equipment, and repair parts, and aids in contracting for services. In most companies the purchasing department also operates the salvage department and sells or disposes of obsolete parts and materials, scrap, and low-value by-products resulting from their operations.

Here are the people whom General Electric's apparatus division purchasing agent (he is a vice president) has reporting to him, together with their specialities:

Buyer and assistant buyer—Fabricated copper, brass, bronze, nickel, silver (except ingot), lumber (including, poles, ties, and the like), packages and packing materials (wood, cleated, corrugated, bobbins, reels, and so on), woodwork patterns.

Buyer—Refrigerator hardware and accessories, asbestos, rubber and rubber parts, molded parts, glass (including globes and lenses), hose, pipe covering, name plates, nonferrous metals except copper.

Buyer—Mica, mercury, polishing and grinding supplies, textiles, rope and twine, springs, leather and leather products.

Assistant buyer—Paper and paper products, transmission appliances (including bearings, gears, and the like), hardware, refrigerator insulation gaskets, packing, and fiber.

Buyer—Large tools and machinery, automobiles, jewels, coal.

Assistant buyer—Steam, gas, and water supplies (except hose, gaskets, packing, and pipe covering), oilers and lubricators, small tools, brushes, and brooms.

Assistant buyer—Oils, greases, and petroleum products, furniture (including typewriters and duplicating machines), roofing materials, steel shelving and racks, partitions.

Assistant buyer—Electrical supplies (including clocks and meters), instruments, microprocessors, carbon brushes, and painters' supplies.

Assistant buyer—Screw machine products, stamping, bolts, nuts, washers, rivets and screws, hospital supplies, stationery and printing, and office supplies.

Buyer—Steel (sheet, strip, and stainless), aluminum (including wire and all forms except ingot), alloys, and nickel.

Buyer—Pig iron, castings, ferro-alloys, chemicals, foundry supplies, factory supplies (except coal, oils, greases, and petroleum products), sand, gravel, and clay.

Buyer—Iron and steel (except sheet, strip, stainless, pig iron, and castings), nails, forgings, railway supplies, iron and steel wire, packages and packing, and tanks.[1]

Purchasing departments are not large, rarely having as many as one half of 1 percent of an organization's employees. But small numbers only highlight the importance of buyers, who spend perhaps $10 million or more each in a year—or up to $5,000 an hour! It costs anywhere from one half a cent up to more than one cent to spend $1. And it costs $20 or more to handle even a small order.

Buyers should know and abide by all laws about purchasing and shipping products—especially hazardous materials such as chemicals. And they should always be on the lookout to see if less costly materials can be used. Naturally, they may not be able to tell whether the less costly materials will do the job (engineering has to decide this), but they should keep materials engineers informed about changes in prices or new materials offered by vendors.

They should also listen to suggestions from industrial sales representatives who may have something new to offer. And, if something sounds interesting they should put these representatives in touch with people in other departments who are qualified to judge new things. Some buyers are reluctant to let a sales person talk to engineers or managers.

MAKE OR BUY

Make-or-buy decisions are nothing less than small vertical integration decisions. But make-or-buy decisions are more specific: this item, this order—does a company make or buy it? As a rule, the more it buys the less a company's investment in machines, and the smaller the company can be. But it also may earn less money because it does a smaller fraction of the total manufacturing activities. In general, the pros and cons of making versus buying are the same as they are for larger vertical integration decisions. But, it does not always pay for a company to "do it yourself."

Purchasing departments are always involved in make-buy decisions because they have to estimate the costs for buying. And, if the decision is to buy, they have to do the buying.

Since most companies specialize in a certain business or service and not in others, some things are obviously going to be purchased or made. It is the choices that are questionable—that are at issue in make-buy decisions. For most items these sourcing decisions are made by committee when each product's original bill of materials is made up by design engineers.

For example, a manufacturer of wind-powered electric generation systems could make the

---

[1] Stuart F. Heinritz, *Purchasing Principles and Practices,* 2d ed. (Englewood Cliffs, N.J.: Prentice-Hall), pp. 65–66.

storage batteries; or it could make the steel required for the propeller or derrick; or make the electronic control circuitry. But more likely, it will buy them all because companies specializing in these items can make them at less cost. These make-buy decisions are more or less permanent, and normally a company does not change back and forth frequently from buying to making.

Since a company usually earns more money on what it makes (if making is advantageous) than on what it buys, there is a question of why it should buy anything which it can make profitably. One reason for buying, in such a case, is that the company is so busy with its main business that it can't make everything it uses. A second reason is that two sources of supply (making and buying at the same time) provide insurance. On difficult-to-make items this is important. If a machine breaks down, stopping a company's internal source, having an outside source will prevent an interruption in production. Third, outside price competition may keep inside producing departments more cost conscious.

Making and buying at the same time has some disadvantages. It cuts the volume both for the inside department and for the outside supplier, which may raise unit costs. And if the buying organization provides tooling to the supplier they will need two sets of tooling, gauges, and so on. Further, it may be difficult to get both the internal and external sources to make the products or provide the services exactly alike.

Sometimes a company buys what it has tried to make because a supplier does it better and cheaper than it can. Ford Motors once tried making automobile tires but went back to buying. Goodyear and the other tire manufacturers can make better tires at less cost than Ford can.

Make-buy decisions are influenced by the amount of money involved. Most metalworking companies could make the paper clips they use in their offices, but for $10 to $20 a year making them is not worth the bother. But add a few zeros and the answer is different. Daisy Company, maker of air rifles, over the years changed from wooden gun stocks (which it made) to plastic stocks (which it bought) for almost all of its models of guns. The day came when it was buying $1 million worth of plastic gun stocks a year, and Daisy then went into the plastics business itself.[2] At IBM, making or buying disc drives is a top-level decision. Firestone Tire used to buy all its nylon cord for tires; now it makes its own.

Make-buy decisions on specific items sometimes depends on workloads.

When a company is busy, it sends orders out, but when they have excess capacity, they may begin making rather than buying. This allows them to have a nonfluctuating work force. Thus, as a company goes from boom to slack and back again, make-buy decisions become matters of strategy and priority. What items or work are purchased or subcontracted first? Which last? Which comes back first? Which last?

Make-or-buy processes and services. Up to here the discussion about make-buy has been largely in terms of products, parts, and materials. But sometimes a decision of this kind is about a process or a service instead of a product. Should a company do its own heat treating? Electroplating? Painting? Should a company buy or do its own research? How about maintenance? And minor construction? Or accounting, data processing, or employee recruiting? The pros and cons for these "do-buy" decisions, and the analysis, are essentially the same as those for making or buying products.

There is probably a bias in most make-buy calculations that favors a make decision. This is particularly true when the question comes up during slack periods. Overhead costs may not be included in the calculation because they are already provided. Making would be a matter of using idle capacity and underused staff and therefore would seem to cost only variable costs. This is true so long as the slack continues. But when normal operations resume, the full costs

---

[2] Recall in our discussion of make-buy analyses using break-even analysis (Chapter 2) the roles that fixed and variable costs and volume play in a decision like this.

of making will be there. Before long, making will be causing its full complement of overhead costs, and switching to buying may also be costly or otherwise difficult—something the analysis may not have included.

Make or Buy in Multiplant Companies

In multiplant companies, divisional plants sometimes make items which are included in make-buy choices for a particular plant. Somewhat different considerations apply here.

If, for example, one division of a company wants to make an item which it has been buying from another of its plants, it will probably be allowed to do so unless this decision would idle a substantial output capacity in the division which formerly made the item. In this case, the buying plant may have to continue buying or take over the formerly used production facility and operate it itself.

Similarly, on items purchased outside the plant, divisional plants are usually given a preference because items are usually transferred at a price lower than outside vendor prices. But, when this is not true, or it is a question of quality or delivery, the buying plant is usually free to buy where it wants to except when large amounts of money or opportunity costs of idle capacity are concerned. Then it may be required to buy from a divisional plant.

PURCHASING PROCEDURES

No one procedure is satisfactory for buying all of the 50,000 items or so that a large organization may buy. Some items (like sheet aluminum for a can maker) are shipped in steadily and, over a period of time, cost millions of dollars. Other items (like the automatic equipment to make automobile motor blocks in a new factory) are one-time orders that cost millions. Between these extremes—steady, high demand or giant one-time contracts—there is every combination of volume, repetition, and variety—all the way down to 10-cent items purchased only once a year. Figure 15–1 shows an overview of purchasing procedures.

Steadily Required Items Used in Large Volumes

For important items that are used all the time, the purchasing department receives its authority to make purchase commitments directly from purchase budgets which are based on approved master production schedules for the months ahead. It does not need requisitions from either production control or the stores department. Purchasing has, in its files, lists of all the things to buy, and it knows how much to buy in order to make a single unit of each of the company's major products. All it has to do is look at the scheduled quantities and calculate the amount of material needed, taking EOQs into consideration. Today computerized MRP systems do most of these quantity calculations and determine the timing for placing the orders.

Most of these items are purchased on "blanket" or "open-end" contracts which may cover a whole year's requirements. Blanket contracts leave quantities and times of delivery (and sometimes price) to be set as the materials are needed. The buying company sends out, several months ahead, estimates of its expected volume requirements but which are not specified in detail. They then follow this up by sending out monthly (or even weekly or daily) purchase order releases telling the vendor how many or how much to deliver and when and where. These releases may be sent to the supplier directly from manufacturing's planning department. Purchasing may not be active in this part of the contract's operation.

Contracts for these steadily used, high-volume items are usually not wide open to competition, except that a company may buy from *two* sources instead of one, just for safety. The buyer-seller relationship is much like that of a company department with a divisional department. Supplying companies often continue certain contracts for years. ELTRA, for example, made most of Chrysler's auto ignition systems for 30 years.

FIGURE 15–1

Chart of a Purchasing System

Step	Activity	Using Dept.	Purch. Dept.	Inventory Control Dept.	Inspect. Dept.	Receiving Dept.	Acctg. Dept.	Vendor
1	Using (or control) department issues PR, TR, or BM.							
1a	Check to see if material is in stock							
2	Investigate potential sources, negotiate, determine price, and select supplier; issue PO.							
3	Vendor acknowledges order.							
4	Follow up activity (as needed).							
5	Vendor ships material.							
6	Receiving department checks material against packing slip and PO; issues RR.							
7	Inspection dept. inspects material; issues IR.							
8	Purchasing department closes order.							
9	Vendor issues invoice in multiple copies							
10	Acctg. dept. checks invoice against PO, RR, and IR, issues voucher and/or check.							

Chart annotations:

Step 1: PR 1; PR 2; File; PR 1.

Step 2: File ← PO 5; PO 1 and acknowledgment form 2; PO 7 & PR 1; Working file; PO 6; Follow-up file; PO 4; PO 3.

Step 4: Acknowledgment form; Follow-up inquiry; Follow-up response; File.

Step 6: Material & packing slip; RR 1, 2, 3; material; RR 4, PO 4, Packing slip, File.

Step 7: Material; Use; RR 3 and IR 3 to using or control dept.; File; RR 1 & IR 1; RR 2 & IR 2; IR 4; File; Invoice.

Step 8: Check; PR 1; PO 6, 7; Acknowledgment; RR 1 & IR 1; Other correspondence; Closed order file; Invoice, PO 3, RR 2, IR 2, Voucher; File.

PR = purchase requisition; TR = traveling requisition; BM = bill of materials; PO = purchase order; RR = receiving report; IR = inspection report.

Source: Lamar Lee, Jr., and Donald W. Dobler, *Purchasing and Materials Management*, 3d ed. (New York: McGraw-Hill, 1977).

Goodyear has never failed to get a good share of General Motors' tire business for over 50 years.

However, this may be changing. Some companies are inducing their current suppliers or new suppliers to locate more closely to them to aid in implementing Japanese-style just-in-time purchasing. Delco Electronics, for example, is doing just that in their revitalized facility in Kokomo, Indiana. "To mesh with Delco's new system more efficiently, many of its 800 suppliers will have to be located closer than previously was necessary. Indeed, Delco has subtly made it clear that those locating nearby will be rewarded."[3]

These large contracts usually do not "travel around" because the sellers treat their customers as well or better on price, quality, and service than anyone else could. Also, these contracts are so large that no competitor could accept one and deliver overnight. He might have to build new factories, tool up, and recruit new work forces.

One exception to this is basic raw materials (materials of nature: cotton, wool, rubber, lumber, wheat, and so on). There are many suppliers of these items, and their prices fluctuate. Here, buyers may not stick to one vendor but negotiate the best deal each time they let a new contract. Buyers should not forget, however, that dependable service is important in these items. It is best not to switch a company's entire requirements to unknown vendors, although they might well be given a trial order now and then to see how they perform.

Large Special Orders

Large special orders are different; they might be machinery for a newly built factory, or equipment for an electric-power dam, or some other construction, or a computer system. These pro-

jects require months or years of planning. Discussions are held with several machinery makers. Alternative designs are considered. Sometimes the advance work takes so much engineering work that the customer pays an engineering fee to prospective bidders. Otherwise a prospective vendor may be unwilling to spend $50,000 on design engineering for a job he might not get. Vendors have to bid separately for every one of these large jobs.

Middle-Sized Orders

Here the buyer in the purchasing department is usually buying something specified in a purchase requisition from the PIPC department. PIPC, for example, may release purchase requisitions for parts needed for making the products specified in the master production schedule (except for the heavy or steadily used items discussed above).

These middle-sized repeat orders are usually placed with the same vendors; but they are not releases against blanket orders. Vendors get specific purchase orders from purchasing for every order. Every new order describes the product and the quantity to be delivered by a certain date. Figure 15–2 shows a typical purchase order, which is often printed by computers.

But whether middle-sized orders are for old or new items, it is common to ask two or three vendors to bid. Generally the contract goes to the low bidder if he is dependable. Sometimes, if middle-size orders are for standard catalog items (and particularly on rush orders), the buyer may not shop around to try to get the best price but simply order the material wherever he can get a reasonable price with an agreement to deliver when needed. Saving 2 percent on an order whose late arrival may cause an assembly line to be stopped is probably suboptimizing.

Small Orders

Small orders are one of the headaches of purchasing specialists. It costs $20 or more in cleri-

---

[3] Robert Johnson, "Just-in-Time Plan to Trim Inventory Can Help Lure Suppliers Near Customers," *The Wall Street Journal,* August 23, 1983, pp. 1, 25.

FIGURE 15–2
A Purchase Order

```
          ALUMINUM COMPANY OF AMERICA          PURCHASE
               PITTSBURGH 19, PA.                ORDER

                              REQ'N NO.      P.O. DATE   P.O. NO.
A-B-C Box Company             510444                    657508
2345 Main Street              AUTH. NO.      DEL'Y REQ'D SHIPM'T PROMISE
Pittsburgh 5, Pa.                                        As Req'd
                              SHIP VIA
                              Motor Freight
                              F.O.B.
Aluminum Company of America   New Kensington, Pa.
Building 242                  TERMS OF PAYMENT
New Kensington, Pa.           1% 10 days - Net 30 days

Please ship the following items as instructed above.

ITEM
NO.   QUANTITY      DESCRIPTION AND SPECIFICATIONS      PRICE

 1    50,000 - No. 3383-24 Alcoa Wrap Cartons,          $183.00 per
              size 12-3/8 inch x 8-3/8 inch x           M
              12-1/2 inch, 175 lb. test, R.S.C.,
              printed 1C - 4 P.

 2            Set-Up Charge for Each Release            19.50

NOTES

 A    Cartons must be manufactured with extreme
      care since they will be filled and sealed
      by automatic equipment.

 B    Cartons must be palletized 400 per pallet,
      with protective cover on corners to prevent
      top layers of cartons from becoming distor-
      ted.

 C    Each pallet to be marked with quantity and
      item number.

KRG:mrw

        NOTE: In accepting this order it is understood the Seller agrees to the terms and con-
        ditions shown above and printed on the back hereof. The Buyer hereby ob-
        jects to any conflicting or additional terms or conditions.

                              ALUMINUM COMPANY OF AMERICA

                      BY _____
```

Source: Aluminum Company of America.

cal costs to process a purchase requisition and to place a purchase order, so it would reduce costs to be able to eliminate all the little orders for one or two items or for 50 cents or $1 worth of materials. Unfortunately, these items are needed and, worse yet, they may be as badly needed as expensive items. They, too, can be rush orders.

Most companies let these orders go through the regular procedure, cost what they may. Some, however, try to reduce their cost. American Can uses the following policies: (1) Don't reorder inexpensive and infrequently used ("C items") things often; order two or three years' supply. It doesn't matter that some day part of the supply of some item may not be needed or obsolete. It is still less costly than buying small quantities all the time. (2) Let departments directly buy all things costing less than $50. Don't

bother the purchasing department about them. (3) Place blanket orders with suppliers; then order by telephone what is needed without making out a purchase order every time.

Kaiser Aluminum sends a blank check (valid only up to a limited amount) along with its order and lets the vendor fill it in. Modern computer systems monitor the levels of these items and, when new orders are required, automatically print out the purchase order and even the blank checks.

Follow-up

Keeping large inventories of materials on hand is so costly that no one wants to do it. This means things are not purchased, or at least not delivered, until shortly before they are needed. But this also means that if anything goes wrong and the vendor doesn't deliver on time, the customer is in trouble. And vendors *do* let customers down more often than either they or their customers would like. So buyers "follow up" or monitor orders for items that are scheduled (perhaps with MRP) to arrive in time to meet master production schedules.

The buyer might call the vendor, write him, or send a telex and ask him about the status of the order. He might even "hound" and annoy him, and repeatedly remind him that he is counting on getting the order on time. All this helps. The vendor may get the order out just to get the buyer off his back. Likewise the buyer should "de-expedite" by telling the vendor the order may be delivered later. This gives the buyer more credibility when he asks to receive his order on time or when asking to "expedite" it in earlier.

Most purchasing departments have a few expediters who do most of the follow-up. Some even go to vendor plants to see if the vendor needs any help. Not only does this follow-up get more orders delivered on time, but, if an order is going to be delayed, the customer knows more quickly—and may be able to change its master schedule.

It might seem that it would be cheaper just

to carry more safety stock to avoid these problems. However, as discussed in Chapter 8, this may not pay because of the investment in extra inventory required to provide this protection. Besides, even with the inventory there will still be occasional stockouts and it would still be necessary to do some follow-up.

Receiving Inspection

Purchasing is not complete until the proper material in the right quantity and of the right quality has arrived. Because the receiving department usually is not under the purchasing department, purchasing must be told (it gets a copy of the receiving report) when materials arrive so that it can clear these "open orders" out of its file and instruct accounting to pay the bill. The bill (or invoice) may have arrived at the accounting department by mail, as well as the freight bill covering shipping costs. At this point, the quality control department becomes involved in incoming materials inspection. They check to see if it is what was ordered, if the quality and quantity are correct, and if anything is damaged. If the material is not right in any way, purchasing is informed, and they usually handle all dealings with the vendor concerning what to do about it.

However, sometimes it is not possible for receiving inspectors to tell if incoming products pass inspection unless they make special tests—chemical, electronic, or other. Normally, for example, a receiving inspector can't tell if a shipment of thermostats for stoves is acceptable. A call to engineering or the laboratory to pass final judgment may be necessary.

HOW MUCH CENTRALIZATION?

When an organization has several (or many) divisions scattered around the country, it is possible to have one central office do all of the buying or only part of it. There is no simple answer as to which is better. Nearly all organizations end up doing some of it centrally and some of it lo-

cally. General Motors decentralizes its buying to about 50 divisions, which in turn decentralize the actual buying to more than approximately 100 purchasing offices. To aid prospective vendors, GM publishes a directory listing all of its purchasing offices and what each one buys.

Buying centrally means dealing in larger volumes, and this sometimes means better prices, possibly up to 10 percent better. And it means more "clout" in periods of materials scarcity. The total volume of any item is not, of course, increased by central buying. But the volume dealt with on a single contract will be the entire company's volume, not just one plant's volume, so this will probably mean a better price, and less time spent negotiating and in order preparation.

Additionally, more specialized people can do the buying when it is done centrally. And, it gives top management tighter control over the entire company's inventory policies and forces more standardization in product design. The American Management Association's report that there is a trend toward more centralization of purchasing in large companies.[4]

Centralized purchasing, however, is often slow and too cumbersome for minor items. The thousands of little things can be purchased more efficiently by separate purchasing departments at the plant level. Also, plant inventories cannot be controlled very well from a central office. The controls are quite likely to become too rigid and not responsive to local needs.

Also, central buying may create a risk if *all* of any important item is purchased from only one supplier. As insurance against strikes and other holdups, it is wise to divide orders for most important items and place them with at least two suppliers. If this is done, however, quantity discounts expected from centralized purchasing are reduced because each supplier places smaller orders.

Freight cost alternatives are also more critical. If high-volume orders are placed with only

---

[4] Reported in *Management's Forum*, November 1975.

one or two suppliers, and if they ship to all of the customer's plants, long freight hauls may cancel out any quantity discount obtained from volume buying. This does not apply, however, if the vendor is also a multiplant company and can ship to a customer's Midwest plant from its Midwest plant, to the customer's Pacific Northwest plant from its Pacific Northwest Plant, and so on. But if the vendor of any item does not have plants close by, it may be wise to let each plant order its needs from a nearby plant just to save freight costs.

Materials which fail inspection and "short" shipments also turn up at times. These can be handled much better locally than centrally. Local buying also gives plant managers more responsibility, and it creates community goodwill.

Large companies usually end up centralizing all buying where large amounts of money are involved or where highly technical knowledge is required. They also centralize most capital-expenditure buying because of the enduring nature of the commitment. Buying is also centrally done where reciprocity (explained in the next few pages) is an issue. Other things are usually bought in the separate divisions. Often some dollar limit is set for local purchasing, and all contracts exceeding this limit must be approved through central purchasing. The central purchasing department also sets up policies and procedures for the decentralized groups to use.

VALUE ANALYSIS

Value analysis tries to reduce the costs of materials by studying the purpose to be served by a part or component being purchased and by seeing if there are other less costly ways of accomplishing this purpose. As mentioned in our discussion of value engineering in Chapter 5, purchasing specialists are usually members of value analysis teams because of their special knowledge of the availability of products, materials, and processes.

KNOWN COST

The known-cost concept is very similar to value analysis and usually includes some value analysis activity. *Known cost* is a term often used to describe a policy of large retail buyers, such as Sears, Roebuck or K mart.

The customer company's buyer decides, for finished products or for parts, what he can afford to pay for an item, considering the resale price. The customer company may want, for example, a man's shirt which will retail for $20. The buyer then searches for a supplier who can produce them for, say, $12. He hopes to get good or even fine quality; yet, the price is often set so low (because of the low retail price) that there is strong pressure to reduce the item's production costs. Sometimes the supplier can't reduce costs to this level without sacrificing quality. If so, a compromise is reached by raising the price, lowering the quality, or changing the order quantity, and so on.

Since the customer company knows the price (or price range) it will pay before negotiations begin, the negotiations are concerned more with the quality it can get for the price than with the price which will be paid for a given quality. If either price or quality has to yield, quality—not price—usually becomes the variable factor.

Buyers for manufacturers as well as retail buyers practice the known-cost strategy.

MASS PRODUCTION PURCHASING

General Motors spends over $2.5 billion a month for materials. It takes over 300,000 tons of steel, costing more than $150 million, for bumpers and springs alone for Chevrolet cars in one year. But a company does not have to be General Motors to find itself buying many items in million-dollar quantities in a year.

These contracts usually are so large that neither buyer nor seller wants to take any chances on price; yet, each wants to be sure of the contract. As a result, these contracts are often written with the price unspecified, and it is settled every now and then during the year. Quantities are also left open and are set as the customer orders week by week. Or the price, if the item is a manufactured product, is often subject to negotiation if raw materials prices change. If steel prices go up, General Motors pays more for its bumper steel, or the reverse if steel prices go down. That way no one suffers much when prices change. Often there are severe penalty charges if the vendor does not deliver or if the buyer cancels.

Quantities required to support mass production are so large that neither buyer nor seller wants to carry enough inventory to last more than a few days, so both try to mesh their schedules exactly to achieve just-in-time coordination. Supplier quality and dependability are often more important than price. In busy times Chevrolet cars require steel for bumpers and springs at a rate of more than 1,000 tons a day; which, at 50 tons to a freight car, means 20 freight car loads a day! Yet Chevrolet rarely carries more than a day or two's supply on hand. In fact, they prefer the freight cars of steel to come in at regular intervals all day long rather than all at once. Both the vendor and the railroad know this and try to time their arrivals to match this kind of schedule.

On the other hand, lead time is very important. To receive steel in July, it needs to be rolled in the steel mills in June. Steel mills plan June's production in May, so General Motors has to place its order in April. But in April, Chevrolet's July final assembly schedule has not yet been firmed up. Of course everybody knows that cars will be made in July but not how many or exactly what kinds. But purchasing must go ahead anyway and place the order and then, in May or even June, ask the vendor to change the quantities to correct for any schedule revisions. All of these revisions require a great deal of flexibility by the purchasing department and in the vendor plant's production control department, but the burden is lessened by the use of computer-based MRP systems.

HOW MANY TO BUY AT ONE TIME

Since nearly everything purchased is bought again and again there is a question of whether to buy few and often or more at a time and less often. For large-volume requirements the answer has already been given: use blanket contracts covering perhaps a year's needs and then get frequent shipments as needed. For the bulk of other items—those bought repetitively but not on blanket contracts—the purchasing department, as we said, usually buys things only in response to specific requests from someone else, perhaps as specified by an MRP system.

Purchasing should not be too passive, though, in following these planned order release requests because they may ask for small quantities to be purchased often. And it is expensive to order small items in little dribbles. But, as we saw in Chapter 12, buying more at one time increases inventory carrying costs, so someone should try to balance out these costs—perhaps by using the EOQ models discussed earlier. Inventory control and purchasing people should work together on problems of how many items to order at a time.

But, sometimes EOQs must be overridden, and companies sometimes "speculate" when buying large-volume, regularly used raw materials. If they think prices will go up, they may contract for even a year's supply in order to take advantage of today's price. This would be risky, quite uncommon, and might need the approval of top management because of the large financial commitment.

Contracting for a year or more's needs is generally called *speculation* for three months to a year is called *forward buying*, and for one month to three months ahead is called *buying to requirements*. Contracting for less than one month is called *hand-to-mouth buying* and is done only when companies are short of money or when they think prices will go down. Of course, such short-term contracting usually results in higher unit costs for the moment because of the small quantities bought on each order.

Standard Quantities

Inventory controllers (and their MRP systems) determine how many of an item they will need in the near future when they release orders to buyers. For items which will continue to be used, however, the buyers should have some freedom to increase (less freedom to decrease) the quantity requested to allow for buying in standard packages, full barrels, and whole bundles. Nearly always, if an order is for less than a standard package, the price per unit is higher. So the quantities actually ordered perhaps should be adjusted when necessary to purchase full standard packages.

On small items, it is often possible to set a fixed quantity (which recognizes standard packages) to reorder every time. Supplies are often ordered this way. So are minor "free issue" items, such as nuts and bolts. Ordering nuts and bolts by the gross (12 dozen), for example, saves clerical time and costs.

Freight Rates and Order Size

This type of savings also applies elsewhere. It often applies where freight or truck rates are consequential. Perhaps the full railroad car freight rate for steel applies to orders of 30,000 pounds or more, but the inventory planner wants only 25,000 pounds right now. The shipping rate per pound is higher on all shipments of less than 30,000 pounds. It might even result that the total freight cost on 25,000 pounds at the less-than-carload rate would be *more* than the cost for 30,000 pounds at the full-carload rate.

Unless the company just does not need the extra 5,000 pounds *at all,* or not for a long time, it may be better off to order 30,000 pounds. The freight cost savings will outweigh the costs of carrying the extra 5,000 pounds a little longer

than usual. Decisions like this, however, should be jointly made between purchasing and PIPC.

PRODUCT DESCRIPTIONS AND SPECIFICATIONS

Purchasing is a matter of buying what the organization needs, but, when a vendor is 500 miles away from a customer, he has to determine from the customer's purchase order what the buyer wants. And if the vendor has several things which are similar, the customer may only generally specify what he wants unless he chooses from the vendor's catalog, where the differences are described.

This situation is not like a customer going into a store to buy a home-use microcomputer, where he can see and try out the various systems. He can ask about them; he can tell the clerk what he wants the microcomputer for and ask for his recommendation; and he can come away with one which suits him. Think for a moment about buying an item like this in any other way. Anyone who has tried to help someone by buying something for them knows all too well that the friend often doesn't like what is purchased.

Actually, describing products is not an easy task. Sometimes, though, it is unnecessary to write lengthy specifications. Often, standards that are generally understood by the trade can be used. Or the customer can specify an item's catalog number, or trademark name, or can furnish a drawing or sample.

Written descriptions of materials or services to be performed are called *specifications,* and they must be used for many items or services which can't be described any other way (see Figure 15–3). Specifications describe an item in considerable detail and list certain requirements, such as chemical content, surface hardness, tensile strength, moisture content, heat content, and so on. Usually the requirements are stated as test scores which will have to be met when the material is given certain tests.

Sometimes specifications have to describe

FIGURE 15–3

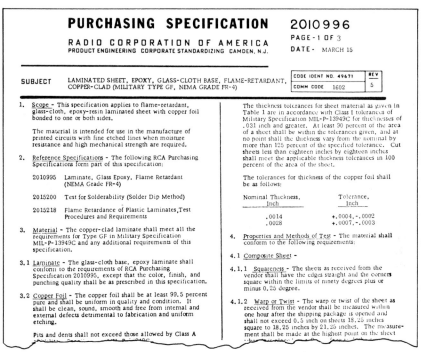

Source: RCA Corporation.

characteristics that are not easy to describe. A surface may be required to be "reasonably free from surface defects"; a finish may be a "smooth satin finish"; a specially made product may have to be "of good and workmanlike quality." These seem to be rather vague instructions, but sometimes it is hard to do any better. Service specifications can also be rather detailed. For example, specifications for subcontracting out janitorial services may include detailed descriptions of what is to be cleaned, how frequently, the kinds of cleaning materials to be used, and so on.

Sometimes, in purchasing, the customer has a choice of ordering a brand-name item or of ordering its generic equivalent by specification. (Industry has used generic brands for years—and now supermarkets are expanding their generic line of products). Choices are available with wire, chemicals, cement, flour, tool steel, cutting oils, grinding wheels, cleaning compounds,

paints, and so on. All of these can be bought by using the vendor's trademark or catalog numbers. Or the customer company can ignore these and write his own specifications, stating what he wants in the way of chemical composition, size, performance requirements, and so on.

When a customer company buys all of its large quantities by specification, it will usually save money. It gets exactly what it wants. Trademark items may not be just right for a given job—maybe they are too good, or not good enough. Also, trademarked items are advertised, and people who buy those items pay for the advertising.

On small orders, on the other hand, specification buying will probably cost more than buying trademarked materials. If the vendor has to make a special run of materials for an order, the cost of the special item may be more than the price of trademarked items. In general, for small quantities of anything, the buyer should choose trademarked items.

Vendor Participation in Product Specifications

There is a trend these days, however, to delegate some of the responsibility for determining the specifications of purchased parts to the vendor. Often, the specifications provided by the company to the vendor are too rigid and specify materials and tolerances which are "over-engineered" for its use. The Japanese have used this philosophy for some time. In a sense, it is a way to make the supplier a partner in value engineering or value analysis, as discussed in Chapter 5. For example, Schonberger reports that:

> Kawasaki [in Lincoln, Nebraska] buyers sometimes ask suppliers for recommendations rather than rigidly specifying. The idea is to let a supplier innovate and also allow the buyer some discretion in evaluating the supplier's proposals. After all, the supplier is the expert. A performance-oriented spec package might consist of only a blueprint with only critical dimensions. Type of material may need to be specified, but sometimes strength characteristics, type of finish, and so forth are sufficient. Even the finish may not need to be precisely specified: Kawaski calls for only "an appropriate polymer coating" on some parts. The spec package avoids restrictions that dictate how the product is to be made, leaving the supplier some freedom of choice on whether to stamp or drill, cast or weld, grind or mill. For example, TRICON [a seat supplier to Kawasaki] buys seat pans based on blueprints that call for 12-gauge cold rolled steel, give key dimensions, and describe the desired finish—but give no other specifications.[5]

Schonberger reports that suppliers sometimes are not used to working this way and sometimes refuse to supply a bid for component parts because they get nervous about the looseness of the specifications. However, in general, it aids

in achieving JIT methods because it gives the supplier more flexibility.

CHOOSING VENDORS

The purchasing department nearly always decides which vendors to buy from. Equipment purchases are usually an exception; so are some trademarked items that engineering or someone else insists on; and so are reciprocity situations where top management tells the purchasing department whom to buy from.

To choose vendors intelligently, the purchasing department's buyers need to know which things are sold by which companies. This they learn from sales representatives who call on them and from advertisements in technical and trade directories and buyers' guides. Also, they maintain an up-to-date file of catalogs of vendor companies and their price and discount lists.

In deciding who gets an oder, buyers should consider several factors. Price, important though it is, is not the only thing. Reliability usually is more important than small price differences. Can and will the vendor company deliver the order on time? Will the materials pass inspection after they arrive? If they don't, will the vendor be responsive without argument? Schedule changes may also be a factor. Can and will the vendor handle schedule changes and rush orders? How about service if something goes wrong? Or will he extend credit? Any of these matters might be important.

Assuming that all other factors are equal, often it is still not completely clear which vendor's price is the lowest. In the following case, for example, which vendor should be chosen? Each of the vendors has submitted a bid in which a separate charge is listed for the special tooling which will be required plus an additional charge per unit with or without volume discounts.

Vendor	Tool Charge	Price per Unit	Discount for Volume	
			Price	Volume over
A	$220	$.80	$.70	1,000
B	320	.72	.60	3,000
C	180	.96	.85	500

---

[5] R. J. Schonberger, *Japanese Manufacturing Techniques* (New York: Free Press, 1982), pp. 165–66.

This problem can be solved with the break-even method described in Chapter 2. The least-cost choice would be the vendor with the *lower tool cost* for all volumes below the crossover point and the vendor with the *lower unit cost* for volumes above the crossover point.

To compare A and B at regular prices:

$$220 + .80x = 320 + .72x$$
$$.08x = 100$$
$$\text{Crossover point} = x = 1,250$$

For volumes at or below 1,250 units, the choice is vendor A; above 1,250 units it should be B. Actually, this particular comparison yields an irrelevant answer because at 1,250 units, B's volume discount price would not be in effect, while A's would be.

In our example there are 12 crossover points required before a decision can be made. Of these 12, only 2 are useful. Figure 15–4 shows the 12 crossover points. The stars indicate nonapplicable points because the price used in the calculation does not apply because of the quantity discount schedules.

In summary, only the two crossover points of A-regular prices with C-regular prices and C-discount prices are feasible. Because of C's low tool charge, orders should be given to vendor C at regular prices for volumes up to 250 units. Above 250 units, orders should be given to A at regular prices. At 500 units (this does not show in Figure 15–4) C's discount price is available ($.85), and orders should be shifted to C. But for orders of 800 or more, A's regular price of $.70 produces less total cost per unit—and at 1,000 units or more it drops even more. There is no volume where B should receive any orders at all, if prices are the main consideration.

Vendor Rating and Certification

Some organizations use vendor-rating systems which monitor vendor performance on a number of factors including price, delivery, quality, service, and geographic location. Figure 15–5 shows the range of factors that purchasing specialists consider to be relevant and their relative importance (at the time this study was conducted). Figure 15–6 shows how these factors vary in importance for various purchasing situations. Some companies—IBM, for example—"certify" their vendors if they meet certain qualifications. This aids buyers in choosing vendors because someone has already evaluated their performance and found them to meet their qualifications. This should not prevent buyers, however, from bargaining hard with these vendors or from using other sources which have superior prices, products, or service. The buyer may try them, and then after they have proven themselves, they too can become certified vendors.

Affirmative Action Purchasing

Most large organizations, both private and public, have established a policy of buying a portion of their goods and services from minority-owned suppliers who can provide as good or better prices and services as nonminority suppliers.

The main reasons for establishing these "affirmative action" purchasing programs are to increase business opportunities for minority firms; to buy from the minority community—not just to sell to it; to generate jobs for minorities; and to fulfill a company's social responsibility.[6]

FIGURE 15–4

| | Break-Even Quantity | | | |
	B Reg-ular	B Dis-count	C Reg-ular	C Dis-count
A Regular	1,250*	500*	250	800
A Discount	−5,000*	1,000*	154*	267*
B Regular			583*	1,077*
B Discount			389*	560*

* Nonapplicable answer.

---

[6] See Thaddeus H. Stratlen, "The Impact of Affirmative Action Purchasing," *Journal of Purchasing and Materials Management,* Spring 1978, p. 6. (Page 8 presents a good outline for developing an affirmative action purchasing program.)

FIGURE 15–5
Vendor Rating Factors

Factor	Mean Rating	Evaluation
Quality	3.508	Extreme importance
Delivery	3.417	
Performance history	2.998	
Warranties and claims policies	2.849	
Production facilities and capacity	2.775	Considerable importance
Price	2.758	
Technical capability	2.545	
Financial position	2.514	
Procedural compliance	2.488	
Communication system	2.426	
Reputation and position in industry	2.412	
Desire for business	2.256	
Management and organization	2.216	
Operating controls	2.211	
Repair service	2.187	Average importance
Attitude	2.120	
Impression	2.054	
Packaging ability	2.009	
Labor relations record	2.003	
Geographical location	1.872	
Amount of past business	1.597	
Training aids	1.537	
Reciprocal arrangements	0.610	Slight importance

Source: In Wilbur B. England and Michiel R. Leenders, *Purchasing and Materials Management,* 6th ed. (Homewood, Ill.: Richard D. Irwin, 1975), p. 436.

Some organizations set minority purchasing objectives—say, 1 or 2 percent of all the value of all their purchases, or some number of minority vendor purchases per buyer per year, and so on. While the amount purchased from minority vendors is still less than 1 percent of total industrial purchases, this percentage is increasing at a rapid rate and will become a more important consideration for purchasing specialists in the 1980s.

Vendor Turnover as a Control Tool

One way for management to keep the purchasing department effective is to measure the turnover of vendors that are used—adding new vendors and discarding others whose service/

price/quality may no longer be competitive. It is only human nature to continue using vendors who have been used in the past. Relationships are formed, procedures are known, friends are made, and Christmas turkeys and liquor are nice to receive from vendors. But, this may lead to both buyer and vendor apathy, and price, quality, and service may deteriorate.

One expert has suggested that a purchasing department should have at least an annual turnover of from 5–10 percent of its vendors, and that this would result in a savings of 1.5 to 3.5 percent of total purchasing expenditures[7]—which could amount to several million dollars

---

[7] See J. Charles Miller, "Supplier Turnover Rate as a Purchasing Management Tool," *Journal of Purchasing and Materials Management,* Spring 1978, pp. 16–17.

FIGURE 15–6
Vendor Rating Factor Importance for Various Purchasing Situations

Importance Rank	Case A: Paint	Case B: Desks	Case C: Computer	Case D: Art Work
1	Quality	Price	Quality	Delivery
2	Warranties	Quality	Technical capability	Production capacity
3	Delivery	Delivery	Delivery	Quality
4	Performance history	Warranties	Production capacity	Performance history
5	Price	Performance history	Performance history	Communication system

Source: In Wilbur B. England and Michiel R. Leenders, *Purchasing and Materials Management,* 6th ed. (Homewood, Ill.: Richard D. Irwin, 1975), p. 436.

for a large company. Setting turnover objectives and monitoring them can aid in pinpointing complacent and incompetent buyers, reduce unqualified suppliers, and guard against collusive and unethical practices.

How Many Vendors?

As mentioned earlier, some companies deal with thousands of different vendors. The Japanese, however, use on the whole many fewer vendors than U.S. firms. They find it easier to deal with fewer vendors and also find it has some economies of scale. If a vendor knows they will be getting a larger share of their customer's business, they tend to give better services, prices, and quality. They become an "extension" of their customer and realize their success depends on the success of their customer base. A vendor, for example, may invest more heavily in automated production and quality control equipment, as a result of higher volumes being made, and pass these economies on to their customers. And, with larger outputs, the labor force may be operating at a lower point on their learning curve (as discussed in Chapter 10) with more savings. While this can be risky for both sides—customers and vendors—because of the "too-many-eggs-in-one-basket" concept, some balance can be struck to gain the advantages of

fewer vendors while minimizing the risky side of having too few.

RECIPROCITY

"Dear Red," wrote FMC Corporation's board chairman to a Ford Motor Company vice president. "This is just a note to express appreciation for the good news we had, that your company had decided to purchase part of your Nashville requirements for soda ash from our company.

"Effective as of now, wherever possible, our people are to purchase Ford products. I believe that our salesman and service fleet now amounts to 600 to 700 cars. As you know, our two company-chauffeured cars are Continentals which we buy new each year, and our family has only Continentals."

It took a court order to unearth this letter in a Federal Trade Commission investigation of reciprocity practices. Thus, reciprocity is industry's version of "You scratch my back and I'll scratch yours"—or you buy from me and I'll buy from you. Back in the old days, when Henry Ford and Harvey Firestone were alive, they were friends; so Henry put Firestone tires on most new Fords, and Harvey used Ford cars and trucks in his tire company.

Buying from each other sounds reasonable, although most people—particularly purchasing agents—condemn it. Most companies even deny they practice it; but, on the other hand, they don't give customers a cold shoulder when they place purchase contracts. That would be a good way to lose customers. Customers are not at all above asking "If we buy from you, you are going to buy from us?

The FMC board chairman, for example, also sent a "Dear Roger" letter to the head of U.S. Steel in which he pointed out that FMC had bought $3,446,000 worth of U.S. Steel products whereas U.S. Steel had bought only $453,000 worth of products from FMC. Then he wrote: "I wish you would send my letter to whoever is in charge of reciprocity for your company and would see that they are alerted to our relationship with your company. There are a number of chemicals which we are in a position to sell your company." He suggested that an FMC vice president meet with the proper U.S. Steel executive. In many companies the reciprocity person is called the *trade relations representative.*

Actually, every company has to buy from someone, so it is not surprising that reciprocity is a common practice. Purchasing agents regard it as a necessary evil. But one might ask what is bad about it? Does it matter what make of steel filing case is used in the office? Or whether salesmen drive Chevrolets or Fords? Why shouldn't purchasing agents face up to the fact that the company has customers?

Purchasing agents don't like reciprocity because they are forced to buy some item where they are told to and can't shop around. They are afraid they might have to accept inferior materials or pay higher prices and receive poorer service. This would not be particularly important for supply items which are consumed in production, but it could be quite important for materials and components to go into finished products.

It is true that all of these things *may* occur— and some of them *will* occur once in a while. But purchasing agents look at only one side of the coin. A company may lose a little on the buying side, but it might also gain on the selling side. Surely a company may receive some sales

where its products are not the very best or least costly because of reciprocity.

If reciprocity harms anyone, it is small companies. They don't buy enough volume to command much attention. Large companies often have to buy from their large customers to keep them. Their big customers demand it! Small customers demanding a share of what a large supplier company buys rarely get very far with their threat to buy elsewhere. Actually, though, even small customers often manage some sales to large companies—which try to satisfy *all* their customers by allocating their ordering at least a little.

Every now and then the Federal Trade Commission strikes out against reciprocity. But, although its interest in reciprocity started a decade or more ago, the FTC has not been aggressive enough to curtail the practice very much.

BIDDING VERSUS NEGOTIATED CONTRACTS

When the government lets contracts, normally it is supposed to ask for bids and take the lowest price, provided the lowest bidder is deemed capable of fulfilling the contract. Private industry is not required to do this. Sometimes private organizations don't even ask for bids but just negotiate with their main supplier and agree on a contract—price and all. This is called *sole source* contracting.

At first sole sourcing does not sound very effective because the company cannot be sure that it is getting the best possible deal. But, in fact, the purchasing agent usually has a pretty good idea because either his own company makes similar items so he knows the company's cost, or he occasionally asks for bids from other companies. Or, possibly, he will have his company's engineers evaluate the vendor's expected cost figures to be sure they are reasonably efficient and that their price is reasonable. In practice, some of the largest purchase contracts are negotiated and not put out for bids.

On the other hand, most middle-size orders

and most large special contracts are put out for bids. And, if the purchasing agent does not give the contract to the lowest bidder, at least the one who gets it has to be near the lowest bid. Buyers, supposedly, should always choose the lowest dollar bid from among those vendors who probably can do the job equally well and on time.

But thousands of little things that are purchased are neither negotiated nor let for bid. They are just ordered from a catalog at list price less the usual discount. About all the buyer does is look in two or three vendors' catalogs and order from the one who quotes the lowest price. The money involved doesn't justify much effort in trying to save a few nickles.

GOVERNMENT CONTRACTS

Billions of dollars a year in government contracts go to companies making defense products and space products. Most of this goes to aircraft, shipyards, missile, and electronics companies.

Often single contracts total hundreds of millions of dollars, and often, too, each individual product (a nuclear submarine, for example) costs many millions of dollars. As a rule the government places a complete contract with one company, and it becomes the "prime" contractor. Prime contractors then buy whatever components they themselves don't make. In a few cases the government will buy and furnish major components, such as jet engines for airplanes. Boeing, Lockheed, and the others do not make these components, nor do they themselves buy them. The government buys them from General Electric or United Technologies and supplies them. But, for the thousands of other items purchased, the prime contractor places the orders.

Prime contracts are usually (but not always) let on a competitive basis. Sometimes, when they are a continuation of previous contracts, the terms are set by negotiation. Prices are usually set to enable the contractor to earn 7 percent or more of the sales price as a profit (10 percent or more for research contracts). The govern-

ment's pricing policies, however, shift from time to time.

In the 1980s, most of the largest contracts are not at fixed prices but are "incentive" contracts. These contracts specify a price that is based upon expected costs, performance, and delivery schedules. But if costs overrun and go higher, the company and the government share the excess. Or, if there are cost savings, these too are shared. Similarly, bonuses are given for performance above expectations and for delivery ahead of schedule. And, in a parallel way, subspecification performance and late deliveries are penalized.

Government contracts differ from most others in that they rule out assessments of overhead not related to the contract. The government will not, for examnple, pay for any assessment of advertising costs. The government also expects the learning curve to operate. Prices on large contracts contemplate that final products will cost less to make than initial products.

The prime contractor, if it is an aircraft maker, probably has to buy such items as aluminum sheets, landing gear, and radar because it doesn't make these items. It is free to buy these items wherever it wants, except that the government requires it to buy American-made items and to give a stated portion of subcontract business to both small and minority-owned companies.

Besides having to subcontract, the prime contractor is responsible for seeing that the subcontractor is capable of doing the work; that the prices paid to subcontractors meet all regulations; that the sub can finance the contract; and that it does not make too much money on the contract. In addition, the prime contractor is responsible for seeing that all subcontractors obey all work-hour, nondiscrimination, and wage regulations; that the quality and reliability of their products meet government requirements; and that they meet their promised delivery schedule. Sometimes subcontractors are so anxious to get contracts that they promise anything the prime contractor asks and then can't deliver. The prime contractor's purchasing department may have to send in various specialists, particularly design and quality control engineers, to get them back on schedule and without major cost overruns.

PURCHASE CONTRACTS

Purchase orders, after acceptance by the vendor, become legal contracts which bind both parties. If either one doesn't live up to the contract, the other can sue. Problems are rare though, because both parties usually do what they agree to. And, if one side violates a small part of the contract (as when delivery of the materials is a few days late), the matter is rarely of enough importance to make much difference. Or if a small part of a shipment is rejected, the customer accepts the balance and pays accordingly. Or if it is all rejected, either the vendor replaces it or the contract is dropped and the order is placed elsewhere. Even if a customer cancels an order or wants to return materials, the vendor is usually willing to do what the customer wants just to keep him satisfied.

It is easy for each side to be agreeable in most minor contract violations because no one is going to lose much. But, if someone has to take a big loss, the contracting parties are not always quite so agreeable. If the prospective loss is great, the two parties sometimes submit their differences to arbitration, or even go to court. In court the *contract as written* is the basis for the decision as to whether an actual breach of contract has occurred. Whichever party is judged to have breached the contract will be liable for damages.

Standard printed contracts are used as the order from when the amount of money is small, but on large orders special contracts are usually written. Such things as the possible return of goods, contract cancellation, price adjustments, and provisions for the arbitration of disputes between buyer and seller are all specified in the contract. If there is any doubt about a contract's wording or interpretation, the purchasing department consults their legal department before contracts are signed.

DISCOUNTS

In the United States at the retail level, we are used to a one-price system. The seller sets a price, and we usually either pay it or don't buy. Discount houses flourish, though, proving that most of us shop around to get the best buy. We rarely bargain with a vendor about price, but in effect we bargain on prices by going elsewhere when we think a price is too high.

In contrast, company purchasing agents rarely buy at retail prices, nor does the one-price system work very well in industrial buying. As we have seen, purchasing agents ask for bids or negotiate prices on all large and middle-size contracts and on all small contracts for special items. On small orders for catalog items, they expect and get discounts from list prices.

Sometimes they get two or three discounts in series (such as 20 percent off, then 10 percent off the balance, and maybe another 5 percent off that) on the same order. Catalog items' list prices are supposed to be retail prices, and they are the prices a manufacturer almost never pays.

Regular discounts are of three kinds: trade, quantity, and cash. Trade discounts are supposed to be a certain percent for retailers and a larger percent for wholesalers, jobbers, or other manufacturers. Manufacturers of items that are sold through distributors at retail sometimes get only as little as one third of the retail list price. Trade discounts are supposed (even required by the Robinson-Patman Act, a federal law) to be the same for all buyers in the same class (as, for example, wholesalers). The law is not too effective in the case of manufacturers' buying from other manufacturers because they ask for slightly different items—items not sold to others at all. So there can be no direct comparison between what they pay and what someone else pays.

Quantity discounts, which are generally offered to customers who buy large quantities, are usually quite small compared with trade discounts. Quantity discounts are in addition to trade discounts and are supposed to be equally available to all customers. Large buyers are sometimes able to coax still greater discounts (for themselves only) from vendors by threatening them with buying elsewhere. Under present laws, vendors are allowed to pass on, in the form of lower prices, the actual savings in cost that large orders make possible, but *no more* than that. The difficulty of documenting the exact savings keeps this law from being very effective, because of the various ways that costs can be calculated—average, incremental, full cost, etc.

In addition, the enforcement of these laws somewhat depends on how aggressive the federal Justice Department is during a particular presidential administration. For example, during the Reagan administration where the mood toward deregulation has been strong, this aggressiveness has been minimal.

Cash discounts are often offered as inducements to pay quickly. Most bills are due in 30 days, but vendors don't want to wait that long for their money. Cash discounts of 2 percent if the bill is paid in 10 days instead of 30 (called 2–10–net 30) brings in most of the money sooner. Besides, they also reduce bad-debt losses. A 2 percent discount for paying sooner is a fine windfall for the customer; it is equivalent to a 36-percent return a year on money. Most customers will pay quickly even if they have to borrow money from a bank to do so. Yet why would a vendor rather have 98 cents in 10 days than $1 in 30 days? He would probably rather wait and receive more, but he has to meet industry customs.

Competition has brought other kinds of concessions that amount to discounts. Freight equalization is common when competing vendors are not located the same distance from the customer. A far-away vendor offers to pay the difference between the freight cost from his plant to the customer's plant and the freight cost from a competitor's plant that is nearer to the company's plant. Other practices, amounting in effect to discounts, including postdating the bill, thus extending credit for longer times; offering to pay part of the customer's advertising costs on the assumption that he will advertise the vendor's product; and offering free engineering or other services.

PURCHASING PROBLEMS

How Much Price Pressure?

Although the same prices are supposed to be quoted to all customers in each class (manufacturer, jobber, wholesaler, retailer), it doesn't always work that way. A large customer in any class can bargain down the price he pays until it is not far above an item's cost to manufacture. All he has to do is threaten to place his order somewhere else or to make his own items. Small customers can play this game, too, although not quite so effectively.

Gifts

Should a vendor show appreciation for getting a contract? That is, should they show it by giving the person who sent the order (another company's buyer) a gift? It is so easy to answer no that we seem to have disposed of the problem. Any other answer opens the door to kickbacks, rebates, and outright bribery—to the detriment of the buying company—because bribe-prone buyers will place orders where *they* get the most out of it, not where the company benefits the most.

But the problem can't be put down so easily. Vendors *are* appreciative, and most of us *like* to be appreciated. We corrupt easily if on the receiving end of gifts. Spending money just seems to breed graft, at least small-scale graft. Most companies have strict policies against their buyers' accepting expensive gifts, but most of them don't object to, say, free meals, a box of cigars, a cigarette lighter, or a few bottles of liquor at Christmas time. But a TV set or an automobile—no. Mink coats, free trips, and lavish entertainment during big-city visits also are out.

Curiously, the ethics of gifts seems to be all one-sided—we always hear about the person who *receives* a gift and whether this is proper. But someone has to *give* gifts. Can a company logically forbid its buyer to receive a gift and at the same time pay the bills for the gifts given by its own sales department?

The very embarrassing disclosures in the

mid-1970s that several American companies had paid bribes to officials in countries around the world in connection with selling airplanes or to win contracts to construct power plants, steel mills, and so on shows what the practice of giving gifts can come to. There are some countries in the world where this is the accepted way of doing business, but it is not according to the code of ethics in most Western countries. And, particularly since these bribery disclosures, surely managers will try even harder to see that none of this goes on in their organizations.

MISCELLANEOUS FUNCTIONS OF THE PURCHASING DEPARTMENT

The purchasing department should always be on the lookout for less costly materials, which is an objective of value analysis, as discussed in Chapter 5. Sometimes this means that they need to try out new materials. This means sample runs in the factory and performance tests to see how the new materials work. Purchasing should follow these trials, noting their success or failure. Purchasing should also keep informed about the quality of what it buys. Whenever the factory has problems with purchased items, they should work with the vendor to eliminate the problem or eliminate the vendor.

Another purchasing function is to handle matters relating to rejected purchased materials—whether they are rejected when received or later in processing. All correspondence having to do with disposing, reworking, or returning anything is handled by the purchasing department. Purchasing also sells a company's salvage and waste materials. It gets this job, rather than the sales department, because these are materials, not finished products. The purchasing department knows materials markets better than does the sales department.

Review Questions

1. How important is purchasing? If wages make up 20 percent of an organization's total costs, how important is it to get greater productivity from workers as against doing a more effective job of purchasing?

2. Suppose that purchasing is regarded as "outside manufacture." In what way does this viewpoint affect purchasing?

3. What part should the purchasing department play in make-buy decisions? Why, if ever, should the purchasing department instigate a change from one policy to the other? How would the purchasing department come to realize that such a change should be made?

4. The text says that expensive, steadily used items are often bought on a more or less continuing basis for years from the same supplier and that contracts for such items are not really open to competition. Is this wise? Discuss.

5. What is the "known-cost" concept? This concept brings purchasing closer to quality determination problems. Should this be? After all, the purchasing department is not highly qualified in the quality area. Or is it? Discuss.

6. Most large companies buy their large volume items by specification rather than by brand name or trademark. How far down the volume scale should this practice be carried? Why?

7. Why is vendor rating important? What factors are most important?

8. How can monitoring vendor turnover improve purchasing activities? Once you find a good supplier, shouldn't you stick with them?

9. What are the general objectives behind selecting minority vendors as suppliers?

10. The Federal Trade Commission does not like reciprocity. Why, then, does it not order it stopped? Discuss.

11. Purchasing agents usually object to reciprocity as a practice. Why? What might the company president's views be? Why?

12. How does the typical American one-price system operate so far as industrial buying is concerned? What part do discounts play in actual pricing?

13. The text says purchasing specialists and inventory controllers should be thought of as investment portfolio managers. Discuss.

14. Why do some companies give loose specifications to vendors and rely on them to design the product?

15. What trade-offs are there in having many versus few vendors?

16. What effect do JIT methods have on vendors' production activities?

Questions for Discussion

1. The president wants to know if his purchasing department is doing a good job, so he calls in a consultant and asks him to investigate and tell him. How should the consultant go about his work?

2. Purchasing and sales are two sides of the same coin. Is there any occasion for having people with different training in these two departments?

3. A large company with government contracts finds from its past experience that small suppliers are so often unreliable that it would be better off in every way to cut way down on subcontracting. Should it do so? Why?

4. When a company buys instead of makes parts, it would seem that it would incur additional transportation and packing costs and that it would have to carry more inventory and be out of stock more often than if it made the items itself. How, therefore, can it ever be wise to buy instead of make?

5. Should one division of a company be allowed to buy from the outside when the same items are made by a division of the same company? (The buying division thinks it can save a little money by doing this.) Discuss.

6. A San Francisco plant manager wants to buy his printed forms locally and not have them printed by the central print shop in the Chicago office. Should he be allowed to do this? Discuss.

7. When a company buys by specifications, it usually writes its own specifications. Isn't there a danger that these may not be rewritten and updated enough to incorporate new developments? How can a company protect itself against obsolescence in the design of purchased parts?

8. Assume that you are the buyer who places orders for all of the blackboard erasers in your school. How do you decide what kind to buy? How do you decide when to buy them? Would you buy them by specification? Write out the item description you would use.

9. In order to convince the vendor of the urgency of the company's need, the expediter wants to go to the vendor plants involved. Should the company send him? What can he do? To whom will he talk? When should outside-of-the-plant expediters be used?

10. The expediter is happy. He got the order through even though it took air express to get some of the parts. Should this please the president? Why?

11. What should the city manager tell the purchasing agent about how much price pressure to put on vendors?

12. It is found that the purchasing agent owns 100 shares of Du Pont stock, a company with which he places orders for paint for the company. What should be done about this situation?

13. The bid from a minority vendor is 5 percent higher than the bid from a nonminority vendor. What should the purchasing department do? What additional information or policy needs to be determined before the decision is made?

Problems

1. Should the company buy or make steel stampings in the following example? They can be bought for $44,000. The company calculates that it will cost $50,000 to make these same stampings, with its costs being as follows: materials, $15,000; direct and indirect labor, $7,500; machine costs, supervising, tool design, handling, labor fringe benefits, and so on, $20,000. These total $42,500. General overhead of $7,500 brings the inside costs to $50,000. The plant is not operating at capacity and could make these stampings if this were the decision. Discuss.

2. Should the company make or buy the following three items?

	Product		
	A	B	C
Quantity needed	40,000	15,000	24,000
Material costs/unit	$ .046	$.0185	$.0275
Direct labor-hours required	360	300	100
Purchase price/unit	$ .141	$ .172	$ .090

The direct labor cost rate is $10 per hour. There are also variable overheads, which go up and down with labor, which cost $6 per labor-hour. Fixed overhead is $4.20 per direct labor-hour (based on 2,000 hours a year).

If the decision is to buy these items, would the fact that the plant is heavily loaded or is working far below capacity change the decision in any way?

3. The steel supplier quotes the following prices for rolls of strip steel:

Number of Rolls Ordered at a Time	Price per Roll
0–24	$24.00
25–74	23.85
75–199	23.75
199 and over	23.70

The company uses 400 rolls of this steel a year. It costs $50 to place an order and 20 percent to carry inventory. How many rolls should be bought at a time? (Note: The economic lot size models explained in Chapter 23 would help here, but it is not necessary for getting an approximate answer.)

4. Two suppliers have sent in bids for supplying component part X. These parts will be needed at the rate of 1,000 a month for a year but not thereafter.

Supplier A is 1,000 miles away and has been known not to deliver on time every time. His quality control is also a little less than perfect, and once in a while a shipment will have to be rejected. His proposal:

Cost of tooling (to be paid by you)	$1,000
Up to 1,000 units	.28 ea.
1,000 to 5,000	.27 ea.
5,000 and over	.26 ea.

Supplier A will ship as many or as few as are required, according to the customer's delivery schedule, but he needs ten weeks' lead time.

Supplier B is 100 miles away and is very dependable. His proposal:

Cost of tooling (to be paid by you)	$1,000
Up to 1,000 units	.32 ea.
1,000 to 2,000	.31 ea.

2,000 to 4,000	.30 ea.
4,000 and over	.29 ea.

B will also ship according to the customer's delivery schedule and needs 2 weeks' lead time. Buying from B saves $.01 per unit in freight costs.

It costs ¼ cent a week to carry product X in stock.

a. What purchasing and stocking policy should the company follow if it expects B never to let it down but A to let it down four times a year, each time costing $200 for the delay?

b. Would your answer be the same as above if Supplier B is a minority vendor?

5. The company is considering making versus buying a heavily used part. This part goes into a new finished product whose total volume is very much a question. The market forecasters estimate that there is 90 percent probability of selling at least 5,000 units. They estimate that there is a 75 percent chance of selling at least 15,000 and a 40 percent chance of selling as many as 30,000.

To make the items, it would be possible to choose between two alternative methods. The first would require an investment of $5,000 in tooling and $1.30 per unit in variable costs. The second would require $15,000 for tooling and $.50 per unit in variable costs.

These items can be bought in quantities up to 5,000 for $3 per unit. For orders of more than 5,000, the price is $2 each. For orders of over 10,000 units, $1.50, and for orders above 15,000, $1.25.

What should the company do? Show your analysis.

Case 15–1

The plant manager is on the telephone calling you, the purchasing agent, about production holdups. He says that several jobs are being delayed in the factory from the failure of purchased parts to arrive. He has just called the supplier, who has told him that there is no reason for the delay. The supplier could easily have got the parts delivered if he had only known that you wanted them.

What happened was that because of production problems with materials, an unusual number of items were scrapped in process and more were needed. The factory's PIPC department, being forbidden to call suppliers directly, had called the buyer in the purchasing department asking for a rush shipment. But the buyer was out sick with a cold for two days and didn't get the call and missed learning about it when he came back.

Should the factory's PIPC department ever call suppliers directly? What reasons are there for and against their doing this?

Case 15–2

The Mississippi Company found that it could buy the wiring systems used in the machines it made for considerably less than its past cost for making them. Since the savings came to $25,000 a year, the company decided to buy instead of make, even though this meant laying off 10 workers and putting others in the wiring department on short hours.

The union said that the company had no right to do this and asked for an arbitrator to decide. The company refused, but the union carried it to court; it lost in the district court but was upheld by the appeals court, which ordered the company to arbitrate. The labor contract said nothing about making or buying.

You are the arbitrator. You decide. Does the company have the right to subcontract work outside in this case?

Case 15–3

The manager of the Lux textile mill looked forward glumly to the next three months. They were the low demand months of the year—months when there would be only four days of work a week for only one quarter of the usual work force.

Then his phone rang. It was a buyer from a large chain store with a proposition. He offered to buy enough material from Lux to keep the mill operating normally through the whole slow period. Furthermore, he hinted at repeating the offer next year if this year's arrangement worked out well.

There was a catch in the deal, however. The chain store buyer quoted a price which was not very much over the cost of materials and labor. If Lux accepted the order it would get back only a small amount of the overhead costs it stood to lose if it refused the order. So if Lux accepted, it would be selling below total costs.

The offer was not easy to refuse, however. If it were accepted, the work force would be kept busy and Lux would be less worse off than if it turned the offer down. In the short run, Lux would be better off to accept the offer. But in the long run the low-price items offered for sale by the chain store would steal sales from Lux's regular customers. To make the choice even more difficult, Lux's manager couldn't prevent his customers' getting hurt by turning the offer down. There were too many other textile mills. Someone, somewhere, would accept the offer.

What should be done in this case?

Section Four

Special Planning and Control Techniques

Operations research techniques use quantitative methods to aid in making many production and operating managerial decisions. These techniques (PERT/CPM, queuing, Monte Carlo simulation, and linear programming) are presented in this section.

Network analyses using such systems as PERT have proved to be of great value in the production of extremely complex products and of large projects whose completion takes many months or years. The whole production activity is viewed as many subsystems of component activities, all of which must, in the end, tie in together as the final product is made or as the project is finished. PERT and its several uses are presented in Chapter 16.

Queuing aids in analyzing problems where waiting lines and service capacities need to be balanced. Monte Carlo simulation can also be used for the same purpose. In addition, it can analyze a host of other situations where a synthetic model of a system that "behaves" according to specified probabilities can aid in understanding the system. These topics are presented in Chapter 17.

Linear programming is an operations research technique, which can be used as an aid in scheduling and capacity planning and control. Chapter 18 introduces linear programming analysis and shows how it can be used in different production planning activities in manufacturing and service situations.

Chapter 16

Project Management with PERT

Special projects are continually being planned and produced in all kinds of organizations. For example, the development of IBM's new "junior" personal computer and Apple's Macintosh microcomputer in the early 1980s were both multimillion-dollar special projects for these companies. Other examples of special projects are building the space shuttle; constructing Disneyworld's Epcot Center in Florida; and planning the 1984 presidential campaign.

The management of special projects requires different scheduling and control systems than those used for managing job shop and repetitive production and service activities.

PERT

The best known and most widely used project scheduling and control method is called PERT, or program evaluation and review technique. PERT is an analytical method designed to aid in the scheduling and control of complex projects which require that certain activities be performed in sequence while others may be performed independently.[1]

---

[1] PERT and a similar variant, CPM (critical path method), are essentially the same. CPM depicts "nodes" as activities and uses arrows to symbolize the logical relationships between the activities. This is called ADM, or arrow diagramming method. Since the terms are used almost interchangeably, we will use the more common term, PERT.

PERT has been used for many kinds of construction activities, for building bridges and unusual buildings such as stadiums, and for coordinating maintenance and installation projects such as refitting ships and installing new computer systems. PERT was used extensively to plan and control the thousands of activities needed in the construction of the Alaskan pipeline for oil. Generally, it is most applicable to rather complex, nonrepetitive projects.

PERT Characteristics and Definitions

PERT's methodology and components have fairly standard definitions, which are as follows:

Activity. An activity is a part of the total work to be done; it consumes time and resources and has starting and ending points. Figure 16–1 depicts a network of activities showing the sequence in which activities (the arrows) must be performed.

Event. An event is a "milestone"; it marks the beginning or the end of an activity. In drawing a PERT network, events are symbolized as circles or "nodes." Events are also numbered, with those at the tail of an activity having lower numbers than events at the head of each activity arrow.

FIGURE 16–1
PERT Network Diagram

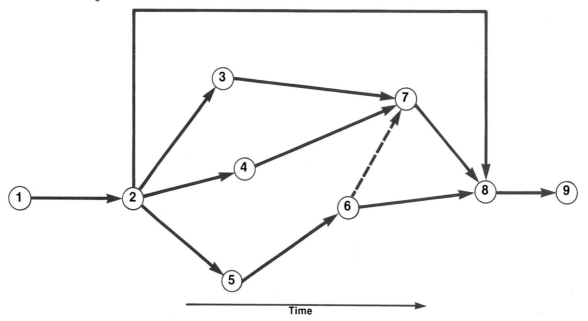

Time

In a PERT network, each activity connects two events whose identification numbers indicate the beginning event and the ending event. No two activities are allowed to have both the same beginning and ending events because there would be no way to distinguish between the two activities. (Computerized PERT systems often identify activities only by their beginning and ending event numbers.)

Activity time. PERT uses three estimates of the amount of time an activity might take to com-

a. Optimistic time: The time the activity will take if everything goes well and no delays are encountered.
b. Realistic time: The time the activity will most likely take under normal conditions, allowing for usual delays.
c. Pessimistic time: The time the activity may take if more than the usual delays are encountered.

PERT weights these three estimates to obtain an "expected time" for an activity by:[3]

$$\text{Expected activity time} = \frac{\text{Optimistic time} + \left(4 \times \text{Realistic time}\right) + \text{Pessimistic time}}{6}$$

plete. These estimates are obtained from people who have some knowledge about the work and how long it will probably take.[2] They are:

Thus, if an activity in a PERT network for building a building were "pour the concrete foundation" and it had estimates of 2, 4, and 12 days, its expected duration would be:

---

[2] Many users of PERT do not actually use three time estimates in this fashion. Rather, they simply use the "realistic" time as the expected time for the activity. We will use three times in our example in order to illustrate their use in anticipating finishing dates.

[3] Note that this formula simply weights the realistic time ⅔ and the other two estimates ⅙ each. This is somewhat arbitrary but does have some logic to it, as we will see later.

Expected

$$\text{activity time} = \frac{2 + (4 \times 4) + 12}{6} = 5 \text{ days}$$

Precedence requirements. Since some activities cannot begin until others are completed (we cannot pour the concrete foundation until we have excavated and built the forms) and others may be performed independently and/or simultaneously (we may simultaneously pour the foundation and order lumber), we must develop the *immediate precedence requirements* of the activities in the project. The easiest way to do this is ask this question of *each* activity: "Which *other* activities must be completed immediately before we can begin *this* activity?"

Start and finish times. The earliest time an activity can begin, considering the expected activity times and the precedence requirements of all prior activities, is called the *earliest start* (ES) time. The latest time an activity can start without delaying the whole project is called the *latest start* (LS) time. The earliest time that an activity can finish is called the *earliest finish* (EF) and is equal to the activity's ES + its expected time. The latest time an activity can be completed without delaying the completion of the entire project is called the latest finish (LF) time. This is equal to the activity's LS + its expected time.

PERT EXAMPLE

To illustrate how PERT works, let us consider the example whose figures are shown in Figure 16–2 and which are depicted in the PERT network in Figure 16–3. We will suppose that our project has 12 activities (11 real activities and 1 dummy),[4] designated A, B, . . . L; a set of immediate precedence requirements; and the three times estimates for each activity.

Looking just at columns 1, 2 and 3 in Figure

---

[4] A "dummy" activity is not really an activity which consumes time or resources. It is indicated on a PERT network diagram by a broken arrow line and is there to preserve proper sequences when one activity does not depend directly on another.

16–2, we can see that activity A is the first activity. It precedes everything else and must be completed before activities B, D, F, and L can begin. This is shown in Figure 16–3 by the "burst" of activities B, D, F, and L not being able to start until after A is completed at node ②.

At the other end of the project, activity K is the last activity, and it cannot begin until activities L, I, and J have been completed. This is shown in Figure 16–3 by a "merge" of these three activities before K can begin. Using only columns 1, 2, and 3 in Figure 16–2 and looking at the graphic representation in Figure 16–3, one can see that all of the immediate precedence requirements have been met.

Next, columns 4, 5, and 6 in Figure 16–2 are the three time estimates for each activity. These have been used to calculate column 7's expected times, using the formula given above. These expected times have been entered on the network in Figure 16–3.

We are now ready to calculate the early and late starts shown in columns 8 and 9 of Figure 16–2. To do this, we turn to the network shown in Figure 16–4. This is the same network as before but with more information on it. On this network we first draw a $+$ ("tee") at each node or event. Next, beginning at event ① and moving to the right in the network, we put the ES for all activities which burst out of each event on the left side of the tee. (Here we will begin with zero at event ①; later we will see that computer systems use actual dates). For example, the earliest possible starting time (ES) at event ② is simply the ES at event ① plus the expected time (of four days) for activity A. It is important to note that these ESs are for all activities bursting from an event. Later we will determine the ES for each activity.

The ES for activity I is the 20th day because it cannot begin until activities C, E, and G (G is dummied through H) are completed. The path through H is longer (20 days) than the paths through C (18 days) or E (15 days), so activity I must wait until G is completed before it can begin. A similar situation occurs at event ⑧. The

FIGURE 16–2
PERT Data

(1) Activity	(2) Immediate Precedence Requirements	(3) Events Begin	(3) Events End	(4) Optimistic Time	(5) Realistic Time	(6) Pessimistic Time	(7) Expected Time	(8) Start ES	(8) Start LS	(9) Finish EF	(9) Finish LF	(10) Total Slack
A	None	1	2	3	4	5	4	0	0	4	4	0
B	A	2	3	4	7	10	7	4	16	11	23	12
C	B	3	7	2	7	12	7	11	23	18	30	12
D	A	2	4	3	5	13	6	4	19	10	25	15
E	D	4	7	1	5	9	5	10	25	15	30	15
F	A	2	5	7	8	21	10	4	4	14	14	0
G	F	5	6	1	7	7	6	14	14	20	20	0
H*	G	6	7	—	—	—	—	20	30	20	30	10
I	C,E,G	7	8	10	10	10	10	20	30	30	40	10
J	G	6	8	15	20	25	20	20	20	40	40	0
K	L,I,J	8	9	2	7	12	7	40	40	47	47	0
L	A	2	8	10	15	20	15	4	25	19	40	21

* Dummy activity.

FIGURE 16–3
PERT Network with Data Added

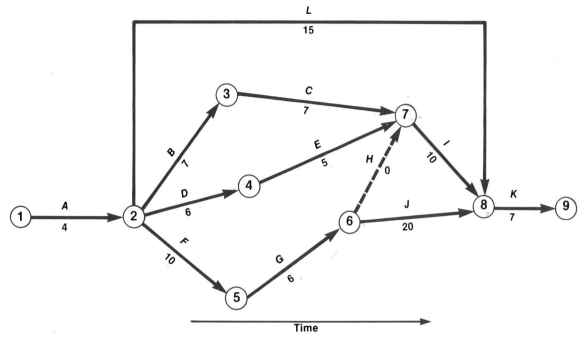

FIGURE 16–4
PERT Network with More Information

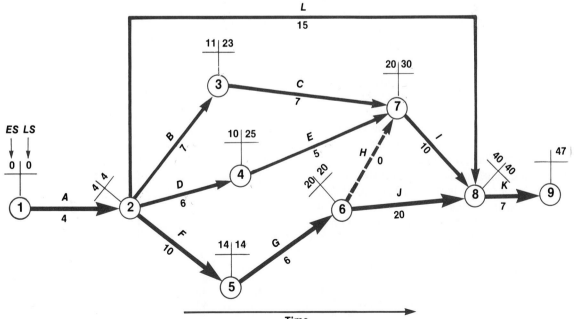

cumulative time through activity L is only 19 days; through I is 30 days. But through J, it is 40 days, so 40 is the ES for activity K. Since event ⑨ is at the end of the project, it does not have an ES. (It would, of course, if this small network were only part of a larger project network that continued on, beyond event ⑨.)

The Critical Path

The *critical path* is the *longest path* through the network and its time becomes the minimum expected completion time for the entire project. In our example, the alternative paths and their expected completion times are:

Alternate Event Paths	Total Expected Completion Time	
1, 2, 8, 9	4 + 15 + 7	= 26
1, 2, 3, 7, 8, 9	4 + 7 + 7 + 10 + 7	= 35
1, 2, 4, 7, 8, 9	4 + 6 + 5 + 10 + 7	= 32
1, 2, 5, 6, 7, 8, 9	4 + 10 + 6 + 0 + 10 + 7	= 37
1, 2, 5, 6, 8, 9	4 + 10 + 6 + 20 + 7	= 47

The longest path, that of ①, ②, ⑤, ⑥, ⑧, and ⑨ takes 47 days. This is the critical path and is indicated by heavy arrows in Figure 16–4.

The project can therefore be scheduled to be completed in 47 days. This becomes the completion goal, and the number 47 is placed on the right side of the tee at node ⑨. From here we begin to work backward through the network, from right to left, placing the latest possible start day number (LS) on the right side of each tee. Again there are LSs for all activities which burst from the event, and we will determine each activity's LS later. The LS at event ⑧ of 40 is simply 47 − 7, the expected time for activity K. Similarly, the LS for activity I is 40 − 10 = 30. This tells us that activity I could start as late as the 30th day and not cause the overall project to be late. Similarly, C could start as late as the 23rd day; E the 25th day; and B and D could also delay their starting.

However, the correct LS for events ⑥ and ② require some further analysis. Since the LS at event ⑥ is for all activities which burst from it, we must choose the most limiting. The LS coming back through H is 30 − 0 = 30; through J it is 40 − 20 = 20. Since the LS through J is smaller, this becomes the LS for event ⑥. The LS for event ② is similarly constrained by the path back through activity F and is 14 − 10 = 4. It can be seen in Figure 16–4 that for all events in the critical path, the ES and LS dates are the same. This is always so since activities can't be started any sooner because earlier activities are not completed; nor can following activities be started later because then the project will not finish in time.

Slack

Slack is the amount of "play" in the system. When one activity can be finished before the next activity has to start, there is a slack time period during which the next activity could be started, but it doesn't have to be started so soon. Slack is thus the time that an activity can be delayed in starting without delaying the completion of the entire project, provided that the activities which precede the activity have not been delayed beyond their earliest finish, EF, date. The total slack for each activity is computed as follows: (LS of ending event) − (Expected completion time) − (ES of beginning event) = Total slack. The slack for each activity in our example is:

Activity	LS at Ending Event		Expected Time		ES at Beginning Event		Total Slack
A	4	−	4	−	0	=	0
B	23	−	7	−	4	=	12
C	30	−	7	−	11	=	12
D	25	−	6	−	4	=	15
E	30	−	5	−	10	=	15
F	14	−	10	−	4	=	0
G	20	−	6	−	14	=	0
H	30	−	0	−	20	=	10
I	40	−	10	−	20	=	10
J	40	−	20	−	20	=	0
K	47	−	7	−	40	=	0
L	40	−	15	−	4	=	21

The total slack for all activities on the critical path is always zero if the desired completion time of the project is the same as the earliest expected completion time. In our example, if the desired completion time for the project were 50 days, instead of 47 days, all activities on the critical path would share 3 days of total slack.

Total slack rarely belongs to a single activity. It is usually shared among adjacent activities along a path. For example, both B and C have slack of 12 days; however, if B is delayed in starting by 4 days or if it goes slowly and takes 4 days extra, then it takes 11 days instead of 7. This uses up 4 days of the 12 days slack and leaves only 8 days of slack for activity C. This also affects I's slack, reducing it to 6 days. If B's completion were delayed 4 days and C were delayed by 7 days more, this would reduce I's slack to −1, and the whole project would fall 1 day behind schedule.

Determining the ES and LS for Each Activity

The early start, ES, for each activity is simply the ES on the left side of the tee at its beginning event. The latest start, LS, for each activity is simply the ES at its beginning event (the left side of the tee) plus the activity's slack. These are shown in column 8 in Figure 16–2.

Determining the EF and LF for Each Activity

Now that we have ESs and LSs for each activity, EF is simply the activity's ES plus its expected time. Similarly, LF is the activity's LS plus its expected time. These are shown in Column 9 in Figure 16–2.

Free Slack

Free slack may also exist in a PERT network. It is the amount of time an activity can be delayed without delaying any succeeding activity's ES. For example, activity C could be delayed until the 13th day without violating activity I's ES at the 20th day. On the other hand, if activity D is delayed even one day, then the ES of activity E is also delayed one day. Thus, there is no free slack in D even though it shares five days of total slack with E. Free slack for an activity is calculated by subtracting its EF from the ES of all activities to which it is an immediate predecessor.

PROBABILITY OF MEETING PERT SCHEDULES

One of PERT's interesting features is that it allows the calculation of the probability that the schedule will be met.[5] Only the critical path is concerned here. For each activity on the critical path, the procedure uses *one sixth* of the difference between the pessimistic time and the optimistic time as an estimate of the standard deviation of the expected activity time (a range of six standard deviations encompasses virtually all the area in a normal distribution).

Since we are concerned only with the likelihood of the whole project finishing on time, we have to compute the probabilities of all of the activities in the critical path, taken together, taking more time or less time than the expected time. To do this, we first (in Figure 16–5) square the standard deviation for each activity to get the "variance" and add these variances cumulatively. Then, we take the square root of these cumulated variances and arrive at the standard deviation of the probable variations in the total time for the project. We can also take the square root of the cumulated variance at any intermediate event in the critical path and get the standard deviation of the expected times up to this event. These standard deviations are shown in Figure 16–5.

It is now possible to see how likely it is that the scheduled completion dates for the whole project or for the successive stages in the critical path will be met. The entire project is expected to take 47 days, and the calculation we just fin-

---

[5] This can be true only if three time estimates are used for each activity. Most organizations use only one time estimate for each activity and thus cannot perform this kind of calculation.

FIGURE 16–5

Critical Path Activities	Pessimistic Time	Optimistic Time	Difference	Activity's Standard Deviation	Variance (σ^2)	Cumulated Variance	Path's Standard Deviation
A	5	3	2	0.33	0.11	0.11	0.33
F	21	7	14	2.33	5.43	5.54	2.35
G	7	1	6	1.00	1.00	6.54	2.55
J	25	15	10	1.67	2.79	9.33	3.05
K	12	2	10	1.67	2.79	12.12	3.48

ished tells us that the standard deviation is 3.48 days.

This standard deviation shows that there is a 68 percent probability that the actual time for the project will be between 47 ± 3.48 days, or between 43.52 and 50.48 days. And there is a 95 percent probability that it will be completed in 47 ± 6.96 days. And it is almost certain that the project will be finished in 47 ± 10.44 days.[6]

Suppose that a manager asks the likelihood that the project will be completed in 44 days, or three days ahead of schedule. We can determine the number of standard deviations this is by:

Number of standard deviations

$$= \frac{44 - 47}{3.48} = -.86$$

Going to Appendix C, we find that −.86 of a standard deviation represents about a 20 percent probability. Thus, there is only a 20 percent chance that the project will be completed in 44 days, unless additional resources are made available to speed things up.

If the manager asks about the chances of the project being completed within 55 days, it would be:

$$\frac{55 - 47}{3.48} = +2.29 \text{ standard deviations}$$

From Appendix C, we find that this results in a likelihood of about 99 percent of the project finishing within 55 days.

The purpose in determining these probabilities is that managers may want to increase the chances of finishing early or on schedule and decide to allocate more resources to activities on the critical path. Conversely, if the project is likely to finish earlier than is needed, resources can be diverted to other work without putting the finishing date for this project in jeopardy. Of course, the validity of these probabilities is based on the assumption that the time estimates are realistic and not under- or overstated. For this (the possibility that the estimates will be somewhat unrealistic) and other reasons, this aspect of PERT has fallen out of favor and is not used much in practice. However, this does not diminish the other useful aspects of PERT. Our purpose in presenting this aspect of PERT here simply is to show the reader how this feature works and to warn of the underlying assumptions.

PERT/COST

Although PERT is usually thought of as a means for scheduling the timing of activities required by complex projects, it also provides a framework for cost planning and cost control. Every activity that is carried on costs money; so PERT/time and PERT/cost go hand in hand. When a company plans for and schedules an activity, it also estimates its cost, so it has cost estimates for each part of the project.

---

[6] Based on the characteristics of the "normal" curve where the mean ±1 standard deviation gives measures which include 68 percent of the cases; ±2 standard deviation will include 95 percent and ±3, includes 99¾ percent. For a discussion of this concept, see Chapter 7.

PERT/cost has become increasingly important over the years as people become more aware of its value. Actually, in many cases managers are more interested in the *cost* of a project than in exactly *when* it will be finished. And, as in the case of PERT/time, PERT/cost provides a good control mechanism while projects are under way. Reports of completed activities tell managers when they reach each event milestone. This gives them frequent opportunities to compare the costs incurred with the expected budget for the work done to date. If the project is running behind the time schedule or is running over the budget, managers learn about it early, perhaps in time to do something to bring the project back on schedule or within the budget.

TIME AND RESOURCE TRADE-OFFS

PERT activities are actually workload assignments and are not directly calendar time assignments. Yet, they are usually shown as work which will take a certain amount of calendar time. These times are based on the expected commitment of normally used resources for the activity.

There is a problem here, however. One hundred labor-hours of work will take 100 hours of clock time if one person is assigned to do the work. But, if 100 people are assigned, this same activity might become a one-clock-hour job. Thus, there is usually a possibility of a trade-off between resources committed to an activity and the calendar time it will take (see Figure 16–6). Workers on noncritical path work, for example, might be transferred to critical path activities and thus shorten the calendar time required and possibly at no additional total resource cost. Slowing down the noncritical activity is possible because of the slack in the noncritical paths.

In many cases, unfortunately, resources are not wholly transferable because they are not interchangeable in use. For example, in Figure 16–7, if an activity could use more engineers, they cannot use purchasing agents even if purchasing is noncritical.

Another problem is that often both the ex-

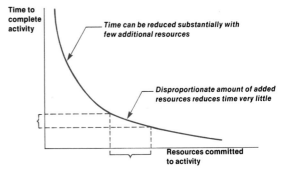

FIGURE 16–6
Time-Resource Requirement Trade-Off

pected time has elapsed and the money set aside for an activity is spent; yet, the activity is not complete. The work is taking longer and costing more than was planned. Time slippages can usually be made up if more resources are assigned to the late activity. Ordinarily, almost any activity can be speeded up by assigning more people to it, by working overtime, by using air express to get needed parts, or otherwise using more resources. However, as more people or resources are added to an activity to reduce its time, the time reduction usually gets more difficult to achieve, and eventually a disproportionately large amount of resources must be added to achieve even small time reductions. Figure 16–6 shows this relationship.

But, almost every activity can be speeded up by relaxing some of the technical specifications. And, occasionally, work which was planned to be done in sequence can, in part, be done concurrently.

Cost overruns, on the other hand, usually can be made up only at the expense of quality in other activities.

"CRASHING"

Sometimes a problem comes up where a manager is willing to trade off the costs of additional resources against the value of the time saved. This is called *crashing* a network. Figure 16–8

FIGURE 16–7
Event Milestones with Activities Shaded to Show the Kind of Resources Needed

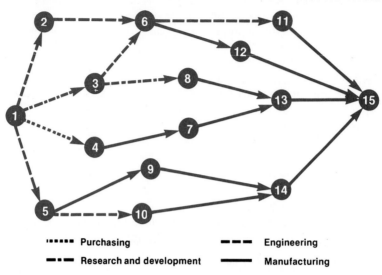

```
······ Purchasing          ▬ ▬ ▬ Engineering
▬ ▬ ▬ Research and development    ▬▬▬ Manufacturing
```

is a simple PERT diagram which we will use to illustrate how time and costs might be related. All but one of the activities can be "crashed" or speeded up, but at an additional cost.

Activity sequence H–K–N is the critical path and requires $3 + 5 + 4 = 12$ days. The analyst estimates that K's time can be reduced (as is shown in Figure 16–9) as much as two days at a cost of $40 for each day saved. Reducing K by 1 day will allow the whole project to be finished in 11 days at an extra cost of $40. Still another day can be cut off K for another $40

in cost. This would reduce the critical path to 10 days.

But at 10 days, paths I–N and H–M also take 10 days, as does path H–K–N. All three paths are now critical to any further time reduction. To reach nine days, it will be necessary to reduce both H and N because K can't be reduced any farther.

Cutting both H and N one day would cost $120, but K would then need to be cut only one day, so there would be an offsetting savings of $40, resulting in a net cost of $80. To reach eight days, it would be necessary to cut M and N another day, each at a cost of $100. To reach seven days, it would be necessary to cut I, K, and M simultaneously at a total cost of $350.

Should the managers make the time cuts proposed for these crash costs? This would depend on the value of the time saved. If we were talking about repairing a machine which is out of production and costing $60 every day it does not operate, then the trade-offs are as shown in Figure 16–10.

The analysis shows that a crash program aiming for a 10-day completion is the best repair

FIGURE 16–8

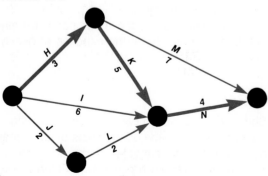

FIGURE 16–9

Activity	Normal		Crash Basis		Cost per Day to Save Days
	Days	Dollars	Days	Dollars	
H	3	$ 50	2	$ 100	$50
I	6	140	4	260	60
J	2	25	1	50	25
K	5	100	3	180	40
L	2	80	2	80	—
M	7	115	5	175	30
N	4	100	2	240	70
Total		$610		$1,085	

FIGURE 16–10

	Days to Make Repairs					
	7	8	9	10	11	12
Cost of repairs	$1,000	$ 870	$ 770	$ 690	$ 650	$ 610
Cost of production loss	420	480	540	600	660	720
Total	$1,420	$1,350	$1,310	$1,290	$1,310	$1,330

schedule. This will hold costs at $1,290, less than the cost of any other alternative.

COMPUTERIZED PERT SYSTEMS

As mentioned earlier, most users of PERT use computer programs to aid both in the development of the initial activities network (which, for large projects, is rarely developed graphically because it would be too complex) and to monitor the progress of the project as it is carried forward. Most computer manufacturers have PERT "packages" available for their customers to use. And several software companies also have PERT packages available. A simple computer-generated PERT report of our earlier example is shown in Figure 16–11.[7]

For large-project management, "batch"-type packages are normally used. *Batch* here means that all of the required information is first developed and entered into the computer. The initial PERT networks are developed and analyzed by means of batch runs through the computer. Figure 16–12 shows the steps in this process.

Further refinements, updates, and changes are then usually made in subsequent daily or weekly batch reruns as the project unfolds. On critical activities, the computer can, of course, print up-to-the-minute reports at any time. Figure 16–13 is an example of a computer-generated PERT report.

Online PERT Systems

Occasionally the few days' delay in receiving timely information from weekly update runs of PERT data are costly, in which case an online

[7] This software is available in a supplemental workbook to this text: T. Hendrick, R. Taylor, and B. Juhlin, *Microcomputer Software for Production/Operations Management,* (Homewood, Ill.: Richard D. Irwin, 1985).

FIGURE 16–11

```
PERT

INITIAL CONDITIONS:
```

ACTIVITY	STARTING EVENT	ENDING EVENT	OPTIMISTIC TIME	REALISTIC TIME	PESSIMISTIC TIME
A	1	2	3.0	4.0	5.0
B	2	3	4.0	7.0	10.0
C	3	7	2.0	7.0	12.0
D	2	4	3.0	5.0	13.0
E	4	7	1.0	5.0	9.0
F	2	5	7.0	8.0	21.0
G	5	6	1.0	7.0	7.0
H	6	7	0.0	0.0	0.0
I	7	8	10.0	10.0	10.0
J	6	8	15.0	20.0	25.0
K	8	9	2.0	7.0	12.0
L	2	8	10.0	15.0	20.0

ACTIVITY	EXPECTED TIME	EARLY START	EARLY FINISH	LATE START	LATE FINISH	TOTAL SLACK	FREE SLACK	
A	4.0	0.0	4.0	0.0	4.0	0.0	0.0	CA*
B	7.0	4.0	11.0	16.0	23.0	12.0	0.0	
C	7.0	11.0	18.0	23.0	30.0	12.0	2.0	
D	6.0	4.0	10.0	19.0	25.0	15.0	0.0	
E	5.0	10.0	15.0	25.0	30.0	15.0	5.0	
F	10.0	4.0	14.0	4.0	14.0	0.0	0.0	CA
G	6.0	14.0	20.0	14.0	20.0	0.0	0.0	CA
H	0.0	20.0	20.0	30.0	30.0	10.0	0.0	
I	10.0	20.0	30.0	30.0	40.0	10.0	10.0	
J	20.0	20.0	40.0	20.0	40.0	0.0	0.0	CA
K	7.0	40.0	47.0	40.0	47.0	0.0	0.0	CA
L	15.0	4.0	19.0	25.0	40.0	21.0	21.0	

* Critical Activity

PERT system might be used so that the project can be monitored in "real time." This allows problems to be spotted quickly and corrective action to be taken. However, online PERT systems can be costly.

As an example of online PERT systems we will look at an IBM package, called MINIPERT, which is designed to plan and control in detail small projects or subparts of large projects of up to 200 activities. All inputs and reports are entered and retrieved through a terminal so the project's status is in real time and the computer's data file is always kept up to date.

Example of MINIPERT. Figure 16–14 shows the PERT network which we will use in an example of online MINIPERT. The problem is as follows:

A construction company maintains a network for each project that it is working on. One of these projects is the construction of a garage which involves 15 separate activities and four types of labor specialties. It should be noted that when using MINIPERT it is usually not necessary to draw the PERT network but rather to directly input the activities as they exist through the CRT terminal. The PERT network is shown only to

FIGURE 16–12
Batch Approach to Computerized PERT

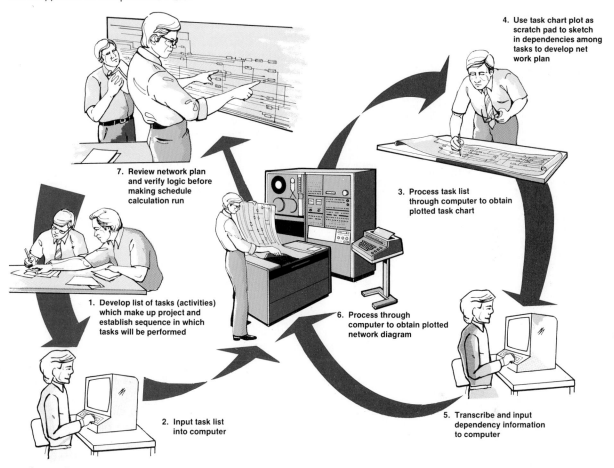

4. Use task chart plot as scratch pad to sketch in dependencies among tasks to develop net work plan

7. Review network plan and verify logic before making schedule calculation run

3. Process task list through computer to obtain plotted task chart

1. Develop list of tasks (activities) which make up project and establish sequence in which tasks will be performed

6. Process through computer to obtain plotted network diagram

2. Input task list into computer

5. Transcribe and input dependency information to computer

Source: Systonetics, Inc. (adapted).

assist in a better understanding of the problem.

The garage construction project is first processed by MINIPERT. Figure 16–15 shows the MINIPERT report for all the activities. A network diagram generated for the project is shown in Figure 16–16.

Next, we wish to insert resource data into the network so that proper work scheduling can be maintained. As mentioned previously, four types of labor specialities are needed. These are *builders* to erect the building; *concreters* to lay the foundation and do the cement work; *electricians* to install the wiring; and *laborers* to pre-

pare the excavation. In actuality, each of these resources could represent a separate subcontractor assigned that portion of the work.

The next step is to input the various labor specialties into the computer. This is done through the terminal by using the following codes:

Labor Specialty Code	Description
LB	Laborer
EL	Electrician
BL	Builder
MA	Mason

FIGURE 16–13
Computer-Generated PERT Report

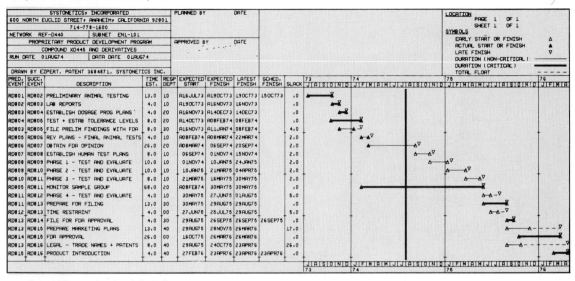

Source: Systonetics, Inc. (adapted).

Using this and previous information, MINIPERT produces a "resource category" printout called CATREPORT, shown in Figure 16–17. The report contains *blanks* where estimated labor-hours required of each type are entered by the planner. For example, the planner has allocated 120 laborer-hours (*LB* column) to the "excavate" activity; and 160 mason-hours *(MA)* to the "pour floor" activity. This information is then typed into the terminal, and a complete CATREPORT is then printed out on the terminal showing the resource allocation just made (or made at an earlier time).

Next, MINIPERT is told through the terminal how to spread the allocated labor-hours over each activity's time.

As an example, the 120 laborer-hours may be evenly spread over the five-day "excavate" activity as 120/5 = 24 hours per day.

After comparing labor specialty requirements with the network starts, finishes, and

FIGURE 16–14
PERT Network for Constructing a Garage

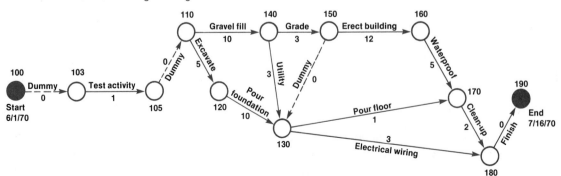

Source: Reprinted by permission from *Introduction to Minipert,* by International Business Machines Corporation.

FIGURE 16–15
MINIPERT Report

```
┌──────────────────────────────────────────────────────────────────────────────────────────┐
│ PROJECT: CONSTRUCTION OF A GARAGE              PRINTED 01/13/   AT 10.55.31                 │
│                                                                                            │
│ TIMENOW DATE USED:                                                                         │
│                                                                                            │
│ SORTED BY ORDER OF INPUT                                                                    │
│                                                                                            │
│ PRED  SUCC    DUR     ES      EF      LS      LF     SLACK   SCHD   DESCRIPTION             │
│ ────  ────    ───     ──      ──      ──      ──     ─────   ────   ───────────             │
│ 100   103       0  02/01/  02/01/  02/01/  02/01/      0            DUMMY                   │
│ 103   105    1.00  02/01/  02/02/  02/01/  02/02/      0            TEST ACT.               │
│ 105   110       0  02/02/  02/02/  02/02/  02/02/      0            DUMMY                   │
│ 110   120    5.00  02/02/  02/09/  02/22/  03/01/    2.80           EXCAVATE                │
│ 110   140   10.00  02/02/  02/16/  02/02/  02/16/     ·0            GRAVEL FILL             │
│ 140   130    3.00  02/16/  02/19/  03/10/  03/15/    3.20           UNDERGROUND UTILITY     │
│ 140   150    3.00  02/16/  02/19/  02/16/  02/19/      0            GRADE FOR SLAB          │
│ 150   130       0  02/19/  02/19/  03/15/  03/15/    3.20           DUMMY                   │
│ 120   130   10.00  02/09/  02/23/  03/01/  03/15/    2.80           POUR FOUNDATION         │
│ 130   170    1.00  02/23/  02/24/  03/15/  03/16/    2.80           POUR FLOOR              │
│ 130 · 180    3.00  02/23/  02/26/  03/15/  03/18/    2.80           ELECTRICAL WIRING       │
│ 150   160   12.00  02/19/  03/09/  02/19/  03/09/      0            ERECT WALLS AND ROOF    │
│ 160   170    5.00  03/09/  03/16/  03/09/  03/16/      0            WATERPROOF              │
│ 170   180    2.00  03/16/  03/18/  03/16/  03/18/      0            CLEAN-UP                │
│ 180   190       0  03/18/  03/18/  03/18/  03/18/      0            FINISH GARAGE           │
└──────────────────────────────────────────────────────────────────────────────────────────┘
```

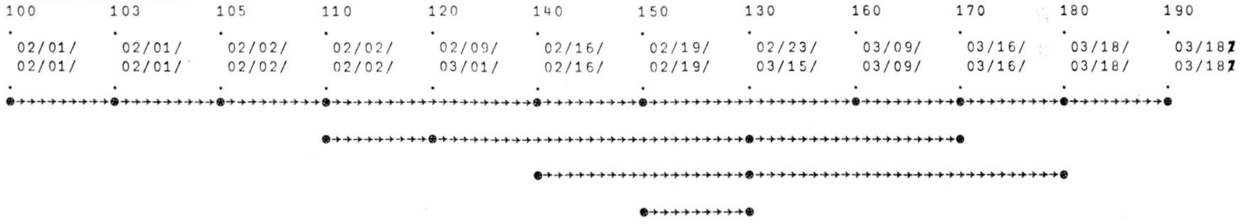

Note: DUR is activity time in days; SLACK is in weeks.
Source: Reprinted by permission from *Introduction to Minipert,* by International Business Machines Corporation.

FIGURE 16–16
Computer-Produced PERT Network from MINIPERT

Source: Reprinted by permission from *Introduction to Minipert,* by International Business Machines Corporation.

FIGURE 16–17
CATREPORT

```
CONSTRUCTION OF A GARAGE
PRINTED 01/13/    AT 10.16.23
ENT  PRED  SUCC       START     FINISH      LT     FI     BL     MA
          DUR      DESC
  1. 100   103      02/01/     02/01/    ------|------|------|------|
            0    DUMMY
  2. 103   105      02/01/     02/02/    --.---|------|------|------|
            1.0  TEST ACT.
  3. 105   110      02/02/     02/02/    ------|------|------|------|
            0    DUMMY
  4. 110   120      02/02/     02/09/   120.0 .|------|------|------|
            5.0  EXCAVATE
  5. 110   140      02/02/     02/16/   160.0 .|------|------|------|
           10.0  GRAVEL FILL
  9. 120   130      02/09/     02/23/    80.0 .|------|-----160.0|
           10.0  POUR FOUNDATION
 10. 130   170      02/23/     02/24/    16.0 .|------|------24.0|
            1.0  POUR FLOOR
 11. 130   180      02/26/     02/26/    24.0  24.0 .|------|------|
            3.0  ELECTRICAL WIRING
  6. 140   130      02/16/     02/19/    ------|------|------|-----.|
            3.0  UNDERGROUND UTILITY
  7. 140   150      02/16/     02/19/    24.0 .|------|-----24.0|
            3.0  GRADE FOR SLAB
  8. 150   130      02/19/     02/19/    ------|------|------|-----|"
            0    DUMMY
 12. 150   160      02/19/     03/09/   192.0 .|------|------|------|
           12.0  ERECT WALLS AND ROOF
 13. 160   170      03/09/     03/16/    40.0 .|------|------|------|
            5.0  WATERPROOF
 14. 170   180      03/16/     03/18/    32.0 .|------|------|------|
            2.0  CLEAN-UP
 15. 180   190      03/18/     03/18/    ------|------|------|------|
            0    FINISH GARAGE
                                TOTALS      0      0      0      0
```

Notes: DUR is "duration" or activity time.
DESC is "description" of activity.
PRED is predecessor event (at the tail of the activity arrow).
SUCC is successor event (at the head of the activity arrow).

Source: Reprinted by permission from *Introduction to Minipert*, by International Business Machines Corporation.

slacks, a report is printed which shows how many *people* are required each week by labor specialty (Figure 16–18).

For example, in the first week (five working days each), four laborers will be required. Looking at Figure 16–17 and the network back in Figure 16–14 shows how this is determined. In the first week of five days, excavation cannot begin until the one-day "test" activity is completed. Presume the "test" takes place on Mon-

day. This means the laborers will do the five days of excavating on Tuesday, Wednesday, Thursday, and Friday of week 1, and Monday of week 2. Thus, only four of the five days of excavation can be completed in the first week. This means that 120/5 × 4 days = 96 hours are required for this activity. But also note that we allocated a total 160 hours of laborer's time to the "gravel fill" activity, which also cannot begin until Tuesday of week 1. Thus the "gravel fill"-hour requirements for the first week are 160/10 days × 4 = 64 hours. Thus, 96 + 64 is 160 hours for the week. And, since laborers work an average of 40 hours a week, we will need 160/4 = 4.0 of them, which is shown in the shaded area of Figure 16–18. This same information is then displayed graphically in a bar chart (Figure 16–19), which is essentially a labor resource "load" report.

Similarity of PERT to MRP

Note the similarity of this approach to that of MRP, discussed in Chapter 11. These reports essentially show "time-phased" resource requirements which have been exploded from the "bill of resource requirements" which are estimated by the manager. They are "time-phased" because of the precedence restrictions in the network.

PERT ADVANTAGES

More than any other technique, PERT gives project managers some degree of control over diffi-

FIGURE 16–18

```
CONSTRUCTION OF A GARAGE
PRINTED 01/13/    AT 10.28.32
                                       STARTING WEEK 02/01/
CATEGORY        1ST   2ND   3RD   4TH   5TH   6TH   7TH   8TH   9TH   10TH  11TH  12TH   TOTAL

LABORER         4.0   3.4   2.4   2.2   2.0   1.2   1.0    0     0     0     0     0    16.2
ELECTRICIAN      0     0     0    1.0    0     0     0     0     0     0     0     0     1.0
BUILDER          0     0     0     .6     0     0     0     0     0     0     0     0      .6
MASON            0    1.6   2.6   1.0    0     0     0     0     0     0     0     0     5.2

   WEEKLY TOTALS 4.0   5.0   5.0   4.8   2.0   1.2   1.0    0     0     0     0     0    23.0
```

Source: Reprinted by permission from *Introduction to Minipert*, by International Business Machines Corporation.

FIGURE 16–19
Bar Chart for Labor-Power Problem

```
CONSTRUCTION OF A GARAGE
PRINTED 01/13/   AT 10.30.21

CATEGORIES ARE:

LR   LABORER
EL   ELECTRICIAN
BL   BUILDER
MA   MASON

 PERIOD        0       .50     1.00     1.50     2.00     2.50     3.00     3.50     4.00     4.50      0
 _START  AMOUNT |-- -- --- --|---------|---------|---------|---------|---------|---------|---------|----------|
 02/01/    4.00+****************************************************************************************
 02/08/    5.00+**************************************************************************************************
 02/15/    5.00+**************************************************************************************************
 02/22/    4.80+***********************************************************************************************
 03/01/    2.00+*******************************************
 03/08/    1.20+*************************
 03/15/    1.00+*********************
 03/22/       0+
 03/29/       0+
 04/05/       0+
 04/12/       0+
 04/19/       0+
         |---------|---------|---------|---------|---+ ----|---------|---------|---------|---------|-------|-
          0       .50     1.00     1.50     2.00     2.50     3.00     3.50     4.00     4.50      0
                                            SCALE       0.05
```

Source: Reprinted by permission from *Introduction to Minipert,* by International Business Machines Corporation.

cult-to-estimate projects and over projects which are surrounded by technological uncertainty. By forcing them to think of the parts of the whole and how they link together, PERT forces managers into making time and cost estimates for individual parts of the project. Doing this seems to produce greater overall accuracy.

PERT also helps minimize the "crash everything" attitude. It answers questions such as: If there is a delay in an activity, will the entire project be delayed? And if so, how much? PERT also provides an alternative to the frequent and lengthy meetings needed for coordination. And it cuts down on cross-checking unrelated activities.

PERT helps detect problems while things are still in the planning stage. It shows, ahead of time, which activities need the most attention so they will not hold up other activities. It also points to bottleneck activities which may have to be speeded up on a crash basis. PERT also reveals the existence of near-critical paths. They, too, need monitoring because a minor holdup in one of their activities will make *them* become the critical path instead of the original critical path. And in the case of slowdowns in noncritical path activities, PERT shows whether the slack in these

paths is enough to absorb the delay or whether costly speeding-up action is needed.

Critical path analyses sometimes surprise managers. On one construction project, Du Pont's engineers thought that labor and overtime would be the factors critical to its completion. However, the analysis showed that these factors were unimportant and that the tight factors were the electrical design time and the delivery dates of certain equipment. As a result, they readjusted the sequence of electrical equipment installation and saved 21 days, enabling them to begin production three weeks sooner.

Aerojet-General found, when developing one of the early Polaris missiles, that its new fiberglass motor casing was taking longer to develop than was planned. PERT showed that this would probably delay the project for three months. The warning came early enough to give them time to switch back to an earlier type of steel casing and avert the delay.

PERT also provides for progress checkpoints. As reports of completed work are made, they are entered into the computer, which compares the progress of each activity with its planned progress. If any chain of activities is falling behind (if there is any "slippage"), PERT reports it. Managers find out about these slippages before much harm to the program has been done. Figure 16–20 shows such a report, called a *Target Bar Chart* report. Look at activity 510—Purchase electrical equipment—in Figure 16–20. The string of "****" shows a target completion date of the fourth week of April 1980. The letters below (which are special codes to show various aspects of actual or projected completion) show that activity 510 is expected to be completed four weeks early. The dashes ("–") to the right show the slack. There are nine dashes for activity 510, which means this activity can be up to nine weeks late without affecting the project's scheduled completion date of March 3, 1981.

Reports like this are extremely useful in keeping a project's completion on target.

Still another advantage of PERT is that it can be used to *simulate* certain conditions so that a manager can see how a project will be affected if less or more time is spent on certain activities. For example, PERT software can display a "resource load" of engineers which are planned to be assigned to a project. Figure 16–21 shows such a load, where five types of engineers are assigned to a project. It shows that the load is very heavy in the early part of the project, with another "mini" peak use of engineers required in December and January.

In a *simulation mode,* the planner can try to level the load (if desired) and see what effect it may have on the cost and the completion of the project.

PERT has the peculiar characteristic (which can be bad as well as good) of being self-validating to some extent. Because it provides dates for subsidiary events, everybody works toward

FIGURE 16–20
Target Bar Chart Report

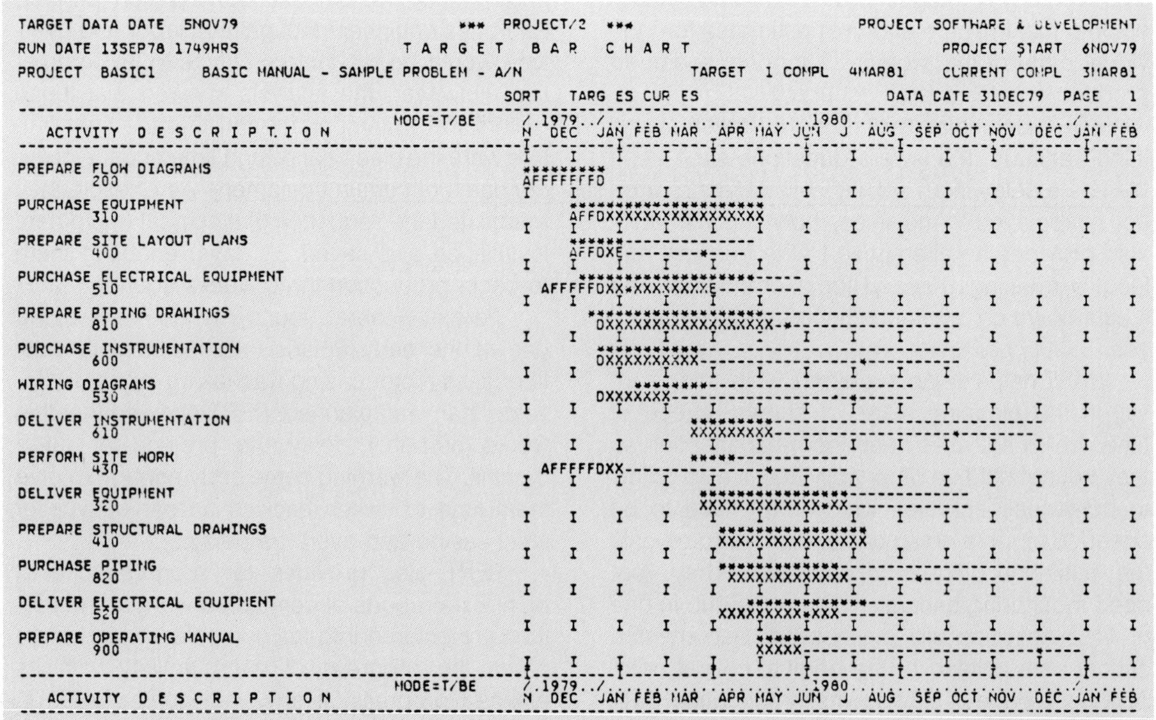

Source: *Project/2 Basic Manual* (Cambridge, Mass.: Project Software & Development, 1980), p. 9.17.0

FIGURE 16-21
Resource Load Report

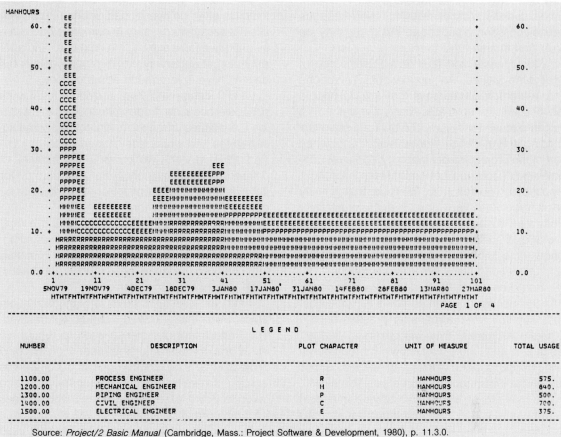

Source: *Project/2 Basic Manual* (Cambridge, Mass.: Project Software & Development, 1980), p. 11.3.0.

them and usually meets them. The bad part is the failure to move as rapidly as they should in case the expected times are too loose.

PERT DISADVANTAGES

By no means is everyone "sold" on PERT. Some building contractors do not seem to like it because they say it doesn't help them. They know how long it takes to build a building. They say that PERT only requires duplicate planning.

There are also critics at the other end of the line, out where projects are near technical frontiers—where PERT is supposed to be at its best. Joseph Freitag of Hughes Aircraft has said

that it is not possible to use PERT to control or coordinate changes in the configuration of complex electronic projects because this work "is just not networkable." Nor do time estimates for uncertain activities become any more certain from statistical manipulation.

Some managers resist PERT because they see it as taking away part of their jobs. Construction superintendents like to be fountainheads of all knowledge about how long work will take and how the delay of one activity might affect the whole project. And it is true that when a project is made the subject of a PERT analysis and put in a computer this takes away part of a superintendent's need to judge. When PERT is first introduced, the resistance it sometimes meets (which may almost amount to sabotage) may make it almost useless. Most companies report that such opposition soon disappears, but there may be problems at first.

Most people find fault with PERT's use of three time values. An International Telephone and Telegraph official says that asking people for pessimistic estimates only gives them a built-in excuse for failure. ITT built a post office building in Providence, Rhode Island, and, when part of the project fell behind, the people responsible said: "I told you that it might take that long."

Another objection to PERT is that usually pessimistic times vary more from the most likely times than do the optimistic times. The weighted average, therefore, is always biased toward a longer time than the most likely time, and this puts unintended slack into all calculations.

Some critics of PERT don't like it because it forces people to estimate times for activities. They say that when a manager presses people to make estimates, they will put in a "fudge" factor and that time estimates will be too liberal. If this happens, none of the ensuing calculations rectify the inaccuracies. Worse yet, liberal estimates may make people work toward minimum performance (since this is all the program calls for) and no more. Perhaps this objection has more validity for PERT/time than for PERT/cost because overliberal cost estimates boost bid prices and lose contracts.

Still another objection to PERT is the cost of reviewing all the reports to see where things stand. PERT can help only when the data are accurate and up to date, and this means frequent computer reviews of the data at considerable cost. Well-run PERT systems, however, generate "exception" reports which highlight problem areas and save considerable review time.

There are still other objections to PERT, but most of them are simply complaints that it is not a perfect tool. PERT does not, for example, show if the company *has* the resources the project will need. Nor does PERT reveal if resources are interchangeable. These must be input to the system.

PERT also makes it look like things have to be done in a strict sequence when, in fact, they can often be overlapped or done in parallel. It is not always necessary to complete one activity *entirely* before starting the next one. And after projects get underway, PERT reports delays but doesn't reveal very much about causes.

PERT does not in itself provide a level work schedule because it doesn't consider the workload it creates in relationship to departmental capacities and workloads caused by other jobs. And, PERT doesn't work well if the priorities of different projects are changed very much. Nor does it solve the problem of low-priority jobs getting pushed back forever.

PERT is limited in the detail it is practical to report. Thus, PERT does not report everything. Nor are networks updated all the time. It is often too costly to produce new reports frequently, even with computer systems.

Yet, in spite of the list of objections just given, PERT has "arrived" and is widely used. The Department of Defense used to require all of its major contractors to use it on all new projects (this is no longer required of companies which plan well). Industry in general has also taken to PERT. Merck, Sharp, and Dohme uses it for new-project planning. Ford Motor Co. uses it when tooling up for new models. Chrysler uses it at every stage in the planning and building of all new plants. United Airlines uses it to prepare their annual business plan. PERT has also been used by builders of apartment buildings, bridges, and roads. Small contractors as well as large are among today's PERT users.

RENEWED INTEREST IN PERT

After being developed in the late 1950s, PERT applications grew in popularity through the 1960s, but then interest in it seemed to wane through the first half of the 1970s, primarily for the reasons mentioned above. However, a rediscovery of PERT seems to have taken place in recent years. Much of the credit for this renewed interest comes from the development and availability of improved computerized PERT systems which simplify the initial development of the PERT network and provide more efficient ways to use this information to manage projects.

One modern system, Project/2, is typical of this generation of project planning and control systems. Project/2 is a sophisticated system that requires a main frame computer such as an IBM 370 to run. It can run PERT networks containing up to 32,500 activities with as many as 100,000 precedence relationships. Each activity can have up to 16,250 different resources assigned to it (for resource allocation reporting). The computational time to run a 30,000-activity network on an IBM 360/40 (the slowest machine it fits on) is three hours. The largest computer it uses— an Amdahl 470/V7—takes only three minutes to compute the entire network of 30,000 activities.[8]

PERT systems such as these are used primarily for large projects, as the software above can cost nearly $250,000. Smaller systems such as the Artemus System can cost the same amount, but it comes installed as a "turnkey" system on a dedicated Hewlett-Packard 1000 minicomputer.[9]

Smaller microcomputer-based systems are now also available for only a few hundred dollars and can provide rather sophisticated analyses, but usually for only a few hundred activities.

For example, the Harvard Project Manager sells for about $400 and runs primarily on an IBM personal computer in an interactive mode. It allows both PERT and CPM to be used, can perform cost allocation, and "automatic recalculation of project duration and cost."[10]

Modularized PERT

Further, new applications are being developed. Fluor Engineering, for example, uses "modularized" PERT to help them prepare bids

for projects such as nuclear power plants. While a power plant may require about 5,000 activities, these can be summarized into perhaps 200–300 "modules" or major components to be built. For example, a power project may need a certain class of pump but with special features required for this particular project.

At Fluor, a catalog of modular or subnetworks has been developed which shows the activities, estimated times, and costs for a number of these generalized major components. The design engineer can look up the modular network for the "generalized pump" in question, see what is involved, and adjust the times and activities for the changes which may be needed for the *specific* pump required. Further, the catalog of modular networks shows "linkages" to other modules. This approach allows design engineers to develop more precise project bids (which include timetables for completion) in a matter of days instead of months.

Review Questions

1. Differentiate between planning for projects and planning for repetitive activities.
2. How is PERT similar to assembly line-balancing methods discussed in Chapter 22? How is it different? How is it similar to MRP I, discussed in Chapter 11? How is it different?
3. Network planning methods such as PERT work best on what kinds of activities? Give a few examples.
4. How far down into detail and subdetails should PERT analyses be carried?
5. Can an analyst calculate the probable time for completing a project covered by a PERT plan if the plan is used only one time for activities? Can the analyst tell how probable it will be that the project might be finished one week earlier even if no effort to speed up is made? Or does the analyst need three time estimates for each activity in order to answer either of these questions?
6. If PERT activities are truly *workload* assignments, why are they so universally spoken of in terms of the calendar time they will take? Isn't the time a direct function of the resource inputs? Discuss.
7. If PERT reports show that cost slippages are occurring, how can managers pick up this slippage

---

[8] *Project/2 Basic Manual* (Cambridge, Mass.: Project Software & Development, 1980), pp. D.05.0, D.08.0.

[9] For an excellent comparative review of the five most popular large-scale PERT/CPM, see J. P. Wilson, "Computer Programs for Planning and Managing Outages," *Power Engineering*, September 1981, pp. 84–87.

[10] P. J. Gill, "Newcomer Debuts Project-Management Package," *Information Systems News*, July 25, 1983, p. 48.

and so end up doing the whole project within the planned cost limits?

8. It is sometimes possible to shorten a project's completion time but at a cost trade-off for the time gained. Explain how this works, and show how far it can be carried.

9. Differentiate between batch and online PERT systems. When is each most appropriately used?

10. Why do many people not like PERT?

11. Why is there a renewed interest in using PERT?

Questions for Discussion

1. How can a system like PERT help in setting time schedules for hard-to-plan activities, such as designing? Is it just not possible to tell how long such things will take? Or is this possible?

2. PERT does not unearth the critical resources needed to accomplish the work along the critical path (or does it?). So it really cannot help to get the work done on time. Is this so? Discuss?

3. How can managers tell, during the *assembly* part of the work on big projects, whether the work is up to schedule or not? Also, how can they tell whether it is running ahead or behind the cost budget? Furthermore, if it is behind either timewise or costwise, what can be done about it?

4. Valuable though PERT is on giant projects, it is still costly to rerun it on the computer every few days. Yet it would have to be rerun often if it were to be a very helpful managerial tool.

   a. How can a manager judge the cost value of reruns of PERT?

   b. Suppose that the manager is not concerned with the costliness of rerunning PERT; in this case how often should it be rerun? Why?

5. Conceivably every path could become the critical path. And near-critical paths may need just about as much attention as the critical path. How does PERT handle the possibility of other paths becoming critical paths?

Problems*

1. The following information covers part of a large PERT diagram:

---
* Calculations to aid in solving most of these problems may be done with provided software or manually. See Preface for explanation of this software.

Starting Event	Following Event	Expected Time (weeks)
A	C	11
A	D	6
B	D	5
C	E	7
C	F	5
D	F	9
D	G	10
D	H	12
E	F	2
F	H	8
F	I	12
G	H	4
H	I	8

What is the critical path, and how many weeks will it take to complete this work?

2. What is the critical path in the following set of related jobs? How long will it take to get the work done? If we could cut three days off the longest job in the critical path, how would this affect the solution? If there is a new critical path, what is it?

Event Sequence	Time in Days	Event Sequence	Time in Days
1–2	6	5–8	7
1–3	4	5–10	8
1–4	5	6–7	7
2–5	7	6–9	3
2–7	6	7–10	9
3–5	8	7–8	3
3–7	10	8–11	8
4–6	4	9–10	6
		10–1·1	5

3. Suppose that in problem 1 there were the following variances?

Activity	Variance (weeks)	Activity	Variance (weeks)
A–C	4	D–H	5
A–D	3	E–F	1
B–D	3	F–H	3
C–E	2	F–I	6
C–F	1	G–H	1
D–F	3	H–I	1
D–G	4		

What are the time limits within which there is a 95 percent chance of the work being completed? What are the extreme times that might possibly occur according to the figures in our problem?

4. Suppose in problem 1, that it would be possible to shorten A–C to 6, C–E to 5, D–F to 6, D–H to 10, and G–H to 3. Which of these changes, if any, would affect the critical path? How long will the new critical path take?

5. Suppose, in problem 1, that it would be possible by putting on extra workers to shorten the times for the activities at the following extra costs:

Activity	Possible Weeks Reduction	Cost per Week Gained
A–C	2	$100
A–D	2	400
B–D	1	300
C–E	3	200
C–F	1	100
D–F	1	300
D–G	3	300
D–H	2	$500
E–F	0	—
F–H	1	200
F–I	3	100
G–H	0	—
H–I	1	300

a. If it were highly important to save all the time possible, regardless of cost, which activities should be shortened? What would the new critical path be? How long would it take? How much would it cost to make the necessary reductions?

b. If there were a $1,000 limit on the amount that could be spent to move things along faster, what would the answers be to the questions in part a?

6. The following data are from a large PERT diagram:

Immediately Preceding	Event	Immediately Following
—	0	1, 2
0	1	3
0	2	3
1, 2	3	4, 5, 6
3, 5, 6	4	8, 9, 10
3	5	4
3	6	4, 7
6	7	9
4, 12	8	13
4, 7	9	11, 12
4	10	11, 12
9, 10	11	15
9, 10	12	8, 13
8, 12	13	14
13	14	15
11, 14	15	—

Here are the estimated times (in weeks) to complete each activity:

Event Sequence	Time
0–1	4–6–8
0–2	6–7–10
1–3	1–1–2
2–3	1–2–3
3–4	3–4–6
3–5	1–3–5
3–6	2–3–5
4–8	5–6–8
4–9	1–3–4
4–10	2–2–3
5–4	1–1–2
6–4	1–1–1
6–7	1–3–6
7–9	3–4–6
8–13	1–2–3
9–11	3–4–5
9–12	1–2–3
10–11	4–6–9
10–12	1–2–4
11–15	2–3–4
12–8	5–7–10
12–13	1–3–5
13–14	1–2–3
14–15	4–6–9

Draw a PERT diagram showing these relationships.

What is the critical path? How many weeks will it take? What are the maximum and minimum probable limits? If this path could be shortened by four weeks, what path would then become critical? How long should it take, and what is its probable maximum?

What are the chances that the project will finish two weeks early without any extra effort having been put forth?

7. Visit a local building contractor, and gather the necessary information for PERT about a small construction project, analyze it, and write a nontechnical report for the contractor explaining your results and how he should proceed in implementing the technique and what costs and benefits are expected.

8. For the following situation (see table below), draw a PERT network, and determine the following (add dummy activities where required):
   a. Critical path.
   b. Early start, late start, early finish, late finish.
   c. Total slack.
   d. Free slack.

e. What would happen if the following time and precedence changes were revised as more information became available:

(1) Activity A's pessimistic time increased to 8?

(2) Activities A, D, G, and F's realistic and pessimistic time each increased 20 percent?

(3) The total time allowed to complete the project was extended four days longer than the duration of the critical path(s)?

f. Given the answers obtained in parts a–d, suppose the project had had fixed costs per day of $1,000. Also, suppose you could reduce the lenght of the project's duration by expediting (shortening) certain activity's expected times at a given cost per day shown to some minimum number of days.

Given the information provided in the last two columns, what would you recommend? Hint: Expedite only those activities which are critical and will produce a net savings in fixed costs. When expediting, other activities may become critical as their slack is eaten away. When this occurs, you may have to reduce two or more activities simultaneously in order to reduce the project's duration and reduce fixed costs.)

9. Develop a PERT network for planning a play which will be produced in your community or college.

Activity	Immediate Precedence Requirements	Optimistic Time	Realistic Time	Pessimistic Time	Expedite Cost* per Day	Minimum Expected* Completion Time
A	—	1	1	1	$ 900	1
B	A	3	6	8	400	2
C	A	4	5	6	700	3
D	A	2	3	4	800	3
E	A	9	9	15	—	—
F	B	7	8	8	300	5
G	B	4	7	9	500	3
H	C	1	3	9	700	3
I	D	5	6	7	—	—
J	H, F, G	3	4	8	1,100	2
K	H, I	2	3	7	650	3
L	H, I	7	7	8	300	4
M	D	8	9	15	—	—
N	M	10	15	17	1,400	7
O	M	3	6	9	600	4
P	D	6	12	13	550	7
Q	M	8	9	12	980	4
R	P, Q	3	6	7	—	—
S	O, R	7	8	12	—	—
T	J, K, L, N	6	7	12	520	5
U	J, K	4	5	5	—	—
V	J, K	2	2	2	100	1
W	E, S, T, U, V	5	6	9	—	—
X	E, S, T, U, V	9	10	10	650	3
Y	W	3	4	6	50	2
Z	X, Y	7	8	9	250	4

* These columns are to be used to answer part f of this problem.

Chapter 17 ⎯⎯⎯⎯⎯⎯⎯⎯⎯⎯⎯⎯⎯⎯⎯⎯⎯⎯⎯⎯

Designing Service Capacities with Waiting-Line Analysis and Monte Carlo Simulation ⎯⎯⎯

In Chapter 5 we said that one of the most important considerations in the design of services concerns decisions involving trade-offs between the cost of the time customers spend waiting and being served against the cost of providing more service capacity to reduce the waits (this being the cost of more idle capacity during lulls in demand). The general methodology used in such analyses is called *waiting-line analysis.*

In this chapter, we will discuss two quite different approaches to solving this kind of cost-balancing problem. One, which might be called "classical" waiting-line analysis, uses "queuing models." This approach uses mathematical calculations which often become quite complex. The second method is to use Monte Carlo simulation.

QUEUING MODELS

Queuing models were first developed by A. K. Erlang, a Danish telephone engineer, in the early 1900s to study the capacity requirements and the performance of early automatic telephone switching systems. There were, however, only a few other industrial applications of queuing until the 1950s when analysts began to apply their skills to analyzing industrial problems.

Queuing models are based on mathematical probability assumptions about how many customers will need to be served and how and when they will arrive to be served at a service facility. They are designed to estimate how long customers wait in line, the length of waiting lines, how busy servers are, and what would happen if service times or the pattern of service demand changes.

Queuing models require a minimum of three kinds of data: *(a)* the average rate of arrival of customers for service, *(b)* the average rate that customers can be served, and *(c)* the number of servers. Other information is also needed in some cases. The variability patterns of arrival rates and of service rates is usually not necessary because the basic queuing formulas include an assumption that these will follow a "Poisson" probability distribution pattern.

Using this information, queuing formulas will provide estimates to such questions as: What will the average waiting time for customers be? How many people (or machines, or airplanes, and so on) on the average will be waiting? How much idle time will the service people (mechanics, airplane landing strips, and so on) have?

Mathematical probability formulas for waiting-line situations with several variables can become quite complex. Here we will deal with a few simplified examples to show how queuing models can be used in designing service systems where waiting lines are involved. In real life, queuing problems are usually much more complicated than they are in our examples.

GAS STATION EXAMPLE (MODEL 1)

The simplest queuing model, which we will call Model 1, can be illustrated by the example of a gas station located in an isolated area which is staffed by one attendant. On the average, customers arrive at the rate of four per hour, although sometimes there are more and sometimes fewer. This *arrival rate's* symbol is λ (the Greek letter lambda).

Service times average six minutes (or a rate of 10 per hour), but this, too, varies. If the attendant is busy serving one customer, then our queuing model assumes that other arriving customers will form a line and wait to be served on a "first-come, first-served" basis. Our model also assumes that the arrival of customers is "independent," meaning that they don't "decide" whether to arrive or not based on whether they see a line. And it is assumed that once they have arrived, even if there is a line of cars waiting, they, too, will get into line and will not defect.

Given these assumptions, it is possible to calculate the probability that any specific number of customers, *P(x),* will arrive during a certain time period, *T.* The formula for the calculation, which uses the Poisson probability distribution, is given in Appendix D where, for our problem, the following probabilities were calculated.[1]

Arrivals in One Hour	Probability P(x)	Cumulative Probability
0	0.018	0.018
1	0.073	0.091
2	0.147	0.238
3	0.195	0.433
4	0.195	0.628
5	0.156	0.784
6	0.104	0.888
7	0.060	0.948
8	0.030	0.978
9	0.013	0.991
10	0.005	0.996
Over 10	0.004	1.000

The next assumption in our problem is that the average service time is six minutes, or, on the average, the attendant can service 10 cars per hour. This 10 per hour is called the *service rate* and is designated μ (the Greek letter mu). As before, the queuing formula assumes that the variations in the service rate will follow a Poisson pattern.[2] The Greek letter μ simply replaces λ in the Poisson formula.

Other assumptions inherent in the formulas are that the possible number of customers is large, that the line can get to be very long, and that on the average the attendant can service more cars than will arrive in an hour—that the average service rate (μ) is *greater* than the average arrival rate (λ).

Using these assumptions, the following equations will provide several useful estimates of the behavior of this service system. Given:

$$\lambda = 4 \text{ and } \mu = 10$$

The average number of cars waiting in line (called L_q) will be:

$$L_q = \frac{\lambda^2}{\mu(\mu - \lambda)} = \frac{4^2}{10(10 - 4)} = 0.267 \text{ cars}$$

---

[1] In typical waiting-line situations, the average arrival rate of customers tends to be small as compared to the maximum arrival rate. In these cases, no individual arrival rate can be very much smaller than the average rate because it can't be less than zero. But, on the high side, it can be several times the average. The Poisson probability distribution is well suited to depicting this situation.

[2] Service *times* are assumed to be explained by the negative exponential distribution, which is the mathematical equivalent of service *rates* (average cars being served per time period) being explained by the Poisson distribution. Since the queuing equations presented require only λ and μ, this relationship will not be explained here.

The average number of cars waiting in line *and* being served (called L) will be:

$$L = \frac{\lambda}{\mu - \lambda} = \frac{4}{10 - 4} = 0.667 \text{ cars}$$

The average time a car spends waiting in line (called W_q) will be:

$$W_q = \frac{\lambda}{\mu(\mu - \lambda)} = \frac{4}{10(10 - 4)}$$
$$= 0.0667 \text{ hours or about}$$
$$4 \text{ minutes}$$

The average time a car spends waiting in line *and* being served (called W) will be:

$$W = \frac{1}{\mu - \lambda} = \frac{1}{10 - 4}$$
$$= 0.167 \text{ hours or 10 minutes}$$

The average proportion of time the attendant spends serving cars (called ρ, the Greek letter rho) will be:

$$\rho = \frac{\lambda}{\mu} = \frac{4}{10} = 0.4 \text{ hours or 24 minutes per hour}$$

The average proportion of idle time of the attendant then becomes:

$$1 - \rho = 0.60 \text{ hours} \quad \text{or} \quad 36 \text{ minutes per hour}$$

Notice that the last two estimates did not need to be calculated by a formula. An attendant serving an average of four cars per hour at an average of 6 minutes per car must be busy 24 minutes and idle 36 minutes. The formulas given here only illustrate that these ratios could be calculated for other combinations of more cars and more attendants, in which case the solutions would not be obvious.

Estimates such as these would be very helpful in providing insight into what would happen if arrivals were to double, as, for example, on a Fourth of July weekend or during a gas shortage. The managers will know whether customers might have to face lengthy waits. Other queuing models could tell them whether or not a second attendant should be added for a busy weekend.

Possibly, too, the managers might try to influence the arrival pattern. In a retail store, three can be a sale on Wednesday and Thursday, normally slow days, but not on Saturday, a busy day. The customers are influenced to alter the arrival pattern, thus reducing the idle time of the servers, the clerks, and shortening the line lengths and waiting time. To reduce the lines at gas stations during the 1979 gas shortage, some states assigned the days on which car owners could buy gas according to odd or even license plate numbers.

AUTOMOBILE REPAIR SHOP EXAMPLE (MODEL 1, CONTINUED)

Many other service design situations can be analyzed with queuing models. In an automobile repair shop, the mechanics arriving at the repair parts issue window have to wait while the service employee looks up the part number in the catalog and its storage location. And the mechanics continue to wait while the attendant gets the part from stock. If the mechanics have to wait while one server does everything, including recording the issue of the part, it might be less costly to have two servers, one to look things up and to handle the paperwork and another to get the item and bring it to the mechanics.

Suppose that mechanics cost $15 per hour and an extra server (the stock chaser) costs $4.50 per hour. If arrivals averaged 4 per hour and could be served by one attendant at a rate of 10 per hour, would it pay to add the stock chaser if this help would increase the average service rate to 12 per hour? The calculations of the answers to this problem are in Appendix D.

They show that the cost of the mechanics' idle time while waiting for parts is $80.16 a day. The stock chaser, if added at a cost of $36 a day, would reduce the mechanics' idle time costs to $60. So the chaser would save $20.16 but would cost $36, and therefore should not be added.

But, a new labor contract increased the mechanics' rate to $18 an hour, and at the same time, because of more business, the arrival rate increased 5 percent to 4.2 per hour. Now, the mechanics' waiting-time cost would increase to $144. Under these circumstances, an added stock chaser would reduce this cost to $102.96, a saving of $41.04 per day. This saving is more than the cost of $36, so the chaser should be added. On an annual basis of 250 working days, the savings would be $1,260.

BANK DRIVE-UP BANKING WINDOW EXAMPLE (MODEL 2)

Our examples so far have assumed that customers needing service, once they have arrived, will always wait in line until they are served.

But people don't always do this. The automobile repair shop mechanics, arriving at the parts issue window and seeing a line, will probably wait because they are being paid for their time. But many prospective customers of a gas station won't wait. They drive on to another station. This is also true of bank drive-up banking windows. Sometimes there is space for only a few cars so there is a physical limitation to the size of the line. But, even if there is room, some prospective customers will not get into line nor will they park and go into the bank on foot. They just go away, usually unhappy with the bank's service.

Our next queuing example is that of a bank drive-up banking window. There is only one window and room for only four cars, including the one being served. This limitation imposes restrictions and makes it necessary to use different queuing models from those we have used before. The average arrival rate is 12 per hour, and the service rate is 15 per hour. The window is open 30 hours per week for 52 weeks per year.

The question posed is, should the bank provide more waiting spaces for cars? Since there is an ample lawn, it is possible, at a cost, to make more waiting spaces for cars by reducing the lawn's size. Now, when a customer arrives

and finds four cars in the line, he has to go away, even if he is willing to wait. This is inconvenient for him and if this happens very often, the bank loses business.

The bank's managers estimate that it loses $1 every time a customer cannot get in line and drives away. More parking spaces can be made available at these costs: one space: $600; two spaces: $900; and $200 each for additional space above two. Assume also that the bank managers want to add enough spaces to receive a one-year or less payback on their investment.

As we said, the limitation of the number of parking spaces requires the use of somewhat more complicated formulas. These and the necessary calculations are given in Appendix D.

These calculations indicate that nearly 19,000 arrivals are expected in a year and that roughly one eighth of them will turn away. This "opportunity" cost, at $1 each, is $2,174. If we assume that everyone who arrives will get into

FIGURE 17-1

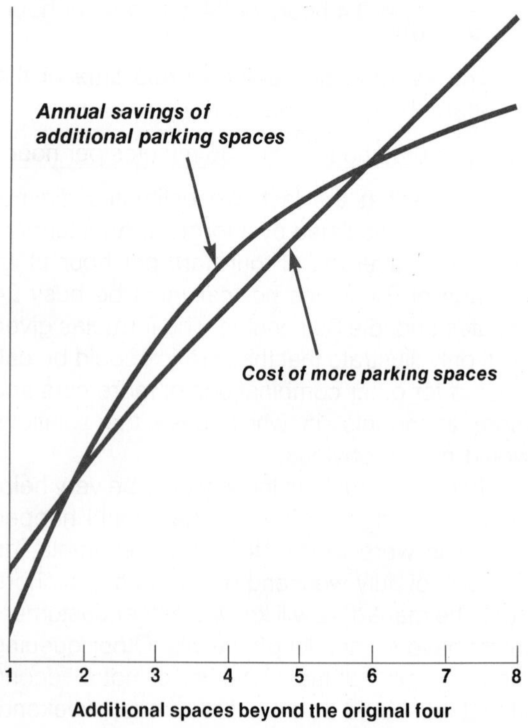

Annual savings of
additional parking spaces

Cost of more parking spaces

Additional spaces beyond the original four

line if there is room, then providing one more space at a cost of $600 would save $507 per year in the reduction of defectors. This is a payback of 1.18 years. Two more spaces would cost $900 and would save $920; three spaces cost $1,100 and would save $1,222; four cost $1,300 and would save $1,444. Paybacks on these added capacities are .98, .9, and .9 years.

From here on, the payback on additional spaces increases. Figure 17–1 shows how one-year payback cost and savings flows are related in this example. Management should probably choose to add either three or four additional spaces in order to meet their payback period and achieve the best return on their investment.

FIRE EQUIPMENT DISPATCHING EXAMPLE (MODEL 3)

Queuing is also useful in analyzing service levels in such places as a city fire department. We will use an example where the alarm headquarters is staffed around the clock by a single dispatcher who answers all emergency calls and dispatches fire engines.

The questions are, how likely is it that a caller reporting a fire will find the line busy, and, if there is a busy signal, how long is the wait for an open line likely to be? Calls come in at the rate of 10 per hour, and it takes from one to three minutes to record where the fire is and to relay the call to the appropriate fire stations.

Here, to illustrate another queuing model, we assume that the Poisson distribution of service rates does not apply, so different formulas are required. These are explained in Appendix D, where the solutions to the two questions are calculated. They show that there is about 1 chance in 10 ($L_q = .095$) that a caller reporting a fire will receive a busy signal and that in that case the average wait until the line is free will be .6 minutes, or 36 seconds. This would seem to be an acceptable level of service.

But, if the calls coming in doubled to 20 per hour, a caller would get a busy signal 76 percent of the time. And, if he or she had to wait, the average wait would be 2.28 minutes. This would be an intolerable average wait when reporting a fire. Additional dispatching capacity would be needed.

MULTIPLE CHANNEL, SINGLE PHASE CALCULATIONS (MODEL 4)

The examples given so far have been with one server doing all of the serving. But, in many actual situations, there are two or more servers, and often there are entire sequences of service activities.

Figure 17–2 depicts several of these different arrangements in schematic form. Our examples so far (Models 1, 2, and 3) have been of the first type, with a single server and a single activity—the "single channel, single phase" model.

If there are two or more servers, each taking customers from a single line and serving them independently, this is a "multiple channel, single phase" case, as is shown second in Figure 17–2. The third case, "single channel, multiple phase" has customers passing by two or more servers. Examples are factory assembly lines

FIGURE 17–2

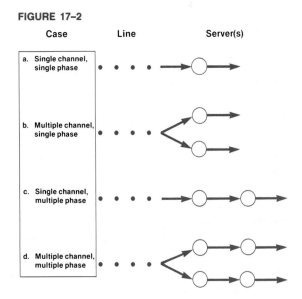

Case	Line	Server(s)
a. Single channel, single phase		
b. Multiple channel, single phase		
c. Single channel, multiple phase		
d. Multiple channel, multiple phase		

with their many servers or cafeteria lines in restaurants.

Finally there is the "multiple channel, multiple phase" case. Here examples would be factory lines where they split for, say, two operations and four assemblers with two on each side of the line working on every other unit. Another example would be college registration systems where the original line splits up into two or more lines for later processes.

In the multiple channel, single phase case in Figure 17–2 (b) the situation is similar to the examples we have given except that the customer at the head of the line is served by the server who is next available. Common examples of this system exist at banks and post offices. Customers wait in a single line and are served by the first available bank teller or postal clerk. (We call this Model 4.)

To illustrate the use of queuing in a multiple channel, single phase serving situation, we will use the Farquhar Company. Farquhar has two Xerox copiers, located in separate office areas where each one often has its own waiting line. There is no common line for the two.

Each machine can handle an average of 15 jobs per hour (although there is a great deal of variation in job sizes). Clerks arrive with jobs for the copiers at the rate of 8 per hour for each machine, or 16 per hour for the two combined. Clerks run their own jobs on the copiers and are thus idle only if there is a line and they have to wait their turn.

With the present system, one machine may be swamped with work while the other is idle. It has been suggested that the machines be moved to a central area where the clerks could wait in a single line for the first machine available. The proposed location is, however, less conveniently located and would require additional walking time by the clerks which would cost 22.5 cents per order, or $3.60 per hour.

The question is, would the saving in the cost of clerk waiting time be more than enough to offset the costs of the extra walking? Clerks cost $6.00 per hour.

The calculations in Appendix D show that with the present system the average cost of clerks waiting is $7.29 per hour. If the two copiers were put together, this would be reduced to $2.60 per hour, but at a cost of $3.60 in extra walking. The new total cost would be $6.20 per hour. The saving of $1.09 per hour, however, would be $2,267 per year so the change should be made.

MACHINE GROUP SERVICING EXAMPLE (MODEL 5)

A different service design problem occurs where a group of machines are required to be set up for new jobs as well as requiring occasional repairs. Often, there is enough of this activity so that one or more service mechanics can be assigned permanently to keeping these machines in operation.

In our problem, we will assume that one mechanic has been assigned to keep five machines in operation. The major difference in this model is that there are a limited number of customers—the five machines in this example. (This is called a *finite calling population.*) Each machine requires service on the average of once every four hours. When service is needed, it averages a half an hour.

The problem here is to answer the following questions: What will be the average number of machines out of production because they are being serviced or waiting to be serviced? What will be the average number of machines waiting to be serviced? What is the average amount of time each machine will spend out of production while being serviced and waiting to be serviced? What will be the average amount of time each machine waits for service?

The solutions to these questions are explained in Appendix D. Figure 17–3 shows a computer printout of these estimates. (Most complex queuing problems are solved on computers or with special-purpose queuing tables and charts.)

This information could serve as a starting

FIGURE 17-3
Computer Solution to Machine Maintenance Example *(using finite calling population model)*

```
QUEUING MODELS


INITIAL CONDITIONS:

AVERAGE ARRIVAL RATE                        0.25
AVERAGE SERVICE RATE                        2.00
*5* SIZE OF FINITE CALLING POPULATION       5


THE SOLUTIONS FOR QUEUING MODEL 5
SINGLE SERVER, SINGLE QUEUE
WITH A FINITE POPULATION

THE AVERAGE ARRIVAL RATE                    0.25
THE AVERAGE SERVICE RATE                    2.00
THE AVERAGE NUMBER OF CUSTOMERS WAITING
AND BEING SERVED                            0.83
THE AVERAGE NUMBER OF CUSTOMERS WAITING
IN LINE                                     0.31
THE AVERAGE TIME EACH CUSTOMER SPENDS
WAITING AND BEING SERVED                    0.80
THE AVERAGE TIME EACH CUSTOMER SPENDS
WAITING IN LINE                             0.30
```

point to an investigation of whether the mechanic should serve more (or fewer) machines and whether he should have a helper or not. Costs of machine idle time could be balanced against the costs of a different number of mechanics or helpers.

SPECIAL-PURPOSE QUEUING TABLES AND CHARTS

In situations where the conditions of classical queuing models can be met, special-purpose tables and charts can be developed to provide precomputed estimates.

TRW company found, for example, that queuing problems came up from time to time but that its employees did not calculate solutions because the formulas looked too forbidding.

TRW solved this problem by developing charts, based on the formulas, from which they could easily obtain estimates to most questions.

Figure 17–4 is a chart used by TRW for various waiting-line problems.[3] Suppose, for example, that there is a group of machines needing occasional service and there is a question of how many service employees are needed. Figure 17–4 will provide an estimate. In Figure 17–4, the horizontal scale is a scale of cost ratios. To find the ratio to use in our example, the cost per hour for an idle machine is divided by the cost per hour of an idle service employee. Suppose that this is $33.75 divided by $9, or a ratio of 3.75.

The vertical scale is another scale of ratios:

---

[3] This chart is one of several presented in *Waiting-Line Pamphlet* (Cleveland, Ohio: TRW, Inc.), pp. 11–20.

FIGURE 17–4

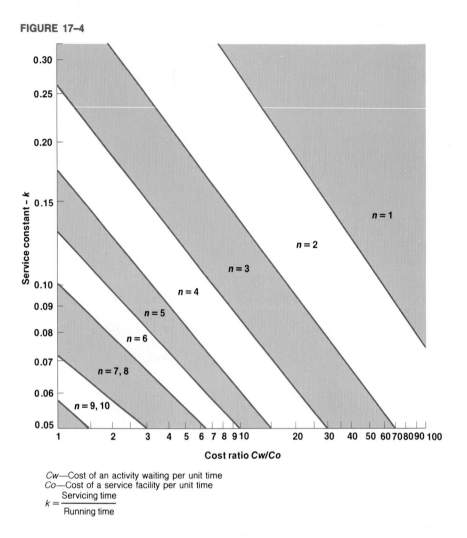

Cw—Cost of an activity waiting per unit time
Co—Cost of a service facility per unit time

$$k = \frac{\text{Servicing time}}{\text{Running time}}$$

the average service time divided by the time the machine runs. If service time averages half an hour per day per machine and if the machines' average operating time is seven hours a day (including the service time), the ratio is .5 divided by 7, or .071. (During the other hour of the day the machines are not operating because the next job is not ready, or the operator is away from the machine, or for other reasons not related to this calculation.)

Reading from Figure 17–4, we find that the two ratios intersect in zone 6. This means that each service employee should service six ma-

chines. If the company has 24 machines of this kind, it will need four service employees.

This chart does not, however, provide solutions to all waiting-line questions. For other questions, such as how many jobs will normally have to wait if there is one server, two servers, and so on, the analyst will have to develop other charts, use queuing formulas, or computer programs designed for this purpose.

TRW has a second chart to use for analyzing tool crib waiting-line kinds of problems. Assume that factory operators arrive and are served at the tool cribs according to the Poisson distribution described earlier. Figure 17–5 shows us how many crib attendants will be needed. Again, the horizontal scale is a ratio scale. This time it is the cost per hour of the machinists who may have to wait, divided by the hourly cost of tool-room attendants who, at other times, may have to wait.

Suppose that machine operators cost $12 an hour and that toolroom attendants cost $6 an hour. Twelve dollars divided by $6 equals 2, which is the ratio to use on the horizontal scale.

The number to use when reading the vertical scale is the product of the average arrival rate

times the average service time. If an average of 12 mechanics per hour arrive and ask for tools, and, if, on the average, it takes a tool crib attendant five minutes (or .08 hour) to find and issue tools, then the average calls for service in an hour total .96 hour, which is the value to use on the vertical scale.

Since the intersection of the horizontal and the vertical ratios, 2 and .96, falls in zone 2, the total idle-time cost of mechanics and crib attendants is minimized by having *two* attendants on duty.

It is often possible, however, to assign tool crib attendants other work to do (grinding tools,

FIGURE 17–5

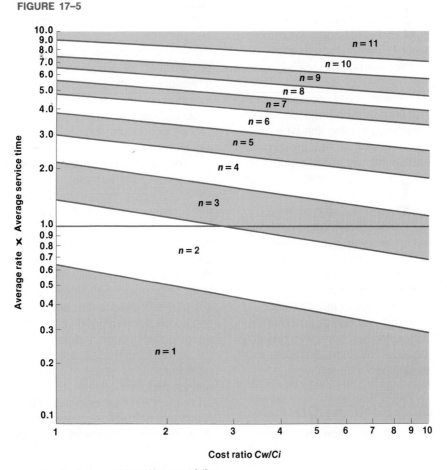

Cw—Cost of an activity waiting per unit time
Ci—Cost of an idle service facility per unit time

cleaning up and repairing returned tools, putting a protective covering of oil on them, and so on) when they are not busy serving machine operators. These odd jobs will reduce idle time, so that the loss when they are "idle" may really be only $3 an hour. In this case, the horizontal ratio would be 4. The vertical ratio remains .96. These two ratios intersect just inside the 3 zone which suggests there should be three attendants although two attendants could almost handle the work.

SUMMARY OF BASIC QUEUING MODELS

The characteristics of the several illustrative queuing models which have been discussed are presented in Figure 17–6. Their formulas are presented in Appendix D. And, although these examples do not cover every possible situation, they do cover a number of situations. Other queuing models, some more complex than these, allow for other conditions and situations.

However, sometimes waiting-line-type problems become so complex that they are impractical to solve mathematically. This would happen, for example, if a company has, say, three enamel-baking ovens whose heating elements burn out occasionally and cause extensive and costly downtime. The question might be, should the company put in all new heating elements every time one of them burns out? Or should it replace only the burned-out element? Or should it replace the others at the same time if they have been in use six months or more? Or should some other policy be followed? A problem like this is too complex for solution with queuing models. It can, however, be analyzed quite satisfactorily with Monte Carlo simulation.

MONTE CARLO SIMULATION

Monte Carlo simulation is an alternative to mathematical waiting-line models. Often it is the only practical way to solve complex problems of the waiting-line type.

Monte Carlo simulation is a logically organized attempt to imitate a real-life situation so managers can test and evaluate various policies. It is a technique whereby a system and its associated possible sequences of events are produced on a make-believe basis. This is usually done by a computer which is programmed to act like the system being studied. Simulation allows managers to investigate changes in a system's behavior without incurring the costs of manipulating real systems. It also helps decision makers develop an understanding of how systems react to certain stimuli.

The name *Monte Carlo* comes from the city on the Mediterranean famous for gambling and, as a method, is based on the same kind of probability laws that govern gambling games.

Our interest in Monte Carlo comes from its usefulness in aiding managers in analyzing a broad range of problems. It has proven to be a helpful tool in the analysis of problems in manufacturing in service companies, transportation organizations, urban planning, health care, education, agriculture, and in any number of other situations.

The major differences between simulation and queuing models are:

1. Queuing models generally presume that the system is operating at a "steady state," meaning that there are no peaks and valleys, no five o'clock rush. Queuing models can calculate the average line length, the average waiting time, and so on, but only for steady-state conditions. In contrast, simulation models can be developed to estimate line lengths, waiting times, and so on, for peak and valley situations as well as for steady-state conditions.[4]

2. Queuing models are, of necessity, based on a number of assumptions about arrival and service patterns, and so on. These limit their use and keep them from being used in more complex situations. Simulation allows much more flexibility in the determination of assumptions.

---

[4] Dynamic queuing models are available—but they are extremely complex to use.

FIGURE 17–6
Characteristics of Basic Queuing Models

Model	Model Name	Channel/Phase	Arrival Rate Distribution	Service Rate* Distribution	Calling Population	Queue Discipline	Other Conditions which Must Be Specified
1	Basic	Single channel, single phase	Poisson	Poisson	Unlimited	First come, first served	None
2	Limited line length	Single channel, single phase	Poisson	Poisson	Unlimited	First come, first served	Maximum length the line can be, including the one being served.
3	Any service time distribution	Single channel, single phase	Poisson	Any	Unlimited	First come, first served	The standard deviation of the service time.
4	Multiple channel service	Multiple channel, single phase	Poisson	Poisson	Unlimited	First come, first served	The number of servers or channels in parallel.
5	Limited number of customers	Single channel, single phase	Poisson	Poisson	Limited	First come, first served	Size of the finite calling population.

* Service *time* distribution is assumed to be negative exponential, which is equivalent to service *rates* being Poisson-distributed. Additional assumptions: $\mu > \lambda$, except in Models 3 and 5. Arrivals are independent.

FIGURE 17–7
Ways in Which Simulation Can Be Used

Air traffic control queuing	Industry models
Aircraft maintenance scheduling	Textile
Airport design	Petroleum (financial aspects)
Ambulance location and dispatching	Information system design
Assembly line scheduling	Intergroup communication (sociological
Bank teller scheduling	studies)
Bus (city) scheduling	Inventory reorder rule design
Circuit design	Aerospace
Clerical processing system design	Manufacturing
Communication system design	Military logistics
Computer time sharing	Hospitals
Telephone traffic routing	Job shop scheduling
Message system	Aircraft parts
Mobile communications	Metals forming
Computer memory-fabrication test-	Work-in-process control
facility design	Shipyard
Consumer behavior prediction	Library operations design
Brand selection	Maintenance scheduling
Promotion decisions	Airlines
Advertising allocation	Glass furnaces
Court system resource allocation	Steel furnaces
Distribution system design	Computer field service
Warehouse location	National manpower adjustment system
Mail (post office)	Natural resource (mine) scheduling
Soft-drink bottling	Iron ore
Bank courier	Strip mining
Intrahospital material flow	Parking facility design
Enterprise models	Numerically controlled production
Steel production	facility design
Hospital	Personnel scheduling
Shipping line	Inspection department
Railroad operations	Spacecraft trips
School district	Petrochemical process design
Equipment scheduling	Solvent recovery
Aircraft	Police response-system design
Facility layout	Political voting prediction
Pharmaceutical center	Rail freight car dispatching
Financial forecasting	Railroad traffic scheduling
Insurance	Steel mill scheduling
Schools	Taxi dispatching
Computer leasing	Traffic-light timing
Insurance manpower hiring decisions	Truck dispatching and loading
Grain terminal operation	University financial and operational
Harbor design	forecasting
	Urban traffic system design
	Water resources development

Source: Reprinted with permission of Macmillan Publishing Co., Inc., from *Design and Use of Computer Simulation Models* by James R. Emshoff and Roger L. Sisson.

3. Simulation can be used for other applications in addition to waiting-line analysis. Figure 17–7 lists examples of the many ways in which simulation can be used.

We will illustrate how simulation works with examples of its use in several different situations.

TRUCK REPLACEMENT EXAMPLE

Air Advance Air Freight is considering discontinuing its leasing of 12 pickup and delivery trucks. If it does this, Air Advance will have to buy 12 trucks right away and then buy replacement trucks in the future, one by one, as the old ones wear out. The question AAAF's managers want to answer is how many trucks they may have to buy during the next five years (including the initial 12 trucks) in order to keep 12 trucks in operation all the time. At the moment, AAAF's managers are not concerned with the fact that at the end of five years they will have 12 trucks on hand, some of which will be relatively new and some of which will be old. The only question is how many will have to be purchased so they can plan their cash requirements accordingly.

Without using a computer, it is possible to perform this simulation by using a random number table. Before using random numbers, however, it is necessary to know how long the trucks are expected to last. Figure 17–8 shows a history of truck life.

Next, a method must be developed to simulate the wearing out and replacement of trucks over the next 5 years, or 60 months. This is done by using "random numbers" from the random number table provided in Appendix E. If we pick a number any place in a table of random numbers and go across a row or up or down a column in any direction, the probabilities of any of the 1,000 three-digit numbers (000–999), say the number 684, being the next number, is 1/1,000. The odds are the same if the numbers are chosen randomly instead of one after the other as they appear in a table of random numbers.

In order to simulate the wearing-out of trucks, we assign blocks of numbers between 000 and 999 according to the frequency distribution shown in Figure 17–9. Since 5 percent of the trucks have had in the past (and we think that this will continue into the future) a life of only 12 months, we assign the first 5 percent of these numbers, 000 through 049, to trucks which will wear out in 12 months. (We could have assigned any 50 numbers from the set 000–999, but we assign the first 50 only for convenience.) Then we assign the next 10 percent of the numbers, 050 through 149, to the trucks which will last only 15 months. Figure 17–10 shows the complete allocation of numbers to the various truck lives.

Next, we read off random numbers successively from the random number table. We started at the top of column 6 of Appendix E. The first number is 027. The number 027 falls in the range 000–049, which corresponds to a truck life of 12 months.

The next random number is 539, which falls

FIGURE 17–8

Truck Life (months)	Percentage of Trucks which Have Worn Out
12	5%
15	10
18	20
21	25
24	30
27	5
30	5
Total	100%

FIGURE 17–9

Truck Life (months)	Percent which Last This Long	Random Numbers Assigned to This Event
12	5%	000–049
15	10	050–149
18	20	150–349
21	25	350–599
24	30	600–899
27	5	900–949
30	5	950–999

FIGURE 17–10

Truck	Random Number				Month (cumulative) when Truck Wears Out and Is Replaced				Excess Truck Life beyond 60 Months
1	027	539	623	485	12	33	57	78	18
2	272	273	852		18	36	60		0
3	850	840	973		24	48	78		18
4	198	523	071	532	18	39	54	75	15
5	025	285	626	890	12	30	54	78	18
6	283	114	116	453	18	33	48	69	9
7	406	539	496		21	42	63		3
8	875	332	963		24	42	72		12
9	032	298	658	308	12	30	54	72	12
10	364	587	310		21	42	60		0
11	123	957	951		15	42	69		0
12	397	687	057		21	45	60		0
Total									114

in the 350–599 interval, indicating that the truck which replaced the first one has a life of 21 months and that it will need to be replaced at the end of the 33rd month. The next number is 623, which indicates a life of 24 months. The cumulative months until the failure of this third truck is 57. So these three trucks, considered together, will last less than five years, so a fourth truck will have to be bought. Its random number, 485, indicates a 21-month life so it will be useful considerably beyond the five-year mark.

Since AAAF is interested only in the next 60 months, we go on to the second truck sequence. This time only three trucks will suffice and will cover the 60-month period. But the sequences for trucks number 4, 5, 6, and 9 will, as in the case of the first truck, require four trucks each in order to last for 60 months.

Figure 17–10 shows how this process works. It shows that 41 trucks will have to be purchased within the next 60 months, or 5 years (12 initially, plus 29 replacements). At the beginning of the sixth year, the 12 trucks then on hand will have, in total, an expected remaining truck life of 114 months.

AAAF can now answer the question first posed: How many trucks will it probably have

to buy each year for the next five years? First, they must buy 12 trucks right away. All of them will last through the first year, but 10 will have to be replaced before the end of the second year. Numbers from 12 to 21 in the cumulative month listing (in Figure 17–10) indicates that the original truck wears out and has to be replaced during the second year. During the third year, six more will need replacing (indicated by cumulative numbers from 24 to 33). In the fourth year, it will be seven, and in the fifth year, six. AAAF will have to buy 41 trucks in all before the end of the fifth year. With the knowledge provided by the simulation, it can plan its truck purchases, having some feel for the necessary monetary needs.

How reliable are these results? It is difficult to say exactly how reliable any simulation solution is since no one can know exactly what sequence of events (in our case, the lives of specific trucks) will occur in real life. But, if the distribution of truck lives in Figure 17–9 continues to be valid, then extended simulations provide a good estimate of what will happen in real life.

If we were to simulate this situation again, starting at another place in the random number table, we would generate a different set of sequences of truck replacements, but the total replacements would probably be very close to 29.

One might ask why we cannot simply use the average life of trucks (which is 21 months) to estimate the required number of replacement trucks. It would seem that if three trucks have an average total life of 63 months, then in 60 months two replacements for each original truck should be enough. It would seem that only 24 replacements would have to be purchased instead of 29. The reason this approach fails is that it does not take into account the irregularities of short- and long-lived trucks which do not dovetail in such a way as to average out in the short run. Nor does it recognize that at the end of five years some recently purchased trucks will still have many months of life in them.

MACHINE SETUP MECHANIC EXAMPLE

This example deals with a waiting-line problem similar to one presented in our discussion of queuing Model 5. It illustrates the interactions of service calls whose time between arrivals varies as does the time it takes a server to take care of the calls.

The Sunray Solar Heating Company has four machines which are used in a variety of operations in producing parts for solar panels. These machines are set up by a mechanic, and then each is run by a machine operator until the job is completed, after which the machine is out of production until the mechanic sets it up for its next job. Whenever no machine is being set up, the mechanic waits. (He does not actually wait but keeps busy on relatively low-value minor jobs.)

The question is: How many mechanics should Sunray have if they cost $15 per hour and idle machines cost $30 per hour in lost production?

From past records, Sunray has determined that setup and job times have varied as shown in Figure 17–11.

FIGURE 17–11

Length of Job		Setup Time	
Hours	Instances	Hours	Instances
4	20%	2	50%
8	30	4	20
16	20	8	15
24	20	12	10
40	10	20	5

First, just as in the truck-replacement problem, it is necessary to assign groups of random numbers so that we can generate simulated job-length times and setup times (see Figure 17–12).

FIGURE 17–12

Length of Job		Setup Time	
Hours	Random Numbers	Hours	Random Numbers
4	000–199	2	000–499
8	200–499	4	500–699
16	500–699	8	700–849
24	700–899	12	850–949
40	900–999	20	950–999

Again we refer to the random number table and generate a simulated list of successive job and setup times. These are shown in Figure 17–13.

In Figure 17–13, the "J" and "S" letters refer to job times and setup times. For each machine they were carried out to simulate the con-

FIGURE 17–13

Machine	J	S	J	S	J	S	J	S	J	S	J
1	4	2	8	4	24	8	24	8			
2	8	2	16	4	40	2	16				
3	16	12	4	2	4	12	40				
4	16	4	4	12	24	2	8	2	4	2	8

tinuing sequence of job time, setup time, job time, setup time, and so on until an 80-hour time period (two weeks) had passed. In our example, we assumed that all four machines were set up and ready to begin their first jobs at the start of our simulation. (This assumption puts a small artificial error into the cost comparisons which follow since the mechanic obviously starts off being idle.)

The next step is to see how it would work to have just one mechanic doing all of the setup work. In allocating his time, we followed the priority rule that in case there are two machines needing him he will first take care of the machine which has been waiting the longest.

In Figure 17–14, the lines and arrows follow the mechanic as he goes about his work. We see that at the start he is idle until time 4 (hours). Then he begins setting up the second job on machine 1, completing it two hours later at time 6. Machine 1 then goes to work on its second

job which will keep it tied up for the next eight hours, or until time 14.

Meanwhile the mechanic has to wait two hours from time 6 to time 8, at which time machine 2 finishes its first job. The mechanic then sets it up in two hours, finishing at time 10. Machine 2's new job keeps it busy until hour 26.

Machines 3 and 4 are still busy so again the mechanic has to wait, this time for four hours. Then he goes back to machine 1 which has finished its second job and starts setting it up for its third job. The mechanic's further work and wait periods are shown in Figure 17–14, as are the several instances when the machines have to wait for him.

As the summary at the bottom of Figure 17–14 shows, the mechanic waits a total of 18 hours which, at a cost of $15 an hour, is $270. But with only one mechanic, the machines wait 56 hours which, at $30 an hour, costs $1,680, bring-

FIGURE 17–14

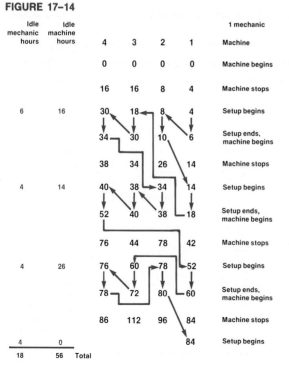

FIGURE 17–15

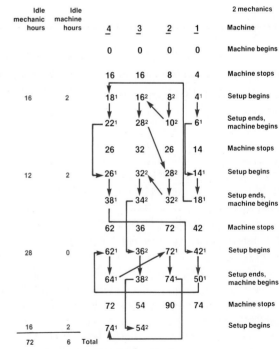

Note: The superscripts on the times (for example, $4^1, 8^2$) refer to mechanic #1 and #2.

ing the total cost of idleness to $1,950 during these 80 hours, or two weeks.

Next we turned to the question of whether hiring a second mechanic woud be cost-effective. Figure 17–15 shows how these two mechanics would shuttle back and forth trying the meet the machines' needs. This time the summary tells us that one mechanic will have 40 idle hours and the other one 32 hours. At $15 an hour, this is $1,080. But idle machine time, six hours, has almost been eliminated. This cost is only $180, which brings the total for the two-mechanic service team to $1,260. Thus, it will save $690 per two weeks, or $17,940 annually to add a second mechanic.

There is no need to consider the question of whether it would pay to add a third mechanic. The most that he could save would be to eliminate all of the $180 cost of machine idle time, but this would be far less than the cost of the added mechanic.

CAR WASH EXAMPLE

The Quick Car Wash Company is concerned about the amount of business it is losing on Saturdays because so many potential customers, seeing long lines, drive on by. Observations show that rarely will the line of waiting cars grow beyond five cars. When potential customers see that many cars ahead of them, they drive away. But, if there are four or fewer, they usually enter the line and wait. Since many car wash customers also buy gasoline and some of the defectors may also be lost future customers, Quick Car Wash's manager estimates that he loses $3 every time a car refuses to wait.

It is possible to change the car wash line controls so that the line can be speeded up on Saturdays. Modifying the controls would cost $900 and would make it possible for the line to operate at either a medium speed (as contrasted with the present slow speed) or a high speed. At medium speed, one extra attendant would be required, and two more for high-speed operation. Attendants cost $4.50 an hour each.

FIGURE 17–16

Service Time (minutes)	Percent of Cars	Random Numbers Assigned
6	10	000–099
7	40	100–499
8	40	500–899
9	10	900–999

The question is: Should QCW modify the controls so that the line can be speeded up on Saturdays, and, if so, should it operate at medium or high speed? This case is similar to the bank drive-up window example in Model 2, except that this time we are using simulation instead of the queuing model.

Past experience with the present line speed shows distribution in service times (the times vary somewhat depending on the kind and size of car as well as how dirty it is in the interior) as in Figure 17–16.

It is estimated that the faster lines will be able to reduce the service times as shown in Figure 17–17.

Past experience shows the distribution of time intervals between the arrival of cars when the long lines might occur on Saturdays as in Figure 17–18.

FIGURE 17–17

Medium Speed—One Extra Attendant		
Service Time (minutes)	Percent of Cars	Random Numbers Assigned
5	10	000–099
6	40	100–499
7	40	500–899
8	10	900–999
High Speed—Two Extra Attendants		
4	10	000–099
5	40	100–499
6	40	500–899
7	10	900–999

FIGURE 17–18

Elapsed Time between Arrivals (minutes)	Percent of Arrivals	Random Numbers Assigned
3	10	000–099
4	20	100–299
5	50	300–799
6	20	800–999

The next step, as before, is to allocate random numbers in proportion to the percent distributions given in our tables. Although we simulated two hours of Saturday operations in order to obtain the figures needed for comparing the alternatives, to save space we will reproduce here only the first half dozen sets of simulated results.

Our first half dozen random numbers for service times were 368, 047, 483, 229, 788, and 096. Those for arrivals were 735, 273, 372, 206, 047, and 252. Translated into equivalent times, these numbers provided service times (for the present slow method) of 7, 6, 7, 7, 8, and 6 minutes. Arrivals were 5, 4, 5, 4, 3, and 4 minutes.

Both sets of times were cumulated in Figure 17–19 so that comparisons could be made. We assumed that there were already five cars in the line when our simulation started. The washing of the first of these cars was completed in 7 minutes, the second at a cumulative time of 13 minutes, the third at 20 minutes, and so on. The

FIGURE 17–19

Time	Cars in Line	Time of Next Arrival	Defect
0–7	5	5	yes
7–9	4	9	no
9–13	5	none	—
13–14	4	14	no
14–20	5	18	yes
20–21	4	21	no
21–27	5	25	yes

cumulations of arrival times showed the first car arriving at 5 minutes, the second at 9 minutes, the third at 14, and so on.

Now the comparisons can be made. From time 0 to 7 the line was full so the car arriving in 5 minutes defected. Then the first car being washed was finished and moved out at 7 so the line was no longer full. When, at 9 minutes, another car arrived, its driver got into line and the line was back up to five. It stayed this way until time 13 when the second car in the original line was finished, thus leaving only four cars in line. But, at 14 minutes, another arrival took the empty space at the end of the line, bringing it back up to five cars. This closed the line until 20 minutes. At 18 minutes, another car arrived but, seeing five cars already in line, it did not stay. Then the next car finished at 20, and the line was down to four until the arrival at time 21 took the space, and so on as is shown in Figure 17–19. In our brief example there were three defections in 27 minutes.

We carried through this analysis to simulate all three line speeds for two hours of operations. The existing method showed five defectors per hour. Their total cost in lost revenues is $15 per hour. The medium speed plus one additional attendent resulting in four defections per hour so this change would not have saved enough ($3) to pay for the added attendant $4.50, and obviously not contribute to the cost of the control modification.

Operating at high speed with two extra attendants reduced defectors to two per hour (a reduction of three over the present method, and a saving of $9, but at a cost of two extra attendants at $9). In this case, Quick Car Wash would break even on the savings versus the labor costs, but there would be no contribution toward the $900 cost of making the change. The company should *not make the change* based on this analysis. However, if they could improve their methods so that the service rate could be increased, it might be economical to install the higher-speed system.

DENVER FIRE DEPARTMENT EXAMPLE

This example presents a description of an actual simulation which was used to aid the city of Denver and the Denver Fire Department in determining how many fire stations it should have, where they should be located, and what type of equipment should be placed in each fire station.[5]

In the middle 1970s, Denver's mayor and fire chief recognized the need to consider the application of modern management analysis for the Denver fire department. A multidisciplinary team was created, consisting of members of the Denver fire department, Denver's Office of Budget and Management, and operations researchers from the University of Colorado. In addition, the team was guided by a specially formed Policy Review Committee, which consisted of the fire chief, several city officials, and a university dean. The research study was funded by HUD's Office of Policy Development and Research by a grant of $117,000.

The major assignment given to the research team by Denver officials was rather straightforward: Can the Denver Fire Department provide approximately the same level of fire protection service but at a lower cost?

Fire suppression accounted for about 90 percent of the activities of the Denver Department's $13-million budget. (The department also answers calls to help people in trouble, heart attack victims, people suffocating, as well as getting cats out of trees, and so on.) Nearly all of the money is for the wages and salaries of firefighters.

At the time of this study, it was costing Denver $250,000 *a year* to staff each fire engine or ladder truck with firefighters around the clock. Labor was the major cost, since the vehicle itself

cost only about $60,000 and a firehouse, a one-time cost, about $400,000. The critical factor, therefore, was simply how many fire "companies" (vehicles with firefighters on board) the city should have and where they should be located.

Static Analysis of Station Location Alternatives

When a city like Denver has a large number of fire companies compared to its fire alarm rate, and all vehicles are typically available to respond to an alarm, then a so-called static analysis can be performed. This was done in Denver by having the members of the Denver Fire Department develop a comprehensive inventory of fire hazards which existed throughout the city. Further, they developed a large number of potential new location sites for fire stations. Next, each of the hazards was graded as to its severity and translated into maximum allowable travel response time standards for the first arriving vehicle.

The last data requirement for this static analysis was the prediction of the response time from each of the existing fire stations and potential fire station sites to each of the hazards. This was accomplished through a detailed time-distance regression analysis study of nearly 1,600 actual runs by Denver fire department vehicles.

The team then had four kinds of data: (1) hazard location, (2) severity of hazards translated into maximum allowable travel response time requirements for the first arriving vehicle, (3) the location of existing and of potential fire station sites, and (4) an ability to predict the response time from any firehouse location to any hazard. With these data, the team was able to analyze a large number of alternative station location patterns. This was done by using linear programming and the "Station Configuration Information Model" (SCIM), a specialized computer model developed by the Denver team to show response time statistics of a given station location pattern.

Several alternative location patterns were

---

[5] Reported in Thomas E. Hendrick and Donald R. Plane et al., *An Analysis of the Deployment of Fire-Fighting Resources in Denver, Colorado* (Santa Monica, Calif.: The Rand Corporation, R-1566/3-HUD, May 1975), and in D. E. Monarchi, T. E. Hendrick, and D. R. Plane, "Simulation for Fire Department Deployment Policy Analysis," *Decision Sciences* 8, 1977, pp. 211–27.

FIGURE 17–20
Static Travel Time Statistics

	Average First-Arriving Pumper Travel Time (minutes)		Average First-Arriving Ladder Travel Time (minutes)	
Hazard Class	Existing Configuration	Proposed Configuration	Existing Configuration	Proposed Configuration
Very high	1.8	1.7	1.9	2.1
High	2.3	2.3	2.7	2.7
Medium	2.2	2.2	2.9	3.0
Low	2.5	2.5	3.4	3.6
Overall average	2.3	2.2	2.8	2.9

analyzed in depth. Each pattern specified where pumper trucks and where ladder trucks were to be located. One configuration stood out as being much less costly than all the others. Not only was it less costly, it even showed a small improvement in the average response travel time by pumper engine and only a slight increase in travel time of the first-arriving ladder trucks. The specific statistics of this configuration are shown in Figure 17–20.

The important characteristic of this configuration was that it provided approximately the same level of service, as measured by response time, but *with five fewer companies.* This configuration required the closing of some stations, the building of certain new ones, and other adjustments in the locations of pumper engines and ladder trucks at various locations throughout the city. This redesigned system with five fewer companies was expected to save Denver more than $2.3 million over a seven-year planning horizon and over $1 million annually thereafter.

Dynamic Analysis of Location Analysis, Using Monte Carlo Simulation

The static analysis described here presumes that each piece of equipment is available to respond to an emergency from its firehouse and is never busy at some other fire when a new alarm arrives. This static assumption may be valid most of the time even though it may not be true all of the time. There are times when equipment has to come from more distant stations because the closest one is already busy on another call.

After selecting what appeared to be the most satisfactory new location pattern, it and several other possible configurations were tested against the existing arrangement by means of Monte Carlo simulation. This "dynamic analysis" allowed the investigating team to systematically study alternative fire station location patterns when fires were simulated to arrive in the pattern of occurrence of Denver's actual fire incident experience.

This dynamic analysis showed how well a given station configuration would perform under various alarm arrival rates; it specifically allowed for a fire truck being busy and already at one fire and so unavailable to go to another fire. The simulation considered, for example, how much travel time would deteriorate (increase) to various places throughout the city if the alarm arrival rate were to increase from, say, an average of 5 calls per hour to an average of 10 per hour?

The Denver study utilized a heavily revised version of the New York City–Rand Institute fire department computer simulation model to perform this dynamic analysis. This model kept track of "arriving" fires and, in the computer, dispatched the closest available companies to them and kept track of travel time, the time it took to put out the fire, and when these companies would be available to go to the next fire, and so on.

To feed this complex model with data that reflected the Denver situation, a comprehensive analysis of over 17,000 actual fires and other emergencies was performed by the research team to determine the location of various emergencies and when they occurred. In addition, a sample of these 17,000 incidents was also analyzed to determine how many vehicles were required to put out the fires and how long each was likely to be busy before it was free to be available to service another emergency.

Using this simulation model and various alarm arrival rates, the research team studied the results of several alternative station location patterns. The alarm arrival rates used varied from 2.5 per hour, the 1973 average, to 9.65 alarms per hour, the projected 1978 rate during the busiest hours of the day (4:00 P.M. to 10:00 P.M.) during the busiest month of the year (July).

The results were surprising: Even at the highest average alarm rate, 9.65 per hour, there was no substantial increase in response times between the existing pattern of 44 companies versus the recommended pattern of 39 companies. As Figure 17–21 shows, the additional time in even the busiest periods, with five fewer companies, was about 10 seconds.

Other analyses performed with the use of the simulation model corroborated the ability of the proposed 39-company pattern to provide approximately the same level of fire suppression protection as the existing configuration of 44 companies.

In summary, using travel time as the measure of the level of the suppression service, the project team produced a redesigned location pattern of pumpers and ladder trucks which left the level of service essentially unchanged with a proposed reduction of five companies. The reduction of four of these companies was accomplished over a 10-year period by closing some stations with obsolete locations and building new ones at better locations which were determined by the study. (Elimination of the last station has not been accomplished as yet for political reasons.)

It is important to note that this 10-year plan was implemented carefully by periodically reviewing the recommendations to see if they were still appropriate in terms of the alarm rate experience, annexations, and other changes in Denver's character. And, although all the recommendations of the study have not yet been implemented, the savings to date have been in excess of $4 million dollars—a return so far of over 3,000 percent on the $117,000 cost of the study.

FIGURE 17–21
Average Travel Time for First Arriving Vehicle (pumper or ladder) Needed to Do Work *(based on simulations)*

Alarm Rate per Hour	Travel Time (minutes)		Difference (seconds)
	Existing	Proposed	
2.50 (1973 average)	1.93	2.07	8
3.22	1.95	2.09	8
4.71	2.03	2.16	7
5.12	2.04	2.19	9
6.60	2.06	2.24	11
9.65 (projected 1978 rate)	2.14	2.33	11

VALIDATION OF SIMULATION RESULTS

Once a simulation has been constructed and decisions are to be made based on the results, it is important to first validate the model to see if it was a good replication of the real system under study. In the case of the Denver Fire Department study, several checks were made to validate the process as the work proceeded to see if the model was providing reliable predictions. For example, the model predicted that the response time using the recommended configuration would be 116 seconds. A check of actual response times showed the average to be 121 seconds, a 4 percent difference, which is tolerable.

A second test, the time of the actual work time spent on call, again was extremely close to the times generated from the simulation. This was true for the system as a whole and for most of the individual companies as well. Three quarters of the companies were busy almost exactly as much as the simulation predicted (there was less than a 10 percent difference).

A third test investigated the question of the distribution of the actual workloads of individual runs by pumper engines to emergencies versus the distribution shown to be expected by the simulation. Again the predicted workloads of individual companies were very close to what actually happened.

In the Denver fire department case, simulation proved to be a very worthwhile tool in the analysis of a difficult problem.

USE OF COMPUTERS IN SIMULATION

Since simulation is usually done on computers, special computer languages have been developed which allow analysts to write simulation programs. While excellent simulation models can be written in such general-purpose computer languages as FORTRAN and BASIC, many analysts prefer to use special-purpose lan-

guages such as GPSS (General Purpose Simulation System) or GASP IV (Generalized Activity Simulation Program), or SIMSCRIPT, the language used for the Denver fire department study. In addition, some of the newer financial planning (spreadsheet) software packages such as IFPS, Simplan, Visicalc, and Supercalc allow some rather complex simulation models to be developed.

Most computer languages have built-in random number generators which can be used in simulating the random arrival of customers, service times, and so on. Many also have "built-in" Poisson probability distributions as well as a number of other distributions of various shapes to match the users' needs. In many simulations, the analyst may combine the use of mathematical distributions such as the Poisson (perhaps for arrival rates) with distributions obtained from observation, such as the car wash time distributions used in the Quick Car Wash example. This is what was done in the fire department study. Arrivals of emergencies were generated through a Poisson process, while work times at the emergencies were determined by analyzing and classifying work times of about 1,100 actual fires and other emergencies.

Computers are thus helpful not only in performing simulations of experiences, but, in the absence of complete data, they can generate approximate data which allows simulation to be used even where more detailed actual data are not available.

Review Questions

1. What are the two general approaches to designing service systems with waiting-line analysis?
2. What kinds of questions do queuing formulas answer?
3. What differences are assumed between the gasoline station, repair shop, bank, fire station dispatching, Xeroxing, and machine setup examples given in the text?
4. Why are the special-purpose queuing tables and charts used? Why not just use the queuing formulas?

5. How does Monte Carlo simulation differ from classical queuing analysis?

6. What would happen to the results of a simulation if we used a different set of random numbers? Under what circumstances, would the results be about the same? Different?

7. Explain the way to use random number tables to help develop simulated results in Monte Carlo simulation problems.

8. Is it necessary to have actual experience data upon which to base Monte Carlo simulations? Explain.

Questions for Discussion

1. If a service operator's calls for service average five calls per hour, and service requires an average of 10 minutes each, would there ever be times when a customer that needs service would have to wait? Why is this?

2. "Although Monte Carlo methods are useful to help managers see what average conditions will be like, they are of little help to a manager who is interested in extremes." Discuss this statement.

3. Waiting-line analysis deals with trade-offs. Discuss.

4. Waiting-line problems pervade our everyday life. Discuss.

5. What is queue discipline?

6. Is validation of simulation applications important? How can it be done?

7. What do you suppose were the "political" reasons that stopped the last company from being eliminated in the Denver Fire Department example?

Problems

*1. Customers arrive at a small bank's teller window at an average rate of 20 per hour and can be served at an average rate of 30 per hour. Both arrival and service rates are approximately Poisson-distributed. What is the expected length of the waiting line? The average waiting time? The average time waiting and being served? How busy is the teller? What other things should be considered in analyzing this situation?

*2. Given the information in problem 1, suppose that the bank's managers were considering adding a second teller's window but requiring arriving customers to wait in a single line until a teller becomes available. Additionally, they wish to add some new services to be handled by the tellers. These new services would reduce the service rate to 25 per hour per teller but would increase the arrival rate to 25 per hour. If adding the second teller will cost $8.00 per hour, and the managers value waiting times of customers at $8.00 per hour, should they add the second teller?

*3. An automatic screw machine department has eight machines. The service needs of these machines are Poisson in pattern, as is the service rate by mechanics. On the average, each machine needs service every 3 hours, and service times average 25 minutes when done by a single mechanic.

 a. How many machines would be running if there were 1, 2, 3, or 4 mechanics? Assume service rates double with 2 mechanics, triple with 3, etc. (Use Appendix D.)

 b. If machine idle time (waiting and being serviced) costs $30 per hour, how many mechanics should be assigned to these 8 machines?

4. Using the information given in problem 3, and using the TRW diagram (Figure 18–4), determine the most economical number of servicemen to have. Servicemen cost $10 an hour. Assume that, except for service time, the machines are in operation.

5. A battery of 16 machines is serviced by 4 mechanics who do both setup and repair work. These mechanics are able to give good service and keep the machines running almost all of the time, but the mechanics themselves are not always busy. Machine time is worth $15 an hour, and the mechanics cost $10 an hour. If they are not busy, there is standby work for them, so that half of their wage loss is salvaged. A work-sampling study showed that the machines typically were in operation 80 percent of the time, were being serviced 10 percent of the time, and were idle from lack of orders 10 percent of the time.

 How many mechanics should be on this assignment in order to hold costs to a minimum? (Hint: Use TRW charts to aid in solving this problem.)

---

* Calculations can be done with provided software or manually using formulas in Appendix D. See Preface.

6. How many service workers should there be at a tool crib which serves machinists who arrive at a rate of 20 an hour and whose service times average 10 minutes? Both arrival times and service times are irregular. The machinists cost $12 an hour (including the cost of their idle machines while they are at the tool crib), whereas tool crib attendants cost $6 an hour. When tool crib attendants are not serving the machinists at the issue window, they spend their time cleaning tools that have previously been returned. This work is regarded as saving two thirds of the cost of what would otherwise be idle time.

What would be the answer to this problem if the people who came to the window were $5-an-hour machinist helpers whose time at the tool crib did not cause any machines to be idle?

*7. Refer to the bank drive-up window example discussed in this chapter. Suppose that a major new company opened up near the bank, and the demand for drive-up services went up substantially, so that λ is now 15 per hour. Also, presume a rearrangement of the equipment at the teller station allowed μ to be now 18 per hour. How (if at all) will this change the solution recommended in the text?

*8. Solve the fire equipment dispatching example presented in the text with the following changes in λ:

$$\lambda = 25$$

$$\lambda = 27$$

$$\lambda = 29$$

What do you conclude from this "what if" simulation?

*9. Suppose in the Farquhar Company example discussed in the text that a new brand of copying machine is being considered whose average service rate is 20 per hour instead of 15 per hour. If these machines were installed (assume they are leased, and they cost the same as the old machines), should they still be consolidated into one location or left in the separate offices?

10. Lavern and Shirley work at Zinger Skateboard Company on a two-station assembly line where they put skateboard wheel subassemblies together. Lavern assembles the axle, and Shirley puts the wheels on the axle. The frequency of

work times for each to perform the operations are:

Time (seconds)	Percent of Time (Lavern)	Percent of Time (Shirley)
10	10	5
15	50	50
20	30	35
25	10	10

a. First, assign two-digit random numbers to the above frequency distribution so you can simulate the movement of assembled axles to Shirley's work station.

b. Simulate this assembly line activity for ten subassemblies moving through the two stations, using the following random numbers (which came from Appendix E). Assume that Shirley must wait until Lavern is finished with her operations before she can put the wheels on the axle subassembly.

Lavern's Operation		Shirley's Operation	
73	25	02	85
27	85	53	28
37	10	62	62
20	67	48	89
04	70	27	11

c. How does this system behave? Is Shirley ever idle? How much? Or does a line of axle subassemblies build up ahead of Shirley?

11. Records of 100 truckloads of finished jobs arriving in a department's checkout area show the following: Checking out time takes five minutes, and the checker takes care of only one truck at a time.

Minutes between Arrivals	Number of Cases
1	1
2	4
3	7
4	17
5	31
6	23
7	7
8	5
9	3
10	2
	100

As soon as the jobs are checked out, the truck drivers take them to the next departments. Using Monte Carlo simulation, determine (a) what percent of the time there is no load at all at the check out station, (b) what is the average waiting time for completed jobs, and (c) what is likely to be the longest wait.

12. A study of 100 unemployed people showed that they arrived at a one-person state employment office during peak demand times to obtain their unemployment compensation check according to the following frequency distribution:

Time between Arrivals (minutes)	Frequency
2.0	10
2.5	20
3.0	40
3.5	20
4.0	10

A time study of the time required to disburse checks yielded the following service time frequency distribution:

Service Time	Frequency
1.5	10
2.0	20
2.5	40
3.0	20
3.5	10

a. Will people have to wait? How many and how long? (Carry out a simulation for 10 arrivals.)
b. How can we assign a cost to people waiting in line?

13. The Standard Automobile Company's home plant can, when everything goes perfectly, turn out 1,000 cars a day. But even when sales are high and the schedule calls for 1,000 a day, production varies because of interruptions. Here is the record during past peak seasons when 1,000 cars were actually scheduled (the problem concerns only the 100-day peak period; there's no problem during the rest of the year):

Production	Percent of the Time
750	3
800	7
850	15
875	25
900	23
925	14
950	9
975	3
1,000	1
	100

Standard has a contract with the Truckaway Company to haul out up to 900 cars a day. (This is all that Truckaway's equipment can handle from March through May, the company's peak period.) If there are fewer than 875 cars to be hauled away in any one day, Standard pays a penalty charge of $1 per car short of this amount. If there are more than 900 to be removed, the excess go into a parking lot (storage cost $.50 per car per day) until they can be taken away.

a. What will be Standard's combined cost for penalties and parking charges for 100 days of operation? What will be the largest number of cars in the parking lot at any one time? (In order to reduce the problem-solving time, carry through a simulation for 25 days only and then multiply the costs by 4 in order to get a reasonable approximation of the costs for 100 days.)
b. Will it pay Standard to buy a parking lot which will hold 50 cars if the cost of operating the lot will be $300 a year? (The 100 days in our problem is the only time that the lot would be used.)
c. Truckaway has proposed a new contract covering this peak period. This contract would reduce the trucking cost $.10 per car for all cars hauled away but would call for 925 cars a day to be hauled away with a penalty charge of $1 for every empty space below 925. Should Standard accept this proposal? Use the Monte Carlo method to solve this problem.

Chapter 18

Scheduling and Capacity Planning with Linear Programming

Linear programming is an analytic method which is a member of a family of techniques called *mathematical programming*. In general, mathematical programming methods are designed to allocate limited resources among competing alternative uses for these resources so that some predetermined objective—usually maximizing profit or minimizing costs—is satisfied or optimized.

The term *linear* in linear programming means that the relationships between factors are approximately linearly related or constant. Linear relationship means that when one factor changes so does another and by a proportionally constant amount. An hourly paid employee's working hours and wages are linear: the more hours, the more total wages. Linearity can also be inverse; the more there is of one thing, the less there is of another. If a person starts with $20 and spends a dollar each day, the *more* he spends, the *less* he has left—and he has spent this money at a linear rate per day.

AUTOMOBILE MANUFACTURE: A GRAPHIC SOLUTION

We will first illustrate linear programming by using an example of production scheduling and capacity allocation in an automobile assembly factory. Later in this chapter, we will apply the method to an oil refinery gasoline-blending situation, and then to the location of fire stations.

To keep our automobile problem simple, we will assume that this factory makes only two models: a two-door four-cylinder car and a six-cylinder station wagon. We will deal with three manufacturing departments: metal stamping, engine assembly, and final assembly. In the final assembly department there are two assembly lines: one for two-door cars and one for station wagons. Both can operate at the same time.

The stamping department can, in a week, produce enough parts for 7,000 two-door cars or 12,000 station wagons. But it can't do both at the same time. It is possible to do one *or* the other or to make parts for *some* two-door cars and *some* station wagons. The same is true with engines. It is possible to produce 9,000 four-cylinder engines which are used only in the two-door cars, or 6,000 six-cylinder engines which are used only in stagion wagons, or to have some fours and some sixes.

The two-door car assembly line's capacity is 6,000 cars as a maximum. And the station wagon line's maximum capacity is 4,000. Here, however, both lines can operate at the same time. Increasing the output of one line does not require reducing the other.

These limitations impose several "constraints" to the possible choices in capacity allocation to scheduled production quantities. In summary, these are:

Departments	Maximum Number for Two-Door Cars		Maximum Number for Station Wagons
Metal stamping	7,000	or	12,000
Engine assembly	9,000	or	6,000
Final assembly	6,000	and	4,000

No one constraint sets limits for a large number of possible combinations. It is possible, at one extreme, to make 9,000 four-cylinder engines, the kind used in the two-door cars, but there is no need to make this many four-cylinder engines since only 6,000 two-door cars can be assembled. Assembly limitations would rule here.

It is also possible, so far as assembly is concerned, to assemble 4,000 station wagons as well as the 6,000 two-door cars. But actually this can't be done because it is not possible to make enough stamped parts or engines. The stamping capacity will allow the production of parts for 6,000 two-door cars, but, if this is done, then there is not enough stamping capacity left to make any parts for 4,000 station wagons. Nor could enough engines be made to permit making the maximum assembly quantities of each kind of car at the same time.

All of the possible maximum quantity mixes can be defined by using the "linear rate of substitution" between two-door cars and station wagons. For stampings, this rate of substitution is 7,000/12,000, or .5833. For every *one* station wagon that we stamp parts for, we could instead stamp parts for .5833 two-door cars. Thus, if we stamp enough parts for 6,000 two-door cars, or 1,000 under the maximum of 7,000, we could also stamp enough parts for 1,715 station wagons (1,000/.5833).

Similarly, for engines, for every six-cylinder engine, we could make instead 9,000/6,000, or 1.5 four-cylinder engines. Thus, if we make 6,000 four-cylinder engines, this would leave enough additional capacity to make 3,000 more four-cylinder engines, or 2,000 six-cylinder engines (3,000/1.5).

These relationships can be stated in the form of constraint equations. If we let T equal the number of two-door cars we can make, and W the number of station wagons, then the stampings department constraint is:

$$T + .5833W \leq 7,000$$

For the engine department, the constraint equation is:

$$T + 1.5W \leq 9,000$$

Figure 18–1 shows the area of feasible solutions for stamping production. The enclosed area encompasses all possible combinations of two-door cars and station wagons which can be stamped. The diagonal sloping line is the constraint and defines the "linear rate of substitution" between the two models. Any combination of numbers of two-doors and station wagons which falls on the diagonal line will keep the stamping department fully occupied. Combinations within the enclosed area are also possible but will not keep the department busy.

FIGURE 18–1
Stamping Department Feasibility Area

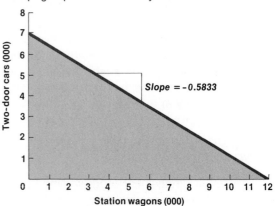

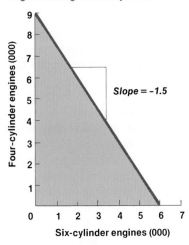

Figure 18–2 shows the solution feasibilities for the engine department. Again, the diagonal line sets off the maximum production combinations. And again, lesser combinations are feasible even though they would not keep the engine department busy, so slack capacity would occur.

The two other constraints, the assembly capacity for each kind of car, are shown in Figure 18–3. These constraint lines are not mutually de-

FIGURE 18–3
Assembly Department Feasibility Area

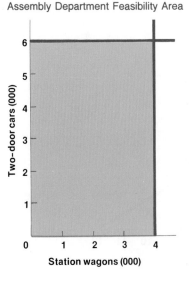

Station wagons (000)

pendent on each other, and one capacity cannot be substituted for the other so there is no rate of substitution. Again, the enclosed area encompasses the feasible combinations so far as these two constraints are concerned. The constraint equations for the two assembly lines are:

$$T \le 6{,}000$$

$$W \le 4{,}000$$

Now that we have determined the maximum capacity of each department, we are ready to determine how many of each model we should schedule for production and how capacities should be allocated. We will assume that we can sell all that we can produce and so want to choose the product mix which will yield the largest total contribution. The contribution per unit, it will be recalled from Chapter 2, is the selling price per unit minus the variable cost per unit. In our example, the contribution is $300 for each two-door car and $400 for every station wagon. This means that the contribution from selling 1 station wagon is the same as it is for 1.33 two-doors (400/300).

Thus, we also have a linear rate of substitution for contribution between the two models of −1.33. This can be depicted graphically by drawing in "iso-contribution" lines, one for each contribution total. There could be any number of such lines, each for different amounts of money. Two of them—showing the sales volume relationships which would produce total contributions of $1 million and of $2 million, are shown in Figure 18–4. For example, selling 3,333 two-doors and no wagons produces $1 million as does the other extreme of selling 2,500 wagons and no two-doors. Similarly, $2 million in total contribution would occur at any combination of two-doors and station wagons along the B line in Figure 18–4. If, for example, we sold 5,000 two-doors this would result in $1.5 million, leaving $500,000 required from station wagons. At $400 each, sales of wagons would have to be 1,250 to produce the $2 million.

There is a whole family of iso-contribution

FIGURE 18–4
"Iso-Contribution" Lines

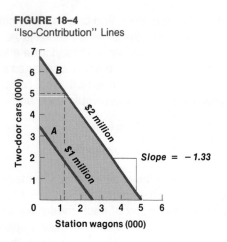

for the iso-contribution line for our problem (which is also called the *objective function*) is:

$$\text{Maximize } F = \$300T + \$400W$$

This says, find a combination of quantities of T and W which, when multiplied by their respective per-unit contributions, will result in a greater total contribution F than that produced by any other combination of T and W. The four equations needed to solve this problem are those shown above.

Figure 18–5 combines the four previous charts into one. The enclosed area A-B-C-D-E encompasses all possible feasible solutions to the problem. Note that some of our earlier feasible-solution areas have been eliminated because some constraints allow fewer units than others. This final-solution area, which is shaded, is called the *feasible region.* The iso-contribution line for $2.591 million touches the feasible-solution area at its maximum point, C.

As we have said, it is feasible to make two-door cars and station wagons in any of the infinite number of combinations in the shaded area. We

lines for this problem, all having the same slope of -1.33. The lines closer to the origin produce less total contribution; those farther out, more. Since we wish to maximize the contribution, we want to find how far out (how far upward and to the right) we can draw the iso-contribution line, yet still have *at least one point* on it touch one point in the feasibility area. The equation

FIGURE 18–5

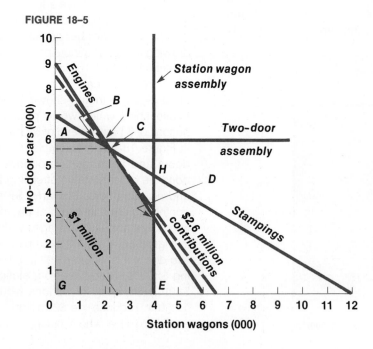

can make 6,000 two-door cars and no station wagons (point *A*), or 6,000 two-door cars and anywhere up to 1,715 station wagons (point *B*). But from there on, in order to produce any more station wagons, it will be necessary to reduce two-door cars because the stamping department is at its capacity. The rate of this substitution as defined earlier is the slope of the line. For each .5833 two-doors we don't schedule, we can stamp parts for 1 more station wagon. By the time we reduce two-doors to 5,727, and increase station wagons to 2,182 (point C), we run into engine department capacity limitations. From this point on, as two-doors are reduced in order to increase station wagons, engine capacity limits us until we reduce station wagons to 4,000, and two-doors to 3,000 (point *D*). From here on station wagons cannot be increased because 4,000 is the maximum capacity limit for assembling station wagons. Even if we cut two-door cars below 3,000, we could not make any more station wagons.

So far, we have seen how the constraints determine capacity trade-offs between two-doors and station wagons. The plant is operating at its full capacity in at *least one* department at any point on the line connecting the corner points *A, B, C, D,* and *E*. At points *B, C,* and *D,* the plant is operating at full capacity in the *two* departments defined by this corner and has excess capacity, or slack, in the other two.

The real objective, however, is not just to keep departments busy but to maximize contributions.

Determining the Optimal Solution Which Maximizes Contribution

To determine the optimal solution, we have to find the value of point *C* in Figure 18–5. This is the point where the stamping department and the engine department lines intersect and where both are working at capacity. They are the constraining capacities since neither of the assembly lines is working up to capacity. As we already know, the equation for maximum engine produc-

tion in Figure 18–5 is $T + 1.5W = 9,000$, and the equation for stampings is $T + .5833W = 7,000$. To find the value of point *C,* we can either graphically determine the solution—as is shown by the dotted lines in Figure 18–5—or, to be more precise, we have to solve these two equations simultaneously. This we do by multiplying the stamping department equation by -1 and adding it to the engine department equation, thus eliminating the *T* factor from the equations:

$$
\begin{aligned}
(1) \quad & T + 1.500W = 9,000 \\
(2) \quad -& T - 0.5833W = -7,000 \\
\hline
& .9167W = 2,000
\end{aligned}
$$

At point *C*: $\qquad\qquad\qquad W = 2,180$

Substituting 2,180 into Equation (1):

$$T + 1.5(2,180) = 9,000$$

At point *C*: $\qquad\qquad\qquad\qquad T = 5,730$

The solution at point *C* is therefore to schedule 5,730 two-door cars and 2,180 station wagons. The total contribution realized from this manufacturing program will be:

$$\$300(5,730) + \$400(2,180) = \$2,591,000$$

To show that this solution is the best, Figure 18–6 shows the contributions from all of the corner points in our problem.

Slack

While the solution defined by point *C* uses all of the capacity of the engine and stamping departments, slack capacity remains in the two assembly lines. To calculate this slack, we simply subtract the number of each kind of product in the solution from its assembly capacity. At point *C,* the two-door assembly department is producing 270 cars less than its capacity, and the station wagon assembly department is 1,820 wagons under its capacity. There is, however, no slack in either the engine or assembly departments.

This kind of analysis can be used to aid in managerial decision making. Suppose that it is

FIGURE 18–6

	Number of		Total Contribution		
				Station	
	Two-	Station	Two-Doors	Wagons	
Point	Doors	Wagons	($300 each)	($400 each)	Both
A	6,000	0	$1,800,000	0	$1,800,000
B	6,000	1,715	1,800,000	$ 686,000	2,486,000
C	5,730	2,180	1,719,000	872,000	2,591,000
D	3,000	4,000	900,000	1,600,000	2,500,000
E	0	4,000	0	1,600,000	1,600,000

possible to sell more station wagons if the engine-making capacity could be expanded. We could then move to point H in Figure 18–5 and could assemble 4,000 station wagons.

At point H, the capacity limitations of the stamping department limit two-door production to 4,670. Thus, we would need 1,060 fewer four-cylinder engines than at point C. In total, the new engine capacity would have to be capable of making 4,000 six-cylinder engines plus 4,670 four-cylinder engines, or the equivalent of 10,670 fours or 7,110 sixes. This would require an increase in engine production capacity of 11.9 percent.

Suppose that the company's managers were considering making this expansion, and they find that if they do, the capital investment would be $350,000. Should they go ahead? The new sum of the contributions would be 4,000 × $400 + 4,670 × $300 = $3,028,000. The present sum is $2,591,000, which shows that this move would increase the contributions by $437,000. This is a 25 percent first-year return on investment (($477,000 − $350,000)/ $350,000). Thus they should proceed if they think they can sell the additional output, and their hurdle rate is as low as 25 percent.

Sensitivity Analysis

Often the most important uses of linear programming are not to find single individual problem solutions, but to use the model to analyze a num-

ber of trade-offs by asking "what-if" questions. This is called sensitivity analysis. It reveals how sensitive the solution is to changes in constraints or values. We might ask, for example, what would happen if we had to cut two-door car prices. Or what would happen if we could reduce the costs of making station wagons. Or we might want to know what the effects would be if we could change the method of producing six-cylinder engines so that as far as capacity is concerned a six-cylinder engine would equal 1.25 four-cylinder engines instead of 1.5 four-cylinder engines.

This would mean that six-cylinder engines would require only 25 percent more resources per unit than four-cylinders instead of the present additional 50 percent. The capacity of the engine department would then remain at 9,000 four-cylinder engines, but the six-cylinder engine capacity would increase to 7,200. How much would our earlier solution change (if at all) and how much would we be willing to pay for this new process?

The new constraint is:

$$T + 1.25W \leq 9,000$$

This analysis is called relaxing the constraint on the engine department's capacity. Plotting this constraint would make point C move downward and to the right (the plot points are 9,000 and 7,200) and point D ove straight upward, as shown in Figure 18–7. Points A, B, E, and F are not affected. The new solutions for points C and D are:

	Number of Two-Door Cars	Number of Station Wagons	Total Contribution
C	5,250	3,000	2,775,000
D	4,000	4,000	2,800,000

As can be seen, the solution which maximizes contribution is now defined by point D, with a mix of 4,000 units of each model. This solution's contribution is $209,000 higher than the previous solution. Thus, if the new engine process costs less than $209,000, and we can sell these quantities of the two models, then we would invest in the new process. Note also that with this solution we now have slack capacity in the stamping department:

$$T + .5833W \leq 7,000$$
$$4,000 + .5833(4,000) = 6,333$$
$$\text{Slack} = 667$$

which would allow the production of 667 two-doors, or 1,143 station wagons (667/.5833), or some similar combination.

We could continue our analysis by evaluating alternatives which might, for example, allow a solution defined by point G in Figure 18–7. This would require us to "relax" the engine de-

FIGURE 18–7
Alternate Solution for Proposed Change in Engine Department Capacity

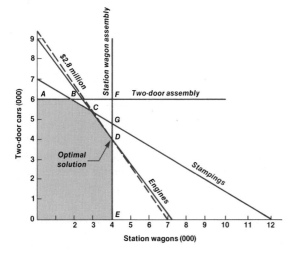

partment capacity constraint even more. These examples are just a few of the things which can be done using sensitivity analysis procedures. Another might be to vary the per-unit contribution of the two models to see how it affects the solution mix, total contribution, and slack capacities.

COST MINIMIZATION

In our automobile example, we found solutions which maximized contribution. Another common use of linear programming is to *minimize total cost*.

Suppose in our automobile assembly plant we now have installed the new process in the engine department, but now, for illustrative purposes, face a situation where we *cannot have any slack capacity* in our engine and stamping departments because of a management decision to fully utilize capacity. However, while the stamping department *can* work overtime, the engine department *cannot* because there would not be enough time for maintenance. For this example, let us assume that there is no such *minimum* constraint on the two assembly departments. This means that our constraints for these departments are now:

Engine department (no slack capacity or overtime allowed)	$T + 1.25W = 9,000$
Stamping department (overtime allowed but no slack capacity allowed)	$T + .5833W \geq 7,000$
Two-door assembly	$T \leq 6,000$
Wagon assembly	$W \leq 4,000$

These constraints are plotted in Figure 18–8. Because the engine department constraint is an equality and the stamping department is a minimum, the feasible region is limited to the line segment A-B. This means the solution must be at point A, or B, or any point on this line segment.

Assume the unit costs to make both models on regular time are $2,000 for two-doors and

FIGURE 18–8
Cost Minimization Solution for Automobile Production Mix Problem

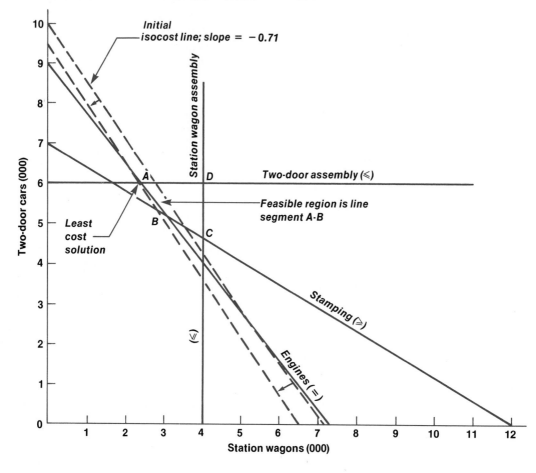

$2,800 for wagons. Using these regular-time costs, our objective function becomes:

Minimize $F = \$2,000\,T + \$2,800\,W$

As before, this says costs will be equal if we produce 1 two-door or .71 wagon (2,000/2,800). Thus, we can plot an initial *isocost* line whose slope is −.71. (We arbitrarily choose the points 10,000 and 7,100 for this initial plot.) Now, instead of moving the isocost line *out* to the extreme corner of the feasible region (maximizing), we move it (the dotted line in Figure 18–8) *into* the feasible region as far as possible (minimizing). The least-cost mix is defined by point *A*,

which is 6,000 two-doors and 2,400 wagons. Thus:

Minimized $F = \$2,000(6,000) + \$2,800(2,400)$
$= \$18.72$ million

But, in order to make this many cars, the stamping department will have to work overtime. The amount of overtime (called *surplus*) can be calculated from this department's constraint:

$$T + .5833W \geq 7,000$$
$$6,000 + .5833(2,400) = 7,400$$
$$\text{Surplus} = 400$$

If overtime costs in the stamping department, in terms of two-doors, are $100 per unit, then total costs are $18.72 million + $100 × 400 = $18.76 million. But what about the solution at corner B where no overtime is required in the stamping department? The solution at B is 5,250 two-doors and 3,000 wagons, for a total cost of:

$$F = \$2,000(5,250) + \$2,800(3,000)$$
$$= \$18,9 \text{ million}$$

Thus, it costs $140,000 *less* to stay with the solution at point A and work the stamping department overtime.

THE SIMPLEX METHOD

In most problems which can appropriately use linear programming (and there are hundreds of them), there may be dozens, hundreds, or, in rare cases, thousands of variables and constraints. These require solution methods which can handle these larger number of variables and which can be programmed for computer solution.

The best known of these methods is the simplex method. It is designed to simultaneously solve a system of linear equations where there are more unknowns than there are equations. Appendix F continues our discussion of linear programming by demonstrating how the problems we have just solved graphically are solved with the simplex method.

GASOLINE BLENDING: PROBLEM FORMULATION

In our previous example of linear programming, we applied it to a piece-part manufacturing situation—automobile parts fabrication and assembly. But linear programming is also used for scheduling and capacity allocation in *process industries,* such as oil refining and other operations which have what are called *blending* problems.

For our example here, we will concentrate

FIGURE 18–9

Crude Oil Grade	Maximum Quantity Available in Barrels per Day	Cost per Barrel
X	3,000	$10
Y	2,000	$16

on the *formulation* of the problem rather than its solution, which cannot be done graphically—but can be solved with the simplex method as presented in Appendix F.

Suppose an oil refinery blends two grades of crude oil (X, Y) into two kinds of gasoline: regular (R) and unleaded (U). Figure 18–9 shows the maximum quantity of each grade of crude pumped per day from their wells, and the cost per barrel to pump it and ship it to the refinery.

In order to maintain the required quality for each grade of gasoline, the refinery's chemists have determined that unleaded gas cannot consist of more than 30 percent of crude X, the cheapest of the two. And, regular gas cannot contain less than 10 percent of crude Y, the most expensive.

Finally, the wholesale selling price at the refinery (not including transportation costs) for U is $25 per barrel; for R it is $22 per barrel.

The Objective Function

In formulating this problem, the objective function becomes:

$$\text{Maximize } F = \$25(G_{ux} + G_{uy})$$
$$+ \$22(G_{rx} + G_{ry})$$
$$- \$10(G_{ux} + G_{rx})$$
$$- \$16(G_{uy} + G_{ry})$$

The subscripts *(u,x)* to the variable G_{ux} (G is for barrels of gas) stand for *un*-leaded gas made from crude x. G_{ry} means regular gas made from crude *y,* and so on.

The first term above, $25 G_{ux} + G_{uy}$), is the selling price of unleaded times the way that unleaded is made—with some crude x and y. The third item, $-\$10(G_{ux} + G_{rx})$, is the cost of crude x per barrel times the way x is used—to make U and R.

Multiplying through and arranging like terms for subtraction in this equation gives us:

$$
\begin{aligned}
\text{Maximize } F = \; & 25\, G_{ux} + 25\, G_{uy} \\
& + 22\, G_{rx} + 22\, G_{ry} \\
& - 10\, G_{ux} - 16\, G_{uy} \\
& \underline{- 10\, G_{rx} - 16\, G_{ry}} \\
= \; & 15\, G_{ux} + 9\, G_{uy} \\
& + 12\, G_{rx} + 6\, G_{ry} \quad (1)
\end{aligned}
$$

This gives us the *contribution* per barrel for each way the two gasolines are made from the two crudes, remembering of course, that each blended barrel may be refined from a mix of each type of crude.

The Constraints

The availability constraints for crude X and Y are simply:

$$G_{ux} + G_{rx} \le 3{,}000 \text{ barrels per day} \quad (2)$$

$$G_{uy} + G_{ry} \le 2{,}000 \quad (3)$$

The blend constraints provided by the chemist are, however, a little more complex. The first blending constraint, limiting the percentage of crude X in unleaded gas, is:

$$G_{ux} \le 30\%\,(G_{ux} + G_{uy})$$

This says that G_{ux}, the amount of X in U, must be less than or equal to 30 percent of the total unleaded gas, which is made up of $G_{ux} + G_{uy}$.

Manipulating this equation algebraically:

$$G_{ux} \le .3\, G_{ux} + .3\, G_{uy}$$

subtracting G_{ux} from both sides:

$$G_{ux} - G_{ux} \le -\, G_{ux} + .3\, G_{ux} + .3\, G_{uy}$$

yields

$$0 \le -.7\, G_{ux} + .3\, G_{uy}$$

Now, we reverse the inequality so the constant of zero is on the right, which is the convention in linear programming:

$$-.7\, G_{ux} + .3\, G_{uy} \ge 0 \quad (4)$$

The second blending constraint, that no less than 10 percent of regular gas can be made from crude Y, is developed in a similar way, but with reversed logic:

$$G_{ry} \ge 10\%\,(G_{rx} + G_{ry})$$
$$G_{ry} \ge .1\, G_{rx} + .1\, G_{ry}$$
$$0 \ge .1\, G_{rx} - .9\, G_{ry}$$
$$.1\, G_{rx} - .9\, G_{ry} \le 0 \quad (5)$$

Summary of Objective Function and Constraints

The problem in summary is:

$$
\begin{aligned}
\text{Maximize } F = \; & \$15\, G_{ux} + \$9\, G_{uy} + \$12\, G_{rx} + \$6\, G_{ry} \quad (1) \\
\text{Subject to: } \quad & G_{ux} \qquad\quad + \quad G_{rx} \qquad\quad \le 3{,}000 \quad (2) \\
& \qquad\quad G_{uy} \qquad\quad + \quad G_{ry} \le 2{,}000 \quad (3) \\
& -.7\, G_{ux} + .3\, G_{uy} \qquad\qquad\qquad\quad \ge 0 \quad (4) \\
& \qquad\qquad\qquad .1\, G_{rx} - .9\, G_{ry} \le 0 \quad (5)
\end{aligned}
$$

The problem is now formulated and ready for solution with the simplex method (explained in Appendix G) which is the assignment of Problem 10 at the end of this chapter.

LOCATING FIRE STATIONS WITH LINEAR PROGRAMMING

Our third example moves to the public service sector, where linear programming is used as ex-

FIGURE 18–10

Hazard	Maximum Response Time (seconds) for First Pumper	Expected Response Time (seconds) from Fire Station Locations:			
		Existing Stations		Potential Stations	
		W	X	Y	Z
Adam Elementary School	120	150	110	90	140
Brown Memorial Hospital	90	60	200	120	80
Chase Retirement Village	90	100	120	200	80
Dalton College Center	180	150	170	90	100

tensively as in manufacturing and service organizations in the private sector of our economy.

In Chapter 17, we said that the Denver Fire Study research team used linear programming to aid them in their static analysis of alternative location patterns for fire stations in Denver.[1]

Data Requirement

First, recall from Chapter 17 that the four kinds of data required for this analysis were: hazard location; severity of hazards translated into maximum allowable response time requirements for the first-arriving pumper engine; the location of existing and of potential fire station sites; and the expected travel response time from any existing or potential firehouse location to any hazard.

To simplify the use of linear programming in this situation, suppose a small town has only four hazards, two existing fire stations, and two additional potential sites for new fire stations. They wish to determine if the two existing stations are correctly located in relation to their hazards, or, if they should have two or fewer or more than two stations. And if so, which ones of the four station sites should be used. They, of course, would prefer not to abandon a station if its location is as good or better than one of the potential sites. In addition, the fire chief has

[1] See Donald R. Plane and Thomas E. Hendrick, "Mathematical Programming and the Location of Fire Companies for the Denver Fire Department," *Operations Research*, July–August 1977, pp. 563–78.

estimated the travel times required and the maximum allowable travel response times to the four hazards. This information is summarized in Figure 18–10.

The Objective Function

The Objective of this problem is simply to minimize the number of fire stations, such that each hazard is "covered" by at least one station within the maximum response time standards. The objective function is:

$$\text{Minimize } F = W + X + Y + Z$$

where W, X, Y, and Z are equal *either* to 1 or 0 in the final solution. For example, if $W = 1$, then station W is to be kept; if it equals 0, it is to be abandoned.

The Constraints

To develop the constraint equations for this problem—and there is one for each hazard—we shall assume that all we care about is if each station's pumper engine can respond to each hazard *within* the maximum response time allowed. If it can, we set the coefficient of the station's variable (W, X, Y, Z) equal to 1; if it cannot, the coefficient is set at zero.

Following this simple rule, the objective function and the four hazard constraints become:

$$\text{Minimize: } F = W + X + Y + Z$$

Subject to:

Hazard	Stations (Constraints)
A	$0W + 1X + 1Y + 0Z \geq 1$ pumper
B	$1W + 0X + 0Y + 1Z \geq 1$ pumper
C	$0W + 0X + 0Y + 1Z \geq 1$ pumper
D	$1W + 1X + 1Y + 1Z \geq 1$ pumper

For example, the travel time from W to A (150 seconds) is greater than the maximum allowed travel time of 120 seconds, so W does not cover hazard A; it receives a zero coefficient (0W) in the constraint equation. But station X's time of 110 to hazard A is less than 120, so it receives a 1.

Solving the Problem

We will not formally solve this problem here with linear programming because it requires a special method, called *zero-one* programming, which takes advantage of the fact that all the coefficients are either zero or one, and attempts to find a solution where *W, X, Y,* and *Z* are *either* zero or one (which was our earlier stated objective) and *F* is minimized.

We can, however, solve this problem by simply looking at it because the alternatives are few. Since no single station can "cover" all four hazards (no stations have all 1s in their column) we know we need at least two stations. And, the two existing stations (W, X) do not cover hazard C, so we know that at least one of the two stations must be either Y or Z. So the two *feasible* alternatives of two stations each that

cover all four hazards are X and Z; or Y and Z. The other combinations do not cover all four.

Thus, the two objective functions for these two solutions would be:

$$Minimized\ F = 0 \times W + 1 \times X + 0 \times Y + 1 \times Z$$
$$= 2\ stations$$

or

$$F = 0 \times W + 0 \times X + 1 \times Y + 1 \times Z$$
$$= 2\ stations$$

Since station Z seems to be in both of these feasible alternatives, it should be built. But, for the second station, should we choose X or Y?

Obviously, since X exists and Y doesn't, X should probably be kept in operation. If this is the case, the solution would be to abandon W, retain X, forget about Y, and buid Z.

Suppose, however, that existing stations do not take precedence over potential ones, because the town has enough revenue-sharing funds to build two *new* fire stations, and this is one of the things these funds can be used for.

Since W seems to be an obsolete location, we won't consider it any further. And, Z seems ideally located, since it alone covers three of the four hazards. So, we are back to considering X versus Y. While we prefer X over Y because it exists, Y seems to, in general, be better located than X, if measured by the differences between expected response time and maximum response time standards. This is shown in Figure 18–11.

Based on the analysis, Y is clearly superior to X if *relative closeness* is a criterion, as well as the ability to respond within a minimum time.

FIGURE 18–11

Hazard	Maximum Response Time	Station X		Station Y	
		Response Time	Difference	Response Time	Difference
A	120	110	+10	90	+30
B	90	200	−110	120	−30
C	90	120	−30	200	−80
D	180	170	+10	90	+90
	Net difference		−120		+10

Use of This Method in the Denver Fire Study

The Denver Fire Study used the zero-one linear programming approach discussed above. A different method, however, was used for breaking ties between existing and potential locations than the one we have just discussed.[2]

While our simple example could be solved manually, the Denver problem had 117 existing and potential station sites, and 246 hazard "focal points" which were reduced from over 800 hazards studied. Picture if you will, a problem with 117 columns and 246 rows of zeros and ones, and one can readily see why a computer was necessary to solve this problem.

INTEGER LINEAR PROGRAMMING

The simplest kind of linear programming is "noninteger" linear programming. This is the kind we used in our automobile-making example. This means that solutions can be fractional numbers and are not required to be whole numbers, including zero. For example, a solution might say that in order to maximize profits and at the same time to meet certain nutritional requirements, we should make hot dogs be: 24.019 percent meat, 68.207 percent cereal, and 7.674 percent other additives.

Here, in order to make 100 pounds of hot dogs, we could just round off the percentages to 24, 68, and 8. This would be all right for hot dogs, and it was all right in our automobile example where we just rounded off the numbers to units. The rounded fractions did not represent very much money.

There are times, however, when rounding the solution values might not give the best answer. Suppose, for example, that an airline company wanted to find an optimal assignment—or schedule—of its jet aircraft to its numerous routes. The goal is to arrive at an assignment which would maximize its profits, yet would meet customer demand for airline service, allow

enough time for maintenance, and other constraints.

Using noninteger linear programming, the solution might say to allocate 2.3 planes to the Seattle–Denver route, 1.4 planes to the Chicago–St. Louis route, and so on. Of course, it is impossible to fly .3 or .4 of an airplane. The Seattle–Denver allocation must be either two or three airplanes. But why not just round off? This cannot be safely done when the problem deals with capital equipment such as airplanes which cost millions of dollars, or other cases which require solutions to be integers. The same is true for our fire station location example. Here we required the solution variables (the stations) to be the integers of either 0 or 1.

Another kind of linear programming, "integer programming," can be used in such cases. There are several varieties of integer programming methods available, such as "branch-and-bound," "zero-one," and network methods. These methods are quite complex and beyond our scope here but are covered in books on mathematical programming.

CAUTIONS IN THE USE OF LINEAR PROGRAMMING

While linear programming is a powerful aid to decision making, with a wide range of applications, it should be made clear that it is one of the most difficult analytical methods to implement and use for either a one-time case or for day-to-day repetitive problems.

For problems of realistic size (often hundreds or thousands of variables), the problem of simply determining the structure of the problem (the objective function and the constraints) and the values of the coefficients can be a major task. Often, by the time these data have been gathered and a linear programming solution found, either the problem has changed, or the data that were assumed are no longer valid. This, of course, is not true in many applications where the problem situation is fairly stable—and there are enough of them to justify using this approach.

[2] Ibid.

FIGURE 18–12

Using Piecewise Linear Constraints to Approximate Nonlinear Relationships

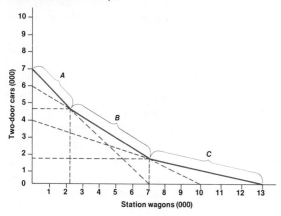

As we have said, linear programming assumes that the relationships in the problem are *linear* which, for a large number of situations, is a reasonable approximation. However, the whole world is not "linear," and where these nonlinearities can be estimated, different methods should be used. One of these methods calls for the use of a series of "piecewise" linear relationships, as shown in Figure 18–12. Suppose, for example, we did *not* have the linear relationship between two-doors and wagons in the stamping department that was shown in Figure 18–5—but had the "nonlinear" relationship shown in Figure 18–12. We could "approximate" this nonlinear trade-off with three linear ones, labeled *A, B,* and *C* in Figure 18–12.

We will not formulate this approach here as it is quite complex. Most large-scale computer programs, however, which are designed to solve linear programming problems allow these "piecewise" approximations to be done rather easily—*if* the analyst can estimate the relationship.

COMPUTER PROGRAMS FOR LARGE LINEAR PROGRAMMING PROBLEMS

All large linear programming problems are solved with special-purpose computer programs. These programs can usually solve problems with thousands of variables and constraints—their only limit being the size of the computer and the cost of computer time. Some of these programs are "mixed integer" programs, which means that they can solve problems where some solution values are required to be "integers," as described earlier, and some may contain fractional solutions. These programs automatically set up slack, surplus, and artificial variables for the user after the "less-than," "greater-than," and "equal-to" relationships have been defined (described in Appendix F); perform "sensitivity analysis," and allow for "piecewise" approximations on nonlinear relationships.

Review Questions

1. What is meant when it is said that linear programming requires linear relationships between factors? What other kinds of relationships are there? Give examples, and show how it may be possible to use linear programming in spite of this difficulty.

2. What are linear rates of substitution?

3. Distinguish between an objective function and a constraint.

4. What is a feasible solution? Feasible region?

5. How is "contribution" defined in an objective function?

6. What is an iso-contribution function? An iso-cost function? Why is there a "family" of them for a given problem, and why are their slopes identical?

7. Outline the procedure for graphing a set of constraints to obtain the area of feasible solution or feasible region.

8. What is an optimal solution, and how is it determined using the graphic method?

9. How is slack determined, and what does it mean? Surplus?

10. What does the simplex method do for us that the graphic method cannot do?

11. What cautions should be heeded in using linear programming?

12. Why is sensitivity analysis such an important part of the use of linear programming for capacity planning and scheduling?

*13. How does the simplex method handle problems where there are more unknowns than equations?

*14. How are inequality constraints translated into equations?

*15. What guides are there for choosing the variables to enter the BASIS? For leaving the BASIS? Do these guides change when we are minimizing costs rather than maximizing contributions?

*16. How do we use the identity matrix to produce a new tableau?

*17. How do we know when we have reached an optimal solution in the simplex method?

*18. How are ranging and shadow prices used in evaluating capacity decisions?

*19. What are the main procedural differences between maximizing contribution and minimizing cost when using the simplex method?

*20. What kinds of things are done automatically when using most computerized linear programming systems?

Problems

1. Suppose, in the text's first example of making automobiles, that any one of the three departments could be expanded by 20 percent. Which one should it be? Assuming that all the cars made can be sold, what would be the new production schedule? How much better would this choice be than the next best choice?

2. Present production is 800 of product A, and it is proposed to produce 1,100 of product B. The two products each require operations on the same three machines, whose maximum capacities for operation 1 are: A, 1,200, and B, 0; or B, 2,400, and A, 0; or proportional combinations of A and B. For operation 2 the capacities are: A, 1,500, and B, 0; or B, 1,000, and A, 0; or linear combinations. For operation 3 the capacities are: A, 2,400, and B, 0; or B, 1,200, and A, 0.

   a. Can the present equipment continue to pro-

duce the 800 units of A and also 1,100 of product B? If not, which operation's capacity will need to be increased and by how much? (Solve this problem graphically.)

   b. If the contribution of A is $100 per unit, and $80 for B, what production combination maximizes contribution?

3. A company making microcomputers and small disk drives has three major departments: stamped parts, machined parts, and assembly. The capacity of each department depends on what they make. The departmental capacities are given below:

	Microcomputers	Disk Drives
Stamped parts	2,000	6,500
Machined parts	1,500	10,000
Assembly	2,500	5,500

   a. Assuming that the Microcomputers contribute $50 each and disk drives $40, what is the optimal combination of output? (Solve graphically.)

   b. How much slack capacity exists in the three departments with the solution obtained in part a?

4. Farnsworth Fidget, Inc., makes Greenones (Gs) and Blueones (Bs). They wish to determine the optimal production and sales quantities for next month. Only $24,000 in cash is available to spend for production and selling expenses in the month. Gs require $4 per unit of cash; Bs require $6.

   Production capacity is 2,000 hours per month. Gs need two hours each; Bs three hours. Production is flexible enough to produce either Gs or Bs, or some of each.

   Marketing doesn't believe they can sell more than 500 Gs and 300 Bs next month.

   a. If Gs have a contribution of $9, and Bs of $16, how many of each should they schedule for production?

   b. Is there any slack in this solution? How much and where?

5. The Orehouse Mining Company owns two different mines that produce limestone used in making cement. After being crushed, the limestone is graded into three classes: high-grade, medium-grade, and low-grade. There is some demand

---

* The questions and problems preceded by an asterisk should not be attempted until Appendix F is read. These problems may be solved with the aid of provided software or calculated manually. See Preface for explanation of this software.

for each grade of limestone. Orehouse has contracted to provide a cement plant with 120 tons of high-grade, 80 tons of medium-grade, and 240 tons of low-grade ore per week. It costs the company $20,000 per day to run the first mine and $16,000 per day to run the second. These mines have different capacities, however. In a day's operation, the first mine produces 60 tons of high-grade, 20 tons of medium-grade, and 40 tons of low-grade ore, whereas the second mine produces daily 20 tons of high-grade, 20 tons of medium-grade, and 120 tons of low-grade ore. How many days a week should each mine be operated to fulfill the company's orders at minimum operating cost? (Hint: Let one variable be the number of days per week that mine 1 operates and the other variable the number of days per week that mine 2 operates.)

*6. Solve Problem 3 with the simplex method, and assume that the quantities in Problem 3 are the output capacities for a 40–hour week. This makes the time requirements for each product become:

Hours per 100 Units

	Microcomputers	Disk Drives
Stamped parts	2.00	.62
Machined parts	2.67	.40
Assembly	1.60	.73

(Hint: Stamped-part constraint is $2T + .62A \leq 40$ hours.)

*7. A company makes four products, A, B, C, and D, which go through four departments: drill, mill, lathe, and assembly. The hours of department time required by each product per unit are:

a. How many of each product should be made?
b. Identify the slack capacity with the solution obtained in part a.

*8. There are two factories and two warehouses in the Core Laboratories production-distribution system. The per-period capacities, demands, and the per-unit shipping costs for one of their major products from each factory to each warehouse are as follows:

	Cost to Warehouses		
Factory	A	B	Capacity (units, regular time)
R	$1	$2	600
S	5	3	1,100
Demand (units)	700	1,200	

Since the demand exceeds regular time capacities, extra capacity can be added as follows:

Factory	Capacity (regular time)	Extra Capacity from Overtime (in units)	Premium Cost per Unit on Overtime
R	600	150	$2.50
S	1,100	160	2.00

If this item sells for $15 each in both markets, but has variable manufacturing costs (on regular time) of $5 at Factory R and $4 at Factory S, what production-distribution plan, utilizing regular and/or overtime capacities, should they use to maximize contribution? Set up as a simplex problem, but do not solve.

*9. Formulate problem 2, Chapter 20, as a simplex problem. (Hint: The variables are the 12 possible shipping routes. We wish to minimize shipping

	Drill	Mill	Lathe	Assembly	Amount Saved by Making Instead of Buying
A	4	0	2	3	$ 9
B	8	3	5	5	18
C	5	7	1	6	14
D	1	8	6	3	11
Maximum hours available	6,000	9,000	8,000	11,000	

costs subject to demand and production capacity constraints.)

*10. Your instructor will supply you with a computer solution to the gasoline blending problem discussed in the chapter.

a. How much of each grade of crude should be allocated to unleaded and regular gasoline?

b. What slack exists, and how should it be interpreted?

Section Five

Designing Production and Service Facilities

Every kind of production requires physical facilities in the form of buildings, machines, and equipment. These have to be designed and arranged to allow for the economical production of products and services.

These facilities should be located advantageously, considering the sources of the company's physical inputs, such as materials, labor, energy, and capital costs, and its outputs, considering freight costs and the location of markets.

Chapter 19 begins this section with the study of basic production processes, automated machine systems, and maintenance of facilities and machines.

Chapter 20 considers locations and the interactions of the various factors which bear upon the proper location of an organization's production facilities.

The buildings which house operations need to be designed to facilitate economical production. They need to provide for housing the facilities used directly to produce products or services and to keep these assets in operable condition. Chapter 21 deals with building design and the internal services. The arrangement of production facilities within a structure to allow for economical production is also considered in Chapter 21. The merits of various layout patterns are presented.

Chapter 22 continues the discussion of the overall designing of operations for economical production. This chapter is devoted to the designing of high-volume repetitive production assembly lines—the kind of work we all associate with mass production. This is where large numbers of workers have adjacent work stations through which products pass from one to the next until they emerge at the end of the line as finished products.

Finally, Chapter 23 discusses energy management and the influence of this scarce and expensive resource on facility design as well as other energy management related topics.

Chapter 19

Production Processes, Automated Machine Systems, and Maintenance

Once products and services are designed, their specifications must be translated into specific processing systems which create the product or provide the service. For example, in manufacturing a keyboard for a new microcomputer, it is necessary to determine what processing methods to use for making its component parts. Some may be stamped from sheet steel, others may be die-cast from aluminum, or they can be plastic parts formed by plastic injection molding.

Decisions must be made about the kinds of machines to use to perform these operations. Questions have to be answered, such as, will "general-purpose" machines (such as drill presses, lathes, and stamping machines) be sufficient to do the work? Or can "special-purpose" machines (perhaps computer-controlled) be justified because of the high prospective volume of parts and products to be made?

How should the keyboards be assembled? Should one worker assemble an entire keyboard, or should assembly be broken down into a number of stages where each worker (or robot) repetitively performs only one or a few steps? Should the products move down an assembly line, or should they be completely assembled at one assembly station? At what stages of the process should inspection or testing take place to ensure the desired quality level?

These and other similar questions have to be answered by manufacturing engineers and systems analysts who work closely with production and operations managers as they develop the necessary production processing systems.

Nor are these activities peculiarly and only associated with factory production. Service organizations, such as airlines or even city governments, have to determine how to integrate people and machines to provide their services in an effective manner.

Figure 19–1 shows the kinds of information flows which are needed in order to translate product design specifications into processing instructions.

PRODUCTION PROCESSING SYSTEMS

Every manufacturer and every service organization already has processing systems for producing its goods and services. These were developed in the past. And, although these usually

FIGURE 19–1
Model of Information Flow from Product Design to Production

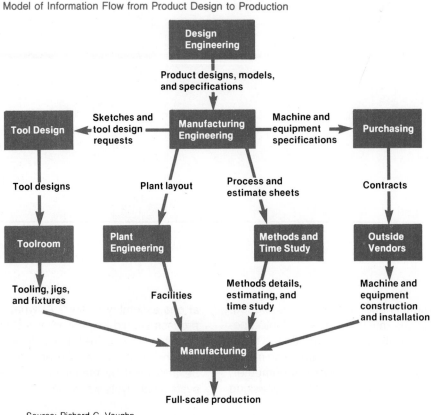

Source: Richard C. Vaughn.

do not change fast, there is often a slow evolutionary process of change going on. Sometimes, however, major changes do come quickly. The steel industry, for example, was revolutionized some 20 years ago by the introduction of the basic oxygen process, which makes higher-quality steel at less cost than other processes. Often, too, a company has to invest large amounts to install up-to-date methods which have been developing over the years but require extensive change to use to their fullest. Chrysler built a new $2-million automatic welding system for welding together the body shells for its small cars. In about 6½ minutes, a "team" of 13 robot welding machines (6 on each side of the assembly line and 1 overhead) perform 504 spot welds on each body shell as it travels along a 140-foot track. Also, GM is, in the mid-1980s, rebuilding entire plants to take advantage of the latest technology in robotry, computer-controlled assembly, and advanced production and inventory control systems.

Some cities are now building prototype plants to process garbage and trash into methane fuel and burnable pellets to use in generating electricity. The process also recovers limited amounts of reusable metals. If this proves to be economically feasible, garbage and trash may not be something to bury but something which, when recycled, has a market value and which will improve our utilization of scarce natural resources.

Systems for delivering services can be just as complex as those in manufacturing. Blood-cleansing processing systems for people whose kidneys are not functioning (kidney dialysis machines) are, for example, quite complex. So also, mountain resorts catering to skiers need to provide ski lifts and ski trail systems which are designed to accommodate skiers with differing abilities. The ski lifts need to be safe yet fast enough to transport skiers up the mountain at rates which keep waiting at a minimum.

BASIC METAL TRANSFORMATION PROCESSES

So many of today's products are made from metal that metal processing methods are perhaps the most pervasive of all systems in modern-day production operations. Consequently they merit brief attention here.

After having been abstracted from ore, metal processing usually starts with molten metal being poured into ingots or sometimes "pigs." In the case of gold or other precious metals the ingots may be roughly a foot long by some four inches by four inches in size. Pig-iron pigs are larger. Steel ingots are much larger, perhaps as large as 2 feet by 3 feet by 10 feet and weighing several tons.

Ingots and pigs are later reheated and processed into specific items. Ingots can, while hot and soft, be rolled between squeezing rollers into billets, bars, sheets, or other standard semi-finished forms. Billets and bars can be cut by shearing, sawing, or flame-cutting into smaller pieces which can be pounded into rough shape for forging. In forging, the metal is heated to a soft state and then pounded into final shape (the head of a hammer is made this way).

Metal can also be rolled out into sheets which can be sheared or stamped into pieces and then folded or bent into desired shapes (the outside of a stove or refrigerator is made this way). Pieces of sheet metal can also be "drawn," or pushed between two dies, to make them take on the desired shape (an automobile fender is shaped this way).

Metal is sometimes made directly into its fi-nal shape by casting, which means pouring it, while molten, into molds, which usually are made of sand. Sometimes molten metal is forced into water-cooled metal molds of intricate shapes. This method, called *die casting,* is used to make many trim and decorative parts out of zinc or plastic. Knobs on television sets, typewriter keys, and a host of other items are made this way.

There are also other less common processes such as extrusion. Metal, particularly aluminum, can be extruded through an orifice which gives it a certain cross section, such as are used in aluminum window and door frames. Another less common process is sintering, where powdered metal is compacted in a forming die to the desired shape. Later this compacted part is baked at close to the metal's melting point, which causes it to fuse into a solid piece.

Sheet metal can be "spun" (Chinese woks are often made this way). A flat piece of metal is put next to a semiball form and rotated, and, as it rotates, force is applied to push it against the semiball. In the end, it will have taken the shape of the semiball form. Another process is "coining," where a forming surface contour is forced against a piece of metal (our coins are made this way).

Most metal forming, however, starts with a rough piece which is oversized, and then the excess is removed, much as a sculptor "exposes" a statue in a stone. The excess metal can be removed in many ways. It can be ground off; it can be drilled out or, with thin metal, punched out; it can be chipped, or sheared, or shaved off.

Of these processes, shaving off the excess is the most common. Except for grinding, which is done by an abrasive grinding wheel, the tool is almost always a steel tool with a carbaloy tip which is harder and tougher than the metal being cut. Usually this process generates considerable heat and requires that a stream of coolant liquid be directed at it constantly.

Sometimes the material being machined is rotated against a stationary cutting tool, as in the case of lathes. One form of lathe is the turret lathe; another is the automatic screw machine. Both of these machines can perform two or three operations on a part in sequence or simultaneously. The cutting tool may be stationary or may rotate in a fixed spot while the material is passed back and forth against the tool as it shaves or chisels off a little more metal at each pass. This is called *milling* or in some variations, *shaping*.

If the tool rotates and makes a hole, it is "drilling," but, if the tool is stationary and the work is rotated around it to make a hole, it is "boring." Sometimes a hole is first drilled to rough size and then finished to more exact size by using a "broach." A broach is a slightly tapered mandrel with sharp ridges at each size expansion, and, as it is pulled through the hole, it enlarges it by gouging off the required amount of metal and making the hole the right size.

A different way to remove excess metal is with chemicals, which eat away the unwanted metal. To control the process, the areas that are not to be thinned down are covered with a chemical-resistant coating. The chemical eats away (etches) the exposed surfaces, leaving the remaining areas untouched. Later the coating is removed, and the piece has the high and low areas as designed (the end pieces for missile fuel tanks are made this way).

Hewlett-Packard, which makes calculators, computers, and other sophisticated electronic devices, uses such a process for manufacturing printed circuit boards. The entire process is monitored by a minicomputer which automatically moves the boards through the proper sequence of dips into the various chemicals (acids, neutralizers, water, and so on). The system can handle several different types of circuit boards at the same time. The computer "remembers" which vat each board is in and how long it is supposed to stay there. At the proper time an automatic conveyor moves down the line of vats and arrives at the vat at just the right time to remove the board and take it on to the next operation.

Other important processes include heat-treating parts for hardening. The parts are heated close to their melting point and then are quenched quickly in a cool liquid. This process hardens the surface. In other cases, just the reverse is done: Castings are heated up close to their melting point and allowed to cool very slowly. This "annealing" process relieves the internal strain originally set up by thick and thin areas cooling at different rates. The unequal cooling rates, by causing the castings to shrink unevenly, creates internal strain. If these are not relieved by annealing the casting will crack more easily. Water glasses which have not been properly annealed will break very easily.

Plating is also a common metal treatment. Chrome is added to steel bumpers, for example, by passing them through a series of acid and water baths and through an electrically charged solution which makes the chrome adhere to the steel.

MACHINING PROCESSING SYSTEMS

Year by year, more and more work once done by people continues to be transferred to machines. In a recent study, the Brattle Institute of Boston estimated that robots and other computerized or intelligent machines could replace up to 30 percent of U.S. manufacturing jobs.[1] This is because machines respond very quickly to control signals and can apply great force smoothly and precisely. They can do several operations at the same time, and they can handle repetitive and routine tasks well. More and more machines are also being developed to do things which people never could do, such as refine oil or to make chemicals or plastics. And in almost all cases the equipment is becoming more fully automatic. (Machines are vastly inferior to people, however, when it comes to reasoning, exercising more than minimal judgment, developing new methods, or in assembling complex products.)

Today's more advanced equipment is being

---

[1] A. M. Senia, "The Factory of the Future," *Iron Age*, January 21, 1983, p. 54.

designed to include closed-loop feedback systems. Machines control themselves. They inspect their own output, and, if they are turning out poor work, they reset themselves.

In order to do these things, they contain minicomputers and microprocessors which contain built-in memory units which allow them to remember what they are supposed to do; sensor units which monitor their output; reporting and judging systems which compare the quality of the work they are turning out with what they are supposed to be turning out; and correction effectuators which reset the machine whenever this is needed (see Figure 19–2). All of this is done quickly and accurately since the computer can store vast amounts of information and can calculate virtually instantaneously.

Automated process controls are now widely used in oil-refining, chemicals, steel-making, cement, and other "process" industries. (Process industries may be contrasted with fabrication industries which assemble products from component parts.) Materials in process industries are processed inside tanks, vats, pressure vessels, and the like, and materials flow from one processing step to another in pipes and ducts. The processing, rates of flow, temperatures, mixture ratios, and so on are controlled largely by computers. In the case of oil refining, complex mathematical models "optimize" the way crude oil (which is by no means always homogenous and, depending on its source, differs in chemical makeup, viscosity, volatility, specific gravity, and

so on) is refined into various finished products, such as premium and regular gasoline, jet fuel, and heating oil.

GENERAL-PURPOSE VERSUS SPECIAL-PURPOSE MACHINES

The best way to make a product depends upon how many are to be made, because machines can be designed to do most manual operations, except complex assembly. Such machines sometimes are very costly; yet, they are so productive that they cost very little per unit of product if a large volume is produced. Thus, the prospective volume determines the proper "depth of tooling," or the extent to which managers should mechanize or automate. In fact, specialized machines are so costly that they are sometimes made in sections so that product model changes will obsolete only part of the whole machine. Automobile fenders, for example, are formed in huge presses that have removable dies. When models change, the companies take out the old model dies and put in the new. They still have a specialized machine, but they do not have to buy a whole new press for every model change.

For low volumes, the large investments in special-purpose machines can rarely be justified, so general-purpose machines which are designed to do one kind of work rather than one job should be used. Usually these machines are not costly, and they are suitable for performing a wide range of operations, such as drilling holes of various sizes. The machines, however, often require highly skilled machinists to set them up as well as to operate them, and they are relatively slow in operation. Special-purpose machines also require skilled people to set them up, but, because many are automatic, they can be operated by semiskilled or unskilled labor.

In using general-purpose machines, a number of things usually have to be done either manually or automatically:[2]

FIGURE 19–2
A Process Control System

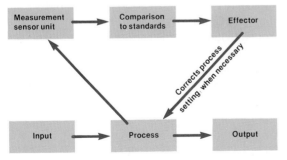

[2] Nathan H. Cook, "Computer-Managed Parts Manufacture," *Scientific American*, February 1975, p. 26.

1. Move the workpiece to the machine.
2. Load the workpiece onto the machine in the right position and affix it rigidly and accurately.
3. Select the proper tool and insert it into the machine.
4. Establish and set machine operating speeds and other conditions.
5. Control machine motion, enabling the tool to execute the desired function.
6. Sequence different tools, conditions, and motions until all operations possible on that machine are complete.
7. Unload the part from the machine.

In the operation of traditional general-purpose machines, lathes, milling machines, drill presses, and so on, all seven of these activities are performed by the operator. But with automated machines, the machines do numbers 3 to 6 of the above activities, and they do them faster and as well or better than the most skilled operator can do them.

As volume goes up, it is possible to justify the use of specialized gadgetry attachments on a machine, such as magazine feeds, special tool guides, and material holding devices (''jigs and fixtures''). These items speed production and lower operating costs.

COMPUTER-AIDED MANUFACTURING (CAM)

The other half of the CAD/CAM ''new industrial revolution,'' as some have called the application of computer technology to manufacturing, is CAM—*computer-aided manufacturing.* (CAD, computer-aided design, was discussed in Chapter 5.)

CAM covers a wide array of machine systems, from the older but widely used N/C or *numerically controlled machines,* to *robots,* to *automated batch manufacturing systems,* to *flexible manufacturing systems,* to *automatic assembly systems* designed for assembling products. Each of these will be discussed in this chapter.

Numerically Controlled (N/C) Machines

Today many—and it will soon become the majority—of metal-cutting machines used to make parts are ''numerically controlled.'' These machines are well suited for complex parts made in small- and medium-sized lots but not for large lots where automated batch-manufactured machines are more effective. Essentially, numerically controlled machines (which may also be classified as general-purpose machines) automate steps 3, 4, 5, and 6 listed above.

Instead of an operator getting instructions to plane a surface, mill a slot, or drill a hole in each item of a lot of 50 steel castings, the directions go directly to the machine. The machine is told, by means of instructions on a floppy disk to advance its planning tool to the surface of the casting and to plane its surface to a set thickness for a certain width. It is then told to change to a tool for cutting a slot, to cut the slot, and then to drill a hole, and so on. Once a process has been programmed and the machine set up with the proper tools in place, all the machine operator has to do is fasten the unfinished casting in place and remove it when the work is done.

The term *numerically controlled* comes from the fact that a machine's instruction program is based on mathematical relationships which tell the machine how far to advance its tools, how many cuts to take, to what depth, and the like. Where necessary, these directions cause the machine to make several coordinated motions at the same time (see Figure 19–3). These directions come from each machine's computers, which may not always be wholly independent but may be satellites of a central computer and receive part of their instructions from the central computer. Local disk controls can even be eliminated in *direct numerical control* (DNC). Or, if the machine has its own dedicated microcomputer, it is called *computerized numerical control* (CNC).

Numerically controlled machines do work much faster and more accurately than skilled

FIGURE 19-3
System for Direct Control of Numerically Controlled Machines

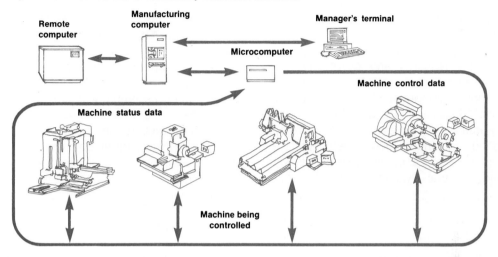

operators in manual operations. And, although it requires skilled programming to program machine instructions from a drawing and to design a machine's setup, once this is done, production is almost fully automatic and little labor is required. The disks and the design of the machine setup can be kept for repeated use in the future. In addition, the same floppy disk can often be used to control operations on different brands of similar machines.

N/C machines can be expensive; most of them cost at least $100,000. Numerical control attachments put on older machines are likely to cost $50,000 or more. Machine programmers are also needed, and castings and forgings cannot have as much minor size and shape variation as with conventional machines. (Castings made in sand molds are only "more or less" identical in size and shape.)

Another disadvantage of N/C machines is that they often require complex and frequent maintenance. Because they operate so effectively, they remove metal a large part of the time they are running, and, consequently, they wear out tools and their own operating parts more rapidly. Also, in order to operate correctly they need to be adjusted to close tolerances. Their

downtime during operations is likely to run over 4 percent, which is higher than for less sophisticated machines.

All of these requirements mean that N/C machines require a substantial amount of highly sophisticated maintenance. Often jobs are so complicated that the machinery manufacturing company's troubleshooters must be consulted to aid in programming the instructions for the part to be processed.

Role of Government in CAM Development

Millions of parts are made with N/C machines. Boeing has "spar mills" and "skin mills" that are nearly 100 feet long where N/C machines mill wing spars and wing skins for their huge aircraft from solid pieces of metal, usually aluminum or titanium. Martin Marietta uses N/C machines to make many of the thousands of parts that make up a Titan missile or NASA's manned maneuvering unit (the device the astronauts used for their spacewalk from the space shuttle in 1984). In fact, aerospace and defense companies have been the leaders in the use of N/C machines, as well as some of the more advanced CAM systems to be discussed later. This is because the Department of Defense (primarily through the Air Force) has invested millions of dollars to stimulate advances in manufacturing automation. While much of it has been directed toward building spacecraft and weaponry, the fallout of this research and development to commercial manufacturing has been substantial. N/C technology development was financed this way in the 1950s, and 60s, and 70s, and now the Air Forces' ICAM (Integrated CAM) project is doing the same in the 1980s. They spent $67 million in 1982 alone on ICAM projects with Lockheed, General Dynamics,[3] and 13 other firms.

ROBOTRY

It is now possible to develop electronic-mechanical robots to do most highly repetitive manual jobs. Only their cost stands in the way of more of them. Curiously, Japan (where labor pay rates are lower than in most other developed countries) apparently has gone farther in this direction than any other country. For example, Kawasaki (motorcycles) in Japan has developed robots which can completely assemble motors and gearboxes. The development of robots in Japan may have been caused by its rapid industrial development in the last 20 years which created a severe labor shortage. This labor shortage is expected to continue in the 1980s.

In the United States, robotry has been uncommon except in the automobile industry. However, this is changing: In 1970 there were only about 300 robots in use. In 1982 alone, about 4,000 were sold. However, during the same year, Japanese manufacturers bought almost 25,000 robots.[4]

A U.S.-made robot costs an average of $60,000 with a range from $10,000 to about $175,000. Operating costs are usually low, running about $5 to $7 per hour compared to $15 per hour for a factory worker.

Robot makers and robot users estimate that ultimately they can make robots that can do 60–70 percent of the jobs done in factories by blue-collar workers.[5] (See Figure 19–4.) General Motors estimates that about 30,000 jobs will be replaced by the nearly 14,000 robots they expect to have installed by 1990; GE expects to replace about 20,000 assembly workers with robots in this decade. Ford expects to have between 5,000 and 7,000 robots in use by the end of this decade. New jobs will be created to maintain these robots, no doubt, but there will still be a large displacement of labor caused by their introduction. Even after one discounts these optimistic estimates by robot makers, the possibilities are still enormous.

Robots are more general-purpose in application than automated machines since they, like general-purpose machines, can be reprogrammed rather easily. Typically they are programmed by having a technician "tell" the robot what to do. Figure 19–5 shows graphically how this is done. Most robots are, however, both blind and stupid; they cannot do "scene analysis." If a robot is supposed to pick up something, it does so whether anything is there or not. Parts and products have to be presented to them "just so" (left side front, standing on end, or what not), and, if they are not, the robot doesn't know it and proceeds to act as if they were.

However, even this problem is being overcome with "vision-oriented" robots. While they are primarily in the R&D stage, the technology exists to make them more flexible.

Most robots in the United States are used in the auto industry to do welding, painting, and some assembly. But some expansion to other industries is taking place, primarily in electronics assembly. Storage Technology is installing six robots to test hard disk drives; Fairchild Camera and Instrument is installing robots to produce printed circuit boards, and Hughes Aircraft uses

[3] Senia, "Factory of the Future," p. 50.

[4] "The U.S. Robot Industry Starts to Come to Life," *Business Week,* November 14, 1983, p. 194.

[5] In General Motors' heavily automated Chevrolet factory in Lordstown, Ohio, robots do 95 percent of the spot welding (there are over 9,000 spot welds in a car body). At one point, two robots make 130 spot welds in 4.5 seconds.

FIGURE 19–4
Individual Robot on an Automobile Assembly Line

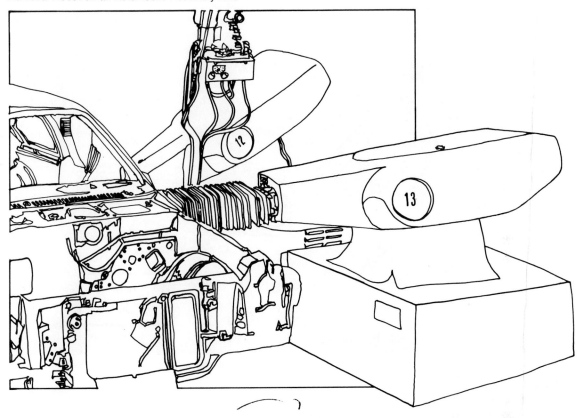

them to assemble wire harnesses (the miles of wire that are woven into aircraft to connect all of the electronics).[6]

Classes of Robots

Robots are generally classified into four kinds: manual manipulators which simply do a fixed sequence of operations; programmable units which can be "taught" to repeat a fixed set of varying sequences (see Figure 19–5); N/C robots that respond to numerical instructions from a preprogrammed disk or computer; and intelligent units which can recognize objects and have some minor capability to "think for themselves."

A robot's movement is essentially either "point to point" or "continuous path." Point-to-point robots have instructions to stop at predetermined points, do their work, and move on to the next point. Continuous-path movement is where the robot's arm or tool moves continuously along a programmed path.

Robots are powered electronically (the most expensive—as much as $175,000); hydraulically, with fluids under pressure used to drive the moving parts (these can cost nearly as much as the electronic-powered systems); and by pneumatics or air-driven (the least expensive, each costing from $10,000 to $25,000).

Industrial robots are an important means for releasing human beings from dirty and onerous labor. They eliminate drudgery. They don't take

[6] *Business Week,* "U.S. Robot Industry," p. 194.

FIGURE 19–5
  Programming an industrial robot is frequently done by using a hand controller to guide the robot through a sequence of operations. The successive positions of all the robot's joints are stored in a memory. By switching from the "teach" to the "playback" mode stored positions are repeated. The robot is now ready to take its place on production line.

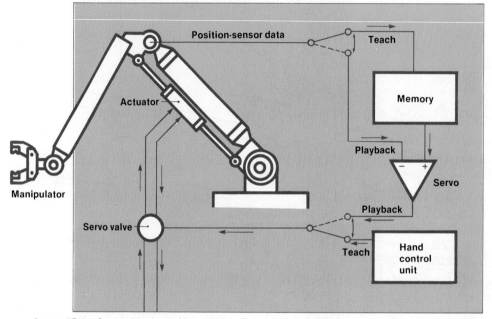

coffee breaks, don't belong to unions, and they work around the clock. They show up for work every day and quickly learn reasonably complex work. They don't get hurt and never complain about dust, fumes, heat, or cold.

AUTOMATED BATCH MANUFACTURING SYSTEMS

For large volumes of similar metal parts, automated batch manufacturing systems (ABMs) or "transfer" machines are superior to numerically controlled machines. ABMs do many operations on a part rather than just one or two. And, although their setup costs are high, the setup cost per part is low because of their ability to produce a large volume of a reasonably wide array of similar products. An ABMS is an electronically controlled collection of somewhat flexible and dedicated machines linked by materials handling equipment in a manner to convert stop-and-go batch manufacturing into continuous or nearly continuous processing.[7]

ABMSs, illustrated in Figure 19–6, are fast approaching the automation stage in metal working. An unfinished part, say a steel casting or a forging, is fastened to a conveyor which moves on a stop-and-go basis from one machine to the next. The part stops long enough at each machine to have one or more operations performed on it. Separate machines, performing successive operations, are lined up on each side of a conveyor, and, as the conveyor stops, each machine automatically reaches out and performs its operation on the part. As the operating parts

---

[7] See Raymond J. Larsen, "Taking the Wraps off Flexibility in Manufacturing," *Iron Age,* November 20, 1978, p. 76.

FIGURE 19–6
Typical Automated Batch Manufacturing System

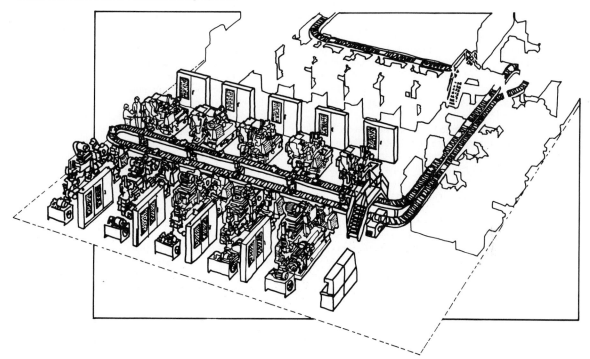

on the various machines move back and out of the way, the conveyor moves another step, and the performance is repeated on the next units. The machines, though actually separate, operate together as if they were parts of a very complex single-purpose machine. Such machine groupings eliminate all product handling except the little that is needed before the first and after the last operation.

An interesting problem arises when one operation takes considerably longer time than others. In such a case the operation must be considerably speeded up or else that particular operation must be broken into two parts. If it is a hole, one drill may drill it only part way, and another drill, at another work station, may drill it the rest of the way. This allows individual operations to be in balance. And, while an ABMS can cost $5 million, it can increase production several hundred percent, as well as require less floor space for storage of work in process and the cost associated with having idle WIP waiting to be processed in a functional machine layout system.

Flexible Manufacturing Systems

Generally, there are two types of ABMSs. The first type, more commonly in use, is the one just described—*dedicated* or *sequential* systems. They are dedicated to processing only one part or parts with small differences and always with the same sequence of operations. The second, and most expensive, are called *random* or *flexible* manufacturing systems because they can handle "families" of similar parts in different process sequences. They use direct numerical control (explained earlier) and are used by Allis Chalmers to make tractor castings; by Rockwell International to make truck axles; and by Avco

FIGURE 19–7
A Look at Some Japanese Automatic Factories

A visitor to Japan these days finds the new manufacturing systems turning out parts for machine tools in Nagoya, electric motors near Mount Fuji, diesel cylinder blocks in Niigata, and many other products elsewhere. In most cases these plants run on three shifts. During the day skeleton crews work with the machines. At night the robots and the machines work alone.

In Fanuc Ltd.'s cavernous, bumblebee-yellow buildings in a pine forest near Mount Fuji, automatic machining centers and robots typically toil unattended through the night, with only subdued blue warning lights flashing as unmanned delivery carts move like ghostly messengers through the eerie semidarkness. This plant, one of two in the Fuji complex, makes parts for robots and machine tools (which are assembled manually, however). The machining operation, occupying 54,000 square feet, is supervised at night by a single controller, who watches the machines on closed-circuit TV. If something goes wrong, he can shut down that particular part of the operation and reroute the work around it.

Some Americans think that Fanuc's Fuji complex is just a showcase. Some showcase. The total cost of the plant was about $32 million, including the cost of 30 machining cells, which consist of computer-controlled machine tools loaded and unloaded by robots, along with materials-handling robots, monitors, and a programmable controller to orchestrate the operation. Fanuc estimates that it probably would have needed 10 times the capital investment for the same output with conventional manufacturing. It also would have needed 10 times its labor force of about 100. In this plant one employee supervises 10 machining cells; the others act as maintenance men and perform assembly. All in all, the plant is about five times as productive as its conventional counterpart would be.

Across the street, 60 machining cells and 101 robots toil in a big two-story facility automatically machining parts and assembling them into 10,000 electric motors a month. There is nothing else like it in the world. Men perform maintenance functions here in the daytime. The robots work through the night, in silence marred only by hydraulic sighs and the sibilance of those automatic carts. The first floor of the plant contains the machining cells and 52 robots. Machining is carried out on about 900 types and sizes of motor parts, in lots ranging from 20 to 1,000 units. Machined parts are temporarily stored in an automatic warehouse; they are automatically retrieved when they are scheduled for assembly on the second floor.

Yamazaki Machinery Works Ltd. operates a flexible automation plant near Nagoya that makes parts of computerized numerically controlled lathes and machining centers; the latter combine several metalworking machines and incorporate automatic tool changers. In the daytime 12 workers man the $20-million plant. At night only a lone watchman with a flashlight is on duty while the machines keep on working.

A conventional machining system with similar production volume, according to Yamazaki, would require 215 workers and nearly four times as many machines, and would take three months to turn out the parts the new plant makes in three days. The company estimates that over five years of operation its plant will produce after-tax profits of $12 million, compared with $800,000 for a conventional plant that size. Yamazaki is now transferring this technology to its machine-tool-making plant in Florence, Kentucky—bad news for Yamazaki's American competitors.

But the most astonishing Japanese automated factory will be started up next month by Yamazaki about 20 miles from its headquarters near Nagoya. This will be what Tsunehiko "Tony" Yamazaki, the personable senior executive managing director, describes as his company's 21st-century factory. The new plant's 65 computer-controlled machine tools and 34 robots will be linked via a fiber-optic cable with the computerized design center back in headquarters. From there the flexible factory can be directed to manufacture the required types of parts—as well as to make the tools and fixtures to produce the parts—by entering into the computer's memory names of various machine tool models scheduled to be produced and pressing a few buttons to get production going. The Yamazaki plant will be the world's first automated factory to be run by telephone from corporate headquarters.

The plant will have workmen, to be sure: 215 men helping produce what would take 2,500 in a conventional factory. At maximum capacity the plant will be able to turn out about $230 million of machine tools a year. But production is so organized that sales can be reduced to $80 million a year, if need be, without laying off workers. The Yamazaki plant illustrates yet another aspect of economy of scope: with flexible automation, a manufacturer can economically shrink production capacity to match lower market demand.

Though Japanese machine tool makers are the most ambitious installers of flexible automation, they are by no means alone. FMS is spreading throughout Japanese

(continued)

manufacturing, with Panasonic, Mitsubishi, and other consumer and industrial goods producers installing the new systems.

So far, nothing even remotely comparable is happening in manufacturing in the United States or anywhere else in the world. Disturbingly, all of U.S. industry can boast only about 30 flexible manufacturing systems in place; in Japan one large industrial company, Toyoda Machine Tool Co., has more than 30. Frets David Nitzan, director of industrial robotics at the research and consulting firm SRI International, "We are facing another sputnik—a Japanese sputnik."

to make U.S. Army XM-1 tank engine components. However, the United States is far behind Japan in their use. Figure 19–7 illustrates just how far this is! Figure 19–8 shows a schematic of a FMS.

Automatic Assembly

In manufacturing one of the last frontiers of handwork is assembly, and putting finished pieces together is still handwork in most industries. Assembly lines for putting shoes together, suits of clothes, automobiles, typewriters, adding machines, stoves, refrigerators, radios, television sets, and so on are characterized by *people* putting things together.

Nevertheless, computer-controlled automatic assembly is slowly becoming more common, although its high initial cost and lack of flexibility stand in the way of faster acceptance. Automated assembly requires costly magazine feeds, indexing turntables, robot fingers, hands, and arms, and all the electronic equipment (electric eyes, solenoid switches, electronic circuity, and so on) that goes along with it. IBM assembles many of its electronic-panel units automatically. Parker Pen assembles ball-point pens automatically. Gabriel Company assembles 2,000 valves an hour automatically. McGraw-Edison assembles 1,500 rollerskate wheels an hour. Sara Lee puts cakes and pies together automatically.

Here, in general, is how one of IBM' automatic assembly machines operates for the assembly of wire contact relays. A supply of every part is loaded into a hopper (or magazine feed) located above an assembling machine along a conveyor or around a lazy Susan revolving table. The first assembling machine automatically picks out one of the frame parts of the relay and fastens it on the conveyor. Then the conveyor "indexes" or moves it to the next work station (a foot or so away). There the next assembling machine puts its part into place in the frame. Then the conveyor indexes again and moves the frame to the next station, where part two is attached. Then more moves and more parts are added. Besides placing the parts, the machine fastens them together, so that finished assemblies come off at the end of the line.

Station 1 feeds molded plastic frames into the left side of a turret fixture. A vibrating feeder positions the frames, which move down inclined rolls to a loading platform. An air cylinder drives a horizontal reciprocating plunger, which pushes frames along a platform one at a time. Jaws lift a frame and place it in the left side of the fixture. A photoelectric cell watches the frames on rails and cuts off the feed if the frames back up. Frames pass through a fixture which stops those with misaligned or bent terminals. If one stops, the frames back up to a photoelectric detector.

Station 2 is the same as station 1 except that it feeds frames into the right side of the turret fixture. Between stations 2 and 3 an inspection device checks the loading of frames in their holding fixtures.

Station 3 probes for the presence and location of holes in the frames, and absence of dirt or "flash" in the holes. If the probe is impeded, work on the frames stops.

FIGURE 19–8

Flexible Manufacturing system is an automated set of programmable machine tools for metalworking. The machines are controlled by a hierarchy of computers and are linked by a conveyor that carries workpieces from one machine to the next. The minicomputer determines the overall sequence of operations to be carried out on each workpiece. When the workpiece reaches a machine, the minicomputer also directs the machine to select a cutting tool and "downloads" a program into a smaller microcomputer that controls the cutting path of the tool. Flexible manufacturing systems have now been built that can run for hours without intervention. Parts to be machined are loaded at the entry to the system during the first shift, and the system operates throughout the second and third shifts. Setup times are so reduced that such a system may be able to manufacture 100 randomly selected rotational parts in 72 hours.

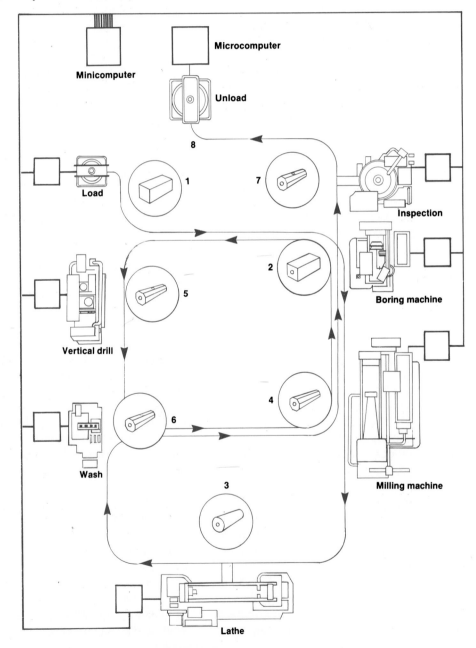

Source: Thomas G. Gunn, "The Mechanization of Design and Manufacturing," *Scientific American*, September, 1982.

Station 4 countersinks holes in the frames for guide pins.

Station 5 taps holes for setscrews.

Station 6 cleans chips from holes with an air blast.

Station 7 ejects frames found substandard at station 3. A memory pin, extended at station 3, closes an electric circuit at station 7, actuating rams that remove the frame from its work-holding fixture.

Station 8 examines tapped holes with photoelectric cells for broken taps. Clogged holes stop the light, and this stops the machine. A signal light shows the operator the trouble spot.

Station 9 inserts rubber bumpers into threaded holes. Vibratory hoppers feed these bumpers in the correct position. Nozzles lift the bumpers by suction and transfer them to holes. When bumpers are seated in the frame, the air flow in nozzles automatically reverses from suction to pressure. Bumpers are released and pushed into position by air pressure.

Station 10 checks with photoelectric cells for the presence of bumpers. When a frame lacks one or both bumpers, the machine stops and a red light signals the operator.

Station 11 inserts a setscrew into a tapped hole in the relay frame in the left side of the holding fixture. A vibratory feeder positions the screw for driving. An automatic screwdriver sets the screw at the right depth.

Station 12 inserts a setscrew into the frame in right side of the holding fixture.

Station 13 inserts guide pins into frames. A transfer arm picks up pins by vacuum and moves them by mechanical linkage to location where it inserts the pins into frames.

Station 14 flares guide pins to secure them in frames.

Station 15 performs final inspection. It probes for guide pins and checks for high, low, or missing setscrews.

Station 16 removes all relays. Those that have passed all inspections slide down a track into a container. Memory pins locate faulty relays, and, when they find a faulty one, they close

an electric circuit, which shifts the track so that it drops the rejected relay into a reject box. This station also probes the fixtures to make sure all relays have been ejected.

In another example, Figure 19–9 shows the layout of a minicomputer-controlled programmable robot assembly system which assembles automobile alternators.

So far, no one puts entire automobiles or any other large product together entirely automatically, although the Japanese have made great strides toward doing so. As this decade ends, we may see it happen.

MAINTENANCE

Because machines and buildings are continually wearing out, they need repairs and sometimes replacement. For machines, wear on shafts, bearings, gears, belts, and other parts makes repair necessary. Electric motors must be serviced. Transportation facilities—elevators, conveyors, gasoline- and electric-powered trucks, hand trucks, hoists, and cranes—all need continual lubrication and repairs. Plant services—electric power, light, gas, water, compressed air and steam lines, washrooms, sewers, pumps fire protection equipment, and heating systems—all need to be maintained. So do the buildings themselves—the roofs, windows, walls, floors, and foundations. In total, keeping everything operable often costs more than one tenth of all of a company's costs. And, as more and more machine systems are introduced to the production process, the role of maintenance becomes essential to keep these expensive systems running.

THE MAINTENANCE DEPARTMENT AND ITS DUTIES

The responsibility for maintenance is usually assigned to the plant engineer who is under the general direction of the chief engineer. The plant engineer often has two main departments: a machine shop and a plant maintenance department.

The machine shop keeps the machines and

FIGURE 19–9

Programmable robot assembly station built at the Charles Stark Draper Laboratory can assemble the 17 parts of a commercial automobile alternator in 2 minutes, 42 seconds. At the far right is a control box through which the robot can be taught a sequence of moves that can then be recorded in the memory of a minicomputer. The robot serves as a test bed for exploring theories, techniques, and costs of computer-controlled assembly systems capable of being reprogrammed for various comparable tasks. The alternator was selected for the assembly experiment because it is an actual industrial product and thus requires mating of component parts that have standard industrial clearances. Alternator was also chosen because it is a "stack" product: All the parts can be added from a single direction.

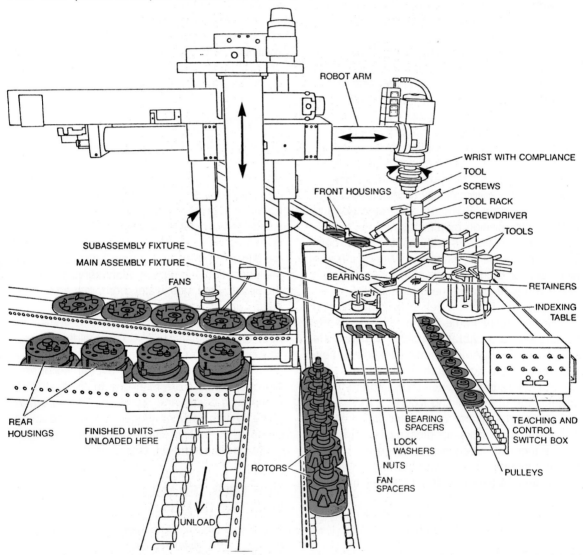

Source: James L. Nevins and Daniel E. Whitney, "Computer-Controlled Assembly," *Scientific American,* February 1978, pp. 62–74. Copyright © by *Scientific American,* Inc. All rights reserved.

equipment in working order. Its employees include millwrights (general mechanics and people who move machines), machinists, sheet-metal workers, welders, oilers, and others who repair machines and keep trucks and conveyors operating.

The plant maintenance group specializes in the building and building's services. Its employees are electricians, tinsmiths, welders, pipefitters, steamfitters, bricklayers, steeplejacks, painters, glaziers, carpenters, millwrights, window washers, and janitors. Also, the maintenance department usually operates its own spare parts stockroom and orders the materials used on repair jobs.

Besides repairing machines and equipment, the maintenance department in most companies does minor remodeling and relayout work. It tears down or puts up partitions between departments, builds new concrete foundations for equipment, and makes mountings for machines and motors. Since some of this work requires construction drawings, as well as compliance with laws, the department should include one or more construction engineers who can make the drawings and who are acquainted with building codes and safety regulations.

The maintenance department has to keep all fire prevention equipment in operating order at all times. To do this, the department must periodically inspect the sprinkler systems, valves, fire pumps, elevated tanks, portable extinguishers, fire doors, and sirens. The department also trains the company's inside emergency fire fighting crews in fire fighting methods and in the use of fire suppressing equipment. The maintenance department is also responsible for the premises outside the building. It maintains truck docks, rail sidings, storage yards, parking lots, fences, and landscaping.

THE INHERENT INEFFICIENCY OF MAINTENANCE ACTIVITY

A considerable amount of maintenance work must be done to take care of emergency break-downs. Such demands for services are irregular and impose variable workload demands on the maintenance department. Often, too, the machines being maintained are highly sophisticated, perhaps with electronic controls, and they can be repaired only by highly qualified technicians. To meet such needs, the department has to maintain a capability of serving at a high-technological level even though this high level of service is not often required.

Such irregularities force the maintenance department to operate at less than its peak efficiency. Maintenance workers can give good service only if there are enough of them to answer calls quickly, but they can do this only if they are not very busy. If they are always fully occupied, they cannot give the best service. This need not be a serious problem, however, because there are usually a few necessary but not urgent jobs of relatively low-skill content which they can work at between emergencies. They can work on these jobs when they are not otherwise busy and then drop them to answer more urgent calls.

This is a case where it is necessary to forgo optimizing the work of one department in the interest of optimizing the performance of the whole organization.

PREVENTIVE MAINTENANCE

Repairing machines after they fail is often *not* the best maintenance policy because *good* maintenance prevents breakdowns. The biggest cost of maintenance is usually not the cost of repairing, even if it is done at high overtime labor rates. More often the major cost is the "down for repairs" cost. Breakdowns, even when repairs are made quickly, stop production for at least a while. Employees and machines are idle, production is lost, and orders get behind schedule. Finally, getting the delayed orders back on schedule may entail overtime.

Breakdown repair jobs are almost always more costly than preventive repair jobs. It costs something to fix a loose front wheel on a car, but it costs more to fix the car after the wheel comes loose on the road. Then the owner (or his heirs) has to pay for a car wreck.

Preventive maintenance means *preventing* breakdowns. Putting new spark plugs in an automobile before winter comes is preventive maintenance. It anticipates likely difficulties and does the expected needed repairs at a convenient time, *before* the repairs are actually needed. Preventive maintenance depends upon knowledge from the past that certain wearing parts will need replacement after a normal interval of use.

In the case of factory equipment, the maintenance needs are sufficiently irregular that it does not always pay to try to anticipate breakdowns and overhaul equipment which doesn't need it badly. Preventive maintenance should be undertaken only if there seems to be need for it. Machine operators and supervisors can pay close attention to their machines and ask for repairs before parts get too worn to do the work. On unusual items, such as air conditioning equipment or elevator motors and cables, the maintenance department inspects them periodically and watches for wear.

Maintainability

Another and quite different kind of preventive maintenance can better be called *maintainability*. Maintainability is concerned with designing machines which will be both trouble-free and easily repaired.

Lubricants and hard-to-get-at bearings for today's machines are often designed to operate without attention for years, possibly for the life of the machine. Temperature detectors and gauges also reveal trouble spots (they usually get hot) before failures occur. And replacement units are modular so that they are almost as simple to replace as a light bulb. When a part goes bad, the whole unit of which it is a part can be taken out, and a new one can be plugged in. Designing machines with replaceable units is particularly helpful in maintaining their electrical control parts, which are themselves so complex that, in many cases, maintenance people

cannot repair them. All they can do is to replace the module.

PREVENTIVE MAINTENANCE ECONOMICS

In general, preventive maintenance wastes the remaining life value of all partially worn parts which are removed during repairs. The repair mechanic takes out worn but still operating parts and puts in new ones before the old ones wear out completely. This is a little wasteful, as are the extra and more frequent repairs. However, repair jobs done on a preventive basis and at a convenient time can be done at low cost, and they do reduce the number of more costly breakdown repair jobs. Considering this important trade-off, the operation of the entire production system may be optimized, albeit at the cost of not maximizing the life of parts and not minimizing the number of repair jobs. In other words, maximizing the life of parts and minimizing the frequency of repairs may be suboptimal.

If a company's maintenance workers spend as little as 25 percent of their time on emergencies and "crash" work, they are probably doing a good job of preventive maintenance. Normally, without preventive maintenance, they will spend more of their time repairing breakdowns. If they spend most of their time on emergency jobs, the company is most likely experiencing costly production holdups which may require overtime. If this is the case, preventive maintenance expenditures should probably be increased.

Preventive maintenance, however, need not be carried too far. A machine doesn't need an overhaul every time a simple bearing wears out. If a car owner lets the garage fix everything they say the car needs, the owner will have a big bill—and it may include some unneeded repairs.

Worse, is the possibility that the repair mechanic, while repairing something that is not critical, unintentionally damages other components or gets something else out of adjustment.

In some cases, a preventive program may not be necessary because a breakdown policy is reasonably satisfactory—when there is little need for immediate repair and little harm will be done by waiting. If an automatic dishwasher gets out of order, the dishes can be washed by hand. This might be a problem in a restaurant but not in a home. A repair would be needed, but it would not have to be rushed at high over-time pay rates.

In a factory a machine may even be used wastefully in the interest of maximizing the whole. Suppose, for example, that a $500 electric motor will be ruined if it is kept running, but an entire production line will be shut down—with a loss of $2,500—if it stops. By all means the motor should be kept running while everything possible is being done to replace the motor before it burns out.

Standby Capacity

Preventive maintenance is less important when production is at low levels than when production is high. At low levels there is excess capacity because machines are not being used to their fullest. When there are several machines, it doesn't matter if one machine breaks down. Production can be transferred to another machine with minimal trouble. The machine which needs repairs can be repaired at the convenience of the maintenance department without suffering any penalty cost because of the breakdown. Excess capacity operates, in a sense, in lieu of preventive maintenance.

This same philosophy can be incorporated into a preventive maintenace program when operations are at high levels. Excess standby capacity can be provided for use in case trouble occurs. This excess capacity can be complete machines, or it can be major parts or components which take a long time to get.

The decision to use this strategy is a matter of cost trade-offs. It may be expensive to carry the replacements, but they reduce total costs by minimizing breakdown interruptions. Suppose, for example, that it is necessary to keep a fleet of 20 forklift trucks in operation and that

it costs $40 a day to own a truck, whether it is in use or not. If only 1 or 2 of the 20 trucks are not in operation, then the work can still be done by using hand lift trucks. Using hand trucks, however, will cost $50 for each lift truck not operating.

But, if three, four, or more of the trucks are out of order, the hand truckers can't handle the work. There will be production holdups during the day and overtime costs at night as the remaining forklift trucks catch up on the work. The costs are $100 per day for the next three forklift trucks out of order. If more than a toal of five are out of order at any one time, certain production work will be seriously affected, and the cost will be $500 per day for each truck over five not in use.

Figure 19-10 shows how these various costs would be affected if the company decided to carry one or more spare trucks as standbys. The column of probability figures is based on the record of how frequent various numbers of trucks have been out of order in the past. The figures in each cost column were multiplied, in turn, by the figures in the probability column. The vertical summation of each cost column shows the expected cost for trucks being out of operation over a period of time. These costs go down markedly with more and more standby trucks. But, when the cost of the standby trucks is added in, their costs quickly become equal to and then greater than the losses from trucks being out of operation. In this example, Figure 19-11 shows that least costs are achieved by owning a fleet of 22 forklift trucks, recognizing that occasionally some will be idle, and that at other times more than 2 of the regular fleet will be broken down.

Preventive Maintenance Repairs

Often preventive maintenance is a matter of over-hauling entire groups of machines rather than letting them operate until they break down. Here, too, it is possible to calculate which policy is best to use.

FIGURE 19-10

CxP   ClxP   *MINIMUM 0*

Number out of Order	Cost	Probability	Expected Costs (no spare)	Costs with 1 Spare	Expected Costs	Costs with 2 Spares	Expected Costs	Costs with 3 Spares	Expected Costs
0	$ 0	.09	$ 0	$ 0	$ 0	$ 0	$ 0	$ 0	$ 0
1	50	.30	15	0	0	0	0	0	0
2	100	.25	25	50	13	0	0	0	0
3	200	.15	30	100	15	50	8	0	0
4	300	.10	30	200	20	100	10	50	5
5	400	.05	20	300	15	200	10	100	5
6	900	.03	27	400	12	300	9	200	6
7	1,400	.02	28	900	18	400	8	300	6
8	1,900	.01	19	1,400	14	900	9	400	4
		1.00	$194		$107		$ 54		$ 26
Add cost of spares			0		40 ← 1 SPARE		80 → 2 SPARES		120
Total			$194		$147		$134		$146

Suppose, for example, that there are 50 machines to keep in service, and they can be overhauled on a preventive basis at a cost of $200 per overhaul. Such a policy, if overhauls were frequent, would prevent nearly all breakdowns (breakdown repairs cost $700). The question

would be whether to repair the machines only when they break down or to follow some kind of a regular preventive repair schedule. And, if a preventive schedule should be followed, how often should the machines be overhauled.

Experience shows that breakdowns after

FIGURE 19-11
Cost Effects of Having Standby Trucks Available

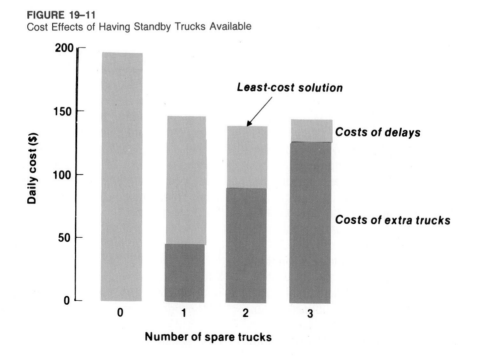

overhaul or repair will occur in the manner shown in Figure 19–12. It shows a slightly greater probability of a breakdown right away than a little later on. This is because once in a while the overhaul is itself faultily done, thus leading to an almost immediate new breakdown. If a machine gets through the first month without a breakdown, there is little likelihood of its needing repair until it begins to wear out from use.

The first step is to calculate what it would cost to follow a repair-on-breakdown policy. This requires only calculating the average length of time that machines can go without repairs. This proves to be 8.42 months. (The calculation is done by multiplying each figure in column 1 by the corresponding figure in column 2 and summing them.) A repair-on-breakdown policy would therefore cost an average of $4,157 per month (50 machines × $700 ÷ 8.42 months = $4,157).

Calculating the cost of periodic preventive overhauls is a little more complicated because it costs $10,000 each time to overhaul all 50 machines, and, in spite of this, there will still be a few breakdowns. Besides this, there will be a few cases where a machine recently overhauled will again break down soon because the repair was not correctly done.

The equation for calculating the expected number of breakdowns (B_n), where n is the policy for the number of periods that will elapse between preventative overhauls, is:

$$B_n = N \sum_i^n p_n + B_{(n-1)}p_1 + B_{(n-2)}p_2$$
$$+ B_{(n-3)}p_3 + \cdots B_1 p_{(n-1)}$$

where

$N =$ Number of machines in the group

$p_n =$ Probability of machine breakdown in period n

For example, the expected number of breakdowns if the preventative overhaul policy is monthly, is:

$$B_1 = Np_1$$
$$= 50(.05) = 2.50$$

If the policy is to overhaul every two months:

$$B_2 = N(p_1 + p_2) + B_1 p_1$$
$$= 50(.05 + .02) + 2.50(.05)$$
$$= 3.63$$

If the policy is to overhaul every three months:

$$B_3 = N(p_1 + p_2 + p_3) + B_2 p_1 + B_1 p_2$$
$$= 50(.05 + .02 + .03) + 3.63(.05)$$
$$+ 2.50(.02)$$
$$= 5.23$$

In words, the above calculation says the expected number of breakdowns (B_3) is the product of N, the total number of machines, times the probability that a machine will break down in periods 1 or 2 or 3 $(p_1 + p_2 + p_3)$, plus the expected number of machines which will break down in period 2 (B_2) multiplied times the probability that B_2 machines will break down again after one period (p_1), plus the expected number of machines that will break down in period 1 (B_1) multiplied times the probability that these machines will break down again after two periods (p_2).

FIGURE 19–12

(1) Months until Breakdown after Overhaul or Repair	(2) Probability of Breakdown	(3) Column 1 × Column 2
1	.05	.05
2	.02	.04
3	.03	.09
4	.04	.16
5	.04	.20
6	.05	.30
7	.08	.56
8	.11	.88
9	.13	1.17
10	.14	1.40
11	.15	1.65
12	.16	1.92
Total		8.42

FIGURE 19–13

2 ÷ 1　　　*(3) × 700*　　　*(4) + (5)*

(1)	(2)	(3)	(4)	(5)	(6)
Preventive Maintenance Every n Months	Total Expected Breakdowns in n Months	Average Number of Breakdowns per Month	Expected Cost of Breakdowns per Month	Cost of Preventive Maintenance per Month	Total Cost of PM Program Including $10,000 for Periodic Overhaul
1	2.50	2.50	$1,750	$10,000	$11,750
2	3.63	1.82	1,274	5,000	6,274
3	5.23	1.74	1,218	3,333	4,551
4	7.44	1.86	1,302	2,500	3,802
5	9.68	1.94	1,358	2,000	3,358
6	12.54	2.09	1,463	1,667	✳ 3,130
7	17.03	2.43	1,701	1,433	3,134
8	23.28	2.91	2,037	1,250	3,287
9	30.90	3.43	2,401	1,111	3,512
10	39.44	3.94	2,758	1,000	3,758
11	48.93	4.45	3,115	909	4,024
12	59.62	4.97	3,479	833	4,312

For a four-month policy:

$$B_4 = N(p_1 + p_2 + p_3 + p_4) + B_3 p_1$$
$$+ B_2 p_2 + B_1 p_3$$
$$= 50(.14) + 5.23(.05) + 3.63(.02)$$
$$+ 3.50(.03)$$
$$= 7.44$$

The cost figures for each maintenance policy (preventative overhaul of every machine every month, or every two months, or every three months, and so on) are given in Figure 19–13.

Column 3 is calculated by dividing column 2 by column 1. Column 4 is column 3 times $700. Column 5 is the total number of machines preventatively overhauled per month times $200 per overhaul. For example,

$$(50/1)(\$200) = \$10,000$$
$$(50/2)(\$200) = \ \ 5,000$$
$$(50/3)(\$200) = \ \ 3,333$$

Total costs, column 6, is simply the sum of columns 4 and 5.

The cost figures which are plotted in Figure 19–14 show that preventive maintenance should be used. The horizontal line is the expected cost of the repair-on-breakdown policy, calculated earlier as $4,157 per month. The dish-shaped curve is a plot of the total costs of the alternatives as presented in the last column of Figure 19–13. The least-cost policy would be to do preventative overhauls every six or seven months, the lowest point on the curve. Such a policy would entail monthly costs of $3,130 and would save $1,027 a month as compared to the repair-on-breakdown policy.

FIGURE 19–14
Relative Costs of Various Preventive Repair Policies

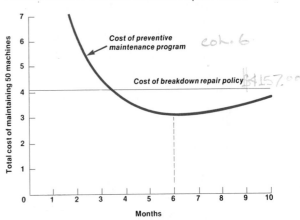

WAITING-LINE ANALYSIS IN PREVENTIVE MAINTENANCE

Often it is difficult to get good evidence about the merits of preventive maintenance—at least by mathematical formulas—because the process is just too complex. Waiting-line analysis with queuing models and simulation can often be used in such cases. Various policies and cost relationships can be evaluated to see which combination will result in the least cost. Examples of these methods were presented in Chapter 17.

CENTRALIZATION OF MAINTENANCE

Large factories are usually so spread out (they may cover 100 acres or more) that it takes along time for maintenance workers to get from place to place. The managers of such plants have, therefore, to decide which things to do centrally and which to decentralize.

Area Maintenance

In general, the closer that maintenance people are to the place where there will be a need for their work, the better service they can give but at an extra cost, because they will not always be fully occupied at their highest skills. The waste in their not being fully utilized is usually less than the time wasted by their travel time to jobs from central maintenance departments. Equipment duplication is also wasteful, but this is usually minor since only small tools are usually involved (most of the specialized costly equipment is kept in the central office).

Decentralized area maintenance people are usually kept busy as members of fixed small crews on routine maintenance. On larger jobs they often receive extra help from the central department.

Area maintenance people may feel more sense of responsibility for their own limited areas, and they become more familiar with the equipment and with each other. Costs sometimes are better controlled when they are directly associated with a given area.

Central Maintenance

Yet, even with area maintenance there is usually a central department to provide back-up service of the kind not called for often. And some organizations—if they are not spread out too much over too wide an area—prefer to have the central department do all of the maintenance. Central maintenance makes it easier to adjust crew sizes and craft mixes to task needs. Crews' work assignments can be more specific and can usually better utilize the workers' skills.

In central maintenance the supervisors are craft-oriented (an electrician foreman supervises the electricians, and so on), but in area maintenance the individual craftsmen seldom receive any craft supervision. Area maintenance sometimes underutilizes particular craftsmen (there is not enough work requiring their specialized skills to allow them to keep busy just on that work), who are nonetheless kept there rather than released to possibly more productive use in other areas.

The slight advantage which central maintenance seems to have over maintenance disappears, however, when facilities become very large: the distances and travel times become too great and cause so much waste that they are usually compelled to go to area maintenance—yet with a central maintenance back-up group.

DOING VERSUS BUYING MAINTENANCE

Normally an organization staffs its maintenance department with enough employees with the necessary skills to do all of its day-to-day repair work except where a very high level of technical competence is required and where the needs are irregular.

Most companies do not, for example, repair

their own elevators or telephones or computers. Nor do they do any major construction work, because large projects would impose heavy extra workloads. Often such jobs as window washing and lawn care are contracted out, as is maintenance work on company-owned automobiles.

Complications can arise over matters of inside versus outside, or contract, maintenance. If a serious breakdown requires extra work, the organization's own maintenance people may object to the company's bringing in outsiders because they could lose considerable overtime pay. The same thing can happen on not-so-minor construction projects: The inside people can do them, but because so much additional work is involved they can do them only on overtime. Again, they may object to allowing an outside contractor do the work. Finally, labor problems can arise when the company decides to discontinue certain work that was formerly done by its inside people and contracts it out permanently.

Labor contracts need careful formulation to cover the company's right or lack of right to use outsiders in any of these cases. If the contract is not clear, arbitrators and courts will usually hold that the company cannot make such decisions without bargaining over them with the union. So, this is often a decision which managers are not wholly free to make on their own.

Repair or Replace

Should a maintenance mechanic repair worn machine parts or replace them with new parts? The answer would seem to be whichever is less costly. When a person gets a small dent in their car fender, they want it straightened out. But, if it is badly dented, it may pay to put on a new fender rather than straighten out the old one. It depends on costs.

But this is only half the story. Old automobiles and old machines that need repairs sometimes keep on needing other repairs. No one ever knows how much added performance life

is being bought when one repairs an old automobile or an old machine.

Here, however, our concern is whether a repair mechanic should repair a faulty part, thus making it operable, or discard it and replace it with a new part. Often the problem is similar to that with automobiles. If the machine is old, the mechanic should probably repair the part at a minimum cost so that the machine will operate a little while longer. It won't have to last very long because the machine will be worn out regardless of whether this part is repaired or replaced with a new part.

Also, the repair-or-replace decision might depend on how busy the maintenance people are. If they are not busy, they might take the time to repair worn parts. But, if they are very busy, they probably should use replacement parts. Because today's maintenance labor costs are so high, there is a tendency (more so than in the past) to replace worn parts with new parts rather than repair worn parts.

Sometimes, we have a situation called *conditional replacement*. Conditional replacement asks the question: If a machine fails and we have it torn down for repairs, should we replace (or rehabilitate) other parts in the machine which are likely to fail in the near future? The trade-offs here are between replacing parts which still have some life remaining versus the downtime costs of possibly having to tear down the machine again in the near future.

For example, if a machine has three critical bearings, and one fails, should only it be replaced? Or should the other two be replaced even though they are not badly worn? Or, alternatively, should we replace only those which have been in service for, say, 1,000 or more hours? The answer depends on the relative cost of replacement parts, maintenance labor costs, the opportunity costs of machine downtime, and the probability of each bearing's failure after being in service for different numbers of hours. In a complex situation like this, and if reasonable life expectancy statistics for component parts can be estimated, Monte Carlo simulation (discussed in Chapter 17) is the most effective way to analyze these alternatives.

Maintenance in Assembly Line Production and Automation

Assembly line production ABMSs, and FMSs in a factory operate like large machines: everything operates or everything is idle, and even a few minutes' delay is expensive. Preventive maintenance therefore becomes very important.

Preventive maintenance should start with the design of machines and equipment with *maintainability* in mind. Machines should be designed to operate dependably, accurately, and steadily for long periods of time without breaking down. And, redundancy, and modular components, as described in Chapter 5, should be included in design decisions. These features allow for automatic switch-over to a redundant component should the original one fail; and if both fail, it allows the quick replacement of the component.

In line production, a maintenance mechanic should be close at all times to take care of minor emergencies. Maintenance supervisors need to think in terms of *maintaining production* rather than maintaining machines. Maintenance mechanics, rather than being on call to make repairs, should be on patrol to anticipate them.

Breakdowns are often caused by the tooling, not by the machines themselves. To prevent the tooling from wearing too much and breaking in use, cutting and grinding tools should be inspected frequently. Some companies even attach counters to each tool (to show how many times it has performed its operation) so they can anticipate its wearing out and replace it before it fails. And in some advanced systems, tools are changed automatically when the computer senses they need it.

CONTROL-PANEL MONITORING SYSTEMS

Process industries (oil refineries, cement, chemicals, and the like) are usually highly automated. The processing is done in pressure vessels, vats, tanks, mixers, and so on that may be automatically controlled by computers. Materials are moved in enclosed pipes or ducts—again, all automatically.

In such cases the entire integrated process is frequently controlled from a central monitoring station whose walls are covered with control gauges, lights, meters, push buttons, and switches, or are controlled by computer systems which automatically make adjustments in the process and signal the monitors when problems arise. Interruptions to operations, wherever they occur, are flashed immediately to the central control, and maintenance people are dispatched by telephone or radio to the point of interruption.

Similar control consoles are sometimes used in other kinds of automated production, such as nuclear power plants or steel rolling mills, where 20 or 30 successive mills operate as a unit and are centrally monitored by the on-line computer systems. In cases like this, teams of highly trained maintenance crews are on alert to "scramble," should equipment fail—because of the extreme cost (and perhaps danger) of downtime.

BUDGETING MAINTENANCE COSTS

Most large organizations—and some small ones as well—try to control maintenance costs by budgets. The expected costs of repairing and keeping production equipment in operation are allocated in separate budgets for each producing department. The supervisor of each department is responsible for keeping maintenance costs within the budgeted amount. Capital expenditures and large repair projects also are covered by separate budgets.

Unfortunately, however, budgets do not keep machines from wearing out: *Maintenance costs can't be budgeted out of existence.* And if budgets are set too low, some things may be postponed until heavy and costly repairs become necessary.

Actually, many maintenance costs *can* be

postponed and money can be saved thereby—particularly in the case of such cosmetic things as painting. Some maintenance jobs are like car washing: One does not *have* to get one's car washed every month. In many cases, however, the apparent savings may be wiped out when a straw—so to speak—breaks the camel's back and a serious breakdown or accident occurs. For example, a person can wait only so long before having to get new brakes or tires. Maintenance should be postponed only as a calculated risk, and the risks should be properly evaluated.

Review Questions

1. In metal-cutting operations in factories, is it, in general, better to have the material or the cutting tool move? Or is this not relevant? Why?

2. Is it possible to get the benefits of costly special-purpose machines which produce low unit costs for high-volume items, yet avoid most of the risks of loss if product designs change before the machines have fully paid for themselves? Explain.

3. Why do numerically-controlled machines operate so economically?

4. How can the 20–80 law be helpful in decisions concerning the depth of tooling?

5. How much improvement in machine-use ratios should be achieved when a company changes from lot production to line production? What conditions would make this an economical move?

6. Is it more important, when comparing machine-use ratios of machines under different production situations, to compare the machines' hours of use ratio or dollars' investment-use ratio? Why?

7. Is there anything that managers can do to reduce either *(a)* the probability of a production line's having to stop or *(b)* the duration of the downtime when a stoppage occurs?

8. Is industrial robotry a reality in industry or of limited application? How about automatic assembly?

9. Why is it that inefficiency is inherent in maintenance activities?

10. Under what conditions is preventive maintenance *not* of considerable importance?

11. Is central or area maintenance better for small factories? for very large factories?

12. What factors should be considered in "make-buy" maintenance decisions?

13. How should materials used by maintenance workers be charged? What ways are available? Discuss.

Questions for Discussion

1. How can machine-design engineers do a proper job of setting the most appropriate depth of tooling when market forecasts of sales volumes of products are often off by 50 percent or more?

2. Why is it that interest in robotry seems to be more general in Japan, where wages are relatively low, than in the United States, where wages are high?

3. Since high volume makes it possible for a company to use production lines which are so economical, how can companies with lower volumes get along?

4. If a company has several machines, each doing its job in sequence on the product, would conveyors probably cause production to go up or down? Why?

5. Isn't the maldistribution concept largely a textbook concept, since every company should know which products are its biggest sellers? Discuss.

6. There seems to be a general acceptance of the Pareto maldistribution curve. Would its principle hold true for the products sold in a K mart or Sears store? If the answer is no, doesn't this suggest that maldistribution curves do not have such universal application?

7. "When my maintenance people have nothing to do, the plant is running well, and we are doing a fine job." Comment on this statement.

8. Does the supervision of maintenance workers differ from the supervision of workers who work on the product? Are maintenance workers of such high caliber that they don't need supervision? What problems arise? How can they be solved?

9. If a plant closes down for two weeks in the summer for vacations, what does this do to or for maintenance activities?

10. What trade-offs are important in the "repair or replace" decisions?

11. Some years ago, when the government made a check, it found that repairing airplanes at Norfolk, Virginia, and Alameda, California, cost just about

the same. Evaluating the figures, however, disclosed that Alameda's labor costs were much higher, but its costs for materials and parts were much less than Norfolk's. Why might this be? Which distribution of expenditure is better? Discuss.

Problems

1. The Roe Company has 20 machines to keep in service. Preventive overhauls cost $100 each. Overhauls from breakdowns in service, however, cost $300. These machines are hard to get into adjustment, and often they need repairs again right after being repaired. If, however, they operate without problems through the initial period, they usually operate a long time before needing repair again. The probability of breakdown since the last overhaul is as follows:

Months after Overhaul	Probability of Breakdown	Cumulative Probability of Breakdown
3	.10	.10
6	.02	.12
9	.03	.15
12	.04	.19
15	.04	.23
18	.05	.28
21	.08	.36
24	.12	.48
27	.16	.64
30	.22	.86
33	.10	.96
36	.04	1.00

What preventive maintenance policy should be followed?

2. Suppose that the following is a sample of the variety in sales volumes of all the items made by the Rio Company. Construct a maldistribution curve, and determine what percent of the company's best-selling products produce 80 percent of its sales.

Product	Annual Sales	Product	Annual Sales
1	$315,000	9	$110,000
2	25,000	10	5,000
3	110,000	11	275,000
4	9,000	12	190,000
5	17,000	13	13,000
6	60,000	14	60,000
7	450,000	15	125,000
8	8,000		

3. Avalon, Inc., is introducing a new butcher-block table which it plans to price at $100 per unit. It is considering five alternative ways to make this product, each having different tooling-up costs and different variable costs as follows:

Method	Tooling Cost	Variable Cost per Unit
A	$10,000	$75
B	15,000	50
C	25,000	30
D	40,000	20
E	50,000	16

The prospective volume estimates are:

Quantity	Probability
1,000	.15
1,500	.20
2,000	.25
2,500	.18
3,000	.13
3,500	.06
4,000	.02
5,000	.01

Which manufacturing process should be chosen?

4. In the text's example of chaining successive machines together (under heading "Vulnerability of Dedicated Machine Lines to Downtime"), we found that the losses outweighed the gains. Suppose we had six machines with the following normal downtimes: .02, .06, .07, .03, .05, .10. This means that machine 1 runs 98 percent of the time, machine 2, 94 percent, and so on. (The machines are of equal capacity.)

By spending $10,000 for equipment, which will last five years, we can reduce the inventory between operations by $3,000 and also save $10,000 annually in labor used to pick up and put down materials. Inventory carrying costs are 20 percent of value per year. The plant operates 2,000 hours a year, and we would like to keep these machines operating; in fact, we lose $8 every hour each is not operating

Should we mechanize? If we do, how much will we gain or lose?

5. The engineers have decided that volume is sufficient to justify setting up a small work center to

work continuously at making part number HCO29436, which is used in the magnetic tape drive of a computer system. This particular job is a drilling operation, and 120 pieces per hour are required.

It takes ¼ minute to unload the drilling machine, ½ minute to load it, and 1½ minutes to drill the hole. The work is done by a machinist whose hourly rate is $15. But the unloading could be done by a $6-an-hour helper. Machine time is calculated to be worth $20 an hour. During the 1½ minutes of drilling time, the machinest could be doing other work, such as loading another machine.

Set up this work station so as to minimize the costs of drilling 120 pieces of HCO29436 per hour.

Case 19–1

The Bow Company (500 employees) has had a maintenance department of 50 employees, but these people have not been very busy. There just is not a great deal of work requiring skilled maintenance activities. Upon investigation, Bow has discovered that it can contract out its maintenance work and have it done by the Jackson Services Company at a savings of $75,000 a year. The Bow Company accordingly has entered into a contract with Jackson and reduced its own group to a skeleton crew.

The union has filed a grievance with the National Labor Relations Board accusing the company of engaging in an unfair labor practice. It claims that changing to contracting out the maintenance work is a bargainable issue and that the company should not be allowed to proceed with this action without bargaining about it.

Discuss this case.

Chapter 20

Location of Facilities

Organizations are continuously building new facilities and expanding existing ones. In most years, over 3,000 new industrial plants and over 7,500 industrial plant expansions take place in the United States. These activities involve a new investment in construction and equipment of almost $125 billion.[1]

However, contrary to what we might intuitively think, an organization's *exact* location is not always of great importance. Nearly all large companies have production facilities in many locations around the country, and many of them are relatively equal in efficiency.

Yet there are differences, and there may be advantages or disadvantages because of location factors. It is even possible for negative factors to be critically important. Several years ago the National Seating and Dimension Company went to Varney, West Virginia, for low labor rates but went bankrupt trying to train coal miners to be good wood workers. And over the last half century, most New England textile companies that did not move South, where costs are less, went bankrupt. Most furniture companies, too, have had to move South in order to remain competitive. So, although a plant's location is often not highly important, there may be critical factors which make it very important.

Some locations are better, sometimes decidedly better, than other locations; yet, good locations are not scarce as is evidenced by the diverse location of the American manufacturing industry. Steel mills are found in Pennsylvania, Ohio, Indiana, Illinois, Alabama, California, and other states (see Figure 20–1). There are shoe factories in Massachusetts, New York, Maryland, Ohio, Illinois, Wisconsin, Missouri, and California. Many other industries show similar dispersions, many with international locations in Europe, Japan, Canada, Mexico, and South America.

There are other examples. Years ago General Electric built its Appliance Park (for household appliance manufacture) at Louisville. Why Louisville, instead of Cincinnati, St. Louis, or Indianapolis? Many other companies have built plants in these cities. And years ago automobiles developed in Detroit, tires in Akron, airplanes in Los Angeles and Seattle, General Electric in Schenectady, and National Cash Register in Dayton. More recently, electronics has centered in "Silicon Valley" near San Francisco. But, electronics also abounds in Texas, Colorado,

---

[1] Source: *Site Selection Handbook,* 1978.

FIGURE 20–1
Location of Steel Production Facilities in the United States

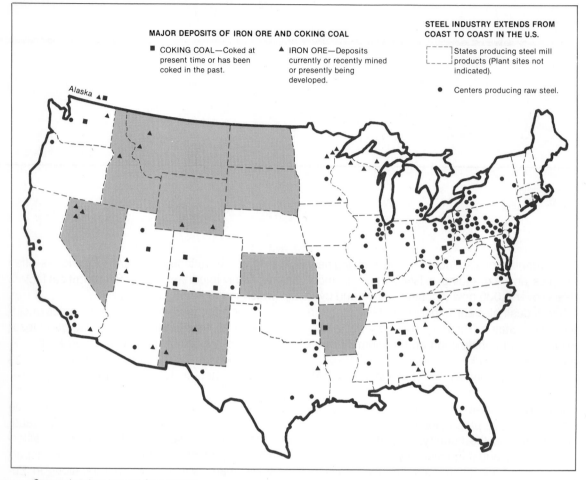

MAJOR DEPOSITS OF IRON ORE AND COKING COAL

■ COKING COAL—Coked at present time or has been coked in the past.

▲ IRON ORE—Deposits currently or recently mined or presently being developed.

STEEL INDUSTRY EXTENDS FROM COAST TO COAST IN THE U.S.

States producing steel mill products (Plant sites not indicated).

● Centers producing raw steel.

Source: American Iron and Steel Institute.

and Arizona. In most of these cases, the original choice of where to locate was largely happenstance.

PITFALLS IN LOCATION CHOICES

Companies sometimes make mistakes in choosing locations. One firm accepted a community's offer of a free site and then found that subsoil conditions were so bad that it had to spend several times a good site's cost on foundations. An-

other company turned down an in-town site at $20,000 an acre and bought outlying land at $4,000 an acre. Then it ran into two years of zoning problems and had to buy two extra lots for "protection," only to have sewer problems. It finally cost $25,000 an acre, plus the delay.

A third company accepted a town's claims that glossed over a poor labor situation. Six months after it moved in, it had labor problems. A fourth company located where there was only one means of transportation—whose charges promptly went up because of the lack of competition. A fifth located in a nice industrial park, then found that it was four miles out of the free city pickup and delivery zone. It paid a penalty of more than $60,000 a year for this oversight. A sixth put up a $15-million paper mill but didn't buy enough space for the disposal of waste chemicals. Now its five-acre lake of waste liquid is filling up, and there is no more land for reservoirs.

Facility location specialists have no end of such stories. The common thread is that some one thing, overlooked, turned out to be seriously disadvantageous. Location choice is perhaps as much avoiding all seriously negative features as it is choosing the most positive factors.

Rarely does an organization locate a new facility today without careful study. Every attempt is made to choose the best location and, in particular, avoid a faux pas. When Chrysler was choosing a place to put a $50-million assembly plant (which opened some years ago in Belvidere, Illinois), it went through a computer analysis of 20 locations. Among the considerations were inbound and outbound freight rates; direct and indirect labor costs; the anticipated percentage of sales in each of 459 economic zones all over the United States for three years and five years ahead; and other factors designed to yield a dollars-and-cents estimate on such things as freight backhauling versus overtime operation.

In the service sector, considerably more effort is also being spent in properly locating branch banks, retail stores, fire stations, community health centers, and solid-waste disposal plants, to name a few.[2]

LOCATION AS AN INDIVIDUAL MATTER

The examples just given of unfortunate location choices would have been unfortunate for any company. But, because most companies are more careful and make better analyses, such mistakes are probably few.

It is more probable that a location is good or bad because of the way its merits relate to the needs of the particular organization concerned. For one organization it may be most important to be located near the organization's customers. But it may be more important to another organization to be near the sources of supply of materials and components parts. Still other organizations may find that the most important thing is to locate where there is an adequate labor supply of the kind needed by the organization. Nor can transportation costs be forgotten. These are high where products are heavy and bulky.

Thus, the major reason organizations choose varied locations is that their needs differ. Consequently, it takes different locations to meet these different needs. So, although the discussion in the remainder of this chapter is in general terms, a good location is an individualized matter. This is called a *situational* or *contingency* approach to decision making—stated simply. "It all depends."

ECOLOGY AND ENVIRONMENTAL VALUES

Manufacturing plants often produce waste in the form of polluted water, air, or solid wastes, and often they are noisy. For the most part noise is within the plant, so its reduction is related to worker safety and comfort more than to community well-being.

Not many years ago, polluted air and water were accepted as facts of life about which nothing need be done, and, indeed, as things about which nothing *could* be done, but not today. Public sentiment, backed by federal and local laws, is putting pressure on managers to improve these conditions. (The ecology wave is not confined to the United States; Sweden, Japan, Russia, and many other countries also have antipollution laws.)

---

[2] A detailed description of a fire station location analysis was given in Chapter 17.

Federal law prohibits companies, and municipal governments as well, dumping waste into navigable waterways without a permit, and such permits are now almost impossible to obtain. Companies and cities which have been dumping contaminated effluents now have to clean up.

The contaminants are of many kinds. Steel plants not only emit sooty smoke and sulphur dioxide fumes into the air but also routinely flush cyanides, phenols, sulphides, and ammonia into adjacent rivers. Electric power plants and many factories return hot water to rivers (thermal pollution). There is apparently no good way to get rid of heat except by means of expensive and gigantic cooling towers. Today's regulations say that warm water discharged into a river may not raise the stream's temperature by more than 5°, or above 87° in any case. (The sun does better than 87° in many places, so there are places where this regulation is unrealistic.) Sometimes this water contains too much oxygen and is harmful to fish.

The job of cleaning up is by no means easy, nor can it be done at low cost. Union Carbide, for example, has been spending $40 million a year trying to stop its air and water pollution in West Virginia. And even at this rate it will take several years to do the job well. Riegel Paper Company spends $10 million a year on cleaning up. Kansas City Power & Light has invested $45 million in a "scrubber" system which is supposed to remove the ash, soot, and harmful gases from the smokestacks of its coal-burning electricity generating plant.

It was estimated by the President's Council on Environmental Quality that it costs some $5 billion annually throughout the 1970s to reduce emissions and solid wastes to a satisfactory level. And this expenditure is expected to rise substantially in the 1980s. Some 20 percent of the cost will be required for air pollution control, 40 percent for water pollution control, and the other 40 percent for solid-waste disposal. Industry will not have to pay all of this cost, however, since sewage, waste, and trash disposal are included in the figures, and these are largely costs to local city governments.

Managers of some factories say—perhaps correctly—that the cost of meeting all the antipollution standards is too great and that they will have to close down some operations. No doubt such statements are, for the most part, exaggerations. But, nonetheless, they will prove to be true in some individual cases. The closing of most of the steel mills in Youngstown, Ohio, for example, was caused partly by the prohibitive costs of cleaning them up.

If, in an individual case, it comes down to relaxing the standards or closing a facility down, most communities seem *not* to want the factory to close down and do without the industry and its jobs. This is a most difficult question for a community. Almost certainly the people who would lose their jobs if this occurred would rather have jobs and dirty air or water, than clean air and water and no jobs.

Yet, with today's regulations, the choice is often not their's to make. Employers sometimes find that the added cost for a plant which is already somewhat uneconomical to operate is too much. Faced with regulations that would force operations at a loss, the decision is to close up. Not only the employees but communities, too, may not have the power to relax state and federal regulations, even if they are willing to endure the old conditions.

A curious situation is also developing in pollution control. In Los Angeles, where a regional pollution control authority sets maximum emission standards for the area, one company is allowed to "sell" its right to pollute a given amount to another company whose emissions exceed the standards—as long as the overall emission level in the area is kept below the permissible level. Thus, pollution "rights" have become an asset with a value, and a market exists for the buying and selling of these rights.

Industry gets some tax relief from the financial burden incurred for alleviating pollution situations. The costs of antipollution equipment receives special tax consideration (in both federal and state income taxes) in the form of faster write-offs and tax reductions to offset part of the expense. And local tax rates on the value of antipollution equipment are often very low. There may be other benefits. The recovered (and reusable) effluent itself, particularly from chemical plants, is sometimes worth enough to offset part of the cost of staying clean.

Besides these positive incentives to clean up, a number of possible punitive actions face organizations which do not comply with the regulations. Penalties that would deny government contracts to noncomplying companies seem likely to be enacted into law. And noncomplying city governments may be denied government grants. It is even possible for the responsible managers to be sued by outsiders, or to be fined, or even jailed. All of these possible penalties may backfire, however, because they make it more certain that old facilities will just be closed down instead of being cleaned up.

Many people believe that this represents overkill and that government regulators are asking for too much too fast and imposing restrictions which can be met only at high cost, which, of course, has to be passed on to the public.

Employees, and frequently their unions, are objecting to the severity of restraints which may result in their losing their jobs. In a few cases, the regulations have been relaxed. The energy crisis of the latter part of the 1970s caused the relaxing of some standards. Prior to this crisis, many electric power generating plants were switched from coal to oil and gas as a means for complying with antipollution standards (to get rid of the coal smoke). Now, many have been given permission to go back to coal in order to save on oil and gas.

Some of the biggest adjustment problems are faced by city governments which have to contend with sewage and trash disposal. Many communities cannot afford to build the facilities needed to meet the state and federal regulations. Some communities, however, are building proto-

type plants which recover reusable materials from trash and which produce methane gas which can be used in place of coal or oil to power electrical generation plants. These attempts have, so far, not proved to be very attractive financially, but as the cost of energy continues to increase, they seem to be gaining ground.[3]

RELOCATION

Several years ago PPG (formerly Pittsburgh Plate Glass Company) built a mile-long modern addition to its glass plant outside Cumberland, Maryland. It was built to use a new process which floated molten glass on a bed of molten tin, a process that was developed in England for producing plate glass at low costs. When the new plant came into production, the company's old Ford City, Pennsylvania, plant went on short hours. Essentially PPG relocated its production and moved it from Ford City to Cumberland.

Whenever an existing organization makes location decisions, they involve either the relocation of existing facilities or expansion by opening facilities in new geographical areas.

Plant relocation is common, with the trend being from cities to suburbs and across country, usually from East to West, or North to South. Some of the causes for this migration are lower taxes, less crime, more recreational activities, and a more relaxed life. Other reasons include the need to expand and increase capacity, to open new markets, or to be closer to raw materials or suppliers. And, more important in the 1980s are the increasing cost of energy, rising labor costs, and the substantial growth in state and local taxes.[4]

---

[3] See W. M. Bulkeley, "After Costly Mistakes in 70s, Trash Processing Is Reviving," *The Wall Street Journal*, February 24, 1984, p. 27.

[4] See Richard L. Wilson, John G. Phelan, and Steven S. Rosen," The High Cost of Making an Industrial Move," *AMA Forum*, August 1978, pp. 31–33.

The relocation of the PPG facilities referred to above was for still a different reason. PPG would have liked to have built its new glass factory at Ford City. It did not want to move, but the labor union at Ford City wouldn't allow this process there, hence the expansion at Cumberland.

Interestingly, if business gets either better or worse, there may be need to relocate. If it gets better, the company's managers have to decide where to build the added facilities. Or, if business gets worse, perhaps the poor location of one or more of its facilities has been a contributing cause of the difficulty.

Actually facility relocations probably should be more common than they are. Many plants are in locations which become more obsolete every year; yet, each year their managers put off moving. Sometimes they even expand production or service facilities in wrong locations because they are already there. They really have a relocation problem, but they don't recognize it, or they don't have the courage to face the task of building a new plant. Examples can be seen in retail stores "hanging on" in decaying core areas of cities; of fire stations built 75 years ago and mislocated with respect to the current hazard characteristics of the city. A&P grocery's rejuvenation program of the mid-1970s consisted of closing down supermarkets in poor locations.

Sometimes the poor location of facilities can be disastrous. Two of the major reasons for the bankruptcy of retailing giant W. T. Grant in 1975 were its rapid expansion a few years earlier into poor locations and their reluctance to close many old stores which were located in what had become obsolete locations.

THE COMMUNITY VIEWPOINT

Most communities are anxious to attract industry because of the jobs and the money industry brings into the community. Besides this, the taxes industry pays helps lower the burden on individuals. People need jobs, and communities without businesses are rarely prosperous. The United States Chamber of Commerce says that 100 new factory workers in a community will make 110 new households and will create 75 more jobs in the community in other lines. One hundred new factory workers in a community also mean nearly $2 million in annual personal income and $1.5 million more in bank deposits in the community.

In fact, so many communities want industry that even a minor objection by anyone in one community can be enough to cause a company to choose another community. Several years ago Columbus lost a new Ford factory to Lorain, Ohio, because a college professor objected to the rezoning of a small part of the site. Columbus lost 2,000 jobs to Lorain.

At the same time, most communities are quite demanding. They want industry but no "dirty" industry—only clean service or light manufacturing industry. They want it to be staffed entirely with high-paid childless executives. And they want the factory to look like a park with no smoke or noise, and no rail or truck traffic in and out. It is not easy to satisfy all their demands. Often these characteristics are not enough. In Boulder, Colorado, the city council debated the rezoning of a piece of land for so long that a major (clean) electronics manufacturer gave up plans to locate there, and several thousand jobs were lost.

Actually, in the 1970s, the ecology and antipollution wave really did dampen the enthusiasm for new industry in some communities. In 1970, residents of the small town of Congers, New York, picketed the site of a future $3-million Reynolds Metal Company plant. They were afraid that it would pollute a nearby state park. So Reynolds built its plant elsewhere. Later, the people of Beaufort, South Carolina, demonstrated against a proposed $100-million chemical plant to be built by BASF, a large German chemical company. They were afraid it would cause air and water pollution. This plant, too, was not built there.

Such opposition to new industry (and there have been other such cases) would never have occurred a decade earlier. But in the 1970s, and stimulated by student-age groups (who were not very job-conscious), many people became aware of potential dangers to the environment, and this feeling frequently played a part in facility locations.

By no means are all people united in such viewpoints. In 1971, the Sierra Club, the United Automobile Workers, and several other groups objected to the building of a nuclear power plant in Midland, Michigan. Whereupon, 15,000 Midland citizens held a football-style rally supporting its construction. (In 1979, however, the Three Mile Island nuclear near-disaster in Pennsylvania restimulated protesters across the country to shut down existing plants. Their impact on the placement of new plants in the 1980s continues to be significant.)

In all three of the cases where there was objection to new industry the local unemployment rate was probably over 7 percent at the time. Turning away new jobs is surely not what everyone wants. The unemployed in Congers and in Beaufort would almost surely have felt the same way as did the citizens of Midland. Given a chance they would have chosen jobs.

In 1976 when Volkswagen was deciding where to put its new assembly plant in the United States, dozens of communities vied for the industry. The choice finally made was New Stanton, Pennsylvania, where VW bought from Chrysler a partially completed assembly plant. Because the plant would add 5,000 jobs, the state of Pennsylvania put up nearly $50 million to help VW buy the property and to improve rail and roadway connections. The state also agreed to see that $150 million more would be made available for borrowing. VW invested $50 million of its own money.

However, in the early 1980s when the auto industry took such a beating, and unemployment was 18 percent in some communities in the auto industry belt, the opposition to new plant locations seemed to lessen considerably. And, in

fact, communities and citizen groups became very aggressive in recruiting new businesses.

Communities as Places to Live

Over the years, companies planning new factories are paying increasing attention to the nature of the community as a place to live. Employees, including company executives, probably do better work when the community is a pleasant place in which to live. Adequate schools, recreation, cultural, and sports activities are an important part of this decision. At the same time, companies avoid many large-city residential suburbs because taxes will probably be high there. For this reason many companies are opening new plants in the relatively unpopulated western states of Colorado, Arizona, Utah, New Mexico, and Texas.

COMMUNITY DOMINATION

Most companies prefer not to put a plant anywhere where it would dominate the community. General Electric does not like to put a plant anywhere where it will hire more than one eighth of the people working in the area. GE has more than 100 factories, so this policy would rule out many locations where GE already is, including Schenectady. Such policies are in agreement with most community objectives; they, too, do not want single-company or single-industry domination.

Seattle, dominated by Boeing Aircraft, is a case in point. In the early 1970s Boeing's business was down, and several thousand employees were laid off. Consequently, Seattle had a double recession. The whole country was in a recession, and on top of this Seattle had its own local recession. Things became so bad that a group of laid-off engineers rented a freeway billboard at the edge of Seattle which said, "Last one to leave Seattle, please turn out the lights." Subsequently, in the late 1970s, Boeing's orders for existing and new aircraft skyrocketed, and Seattle was once again a boom town.

Another General Electric policy is not to locate a small plant in a big metropolitan area where its corporate voice would be muffled or lost.

Still another policy is not to put plants too close together. Ford Motor Co. likes to have its plants 15 miles or more apart (although its Detroit plants are not that far apart). Westinghouse says 20 miles. These reasons are tied in with the above reasons, but a company also avoids having two of its plants drawing from and competing for the same labor pool.

LABOR LAWS AND RELOCATION

When a company relocates and closes down its old plant, it may have a legal obligation to offer jobs in the new location to employees in the closed-down plant. Laws and court decisions are ambiguous on this matter, but they are moving in the direction of giving employees in a plant that is being closed down a vested right in a similar job in the new plant.

Companies should clarify this matter by spelling out in their labor contracts what, if any, obligation they have in case of plant relocations. Practically speaking, this usually means that they agree to offer either (1) employment in the new plant, and possibly some moving expenses, or (2) substantial severance pay to employees who are not offered jobs in the new location. Retraining programs are often set up for severed employees. Also, employees near retirement age can retire early on liberal pensions.

If employees are given a chance to move with the relocation, the number of employees who accept drops off sharply with the distance of the move, and even more sharply if the new plant's pay rates will be less. Several years ago, when Armour closed its Sioux City, Iowa, meat packing plant (1,200 employees), it gave three month's notice and set up both an employment and retraining office. One hundred displaced workers who were more than 55 years old and had 20 years' service retired. Six hundred others took severance pay equal to about $125 per

year of service. Only 400 asked to be transferred to Armour jobs elsewhere. And at an earlier plant closing at Fort Worth, Texas, only 155 out of 1,000 asked for transfers. The geographic choice of relocation, of course, can make a difference. When Western Electric, a few years ago, relocated one of its plants from New Jersey to Colorado a substantial number of employees made the move.

LABOR

Wherever a company locates, it must have employees, so an ample supply of labor is essential. It helps if the available labor is already skilled, but for most companies this is not necessary. Most companies expect to train new employees because jobs are so varied and so highly specialized that a company will never find very many new employees who already know how to do most of its jobs.

For regular factory or office jobs the work habits and attitudes of prospective workers are much more important than the skills they already have. People in some areas are just better workers than those in some other areas. Absentee rates differ, and so does the willingness to work.

If a company moves to a new location, it may have to move a few of its skilled workers and some supervisors, but it will usually recruit most of its new work force from the area of the new plant. It it moves to a lower-wage area, this can often cause problems about what pay rate to use for transferred workers. If they are paid their old high rate, they are out of line with the new workers. But, if they are to get the local-area rate, they take a pay cut, which of course they do not like.

An effective new labor force cannot be recruited quickly. When a factory moves into a community, it will take time to build up a good work force. Good workers are rarely out looking for jobs in great numbers. In fact, it is well to build up employment slowly and thus not to have to hire too many marginal people.

One should also pay attention to quantity

and distance. The personnel planners for a new factory should not plan to hire more than 5 percent of the area population or 20 percent of the elibigle labor force. Nor should they plan to recruit beyond 20 miles from the new plant. If there are not enough people to fill the factory's needs within 20 miles, it will probably have trouble finding employees. And this has become more critical as the price and availability of gasoline become a factor.[5]

It is possible, however, that in the future, employers may not be as free to make this decision. In 1976, the government's Equal Employment Opportunity Commission ordered Timken (maker of bearings) to recruit in a radius of 25 miles. In Bucyrus, Ohio, where Timken has a factory, there were very few blacks. The EEOC ordered Timken to go 25 miles away and hire blacks who lived in Mansfield.

FREIGHT COSTS

Freight costs as a location factor are of little consequence for companies making high-value products such as watches, cameras, or computers. Their freight costs (which is often air freight) amount to only 1 or 2 percent of their total costs. So far as freight costs are concerned, it doesn't matter where they locate. But for larger, heavier products it matters more. In some cases (cement, plaster, gypsum), freight costs are much higher. Johns Manville and U.S. Gypsum spend close to 20 percent of their sales dollars on freight costs.

For most companies, freight cost differentials are not as important as wage differences. If wages in one location are noticeably lower than in another, it will pay to go there even if freight costs are a little higher. This situation may, of course, be reversed as the price of transportation fuel increases.

So far as freight costs are concerned, one might think that a plant should be located where

total freight costs are the least. But this is easy to say and hard to do. Companies buy thousands of different raw materials from suppliers in many locations. And they sell nationwide. It is hard to discover the location where freight cost is least. Besides, in 10 years' time suppliers will not all be where they are today nor will a company's customers. So the rule to locate where freight costs are the least is usually not too helpful.

Freight costs cannot be eliminated no matter where a factory is located because, in one form or another, the product has to be moved from the raw material producer to the final user; thus, a facility should be located somewhere between the raw material source and the market. Locating near raw materials reduces raw materials freight, but freight costs for delivering products increase. Locating near the market saves on finished products freight but increases on raw materials freight costs. Being near the supply source, however, is not always important because vendors often "equalize" or absorb freight differences. They pay all freight costs above the cost from the customer's nearest conpetitive supplier. Sometimes they pay all the freight costs, in which case a company might as well locate its factory near its market.

NEARNESS TO MARKET

Being near the market lets an organization give better service to customers, and it often saves on freight costs. Of these two advantages, giving better service is usually the more important.

But, as we have noted, a facility can't always be near its market—its whole market—because this market is too widespread. It may be nationwide or international. Large companies with worldwide markets may put plants in many parts of the country or the world to get close to these markets. Bucyrus-Erie, which manufactures gigantic earth-moving equipment for the coal mining industry, opened a new plant in Pocatello, Idaho, to be near the vast coal reserves in Idaho, Wyoming, and Colorado.

---

[5] See "What Management Needs to Know before Picking a Plant Site," *Dun's Review,* October 1979, pp. 14–16.

Smaller companies must either give up the idea of being close to all their customers or must concentrate their selling in the area near their factory so that they can be close to their market. Small plants in New England serve the northeastern states; those on the West Coast serve the Pacific states. Most small plants are started close to the owner's home, and, as they grow, they develop their market nearby. In many cases, the location of a facility determines its market area more than the market area determines the facility's location.

In the service sector, the market area is usually determined by travel time of customers to the facility (banks, recreation facilities, restaurants, hospitals) or of travel time of servers to customers (fire trucks and ambulances to houses, telephone installers, appliance repairers).

NEARNESS TO RAW MATERIALS AND SUPPLIERS

Being near its raw materials allows a company to get better supplier service and to save on incoming freight. But—like being close to the market—this is not always possible. No one facility can be close to 5,000 suppliers. General Motors buys from 50,000 suppliers in at least 1,000 different locations. On the other hand, no matter where a factory is located, it can probably find nearby suppliers for most of the things it buys, so every factory can be near many of its suppliers. General Motors' buying is spread out primarily because its own manufacturing is spread out. Its plants are near most of their suppliers.

Just-in-Time and Location Decisions

In Chapter 14 we mentioned that one of the conditions for a JIT production/inventory system was that suppliers are able to make many frequent deliveries of small lot sizes. This, of course, affects location choice for some companies who supply JIT-oriented companies. As a result, some companies are locating their plants (or warehouses) near their customers for this reason. Further, some industrial parks are developing to accommodate the JIT philosophy. Buick City is an example. The park is designed to allow automobile component suppliers to have even closer access to Buick, their customer, so that they can provide parts on an hourly basis much as is done in Toyota City in Japan.

Companies that use iron ore or other materials which create waste often locate near their raw materials so they can minimize the transportation of the heavy bulky waste. Similarly, where finished products are heavy, bulky, and of low value, freight costs limit the area the companies can serve. Cement plants, for example, mostly serve local areas and are found in many parts of the country where limestone, cement's key ingredient, exists in sufficient quantities.

NEARNESS TO OTHER PLANTS AND WAREHOUSES

Companies usually try to locate new plants where they will complement their other plants and warehouses. The best location for a facility, therefore, might depend on where its other facilities are. New locations should fill a hole where the company has no facility and where its markets are now not adequately served or are being supplied by costly long-distance hauls.

The location of competitors' plants and warehouses also need to be considered. Each company should develop location strategies where they will have the advantage over competitors both in freight costs and fast customer service.

WATER

Some companies need a great deal of water—more than is available at low costs in some places. U.S. Steel's Fairless Works uses 250 million gallons of water a day, and only a large river (the Delaware) could supply this much.

For industries that need such large quantities

of water, most locations cannot be considered. These industries include paper, sugar refining, steel, rubber, leather, chemical, rayon, food processing, aluminum, and nuclear power plants. Producing a ton of synthetic rubber requires 60,000 gallons of water, a ton of aluminum takes 300,000 gallons, a ton of rayon 200,000 gallons, and steel 40,000 gallons per ton. Water is used directly in the processes, or for cooling products or machines, for condensing steam, or for washing, cleaning, quenching, and for air conditioning.

Companies that use these quantities of water need to be very sure that future supplies will be ample for their needs. This becomes a more critical factor in plant location year by year because the use of water is increasing, and environmental pressures are more and more stringent on the use and pollution of water.

Water used in these processes is often contaminated, or it is hot after its use and needs to be decontaminated or cooled before it can be returned to rivers or lakes. Since nearly all cities and states have laws against dumping waste of harmful nature into waterways, the costs of returning water to its natural state are often very important factors to consider in any location decision.

LAND COSTS

Land costs and local taxes are sometimes deciding factors in factory location choices, although on the whole they are relatively unimportant. The total cost of a site, including taxes and landscaping, may be as little as 3 percent and is usually less than 10 percent of the total cost of a facility. Of this total, the land itself is often less than half. Since it is only a one-time cost, it is usually relatively unimportant in the choice of a location. In fact, it is sometimes such a minor factor that communities wanting industry often donate land (or offer it at a reduced price) to an organization which it would like to have locate in the area. Often they rezone the land to accommodate the user.

LOCAL TAXES AND LOCATION INCENTIVES

Local real estate and property taxes also are usually relatively unimportant, and, except where other considerations are nearly equal, neither should be the deciding factor in the choice of a location. Most manufacturing companies have investments in plant and equipment and inventory of $14,000 or more per employee. (General Electric's, General Motors', and National Cash Register's investment per employee ranges from $16,000 to $19,000.)

Large cities usually have tax rates of from 2 to 6 percent of the value of property, so it would seem that taxes might be anywhere from $300 to $1,100 per year per employee. But rarely are taxes as high as, say, 6 percent, because assets are almost never appraised at their full value (although legally they are usually supposed to be).

A company usually ends up paying perhaps 2 percent of its assets' real value. This amounts to somewhere around $500 per employee, with differences between areas rarely being more than $100 per employee per year. This could be important, but, taken by itself, it is seldom a decisive factor, particularly since low tax rates often don't stay low.

This generalization, that taxes should count little in location choice, does not *always* apply, however. U.S. Steel has investments in plant, equipment, and inventories of over $44,000 per employee. Du Pont's total plant, equipment, and inventory investment exceeds $42,000 per employee. To them even small tax rate differences are of consequence.

Communities that furnish free sites or even rent- and tax-free buildings to new companies for a period of years usually get new companies. Generally these "incentives" are for limited periods, after which a company pays regular rent and taxes (or even more to support incentives for others). Companies should not allow temporary inducements to overshadow the basic merits of alternative locations. If they do, they may find themselves located where, in the long run, overall costs are higher.

Most large companies regard location-free offers as a relatively minor factor. By no means, however, are they opposed to accepting such offers, and they frequently do accept them. They do so, however, only where the other factors for alternative locations are more or less equal.

FOREIGN LOCATIONS

With domestic production costs increasing and foreign markets expanding rapidly, many American companies are locating facilities abroad. Most of these are primarily to supply foreign markets; however, some of these are to take advantage of lower labor costs (especially in countries such as Mexico, Korea, and Taiwan) to produce products for the American market. The movement is slowing down a little, however, because wages in almost every part of the world have gone up faster in recent years than in the United States.

But in the very low wage-rate areas, the wage savings overseas are great enough so that, in spite of the many difficulties caused by learning local customs and complying with local laws, and by great distance, it is still likely that labor-intensive items will be made abroad in the years ahead.

URBAN, SUBURBAN, AND SMALL-TOWN LOCATIONS

The movement away from the cities is still on so far as many facility locations are concerned. Today there are few small towns that do not have one or two factories. But—and this is sometimes not appreciated—most manufacturing is still done, and most new buildings are still being built, close to cities. Today's trend is toward moderately small factories, so small towns with small labor pools are suitable. But new plants, large and small, are also being built on the outskirts of big cities.

Wage rates in small towns are usually a little

lower than in cities, although not as low as they used to be. Even so, they are sometimes as much as one-fifth lower. Labor relations are often better in small towns since they are less influenced by other companies' labor problems.

Small towns have some disadvantages, but most of them are minor. It takes a while—possibly a year or two—to train new workers to get used to manufacturing activities. Inventory investments are likely to be larger, particularly for spare parts for maintenance. And the company will need to have a fairly complete maintenance department because it cannot draw on outsiders. Fire insurance rates may be higher, and absenteeism during hunting seasons will be greater.

Many companies, wishing to leave congested city locations, go only as far as the suburbs and not to rural locations. If they move to a nearby suburb, they may not have to hire very many new employees. Suburban locations usually give a company most of the advantages of both city and country. Labor is plentiful and the plant is not far from the market provided by the city, which, in the case of small plants, is often its main market. Land for present and future needs is usually available at reasonable prices and taxes are generally a little lower than in cities.

Suburbs usually have better rail and truck connections than small towns—almost as good, in fact, as those of cities. Suburban plants are also close to service industries. Located in a suburb, a company does not need to have so many of its own maintenance people—electricians, plumbers, and so on—as it would in a small town.

ORGANIZED INDUSTRIAL DISTRICTS

Factories, stores, and homes don't mix very well; they ought to be in separate areas. Factories need railroads and superhighways, and they create truck traffic. Among other things, they need high-power electric lines. All these things are undesirable in residential areas. Whole industrial districts—of factories and only factories—constitute a happy solution to the problem of mixed areas. To meet this need, over 2,000 industrial parks have been set up in the last 30 years.

The advantages of industrial parks include lower construction costs, because preliminary site work is done, and site preparation pitfalls are few because the land is already prepared. Financial and transportation services are close. The site is already favorably zoned, and it is in a prestige area where land values are likely to go up because of the controlled programs.

On the negative side is the small acreage available for expansion (usually 5 acres and rarely more than 25 acres). The facility also becomes part of a community and may have to submit to control of its architecture, design, and construction, or even to using a "suggested" contractor. It has close neighbors whose labor problems may spread to other organizations in the industrial park. Traffic flow in and out of the park and from and onto roads and highways may be congested during rush periods, although some of this can be eliminated by staggering shift times.

Space Requirements

Inasmuch as the amount of floor space needed in a new plant varies a great deal between industries, a company's old operations will suggest how much space is needed. Here are some general guides: compact operations, not much extra space anywhere; 200 square feet per worker (this includes all floor space, not just the space at a person's workplace). Ordinarily manufacturing, with ample aisles and storage areas, needs perhaps 500 to 700 square feet per worker. Spread-out manufacturing might require up to 1,500 square feet per worker.

When a company is building a new factory, it should prepare for the future and choose a site with more space than it needs for the present. Westinghouse Electric uses a 5-to-1 or 50-acre rule, whichever is greater. It tries to get a site five times as big as its present-building floor space requirements, or at least 50 acres. Some companies use even a 10-to-1 ratio. If they end up not requiring all the land, they may want to control the land next to their new facility to minimize the build-up of hot-dog stands, bars, loan companies, gasoline stations, and small stores, which add to the traffic congestion. Excess land can usually be sold or leased at a profit to other organizations which compliment the parent organization.

Most companies acquire enough land to let them double their initial capacity. Actually, a 4-to-1 ratio will often provide enough land for this much expansion.

The 1970s saw a reversion away from such substantial provision for the future. Many companies found that they had been wasting their money by investing in real estate that they did not need at the time and not in the future either. Often, too, the companies that did need to expand found that because of changed conditions they wanted to expand somewhere else and not where they had bought extra land 10 or 20 years earlier.

SITES

Choosing the general area is the most important job in selecting a location, but the site within the area must also be suitable. It must have, to some extent, all of the characteristics already discussed. It probably should be near a residential area where workers can live. And it should be near main streets or roads and be served by the public transportation system. Often land that has been zoned for industrial use is the poorest available; it is sited on an old dump, or it is swampy or subject to floods, or it is inaccessible.

Land for a site should be dry and able to carry the building's weight without much settling. The site must be zoned for industrial use, and it needs to have good police and fire protection.

If the facility's operations unavoidably create smoke or fumes, it should choose a site where the prevailing winds will carry them toward the open country—although a company may have to put in antipollution equipment to stop smoke and fumes even in rural locations. If the plant's processes produce large quantities of waste which have to be carried away by water (common in chemical companies), the site must be next to a river or some other large body of water. And, again, antipollution regulations must be met.

The cost of alternative sites will be important only if there is a great difference in the prices and little difference in the merits. Besides the cost of the land, some sites will require more filling, grading, and expensive foundations, or more costly connections to utilize than other locations.

It is desirable to have a railroad siding and a truck dock, and, for some companies, a dock for ships. Being near a superhighway is also very desirable and may be more important than being near a railroad. (Half of everything Ford Motor Co. buys comes in on trucks, and half of Ford's finished cars leave by truck.)

There should be enough room for the present buildings, for future expansion, and for parking employees' automobiles. In size, the parking lot may approximate the total area of the plant itself; however, a good public transportation system (often with fares subsidized by the company) reduces this need and this cost.

Any company that is planning to build a new facility should not look only at communities that are aggressively going after new industry. Communities that are not actively seeking industries may have greater advantages than those which try to attract new plants. And both "active" and "passive" communities will often, if asked, make concessions equal to those offered by other places. Parke-Davis wanted to build a research facility in Ann Arbor, Michigan, on a site which would require new sewer construction, and when the company objected to bearing the nearly $100,000 charge, the city cut it to less than half. When Chicago Pneumatic Tool Company was thinking of moving from its Cleveland plant, Utica, New York, was its choice until the com-

pany found that New York tax laws were unfavorable. When Utica's city leaders went to Albany and in two days got the laws changed, Chicago Pneumatic found the new laws satisfactory and moved to Utica.

When the search for a new location gets down to picking the exact site, it is well to have either expert consultants or real estate brokers do the final investigating of good and bad points of different sites. Better yet, they should first get an option on the most likely site. The point is that the company needs to keep its identity secret. Any time a well-known company becomes interested in a plot of ground and people find out about it, its price skyrockets. Options protect a company against such price increases.

8 14 85

MAKE-BUY ALTERNATIVES IN NEW FACILITIES DECISIONS

Obviously a new facility need not be built if an existing facility is available whose size and other characteristics fit the organization's requirements. In fact, many organizations begin their operations, relocate, or expand by buying or leasing an existing facility. W. T. Grant, which went bankrupt in 1975, sold over 100 of its empty stores to K mart, Sears, and J. C. Penney. And in the early 1980s when Woolco closed down their discount operations, several hundred of these spaces were picked up by new operators. The new Bucyrus-Erie facility in Pocatello, Idaho, mentioned earlier, in which Bucyrus-Erie planned to make large earth-removing equipment, was actually an existing plant. It had been built in World War II to manufacture huge battleship guns. In another case, the Michelin Tire Co. purchased an empty Gates Rubber plant in Denver rather than building a new facility, but then later sold it to Martin Marietta for aerospace manufacturing.

In these times of inflating building costs, buying an existing facility is often the most advantageous thing to do. Since empty facilities (especially large ones) have few alternative uses and their carrying costs are substantial, the owners

FIGURE 20–2

	Labor Cost	Market Potential	Taxes	Water Supply	Recreational Opportunities
Seattle	3	2	3	5	4
Denver	3	5	2	1	4
St. Louis	4	3	5	4	2

of such buildings (often including specialized equipment) are usually willing to sell or rent them at very reasonable prices.

COMPARING ALTERNATIVE LOCATIONS

An analysis of location alternatives should consider both objective factors (such as taxes, labor, transportation, and material costs, and market potentials) and subjective factors (such as schools, recreation, labor union activities, political climate, and even weather conditions).

Companies needing new locations often set up search teams to seek out and evaluate location alternatives. When A. H. Robins (chemical manufacturer) decided to expand its capacity for producing chemicals, it set up a task force of two teams; one to consider the building of a new facility and the other to study buying an existing plant. Because of other considerations, the search was to be limited largely to the state of Virginia.

The "build" team had an engineering firm make a preliminary design of the plant. Then it asked the state of Virginia's industrial development department to help choose a site. The search soon narrowed down to nine possible locations. Meanwhile the "buy" team narrowed its search to 20, of which 3 became serious candidates.

Robin's first decision was to build a new plant. But, one of the three final candidates for buying was a company which was interested in merging with Robins, and this is eventually

what happened. Robins expanded its capacity through this merger and did not build after all.[6]

Rating Location Alternatives

A simple method which can be used to aid in choosing among location alternatives is to have decision makers evaluate the relative desirability of each location on a number of factors and to evaluate the relative importance of each of the factors in the location decision. For example, suppose the following sites are being considered in terms of the five listed factors. For each factor, each of the team members distributes 10 points among the alternative sites in terms of their relative merits. These several point distributions are then averaged to get a composite distribution. Figure 20–2 shows one company's composite ratings for Seattle, Denver, and St. Louis.

The figures in Figure 20–2 could be added horizontally to get a total score for each city, but, if this were done, it would impute equal weight to each of the five factors. Actually, in this analysis, the company decided to assign weights as follows: labor costs 20 percent, market potential 30 percent, taxes 10 percent, water supply 30 percent, and recreational opportunities 10 percent. The ratings in Figure 20–2 were accordingly multiplied by the weights, producing the numbers in Figure 20–3.

When the weighted point credits for each

---

[6] The story of this merger is told in "Planning a Plant: How a Drug Firm Decided to Build a Chemical Facility," *The Wall Street Journal,* October 22, 1975, p. 1.

FIGURE 20–3

	Labor Cost	Market Potential	Taxes	Water Supply	Recreational Opportunities	Total
Seattle	60	60	30	150	40	340
Denver	60	150	20	30	40	300
St. Louis	80	90	50	120	20	360

city are added horizontally, we find that St. Louis has the edge.

The method illustrated here uses the composite of the judgment of several people. Obviously such a mechanical procedure would not be used as the sole criteria for making a decision. Rather, the panel of people asked to participate in the analysis sits down and discusses other factors not included in this calculation before arriving at a decision, or they use the results of the calculation as a basis for further discussion and rating, or until they reach a consensus. This approach is sometimes called the *Delphi* method.

Grid Method of Determining Locations

The grid method is used to determine a central location which takes into account a company's principal markets and/or its principal material supplies. The steps involved in this method are as follows:[7]

1. A large-scale map of the area to be examined is superimposed over standard graph paper.
2. A uniform scale is marked on both the horizontal *(x)* axis and the vertical *(y)* axis.
3. Customer locations are entered in column 1 of the analysis sheet and pinpointed on the map.
4. In column 2 the weight of annual shipments anticipated from the new plant to each of the customer locations is entered, and in column

3 the percentage of each location's weight to the total is entered.
5. In columns 4 and 5 the *(x)* and *(y)* coordinates for each customer location are then entered.

The weighted center of markets, based upon tonnage, is determined by multiplying the number of distance units along each axis for each market location by percentage of the total weight of all shipments from the plant. The total of columns *Fx* and *Fy,* divided by 100, produces the coordinate of the weighted center of markets. An example is shown below.

Let us assume a manufacturer of equipment used by the electric utility industry is planning a new facility to serve customers in eight market areas. First, the eight markets are listed in column 1 in Figure 20–4 with the tonnage to be shipped to each market itemized in column 2. The percentage of the total tons to be shipped to each market is shown in column 3. A map of the total geographic area is prepared with a grid overlay and the exact market locations plotted. See Figure 20–5.

The grid coordinates along axis *(x)* and axis *(y)* are determined for each market and entered in columns 4 and 5. *Fx* and *Fy* can then be calculated. Total all *Fx* values and all *Fy* values. The sums of these two columns, divided by 100, produce the coordinates for the weighted center of market based upon the weight of shipments. In this example, the center of the market is near Cambridge and Zannesville, Ohio.

Once this analysis has been done, other things such as transportation rates, modes, and other variables should be considered.

---

[7] This example is reproduced from *How to Find a Plant Site without Losing Your Mind* (Columbus, Ohio: American Electric Power Service Corp., 1983).

FIGURE 20–4

(1)	(2)	(3)	(4)	(5)	(6)	(7)
Market Areas	Tons Shipped	Percent of Total Weight (F)	x	y	Fx	Fy
Roanoke, VA	88,197	25.3	19.3	6.5	488.29	164.45
Kingsport, TN	5,230	1.5	15.3	4.7	22.95	7.05
Ashland, KY	19,870	5.7	14.0	9.3	79.80	53.01
Canton, OH	130,726	37.5	16.4	14.6	615.00	547.50
Columbus, OH	39,741	11.4	14.0	13.0	159.60	148.20
Wheeling, WV	9,412	2.7	17.5	13.0	47.25	35.10
Fort Wayne, IN	52,639	15.1	9.8	14.9	147.98	224.99
Three Rivers, MI	2,789	0.8	9.0	17.0	7.20	13.60
Total	348,604	100.0			1,568.07	1,193.90

This example is calculated as follows, starting with Roanoke, VA:

$$25.3(F) \times 19.3(x) = 488.29(Fx)$$
$$25.3(F) \times 6.5(y) = 164.45(Fy)$$

Follow the same steps for all other market areas. The total of Fx is 1,568.07, and the total of Fy is 1,193.90. Divide these figures by 100 to arrive at 15.7 for the x axis and 11.9 for the y axis, which are the grid coordinates for the center of these particular markets based on tons shipped.

THE TRANSPORTATION METHOD IN LOCATION DECISIONS[8]

The transportation method is an operations research technique which can be helpful in making

factory and warehouse location decisions. When a company has several plants and several warehouses and is thinking either of putting in added capacity in one place or another or of reallocating the territories served by each factory, this method can be used.

It is easier to understand the transportation method if we start with a reallocation problem, where it must be determined which factories should supply which warehouses and with what quantities. The assumption here is that both factories and warehouses are already in existence. Later the method can be switched to the question of whether or not to build new facilities and where.

In its initial form, the transportation method assumes that each warehouse should be supplied from the nearest factory. There will be times, however, when individual plant capacities and nearby warehouses needs do not match up, and shipments have to be made from more distant plants. The transportation method will show the most economical pairing up of capacities and demands.

---

[8] Transportation problems are special cases of linear programming problems. Alternative methods for solving transportation problems to the one described here (the "northwest corner" or "stepping-stone" method) are the modified distribution method (MODI) and Vogel's approximation method (VAM). These methods are described in operations research books.

FIGURE 20–5

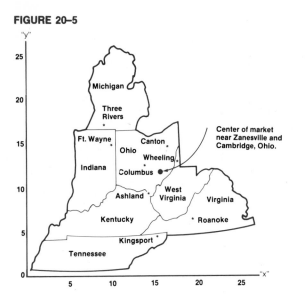

The transportation method is suitable for both small and large problems although, of course, all large problems would be handled on computers. A company such as H. J. Heinz, for example, might use it to control tomato canning and the shipment of canned tomatoes. Heinz could determine which canning factory should ship what quantity to which of its many warehouses, or from which of its many warehouses to customer companies, and make these assignments in such a way that shipping costs are minimized. Cities have also used a sophisticated variation of this method to determine how to "ship" trash to alternative processing facilities and to landfills at least cost.

The transportation method is a trial-and-error process—but with certain rules to follow. It does not, at first, produce the optimal least-cost solution. Rather, it first produces a feasible solution and then improves on it until the best solution is found. The method is an "algorithm" since it consists of several recurring mathematical steps which attempt to allocate the supply to the demand at the lowest cost while meeting the individual warehouse needs without exceeding any factory's capacity.

Often transportation method problems con-

sider only relative freight costs, but, if different factories produce at different costs, then the two (factory costs and freight costs) can be added together to get relative delivered unit costs for use in the analysis.

To illustrate this method we will assume that the Goodride Tire Company has four plants and five warehouses and is concerned with only one line of tires. Any plant can ship to any warehouse, but the costs are different. The costs used in this example include each factory's unit cost *and* the freight costs per unit for shipping products to each warehouse. Daily plant capacities and warehouse demands are shown in Figure 20–6. Factory costs plus freight costs from the plant to each warehouse are shown in Figure 20–7.

FIGURE 20–6

Plant	Capacity	Warehouse	Quantity Needed
A	200	1	150
B	100	2	300
C	400	3	100
D	400	4	200
		5	300
Total	1,100		1,050

When a problem of this kind is solved manually and without a computer (large problems would always be solved by a computer), normally the first step is to subtract the least-cost figure ($20 as shown in Figure 20–7) from every cost figure, thus producing Figure 20–8. This is not an essential step and is taken only to make the numbers small (so that the analyst can see the differences more readily) and to reduce the size of the numbers used in later manipulations.

Partial matrix A is then set up (see Figure 20–9). The cost differences are put into small boxes in the upper right corner of each box in partial matrix A. A column to show the plant capacities is added at the right. Similarly, a row showing total warehouse needs is added at the bottom.

FIGURE 20–7

From Plant	To Warehouse				
	1	2	3	4	5
A	$22	$30	$25	$20	$24
B	20	29	21	25	20
C	24	30	24	24	24
D	23	28	24	22	23

Partial matrix A also contains an added column for "warehouse 6" because in our example the four factories can supply more tires per day than are needed (their total capacity is 1,100, whereas the demand is only 1,050 units). Warehouse 6 is an imaginary or "dummy" warehouse, which would receive the 50 units the four factories can produce but which are not needed. In the final allocation of orders to factories, one or more of the plants will not have to supply all the tires it could. This will show up as an allocation of 50 units of this plant's capacity to the imaginary warehouse 6. Also, because warehouse 6 is imaginary, there are zero costs associated with it.

FIGURE 20–8

From Plant	To Warehouse				
	1	2	3	4	5
A	2	10	5	0	4
B	0	9	1	5	0
C	4	10	4	4	4
D	3	8	4	2	3

Solving the problem begins by arbitrarily allocating warehouse needs to plants so that the demand and capacity constraints are met. Starting at the upper left of Figure 20–10, plant A is first assigned 150 units from warehouse 1. (Ignore the arrows in matrix A for now.) This is all that warehouse 1 needs. So the remaining 50 units of plant A's capacity go to warehouse

FIGURE 20–9

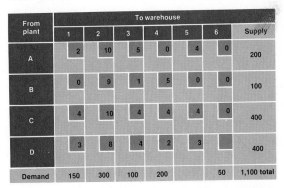

From plant	To warehouse						Supply
	1	2	3	4	5	6	
A	2	10	5	0	4	0	200
B	0	9	1	5	0	0	100
C	4	10	4	4	4	0	400
D	3	8	4	2	3	0	400
Demand	150	300	100	200		50	1,100 total

2. But warehouse 2 needs 300 units altogether. So plant B's entire capacity of 100 is also allocated to warehouse 2. Warehouse 2's remaining needs, then, are to be furnished by plant C.

This arbitrary allocation process continues down each column, moving from left to right, until everything demanded is allocated.

The way we have started to solve the problem is called *the northwest corner method* simply because it starts in the upper left corner (the northwest corner on a map). With this allocation, matrix A is complete. Demands and capacities are matched in a feasible way, although alternative allocations almost surely exist which produce lower costs.

Since no attention has been paid to the costs of this allocation, the next step is to multiply the cost differentials in each little corner box by

FIGURE 20–10

From plant	To warehouse						Supply
	1	2	3	4	5	6	
A	2	10	5	0	4	0	200
	150	50 ── 0 → 0			0	0	
B	0	9	1	5	0	0	100
	0	100	0	0	0	0	
C	4	10	4	4	4	0	400
	0	150 ← 100 ── 150			0	0	
D	3	8	4	2	3	0	400
	0	0	0	50	300	50	
Demand	150	300	100	200	300	50	1,100 Total

the quantity allocated and then add them up. The calculation is $(150 \times 2) + (50 \times 10) + (100 \times 9) + (150 \times 10) + (100 \times 4) + (150 \times 4) + (50 \times 2) + (300 \times 3) + (50 \times 0) = \$5,200$. This allocation therefore entails total costs of $5,200 in excess of the base $21,000 ($1,050 \times \$20$), which would be the inescapable minimum.

It is obvious from looking at matrix A that some allocations have been made to high-cost blocks whereas lower cost blocks are available. So the next step is to set about improving this preliminary allocation.

Looking first at plant A's allocations, can we see any shifts that can be made that would save costs? It costs zero excess dollars to ship from plant A to warehouse 4, whereas this initial allocation of plant A's capacity to warehouses 1 and 2 entails excess costs of $2 and $10 respectively. Is it possible to ship warehouse 2's allocation of 50 units to warehouse 4 instead and save $10 excess costs per unit? Yes, but to do so we must somehow reduce the amount allocated to warehouse 4 so its amount remains at 200. This can be done by transferring either 50 units of plant C's allocation to warehouse 4 to warehouse 2 or 50 units of plant D's allocations to warehouse 4 to warehouse 2. Either transfer would, in itself, lose $6 per unit transferred. (Block C–2's cost is $10 per unit minus block C–4's cost of $4 = $6; similarly, the $8 unit cost in block D–2 less D–4's cost of $2 = $6.) But the $10 savings from shifting plant A's allocation to warehouse 2 to warehouse 4 would result in a net savings of $4 ($10 − $6) for every unit so shifted. Accordingly, as shown in matrix B (Figure 20–11), the 50 units from plant A are shifted from warehouse 2 to warehouse 4 and 50 units from plant C are shifted from warehouse 4 to warehouse 2. (The alternative shift of 50 units from block D–4 to D–2 could have been made instead; the decision was arbitrarily since the savings both equal $4 per unit transferred.)

Matrix B can now be made by incorporating these changes in the original allocations. Since 50 units were shifted at a savings of $4 each,

FIGURE 20–11

From plant	To warehouse 1	2	3	4	5	6	Supply
A (cost)	2	10	5	0	4	0	200
A (alloc)	150	0	0	50	0	0	
B (cost)	0	9	1	5	0	0	100
B (alloc)	0	100 → 0 → 0 → 0			0	0	
C (cost)	4	10	4	4	4	0	400
C (alloc)	0	200	100	100	0	0	
D (cost)	3	8	4	2	3	0	400
D (alloc)	0	0 ← 0 ← 50 ← 300			50		
Demand	150	300	100	200	300	50	1,100 total

the total costs are reduced $200, from $26,200 to $26,000. From here on, the procedure is repeated by evaluating each empty block to see if more cost savings can be made. The answer is yes, if factory B's 100 units for warehouse 2 were instead sent to warehouse 5 for a $9 savings per unit ($9 − $0). This can be done by shifting 100 of factory D's allocation from warehouse 5 to warehouse 2 at a loss of $5 per unit ($8 − $3). But, there is a net gain of $4 per unit shifted ($9 − $5), so it would be done and a new matrix would result. Total costs would be reduced an additional $400, to $25,600.

There prove to be several other changes which will reduce costs still further. The intermediate matrices are not shown, but in due time the final matrix emerges, as shown in Figure 20–12. Since problems even this small are somewhat tedious to calculate by hand, Figure 20–12 shows the solution to this problem calculated by a typical transportation method computer program. This final matrix reduces the total cost to $4,100 above the $21,000 inescapable minimum.

This solution shows that plant C, with a capacity of 400 units, will actually ship only 350 and will either not produce the other 50 that it could produce or will hold them in inventory for the time being.

Had the warehouses needed more than the factories could produce, we would have had to put in plant E, an imaginary factory, instead of

FIGURE 20–12
Computer Solution to Goodride's Problem

```
TRANSPORTATION PROBLEM     1
NUMBER OF ROWS        4
NUMBER OF COLUMNS     6
```

ORIGINAL COST MATRIX

SUPPLY	DEMAND 1	2	3	4	5	6	
A	2.00	10.00	5.00	-0.00	4.00	-0.00	200.00
B	-0.00	9.00	1.00	5.00	-0.00	-0.00	100.00
C	4.00	10.00	4.00	4.00	4.00	-0.00	400.00
D	3.00	8.00	4.00	2.00	3.00	-0.00	400.00
DEMAND	150.00	300.00	100.00	200.00	300.00	50.00	

THE COST FOR THIS SOLUTION IS   4100.00

SOLUTION

SUPPLY	1	2	3	4	5	6	
A	0.00	0.00	0.00	200.00	0.00	0.00	200.00
B	0.00	0.00	0.00	0.00	100.00	0.00	100.00
C	150.00	0.00	100.00	0.00	100.00	50.00	400.00
D	0.00	300.00	0.00	0.00	100.00	0.00	400.00
DEMAND	150.00	300.00	100.00	200.00	300.00	50.00	

imaginary warehouse 6. Allocations of products to be shipped from plant E would actually be shortages and would tell us which warehouse would have to do without and how many units it would be short of its total needs

General rules for making reallocations. The general "path" of moving units around the matrix to evaluate different allocations need not be of the rectangular shape of those shown by the arrows in matrices A and B. They should, however, start with the empty block into which units are first being moved and eventually end up back at this block. Care should be taken so that what is added or subtracted from a warehouse's allocation is subtracted or added elsewhere in that

warehouse's column to keep the total allocation the same. Likewise, any changes to a plant's allocation to warehouses should be counterbalanced some other place in the plant's row. The only restrictions on the "path" of reallocations is that it cannot go diagonally, nor can right-angle turns be made on blocks which have no units allocated to them. Otherwise, blocks with units allocated to them may be skipped to get to other blocks. And, paths may cross and may go clockwise, counterclockwise, or both. When no more improvements in cost can be made by evaluating the reallocation of units to empty blocks, then an optimum (least-cost) solution has been found. It should be noted that, often, alternative optimum solutions may exist in a prob-

FIGURE 20–13
Alternate Optimal Solution

From plant	To warehouse						Supply
	1	2	3	4	5	6	
A	2 0	10 0	5 0	0 200	4 0	0 0	200
B	0 100	9 0	1 0	5 0	0 0	0 0	100
C	4 0	10 0	4 100	4 0	4 250	0 50	400
D	3 50	8 300	4 0	2 0	3 50	0 0	400
Demand	150	300	100	200	300	50	1,100 total

lem—that is, ones which have different allocations but have the same cost. For example, Figure 20–13 shows such an alternative optimal solution whose cost is also $4,100 above the $21,000 minimum. Note that allocations are different for warehouses 1 and 5. Other factors can be considered in choosing which of these two solutions is best for Goodride.

Other Applications

Our example of how to use the transportation method has been confined to how best to use existing facilities. This same method can also be used to weigh the merits of expanding one plant as against another. All that is necessary is to work out the problem as if the expanded capacity were already in existence and use cost figures that are estimated to result from the change in capacity.

The transportation method can also be used to weigh the merits of building a new factory versus expanding some existing facility.

Finally, it can also compare building new factories in different locations. All that is necessary is to work through the calculations as if the new facilities were in existence and operating at their probable costs.

For example, if plants A, B, and C exist, plant D could be one of the candidates under consideration. After the analysis is complete, D would be replaced with another candidate with its costs and capacities, and the analysis re-

peated. The resulting costs of the two analyses would then be compared.

Review Questions

1. How stringent are antipollution laws? Will they, in fact, cause companies to do anything which they would not otherwise do if there were no regulations?

2. What part do labor laws and union contracts play in factory relocation decisions?

3. Both nearness to good transportation and the availability of an adequate labor supply are almost always listed as musts in discussions about location. Yet if these are so important, how does it happen that industry is so spread out across the United States?

4. How important are local taxes in the choice of locations?

5. What advantages should a company expect to gain if it locates in an industrial park? What bad features might there be?

6. What characteristics should an ideal site have? What should the relationship be between the size of the building and the size of the site?

7. When building a new factory, many companies buy 50 acres or more of land. Why do they waste money buying land they may not need?

8. Summarize the data requirements and process for using the grid method for determining locations.

9. Could the transportation method be used if demands exceed capacity? How? Could it be used to help decide whether or not to build a new factory of facility? How?

Questions for Discussion

1. How can an organization go about picking a location which will be good over the years? Explain.

2. How could a city or other governmental agency go about picking locations for fire stations, health clinics, or state employment offices?

3. How can one location be much better than others if it takes a computer to figure out which one is better?

4. Each year, *Factory* magazine surveys new plant construction in the United States; the results of its studies are reported in the May issue. As part of this activity, the reporters ask company officials why they put their new factories where they did. There is no general agreement, and the most popular reasons given one year shift a bit from those of the year before. Why do experts differ so widely on the relative importance of location factors?

5. If a company moves to a lower-wage area, should it offer its former wages to employees who are invited to move, or should those who are invited to move be offered wages comparable to those in the area where the new operations will be located?

6. If a company happens to locate in an area where the labor attitude is poor, is there anything its managers can do about it?

7. How do labor laws affect location choices?

8. How can location be so important if a college professor's objections are enough to cause a company to choose a location 150 miles away? (See under heading, ''The Community Viewpoint.'')

9. If a small town gave a company a free site and tax exemption for 10 years, should the company accept? Discuss fully.

10. A small toy manufacturer, who sells nationally and is located in the Chicago area, is thinking of moving the plant either to Fayetteville, Arkansas, or to El Paso, Texas. Advise him and support your position.

Problems

1. A location consulting firm has produced the following analysis comparing six alternative locations for a company which will have 1,000 employees:

a. If the company were to choose on the basis of this evidence, which location should be chosen? Why? If more information is really needed, what information?

b. Devise a numerical rating scheme to quantify this information into an overall rating for each location.

2. Suppose the tons shipped to the various market areas for the Zenig Corporation are as follows:

	Tons Shipped (1000s)
Roanoke, VA	100
Kingsport, TN	50
Ashland, KY	40
Canton, OH	125
Columbus, OH	60
Wheeling, WV	12
Fort Wayne, IN	65
Three Rivers, MI	20
Total	472

Using the grid method presented in the text, where should Zenig locate their distribution center? (Presume they use trucks for distribution and need good access to the interstate highway system. Use a current road atlas to aid you in determining the city or town you would choose.)

3. Once you have determined the city or town in which you think Zenig should locate their distribution center (from problem 2), outline the next steps you would take to further investigate the suitability of this site.

4. Minimize the shipping costs in the following situation. The numbers in the body of the table are the shipping costs per unit.

From Factory	To Warehouse				Factory Production
	D	E	F	G	
A	$9	$12	$5	$ 9	300
B	8	8	6	12	400
C	6	11	8	6	500
Warehouse needs	200	600	100	300	1,200

Locations						
	A	*B*	*C*	*D*	*E*	*F*
Hourly cost of labor	Low	Moderate	Very low	Moderate	High	High
Productivity of labor	Moderate	Moderate	Moderate	Low	Moderate	Moderate
Freight cost	High	Moderate	High	Moderate	Moderate	Low
Labor supply	Adequate	Adequate	Plentiful	Plentiful	Adequate	Plentiful
Union activity	Moderate	Active	Negligible	Active	Active	Significant
Living conditions	Good	Very good	Rural	Very good	Excellent	Good

5. Suppose that in problem 2 (on page 487) competition between trucks and railroads reduces shipment costs from plant C to $4.00, $8.00, $6.00, and $4.00, respectively. What is the solution to the problem?

6. The Sun Company has plants in Cleveland, Chicago, Houston, San Francisco, and Seattle. It ships sun lamps from these plants to warehouses in Los Angeles, Denver, Omaha, St. Louis, and Atlanta. In the table below are given the freight costs per unit for shipping sun lamps from each plant to each warehouse.

From which plant should sun lamps be shipped to each warehouse? What is the total freight bill?

7. If in problem 4, Sun enlarged its Chicago factory so that it had a capacity of 500, how should the shipment pattern change? How much freight costs would Sun save? If these were weekly savings, how long would it take freight savings alone to pay for the Chicago factory's $5,000 expansion cost?

8. Sales have been increasing in areas distant from Sun's present plants in Chicago and New York,

	Warehouse					
Plant	Los Angeles	Denver	Omaha	St. Louis	Atlanta	Plant Capacity
Cleveland	$14	$10	$9	$ 7	$ 7	800
Chicago	12	8	5	5	7	200
Houston	9	7	8	6	6	600
San Francisco	4	7	9	9	15	100
Seattle	8	9	9	10	16	400
Quantity required	300	500	300	400	600	2,100

so the company is considering putting a third plant in Denver or Dallas. After study it has reduced the pertinent remaining data to that shown below. Where, on the basis of the figures, should Sun put the new plant: in Denver or Dallas?

	Distribution Costs per Unit				
	From Existing Plants		From Proposed Plant		Expected Annual Demand Units
To Warehouses	Chicago	New York	Denver	Dallas	
Washington	$1.62	$.92	$2.71	$2.51	24,000
Atlanta	1.78	1.95	2.12	1.72	18,000
New Orleans	2.05	2.41	1.93	1.17	27,000
San Francisco	3.22	4.69	1.67	2.14	17,000
Los Angeles	3.32	4.78	2.25	2.38	22,000
Plant capacity (units)	40,000	45,000	25,000	25,000	
Production cost per unit	$3.66	$3.79	$4.19	$4.13	

Case 20-1

The Costello Company, with 1,500 employees and located in Terre Haute, Indiana, makes hinges for all kinds of doors, from house doors to automobile doors. It also makes related hardware items such as door latches and catches. Business has been good, and the company has to expand. Several members of the board of directors favor moving all automobile parts to a site near Detroit in Mt. Clemens, Michigan. Several key personnel, however, don't want to move their families to or near a big city.

They propose, instead, moving to Jackson, Michigan—75 miles from Detroit. Labor rates would be 10 percent lower, but extra freight costs would offset half of this gain. Also favoring Jackson is relative freedom from labor problems. Satisfactory sites and ample labor supplies are available both in Mt. Clemens and Jackson. Transportation is also satisfactory in both places.

What should be done? Why?

Case 20-2

A few years ago the Fisher body division of General Motors decided that it needed to build a factory east of Chicago, west of Pittsburgh, and north of the Ohio River. This was to be Fisher's 10th and, at the time, largest factory.

Fisher picked Kalamazoo, Michigan—150 miles east of Chicago and 150 miles west of Detroit. At the time, the head of Fisher said that Kalamazoo was picked because of "its progressive business climate. We took a good look at Kalamazoo and its people, and we liked what we saw."

What characteristics give a community a "progressive business climate"? How might a mayor of a city go about helping to create a climate which will attract business? Could a company's management *create* a favorable attitude in its new employees? What makes a community appeal to a prospective employer so that he "likes what he sees?"

Case 20-3

In the past decade, the movement out of large cities has extended to large company home offices as well as factories. Literally hundreds of major companies have deserted the U.S. major cities for surrounding suburban areas. Among others, for example, American Can and U.S. Tobacco have moved to Greenwich, Connecticut, and PepsiCo has moved to Purchase, New York, Olin Corporation to Stamford, Connecticut, and American Cyanamid to Wayne, New Jersey. Several other companies have also moved their headquarters west to the Rocky Mountain region and to the West Coast.

Yet all is not well, and now a different tune is often played. Working in suburbia or isolated areas is not all it was cracked up to be. Executives miss the excitement and stimulating contacts of the city. They complain about being company captives and smothering in a cocoon of paternalism in suburbia. "You get awfully tired of seeing those same faces every day, and all day, and evenings, too."

Once many large home offices move into a small town, it soon begins to develop big-city problems. Crime rates rise, 5:00 P.M. traffic jams develop, pollution often becomes a problem, and green trees and open spaces turn into parking spaces and big buildings. The local labor supply is frequently inadequate, and the company often has to hire almost a whole new office staff since its former staff people will neither commute to a distant new location nor will they sell their houses and move to the new location. Should they want to move, their problem is worsened by the high housing costs in nice suburbs.

The company officials, too, are somewhat isolated. They are not as close to lawyers, bankers, accountants, consultants, and advertising agencies.

As a result of all these factors working together and at the same time, there has been a slowing of the exodus and, in fact, a slight reversal of the outward movement. This has been stimulated by rising office rental rates in suburban locations and lower rates in the big cities.

Yet Caterpillar operates successfully in Peoria, Illinois. The same is true of Maytag in Newton, Iowa, and Kellogg in Battle Creek, Michigan. And Hewlett-Packard has located in smaller cities in Colorado, Oregon, Washington, and California.

Discuss the merits of being located "where the action is."

Chapter 21

Designing Facilities

FACILITIES DESIGN CONSIDERATIONS

The management of production and operations includes providing and maintaining the buildings and services needed to house and serve the people and machines used to make products and provide services. Most of the time buildings and services are probably regarded as merely being present and not needing managerial effort. Yet, they constitute part of the productive asset base of every manufacturing and service organization. They require a great deal of managerial attention during design and construction, and they continue to call for a considerable amount of ongoing managerial effort to keep them operating so that they contribute to effective operations.

The main job of facilities is to house manufacturing and service operations. But they must also house a multitude of supporting services, which may take up to half of the total space.

There need to be aisles, elevators, stairways, offices, a cafeteria, a dispensary, stockrooms, tool rooms, dispatching stations, time-card racks, locker rooms, and restrooms. There is need for telephones, intercom systems, computer data input and printout stations, electricity of various voltages, hot and cold purified water, unpurified water for processes, compressed air, high- and low-pressure steam, natural gas, lights, heat, ventilation, and air conditioning. Some services need wires, pipes, or ducts. Out of doors there is need for shipping and receiving docks for rail cars and trucks. Also needed are a parking lot for cars and storage space for coal or other materials. The list is long.

Productive facilities should be flexible and easily adaptable to changes in operations. Built-in flexibility is the best way to make changes easily. Some things which help are: (1) wide bays (open areas between rows of posts or walls); (2) ceilings high enough for overhead conveyors, or mezzanines, whether they are needed now or not; (3) space (or installed wires) for high-voltage electricity for areas that do not need it today; (4) heavy-duty floors; and possibly (5) machines (in some areas) on easily detachable mounts so that departments can easily expand.

BUILDING DESIGN

Single-Story Buildings

Single-story buildings are the most common kind today. They can be as wide or long as needed and can easily be expanded. Single-story buildings have no stairs, elevators, elevator wells, or ramps to connect floors. There are few posts to interfere with overhead cranes or to reduce light. It is easy and inexpensive to move materials from job to job because all the moving is horizontal, not up and down. Heavy equipment can be put on separate foundations.

There are some disadvantages though. Single-story buildings require more ground space. And, if there is a flat roof and no glass skylights, it is necessary to use artificial light in most of the plant. Also, a forced ventilation or air-conditioning system will usually be required.

Architecture and Styling

A facility's architecture can have an important impact upon its fixed and variable cost structure, as well as upon the attitudes of the people who work there. Because of the nature of many industries and because of heavy fixed investments in a physical plant, many organizations have historically taken a utilitarian approach to the appearance and design of ther production facilities. The industrial sections of many communities have consequently been less attractive than residential sections.

However, things ar changing. Many organizations are spending much more money on the design of their facilities, trying to make them at the same time both economical functionally and attractive architecturally.

Westinghouse's plant which makes electrical transformers at Jefferson City, Missouri, is a good example of this trend. This 570,000-square-foot facility sits on a 100-acre site at the foot of a high bluff. It was designed to blend into the area where the state capital buildings and a residential area (on the bluff above the plant) are within view. Its contemporary design contains extensive landscaping (including an eight-acre lake which doubles as a storm drainage basin) and a relatively uncluttered roof for the benefit of the residents on the bluff.

The plant is also designed to appeal to employees, with the objective of higher motivation and productivity. The trapezoid-shaped office areas have views of the lake, capitol, and a nearby river. There is an extensive use of carpeting, wood, and coordinated color schemes in the offices. The plant was also designed for expansion, should extra capacity be required. Westinghouse believes that this plant is one of their most productive facilities.

Although new buildings are usually the most attractive, a great deal of plant remodeling is always being carried on. For example, the huge 560-building Dow Chemical plant complex at Midland, Michigan, has been undergoing extensive refurbishment for several years. Dow is trying to change its plant appearance from a fortress-like structure to one which its employees will find more pleasing.

BUILDING COSTS

A new facility's cost depends on what is required. In 1985 a simple building with a 10-foot ceiling might be built for about $30 a square foot. But it would be necessary to go above $50 a foot to get very many "trimmings." Costs vary, of course, in different parts of the country. Size also affects the square-foot unit cost. Large facilities can cost a little less per square foot than smaller ones. Worker density also affects the costs. Less space per worker often means more machines per foot, more electrical connections, and more of all of the accessories that equipment requires. At the same time, greater worker density requires more locker rooms, cafeterias, entrance ways, and so on, increasing the cost per square foot.

Leasing is an alternative to buying. One year's rent is likely to cost more than one tenth of the total cost of a new building (including land). Normally it costs more to rent than to own, but there may be tax advantages to leasing. Rent is fully tax deductible, whereas owning allows only depreciation and property taxes to be deducted.

FACILITIES LAYOUT CONSIDERATIONS

A plant's internal arrangement of facilities—its layout—should be designed to permit the economical movement of people and materials through processes and operations. Travel distances should be as short as possible, and picking up and putting down products or tools should be held to a minimum—as should paperwork and instructions to operators and truckers. This should result in the minimization of handling and transportation costs, as well as holding down work in process time and machine idle time.

The never-ending struggle to keep the productive capacity of operations in balance with current needs means constantly adding machines in some places and taking out old machines in other places. Because businesses grow, more machines are usually added than are removed. In any case, the layout of machines often must be rearranged and materials handling systems must be redesigned.

SPACE REQUIREMENTS

Machine Space

Machines need floor space plus space for their electric motors and control panels, as well as for any operators and conveyors. They also need space for the storage of materials before and after the operations have been performed. Furthermore, maintenance and machine repair people need enough room to work. There is also need to consider the shapes of the machines. Some are long and narrow, others are round, and some are nearly square. Some extend upward 10 feet or more above floor level; others have beds or foundations extending several feet below floor level.

In total, machines will usually require more space than the total of their separate space needs because these spaces never dovetail exactly. The actual placing of machines is generally decided after experimentally placing machine

FIGURE 21–1
Mock-Up of a Plant Layout

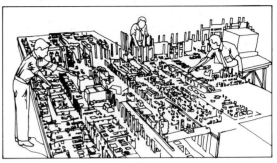

Source: Westinghouse Electric Corporation.

templates (paper cutouts or even three-dimensional models made to scale) in position on a floor plan. (See Figure 21–1.)

Product Space

In most organizations the space allowed for storage, machines, conveyors, and aisles provides enough room for work in process, but companies that make large assembled products such as locomotives, freight cars, or aircraft need extensive assembly or erection floors. Acres of floor space are sometimes needed.

Usually, large products are partially assembled in one part of the assembly area and then moved to another area where more work is done to them. Each area needs to be large enough to hold several products at a time.

Service Area Space

Service areas—washrooms, locker rooms, restaurants, medical facilities, offices, tool rooms, stockrooms, storage areas, weighing scales, elevators, stairs, and aisles—are important support facilities to manufacturing operations. They should be close to work areas where they can be most useful, yet not be where they will disrupt production.

Overhead Space

Overhead space, as well as floor space, should be considered in layouts because overhead space saves floor space (and floor space costs more than overhead space). Overhead conveyors and cranes can take materials directly to workplaces, which is something that trucks operating in aisles cannot always do as easily. Overhead conveyors are often used for the temporary storage of materials between operations, which will cut handling costs considerably and free floor space at machine centers.

Today-s high-stacking lift trucks allow for the economical use of floor space. They can, despite narrow aisles, stack materials up to 20 or 30 feet at almost no cost above that of setting loads on the floor. Floor-space requirements are thereby reduced drastically. And, some computer-controlled "stacker cranes" can place and retrieve items in bins that are over 100 feet high.

LOT VERSUS CONTINUOUS PRODUCTION

Many companies make finished products which are assemblies of separate pieces or components. Raw materials are first made into parts which are later assembled into finished products. In this kind of manufacturing, products can be made continuously or in lots. This applies to individual parts as well as to finished products. A company uses "lot production" when it makes up, as one order, enough products or parts to meet the needs of, say, one month. Then it turns to other parts or products, which also are made in lots to meet final assembly requirements.

When parts or products are made in lots, there are several decisions to make. How many units should be made at one time as one lot? Only a few at a time and frequently? Or larger lots less frequently? These are important questions because they result in different unit costs. If the lots are too large, they result in excess inventory costs; if they are too small, they result in too many small reorders. The number that

should be made in order to produce the lowest unit cost is called the *economic lot-size* and is discussed in Chapter 12.

Here we are not interested in the size of the reorder lots, or with lots as such, but with the fact that lot production and continuous production need different layouts of machines and equipment. Lot production requires a "functional" layout, whereas continuous production requires a "product"-oriented layout.

LAYOUT PATTERNS

There are four basic patterns of layout. First, *functional layout* refers to the grouping of similar machines into work centers which perform similar functions. Second, *product layout* refers to the grouping of machines required to make certain products along lines down which the products move continuously, as in an assembly line. Product layout is oriented toward the products being manufactured—to achieve high-volume production. Chapter 22 deals with the design of product layout or assembly line systems.

Third, *group technology layout,* sometimes regarded as a separate kind of layout, is really a variation of product layout. In group layout, parts and components being made are grouped into "families," and areas or departments are set apart to work only on such parts and to do everything needed to make them complete. (See Figure 21–2.)

Fourth, *fixed position layout* applies to complex assembled products being put together on one spot such as a Boeing 767 aircraft or the space shuttle. Most companies use predominately one or the other of these layout patterns but may include all four to some degree.

Functional Layout

Functional layout (sometimes called *process* or *job lot* layout) is a grouping together of machines and people to do similar work. Grinding is done in a grinding department, painting in a paint department, data processing in the computer de-

FIGURE 21–2
Layout Patterns

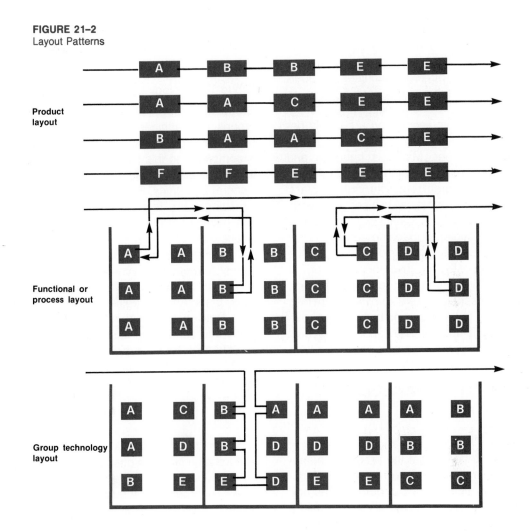

partment, and bills paid in the accounts payable department.

Advantages of functional layout. The goal of a functional layout is to make the best use of the specialization of machines and people. But functional departments are also flexible and are able to handle a variety of products. The machines are general-purpose machines which allow products or services requiring diverse operations to easily follow diverse paths through the facility.

Functional layout facilities are less vulnerable to shutdowns than product layout patterns. If a machine breaks down, its next assigned work can often be transferred to a nearby similar type of machine, and the delay may not interfere with the progress of other orders through the plant. If the products are varied and are made in small quantities, costs are lower with functional layouts than with product layouts. And since the machines and workers are somewhat independent of each other, this method is suitable for incentive pay systems.

Disadvantages of functional layout. A functional layout has certain disadvantages. General-purpose machines usually operate much more slowly than special-purpose machines, so operation costs per unit may be higher—often much higher for small lot sizes. Setup, work routing, scheduling, and cost accounting are costly because these things have to be done separately for every new order. Materials handling and transportation costs are high. Since different products follow different routes through the plant, it is usually not economical to use conveyors, so material movers have to haul work in process from machine center to machine center.

Materials usually move slowly through the plant. Consequently, the inventories of work in process are higher, and a large amount of storage space is needed. Orders sometimes are lost. It is also difficult to keep a good balance between labor and equipment needs. Functional layouts are best for small volumes of a wide variety of products. In addition, idle WIP has a high monetary opportunity cost.

Product Layout

Product layout means that the product's manufacturing requirements and higher volume dominate and determine the layout of machines and equipment. Products move, usually continuously, down a conveyor line past successive work stations where people and/or machines do work which results in the finished product (See Figure 21–2).

Continuous production is the best kind of layout pattern for products, whether they are large or small, which are made in large quantities. Products are moved by conveyor from work station to work station either steadily or on a stop-and-go basis. This is how television sets, kitchen stoves, and automobiles are made. At individual work stations the work may be manual, as it usually is in assembly work, or it may be machine work, as it usually is in the making of parts. This kind of production is often called *straight-line layout,* although the line sometimes turns a corner and goes on in another direction.

Group Technology Layout

Group technology layout sets apart areas and groups of machines for making "families" of parts which require similar processing. Each part is completed in this small specialized area with the entire machining sequence being done there. General Dynamics, Bell Helicopter, and Otis Engineering are a few of the many organizations that have, or are, moving toward this type of layout.

Among advantages claimed for group technology layout are a saving in handling costs: parts do not have to be hauled to far corners of the plant. And it is easier to know where each lot is. Delivery times can be estimated more precisely and scheduling is simplified. Setup costs can often be reduced since next operations on machines may be much like preceding operations, thus making it possible to use part of the former setup.

Fixed Position Layout

Fixed station layout is often used for large, complex products, such as factory machines themselves, hydroelectric turbines, locomotives, airplanes, ships, and prefabricated houses. The product may remain in one location for its full assembly period, as in the case of a ship. Or it may stay in one area for a long time, perhaps several weeks, while considerable work is done on it. Then it is moved to another assembly area where more work is done. In total, it may be moved only four or five times.

There really are few economic advantages to the fixed work station method except that it avoids the prohibitively high costs which would be entailed if the product were moved from one work station to another very often. Indeed, the fixed station arrangement is probably the only feasible way to put these large products together.

However, because some workers don't like paced moving assembly lines with their small repetitive tasks, some manufacturers use a semi-fixed position assembly layout. Hewlett-Packard's assemblers of desk-top computers, for example, work at benches where they do a number of tasks on each unit, including their own testing. Their total assignment can take an hour or more. When one worker completes the assigned tasks, the product is moved on to the next bench where another worker has another large collection of assembly tasks to perform, and so on.

This approach requires a bank of one or two partially completed units at each work station to "decouple" assemblers from each other so delays will not hold up later assemblers. Unfortunately, this type of assembly may increase assembly costs rather than decrease them as compared to the costs of regular assembly lines. It is not clear that the higher morale and fewer problems of absenteeism and turnover which can result are always enough to offset the less efficient method of production, but Hewlett-Packard thinks it is.

LAYOUT METHODS

Companies that build new facilities often spend two or three years in preliminary work, part of which goes into searching for improved methods to use in the new plant. The building of a new plant provides an excellent opportunity to make far-reaching improvements. With a new layout, it is possible to eliminate many wasteful practices.

One way to begin a layout analysis is to start with an assembly diagram (or process chart) that shows the way the finished products are made from subassemblies and how the subassemblies are, in turn, made from parts. Next, lists of the operations required to make the parts should be obtained from the engineering department. These lists show the sequence, or "routing" of machines needed for successive operations to be done on a part or product. If the layout is to be product-oriented, the lists provide a pattern for setting up work stations along assembly lines for people and for placing machines.

A second way to begin a new layout is to consider products from a materials handling point of view. Are the products heavy and dense (castings, forgings) or bulky and light (hollow sheet-metal items)? How about their shape? Are they long and slim, or floppy, or readily stackable? What about the risk of damage? Are they easily broken or marred, or dangerous or hard to contain (acids), or are they immune to harm (scrap iron)? Are they covered with grease, or are they dry and clean?

Next, the quantities of each product need to be considered. If the expected volume requirements will justify it, a product layout for the hard-to-handle items can be developed. But, if the volume is small, it may be necessary to stay with a functional arrangement. In any case, cutting the transportation cost of hard-to-handle items is an important consideration in layout.

A third way to begin a layout analysis is to begin with floor space drawings showing all permanently or semipermanently fixed items—everything that cannot be changed or moved easily. Then, all proposed new machines and equipment can be marked in at their ideal positions.

THE TRAVEL CHART OR LOAD-PATH MATRIX METHOD FOR FUNCTIONAL LAYOUT

A quite different way to solve a functional layout problem is to focus largely on trying to reduce the transportation of work-in-process materials from work center to work center.

The "travel chart" method tries to place work centers close to each other between which there will be an expected heavy flow or products. A simple example will show how this works. We assume that a factory which makes a variety of metal fasteners is to be laid out and that, in total, the factory will produce 100,000 pounds

FIGURE 21–3

Thousands of Pounds from Departments	Thousands of Pounds per Week to Departments											
	2	3	4	5	6	7	8	9	10	11	12	13
1	90									10		
2		75	15									
3				20	45	5					5	
4							13				2	
5									5	12	3	
6								35		10		
7									5			
8								3	5	5		
9									18	20		
10										33		
11												90
12												10

of metal fasteners every week. There are a variety of paths the various fasteners may take through the different departments, depending upon the item.

First, it is necessary to construct a "from-and-to" matrix showing the flow of materials from department to department. These figures would come from order routing sheets and from projections of the quantities of products to be produced in the future. Figure 21–3 shows this expected volume of flow.

Next, an *initial* schematic diagram is developed, showing the sequence of departments through which the materials will have to move. Ideally, the ultimate solution should be the one where most materials would move along a line drawn directly from the first department to the last department. If it were possible, then a product layout would probably be more appropriate.

In Figure 21–4 (our first attempt to develop such a schematic diagram), the numbers in the circles are department numbers. The numbers along the connecting arrows are the pounds (in thousands) of products which move from one department to the other each week, on the average. In Figure 21–4 the circles have been initially drawn in a uniform grid. This will be changed later as departmental square-footage requirements are considered. As can be seen in Figure 21–4, there are many situations where material

leapfrogs several departments to get to its destination. Whenever this happens, it usually results in long, costly movements of materials.

The next step is to reconstruct Figure 21–4 by moving departments around to reduce the long hauls where the traffic is heavy. Departments between which there is heavy traffic should be placed next to each other in as many cases as possible. As Figure 21–4 is drawn, ad-

FIGURE 21–4

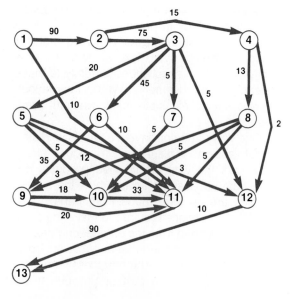

jacent departments (short hauls), for example, are those between 1 and 2, 1 and 5, and 3 and 6. Nonadjacent departments (long hauls) are 1 and 11, 2 and 4, 9 and 11, and so on.

In an example as simple as this one, an analyst can soon arrive by trial and error at a reasonably good rearrangement of departments to meet this objective. One obvious improvement, for example, would be to move department 13 to the right so that it is below department 11. However, after trying other combinations (and there is a very large number of them), this move may later be discarded.

It took us five stages of improved layouts to arrive at Figure 21–5, in which all solid lines are transportation routes to adjacent departments and are therefore short hauls. The dotted lines are time-consuming long hauls among nonadjacent departments. Figure 21–5 still shows 35,000 pounds moving nonadjacently, but this is low compared to the 499,000 pounds moving adjacently among departments.

Having arrived at the schematic arrangement of departments, our next step is to consider each department's size. This has been done in Figure 21–5 by the size of the blocks being in

FIGURE 21–5

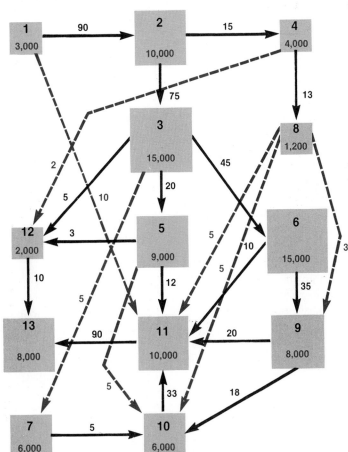

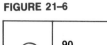

FIGURE 21–6

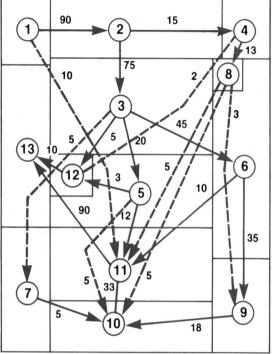

accord with each department's required square footage. It is not necessary, however, that departments be square in shape. The next step is to try to fit the departments into a building, either an existing building or a new one. If the building is to be new, then the departmental requirements will determine its size and have a part in determining its shape. Figure 21–6 shows how the 13 departments in our example might fit into a 560-by-700-foot floor plan.

The travel chart method does not consider all of the problems that engineers face in layout analyses since it pays attention only to the flow of products between departments and not to transportation within departments. It also pays attention only to the material which has to be moved, but only as loads. Implicitly it assumes that distance and costs vary together. There may also be other things which are important, such as bulk, fragility, the need for departments to

be close together in order to help coordination, their need for common service and supporting facilities, or the isolation of noisy or hazardous operations.

COMPUTERIZED LAYOUT METHODS

Because of the large number of combinations of departmental patterns which must be considered in larger, more realistically sized problems, computer programs have been developed to aid in this analysis.

One of these systems is CRAFT, which stands for computerized relative allocation of facilities technique. CRAFT uses a heuristic (trial-and-error, but with guiding rules) approach to determine a solution, much as we did in our example but without a computer. CRAFT requires essentially the same information (plus the cost of handling materials between departments) and an initial feasible solution layout on which it tries to improve.

CAD in Facilities Design

Computer-aided design can also be used to design facilities and their layout. Figure 21–7 depicts a Calcomp system which allows a facilities designer to call up a data base of information about the facility, to design it (or reuse its design), and to print drawings for construction once the layout design is completed.

LAYOUT IN SERVICE ORGANIZATIONS

Banks, restaurants, hospitals, and offices face many of the same layout problems as do manufacturing organizations. For the most part, the same layout methods can be used. Instead of loads moving among departments, the analyst must consider the movement of people and the movement of paperwork. In the cases of restaurants, it is the movement of raw materials (uncooked food) through processing centers (refrigerators, stoves, ovens, and the like), and the

FIGURE 21–7
Computer-Aided Design Systems Can Be Used to Design Facility Layouts

Source: Calcomp.

MATERIALS HANDLING

An important part of the design of a production system is the design of the materials handling system. Every company is, in effect, in the materials transportation or materials handling business, whether it wants to be or not. Materials have to be moved from incoming freight cars or trucks to "receiving inspection" and then on to raw materials storage. From there they go to the first operation, then to other operations, and to and from temporary storage points between operations, and to finished stores, to the shipping room, and, finally, to the outgoing freight car or truck. During their trip through the plant they are picked up, moved, and put down many times. In and of itself, every kind of materials handling or transportation is unproductive in that it does not change the form of the product. Eliminating any part of such movement or idleness increases efficiency.

Companies which make materials handling equipment report that few companies spend less than 15 percent of their labor costs for handling materials. Most companies probably spend from 20 to 30 percent of their factory payroll for materials handling—or something well over $5,000 per employee per year! A company with 1,000 employees probably spends more than $5 million every year moving things around! Large companies spend hundreds of millions, annually, moving things around.

Few companies know the extent of their materials handling costs because accounting reports rarely show all of these costs. They know the cost of handlers and truckers, but besides this a great deal of materials handling (picking things up and putting them down) is done by machine operators and assemblers incidental to their work. These employees are classified as production workers, and all of their pay is recorded as pay for productive work, ignoring the fact that part of it is for materials handling costs. In addition, although neither stockroom employees nor inspectors are classed as materials handlers, they too spend time picking things up and

movement of finished products (cooked foods) to customers.

A McDonald's fast-food store, for example, is really a highly engineered "food factory" with a combination of functional and assembly line layouts. McDonald's restaurants are designed so that raw materials move in the most efficient manner from machine center to machine center (such as french fryer, grill, and shake machines) and into finished goods inventory—which turns over, sometimes, in a matter of a few minutes. (The next time the reader is in a fast-food store, watch their "manufacturing" activities for a moment.)

putting them down. Many companies, particularly small companies, do not give handling costs the attention they deserve.

The best way to handle materials is *not* to handle them; but, if this cannot be avoided, then "hands-off" handling is next best. Materials handling costs can be cut by (1) eliminating the handling whenever possible, (2) mechanizing—largely by conveyors and power-driven trucks—whatever handling still remains, and (3) making the necessary handling more efficient by reducing movement distances. (This is the objective of the "load-path matrix" method, presented earlier.)

Often there is a question of what to move—people, tools, or materials and products. In parts making, it is almost always more economical to move materials and parts to machine operators. But for large items such as airplanes, or ships, or locomotives it is more economical to do assembly work in one or only a few areas. The product remains stationary as workers with portable tools assemble the product's components.

SUPPLYING PARTS TO ASSEMBLY WORKERS

Supplying parts to assembly workers along assembly lines is more than a matter of just moving materials. In all, it is necessary to bring hundreds of different parts to dozens of assembly stations. Each part has to go to the station where it is attached to the product; yet, except for very small items, very few parts can be stored at these stations.

The object is to keep a steady, though small, stream of parts arriving at the assembly stations just before the assemblers need them but to do it so that materials suppliers are not carrying one and two parts around all the time. This can be done economically by using service conveyors with pans or trays which are loaded in behind-the-scenes stockrooms and which pass by the assemblers who take what they need from

them. Parts may also be gathered into sets in the stockroom and, by conveyor or truck, taken in pans to the assemblers. The pans can have sections for separate parts so that assemblers do not have to fish around for the part they want next.

Small inexpensive items (washers, cotter pins, and the like), however, should be stored in ample supply at the assemblers' work stations. This saves expensive stockroom handling of many minor inexpensive items.

ECONOMICS OF MANUAL HANDLING

When a large volume of products is to be handled, it is usually possible to calculate how best to do it. Suppose, for example, that incoming materials are typically received and stacked near the receiving point. Later they must be moved to another storage point closer to the operations. We will assume that there is a pile of cased products, each case weighing 30 pounds, and that they are to be moved and stacked again.

The various methods for moving them are *(a)* by hand, with a laborer carrying one case at a time; *(b)* manually, with a laborer pushing or pulling a two- or four-wheeled truck; *(c)* manually and mechanically, by putting the cases on a pallet and then using a forklift truck; *(d)* mechanically, by using a fork truck with the cases already on pallets; or *(e)* by using a conveyor.

At the moment, we are calculating only worker costs and are not concerned with equipment costs. The handler costs $4.50 per hour, or $.075 per minute.

If the laborer carries the cases, he will take ⅓ of a minute to get a case off the pile, will walk at the rate of 250 feet per minute, and will take another ⅓ minute to put the case on the new pile. This costs $.025 per case for "unpiling," $.03 per 100 feet per case for carrying, and $.025 per case for piling—or $.05 + $.03 per 100 feet per case. Using a two-wheeled hand truck requires the following: unpiling, ⅓ minute;

piling on truck, ⅓ minute; travel at the rate of 200 feet per minute for a load of five cases; unpiling from truck, ⅓ minute; and piling onto stack, ⅓ minute. This amounts to 1.33 minutes for handling each case plus .5 minute of travel per five cases. The cost is $.10 + $.0375 ÷ 5 = $.10 + $.0075 per 100 feet per case.

The four-wheel truck requires the same handling as the two-wheel truck, but travel is at the rate of 150 feet per minute for loads of 20 cases. The time requirements are 1.33 minutes' handling plus .666 minute per 100 feet per 20 cases. This costs $.10 + $.05 ÷ 20 per 100 feet, or $.10 + $.0025 per 100 feet per case.

Using a forklift truck requires unpiling the cases (⅓ minute each) and piling them on a pallet for the truck at another ⅓ minute per case. They travel at the rate of 600 feet per minute in a 15-case load. At the depositing end, the fork truck puts a loaded pallet on the stack in ½ minute. Handling at the beginning is ⅔ minute per case; travel is ⅙ of a minute per 100 feet per 15 cases; handling at the end is ⅓ minute per case. In total, handling time is 21/30, or .7, of a minute. This costs $.053. Travel costs are $.0125 per 15 cases, or 1/12 of a cent per 100 feet per case.

The stacked cases could, however, already be on pallets. If this is so, getting the cases onto the truck would be reduced to ½ minute per pallet, or 1/30 minute per case. Handling at both ends would be 2/30 of a minute, or $.007 per case. Travel would continue to cost 1/12 of a cent per 100 feet per case.

If a conveyor were used instead of a forklift truck, the travel cost for the employee would be eliminated. Unpiling cases and putting them onto the conveyor would take ½ minute per case. Taking them off at the other end and piling them there would take another ½ minute. Handling time would then total 1 minute per case, at a cost of $.075 per case, with nothing extra added for distance.

A summary of the relative costs of these methods shows these costs per case:

	Handling Cost	*Travel Cost per 100 Feet*	*Total Cost for 100 Feet*	*Total Cost for 300 Feet*
Employee walking	$.05	$.03	$.08	$.14
Two-wheel truck	.10	.0075	.1075	.1225
Four-wheel truck	.10	.0025	.1025	.1075
Forklift truck	.053	.00083	.0538	.0555
Truck and pallets	.007	.00083	.0078	.0095
Conveyor	.075	.000	.075	.075

Figure 21–8 shows how these alternatives compare. It shows (rather dramatically) the cost savings possible from using palletized loads, which eliminates the costly handling of cases one by one. Figure 21–8 also shows that although the distance hauled adds to the cost, it is, at least for short distances, only a minor cost. The major costs are for the manual handling at each end.

Also, note the similarity of Figure 21–2 to Figure 2–2 in Chapter 2. Both show the break-even or crossover points among alternatives.

This example deals only with labor costs and assumes that the various kinds of equipment are already available at no extra cost. In a real-life problem the alternative equipment cost would have to be included and the total volume of cases

FIGURE 21–8

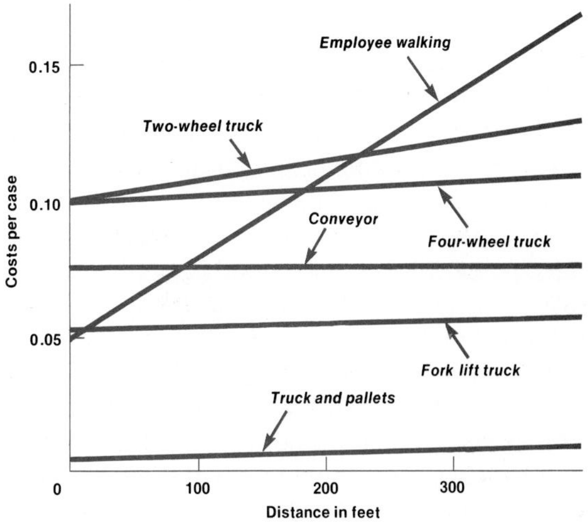

to be handled would also be a factor. For very low volumes it might pay to choose hand trucks rather than trucks and pallets.

FIXED VERSUS VARIED PATH EQUIPMENT

Equipment for moving materials may be divided into "fixed path" and "varied path" equipment. Varied path equipment (forklift trucks, for example) handles material in separate lots whereas fixed path equipment (such as conveyor belts) usually handles material continuously. Varied path equipment is flexible, and fixed path equipment is relatively inflexible. Fixed path equipment is more economical if large quantities of material follow the same path, but it is uneconomical if materials follow diverse paths. Varied path equipment must have portable power units for each piece of equipment, or each piece of equipment must be hauled by a worker. Fixed path equipment is usually driven electrically or, in the case of materials transported downward, by gravity.

Since fixed path equipment fixes the path that materials follow, it reduces the need for identification tags, separate work orders, and records of individual operations. Also, conveyors can be used to pace the worker; in assembly lines, workers must keep up with the work.

Fixed Path Equipment

Conveyors are the main kind of fixed path equipment for moving materials. Large facilities often use several miles of conveyors.

Conveyors can be put overhead, or at work level, or on the floor. Overhead conveyors generally operate by chain, cable, or connected links suspended from a monorail and have separate pans, hooks, or carrying cradles in which or on which materials are placed. Overhead conveyors are used primarily for horizontal transportation, but they can also go up or down to other floors. Generally, they move continuously rather than stop and go.

Both overhead and work-level conveyors are frequently an integral part of the producing process, and operations are often performed automatically or by a worker as the conveyor moves the material along. Painting, baking, cooling, cleaning, degreasing, electroplating, washing, and many other operations can be done in this way.

Conveyors are also often used in raw materials stockrooms and warehouses, where materials are stored on sloping roller conveyors. As they are demanded, quantities are released automatically by computer and electronic controls—as orders come in. The quantity slides off the storage conveyor onto a collecting conveyor which moves the items to an order makeup area. The savings possibilities are great where large numbers of items are stored and the volumes received and issued are high.

Fixed path conveyors at floor level are often used in assembling large products—for example, automobiles and farm tractors. Depending on the kind of conveyor used, the products may be set on the conveyor, or they may be towed or dragged by cable arranged below the floor. Most car washes use this method. Often wheeled cradles are attached to a tow line and materials are put in them. In still other cases, the frame of the product is fastened to the conveyor, and, as it moves down the line, parts are added to the frame. In the service sector, ski lifts, roller coasters, and department store escalators are also fixed path conveyors.

Automated batch manufacturing systems, like the one depicted in Chapter 19, use conveyors. Products are fastened in exact position to the conveyor at one end, which moves a fixed distance to the first machine and stops while the machine does its work. Then it takes the product to the next machine, where it stops again. This goes on until the product is completed. The conveyor is a very important part of this process, even though it is only supporting the automatic machines that do the operations.

Interestingly, Japanese manufacturers dislike using conveyor systems because they hold idle inventory; the quantity on a conveyor system at any point in time is variable (they like completely accurate counts of quantities); they say they are inflexible (they push inventory forward which is in contrast to the "pull" philosophy of Kanban); and they are expensive.[1]

Cranes are a second type of fixed path equipment for handling materials. Overhead cranes, operating on tracks running the entire length of a work bay, are common. They can service any point in an area, whether at floor level or above and whether it is accessible from aisles or not. They carry materials by means of hooks, buckets, or magnets. Large overhead cranes are operated by an operator in a suspended cage that is attached to the crane. Operators of smaller overhead cranes control them from the floor by means of suspended controls.

There are many other kinds of fixed path conveying equipment besides conveyors and cranes. Automatic and nonautomatic elevators are commonly used to move materials as well as people in multistory buildings. Chutes can frequently be used to advantage where material is moved downhill, but, if the materials can be easily damaged, the slope must be moderate. Pipes, ducts, and tubes are often used for bulk materials (particularly liquids). Air pressure and vacuum systems are used for dry bulk materials. Often entire materials handling systems are designed around the fixed size of the items being moved. For example, the shoe industry has its equipment designed to carry shoe boxes. This homogeneity of size allows for greater efficiencies in handling. In another example, luggage manufacturers have their fixed path in-process inventory handling system designed to carry parts around the plant in tote boxes about the size of a child's wagon.

Varied Path Equipment

Practically all moving equipment which can follow a varied path is some kind of truck. These trucks are generally four-wheel platform trucks which also must be loaded and unloaded manually. One variety of hand truck, the lift truck,

hoists previously loaded skids and eliminates the truck's being idle at loading and unloading points. Many variations of dolly trucks (a "dolly" is almost any kind of four-wheel carrying rack) and mobile racks are used. Some are especially designed for particular purposes and are generally used for short-distance moves. Even supermarket pushcarts are sometimes used. Today, most lift trucks that are used for heavy loads are powered by gasoline, propane, or electricity, although they require a trucker to operate the controls and guide them.

Hand trucking is generally confined to short-distance hauls, perhaps from a machine to temporary storage. Trucks that are powerd by gasoline motors or electric storage batteries and driven by truckers are faster and generally more economical for long hauls. Hand trucking is not only slow but, with heavy loads, somewhat unsafe. Truckers may try to pull overloads or may start and stop heavily loaded trucks too quickly and so may injure themselves. There is also more likelihood of damage to materials that are moved on hand trucks. Smooth and level floors are desirable for power trucking but are absolutely necessary for hand trucking. If hand trucks are used, elevators must be large enough to hold the trucks so as to move them from floor to floor. If power trucks are used, ramps can connect the floors. Where the path of transportation varies, most plants use powered and driver-operated industrial trucks.

Most industrial trucks have power-driven pickup devices. The metal forks in front of forklift trucks can be lowered almost to floor level and run under skids or pallets to hoist them and carry them to their destinations, then set them down on the floor or stack them on top of each other. This is done mechanically and fast. Although forklift trucks are very common, they require 12-foot aisles, which are wider than the aisles in some plants. Walking forklift trucks (where the trucker walks and guides the truck by a handle), being smaller and more maneuverable, require less room and can be used where aisles are narrower. One-way aisles can also be used.

Tractors and trailers are used by some com-

---

[1] R. J. Schonberger, *Japanese Manufacturing Techniques* (New York: Free Press, 1982), p. 142.

panies for the transportation of materials. The trailers can be parked and left to be loaded or unloaded whenever it is convenient. When they are to be moved, a trucker hooks them, one behind the other, to a power-driven truck and hauls them to their destination.

MATERIALS HANDLING DEVICES

The amount of materials handling for production operations is often reduced by mechanical lifting devices, such as jib cranes, chain hoists, compressed air hoists, block and tackle, and winches. Specialized devices at the machines include materials holding fixtures, magazine feeds, automatic product ejectors, welding positioners, elevating sheet-feed tables, and automatic scrap disposers. Robot fingers and arms are used wherever there is excessive heat, exposure to acid, or dangerous emissions of fumes or rays from processes or products.

Many kinds of devices are used to reduce the handling required to get materials on and off trucks and conveyors or transferred from one conveyor to another. They include up-enders, down-enders, turn-overs, rotators, transfer equipment, positioners for materials and platforms, regular and portable elevators, and conveyor unloaders. There are also many devices which permit the handling of loads rather than individual pieces. Tote boxes, skids, and pallets are universally used. Carrying cradles, wire baskets, collapsible wire containers, wirebound wood slat containers, sacks, and movable racks also are used. Steel strapping is sometimes used to hold loads or packs on their pallets. Tote boxes, skids, pallets, and other types of materials holders should be "tierable" even if special corner posts have to be provided.

AUTOMATIC GUIDANCE SYSTEMS

More and more companies are installing automatic guidance materials handling systems in their facilities—primarily in their warehouses.

Automatic guidance systems control the movement of specially designed trucks throughout the facility. Usually, though, an operator is still needed to operate the truck; but these systems—depending upon their sophistication—either aid or virtually eliminate the need for steering, for finding the location to put or retrieve the load, and to control the speed of the truck.

The two major types of automatic guidance are called *guide rail* and *guide wire* systems.[2]

Guide Rail Systems

Guide rail systems are mechanical and simply have rails mounted on the sides of the aisles which keep a truck on a controlled travel path by means of wheels which mesh with the rails—not unlike how a modern roller coaster is designed. And, like a roller coaster, trucks can travel at much higher speeds, while reducing materials handling costs, requiring less floor space for aisles, reducing accidents, and allowing the operator to concentrate on tasks and not on driving. While these systems are much less expensive than guide wire systems, they do require more judgment and decisions on the part of the operator (see Figure 21–9).

Guide Wire Systems

On the other hand, guide wire systems allow materials handling to be more fully automated. Electronic in nature, they consist of grids of wires buried in the aisles of the facility. These wires can "communicate" electronically (often through computers) with the truck and with the operator to determine its path, steer it, control its speed, determine where it is to stop next, and what to put where, or what and how many are to be "picked," and where to deliver them. Most guide wire systems do not have *all* of these capabilities, but they are becoming more prevalent each

---

[2] See "Automatic Guidance: Making Operators More Efficient," *Modern Materials Handling,* Spring 1978, pp. 58–61.

FIGURE 21–9

Order Picking in Stockrooms with Narrow Aisles and High-Rack Storage from a Truck Controlled by a Guide Rail System

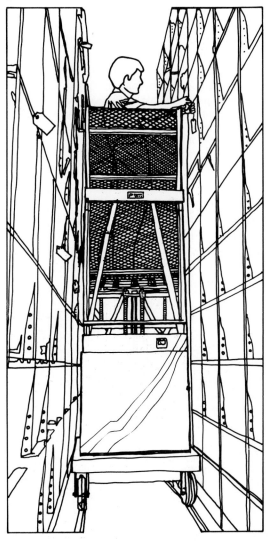

Robins Air Logistics Center at Robins Air Force Base in Georgia.[3] (See Figure 21–10).

This 320,000-square-foot facility contains 217,000 storage locations which hold about 200,000 different items.

The guide wire system, utilizing a variety of computers, microprocessors, and CRT terminals, performs the following tasks:

Assigns storage locations randomly, based on the size and quantity of each item.

Maintains complete inventory records.

Identifies parts for storage by "module" number, and by the shelf for each module.

Controls the speed, shortest path, and positioning of each orderpicking truck.

Receives requests for materials from remote data terminals.

Processes priority and routine pick requests simultaneously.

Arranges store and pick "lists" by location sequence.

Displays store and pick instructions on a CRT terminal on each orderpicking truck.

Generates a routing document for each picked part through a printer on each orderpicking truck.

Creates one of two types of shipping documents based on the exact quantity of each item picked and its destination.

Communicates with remote data processing equipment.[4]

AUTOMATED PARTS RETRIEVAL SYSTEMS

The job of retrieving or picking parts from inventory for assembly has been automated in many electronics firms and other firms as well. Often, tens of thousands of different electronic parts are in inventory, and, when a bill of materials

year because of their high economic benefits. They also save aisle space, require less labor, reduce mistakes and "lost" materials and parts, reduce damage, and are safer.

One example of the level of sophistication that computer-controlled guide wire systems have achieved is the system installed at Warner

---

[3] See "At Warner Robins Computers Control Just About Everything," *Modern Materials Handling,* May 1978, pp. 110–19.

[4] Ibid.

FIGURE 21–10
How Warner Robins Maintains Control through Every Step in Materials Flow

Information flow is controlled through a distributed controller network from the warehouse control room. There are four central processing units (CPU). One contains the master inventory files and is data-linked to the Air Force Base computer as well as to the second and third warehouse CPUs. The second CPU is an orderpicking truck controller. It communicates online with a microprocessor on each of the 19 orderpicking trucks and also controls the trucks' movements. The third CPU is a data-terminal controller which communicates with 40 data terminals—each with keyboard, CRT display, and card reader—in the warehouse and maintenance areas. The fourth CPU is a back-up unit. For local equipment control, microprocessors are installed at key points, and in all trucks along the materials flow path.

Materials flow at Receiving where incoming parts are put on conveyors to the module-loading area. There, filled modules are picked up by orderpicking trucks and moved to the warehouse to be stored. Operators stock and pick as they move through the aisles. Put-away commands for all items in the module are transferred to the truck's microprocessor as it enters the warehouse. Issue, or picking, commands are transmitted to the microprocessor as the truck enters each aisle. The central processor directs the truck to each storage location and causes stocking or picking commands to be displayed on a CRT. During picking, routing documents are printed and attached to the items. Items are then put on a take-away conveyor, to go to the issue station. There, shipping documents are printed, and items are sent to maintenance or shipping.

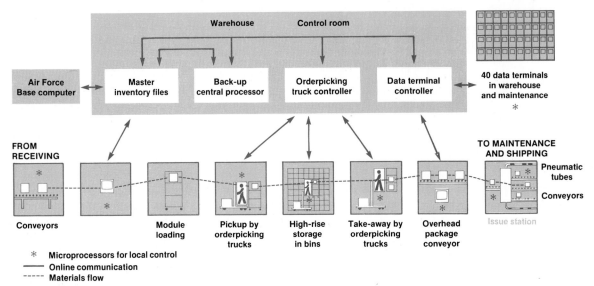

Source: Reprinted from *Modern Materials Handling,* May 1978, pp. 112–13. Copyright 1978 by Cahners Publishing Company. Division of Reed Holdings, Inc.

is exploded which requires several hundred or thousand parts, they must be pulled from inventory and sent to assembly. Modern computer-based retrieval systems can be operated by just a few workers. Here is the sequence of what a typical computerized parts retrieval system does: First, the computer receives information from the MRP computer for "planned order releases" which indicate how many of each part are to be pulled, and when. The computer dis-

plays the part number, a description, and the quantity required on a CRT in front of the storage facility. The operator pushes a button, and a retrieval device moves down to the correct isle, then goes down the isle and up to the correct tier. It stops, retrieves a standard-sized tote box with the parts in it, brings it down to the operator, where the requested number of parts are removed and put in a container (or often just a plastic bag for small parts). The computer prints out an identification tag which is attached to the part(s), and it is placed on a conveyor which sends it to the material movers. When the entire order of parts has been pulled, the mover takes the "kit" of parts to the assembly staging area. The system then returns the tote box to its location and deducts the amount of parts on hand by the amount pulled. These systems can have several "movers" going simultaneously, so the operator is continuously picking from tote boxes and not waiting for the system to retrieve the boxes. Interestingly, the operator is occasionally asked by the computer system to do an actual count of the items remaining in the tote box (after the pick). The quantity counted is keyed in and compared with the computer's count, and where there are differences, the balances are revised. This is an automated form of "cycle counting," as discussed in Chapter 8.

Review Questions

1. If a company's estimates show that it can save 10 percent of its direct labor costs by building a new factory, should it go ahead and build or not? Why?

2. When a company is planning to build a new factory, should it make improvements in the old plant, or should it wait until it gets into the new plant?

3. Obviously, a new facility is built only if it will allow for more effective operations. Where do these savings come from?

4. What trends are taking place in the design of facilities?

5. What things can organizations do to provide security to their facilities? Their processes and formulas?

6. What are the four basic layout patterns for facilities? What are the advantages of each? When should each be used?

7. How should a company's practice of producing by lots or continuously be related to the layout pattern used in the facility? Why?

8. What steps do layout engineers follow in devising a factory's layout if they use the travel chart method?

9. Compare (give good and bad points) of using fixed and varied path materials moving equipment.

10. In general, are costs higher for moving materials over considerable distances or for handling them at both ends of a move?

11. What are the pros and cons of using tractors and trailers to move materials? Where are they most suitable? Where are they poorly suited?

12. How does it happen that many companies do not really know what it costs to move products around and to handle them?

13. How are computers being used in materials handling?

Questions for Discussion

1. The engineer for the construction company which wants to convince a company to build a new plant has just looked over the present layout. "Your layout is very poor and is no doubt resulting in your costs being from 8 to 10 percent more than they should be," he tells the company president. How can anyone tell if the layout is poor?

2. If the engineer in question 1 says the present layout is quite inflexible as one piece of evidence that it is poor, how important is this? Does inflexibility matter today? He says that if his company were to build the new plant, it would build in flexibility. How does one "build in" flexibility?

3. Under what conditions should the layout be based on moving the workers and not the products? What diseconomies would this method cause?

4. When, if ever, should a factory's offices be put on mezzanines rather than on the ground floor?

5. Are methods for laying-out services similar to those for manufacturing?

6. How should an analyst go about the task of producing an estimate of the costliness of a company's materials handling?

7. Suppose that the analyst in the question above is also asked to develop a program for reducing the costs of materials handling. How should he go about this assignment?

8. Under what conditions should things be moved to people? People moved to things?

Problems

1. A company needs to expand and is considering a metal prefab, a wooden building, and a cinderblock building. The figures are as follows:

	Metal Prefab	Wooden Building	Cinder-block Building
Initial cost	$10,000	$12,000	$25,000
Years of expected useful life	10	20	30
Annual maintenance	400	300	150
Interest cost	18%	18%	18%

Which type of construction should be chosen, and how much will this type save as against the other methods?

2. What would it cost to build a factory for 750 workers who need 450 square feet of space each? (Service areas take additional space equal to 40 percent of the space needed per worker.) There is no need to build a building with many fancy trimmings, but on the other hand, there is need for something better than the simplest construction.

3. Suppose, in problem 2, that land was an additional capital cost and is $10,000 per acre (43,560 square feet) and that the company wants a 4-to-1 ratio (land space total is to be 4 times the new building space). What will the real estate tax be on the land and building (not including machinery or inventories) if appraisals are about 40 percent of the costs, and the rate is $3 per $100 of valuation?

4. Suppose, in problem 3, that land costs $20,000 an acre, and the tax rate is $3.25 per $100 of valuation (valuation being 50 percent of true market value). Labor costs $12 an hour in both cases, but in the second case labor is more efficient. How much more efficient would labor have to be to make these two choices equal so far as taxes are concerned?

5. An air-conditioning company estimates that it will cost $4 a square foot to install air conditioning and $2 per square foot a year to operate it on the days when it will be needed. The equipment will have a 10-year life. Money is worth 15 percent.

This company claims that air conditioning will cut labor turnover by half (it is now 25 percent per year, and each turnover is estimated to cost $1,000). The air-conditioning company also claims that labor productivity will go up 5 percent.

At the Roy Company, workers earn $9 an hour and are provided with 350 square feet per worker. People work $2,000 hours a year.

a. On the basis of these figures, should Roy put in air conditioning?

b. Roy's managers suspect that the air-conditioning company is exaggerating and that the savings will only be half of those claimed. If this were so, what would the answer be?

c. Suppose, on the other hand, that Roy's managers believe they will get the gains but that air conditioning will cost 50 percent more than they have been told. Is the answer the same? Show the figures.

d. If the savings estimates are accepted, but the turnover reductions are not believed, how much productivity gain will be required to break even on installing air conditioning?

e. Because business is picking up, Roy is hiring more workers and expects soon to have one worker for every 250 square feet. What would the answer be for this worker density?

6. The following departments are to be fitted into a 200-by-300-foot building which is being bought. The building has a railroad spur along the west side, the long side, of the building. Along the tracks is a loading platform for both rail and truck traffic. It is outside the building and not part of the space allocation problem. The layout has to meet the following space requirements inside the building:

	Department	Space (square feet)
A	Receiving	750
B	Raw materials storeroom	1,500
C	Manufactured parts storeroom	1,250
D	Subassemblies storeroom	3,000
E	Finished products storeroom	3,750
F	Supplies storeroom	1,000
G	Machine shop I	200′ × 30′
H	Machine shop II	150′ × 45′
J	Bench operation	50′ × 45′
K	Subassembly I	150′ × 45′
L	Subassembly II	70′ × 50′
M	Final assembly*	245′ × 50′
N	Packing and shipping	2,500

* Includes 3,000 square feet for subassembly storeroom department D.

	Department	Space (square feet)
P	Production and engineering office	1,200
Q	Factory manager's office	400
R	Cost accounting office	1,700
S	General accounting office	1,700
T	General offices	2,400
U	Secretary and treasurer's office	300
V	Vice president and general manager's office	400
W	President's office	600
X	Sales office	1,100
Y	Purchasing and traffic office	825
Z	Personnel	625
AA	Reception room for departments Y and Z	750

Lay out the departmental arrangement on a scale of 1 inch = 40 feet.

7. The new engineers, recently hired, are crowded for office space. It has been necessary to put them five to an office. Since the offices are only 16 by 20 feet, they are somewhat crowded. The average salary of these engineers is $20,000. More space can be built for $40 a square foot. Newly built space would have a life of 25 years and would then be worth 10 percent of its original cost. Taxes, insurance, maintenance, and interest cost 10 percent a year. Janitor service, heating, and lighting cost $3 per square foot.

How much would the productivity of the engineers have to increase to justify assigning four, three, two or one to a 16-by-20 foot office?

8. Three alternative plans for a revised layout show the following expected results:

	A	B	C
Initial investment	$8,000	$10,000	$13,000
Annual saving	2,200	2,600	3,200

The new layout will probably be used for five years before it will be changed. The hurdle rate is 12 percent.

a. Which plan should be chosen?

b. How much higher an internal rate of return will the selected plan yield than the other two alternatives?

9. The Midland Insurance Company needs a new layout which will meet the following conditions. The problem is to suggest a general pattern and arrangement of departments which facilitates face-to-face communication and minimizes walking time of people from department to department. Department sizes are to be approximately as follows:

Department	Size (square feet)
A	3,000
B	7,500
C	6,000
D	2,500
E	3,500
F	4,500

On the average, the face-to-face communication requirements between departments every day are as follows:

From	To	Number of Contacts
A	B	22
A	C	11
A	D	1
A	E	5
A	F	6
B	A	4
B	C	15
B	D	6
B	E	7
B	F	2
C	A	1
C	B	6
C	D	6
C	E	3
C	F	9
D	E	1
D	F	10
E	B	2
E	F	12
F	B	2
F	C	3

Assuming Midland uses movable office partitions and modules, draw a proposed office layout for a single-story rectangular building that can be nearly square but should not be long and narrow. Do not worry about aisles.

Indicate how many contacts will have to pass between nonadjacent departments. Do not, however, make departments into corkscrew shapes just so they will touch many other departments.

10. The analysis of work loads at the Exo Company has proceeded to the point where the area requirements for each work center have been established. These space needs are:

Work Center	Department Number	Square Feet
Centering	1	1,000
Mill	2	5,000
Lathe	3	6,000
Drill	4	3,000
Arbor press	5	1,000
Grinder	6	2,000
Shaper	7	2,000
Heat treat	8	1,500
Paint	9	1,000
Bench assembly	10	1,000
Inspect	11	500
Pack	12	1,000

a. What handling methods would you choose for various distances that materials are to be moved?

b. What other considerations should be factored into these alternatives?

12. The Dow Company, to remove cases of bottled detergents from the end of the container line, has to build pallet loads for fork lift trucks. Cases may contain 9, 12, and 24 plastic or glass bottles. Because plastic and glass bottles differ in shape, they take different amounts of handling time. This information is available about the operation:

Type of Case	Handling Time (in hours) per 100 Cases		Annual Volume (thousand cases)		Cases per Load	
	Plastic	Glass	Plastic	Glass	Plastic	Glass
9-bottle	.286	.536	1,125	130	75	45
12-bottle	.286	.386	2,500	550	84	50
24-bottle	.327	.410	2,400	410	70	42

Production in those departments is confined to the following seven products, which are "routed" through these departments in the sequence shown:

Product	Units per Month	Units per Load	Routing Sequence
A	500	2	4,7,8,10,11,12
B	500	100	1,3,8,4,6,2,11,3,10,12
C	1,600	40	1,2,4,6,3,11,10,12
D	1,200	40	4,10,2,12
E	400	100	4,6,10,5,12
F	800	100	3,9,10,12
G	400	2	1,2,3,4,5,6,7,8,9,10,11,12

Using the method described in this chapter, develop a proposed arrangement and layout of departments for the new plant expansion. Aim for a rectangular plant.

11. Suppose that the data for the materials handling example under "Economics of Manual Handling" in this chapter were as follows:

	Handling Cost	Travel Cost per 100 Feet
Employee walking	$.07	$.03
Two-wheel truck	.10	.0075
Four-wheel truck	.10	.0025
Fork lift truck	.08	.00083
Truck and pallets	.09	.00083
Conveyor	.075	.000

The employees who do this work are paid $7.40 per hour (plus fringe benefit costs of 25 percent more), and fork lift truck time (including pay for the trucker) is calculated as $10 per hour. It takes .078 hour per load to haul loads from the conveyor to the point of shipment.

There are two ways to mechanize this load-building work, and either method would eliminate the employees now building truck loads. One is to use a 3-lane accumulating unit system capable of handling all kinds of plastic bottles and the 12- and 24-glass bottle cases (9-unit glass bottle cases would be continued as at present). The second alternative uses 4 accumulating lanes and can handle all 6 combinations. The automatic load accumulators would be located closer to the point of shipment and would reduce trucking time to .043 hour per load.

The automatic methods would require one full-time employee (2,000 hours a year at $7.50 per hour) to attend each lane and would cause the following additional annual costs:

	3 Lanes	4 Lanes
Maintenance	$9,300	$10,200
Extra insurance and taxes	1,080	1,200

The installed cost of the 3-lane arrangement is $312,000 and that of the 4-lane arrangement is $336,000. The equipment life is calculated at 15 years with no salvage value. The hurdle rate is 12 percent.

Should Dow put in either of the proposed automated load accumulators? What would be their internal rate of return on the investment?

13. A conveyor costing $3,500 to connect operations A and B would save half an hour a day of labor which costs $7.30/hour. It would also boost the productivity of machines A and B by 5 percent. Machine operating time is $12 an hour. Will this conveyor pay for itself in one 2,000-hour (250-day) year? What first-year rate of return will the conveyor yield on this investment?

14. The Sunbeam Company wants to know how many pallets to buy and whether to leave loads on them in storage, thus tying them up, or to unload them and keep them circulating. For the purpose of this calculation, it is not necessary to consider whether the materials are to be kept in stock very long. It is to be assumed that, so far as pallets are concerned, this is a matter of buying more pallets versus unloading them. The relevant figures are:

Cost per pallet	$5
Pallet life	5 years
Pallet maintenance	$.03 per use
Space costs	$.08 per cubic foot per year
Pallet size when loaded	48″ × 40″ × 6″ (loaded pallet occupies 6.7 cubic ft.)
Cost to unload and load	$.50
Total loads per year	1,000

How many pallets should Sunbeam have? How much floor space will be needed? How long will the pallets stay in storage?

Chapter 22

Designing Repetitive Production Facilities

The high-volume repetitive assembly of products from components parts is a mix of manual and machine operations. People attach parts and components manually or with the aid of portable hand tools and specialized machinery (such as welding robots) as the product moves by them down assembly lines.

ADVANTAGES OF ASSEMBLY LINE LAYOUT

The main advantage of an assembly line (product-oriented layout pattern, as described in Chapter 21) is its low cost per unit, provided there is enough volume and standardization. Low costs result from the use of automatic fast-production equipment, and, because of the use of fixed routes for materials, almost everything can be moved quickly by conveyor. Materials handling costs, travel distances, and storage space can be reduced substantially. Production-control paperwork is also simplified. And the comparatively simple machine-tending jobs simplify the training of new workers. Supervision is also easier since the jobs are routine and supervisors can oversee larger numbers of subordinates. In economic terms, these advantages usually far outweigh the disadvantages of lines.

DISADVANTAGES OF ASSEMBLY LINE LAYOUT

There are, however, several disadvantages. The large investment in special-purpose machines requires high volume in order to achieve low unit costs. Furthermore, a product layout with continuous manufacture is vulnerable to stoppages because there is usually only enough storage room for small supplies of products between operations. When work stops at any point, everything stops quickly. Also, the rate of output is quite inflexible. The only way to get more output is by working the entire line overtime or by putting on more shifts. To reduce output, the entire line goes on short hours.

Product design changes often cause problems. Such changes change operations and operation sequences. They may reduce or eliminate the work of some work stations or they may add to the work of other stations. The whole line may have to be restructured. Because this is costly, desirable changes in the design of products may not be made as often as they should be.

Continuous production does not handle product variety easily. Variety upsets the exact work assignments at work stations. Some automobiles have tinted glass windshields, others do not; some have blue wheels, some white, and so on. Some Samsonite luggage has brown covers, some red. Even small variations in finished products make a great deal of extra production control work. The continual inflow of parts and components to the assembly line must be carefully directed and monitored. The flows of parts and components to assembly lines have to be carefully coordinated, not only as to quantity, but also as to type, kind, and sequence.

Parts must also fit. It is not possible to rework parts along an assembly line. And even laying aside a nonfitting part and using the next one is often not possible because the exact sequencing of arrival of parts (blue doors to match a blue car body, for example) would be upset.

The capital investment is usually high in product layouts because of the special-purpose machines and conveyors. Also, even though a machine may only be needed part of the time, it is often necessary to commit an entire machine, even though similar machines are also used part time elsewhere in the plant. And because entire sets of operations are tied together, line production is often not suitable for incentive pay systems, unless the incentive is tied to the performance of the entire group working on the line. Samsonite does, in fact, use a group incentive pay plan for the workers on its luggage assembly line.

There can also be problems with labor. Absenteeism is hard to handle since every work station *must* be staffed and with one or more employees who can keep up with the line's pace even though the task may be new to the replacement employee. It is necessary to anticipate absenteeism by having a few extra employees on the payroll just for fill-ins.

The highly repetitive work along assembly lines also does not appeal to everybody. And most of the jobs are machine-paced, which some workers find objectionable. There are, however, several possibilities for designing assembly line jobs which "enlarge" or "enrich" them and make them a little more interesting.

Behind-the-scenes labor costs are also generally high. The operators who tend the ma-

chines are relatively few, but they are only a part of total labor costs. Machine designers, methods engineers, setup mechanics, materials supply and maintenance people, and others add substantially to these costs.

Perhaps the most important problem in line production is to align the jobs so that they all require almost identical times to perform because the output of a line is limited to that of the individual "bottleneck" work station which takes the most time. If one work station assignment takes more time than the others, its rate of output will determine the line's maximum production. Workers at other work stations with shorter work assignments will be underutilized. It becomes highly important, therefore, to try to develop equal work assignments for every work station. This is called *line balancing.*

AUTOMOBILE ASSEMBLY JOB DESIGN

In General Motors' Willow Run plant outside Detroit, Walter Jones, at work station 15, picks up a long, slender metal tube which is bent into an odd shape. Jones fastens this tube with four clips to the underside of a Chevrolet automobile body that is hanging from an overhead conveyor as it slowly passes over his head. The tube is part of the car's hydraulic brake system, and the bends in it allow it to follow the contours of the underside of the car.

Jones does not, however, fasten either end of the tube to anything, because this is not part of his job. Fastening the ends is part of someone else's job, because either (1) Jones already has all the work he can handle (this is true in any case, because if Jones fastened the ends he would *not* do some of the other work he now does), or (2) the parts that the hydraulic tube is to be fastened to are not on the car yet, or (3) Jones's working position would make it hard or awkward for him to do the fastening, whereas some other worker farther down the line can do it more easily.

Jones has a collection of small tasks to perform on every car that passes by him at the rate of one a minute. His collection of tasks adds up to enough to keep him busy for about one minute (probably a little less, but definitely not more than one minute).

Jones does not have the work station to himself; he works only on the left underside of the Chevrolet. Jill Hamett, who works at the same station, works only on the right underside.

Neither Jones nor Hamett is hurrying with the task, yet each works steadily. The duties which make up each person's one-minute job package were selected to add up to almost one minute's work when he or she works steadily, yet not at a rapid pace. (Employees on a typical automobile assembly line are allowed two 23-minute paid breaks per 8-hour shift besides the 30-minute lunch break, which is unpaid. Besides this, relief workers—one for each seven on the line—fill in from time to time.)

A visitor walking along this assembly line would find everybody working at about the same pace. At every work station people, sometimes one, sometimes two, perform their near one-minute collection of tasks as cars move down the line by conveyor. And as the conveyor moves, the Chevrolet begins to look more and more like a finished car as more parts are added. Somewhere along the way, someone fastens one end of the hydraulic brake tube to the car's master brake cylinder, and someone else fastens the other end to the brake for a wheel.

17/3/85

RATE OF OUTPUT AND NUMBER OF WORK STATIONS

To justify the use of assembly lines for production, the demand must be rather high. If, for example, there is need for 2,000 assembled products a week, they probably should be produced by the line production method. The line could be designed to turn out about one unit a minute. (Although there are 2,400 minutes in a 40-hour week, some time is lost for rest breaks and starting and stopping each day.)

Both the people and the machines along the line would be geared to work one minute on each unit of product, so that the total work to be done would have to be broken up into one-minute jobs. If, in total, it took 120 minutes to assemble a product, this work might well be divided into, say, 130 slightly-less-than-1-minute jobs. The plan, then, could be for a line with 130 work stations, because the bits and pieces of work which are to average one minute or less may not sum exactly to one minute, or because their work time may vary a little. (See Figure 22–1.)

So, the first step in determining work station assignments is to determine the workload of the line. The number of units required per hour, multiplied by the labor-hours required per unit, gives the total labor-hour workload per clock hour. So, if it takes a total of 2 labor-hours, or 120 labor-minutes of assembly time per unit of product, and 60 units an hour are required, something like 130 employee-hours must be provided along the line every hour.

The matter of line speed and job cycle time is discussed later in this chapter; here, however, it should be said again that line production usually is not very satisfactory for low production—say 25 units per week. In such a case each person would have nearly an hour-and-a-half job, assignment on every unit. Proficiency at doing all of the small tasks in this hour-and-a-half assignment would probably be low. It would be better to use job shop production for only 25 units a week rather than set up an assembly line.

Cycle Times and Number of Work Stations

It is also necessary to determine the cycle-time and number-of-work-stations (or work zones) relationships. If 60 units an hour are required in the example above, 65 work stations through which 1 unit of product moves every minute would do the job, provided that there were two people at every work station, each with almost a 1-minute collection of duties.

But a 65-work-station arrangement is not the

FIGURE 22–1
Assembling Refrigerators and Freezers at Whirlpool, Where the Minor Tasks Add
Up to Nearly Full Use of the Operators' Time *(average 82 percent)*

**A. Putting insulation on cold plate tubing
(79.2 percent)**

**B. Driving 3 screws in shelf and liner
(94.8 percent)**

**C. Installing crisper pan
(85.5 percent)**

**D. Positioning suction line in clips
(69.3 percent)**

only alternative to the 130-work-stations with 1 employee at each. Another choice would be to have 80 or 90 stations with one worker at some stations and two workers at others. Or the line could have 45 stations with three people at most of them. Or, if the assemblers would not get in each other's way, there could be fewer stations with more people.

It is also possible to change the cycle time. There could be two lines with 30 units coming off each line per hour. This would double the amount of specialized equipment needed, but it would open up other possibilities of line speed, number of stations, and number of people at each station. In any case, there are many possible choices and not just one or two.

When the cycle-time and number-of-work-stations relationships have been decided, this automatically sets both the line speed and the amount of space which will be needed along the line. If the products are automobiles and one per minute is required, it may be necessary to provide as much as 25 feet per work station along the conveyor. And the conveyor will have to move at a rate of 25 feet per minute. Assuming two workers each, at 65 stations, at least 65 × 25 feet (or 1,625 feet) of work space, will be needed for the line.

But, if a line normally moves 25 feet during the minute it is a good idea to allot a little more than 25 feet to the station. Then, if one of the assemblers needs to stay with the product a little longer, he or she can do so. This gives a little latitude in balancing out the long and short work cycles. It also gives the job designer the opportunity to assign employees work packages which contain almost a full minute's work instead of something less. In addition, space between stations may also be needed to provide for storage of parts or for other reasons.

The discussion so far has assumed that the number of work stations and the space required can be determined as the first step in setting up a line. This is not always the case, however, because the exact number of work stations and the number of assemblers needed must await the development of "work packages" for each employee. This is because the final number of workers and work stations depends on how the work tasks are combined into work packages. We will see later that there can be complications here, depending upon the sequence in which the assembly tasks must be performed.

Desirability of a Single Line

It might seem that when a total assembly job is made up of a thousand or more small elements of work which add up to 120 minutes there would be an almost limitless number of combinations of how these tasks can be made into work station assignments.

At one extreme, one person could do the entire job. In this case it would seem that 130 or so assemblers could be working at the same time, each assembling a complete product. At the other extreme, 130 or so people (or even more with still shorter assignments) could each be doing just about one minute's work on each product as it passes a work station. Between these extremes there could be any number of combinations. There could be, for example, 24 people each doing 5 minutes of work on every 24th product in one place along the line, or there could be individual workers doing 2 minutes of work on every second unit, or there could be only 40 assemblers along a line, each doing 3 minutes work on every third product, and so on.

A moment's thought, however, reveals how impractical almost every other possible combination is when compared to a line with each person doing about one minute's work. Other arrangements usually multiply both materials handling costs and tooling costs, and this must be considered when evaluating more complex line configurations.

If 130 people each made entire products, supplies of the hundreds of parts would all have to be brought to each of the 130 work stations. At each work station, therefore, there would have to be bins for each of these hundreds of parts, and they would have all to be replenished from time to time.

Each worker would also need every tool that would be required for assembling the complete product. They would need nut and bolt tighteners, soldering irons, riveters, and everything else. If any operation needed special work area conditions, such as heat removal from welding, each work place would have to have this too. One hundred and thirty sets of everything would have to be provided!

Truckers would also have to truck away finished units: 1 every 2 hours from 130 different work stations, or else let them pile up. In any case, the inventories of parts and finished products and the materials handling costs would be exorbitant.

When all these factors are considered, the *economical* choice is almost always one production line, with each worker doing a part of the total work and doing it on every unit. No one else does this work. Each element of work belongs to a single employee's work assignment. However, other considerations such as "job enlargement" or "job enrichment" programs (which are discussed in Chapter 25) sometimes make it necessary to make some concessions in order to reduce extreme boredom and monotony.

INFORMATION NEEDED FOR DEVELOPING WORK PACKAGES

Before work packages can be developed to balance work assignments along an assembly line, it is necessary to gather certain information. The kind of information needed is the same for washing machines, television sets, automobiles, or whatever. We will continue to use automobiles as an example.

Defining Task Elements

First, it is necessary to make a list of every minor task required to assemble a car. As was said earlier, "minor" means job elements as short as 5/100 or 10/100 of a minute, not 2- or 3-minute job parts. This list may well run into thousands of minor tasks (which a time study analyst calls *elements*). The list must also show how much time it will take a person to perform each element. All of these things need to be known before work station assignments are developed and long before any cars have been assembled along the line.

Yet how can an industrial engineer know ahead of time what minor tasks have to be done in order to assemble a washing machine or an automobile? And how can he know before a line is set up just how long each element will take? For the most part the engineers who do this work rely on past experience with similar products to provide this information because the work on this year's products is often much like that on last year's models.

If, however, a company is going into totally

new kinds of products, this is a difficult task. Here, companies often assemble a few pilot items in an experimental area so the methods engineers can learn as much as they can from seeing the work done.

In any case, the engineers try to visualize the sequence of how the work is going to be done along the line and they develop the list of tasks it takes to do the entire job. Then they try to determine about how long it will take to do each part of the whole task. (Chapter 27 will discuss how industrial engineers do this, using catalogs of scientifically determined data on how long it takes to perform basic human movements.)

Determining Element Precedence

Some tasks, or elements, have to be done before others, whereas in other cases it doesn't matter. A man putting on his clothes in the morning has to put on his shirt before his tie, but it doesn't matter whether he combs his hair and then puts on his shoes or the other way around.

And it is the same with cars and television sets. Sometimes the element sequence matters and sometimes it doesn't. A hole has to be drilled before it can be threaded, and an automobile wheel has to be put on before the bolts that hold it can be put on. But it doesn't matter whether a storage battery is installed before or after the carburetor or whether a front wheel goes on before a back wheel. The order of sequence is sometimes "must do" and at other times is "can do," depending on the situation.

"Must do" is a positive and a negative restraint at the same time. The wheel must be put on the car before its bolts can go on. Similarly, the bolts cannot be put on ("must not do") until the wheel is on.

All "can do" elements finally become "must do." It doesn't matter whether a front wheel goes on before a back wheel or the other way around; they are "can do" with respect to each other. And in the early stages of assembly, it doesn't matter when the steering wheel is put in. But,

FIGURE 22-2

Zoning sketch indicating possible zones for assembly operations along a conveyor. (Conditions for a specific situation will determine "can do" for a given work element in several zones or "must do" in a particular zone.)

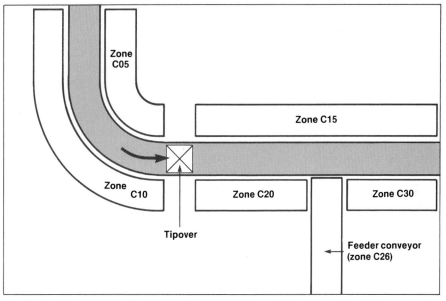

Source: General Electric Company.

finally, and well before the car is finished, the steering wheel has to be installed.

Often it is a good idea to think of "must do," "must not do," and "can do" elements as they apply to zones or general areas along the line rather than as they relate to particular work stations. An element may well be "must not do" for early zones (a car can't be washed until it is assembled); then it may become "can do" for several zones; and, finally, if it has not been assigned earlier, it is "must do" for some particular zone. (See Figure 22-2.)

Sometimes there are "must not do" constraints because of the nature of the work. Some elements are dirty whereas others are clean, and they should be kept apart. The car should not be greased, for example, adjacent to putting in the upholstery.

HEURISTIC LINE BALANCING

Years ago it was a tedious task for engineers to determine the balance between assemblers' assignments along production lines so that they were equally busy and so that everything was kept moving evenly. The engineers had to make long lists of the 5/100- and 10/100-of-a-minute elements of the total task of assembling a car. Then, mindful of the sequence in which elements had to be performed (the windshield trim could not be put in place until the windshield was installed) and how long the minor tasks took, they developed work packages of close-to-one-minute duration for the assemblers who were to work along the line.

Today this method has not changed, but it is no longer the tedious task it used to be because computer programs are available to analyze the millions of possible combinations which exist in assembling a complex item like an automobile.

Computers do not, however, search out every possible combination of the thousands of elemental tasks before settling on certain collections of tasks which become the work packages along the line. Instead, they search for near-perfect collections or "bundles" of elemental tasks. This is called a *heuristic* (trial-and-error, with guiding rules) approach. In a heuristic approach, once the computer finds a near-perfect set of tasks, it sets these tasks apart as the job assignment for work station 1, then it does the same for work station 2, and so on down the line.

The computer also does not just take the first duties it comes to which add up to less than or equal to the limit time (which in our example is one minute). If these happen to add to .65 minute and the next element considered takes .40 minute, it would reject the .40-minute element for the moment because this element would make the work package exceed 1 minute. The computer does not "close" the package at .65 minute because this would leave the work station with .35 minute of idle time. Instead, the computer sets the .40-minute activity aside momentarily while it searches for other short-time elements to bring the work assignment for work station 1 up to or close to a minute. When it can find no more elements which fit within a minute, it regards the assignment for work station 1 as complete and sets it aside. Next the computer may return to the .40-minute activity and use it as the first part of the assignment it will develop for work station 2, if this is one of the heuristic rules the program follows.

In heuristic procedures the computer is programmed to follow logical rules, such as task element A must come before B, work on the frame of the car must be done before the body shell goes on, work on the top of a car should not be combined with work on the bottom, the total time in a job assignment cannot add up to more than a minute, and so on. The computer

is given all of these instructions; then its job is to find combinations of task elements which fit the restrictions.

Electronic Calculator Assembly Example

The assembly of a small hand-held calculator will illustrate how job packages are developed. A listing is first made of the assembly task elements, their required time, and their assembly precedence requirements. These are shown in Figure 22–3. Element 1 takes .2 minute and has no predecessor elements. Element 2 takes .4 minute and cannot be started until element 1 is completed. This means that both can be done at the same work station or that element 2 can be performed later. Figure 22–4 shows in schematic form the sequential relationships that are listed in Figure 22–3.

We will suppose that an output of approximately 65 units per hour is required, and the plan is to produce them all on one assembly line. This translates into a maximum work package time, or job cycle, for each job station of approximately .9 minute per unit, (60 minutes per hour/65 units per hour = .92 minute per unit at each work station). Thus, our objective is to assign task elements to work stations such

FIGURE 22–3
Data for Calculator Assembly Example

Task Element	Element Time (minutes)	Preceding Elements
1	.2	—
2	.4	1
3	.7	1
4	.3	2
5	.8	3
6	.6	3
7	.2	4
8	.2	4
9	.8	5
10	.3	6
11	.5	6
12	.1	7,8
13	.3	10,11
14	.6	9,12,13
Total	6.0	

FIGURE 22-4

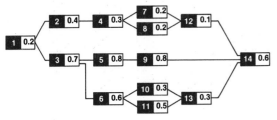

that the maximum time of every station assignment is less than or equal to .9 minute.

A simple solution like our example can be solved without the aid of a computer. All one has to do is, through trial and error, try different combinations until a combination is developed which minimizes the number of stations and the slack time of assemblers. This is shown in Figure 22–5. There are seven work stations, and a total of .3 minute of idle or slack time among stations 3, 5, and 8. In an hour, 65 units representing 390 minutes of work will be finished by seven workers putting in 420 minutes of time. So this arrangement is 93 percent efficient (390/420), and, if assembly labor costs $9 per hour, direct labor per unit is: ($9/60) × (420/65) = $.97.

Using the Computer

Although this problem was solved manually without a computer, we ran it on one to generate work station assignments for two other production rates: 75 per hour and 46 per hour. The computer output for these two rates and for the original problem of 65 per hour is shown in Figure 22–6.

At 75 per hour, the computer arrived at 9 work stations combining elements as shown in

Figure 22–6. This results in .8-minute work station cycles. In an hour, 9 workers put in 540 minutes and do 75 × 6.00 = 450 minutes of work. This arrangement would be 83 percent efficient.

The 46-per-hour rate produced a 5-station solution with a 1.3 minute work station cycle time. It combined elements as shown in Figure 22–6. In an hour, 5 workers put in 300 minutes and do 276 minutes of work, resulting in a 92 percent efficient layout.

With computers it is easy for the analyst to investigate a large number of interrelationships and to compare their costs. It is only necessary to have good estimates of labor times and the costs of operating the work stations, including tools, conveyors, and so on.

As mentioned earlier, sometimes a given heuristic analysis does not arrange the minor tasks into the very best combinations. Once a minor task is assigned to a work package for job 1, for example, the computer regards this as disposed of and does not consider it in its further searching. It removes all job 1 duties from its list of remaining duties and goes on to search for another set of duties for the next work station.

Unless all of the millions of possible combinations are analyzed (which is impractical) a perfect set of job assignments is not guaranteed. The perfect set might, for example, require assignment of some of the elements initially put into job assignment 1 elsewhere, where they would fit even better, enable the reduction of work stations, or reduce slack time.

Heuristic Priority Choice Rules

In order for the computer to do a good job of developing work station assignments, it is neces-

FIGURE 22-5
Work stations

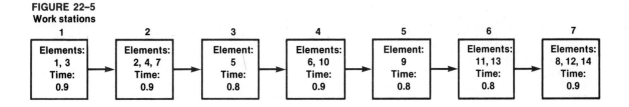

FIGURE 22–6

LINE BALANCING

INITIAL CONDITIONS:

PRECEDENCE RESTRICTIONS		TIME TO COMPLETE EACH TASK	
1	2	1	.2
1	3	2	.4
2	4	3	.7
3	5	4	.3
3	6	5	.8
4	7	6	.6
4	8	7	.2
5	9	8	.2
6	10	9	.8
6	11	10	.3
7	12	11	.5
8	12	12	.1
10	13	13	.3
11	13	14	.6
9	14		
12	14		
13	14		

FOR A CYCLE TIME OF .8
AND AN OUTPUT RATE OF 75

STATION NUMBER	TASKS TO BE COMPLETED			TOTAL TIME	SLACK TIME
1	1	2	0	0.60	0.20
2	3	0	0	0.70	0.10
3	5	0	0	0.80	0.00
4	9	0	0	0.80	0.00
5	6	0	0	0.60	0.20
6	11	4	0	0.80	0.00
7	10	13	7	0.80	0.00
8	8	12	0	0.30	0.50
9	14	0	0	0.60	0.20

FOR A CYCLE TIME OF .92
AND AN OUTPUT RATE OF 65

STATION NUMBER	TASKS TO BE* COMPLETED			TOTAL TIME	SLACK TIME
1	1	3	0	0.90	0.02
2	5	0	0	0.80	0.12
3	9	0	0	0.80	0.12
4	6	10	0	0.90	0.02
5	11	2	0	0.90	0.02
6	13	4	7	0.80	0.12
7	8	12	14	0.90	0.02

FOR A CYCLE TIME OF 1.3
AND AN OUTPUT RATE OF 46

STATION NUMBER	TASKS TO BE COMPLETED			TOTAL TIME	SLACK TIME
1	1	3	2	1.30	0.00
2	5	4	0	1.10	0.20
3	9	7	8	1.20	0.10
4	6	11	12	1.20	0.10
5	10	13	14	1.20	0.10

* The computer produced an alternative, but acceptable solution to the one shown in Figure 22–5.

sary to develop a set of rules or policies to guide it as it assigns job elements to work stations. It is unlikely to develop the best sets of assignments if it makes its selection only on how long task elements take as compared to the unfilled work station time (largely the procedure was described above).

Fred Tonge, in an extensive simulation in which he tested several heuristic rules, found that indeed it did not. Tonge tested the following eight rules (as well as others which produced poorer results)[1] for choosing which *next* task element to assign to a work package:

1. Choose the task with the longest time.
2. Choose the task with the most immediate following tasks.
3. Choose tasks randomly.
4. Choose tasks which first became available for assignment.
5. Choose tasks which last became available for assignment.
6. Choose tasks with the most following tasks.
7. Choose tasks with the greatest work time for following elements.
8. Choose tasks with the lowest priority index.[2]

---

[1] This list is adapted from a list in Fred M. Tonge, "Assembly Line Balancing Using Probabilistic Combinations of Heuristics," *Management Science* 11, no. 7, pp. 727–35.

[2] General Motors' engineers assign a quality or priority index number to help the computer assign elements into their most desirable work package. The quality index for each element, which is set by the industrial engineers, reflects their view of its overall priority in the assignment of elements to first jobs along the line.

FIGURE 22–7

Rule: Choose Task	Number of Work Stations (percent of time listed)			
	21	22	23	24
1. With largest time		100		
2. With most immediate followers		44	56	
3. Randomly		3	65	32
4. Which became available first		100		
5. Which became available last				100
6. With most followers	1	93	6	
7. With largest positional weight		100		
8. With highest distinct number			100	
9. With highest positional number			43	57
10. With least time				100
11. With fewest immediate followers		31	48	21
12. With fewest followers				100
13. With smallest positional weight				100
14. With lowest distinct number			100	
15. With lowest positional number		17	83	

Using hypothetical figures and a large number of simulated computer runs (the original data were rearranged randomly after each run), Tonge tested these rules and found that the heuristic did not always create the same number of work stations. As Figure 22–7 shows, repeated reruns of newly randomized sequences of element listings produced job packages which (except in one instance of 21 work stations) assigned the work to 22, 23, and even 24 work stations.

Since each station required one worker, these differences represented differences in the efficiency of the use of labor. Several of these priority choice rules always yielded 24-station assignments whereas others always yielded 22.

Tonge went further in his analysis and gave the computer simulation pairs of priority rules, with the second to be used to break ties. Figure 22–8 shows that this produced a noticeable improvement. Although 22- and 23-station work sets were still the most common, 24-station assignments were fewer. And 21-station assignments were common. In one combination, where policy 1 and policy 7 were used together, 21-station assignments resulted in 60 percent of the simulations.

Tonge's research verifies the seemingly obvious conclusion that the quality of the computer's ability to find minimum station assignments depends on the quality of the priority rules given to it. Thus, computer-based line-balancing programs are usually designed to allow the analyst to experiment with different priority policy rules.

FIGURE 22–8

Rules	Number of Work Stations (percent of times listed)			
	21	22	23	24
1 and 7	60	40		
6 and 7	31	69		
1 and 6	24	76		
1 and 11	14	40	45	
1 and 9	7	43	40	10
1 and 8	1	39	55	5
1 and 15		69	31	
1 and 14		51	49	
1 and 10		17	71	12
8 and 9		5	56	39
10 and 11			28	72

The best policy may produce a solution which saves a station or two and results in less idle time.

LABOR CONSIDERATIONS

Normally work station assignments should not be used just as they come from a computer analysis because a good methods engineer can usually improve upon them here and there. Rearrangements can often be made to avoid having an operator work in an awkward position by moving the assignment of some other assembler whose duties have him or her in a better position.

Also, knowing the person's (or a robot's) work assignments lets the methods engineer visualize where an operator will be standing and which direction he or she will be facing. Instructions for the people loading parts on parts-supply conveyors can be analyzed so that the operator does not have to turn things around. Supply conveyor employees can load suspension springs, axles, differentials, engines, and so on, in the right position and save the assembler's time. Computer programs cannot see these needs.

Besides purely physical element-precedence restrictions, methods analysts need to consider how elements will combine into job packages for the assemblers. The analyst should try to limit "nonproductive" activities, such as picking up wrenches or having a worker move from one side of the car to the other. Nor should a worker work first under a car then on its top, or walk while not working, except in a direction opposite to the line's movement. If a worker is to have a one-minute set of tasks to perform while the product takes a minute to move through the work station, he or she has to work on a moving product. If all the work is done on the product at the same spot, the assembler will have to walk along with it for 25 feet to the end of the station, then walk back and repeat the cycle, walking all day long. This often happens in the assembly of automobiles, refrigerators, stoves, and television sets. Sometimes, with floor-level conveyors, the assembler rides along with the product and only walks back.

It might seem that it would be possible to eliminate this nonproductive walking back and forth the length of the work station. One way to do this would be to use a stop-and-go conveyor and give each employee a work package of elements which can be performed while remaining in one spot. Yet, if a stop-and-go conveyor is used, everyone is idle during the time the conveyor is moving the product to the next station. And, if anyone is not finished by the time the product moves on, he has to go with it into the next station, and this is likely to interfere with the worker there.

Another possibility is to try to put together tasks into assignments so that they go from the front to the back of the product. On a car, the first tasks would be on the front end, then the middle, and finally on the rear end of the car. The assembler can then stand relatively still as he does his work.

Above all, tasks should not be in reverse. Work should not begin at the rear end of a car, followed by work in the middle, and finish with work on the front end.

A methods analyst also needs to consider "closed" and "open" work stations. In a closed station, all the work must be done in the regular area, as, for example, a spray painting booth. Nor can other work be done in this area. In an open station, a worker from the previous station can follow the product into the next area if there is any delay. Finishing the work there would not interfere with the next station's workers. Closed-area work assignments need to be shorter than the average for other jobs so that the assembler will be finished by the time the product moves out of the area. Open-area assignments can be closer to the maximum cycle time since the assembler can follow the product, should a delay occur.

Try as one may, however, to foresee everything and to balance the work, there usually will be many bugs (unequal workloads, parts can't be fastened as quickly as was expected, quality troubles, and so on) to straighten out when a line starts production, so some rearranging is almost always required.

SUBASSEMBLY LINES

Assembled products are usually made out of subassemblies. Valves, pumps, carburetors, generators, gear sets, wheels, and other components are first assembled into final products.

Figure 22–9 is a diagram of Western Electric's telephone assembly process. It illustrates subassembly and final assembly work being carried on as a single coordinated activity. In such a case, the output rates of subassembly lines have to be geared to the final assembly line's needs.

It often happens, however, that it is uneconomical or impractical to operate subassembly lines at rates coordinated with the final assembly line's needs. When this is so, subassembly lines perhaps should be decoupled, so each could operate at its own most economical rate. This can be accomplished with different working hours and with between-operations balancing inventories whenever they are needed. (As we shall see later in this chapter, Japanese assembly systems strive to rebalance flow rates from subassembly lines so as to minimize the buildup of banks of inventories between operations.)

Not only can subassembly lines operate different hours, they can be located in other departments, other plants, or even in other companies. Magnavox assembles television sets using color tubes it buys from RCA. Both the finished sets and the tubes are made on production lines, but the tube lines for Magnavox's TV sets are made in RCA's factories. RCA's tube-production lines do not produce at the same rates that its finished products lines operate.

Often, and aside from possibly differing output rates, it may be best to do subassembly work in its own area away from final assembly. Subassembled components often need inspection and performance testing, so there is need for a break before final assembly. Furthermore, subassembly lines always have to produce more units than are required for final assembly. Often two or more identical subassemblies are required for a unit (a tricycle requires two rear wheels). Further, there are usually extra requirements for spare or replacement parts or, as in the case of RCA making tubes for Magnavox, parts for sale to other companies. Finally, within the same company, one plant may produce components for one or more of their other plants, so that—again—the assembly lines' output quantity often exceeds its own plant's final-line needs.

PROBLEMS WITH LINES

Lines create numerous problems. One, of course, is the matter of *job monotony* which has received a great deal of publicity and has been the subject of considerable research. This subject is considered more fully in Chapter 25.

A different kind of personnel problem results from line jobs always needing to be filled. Since lines need one or more workers at every work station, if anyone is absent, someone else has to fill in. Furthermore, the substitutes have to keep up with the line's pace although they be unacquainted with the work. Fortunately, job assignments are usually so simple that inexperienced workers can step in with little preparation and do reasonably well. It might, however, be necessary to put in an extra operator at a work station in order to maintain production.

Product-Mix Problems

Product variety introduces a second kind of problem. Lines can handle minor but not major variations in products. Some products require operations which are not needed for other products. Or an automobile assembly line, four-door cars require people to work on the two rear doors—work which two-door cars do not need. In order to operate economically, a line's output must be confined largely to one main kind of product, with variations being confined to minor differences. It would be quite uneconomical to

FIGURE 22–9
Schematic Diagram of Subassembly and Final Assembly of Telephones

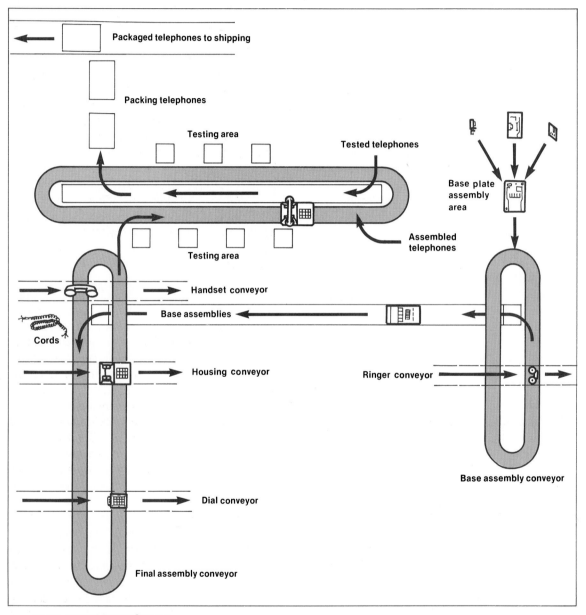

Source: Western Electric Company.

assemble trucks on the same line with passenger cars; they are too unlike and require too many dissimilar operations.

In the case of line work on smaller items (radios and kitchen clocks), a great deal of flexibility in variety of products can be achieved by *not* fastening them to conveyors. Operators can simply sit at fixed work stations where they work on the products that come to them, as shown in Figure 22–10. If the products are not fastened to a conveyor, the operators can keep an inventory of two or three products at their work stations. Then, if some kinds of products require an operation which others don't need, those not needing it can proceed to their next operation. But, if two or three products needing one operation arrive at one time, the operator just pulls them off the conveyor and works on them until caught up.

Product-mix variations can also cause other problems. Customer demands force some variety, so lines need to be flexible enough to handle a limited amount of change in line balancing and model sequencing.

Variety changes the work elements done at work stations along the line. It subtracts from, or adds to, a worker's assignment and often creates imbalances from unequal work assignments. A nominal amount of variety will not create undue imbalances and can be tolerated. But, if substantial product-mix variations seem to be permanent or if they are to last for several weeks, it may be worthwhile to rebalance the work along the line. It is a good idea to have in the file two or three alternative work assignment lists prepared ahead of time so that the supervisors can change to new job assignments whenever the product mix changes, thus avoiding excessive idle changeover time.

Volume Variation

Volume variation may also cause problems. Normally, if there is need for less (or more) output from a line, the entire line works fewer (or more) hours. It would seem to be possible, however, to use fewer workers and to send products down the line at a slower rate. Unfortunately this would necessitate rearranging the work elements and changing the work packages. Such changing is usually impractical for large items such as automobiles, but it is feasible for small items whose total assembly time is as little as 15 or 20 minutes.

Again, as in the case of product-mix variations, it is possible to precompute the worker-package assignments suitable for several production levels. The supervisor could use the assignment list which is appropriate to the volume changeover. It is a difficult job, however, and is not often done. It would mean regrouping job elements, rearranging work tools to different work stations, and resetting the line's speed and/or reallocating the line space allocated to work stations.

FIGURE 22–10
A Loop-Type Assembly Conveyor and Work Stations

Task Performance Variability

Another problem is that average task performance times do not always average out in an offsetting way. If, for example, operation B follows operation A, and each averages two minutes but has some variation, will it be difficult to complete one product every two minutes.

Even though each operation averages 2 minutes, individual operations in this example might sometimes take as long as 2.25 minutes. So, whenever A takes 2.25 minutes, B has to wait .25 minute. Then, and only then, can he go ahead with his operation, which then takes 2 minutes. Except in the rare case where B's shortest time dovetails with A's slow time, 4.25 minutes will pass before the two operations are completed. The average time the product spends in these two operations in this example is 2.125 minutes per operation, not 2 minutes. In practice, the average time would be closer to, but nevertheless more than, 2 minutes. This would not be a problem if long and short performance times for operations A and B always dovetailed and offset each other, but this rarely happens. Since these irregularitis are bound to cause a certain amount of lost time, it may be possible to take care of such variations by allowing for a small work-balancing stock of products between operations. This is not, however, a feasible solution to the problem of time variations along a line where the products are physically large and there are many work stations.

Multiple Stations

Sometimes a particular job cannot be economically subdivided into one-minute assignments and must be treated as a two- or three-minute job. In this case, two or three work stations may be needed and the assembler at each station will work on only every second or third product.

In order for this to work well, it is usually desirable for the products coming down the line to split into two or three lines at such stations. Then each person can do their two- or three-

minute jobs. The product can then move on and resume its place in the regular flow to the following work stations. This is not absolutely necessary, however. The work station can be two or three times as long as usual, and each person can take the second or third product in turn and walk along with it for two or three minutes as they perform their assignment. When they are finished, they can walk back past their one or two fellow workers to the next unit.

FIXED POSITION ASSEMBLY

Large products, such as large factory machines, airplanes, or locomotives, are not put together along assembly lines in the usual sense. Instead, they are more or less constructed in one spot in the assembly department. They are usually moved only occasionally from one specialized assembly area to another.

With fixed position assembly, workers come to the work rather than having the work brought to them. Often whole crews work for days or weeks on a product in one location before it is taken to the next general assembly area where the next several crews take over, one after the other.

Job design is very different from what it is along the more usual kind of assembly line. Instead of workers performing a limited collection of job elements which may add up to only a minute, they have general overall job-accomplishment assignments. It is like an electrician putting in the electrical wiring in a house. The workers themselves have to determine the work that needs doing and then do it. Usually they work with portable tools because the total number of any one product does not justify extremely specialized equipment, and several successive kinds of work are done at each work station. Specialized equipment, if used, would have to be portable, because although it is needed by the one specialized crew today it would just be in the way of the crews doing other work tomorrow.

FIGURE 22-11
Production Lines: Western versus Japanese

Western	Japanese
1. Top priority: line balance	Top priority: flexibility
2. Strategy: stability—long production runs so that the need to rebalance seldom occurs	Strategy: flexibility—expect to rebalance often to match output to changing demand
3. Assume fixed labor assignments	Flexible labor; move to the problems or to where the current workload is
4. Use inventory buffers to cushion effects of equipment failure	Employ maximal preventive maintenance to keep equipment from breaking down
5. Need sophisticated analysis (e.g., using computers) to evaluate and cull the many options	Need human ingenuity to provide flexibility and ways around bottlenecks
6. Planned by staff	Foreman may lead design effort and will adjust plan as needed
7. Plan to run at fixed rate; send quality problems off line	Slow for quality problems; speed up when quality is right
8. Linear or L-shaped lines	U-shaped or parallel lines
9. Conveyorized material movement is desirable	Put stations close together and avoid conveyors
10. Buy "supermachines" and keep them busy	Make (or buy) small machines; add more copies as needed
11. Applied in labor-intensive final assembly	Applied even to capital-intensive subassembly and fabrication work
12. Run mixed models where labor content is similar from model to model	Strive for mixed-model production, even in subassembly and fabrication

Source: R. J. Schonberger, *Japanese Manufacturing Techniques* (New York: Free Press, 1982), p. 133. Reprinted by permission.

Japanese Assembly Methods

Once again, the Japanese are doing some innovative things to increase the productivity of assembly line manufacturing. In general, they prefer to design more flexibility into their assembly lines than do U.S. manufacturers. They do this by developing methods for quick changeovers from one product to another, and by involving the assembly line supervisors and workers more directly in the design and balancing (or rebalancing) of the line. In addition, as mentioned in Chapter 14, Japanese production workers are encouraged to cross-train to do multiple jobs and to help others on the line if they are falling behind or have a quality problem. A summarized comparison of these (and other) major differ-

ences between Western and Japanese production line design is shown in Figure 22-11.

Review Questions

1. What is the fundamental relationship between the number of units per hour an assembly line will turn out and the design of work stations along the line? How should an analyst determine the number of work stations and the length of time each person's work assignment should be?

2. When a computer is used to aid in setting up job packages for workers along assembly lines, the process is often called heuristic. What does this mean?

3. How are policy decisions concerning job element

choices used in setting job assignments for people along assembly lines?

4. What kinds of information are required before a computer (or an analyst) can properly group elements of work into job assignments along a line? How are these job elements determined?

5. How is element precedence established? How is it made effective in the process of setting up work packages?

6. What kinds of improvements can a good analyst usually make in the collections of work elements first determined by a computer?

7. Contrast Western and Japanese assembly line design philosophies.

Questions for Discussion

1. How finely should the analyst try to break down job assignments along an assembly line? If the object is to produce 450 units a day, and if there are 450 labor-minutes of work to be done on each unit, should there be one line with 450 workers each having a one-minute task? Or would it be better to have five lines, each turning out one unit every 5 minutes, and each line with 90 workers who have five-minute job packages? Or would some other combination be better? What factors enter into these decisions? Discuss.

2. Bill Parker, a newly hired man for an assembly line job, looked at the forever advancing line bringing him one more product as fast as he could finish the last one. When the foreman came by, Bill said to him: "I'm getting mighty tired of this job. When do we change to something else?" "Next year," said the foreman. "Next year!" said Bill, "Then I quit. I ain't never worked on a job that hasn't got any end." Discuss.

3. When Motorola redesigned a small radio receiver and reduced its number of parts from 210 to 80, it changed (in its Fort Lauderdale factory) from a regular repetitive assembly line back to individual product assembly. Each worker assembles the whole product at a work bench. The result has been a great improvement in pride of work and quality and a reduction in absenteeism. Is there a "message" here? What costs may have increased?

4. Tom Manly had been a materials supply man in the stock room, a low-paid job, for six months. When a higher-paying opening occurred along the assembly line, Tom asked for the job, but the personnel department refused to recommend his transfer. The job was to work on the underside of cars passing overhead which, because Tom was a short man, would mean quite a reach for him. He filed a grievance, claiming that he had been wrongly denied an opportunity to earn more pay. Should the personnel department's desire to put people on jobs for which they are well-suited prevail in such a case?

5. Suppose that a company would like to operate an assembly line at different rates of output and use fewer or more people. Wouldn't it have to have different sets of work packages for each change? If so, wouldn't this create problems because the workers would have to learn other sets of duties? Also, what would happen to work stations and sets of tools? Would the number of stations and the allocation of space along the line need to be changed? And what would happen if the output rate were changed in only a minor way, such as reducing it two or three units an hour? How big a change would it take to justify changing the number of workers?

6. How can absenteeism be handled along assembly lines? Is there any way to avoid having workers not accustomed to the work having to step in and try to keep up with the line?

7. Folklore says you should not buy a car which was assembled on a Monday, Friday, or during the hunting season. Discuss.

8. Many people say that paced assembly lines are inhumane. "Let machines do it," they say. These same people often complain that mass-produced consumer goods are too expensive and that automation eliminates jobs. Who is right? Is there a "solution?"

Problems

1. It is necessary to set up an assembly line to assemble 3,000 units in a so-called 40-hour week. (Because of start-up and put-away time, as well as rest periods, the workers will lose a half hour each day, so there are only 37.5 productive hours.) There are 6 operations to be done whose

operation times are 1, 1.35, .75, .80, 1.70, and 3 minutes, respectively.

a. How many workers will be needed if each job is done at a separate work station? Is it possible to have more than one person at a work station even though, if they are not fully busy, they do not do anything else?

b. How much loss of labor time because of lack of equal work assignments will this program entail?

c. How will this program be affected if it is possible to group operations in various ways, or to shift people around, or have people do two or three operations, and it is not required to use six work stations with everyone assigned to one work station? How does this compare to the solution in a and b?

*2. General Products Company is planning an assembly line for one of its small products. The plan is for a line which will turn out 75 units an hour, or at the rate of 1 every 48 seconds. Work elements may be grouped in any combination, provided only that the required preceding elements are done, even if in the same work package. They don't need to have been done at an earlier work station. Preceding elements can also be performed several work stations before a following element. The line operates 60 minutes per hour.

a. Using the work element information below, determine how many assemblers and how many work stations will be needed.

b. What average percent utilization of assemblers' time does the plan call for?

Work Element	Time in Seconds	Must Follow	Work Element	Time in Seconds	Must Follow
1	5	—	19	16	2
2	13	1	20	24	19
3	31	2	21	12	11,13
4	7	2	22	6	21
5	26	2	23	6	19
6	7	2	24	9	19
7	6	2	25	22	19
8	11	5	26	17	25
9	11	5	27	25	19
10	11	5	28	9	19
11	24	3,5	29	17	20
12	11	5	30	16	8,10,12
13	24	3,5	31	20	27
14	14	8,12	32	19	27

---

* May be solved with the aid of provided software or manually. See Preface for description of software.

Work Element	Time in Seconds	Must Follow	Work Element	Time in Seconds	Must Follow
15	12	2	33	18	27
16	14	2	34	15	33
17	13	2	35	10	34
18	34	2			

3. In problem 2, could the efficiency of the assembly line be improved by letting small banks of work accumulate between jobs? Which jobs? How much improvement in the use of labor could be expected by doing this?

*4. Below are task times and precedence restrictions for 37 job elements for part of the work to be done along a line which assembles suitcases. (Elements may be put into the same work package with other elements which they must precede or follow.)

a. Arrange these work elements into appropriate job packages in order to assemble 100 finished suitcases per hour. Show which elements go into which work assignments. Show also how much idle labor time this program's assignments contain because of the failure of job packages to all be equal. (Suggestion: Note that 100 units an hour means 1 unit every 36 seconds, or .60 minute. Try to develop work packages of a little less than .60 minute.)

b. Do the same for 150 finished products per hour. How much has the idle labor time been reduced?

c. Assume that methods study analysts are able to put in improvements which reduce the time on all elements which are 16/100 of a minute and over by 25 percent. Answer part a with this assumption.

d. Suppose that time for element 6 is quite variable because of problems which engineering has not been able to solve as yet. A sample of the actual times that element 6 has taken recently and their frequency is:

Time	Percent Frequency
23	2
24	5
25	15
26	60
27	15
28	3
	100

How should this element be handled?

Element Number	Time in Hundredths of a Minute	Must Precede Element Number	Follow Element Number
1	5	3	—
2	80	17,18	—
3	13	7,16,17,18,19,21	1
4	31	12,14	3
5	7	12,14	3
6	26	9,10,11,13	3
7	7	—	2,3
8	6	—	3
9	11	15,32	6
10	11	—	6
11	11	32	6
12	24	23	4,5,6
13	11	15,32	6
14	24	23	4,5,6
15	14	—	9,11,13
16	12	—	2,3
17	14	—	2,3
18	13	—	2,3
19	34	—	2,3
20	29	22,29,30	3
21	16	25,26	3
22	24	31	21
23	12	24	12,14
24	6	34	23
25	6	—	21
26	9	—	21
27	22	21	24
28	17	—	27
29	25	35	21
30	9	—	21
31	17	—	22
32	16	—	9,13
33	20	—	29
34	19	—	24
35	18	36	29
36	15	37	35
37	10	—	36

Chapter 23

Energy Management

The United States has only about 6 percent of the world's population yet uses approximately one third of the energy consumed. We are an energy-intensive economy, and its abundance and low cost has been a major factor in our successful economic growth. In 1946, we consumed 30 quadrillion BTUs of energy: by the 1980s our use of energy had tripled. (A BTU is a British thermal unit, which is a standard measure of energy. A quadrillion is 10^{15}.)

Even with cheap energy, many organizations have always considered the cost of energy in their production and operations activities. The 1973 Arab oil embargo, the rapid rise in oil prices caused by the OPEC cartel, and the high cost of natural gas has made energy a much more important and expensive input to production and service activities. As a result, many organizations have begun formal energy management and conservation programs. These programs are turning out to be as aggressive in the conservation of energy use in production activities as those programs which have always tried to improve the productivity of capital investment, labor, and materials.

Industry consumes about 36 percent of our total energy consumption in the United States. As a result, the success of these energy management programs is an important factor in enabling us to become less dependent upon foreign oil, and to control runaway inflation. Actually, industry has done a credible job in reducing their consumption of energy in recent years. In recent years, for example, while the economy has grown at the rate of about 5 percent, industry's consumption of energy only has grown about 1 percent. AT&T has grown at about 9 percent per year recently, but its energy consumption has decreased about 2 percent per year because of their energy conservation programs. TRW's sales doubled between 1972 and 1978, and yet their energy consumption was down about 19 percent.

RESPONSIBILITY FOR ENERGY MANAGEMENT

Energy management activities require the effort of everybody in an organization. While production/operations managers and engineers may be directly responsible for searching out ways to decrease the use of energy or to use energy in more effective ways, no effective program of energy conservation is likely to succeed unless *all* people become and remain energy conscious.

Within industry, only six major types of producers use about two thirds of the energy con-

FIGURE 23–1
Major Energy Users in Industry

	Total Energy	Electricity
Primary metals	21%	23%
Chemical and allied products	20	29
Petroleum refining and related industries	11	4
Paper and allied products	5	5
Food and kindred products	5	6
Stone, clay, glass, and concrete products	5	5
Total	67%	72%

Source: J. N. Fowler, "Energy Conservation in Industry," *Building Systems Design*, October–November 1978, p. 4.

sumed by all industry (see Figure 23–1). While the greatest savings can be achieved through improved efficiencies in these industries, *all* other organizations, including the public sector and consumers, must do their share.

ENERGY MANAGEMENT PROGRAMS

Many organizations, including General Motors, AT&T, 3M, Dow Chemical, IBM, Peabody Coal, and most governmental agencies, have all implemented formal energy management and conservation programs. 3M's energy management program, for example, has the following objectives:

1. Develop an *action plan* for all energy systems that might be converted from one energy source to another and/or provided with a dual fuel energy system.
2. Conduct total *energy audits* of each 3M facility. These audits document total energy use and cost; evaluate each energy-using system; and document pertinent technical characteristics of each system which uses electric power, natural gas, fuel oil, propane, steam, water, and compressed air.
3. Set plant energy reduction *goals* for fossil fuels and electrical energy use. As a corporation, 3M has set a goal of reducing energy

by 25 percent by the end of 1982 (using 1973 as their base year).
4. Implement energy *conservation programs* by improving operating and maintenance procedures.
5. Implement a meaningful and timely plant *reporting system* of energy use, energy cost, energy use per unit of production, and conservation project evaluation measures to monitor results of their energy conservation programs.[1]

Peabody Coal Company, the nation's largest coal producer, has a similar energy management program. Its annual goal was to reduce the company's present energy consumption and energy costs by 10 percent without affecting its coal production. This would translate into an annual savings of 5 million dollars in operating costs. In all, about 400 people throughout the company are involved in some way in Peabody's energy management program. Figure 23–2 lists the energy conservation ideas it has developed.

At General Motors, an energy conservation program has been in effect since the 1950s. Prior to expensive energy costs, its program primarily emphasized cost reduction. More recently, its program has strongly emphasized reduction in the use of energy. GM has two programs for energy conservation. The first includes programs for the elimination of wasteful uses of energy by people. The second is oriented toward more efficient use of energy through engineering improvements to products, processes, and facilities. These improvements are in the following five general areas:

1. *Elimination or reduction of energy-consuming specifications.* Downgrading unnecessary heat treating or use of energy-intensive materials.
2. *Process changes.* Using, for example, cold-wash detergent in component part washing machines.

---

[1] Richard L. Aspenson, "3M Energy Management Program," *Building Systems Design*, February/March 1979, p. 4.

FIGURE 23–2
Energy Conservation Ideas

1. Review utility rate structures.
2. Use energy-efficient lighting.
3. Use infra-red heating for large areas.
4. Use thermograms to check on poor insulation and energy loss in buildings, electrical connections, etc.
5. Use power demand controls to reduce demand charges.
6. Use insulation on walls and ceilings of all buildings.
7. Use insulating glass on windows.
8. Seal and caulk doors, windows, etc.
9. Consider alternate, more efficient forms of energy. (Electric lift trucks?)
10. Conduct micro audit to determine energy usage levels for individual items.
11. Keep records on energy usage by type, by unit, by building, etc.
12. Purchase energy at least possible cost.
13. Don't spill fuel.
14. Fix fuel leaks on equipment, pumps, tanks, etc.
15. Stagger startup of electrical motors to keep demand charges lower.
16. Post energy management posters, etc.
17. Recognize successful attempts at energy management.
18. Consider more efficient engines and electric motors.
19. Purchase vehicles that get more miles per gallon.
20. Reduce thermostat settings in winter and raise in summer.
21. Install storm windows.
22. Clean or recondition heaters and air conditioners.
23. Check on size of HVAC equipment.
24. Replace pilot lights with electric starters.
25. Seal off unused areas in buildings.
26. Turn off lights when not needed.
27. Reduce unnecessary lighting.
28. Improve power factors.
29. Restrict use of compressed air.
30. Use compressor air discharge to heat.
31. Close shop doors.
32. Reduce heat used to keep prep plants from freezing.
33. Turn off idling equipment.
34. Reclaim any lost heat.
35. Install automatic "turn-off" devices for lights, heaters, etc., when not needed.
36. Shutdown air compressors when not needed.
37. Use waste oil for fuel.
38. Reduce air pressure from compressors to minimum required.
39. Shut off fans when not needed.
40. Check condition of thermostats.
41. Install blowers in top of large bays to circulate air.
42. Reduce temperature on water heaters.
43. Do janitor work during normal office hours.
44. Transfer operations to lower-cost times of day (two and three shifts).
45. Reduce horsepower required on motors to lowest feasible level.
46. Use portable spot heaters in shops.
47. Eliminate gas-burning barrels in shops.
48. Insulate duct work.
49. Use cog belts from Dayco for more efficient power transmission.
50. Eliminate unnecessary ventilation.
51. Reduce rehandle.
52. Shorten haul runs.
53. Shut down equipment when not in use.
54. Repair air compressor leaks.
55. Do not use compressed air for cooling.
56. Install air locks or curtains on large doors.
57. Keep filters clean or replace regularly.
58. De-energize excess transformer capacity.
59. Increase electric conductor size to reduce distribution losses.
60. Reduce viscosity of lubricants (if safe).
61. Maintain constant speed on haul roads.
62. Eliminate unnecessary stops on haul roads.
63. Carry full payloads.
64. Eliminate unnecessary trips.
65. Use the smallest unit that will do the job required.
66. Reduce engine warm-up time to minimum required.
67. Check engine fuel injector settings and pump pressure.
68. Check tire inflation.
69. Do not overfill fuel tanks.
70. Clean light fixtures.
71. Increase light reflectance of walls and ceilings.
72. Reduce window area.
73. Unplug water coolers.
74. Plant trees to shade windows.
75. Use spot lighting instead of area lighting in shops.
76. Lower light fixtures in high-ceiling areas.
77. Tint windows.
78. Provide proper maintenance and lubrication for motor-driven equipment.
79. Install air dryer on compressed air lines to eliminate blow-down.
80. Install compressor air intake in coolest location.
81. Reduce days worked per week.
82. Evaluate lubricants with respect to reducing amp draw on motors.
83. Maintain equipment at a high-efficiency level.
84. Reduce travel in company vehicles.
85. Use correct fuel for diesel engines.
86. Keep exhaust systems open.
87. Avoid Jack-Rabbit starts.
88. Operate transmission efficiently, avoid lower gears.
89. Avoid excessive road speed.
90. Do not overuse air conditioner.
91. "Car pooling" company vehicles.
92. Install light switches to allow smaller area control.
93. Purchase fuel-efficient vehicles.
94. Burn waste oil.
95. Turn down heaters or air conditioners on weekends.
96. Eliminate weekend operations.
97. Restrict number of door openings.
98. Install storm windows.
99. Relocate thermostat away from outside doors.
100. Reduce number of electric heaters.

FIGURE 23–2 *(concluded)*

101. Put drapes on windows.	108. Maintain hydraulic systems at recommended pressures.	114. Doze downhill.
102. Operate diesel engines in the "economy range."	109. Check engine compressed air systems for leaks.	115. Load on downhill slope.
103. Operate diesel engines in correct temperature range.	110. Reduce rolling resistance on roads, ramps, pits, etc.	116. Start equipment slowly.
104. Operate power shift haulage equipment in lockup.	111. Lay out haul roads to minimize grades, crossings, curves, length, etc.	117. Check battery on diesel-powered equipment.
105. Operate diesel-powered equipment in high gears.		118. Adjust track sag on dozers.
106. Operate hydraulic machines above stall speed.	112. Replace worn digging tools.	119. Stop push loading by dozers when normal load is obtained.
107. Derate engines where possible.	113. Do not spin wheels.	120. Do not idle engines over lunch periods or other long-wait periods.

Source: N. P. Chironis, "Peabody Tackles Energy Reduction," *Coal Age,* April 1979, pp. 68–69.

3. *Heat recovery applications.* Utilizing waste heat from one process to heat another, or to reduce waste heat within the process.
4. *Improved equipment controls.* Assuring more effective startup and shutdown of equipment to optimize operating performance.
5. *Materials conservation.* Recycling energy-intensive materials or burning waste materials as fuel.[2]

Specific examples of these conservation areas will be presented later in the chapter.

ENERGY AUDITS

An important activity in the design of an effective energy management program is the *energy audit.* An energy audit is a thorough inventory and evaluation of energy uses in an organization to determine where opportunities might exist for energy conservation and cost reduction. A typical audit includes the gathering of information of where energy is used, how much is used, and for what purpose. Cost information and opportunities for improving the efficiency of energy consumption are often identified as a result of this audit.[3] Energy audits are usually performed by

teams consisting of accountants, production/operations managers, and engineers. Figure 23–3 is a flowchart of the steps involved in an energy audit.

An important part of the energy audit is understanding the rate structures that public utilities use to charge their customers for electricity. First, separate rates prevail for different users—commercial, residential, and governmental organizations. Curiously, a utility is not obliged to guarantee that customers are being given the lowest rates to which they are entitled.[4] This determination is the responsibility of the customer. Most utility rates consist of a *demand* charge, and *energy* charge, a *fuel adjustment* charge, and *taxes.* While little can be done about the last two components of the rate, the first two can be managed.

The *demand* charge is the cost to the customer for the public utility providing the maximum (peak load) electrical power required. Essentially, it is a payment for the utility company's obligation to be prepared to meet customers' peak requirements. This charge can be as much as 40 to 45 percent of the total utility bill. Interestingly, this charge is calculated by periodically measuring the total kilowatt hours of electricity consumed by the customer at various times dur-

---

[2] H. H. Kehrl, "Industrial Energy Conservation: 101 Ideas at Work," *Building Systems Design,* December/January 1978, pp. 18–19.

[3] Stevan Simich and Robert Strauss, "The Energy Audit," *Journal of Accountancy,* November 1978, p. 53.

[4] See C. G. Anderson, G. Harwood, and R. Hermanson, "Energy Audits," *The CPA Journal,* January 1979, pp. 35–41.

FIGURE 23–3
Flowchart for Energy Audit

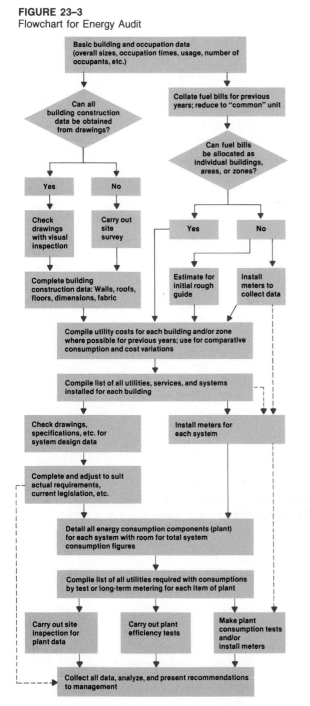

Source: R. A. Edwards, "The Energy Audit—Its Procedure and Potential," *Chartered Mechanical Engineer,* June 1979, p. 62.

ing the day, and then using the *highest* usage of electricity during this period as the basis for the demand charge. Thus, while the demand for electrical use for most customers is rarely constant throughout the day, the rate they pay is based on the highest use rate for the day. As a result, if the customer could somehow reschedule high-energy-use activities to off-peak-load hours, the energy bill can usually be reduced. Methods for managing peak loads will be discussed later.

The second charge, the *energy* charge, is based on how much energy is actually used. Typically, one would think that the larger the customer, the lower the price charged per kilowatt hour. While this is true with many public utilities, some are moving in the opposite direction. Large users of energy must pay more per unit than small users. This measure, of course, is a conservative move and is intended to make large users of energy pay more for the capital equipment required to provide this energy.

ENERGY SUBSTITUTION

A major strategy for conserving energy is to substitute one kind of energy for another. These substitutions range from those that are quite easy to implement to those that are very exotic and whose practicality is uncertain. Forest products companies, for example, now use waste wood and pulp liquor in place of oil and gas as fuel in their operations. One California firm installed $11 million worth of equipment so that these waste materials could be used. Not only does this process provide all the plant's energy needs, but also surplus energy is generated that is sold to a local public utility.

Other substitutes for traditional fossil fuels (oil, coal, natural gas) include solar energy, geothermal (natural underground) steam, synthetic fuels (for example, gasohol) nuclear, wind, biomass (producing methane gas from waste), ocean thermal electrical generation, burning trash as fuel, and oil shale.

Of those alternatives mentioned above

(other than nuclear), solar energy devices seem to be of most interest to individual companies and organizations. The others are being researched and in some cases used successfully in isolated cases, but for the most part, these alternatives are still experimental and will require large investments by companies and governments to make them practical.

Solar Energy Systems

Solar energy systems have always been around. Generally, there are two kinds of systems: passive and active. Passive systems are those in which skylights and large windows are utilized to capture heat for the building. Active solar systems are those which capture the sun's energy with "collectors"—usually on the roof of a building—directed toward the sun. The sun's energy heats water, or a special liquid, or air, which is used in industrial processes, space heating and cooling, and heating water.

Honeywell's new eight-story office building in Minneapolis, for example, uses 252 trough-like collectors located on a nearby parking ramp. The sun heats liquid which flows through pipes in these collectors, and this liquid becomes the source of energy. This system is expected to provide 50 percent of Honeywell's heating, 80 percent of their cooling, and all of its hot water requirements for the 106,000-square-foot structure. Honeywell expects that its solar system will save about 17,000 gallons of oil annually.[5]

In another example, General Extrusions of Youngstown, Ohio, has installed a 100-collector roof-top solar system to heat water for use in its manufacturing operations. Extruded aluminum parts manufacturing requires a substantial amount of energy. This energy is needed for the extrusion process, heat-treating ovens, billet heating, and the annodizing (coloring) process. The annodizing lines require electrical current to chemically color the aluminum. Annodizing

also requires gas for heating water tanks used in cleaning parts. General Extrusions' solar panels, shown in Figure 23–4, provide a half million BTUs per hour on sunny days and save gas required to heat water for cleaning aluminum parts.

Computer-based solar analyses are available to aid in deciding if a solar system is practical from an economic point of view. Figure 23–5 shows a portion of the output from Martin Marietta's solar energy design system to heat water for an indoor swimming pool, hot tubs, and showers for a proposed health club. Assuming a solar system that will provide about 38 percent of the energy for heating water (backup energy for the other 62 percent is natural gas), Martin's model calculates that 900 square feet of solar collectors are required, at a cost of $35,525.

FIGURE 23–4
General Extrusion's Solar Panels

Solar panel array on the roof of the anodizing line building is made up of 100 units containing five rows of half-parabolic reflectors concentrating sunlight on finned-aluminum tubing. The 500,000 BTU per hour (146 kw) developed on sunny days is used to provide hot water for use in degreasing tanks.

Source: A. Berv Hi, "Saving Energy by Using Electricity," *Electrical Construction and Maintenance*, June 1979, p. 61.

---

[5] "Design and Operation of the Honeywell General Offices Solar Heating and Air Conditioning System," *Building Systems Design*, April/May 1979, p. 3.

FIGURE 23–5

Sample Computer Output of a Technical and Economic Analysis of a Proposed Solar Hot Water System

```
ENERGY BALANCE BY MONTH FOR    900.0 SQ. FT. COLLECTOR
```

MONTH	FRACTION BY SOLAR	AVERAGE USEFUL SOLAR PER DAY (BTU/DAY-SQ FT)	TOTAL USEFUL SOLAR ENERGY (MIL BTU/MO)	AUXILIARY ENERGY (MIL BTU/MO)	CONVENTIONAL SYSTEM ENERGY (MIL BTU/MO)
1	.316	702.1	19.59	67.28	98.41
2	.347	771.1	19.43	58.24	88.89
3	.428	950.3	26.51	56.09	98.41
4	.408	907.4	24.50	56.45	95.24
5	.367	814.6	22.73	64.53	98.41
6	.407	903.4	24.39	57.59	95.24
7	.427	948.9	26.47	57.69	98.41
8	.405	900.6	25.13	58.39	98.41
9	.448	994.8	26.86	52.92	95.24
10	.414	919.0	25.64	57.64	98.41
11	.351	779.0	21.03	61.66	95.24
12	.314	698.0	19.47	67.57	98.41
ANNUAL	.386		281.76	716.04	1158.73

```
BEST SOLAR COLLECTOR SIZE FOR TILT ANGLE OF 45. DEGREES IS   900. SQ. FT.
FINANCIAL SCENARIO--BUSINESS
```

```
                    $$$ CASH FLOW SUMMARY  $$$
```

YR	(A) FUEL/UTILITY SAVINGS	(B) MAINT,INSUR PROP. TAX	(C) DEPRE- CIATION	(D) LOAN INTEREST	(E) INCOME TAXES	(F) LOAN PAYMENT	(G) NET CASH FLOW
0							-3553.
1	895.	923.	5290.	4156.	-11842.	4947.	6868.
2	1119.	979.	2885.	4053.	-3399.	4947.	-1407.
3	1399.	1037.	2885.	3937.	-3230.	4947.	-1354.
4	1749.	1100.	2885.	3806.	-3021.	4947.	-1274.
5	2187.	1166.	2885.	3657.	-2761.	4947.	-1165.
6	2624.	1236.	2885.	3490.	-2493.	4947.	-1065.
7	3149.	1310.	2885.	3300.	-2173.	4947.	-934.
8	3779.	1388.	2885.	3086.	-1790.	4947.	-765.
9	4535.	1472.	2885.	2844.	-1333.	4947.	-550.
10	5442.	1560.	2885.	2571.	-787.	4947.	-277.
11	6531.	1654.	70.	2262.	1272.	4947.	-1342.
12	7837.	1753.	70.	1913.	2050.	4947.	-913.
13	9405.	1858.	70.	1518.	2978.	4947.	-379.
14	11286.	1970.	70.	1072.	4086.	4947.	282.
15	13543.	2088.	70.	569.	5407.	4947.	1100.
16	16251.	2213.	70.	0.	6983.	0.	7054.
17	19502.	2346.	70.	0.	8542.	0.	8613.
18	23402.	2487.	70.	0.	10422.	0.	10493.
19	28083.	2636.	70.	0.	12688.	0.	12758.
20	33700.	2794.	70.	0.	15417.	0.	15488.
	196418.	33970.	31955.	42234.	37016.	74205.	47677.

Source: Martin Marietta Corporation, Denver, Colorado.

Taking discounted cash flows, tax rates, investment tax credits, solar tax credits, rising natural gas costs, depreciation tax shields, and other factors into account, the model predicts a discounted payback of 11.3 years.

Experts believe that, given the proper tax incentives, solar systems could provide between 20 and 25 percent of our nation's energy requirements by the year 2000.[6] The reason that tax incentives are required is that solar systems have a fairly long payback period (about 9 to 12 years) and do not compete favorably as yet with elec-

tricity and natural gas. As these energy sources become more expensive, solar is expected to become more widely used.

ENERGY CONSERVATION METHODS

In the short run, most organizations can conserve energy simply by reducing their use of electricity, oil, natural gas and other common energy sources. Energy reduction activities are broadly categorized as follows: improved housekeeping; energy recycling; building design and building retrofit; product design; process design; physical distribution management; lighting design; and load monitoring.

Improved Housekeeping

Reductions in the use of energy can be achieved by such simple measures as replacing incandescent light bulbs with flourescent bulbs. Or, energy used for lighting can also be reduced simply by removing from 10 to 30 percent of the lightbulbs in an area, and by assuring that lights are never left on when unnecessary.

In addition, thermostats can be lowered and controlled so that temperatures during the winter are held to about 65 degrees, and to about 78 degrees during the summer. Machines should not be left running when idle, and maintenance of heating, ventilation, and air-conditioning systems should be done on a periodic basis to keep them performing efficiently. Holiday Inns assigns the responsibility for turning lights out when not in use and turning thermostats down when the rooms are unoccupied. Many other firms do their janitorial activities during the day to avoid lighting, heating, and cooling at nighttime. Those that still have their cleaning done at night require their custodial staff to move from floor to floor turning on only the lights needed to clean.

Simple devices can also be installed to reduce energy consumption. European hotels have had, for many years, timing switches on hallway lighting which go off after a few minutes

---

[6] C. Robert Stobaugh and Daniel Yergin, *Energy Future: Report of the Energy Project at the Harvard Business School* (New York: Random House, 1979), p. 183.

to save energy. Central switches (some with timers) which automatically turn off lights and machines at the end of a workshift are also becoming more common. Some companies do not turn on air-conditioning systems until an hour after the workday has begun, and similarly, turn them off an hour early because of the sustained coolness of the building. Raytheon is so serious about energy conservation that it has inspectors who roam the production facilities and give "tickets" to machine operators who have left their machines on when not working and for similar wasteful energy practices.

Energy Recycling

Energy recycling means to use heat and steam and other energy generated by a manufacturing or service process for other energy needs. One activity, called *co-generation,* uses the heat produced by diesel engines which run electrical generators to heat buildings. Cummins Engine is experimenting with such a facility in a Manhattan office building. Several diesel engines are generating the electrical power for the office building, and the heat that comes from the engines is used to heat the building. Since these systems can generate more electricity and heat than is required for the building, they are even considering a plan to sell excess electricity and heat to neighboring buildings.

AT&T has installed special ducts in the ceilings of its office buildings to capture heat thrown off from copy machines, typewriters, and even the people who work there. AT&T engineers estimate that each person generates as much heat as a 100-watt light bulb! Similarly, General Motors invested $320,000 to install duct work to redistribute and redirect air heated by flue gases in one of their foundries. General Motors estimates the annual savings to be about $193,000, which is a payback of less than two years.

There are other examples of the way heat generated by one process can be used for other purposes. Computers generate a considerable amount of heat. Some companies have installed ducts which redirect computer-generated heat to other parts of the building. Other organizations, whose processes create steam, direct the steam to drive electricity generators. Another method is to install "heat pumps," which remove the heat that exists in outside air or in, for example, the warm humid air in an indoor swimming pool and use it to heat other parts of a building. Heat pumps can be "reversed" to use cool nighttime air for air conditioning.

Building Design

One of the most fruitful areas of energy conservation is in the design or redesign of existing buildings and factories. Increased insulation; double-thickness windows; "balanced" heating, ventilation, and air-conditioning systems; buildings buried in the ground; lower ceilings; and the use of alternative energy sources (such as solar) are but a few examples of the hundreds of ways which buildings can be more energy efficient.

Insulation. One area that provides much promise is improved insulation. One engineering company, for example, has renamed "ROI," which usually means "return on investment," to "return on insulation." This company has developed a computer analysis to aid in the design of optimal insulation investments as a trade-off against energy savings.

Heating, ventilation, and air-conditioning (HVAC) design. In the case of HVAC systems, architects and engineers are designing systems that are more balanced and which require less energy. Traditionally, before energy was an expensive resource of production, HVAC systems were designed to handle peak load requirements—for the coldest or warmest days of the year. This generally results in large centralized systems that operate inefficiently during most of the year, but have the *capacity* to handle those few days during extremely cold and warm months. Now, engineers are designing smaller, more efficient modular HVAC systems which are hooked together in series and can be brought online as temperature conditions vary. For example, in a system that has five modular units, perhaps only three of these would operate in the fall and spring. Then, a fourth might be turned on as winter approaches or as summer approaches. Finally, when summer and winter demands are at their peak, all five systems would be operating. Systems designed this way have been found to be much less energy hungry because each of the smaller units is designed to operate optimally.

Burying buildings partially underground is also a way to reduce building energy consumption. For example, in Sacramento, the state of California plans to construct a 183,000-square-foot office building that will combine the advantages of underground coolness and a sunny climate. About half the office space will be in a two-story underground structure, and another part of the building will be a six-story structure with a south-facing sloping surface for solar collectors.[7]

Product Design

Products for the consumer and products used in industry itself are also being redesigned to save energy. General Motors, for example, announced that it expects to have a battery-operated car available in the near future. And, the lightbulb industry has been working on an electronic incandescent bulb that will save as much as one third the electricity as conventional bulbs. This bulb will last five times longer than an ordinary 1,000-hour-life bulb and will produce about the same amount of light. General Electric, one of the leaders in the development of these bulbs, estimates they will sell for about $10. GE, which plans to introduce their bulb in the 1980s, thinks that, by 1990, 10 percent of the 840 million screw-in sockets that are now burning 100-watt

bulbs or larger will be using their new invention. If this objective is reached, the savings could amount to about 14 million barrels of oil per year. Investments in new product designs like this, however, are extremely expensive. GE plans to spend more than $20 million over the next five years on R&D for their new electronic bulb and another $24 million on manufacturing facilities.[8]

Electric motors are also a prime source for energy savings. Arthur D. Little, Inc., a management consulting firm, has estimated that 64 percent of the electric power consumed in the United States is used to drive electric motors. Further, the firm estimates that in U.S. industry, 75 percent of the electric energy consumed is for powering motors. In addition, 50 percent of the electricity used for motors is concentrated in only five industries—chemicals, primary metals, paper, food, and petroleum.[9]

Newer, more efficient motors have been designed which can save substantial amounts of energy. Exxon Chemical says it has already realized a 5 to 10 percent savings in kilowatt hours of electricity by its motor replacement program. Monsanto requires motor suppliers to pay them a penalty if the motors purchased do not meet Monsanto's specified efficiency standards. Monsanto also has a "motor efficiency program" which urges plant managers to consider using the more efficient motors.

Generally, energy-efficient motors pay back the additional cost over standard motors in less than one year. For example, a new one-horsepower motor has an efficiency factor of 81.8 percent and costs $19.78 more than a standard motor with only 75.9 percent efficiency. According to one motor manufacturer, the $19.78 is paid back in 9½ months of continuous running, assuming a cost of 4 cents per kilowatt hour.[10]

On the consumer side, refrigerators are con-

[7] Michel J. Bartos, Jr., "Underground Buildings: Energy Savers?" *Civil Engineering-ASCE,* May 1979, p. 81.

[8] "From GE, a $10-Bulb That Saves Money," *Business Week,* June 25, 1979, pp. 35–36.

[9] Stephen C. Stinson, "Chemical Firms Seek Higher Motor Efficiency," *Chemical and Engineering News,* February 12, 1979, p. 18.

[10] Ibid., p. 19.

sidered to be one of the most energy-expensive home appliances. California has even set a rigid standard which will not allow 16-cubic-foot refrigerators to be sold if they consume more than four kilowatt hours per day. (General Electric actually withdrew its 16-cubic-foot refrigerator from the market because it felt it would cost too much to redesign it to meet the California standards.) However, a new refrigerator has been designed with research funding from the Department of Energy, which runs on only two kilowatt hours per day and costs $44 more than the older, less efficient refrigerators. This refrigerator has an improved evaporator, uses polyurethane foam, and has a new door design.[11]

Battery-powered cars for highway use also are on the horizon. Among the leading contenders are a nickel/zinc battery and a lithium/iron sulfide battery; several others are also under development. The nickel/zinc battery, while it has excellent power, does not have a very long life. On the other hand, the lithium battery is both powerful and has a longer life. It needs to operate at temperatures which exceed 400 degrees centigrade. Although the nickel/zinc battery is expected to be in commercial operation in the late 1980s, the more advanced lithium battery may not be commercially available until the year 2000.[12]

Often, component parts for products can be made from substitute materials or in other ways which reduce energy consumption. For example, at GM, the entire length of auto steering columns had been painted for rust resistance as well as with the finished color. GM changed this so now only the upper portion of the column that protrudes beyond the dash panel is painted. There is no effect on quality and the heat lamps used to dry the lower portion of the steering column no longer are needed. The cost of this change in product specification was nothing, while the savings are over $1,700 per year.

As another example, GM also changed the material used to make horn housings. Traditionally, they were die cast from zinc. But GM redesigned the housing to be made from lower-costing plastic and reduced the energy consumption required for die casting—saving over $62,000 per year.

Even computers with their microprocessor chips and memories require much less electrical energy to do the computations than did the older, larger (and slower) computers of the late 1970s. (Many microcomputers plug into a normal wall electrical outlet.)

Process Design

Changing the processes by which things are manufactured or services are delivered also can reduce energy consumption.

Experts estimate the installation of energy-efficient processing equipment would conserve up to 25 percent of our industrial energy requirements projected for the late 1980s.[13]

For example, when the steel industry switched from "open-hearth" to "basic oxygen" furnaces, not only was the productive capacity of steel making increased, but the cost per ton of steel was reduced so that the United States could become more competitive with the rest of the world in steel making. Estimates are that the basic oxygen furnace installations at some plants have saved as much as two thirds the energy consumed by the older open-hearth furnaces.

In addition, the newer "continuous casting" process which substitutes for die casting and sand casting saves natural gas because it eliminates much of the heating and cooling required for these older kinds of casting processes.

The aluminum industry, which is an extremely large user of electrical energy, is experimenting with a newer chemical process which may replace the electrical process in aluminum

[11] "Prototype U.S. Refrigerator Puts Energy on Ice," *Electrical Review*, June 22, 1979, p. 23.

[12] "Practical Electric Car Battery Likely by 1990," *Chemical and Engineering News*, May 7, 1979, p. 20.

[13] G. N. Hatsopoulos et al., "Capital Investment to Save Energy," *Harvard Business Review*, March–April 1978, p. 111.

making. If successful, the industry believes that energy usage may be reduced by up to 50 percent. Cement production is also a high energy user. Cement producers are developing a steam process which might save as much as 1/10 quadrillion BTUs by the late 1980s. In addition, cement makers may change the product itself and make cement from a blend of fly ash and portland cement (which currently is done in Europe). If successful, this product redesign would produce substantial energy savings.[14]

General Motors, in its Energy Management Program, has done numerous things to either change or eliminate production processes to save energy. For example, truck bodies had been dried in ovens after being coated with phosphate and rinsed in water. GM installed a water-based paint facility which made it possible to dip auto bodies directly into the paint tanks while they were still wet. As a result, two natural gas drying ovens were eliminated at an annual savings of almost $40,000 per year.

In another GM example, 19 industrial washers which cleaned and degreased parts at one facility were operating at temperatures which ranged from 160 to 180 degrees Farenheit. By switching to a cold-water wash and using low-temperature detergents, the operating temperatures of the 19 washers could be reduced substantially, and in some cases the steam which heated them was completely turned off. GM is saving about $123,000 per year in steam generating costs from this simple move, and no additional capital investment or operating costs were incurred.[15]

Physical Distribution

The physical movement of goods has always consumed a considerable amount of energy. Movement by materials handling devices of raw materials, work in process, and finished goods around the factory as well as the transportation of raw materials, purchased parts, and finished goods to and from regional distributors and wholesalers adds up to a large energy bill.

Within the plant itself, the layout of the facility can do wonders in minimizing the energy-related costs of materials handling. In Chapter 21, the "load-path matrix" method as a way to help solve the problem was discussed. The method aids in minimizing long hauls of large loads of materials.

In moving raw materials from manufacturing facilities to customers, transportation companies—faced with high fuel costs and shortages—are taking more measures to conserve energy by minimizing the number of less-than-full truckloads and rail cars. Truckers are trying to get more payloads on their return trips or backhauls rather than running empty. One major trucking company, for example, estimates that the cost of their empty backhaul problem amounts to over $30 million per year. Methods are under development, for example, which will allow trucking dispatchers to reroute empty trucks as they move toward home base to areas where they may pick up a load. Using online computer systems to do this, the computer will analyze the trade-offs between the expected revenue from picking up a load which is "out of the way" versus the energy and other costs required to deviate from the route to home base to pick up the load and take it to its destination and then return home.

Lighting

The energy required for lighting facilities can be substantial. GM found they could save $900,000 per year simply by turning off a third of the lights. But to achieve further reductions, the design of lighting systems must be analyzed. Generally, fluorescent lighting is less energy consuming than standard incandescent lightbulbs. As a result, most new structures have fluorescent lighting, and many existing facilities are replacing incandescent lighting with this cheaper form of illumination.

[14] Fowler, "Energy Conservation," p. 6.

[15] H. H. Keahrl, "Industrial Energy Conservation," pp. 22, 25.

Coordination of lighting design, maintenance, and bulb replacement can result in still further reduction of energy costs. Lighting designers know fluorescent bulbs lose their lighting ability as they age and as they get dirty. As a result, designers overcompensate for these two factors by designing light systems with more lighting capacity than required for the tasks being done in offices or in manufacturing facilities. In general, this means they provide an excess of 42 percent of lighting capacity over what is actually needed to do particular tasks. This means that the lighting system will require 42 percent more lamps and will consume 42 percent more energy. When energy was cheap this design practice was considered acceptable. But now, with high energy costs, it is usually more cost effective to install smaller lighting systems, replace lightbulbs before they burn out, and clean them more frequently to maintain the proper level of illumination. The trade-off costs are *less* capital costs for smaller lighting systems, and *lower* energy costs versus *higher* bulb replacement costs (replacing bulbs before they burn out) and *higher* cleaning maintenance costs.

Economic studies have shown that generally the least cost of these trade-offs is provided by installing smaller systems and by replacing lamps that have been in service for only 50 percent of their rated lamp life, even though they have not burned out. Second, that the least-cost time span between cleaning of fixtures and bulbs should be approximately one year. Thus to implement a program like this in a large facility, one maintenance person might be assigned to cycle through the entire facility and do nothing but change fluorescent bulbs whose rated life is down to approximately 50 percent. While this is being done, each light fixture can be thoroughly cleaned.

LOAD MONITORING AND LEVELING

As mentioned previously, public utility companies charge for energy based on the peak load requirements of a manufacturing facility, office

building, school, or other commercial users. Thus, if an organization's peak load requirements for electrical energy are substantially higher than what they use during the rest of a day or week, then it is usually cost effective to try to reduce the peak demand by various means.

Public utilities have active load management and load leveling programs. They do this in order to reduce their own peak loads, which may allow them to invest less capital for electrical generation equipment. Load leveling also allows them to utilize their existing capacities more fully. Public utilities continuously monitor the demand for their electrical energy. When they near capacity, they occasionally have to cut back on the amount that is flowing out over their electrical distribution system by asking a few of their large users of electrical energy to let them interrupt their service. This is only done when demand gets extremely high, say, on a very cold or very hot day. Figure 23–6 shows the average weekday megawatt loads by time of day for December and July for Niagara Mohawk.[16] This figure shows that, on the average, Mohawk is operating at about 85 percent of their capacity during July and December, and the additional 15 percent of capacity can be thought of as "safety capacity" for extremely cold or extremely warm days.

This wide variability in use is why public utilities charge their customers for the extra capacity that is required to meet these high-demand times. Thus, anything that their customers can do to reduce their own peak load requirements can result in lower energy rates. As a result, many customers are analyzing the demand for energy throughout their own facilities. Some reschedule activities or simply cut down on the use of energy during these peak times.

As already mentioned, some companies are having their custodial work done during the day to avoid additional nighttime heating and lighting costs. Scheduling of second and third shifts for

---

[16] Martin N. Duggan, "A Perspective on Load Management," *Electrical World*, August 1, 1979, p. 38.

FIGURE 23–6

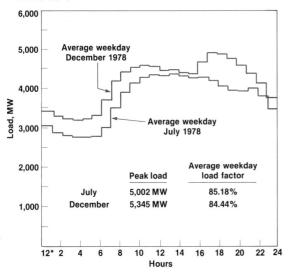

High average weekday load factors can make shifting loads from peak to off-peak periods extremely difficult.

Source: Niagara Mohawk.

certain manufacturing processes is also increasing because these shifts are during off-peak energy demand times.

Computer-Controlled Load Management

More and more individual organizations are using minicomputer controllers to monitor and control various energy-using systems. The computer automatically turns systems on and off at the correct times to both keep the overall load at a lower level and to make individual systems operate more efficiently. Figure 23–7 shows the kinds of items typically under the control of one of these systems.[17]

One of the heaviest energy users in most facilities is the HVAC system. And, because of the seasonal variability of the weather, HVAC systems are usually the most variable users of energy throughout the year. As a result, they are prime candidates for load leveling. This level-

ing is done by "shedding" (reducing energy consumption) or "restoring" (turning it back on) energy at predetermined times when it is known that other energy demands will be high in the facility. This is shown in Figure 23–8.[18] The "ideal rate" of usage is the top line in Figure 23–8 and shows the amount of energy that would be consumed if energy was not costly. The "shed" line shows an upper control limit where energy is turned off or turned down. This point is based on peak load energy, costs from public utilities. Notice in Figure 23–8 that after the energy is shed, its usage falls and is not restored until it reaches the lower "restore" control limit. All of this, of course, is handled by automatic sensors and other instruments which are hooked directly to a computer which automatically starts, sheds, and restores the energy used by the facility's HVAC system.

The forecasting techniques that might be used to estimate energy demand each time period could be methods similar to those discussed later in Chapter 9. Specifically, exponential smoothing model 3 would be well suited to this kind of forecasting task.

The computerized systems that do load monitoring can also automatically turn things on and off according to predetermined occupancy schedules of workers. Some have outdoor sensors which measure the air temperature and then turn on specific equipment to take advantage of warm or cool outside air. But these computer-based systems can do more than simply turn things on and off. They can also calculate the optimal length of time that systems should be on and off so that the right amount of energy per unit of heating, air conditioning, or other "output" from the systems is used. For example, if an HVAC system has been designed with modular units, rather than one large system, the computer automatically turns off and on the correct number of modularized subsystems to match the variability in demand for heat or cooled air.

---

[17] William R. Nieman, "Energy Management System/Power Costs," *Electrical Construction and Maintenance,* June 1979, p. 64.

[18] Stephen M. Zvolner, "Conserving Energy through Computerized Building Automation," *Instrumentation Technology,* March 1979, p. 36.

FIGURE 23-7

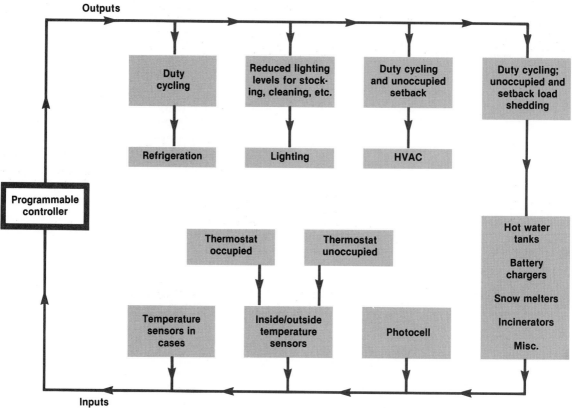

Block diagram of typical "programmable controller" type of energy management system shows how various loads are controlled. System is especially effective and economical for occupancies such as commercial buildings, schools, colleges, public buildings, banks, offices, and apartment buildings.

In manufacturing processes themselves, microcomputers also control the heat and energy consumption in furnaces and other intensive energy users so that optimal conditions are maintained with a minimum amount of energy use.

Load Control Methods

Several load control techniques exist which are graphically shown in Figure 23-9.

Figure 23-9A shows the original profile of demand used in this example. Figure 23-9B shows the use of a "demand limit" load control method. This method simply sheds loads for short intervals at the peak usage times. Figure 23-9C shows the concept of a "fixed start-stop" method which is commonly used for air-conditioning systems. Air conditioning is not started until a half hour or hour before the workday begins, and it is automatically shut off an hour or so before the day is over. Figure 23-9D depicts an "optimized stop-start" method. This method optimizes running time of equipment by monitoring temperatures both inside and outside the facility. If the weather changes then the system responds accordingly. Some optimizing control systems also automatically open or close air dampers to draw upon outside cool air for air

FIGURE 23–8

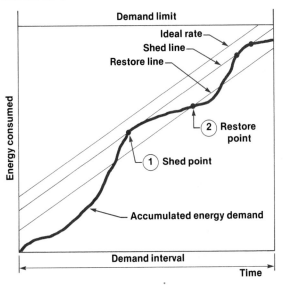

Loads can be shed or restored based on calculations made during predetermined demand intervals: *(a)* the prediction technique forecasts demand at the end of the interval based on accumulated usage and rate of change; *(b)* the ideal-rate principle removes or enables loads according to departures of usage values from an established profile.

FIGURE 23–9
Alternative Load Control Methods

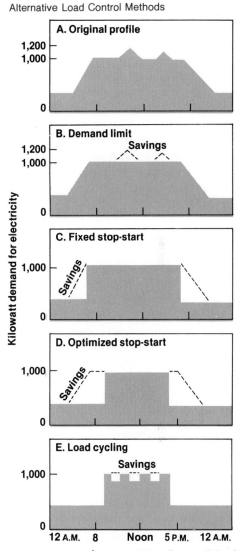

Source: D. Foléy, "Reduce Waste Energy with Load Controls," *Industrial Engineering,* July 1979, pp. 23–27.

conditioning and close them when this air becomes too warm. Finally, Figure 23–9E shows the "load cycling" approach. Here, the control system automatically shuts off fans and other energy-using systems for short periods throughout their normal operating time. Each of these energy users has its own on/off schedule (which is called a *duty cycle*) and is controlled separately—yet coordinated—by the control system.

Load Management Equipment

Load control equipment varies from expensive central minicomputers to medium-priced microprocessor systems down to very simple and relatively inexpensive "black box" systems—essentially timers. Minicomputer systems are best for large office buildings and manufacturing facilities. They automatically gather data, analyze it, and control several different kinds of loads. They eliminate energy waste which might result from equipment being overdesigned for its intended use. (This means having a system which has too much capacity and runs inefficiently at less-than-capacity levels.) In addition, these systems often have fire warning and security systems built into them and can simultaneously control industrial processes to maintain product quality. Mini-computer-based systems can be programmed to use any of the load control techniques shown in Figure 23–9, and can be programmed to perform complex load shedding and restoring activities as shown earlier in Figure 23–8. Also, a minicomputer can control several buildings from one central location and can collect data as energy is consumed so that the analyst can evaluate energy consumption in each process or system. This can identify high energy users as targets for possible energy reduction methods. Centralized minicomputer systems, however, are relatively expensive and can cost from $60,000 to $1 million.

Microcomputer systems are much cheaper (in the $30,000-to-$100,000 range) and usually are used only to manage energy activities and not the other kinds of data processing functions that minis can do. They too, however, can provide fixed schedule, start-stop, load cycling, optimizing, and demand limit load shedding and restoring activities.

Other less expensive systems are available which are much cheaper but are less automatic.[19]

Review Questions

1. Why is energy management becoming an important part of the design of products, facilities, and processes?

2. What are the main activities of an organization's energy management program?

3. What are "energy audits," and how are they performed?

4. Who are the major energy users in industry?

5. What five areas does General Motors concentrate on in its energy management activities?

6. What seem to be the most promising substitutes for fossil fuel energy?

7. Differentiate between passive and active solar energy systems.

---

[19] Foley, "Reduce Waste Energy."

8. What are the main energy conservation methods discussed in the text?

9. Why should HVAC systems and electric motors receive so much attention when it comes to energy conservation?

10. What are the trade-offs in lighting design?

11. Briefly describe how public utilities determine the rates they charge to industry, and why.

12. How can load monitoring and leveling reduce energy costs?

13. What are the different methods for controlling energy usage loads?

14. What equipment is available to do load monitoring and control, and what kinds of things does this equipment control?

Questions for Discussion

1. Is the "energy crisis" over? Discuss.

2. Do you believe energy costs should be measured and separately accounted for as direct costs along with labor, materials, and overhead in the calculation of costs? Why? Why not?

3. What kind of behavioral problems are likely to be encountered in the implementation of a formal energy management program?

4. What major changes can you foresee in the way industry and government operates if energy costs continue to rise faster than normal inflation and as energy becomes scarce in the 1980s?

5. What role do you believe the federal government should play in encouraging alternative energy uses in organizations?

6. Do you think public utilities should charge their large customers more or less per unit of energy than small users? Why?

7. Doesn't it seem wasteful to replace light bulbs before they burn out? Why? Why not? What about the energy required to manufacture the light bulbs themselves?

Problems

1. The average daily demand for kilowatt hours of electricity for Harper Industries is shown below. The public utility charges Harper for electricity at

a rate of 4 cents per kwh, which is the rate for their peak usage from 1:00 P.M. to 2:00 P.M. Harper's energy manager is considering two alternative load leveling plans, each of which requires some capital investment and additional operating costs. The two alternatives are:

a. Install a fixed stop/start system on the HVAC system which would reduce usage to the daily usage pattern shown in column 3 below. This system costs $75,000 and has additional operating costs of $15,000 per year.

b. Install a minicomputer system which optimizes (online) stop and start times and promises to reduce hourly demand to the pattern shown in column 4. This system costs $150,000 and has annual operating costs of $10,000.

Time	Current Usage (thousands)	Alternative 1	Alternative 2	Cost per kwh
8 A.M.–9	100	75	75	
9–10	110	105	105	
10–11	120	115	115	$130 = 3\frac{1}{2}¢$
11 A.M.–12 P.M.	135	120	118	$135 = 3\frac{3}{4}¢$
1 P.M.–2	145	135	130	$145 = 4¢$
2–3	140	130	128	
3–4	130	125	122	
4–5	120	115	110	

If the rate for two alternative peak demands of 135 and 130 are 3¾ cents and 3½ cents per kwh, what should Harper do if their hurdle rate for energy investments is a low 10 percent, the company operates one shift for 250 days per year, and the above rates are expected to increase 10 percent per year for the next 10 years?

2. Vaughn Vibrators, Inc., is designing a new production facility and wishes to install a lighting system which is energy efficient. They know that lighting engineers generally install light systems which have about 40 percent extra capacity, because most companies do not replace bulbs until they fail and rarely, if ever, clean them. The additional 40 percent of lighting compensates for burned out and dirty bulbs.

a. What are the trade-offs to be considered in designing a lighting system which is more energy efficient?

b. If you were the analyst assigned to work with the lighting engineers, what data would you need to make an intelligent decision about lighting capacity, bulb replacement, and cleaning schedules?

3. Visit a local manufacturing firm or service organization and write a brief report on their activities to conserve energy. Consider the topics discussed in the text in your investigation and in writing your report.

Case 23–1

The University has installed a formal energy management program. One part of this program is to make the faculty and staff more aware of energy used for classroom and office lighting. "Awareness tickets" are issued when, for example, a professor leaves an office light on after leaving for the day. When it happens again, the professor is called by the campus energy office and asked to comply.

If the professor continues to "forget," a report is made to the professor's department head. What do you think of a program like this? Suggest alternatives.

Case 23–2

Co-generation of electricity and heat from diesel engine-driven generators is considered to be a promising way to conserve energy. Hoffman Towers, a large downtown office complex, is considering installing such a system to generate its own electricity and to use the heat from the diesel exhaust to heat steam for the building's heating system.

Hoffman Towers is located in a city where "thermal inversions" are common, and a local environmental group is trying to stop the installation of the system because of the pollution the engines will release into the city's atmosphere and because they burn fossil fuel. Hoffman argues that their pollution is no worse than that emitted by the public utility which burns natural gas and is located less than a mile away. In addition, they argue that they would consume less total energy with their system.

The public utility is also against Hoffman's installation of the diesel system, because it claims that if other downtown buildings follow Hoffman's example, they will lose business, and rates for their remaining customers will have to rise to cover their investment in electrical generation equipment. The situation is further complicated by the fact that Hoffman's system produces electricity cheaper than the public utility, and may have enough extra capacity to sell power and steam to surrounding buildings.

You are an analyst for the city's energy management office and have been asked to make a recommendation to the city's public utility commission as to what to do. Outline your approach in preparing this recommendation.

Case 23–3

Following the company's energy conservation plan to hold the offices to 65° in the winter and 80° in the summer, Midstates Manufacturing has received a number of complaints from employees about their working environment. The typists complain that in the winter their typing mistakes are up and their feet are cold, and in the summer they get sleepy in the afternoon.

Production supervisors also complain that factory workers' productivity is down so much that Midstates is forced to work overtime to meet their demands. This results in their having to run the HVAC and lights 10 percent more than before the temperature order was mandated.

To complicate matters, Midstates has always been a very formal company and executives, managers, and office workers tend to dress conservatively. Top managers, for example, continue to wear a coat and tie year round.

Outline a suggested program which combines technical and behavioral approaches to reducing the negative effects of the uncomfortable temperature requirements.

Section Six

Managing Productivity

Society looks to managers of production and operations to produce goods and services in the most economical way possible. Our competitive system in the United States provides for the survival of effective producers and the ultimate elimination of organizations (at least in the private sector of our economy) which do not produce effectively.

Chapter 24 discusses productivity management both in broad terms and in specific recommendations for its improvement. Chapter 25, "Improving Labor Productivity through Job De-sign" continues this discussion, but with more details about the possibilities, the limitations, and the objectives of job design. Finally, Chapter 27 discusses the methods by which productivity standards are developed for specific jobs.

Job design includes the safety and health of workers on the job. The obligations of managers to society for worker safety and health and the methods of carrying out these responsibilities are considered in Chapter 26.

Chapter 24

The Management of Productivity

The only way a society's standard of living can be increased is to increase its productivity. We can consume more only if we produce more. Increasing productivity is essentially the mission of production and operations managers. Peter Drucker has said, "Productivity is the first test of management's competence."

In order to increase productivity, managers, technicians, and workers all have to produce more output (dollar value and/or units of product and units of service) from each unit of input. They have to produce more output from each *labor-hour* used, from each *dollar of capital investment,* from each *unit of material,* and from each *unit of energy* consumed in production. This last input—energy—has become so expensive that it ranks with labor, materials, and capital as major inputs and thus deserves special attention. Energy management was discussed in Chapter 23.

OUR PRODUCTIVITY "CRISIS"

Many economists believe the United States has been experiencing a productivity crisis, and that drastic measures must be taken to bring us out of our slump. One economist calls us an "undeveloping country!" While it is still the most productive nation in the world, U.S. productivity gains (as measured by value of output per labor-hour) have, in recent years, lagged behind those of Japan, West Germany, and France (see Figure 24–1).

The productivity of *capital investment* in machines and equipment has not done much better, and, until recent years, the productivity of energy has been neglected. Managers are trying to use energy more efficiently. As we reported in Chapter 23, many organizations have established energy management programs along with their productivity improvement programs.

REASONS FOR PRODUCTIVITY PROBLEMS

Several factors are believed to be behind our previous poor record of productivity. Some of these are the decline in the amount of capital investment in relation to labor, along with more investment required by EPA for antipollution equipment, and by OSHA for workers' safety and health protection; a younger and less experienced work force; reduced investment in research and development; a switch to more labor-intensive production activities to reduce higher energy costs of labor-saving equipment; more people working in government and services, where productivity gains are usually more diffi-

FIGURE 24–1
The U.S. Trails Its Foreign Rivals in Productivity Growth
(output per employee hour in manufacturing)

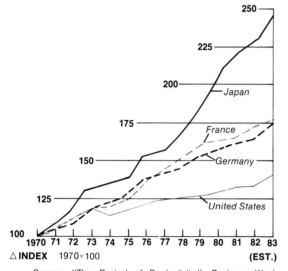

△ **INDEX**   1970 = 100   **(EST.)**

Source: "The Revival of Productivity," *Business Week,*
February 13, 1984. Data gathered and estimated from Bureau of
Labor Statistics.

cult than in manufacturing; increasing import tar-iff barriers which prop up industries such as steel and textiles; inefficient "cost plus" contracts from the federal government; labor union de-mands for more job security and higher wages for unequal gains in productivity by their mem-bers; and, some sociologists say, a decline in the "work ethic," which is a nice way of saying that people don't want to work as hard as they used to—even if the proper incentives are there to motivate them.

While the impact of this list of factors on productivity is debatable, one can see that, with these pressures, productivity improvement is dif-ficult but hopefully not an insurmountable task for management.

One last factor needs mentioning: Perhaps we have simply done such a good job in improv-ing productivity over the years that the law of diminishing returns is at work, which makes productivity improvement possible only with an extremely disproportionate amount of manage-

ment effort and capital investment.[1] In short, maybe all the *easy* productivity gains have been made, and perhaps Japan, West Germany, and others are still in this "easy" stage, and their gains will decline as they catch up with us. While this argument has its proponents, we think there is *substantial* room for more productivity im-provement in all sectors of our economy, includ-ing manufacturing and service, private and pub-lic.

The Picture Is Improving

The productivity picture, while it has been quite dismal in the late 1970s and early 1980s, seems to be improving in the mid-1980s, and prospects through the end of the decade look promising, with most predictions forecasting a gain of about 2.5 to 3.0 per year. The reasons primarily cited for these gains are improvements in the problem areas cited earlier—plus the vigorous activities of U.S. business to focus on productivity im-provement programs. The work force is matur-ing; we have done much of our spending on antipollution equipment; we are spending more on research and development; there is more co-operation between labor unions and manage-ment; and there even seems to be an improve-ment in the "work ethic." People have been asked to help make their jobs more productive and their products of higher quality, and they have responded with many "working smarter" ideas rather tham simply "working harder."

MEASURING PRODUCTIVITY

One of the hardest problems in productivity man-agement is measurement. Companies seem to have had a dollars-and-cents accounting mental-ity for so long that it is difficult to get them to think in terms of productivity other than profits,

---

[1] Interestingly, this "diminishing return to capital" theory was first proposed by Karl Marx as the reason that capitalism would even-tually fail.

return on investment, and other financial ratios which *do* measure the relative productivity of capital investment in plant, equipment, and inventories.

The president of Alcoa, for example, was shocked to see an output per labor-hour ratio report which showed from 1958 to 1965 an increase of 20 percent for Alcoa, but an increase of 60 percent for the entire aluminum industry! He immediately installed a productivity monitoring program which tracked a series of ratios of dollar output value per cost of converting aluminum into specific mill products. Alcoa's ratios are now *above* the industry averages.[2]

Honeywell measures employee productivity as the ratio of dollar sales to dollars of wages, salaries, and fringe benefits. Detroit Edison, an electric utility, measures theirs both as BTUs per pound of coal and megawatt output of electricity per employee.

In the wholesale grocery warehousing industry, the accepted measure of productivity is tons of merchandise handled per labor hour. At colleges and universities, one measure of productivity is student credit hours taught per full-time equivalent faculty member. State highway patrols use several ratios, including "contacts" per mile of patrolling (contacts such as giving a ticket, aiding a motorist, and investigating an accident) and accidents per patrol hour. Other measures can be such things as pages (or pounds) of drawings per hour of drafting labor; accounts receivable per labor-hour of credit employee; tons of trash collected per labor-hour; or value of output per month compared to a company's monthly utilty bills.

TRW measures their productivity (in deflated constant dollars per employee) as follows:[3]

Sales divided by total deflated employee compensation costs (labor-dollar productivity)

Value added: Sales minus direct material cost divided by the number of employees (labor-quantity productivity)

Sales divided by deflated materials costs (material productivity)

Sales per unit of energy consumed (energy productivity)

Sales divided by plant and equipment replacement costs less depreciation (capital productivity)

Composite (Total Firm) Productivity Measures

Some organizations combine these various individual measures of productivity into "composite indexes" by placing various weights on each component according to its importance. This allows them to track overall performance as well as component performance.

In addition, some firms are using a total firm index approach developed by the American Productivity Center which separates the value of output caused by *increases in productivity* and that caused simply by *inflation*—charging higher prices for the same or higher (or lower) output quantity.[4] This allows them to measure and track the effects of both of these components of their changes in the dollar value of output to the values (quantities and their dollar cost) of inputs of labor, materials, capital, and energy.

But, no matter how productivity is measured, what is important is that it *is* measured and monitored, so that management can determine its direction, up or down; to take corrective action where needed; to be able to compare their organization's productivity with their competitors' (usually with data supplied by their trade association); and measure the impact of productivity improvement or cost-reduction programs which they undertake.

[2] *Improving Productivity through Industry and Company Measurement* (Washington, D.C.: National Center for Productivity and Quality of Working Life, October 1976), p. 3.

[3] "The New, Broader Guages of Productivity," *Business Week*, April 19, 1982, p. 44J.

[4] See William A. Ruch, "Productivity Measurement," *Arizona Business*, February 1981, pp. 20–25; also see John W. Kendrick, *Measuring and Promoting Company Productivity*, The Johns Hopkins Press, 1983.

LABOR CONTRACTS AND PRODUCTIVITY

Managers are not entirely free to use the organization's resources as they think best because there are restrictions in the labor contract. They, or previous managers may, for example, have given up some of their rights to make methods improvements which might result in a more economical use of resources. Usually these restrictions on management's right to act result from collective bargaining or even from a strike at some time in the past. Such restrictions are unfortunate in that they often stand in the way of using resources to the best advantage.

Worse, however, are situations where managers lose their right to do certain things by failing to exercise their rights to manage. Dana Corporation lost an arbitration case when it tried to install a permanent production standard for an assembly line because it had used a temporary (and too loose) standard too long. Because Dana had let this inefficient operation prevail, the arbitrator denied them the chance to improve the situation.

In another case Dana agreed to review new production standards with the shop steward before they became effective. This precedent required the steward's initialing of all standards as evidence that he had seen them, and as a result, standards did not go into effect without his initials. From then on the company found it couldn't set a job standard without union approval because of the steward's refusal to initial those he didn't agree with. The labor board upheld the union's position and agreed that the right to initial meant the right to approve or disapprove a standard. Later, at the bargaining table, the company had to win back its right to set standards.

Usually, any kind of job control by a union stands in the way of possible job improvement. A company can rarely make the best use of its resources and have low operating costs if its bargainers give away the managers' rights to set standards or to change methods, or if, by their practices, they abdicate their rights to make improvements. This is because, over the years, unions have been primarily interested in job security for their employees and have opposed productivity improvements which might reduce the number of jobs.

However, this seems to be changing somewhat. Some unions have voluntarily given up wage and benefit increases to save their ailing companies. The United Auto Workers helped Chrysler in the early 1980s; but when Chrysler showed a huge profit in 1984, they wanted their share. Eastern Airlines pilots and flight attendants took substantial pay cuts to help save their jobs. But all is not rosy between unions and management. Continental Airline's bankruptcy (and subsequent startup with nonunion employees working more cheaply) has infuriated their union members, who charged they simply used it as a way to void their union contract so they could lower wages.

PRODUCTIVITY IMPROVEMENT

In order to maintain or improve productivity, many organizations have installed special productivity improvement programs. Beech Aircraft, Detroit Edison, Honeywell, U.S. Steel, and Alcoa, to name a few, have established programs of this type. Following are some examples of the results from these programs, as experienced by Alcoa.[5]

A new, mechanized material-handling system costing $250,000 was installed to load, unload, and quench steel sheets in their large sheet heat-treating furnace. Operating around the clock, the crew was reduced from 36 to 14 workers. The payback period was about six months!

A tempering line (continous) for treating aircraft sheet products (wing skins) was installed, which reduced the crew from 138 to 48.

At no capital cost, Alcoa combined operations and modified work practices in inspection,

---

[5] *Improving Productivity*, p. 42.

packaging, and shipping of sheet aluminum. The result was a crew reduction from 300 to 225.

Again, with no capital expenditure, a materials handling group was decentralized, resulting in a 20 percent reduction in material handlers, or 55 people.

Integrating the packaging of extrusions into the fabrication sequence, instead of having a separate packaging station, reduced labor by 25 percent and improved productivity 21 percent, at a cost of $100,000.

In the auto industry, productivity improvements are taking place through a number of programs, some based on replacing workers with more efficient capital equipment (such as robots), and others based on improving the productivity of workers. In fact, there seems to be an "industrial miracle" taking place. At Ford, their employee involvement program in quality and productivity improvement seems to be working well, *with* the support of the United Auto Workers Union.

The service sector is also active in their use of productivity improvement programs. American Express, for example, has identified 50 services the company provides and is working to improve them. They used to take an average of 35 days to process an application for a new credit card. By evaluating and improving the paper flow process, they trimmed this to two weeks. In addition, responses to cardholder inquiries has gone from 16 to 10 days; and responses to merchants' questions from 14 days to 4 days. American Express estimates they increased revenues by $2.4 million per year (and profits of $1.4 million) simply by speeding up the replacement of lost cards and issuing new ones more quickly.[6]

Impact of the Computer

As one would guess, the impact of computer technology with CAD/CAM, MRP, PERT, and the general computerization of paperwork is a major contribution to productivity improvement. Kemper Insurance is fully computerizing their insurance claims activities and expects to save $24 million a year by doing so. And the revitalized Chrysler Corporation is linking showrooms around the country to their factories with a computer network to enable dealers to input their specific orders, which will enable a more responsive update of their master production schedules.

Even microprocessor-based automatic teller machines are having a huge impact on productivity. Wells Fargo cut 9 percent from its work force of 8,000 and closed 30 of its 400 branches in California in the early 1980s when they installed these machines.[7]

Programs like these cost a certain amount of time and effort, but top management must be committed to spend some money in order to save more money. Also, these programs may not produce substantial results right away (it may take months or years), but the gains from having trained people to become more productivity-conscious usually persist for a long time.

Cautions

Some companies approach productivity improvement with edicts. The president tells the vice presidents to cut 10 percent off their costs. The vice presidents tell their plant managers, the plant managers tell the superintendents, and the superintendents tell the supervisors: "Cut 10 percent." The order goes down the line to every manager at every level. Lower-level managers are told to cut costs and still maintain the same output. The assumption is that the cuts will be made where they will harm operations the least.

Ruthless edicts usually backfire. Yet expenses *are* reduced, and they do often stop a certain amount of wasteful use of resouces. Ed-

[6] "Boosting Productivity at American Express," *Business Week*, October 5, 1981, p. 82.

[7] "The Revival of Productivity," *Business Week*, February 13, 1984, p. 99.

icts, however, can be unwise because worthwhile productive activities may also be cut in the process. Some years ago, Beckman Instruments cut costs 7 percent across the board, including its sales force. But 7 percent fewer sales people sold fewer products, so it was a poor strategy. Productivity programs should pay close attention to the essentiality of activities before they are reduced.

Labor-Management Committees

Some companies implement productivity improvement programs with participative programs consisting of labor-management committees. This not only helps to lessen some of the union-management competition mentioned earlier, but if management gets productivity gains, they share these cost savings with labor in the form of incentive pay and other benefits.

For example, Dana Corporation, in a move to improve its labor relations and productivity, installed a "Scanlon Plan" at a Wisconsin plant which uses labor-management committees extensively:

Scanlon plans have a long history and have been fairly successful. They are productivity improvement sharing plans where labor-management production committees solicit suggestions for productivity improvements from employees. The cost savings from these suggestions are shared between the company and its workers.

The initial reaction to this plan at Dana's Edgerton, Wisconsin plant has been favorable. The local union president said,

I like the Scanlon Plan because it gives a guy or gal a chance to have a say about what goes on. If I have an idea about how to better my job, I have the opportunity to submit the suggestions which make my job (1) possibly easier, (2) sometimes safer, and (3) possibly allowing more time for production. All of our people benefit from suggestions of other people, and the guy on the line

FIGURE 24–2
Objectives of Labor-Management Committees on Productivity

1. Conserve energy and fuel.
2. Reduce equipment downtime.
3. Eliminate waste of materials, supplies, and equipment.
4. Reduce scrap, rejects, and customer returns.
5. Improve housekeeping, eliminate excessive litter.
6. Improve quality of workmanship.
7. Use production time and facilities more efficiently.
8. Improve the scheduling of work.
9. Improve work methods and plant layout.
10. Improve product design.
11. Inform employees about business conditions and other changes which may affect the organization.
12. Dispel rumors that create anxiety and dissatisfaction.
13. Develop flexible work schedules.
14. Develop mutually acceptable ways of setting and meeting work standards.
15. Reduce sources of employee dissatisfaction.
16. Provide more opportunity for employee participation in decision making.
17. Eliminate physical and other stress conditions.
18. Develop skill training for employees and supervisors.

Source: *Starting a Labor-Management Committee in Your Organization* (Washington, D.C.: National Center for Productivity and Quality of Working Life, Spring 1978), pp. 6–7.

who submits them tends to feel a little more a part of the plant.[8]

Labor-management committees can usually consider matters which are not a part of normal collective bargaining activities between the union and management. Some of the problems these committees deal with in finding ways to improve productivity are shown in Figure 24–2. Care should be taken, however, that management not abdicate its rights to the union to make decisions.

On the other hand, with a "new era" of labor-management cooperation seeming to be at work in some sectors of the United States, both sides

---

[8] *Starting a Labor-Management Committee in Your Organization: Some Pointers for Action* (Washington, D.C.: National Center for Productivity and Quality of Working Life, Spring 1978), pp. 12–13.

should probably not stand so firmly behind their traditional adversary roles.

Requirements and Characteristics of Successful Participative Productivity Improvement Programs

There are several requirements for and benefits from successful participative-type productivity improvement programs, some of which may include workers, while others may be made up of only managers and supervisors.[9]

Source: *Business Horizons,* Joel W. Pett, © 1982.

Top management support. First, the program needs top management interest—and active interest. Everybody thinks that they have been doing a good job, have been working hard, and have done all they can. In spite of this, people will usually do even better if top management works with them and if they know that management is watching over their accomplishments. People will try specially hard if the top managers make it clear that productivity improvement is part of the basis for judging promotions and pay raises.

A program probably should start with the top managers calling a meeting in the board of directors' meeting room to announce the general idea that, "We must increase productivity." The challenge is put before everybody, and all are asked for their ideas as to how to go about it. If the crisis is serious enough, it helps for the executives to take salary cuts. This is what Chrysler executives did in 1979 when Chrysler was losing several hundred million dollars per year. In fact, Chrysler's two top executives pledged to cut their annual pay to $1 each until Chrysler was back in the black. In the mid-1980s, Chrysler was again profitable; and payoff to their

chairman, Lee Iacocca, was worth several million dollars in salary, stock, and benefits.

This original high-level committee will probably decide to set up several subcommittees to handle different areas (product design, materials, manufacturing methods, office costs, and so on). Usually one of the top managers will be a member of these subject or area subcommittees, along with middle managers and representatives from labor, if appropriate. Committee membership will also often cut across departmental lines. This often increases the success of a program. (See Figure 24–3.)

In some companies, the productivity effort is headed by a productivity manager who has been trained to install and monitor these programs.[10]

Commitment to implementation. Second, the committee members (with the help of the productivity manager) will, in the end, have to implement the things which will result in productivity improvements. They will not do this as committee members but as heads of their own departments or as workers in a department. As individuals, some of them might have hesitated to do anything about costs, or defended the pres-

---

[9] For a good discussion of these requirements, see Y. K. Shetty, "Key Elements of Productivity Improvement Programs," *Business Horizons,* March–April 1982, pp. 15–22; and W. B. Werther, "Out of the Productivity Box," *Business Horizons,* September–October 1982, pp. 51–59.

[10] See T. J. Murry, "The Rise of the Productivity Manager," *Dunns Review,* January 1981.

FIGURE 24–3
Tips for Planning a Productivity Improvement Program

These practical ideas can be useful in getting a plan going in your organization:

1. Establish a productivity council made up of representatives of major operating units.

2. Define, develop, and maintain a data base for measuring productivity and productivity improvement.

3. Develop and publish a brochure telling the purpose of the program and why everyone in the organization will benefit.

4. Develop a realistic system for measuring progress toward goals—including "deflators" that correct for price increases and inflation.

5. Distribute newsletters that disseminate ideas, techniques, and methods.

6. Establish liaison with professional productivity associations outside your own organization.

7. Set up a reference libarary and information-retrieval system.

8. Attend outside seminars, workshops, and training sessions on productivity and ways to improve it.

9. Find out, through personal contact what others are doing to increase productivity.

10. Develop a set of case histories of successful productivity examples. Support them with detailed descriptions, pictures, guidelines.

11. Determine whether outside authorities such as industrial engineers, industrial psychologists, or communication experts can be helpful in carrying out an industrywide program.

12. Plan and coordinate an internal information program via newspapers, magazines, and radio-television media to make sure people know about your productivity improvement efforts: what they're intended to accomplish and why they're important to employees, your members or customers, and the public.

Reprinted with permission from the September, 1980 issue of *ASSOCIATION MANAGEMENT,* © 1980, by the American Society of Association Executives.

ent practices. Being on the committee lets them be involved in improvement suggestions, and they usually become more committed to their implementation.

Monitoring productivity performance. Third, no program keeps going by itself after it is started. After productivity improvement goals are set, and as time unfolds, reports are made of what is done and comparisons are made against the goals. These comparisons should be made in *all* areas of resource use—labor, machine and equipment, energy and material utilization, and cost savings. The committees often make these comparisons and pay particular attention to unmet goals. Where did someone fail? Why? What else can be done to reach the particular goal? And so on. The committees review these matters as an important part of making the program work.

Productivity appreciation. Fourth, productivity teams (and managers) help develop a climate in which people will learn to appreciate

that resource inputs either are money or they cost money. They will learn how to reduce costs and improve quality. The committee meetings should be educational. Managers who are not experienced in cutting costs can receive ideas from their fellow committee members. Members also come to identify themselves more with the company and to think and work toward overall company goals; and, as a result, they are more willing to work out solutions which are best for the company, not just best for their own department or job.

Productivity competition. Fifth, committees work in an ambience of social pressure. Team members don't look good if they say that they can't cut costs when everyone else has agreed to do the same. Nor do they look good if they don't cut the costs that they told their fellow committee members they thought they could cut.

Committee organization. Finally, high-level productivity committees don't do all this by themselves. Each committee usually accepts the responsibility for overseeing a major resource expenditure area, then each member of these committees takes the responsibility for setting up one or more committees with the same kinds of assignments, but in a lower and smaller part of the organization. They then report their own committees' cost-cutting successes back to the higher-level committee.

Members of these lower-level committees agree to set goals for cutting expenses under their jurisdictions and to get their subordinates to do the same. The program results in the participation of everyone, including supervisors and workers. Some companies discuss programs with union officials before they proceed. Union officials often appreciate the problem and are willing to "go along," but they may not be able to give visible support. If they did, they probably would not get reelected because some of the expected savings are in labor costs.

Having so many people involved in committee meetings would seem to be a costly offset to the gains produced by productivity improvement programs. It is hoped, however, that the benefits will outweigh the costs. Productivity improvement programs are always important. People find the time to work at productivity improvement by cutting down on less important things that they have been spending their time on. They, themselves, often become more efficient.

LIVING WITH ECONOMIC DOWNTURNS

When sales go down and stay down, resource conservation and productivity improvement assumes even greater importance. It may be necessary to shrink the organization to the size which today's sales will support. Failure to do this may well bankrupt the organization. In a factory, direct labor and material costs will go down almost automatically because they are closely tied to production, but with other factors it is different.

The severe recession experienced in the early 1980s saw bankruptcies rise to a rate not seen since the depression of the 1930s. Companies laid off thousands of workers (both blue- and white-collar), and unemployment hit 20 percent in some areas of the country. This "shakeup" has stimulated productivity improvement like nothing else could have done, and some say it has been a healthy "awakening" for U.S. industry that it is time to really pay attention to the problems causing poor productivity and do something about them.

BUDGETS

Budgets are an important tool in planning and control systems and in implementing productivity improvement programs. The budget contains plans for spending to make money and to save money. They can be expressed both as plans for money expenditures and as productivity goals. In a factory, budgets are often both. Yet one can ask: What good is a spending or productivity plan? Will it help cut spending or increase productivity? Viewed just as a plan, a budget will not do these things automatically, but it is *more* than a plan. See Figure 24–4 for the flow of information in the budgetary process.

A budget should include a maximum limit on money expenditures and a minimum limitation on output. Department heads should have to work hard to get the work done without spending more than the budgeted amount. A budget motivates them. A budget is also a yardstick. Actual costs and output will be compared to the budget to see where, and by how much, subordinate managers did better or worse. These comparisons form the basis for answering "why" and "what" can be done to keep unplanned cost excesses or underachieved production goals from happening again in the future. This allows top management to achieve their real goals: controlled and lower costs and higher productivity per unit of input of labor, materials, capital, and energy.

Budgets do not, however, solve all problems. A budget or plan to increase sales or output or to cut costs does not, by itself, do either.

FIGURE 24–4
Budgetary Information Flow System

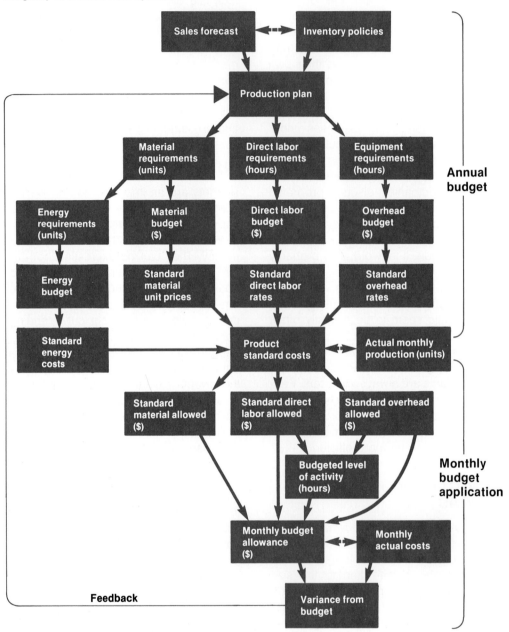

With or without budgets, managers should already be doing their best to achieve these objectives. And while a company can't exactly budget itself into a profit, most people do a better job with budgets than when they don't have them.

Zero-Based Budgeting

Budgets are usually developed for the future year based on some addition or subtraction of money (and the output that it buys) from the current year's budget. This is called *incremental* budgeting. With this approach, managers are asked to justify only the change.

Another approach—zero-based budgeting—is being used more by both private and public organizations, including the federal government. Using this approach, managers must justify their "first dollar" as well as the rest of their budget. Top management, in essence, presumes that next year's budget for a department is zero, unless they can be convinced to the contrary. This forces managers to evaluate their entire operation each year for productivity improvements and cost savings. This avoids their natural tendency of concentrating only on the justification of additional expenditures for labor, materials, capital, and energy—and does not automatically presume that their use was productive and cost-effective.

Review Questions

1. What is the current productivity "crisis" in the United States? (Review recent productivity statistics at the library in answering this question.)
2. In what ways is productivity defined?
3. Differentiate between productivity of labor and capital. How are they interrelated?
4. Why has productivity been doing so badly in the past few years in the United States?
5. What are some of the ways productivity can be measured? Can you think of others beyond those discussed in the text?
6. What role do labor contracts play in productivity?
7. What are labor-management committees, and what do they do?

8. How can a manager go about getting a supervisor to cut costs? Why do supervisors need special attention?
9. The text warns of certain problems in cost reduction; enumerate some of these and tell how to avoid them.

Questions for Discussion

1. Do you agree or disagree with the reasons cited in the text for our productivity problems? Take a stand on each reason, and be prepared to defend it in class.
2. "It's not fair to measure our productivity improvement against Japan and West Germany, because they are still catching up to us." Discuss.
3. "Trying to get people to improve doesn't always get them to do it. There is a low compliance with management's requests for improvement. Foot-draggers show considerable ingenuity in defeating the purposes of a productivity improvement program." Discuss the validity of these statements. What can be done about them?
4. After the meeting where the agriculture department expert told of new and better farming methods, one farmer said to the other: "It sounded pretty good. I think I'll give it a try. How about you?" "Nope," said his neighbor, "I ain't farmin' now half as good as I know how." How can business leaders get their subordinates to "farm as well as they know how"?
5. "It's the people near the bottom who have to make the cuts anyway, so why not just issue edicts from the top, and let these people figure out where and how to make them?" Discuss.
6. "Unions have little or no interest in productivity improvement." "Unions have much to gain from productivity improvements." Discuss.
7. "Look, boss," said the supervisor, "how can I ever satisfy you? You are always beefing about too much overhead, so I get my overhead ratio down, and now you yell because unit cost went up. I thought you'd be happy to see that lower overhead ratio." Discuss the supervisor's position.

Problems

1. The purchasing agent wants to go outside to buy a product which costs $10 per unit to make. The

$10 is made up of $3 for materials, $3 for labor, and $4 of overhead. The purchasing agent can buy the item from a vendor for $8 and save the company $2. Some 5,000 of these items will be used per year. Can the company afford to pass up these savings?

2. The following figures show certain information about three products. Red Ones, Blue Ones, and Orange Ones.

	Red Ones	Blue Ones	Orange Ones
Sales price per unit	$120	$100	$75
Raw material cost per unit	35	30	20
Production hours per unit	4	3	2

These products are all made at the same production facility and so are, in fact, alternative uses of that facility. Direct labor costs $7 per hour. All overhead, including depreciation, is $14,000 per year.

Which product should the sales department promote? How much will the best choice gain for the company as against each of the two less profitable choices?

3. Company A applies overhead as 100 percent of direct labor costs; company B applies overhead at 100 percent of material cost; and company C applies overhead at 50 percent of the sum of direct labor and material.

The companies make the same products. In setting their prices, each company adds 50 percent to factory costs to cover selling and administration costs and to provide a profit.

What will the prices of each company be if direct labor costs $2 a unit and material $8 a unit? What will they be if labor is $8 a unit and material $2 a unit?

Would you expect there to be an industry problem here? How can you resolve it?

Case 24–1

"We can't make any money on that job; it has too much labor in it," says Joe Guzik, the foundry foreman, to Harry Taylor, the cost estimator for the Doe Iron Foundry. The foundry, *like its competition,* always estimated costs (on which prices for jobs were based when quoting prices on prospective orders) on a per-pound basis.

Complex castings were regarded as class A castings and were quoted at a higher price per pound than more simple castings. Somewhat complex castings were class B and were quoted at a lower price per pound. Still simpler castings, class C castings, were quoted at the minimum per pound price.

In the case of the order at hand, Guzik felt that the class A price would not be high enough. It would almost surely cover all variable costs but would contribute little to carrying overhead.

Should Doe start quoting higher prices for castings requiring extra labor? What will happen if it quotes prices that fully cover all costs? Should the estimates be based on the cost of the labor-hours required plus materials costs?

Case 24–2

You are the president of the company, and you find this clause in the proposed labor contract:

"The company shall have the right to change or eliminate any local working condition if, as the result of action taken by Management under Article Fifteen—Management—of this Agreement, the basis for the existence of the local working condition is changed or eliminated, thereby making it unnecessary to continue such local working condition; provided, however, that when such a change or elimination is made by the Company, any adversely affected Employee may process a grievance on the ground that the changed condition did not warrant the change or elimination of such local condition."

How would this clause affect your operations? Would you sign the contract? Give your reasons.

Case 24–3

Central Valley University evaluates the productivity of its faculty members according to three factors: teaching effectiveness; research and publications; and service to the University and community. Each year these productivity evaluations are used as the basis for individual faculty salary increases, promotions, and tenure decisions.

Also, being a state supported university, the state legislature is becoming more interested in the "productivity" of faculty. They often complain that faculty only teach from 6 to 12 hours a week. "What do they do with the rest of their time?" one legislator from the rural western part of the state complained. "I propose we require the University to provide us with productivity measures similar to those I get in my company," said another legislator, who was a manufacturing executive. And, yet another legislator proposed that productivity of faculty be measured by how successful their graduates are at getting jobs—"after all, isn't that what education is all about?"

What difficulties might there be in measuring individual faculty productivity by the three factors that Central uses? What would you suggest?

What do you think of the legislature's desire to measure faculty productivity? Do you agree or disagree with the proposals and comments from the three legislators?

How is productivity measurement likely to be different between manufacturing, public, and service organizations?

Chapter 25

Improving Labor Productivity through Job Design

The task of improving jobs never ends. And the improvement of jobs leads to higher productivity. The time rarely comes when it is not possible to make any more improvements. The payoff from the effort directed at improving jobs can be substantial since a great deal of unnecessary work is often eliminated.

Good job design reduces human effort by determining how to do things more quickly; yet, curiously, many people dislike the thought of saving human effort. To many people, *efficiency* is a bad word. They seem to think that when anyone redesigns a job so that more productivity results this somehow takes advantage of the worker because—using the new method—he turns out more production.

And the worker on the job often thinks so, too. A yard worker who is provided with a power lawn mower can probably mow twice as much grass as he did before with his old hand-pushed mower and without working as hard. But he is still likely to think about it as if *he* were doing twice as much work (spending twice as much effort) as he did before. The same thing often occurs in organizations. Workers often oppose job improvements (or even any change) because they are sure that they must be working harder when more output results. They are also op-posed because improvements sometimes eliminate jobs. Curiously, the same worker who objects to job improvement in a factory will buy a power saw for his basement workshop at home. He can see there that the power saw saves his energy and lets him do a better job and more of it—and without working any harder.

Negative attitudes toward productivity improvements in jobs can often be turned into positive attitudes through such "participatory" programs as quality circles (discussed in Chapter 6) where people aid in the designing and reshaping of their jobs. Workers are encouraged to suggest improvements and are often rewarded for suggestions which can be applied. They may be given money or a certificate, or have their picture in the company paper. Or they may simply become more motivated because they have made a suggestion and it was approved and put into use.

Management often find that they win support for improvements by getting both workers and supervisors involved. Participation and involvement often cause them to become interested in improving the way they do their jobs. Managers, however, may have to "plant" ideas about improvements in people's minds and wait for the seeds to germinate.

JOB ENLARGEMENT AND JOB ENRICHMENT

Sometimes jobs can be made more interesting by enlarging or enriching them. Job enlargement means expanding a worker's job horizontally, adding a few more duties to increase the variety and reduce the monotony, but not substantially increasing the knowledge and skill required to do the enlarged job. Job enrichment, on the other hand, is vertical job and responsibility expansion, and is a planned change of the job's activities to give a person a greater variety of work which requires more knowledge and skill— and, it is hoped, provides the worker with more satisfaction and chance for personal growth. Workers are given the opportunity to participate in the planning, organization, and control of their work through quality circles or similar productivity improvement programs instead of just the execution of the work.

Job Enlargement

In the case of job enlargment, the issue is one of giving up extreme specialization, with a probable small loss in efficiency, for a reduction in boredom and monotony, which makes for more satisfied and effectively motivated workers.

The simplest kind of job enlargment is just giving the workers more duties to perform. Machine operators might, for example, get their own materials or sharpen their own tools, things formerly done by someone else.

Another fairly common practice is to have workers rotate among jobs. This can be done where there are groups of nearly identical machines doing much the same kind of work. Drill press operators, for example, sometimes change machines week by week or even daily. Each week they move over to the next machine. This introduces a little variety and reduces complaints about favoritism.

Another way to enlarge jobs is to use "work modules." A work module approach breaks a worker's job into several kinds of tasks and lets him do one kind of work for, say, an hour or two, as he sees fit. For example, a supermarket employee's task may be stamping prices, stocking shelves, running a checkout cash register, and performing inventory control work. The employee may choose, within limits, which modules he does and when. Some days he may stamp prices and stock shelves most of the day, whereas on other days he spends less time on these activities and more on inventory control.

In a factory, a stockroom employee may open and check in newly received materials for an hour or two. Then he may switch and trade off with another employee and service the stock issue window for a while. Or he may change and do clerical work for an hour or two, bringing the stock records up to date. Being able to change from one kind of activity to another largely as he wants to improves a job's acceptability.

On factory production lines, the evidence is not clear on just how much less boring a three-minute job is than a two-minute job. Nor is the evidence conclusive that less specialized but more strongly motivated workers turn out more work. Often the benefits claimed to have resulted from job enlargement are phrased in terms other than increased output or lower costs as such. Job enlargement is said to result in more motivated employees, lower labor turnover, and lower absenteeism. Yet even these gains do not always materialize. The Internal Revenue Service redesigned clerical jobs to give them increased autonomy, variety, and wholeness. Error rates did not improve and production went down as a result of the more complicated methods.[1]

Industry in general is experimenting with job enlargement; however, the gains have not been great or else we would see more of it.

Job Enrichment

Job enlargement, obviously, offers only limited possibilities for making jobs more interesting and

---

[1] Reported in Mildred E. Katzell, *Productivity: The Measure and the Myth* (AMACOM, 1975), p. 6.

more meaningful, but the horizons are broader with job enrichment programs.

Job enrichment is advocated by many social scientists as a way for allowing people to fulfill their need for "esteem" and "self-actualization." According to these social scientists, all of us have, deep within us, a desire to be esteemed by others and to work at our highest skills levels and to accomplish something which we can claim as our own accomplishment. If jobs can be designed so that these needs can be fulfilled, the result will be more motivated employees who produce more and better work and who are absent and quit less often than if these needs are not fulfilled.

In trying to carry out this philosophy, the Eaton Company (maker of door locks and automobile parts) has found that many of its employees want to be involved in deciding the minor details of the makeup of their jobs. They want to participate in the measurement of the quality of their work by doing their own inspection instead of having others do it. Eaton found, too, that its factory workers wanted to do their own minor machine maintenance and wanted to aid in determining work schedules and such matters as the use of assembly "teams" of workers instead of production lines.

Another area where job enrichment might be used is in the operation of numerically controlled machines. Often these machines are so automatic that all the operators have to do is load the machine and push a button. While the machine is operating, the opertors have nothing to do. Their job would surely be more interesting if they were given something to do during the waiting time. Perhaps they could operate several machines; be given the responsibility for inspecting their own work; plan their daily or weekly workload; or modify instruction programs for N/C machines.

Obviously, however, since people differ from each other, not everyone wants an "enriched" job. Some people avoid creative-type jobs in favor of security as long as the physical work environment, fringe benefits, and pay are satisfactory. To many, their personal lives and recreational activities, *not* their jobs, are of primary interest to them. This point is often overlooked by managers and social scientists as well.

Other innovations which are being used to enrich jobs are the use of teams to assemble products, and variable work schedules.

Assembly Teams

In the early 1970s, Sweden's Volvo and Saab-Scania automobile companies received a great deal of favorable publicity from their innovation of discarding the traditional line assembly method and substituting teams or small groups of workers who collectively assemble such subcomponents as a car's electrical wiring system or its spring suspension system. These teams are free to organize themselves as they see fit and set their own work speed and coffee break times so long as they meet their production goals. Rather than utilizing a moving conveyor, the plant has 18-foot-long computer-controlled "carriers," which move the cars around the plant to the 25 work teams. Each team's progress toward its production goals is computer-monitored and flashes a yellow light if they are behind and a green light if they are ahead.

Reports were that this method worked better than had the older, conventional production lines.

Naturally, these reports interested both American employers and American unions as well as the Ford Foundation. In November 1974, the Ford Foundation sent a group of six Detroit automobile workers to Sweden to work in one of these groups in a Saab-Scania factory for four weeks.[2]

The Detroit workers did not like the experience and felt that the pace was too fast and that the atmosphere was not free and open. Some of the comments were:[3]

"If I've got to bust my ass to be meaningful, forget it; I'd rather be monotonous." "Group assembly becomes boring after a while."

---

[2] Their reactions are reported in *A Work Experiment: Six Americans in a Swedish Plant* (Ford Foundation, 1976).

[3] Ibid., pp. 33–37.

"Things are more open at home and you have better counsel from your foreman. The workers associate better too. They're more part of it. Here it is separate." "In the States you have your boredom, but you still have your more outward-going, more happy-go-lucky [attitudes]. We make the workplace happy while we are there."

"Somehow, I have the feeling, you're being had! They knock themselves out to make this place [good] for you to be able to work in and like it, even though it's really—how can I say this—they make it easy for you as possible to swallow a hard pill. In the States, even though it's dirty, and even though it's noisy, there you don't have to swallow anything." "Here you see the foreman, and that's it. You're on a last name basis with him. [At home] I call my general foreman, 'Hey, Jasper.' [Here] I don't even know his name." "It's a family here . . . but it's a type of family where the father will provide for all of the comforts of his children to see that they get everything they need. But they have no freedom, really, to go against his wishes."

This experience does not give good marks for assembly teams. However, a general indictment against them is probably too harsh, as there have been other, more successful experiences in other industries than the one stated here. In a sense, of course, the "teamwork" approach the Japanese take in assembly can be considered a variation on this theme, as we discussed earlier in Chapter 14.

Variable Work Schedules

Another approach to making jobs more attractive is to allow for variation in the work hours. Sometimes it is possible to adjust work schedules and to allow employees a certain amount of freedom to work whatever hours they want.

Several arrangements are possible. In its extreme form, workers would be free to work whatever hours they care to. Rarely are operations so flexible that they can be carried on effectively with such irregularities.

Often, two part-time employees share a job, one working the first half-shift and the other working the second half-shift. This has been tried at times in areas where full-time workers are scarce but vacationers and older people are available.

"Flextime"

Another variation, called *flextime,* is gaining acceptance. With flextime, workers may come early or late and leave early or late just so they put in eight hours of work in a day. They may even take time out during the day for shopping or going to the dentist.

Flextime, which originated in West Germany in the late 1960s, is a growing practice and is now being used by a number of organizations in the United States, among them, General Motors, Montgomery Ward, NCR, and others. The federal government has also been using it more and more in the armed forces, in the Social Security Administration, and in certain other civil service jobs. Several states also endorse flextime and allow it to be implemented in appropriate organizations. Its use has doubled in the last few years, encompassing about 15 percent of all organizations and about 8 percent of all workers (not counting professionals, managers, and salesmen, many of whom have always had it).

As it is used at Hewlett-Packard, flextime allows workers on this system to arrive at work any time between 6:30 and 8:30 A.M. and to leave from 3:00 to 5:00 P.M., with as much as 2½ hours out during the day for lunch, shopping, or other personal business. Hewlett-Packard reports only good experience with this program, with greater productivity, better morale, and so on. There have also been numerous reports of good results in Europe and Japan from using flexible work hours. It has been particularly helpful to working mothers with school-age children whose time demands often conflict with regular eight-to-five workdays.

In spite of these favorable reports, one needs to discount them a little. Obviously most workers would like the extra freedom it gives them. As against this, tardiness and absenteeism usually interfere with effective operations. And it doesn't matter whether the absent workers are out shopping or have gone home early; their not being on the job when others are there may make joint work more difficult. Nor, in some situations, can a worker who comes in early be very productive working alone.

Flextime may make it necessary for white-collar workers to punch time clocks, and most of them do not like this. Administration costs are also higher. Some labor union leaders regard flextime as a "back-door" attempt to deny workers overtime pay and eliminate the eight-hour day.

In addition, flexible hours are often difficult to arrange in organizations which have to provide 24-hour service, in some maintenance work, in long-haul truck driving, in hospital emergency service, in many airline services, and so on. Nonetheless, the growth of flextime is expected to continue throughout the 1980s.

Four-Day Work Weeks

Another variant from ordinary work schedules, the four-day work week, is regarded by some people as a method of job enrichment. The four-day work week is composed of four 10-hour days. This has been tried, and, although it has received a good press, four-day work weeks are not common. Its use has not increased in recent years, and only about 2 percent of the labor force is on a four-day work week. In addition, about 28 percent of the firms that have tried it have given it up. It has enjoyed its greatest success in small service-type organizations where the days off can usually be arranged to correspond to slow periods in calls for service.

The four-day work week saves workers from working a fifth day and gives them a long weekend. With high fuel costs this could reduce energy consumption. On the negative side, everyone's children have to go to school five days, so there can't be long weekends for the entire family. And, many workers do not like to leave home shortly after 6:00 A.M. and get back shortly before 7:00 P.M. Besides, many people do not know what to do with Friday off.

And, from the employer's point of view, having the establishment closed on Fridays may disrupt service. Shipments in and out on Fridays are delayed. Staggering the four days so that some workers work Monday–Thursday and others work Tuesday–Friday may help. This is, however, quite an unsatisfactory arrangement most of the time in a factory because some machines and production lines need to be staffed with full crews if they are to operate at all. Also, productivity per hour will drop from fatigue during the long 10-hour days.

Unions usually oppose the four 10-hour day arrangement unless they get time-and-a-half pay for the last two hours each day (11 hours' pay for 10 hours of work). This would increase labor costs 10 percent, to say nothing of the slightly lower productivity which can be expected during the long 10-hour days. Unions are, however, strongly in favor of four 8-hour days in a week with 40 hours of pay. With this method's 25 percent increase in costs, it is understandable that this arrangement is probably nonexistent, and certainly so in unionized organizations.

Other unusual schedules are occasionally used. Where seven-day-a-week operations are needed, workers might work four 10-hour days, then have four days off. Different workers can have different sets of four days which can be staggered so that out of any seven workers, four are always working and three are off on any given day.

In other cases, and this is a little more common, workers alternate shifts; perhaps one week on the day shift, one on nights, then back to days, and so on.

These various alternating arrangements may enrich jobs in that they spread favorable and unfavorable situations around. Usually this is at least a little uneconomical from a production point of view, and some workers do not like to have their schedules vary so much.

Permanent Part-Time Jobs

Part-time jobs have always been an important way to provide flexibility to both employees and employers. Employers can use part-timers during peak demand times; and employees are able to have a job, yet do other things, like go to college or be a housewife. A growing trend is to make part-time jobs more permanent and not use them simply for low-level kinds of activities.

Some organizations are hiring professionals and skilled workers on a part-time basis and giving them full or partial fringe benefits—a practice which has been avoided in the past. Employers find that part-timers often get more done proportionally in their 20 hours a week than full-time employees. And it allows them to tap labor pools that have special skills who ordinarily would not be available if they could not work part time.

JOB IMPROVEMENT LIMITATIONS

Jobs are not always improved as much as they could be, partly because there is so much change. There is always a need to start new jobs by performing them at first as best one can and then improving them as time goes along. Also, some jobs are not of much consequence, or they won't be performed very often. It costs less to let them be done inefficiently than to study them carefully to improve them when they are done for only 15 minutes a day.

Nor does careful job study pay off unless jobs are standardized. All of the relevant factors—products, processes, materials handling methods, working conditions, workplace arrangements, as well as methods and the worker's motions—need to be standardized. The improvement and standardization of these factors are two of the main objects of all job improvement analysis; but, if they vary continually and cannot be standardized, improvement possibilities are limited.

It would seem to be unnecessary to add that top-level management support is needed in order for job improvement to be very successful. Yet such support is often not provided. When this is so, lower-level people find it easy not to implement job improvement suggestions made by industrial engineers if doing so requires extra work, even though the savings may be great.

Thus, organizational lethargy and ineffective leadership can severely limit job improvement.

DESIGNING NEW JOBS

Job design is directed toward improving jobs; yet, it may be wasteful to start doing a job one way and then change it. Also, since many people are opposed to changing, it is better to determine the best way to do an operation *before* starting to do it all.

This is where job design and methods study can be useful. Admittedly, it is hard to see ahead of time how a new operation might be done and then improve it before it is actually done. Nonetheless, this is the approach that mass producers of consumer products take. Before production lines are constructed, industrial engineers try to visualize the bits and pieces of work to be done at successive work stations. They sometimes use workplace mock-ups. They try to divide the work evenly among workers; to arrange the workplaces; and to develop tools—all ahead of time. Improvements developed this way avoid the costs of making major changes later, and at the same time avoid much of the opposition to change.

JOB DESIGN OBJECTIVES

Just as product engineers design products, industrial engineers, supervisors, and workers themselves design jobs. They study the needs of operations and the capabilities of people and machines and develop jobs to strike the best balance which satisfies all of the relevant factors.

Usually, the main objectives are to save human effort, to develop the most economical mix of labor and machines, and to design the job so a reasonable amount of satisfaction can be obtained by doing it. Yet, job designers should not strive for ultimates. Frequently, if a person were to ask an industrial engineer what he is trying to do, the time-honored answer will come back: "I try to find the one best way to do every job." This is not really what he should be trying to do, though. He should be trying to find a *better* method. The difference is important. If he always tries to find the *best* way, he will spend all his time seeking ultimates on too few jobs. Job designers usually have to be satisfied with developing a *better* way at reasonable expense. It simply costs too much to be a perfectionist.

In trying to improve jobs, and make them easier for workers, the analyst tries to do three things: (1) eliminate as many human movements as possible, (2) shorten the movements that cannot be eliminated, and (3) make the necessary movements less tiring.

But the job designer should not focus entirely on human movements and overlook other possibilities for improvements. A person's movements often cannot be simplified unless the workplace is rearranged, or the person is given some special tools, or the machine is changed or even the product itself. In fact, the analyst should not study a person's motions at all until the job is improved as much as it can be in other ways.

Suppose, for example, the worker's job is to paint a part. The reason for the operation is to cover a surface—to protect it or to make it look attractive. The analysts should *not* start with the way the worker handles the paint brush; they should start by asking: Does the job have to be done at all? Product engineers should be able to answer that question. Assuming that they say yes, the analysts should ask when, where, and how the paint should be put on. Perhaps the part should be painted when the assembled product is painted—at no extra cost. But if the part must be painted by itself, how should the worker paint the part? By using a spray gun or a brush, by dipping the part in the paint, or by smearing the paint on with a sponge? (Or replacing the painter with a painting robot?) The analysts should pick the best method, and then—not before—begin considering the worker's movements and *how* they should be made. Job design analysis should not be confined to a study of the motions of workers. (See Figure 25–1).

Often, the first questions about a job's de-

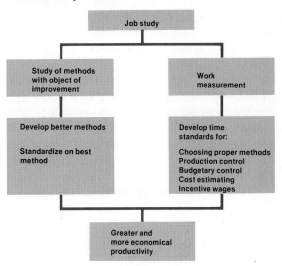

FIGURE 25–1
How Job Study Leads to Greater Production

sign must be answered by product design or tool or machine design engineers. If the job is to drill a hole in a steel casting, an early question might be: Why not make the part out of a steel stamping and punch the hole instead of drilling it? Or suppose that a worker is putting pieces of material, one after the other, into a machine. The natural question to ask is: Could the tool engineers design an automatic feed? Again, the study of the workers' movements should be the last step in methods improvement.

METHODS FOR IMPROVING SPECIFIC JOBS

We have been discussing "macro" or overall job design matters. However, in order to design specific new jobs or redesign old jobs, analysts have to come down to the "micro" level. They have to study the minor parts of the job. In order to do this, several "tools" are available.

The first tool that methods analysts need is an inquiring mind. They will not get far if they accept such ideas as "We've always done it that way"; "The present method works, doesn't it? So it must be all right." Methods which "just grow'' are rarely as good as those which have been analyzed. Instead, analysts should assume that the usual way of doing a job is the wrong way. Or that, if we are still doing a job the same way we did it two years ago, we are probably doing it the wrong way.

If wasted motions flew red flags, it would be easy to improve jobs. But they don't. The analyst must scrutinize the job—and look at it minor part by minor part, not as a whole—to see what movements the worker makes. Then the analysts must decide where improvements can be made.

Analysts have certain working tools (beyond an inquiring mind) to aid in job design or redesign. These are:

1. Process charts.
2. Motion study guidelines.
3. Micromotion study.
4. Therblig analysis.
5. Thought-provoking questions.
6. Quality circles.
7. Ergonomics.

These tools can be used separately or together. Of the six, numbers 1, 2, 5, 6, and 7 are the most often used.

Process Charts

There are a wide variety of charts which analysts can use to aid in visualizing a job and to see ways of improving it. Like a picture, a chart holds things still—so to speak—so they can be studied. And it lets analysts see the entire job, not just one thing at a time. Often things can be better analyzed on a chart than out on the factory floor, or in the bank or clerical office. Charts for new jobs allow analysts, within limits, to see in advance how the jobs might work. If improvements seem possible, they can be made and a new chart developed—all before the new job is started.

Nonetheless, one cannot expect too much from charts. A chart, by itself, does not design a job nor does it improve a job; it takes a creative analyst to make improvements. All a chart can

do is to depict arrangements. Nor do charts need to be precisely drawn to be useful. They should, however, contain considerable detail because some of the opportunities for improvement are in the details. The important things, the obvious things that required improvement in the past, have probably already been taken care of.

Process charts of all kinds show the details of some action. They describe what is done. Besides this, nearly all charts have a symbol for each kind of detailed action. The time it takes to do tasks and the distance things are moved are also commonly shown. Summaries of how often each kind of action occurs are also common.

But, one might ask, why symbols? What good are little squares, circles, flat-sided circles, arrows, triangles, and so on? They are the analyst's shorthand for details. Large circles are usually operations; they show that something is being done to the product or a service is being rendered. Small circles or arrows mean that the product is moved. Triangles or flat-sided circles mean the item is being stored. Squares indicate inspections.

Classifying the details with symbols as codes allows analysts to see how often each kind of activity happens. It also points out where these things are done. This is useful as analysts try to rearrange details to combine some things and eliminate others.

When constructing a chart, analysts should be sure that it shows what *is* happening—not what *is supposed* to be happening. An exception, of course, is in designing future jobs which show how a job is to be done.

As part of the design process, analysts may need to construct one or more working charts depicting interim stages of improvement before they settle on a final method.

It is unfortunate that names for the different kinds of charts are not standardized. However, those we use are fairly common and are listed below:

1. Charts which show the complete processing of a product.

a. *Flow diagrams.* A flow diagram shows, on a floor plan, how a product (or steps in a service activity) moves through the facility. Symbols show where operations are done. This kind of chart is often used with another sheet of paper describing the individual operations and other details shown on the chart by symbols.

b. *Flow process charts* (see Figure 25–2). This kind of chart tells the same story as a flow diagram but as a list without a floor plan. It also provides spaces for showing

FIGURE 25–2
Flow Process Chart

Summary					Analyze present method to
		Present	Proposed	Saved	1. Eliminate
	Distance	50 ft.	40 ft.	10 ft.	2. Combine
◯	Operation	13	11	2(17 min.)	3. Improve
▷	Transportation	3	2	1	4. Change–
▢	Inspection	1	1	0	a. Sequence
▽	Storage	0	0	0	b. Person
D	Delay	1	0	1(10 min.)	c. Place

ASK–Where, When, What, Who, Why, How

Fill in symbol	Proposed detail description	Time or distance	Reasons
1 ▷	Deliver packed valves to stockroom on caster table	20ft.	Delivers valves without carrying
2 ◯	Clear up table for next order	1/2 min.	
3 ◯	Pick up and arrange packing supplies ordered	1/2 min.	Ordering ahead saves delay time
4 ◯	Requisition supplies for next order	3 min.	Helps stock man plan
5 ▷	Push caster table back to packing room	20 ft.	Saves carrying valves
6 ◯	Pick up tote box of valves	1/4 min.	
7 ◯	Dump tote box on table	1/4 min.	
8 ◯	Put prefolded cartons in jigs (2)		New cartons cost 4c more per 100
9 ◯	Place flat instruction sheet over carton		Use instruction sheet as wrapper. Saves paper–9c per 100
10 ▢	Inspect 2 valves at a time	Total of	More complete visual inspection
◯	Place valves in cartons (2)	8 sec. per valve;	Use both hands
12 ◯	Close cartons (2)	13 1/3 min. per	Handles 2 at a time
13 ◯	Put on pressure - sensitive labels	100 valves	New labels 3c per 100 more
14 ◯	Place cartons in shipping carton		Approval to proceed: *James Carlson*

Action taken and resultant savings–

Put casters on table, changed sequence, simplified packing, did 2 at a time, smoother motions, eliminated motions, eliminated some packing supplies.
Better labels.
Saved 27 min. per order of 100, and 2c per 100 in supplies.

how much time it takes to do things and spaces for showing the distance materials (or paperwork, or people, if a service) are moved. Figure 25–2 is actually the "after" chart of a "before-and-after" pair of charts. As a result of a study, the analyst, in this case, reduced the number of operations from 13 to 11. The moves were cut from 3 to 2 and delays from 1 to 0. The 1 inspection and zero storages remained unchanged.

c. *Operation process charts.* These are simi-

lar to the first two charts, but they emphasize how and where parts are joined together and what happens before and after they are assembled.

2. Charts showing details of single operations.

a. *Operator-machine charts.* These charts list the activities of a machine operator (or more than one operator) and the machine operated. The vertical part is a time scale, and activities are listed at exactly the time they have to happen. Doing this makes sure that the operator does not have to

FIGURE 25–3
Operation Chart

Operation: Press insert into sleeve
Equipment: #20 bliss press - 2 position
Punch and dieholder for sleeve

Left hand	Right hand
Carry sleeve to holder	
Position sleeve in holder	Reach to insert
	Pick up one insert
	Move to sleeve in holder
	Position insert in sleeve
Idle	Release insert
Reach to sleeves	Reach to holder handle
Grasp one sleeve	Grasp handle
	Move holder under 1st punch
	Position holder under punch
	Press insert into sleeve
	Move holder under 2d punch
	Position holder under punch
	Press assembly out of holder
	Move holder from under punch
Idle	Release holder

Assemblies (on floor)
Insert
2d 1st
Holder
Sleeves
Sleeve (steel)
Insert (brass)

Source: H. B. Maynard & Co.

be in two places at once. Symbols are not often used in operator-machine charts.

b. *Operation charts.* Figure 25–3 is a left- and right-hand chart without a time scale. Each hand's activities are listed opposite each other whenever they are done at the same time. Small circles are used for every activity, no matter what kind. (This is for counting and highlighting the lack of balance of work between the two hands.)

c. *Simo charts.* Simultaneous motion charts are used in rare cases. They are extremely detailed and depict in detail what each hand or even what each finger does.

3. *Office procedure charts.*

Charts of the type described here can be used to analyze office and other service jobs as well as factory jobs. Office procedures, however, introduce a problem not found in factory charts. Office forms are often made in several copies which go to different departments, so the analyst has to devise charts which track the movement of these multiple copies.

Motion Study Guidelines

Motion study guidelines, the second kind of job improvement tool, provide general rules to follow for improving jobs. Some of these are listed below.

1. *Rules for minimizing human movements.* Never do a job the hard way if there is an easier way.

   a. Don't do jobs by hand if machines can do them. Transfer everything possible to machines when practical. In particular, try to design machines which not only will do the operation, but which will first place the product in position and then eject it after the operation.

   b. Eliminate handling. Bring materials as close as possible to the point of work and remove them by gravity if possible; if this cannot be done, do it mechanically. If materials must be handled by a person, handle as many as possible at one time. De-

sign machines to do two or more operations once the material has been put in position.

   c. Use the fewest motions possible. Move as little of the body as is necessary to do the job; in fact, move only the fingers if finger motion will do. Don't reach; put things where little reaching is necessary.

   d. Use fixed positions for all materials and tools. Put them close to and in front of the worker to reduce searching as well as reaching for them. Motions then become automatic.

2. *Rules for making the best use of people.* A whole person produces more than part of a person.

   a. Use two hands but avoid using hands purely as holding devices. Idle hands do no work. If both are not busy, redistribute the work between them. On light assembly jobs mechanical holding devices can often make a job into a one-handed job, in which case an identical job can be done with the other hand. The worker will not do twice as much work as with one hand, but he is likely to do half as much more. Working with two hands may take practice, but it is quite possible. Typists and pianists do it all the time.

   b. Use the feet as well as the hands if they can be used to push a pedal or do some useful movement. Hands and feet can both be used at the same time. Does it sound impossible? Fifty million of us do this every day when we drive our cars.

   c. Study and analyze all hesitations and short delays within jobs and eliminate them when possible.

   d. Where unavoidable delays occur, give people other work to keep them productive.

   e. The time an expert takes to perform a task is possible for everyone. Try to get all people to do as well.

3. *Rules for saving human energy.* Tiring movements waste energy.

a. Transfer all heavy lifting to mechanical lifting devices.

b. Use momentum where possible, rather than force. A person cannot, for example, push a nail into a board even with a hammer. But, if he swings the hammer, its momentum does the job. Avoid momentum, however, if muscular effort has to be used to stop it.

c. Continuous, curved motions are easier and less tiring than motions involving sharp changes in direction.

d. Assign all work to the body member best suited for it; in typing, for example, don't do it all with the little finger.

e. Use the body to the best advantage mechanically. If force must be exerted, exert it at heights and in positions where the body can employ the most force.

f. Eliminate working conditions which add to fatigue. Use power-driven tools; improve lighting, ventilation, and humidity; eliminate dusty conditions, temperature extremes, and extreme noise. If possible, provide a comfortable chair, and arrange work so the operator can stand or sit as he or she wishes.

g. On fatiguing jobs, allow rest periods. The heavier the task, the more necessary are frequent (but short) rest periods. Many short rest periods are better than a few long rest periods.

h. On monotonous jobs, provide an occasional break; monotony, fatigue, and scrap are related. Consider job enlargement and job enrichment to lessen monotony.

4. *Rules for placing people.* Use labor to its best advantage in view of the jobs to be filled and the people available.

a. Where several workers do the same job day after day, break the job up into small tasks and let each worker specialize but with some rotation allowed. Each will acquire greater proficiency, and the group will usually produce more.

b. Put workers on jobs well suited to them, and place only well-suited people on the jobs.

c. Avoid using high-priced labor on low-priced work even if this work is but a small part of a high-priced worker's job. Divide the job and assign work to the grade of worker required.

Micromotion Study

This way of analyzing motions takes videotapes of jobs and then runs them slowly and even stops the film to look at each frame separately—much as is done in the "stop-action" video we see on TV in sports events. Since we can time the video, we can see how long an activity takes as well as analyze the slowed down (or stopped) subactivites to see what is happening.

It is possible to analyze jobs by using time-lapse photography. This means taking perhaps 1 picture per second instead of 16–20 per second. An even lower frequency may also suffice. (This is what is done in pictures of flowers blooming—a three-day growth can be condensed into a one-minute movie segment.)

Making usable videos is not an amateur's job. It is expensive to do all of this, and most of the people concerned—supervisors and workers on jobs—don't like the idea. Unions nearly always oppose it. It is small wonder that micromotion study is not widely used in industry.

Videos of jobs, however, can be useful in other ways. They furnish an enduring record of how a job is done, and they can be used to help train new people. And micromotion study can be used to advantage in large companies for short-cycle jobs that are done millions of times a year.

Therblig Analysis[4]

Therblig analysis, like micromotion study, is not commonly used. It is just too detailed and costly

---

[4] The term *therblig* was coined by Frank and Lillian Gilbreth, who were pioneers in the study of work design. Therblig is Gilbreth spelled (almost) backwards.

except for very short-cycle jobs which are done thousands of times. A *therblig* is a small part of a job—a very small part. It is usually much too short to time with a stopwatch.

When time study analysts set production standards (discussed in Chapter 27), they analyze jobs part by part, but their parts of a job (they call them *elements*) would stop at, say, "tighten bolt." "Tighten bolt," however, is made up of several very short therbligs: Move hand, get ready to pick up wrench, grasp wrench, move hand with wrench, position wrench, and turn wrench. Other therbligs are: Search, select, grasp, move hands empty, move hands holding something, hold, release load, position something, preposition something, inspect, assemble, take apart, use, unavoidable delay, avoidable delay, plan, and rest.

Therblig analysis, when used, can help analysts because it forces them to look at minor parts of a job. True, sometimes it is possible to cut out large parts of jobs or even whole jobs, but sometimes more time can be saved by looking at the therbligs, one by one. It is often possible to work out job improvements quite effectively with therblig analysis if such analyses are combined with predetermined times for fundamental movements such as methods time measurement (MTM) provides (see Chapter 27). Using this approach, analysts can evaluate alternative methods before production is begun.

But let us return to the "tighten bolt" part of a job. The worker reaches for the wrench and for the bolt; then reaches again when laying the wrench aside. If the wrench and the bolt are put closer to him, reaching time will be saved. Next, if the wrench and bolts are always put in the same places, they can be picked up more quickly, without groping around for them or looking each time to find them. Putting the wrench in a slot or holder so that it sticks up lets the worker grasp it more quickly.

And it is the same with every therblig. Each needs to be looked at separately because different things are needed to improve each one.

After the analyst has done all this, the "tighten bolt" element will probably take less time than it did before. But the improvement will be the result of looking at the details, not the overall job.

Thought-Provoking Questions

Thought-provoking questions are the next job improvement tool. They are much like guidelines, but they are more numerous and detailed. Merely asking some of the following questions about almost any job is likely to make analysts think of one or more ways to improve it.

First, there are general questions which apply to all jobs. They include: By whom, where, why, and how is the job done? Is this movement necessary? What does it do? What would happen if it were eliminated? Can it be shortened? Can it be transferred to a machine? Can it better be done at another time? Can it be combined with another movement or operation?

These questions would start almost anyone thinking, but they are not really what we mean by thought-provoking questions, which are more specific. Here are a few (which apply mostly to metal products):

If the operation is performed to improve appearance, is the added cost justified by adding salability?

If the operation is to correct a subsequent difficulty, is the corrective operation less costly than the difficulty?

Is this operation made necessary because of the poor design of tools that are used in a previous or a following operation?

Is the matching of a surface done merely to improve appearance, and, if so, can a suitable appearance be obtained in some less costly way?

If design requires special tooling, can it be altered so that standard cutters, multiple drilling heads, jigs, and the like can be used?

Is the job inspected at the critical point instead of after the job is done?

Are the suppliers furnishing material on

which they have performed an operation that is not necessary for its use?

Could molded or cast parts be substituted to eliminate machining or other operations?

Are closer tolerances specified than are necessary?

Both the process of generating the questions as well as answering them aids in bringing opportunities for improvement to the analyst's mind.

Quality Circles

Another way to improve jobs (and productivity) is by using quality circles. Usually they are set up as part of a special productivity and quality improvement program, as discussed in Chapters 6 and 24. The people actually doing the work form a task force to "brainstorm" the activities in their work center to see what improvements they can think of. Often they see opportunities for improvements which were missed before.

Ergonomics

The science of ergonomics (from the Greek word for *work*) or human factors engineering is a growing profession. While it is used primarily for product design, it naturally can be applied

FIGURE 25–4

In the ergonomics lab at Burroughs Corp., an operator puts a mock-up of a check encoder through its paces. Researchers studying the operator's movements will adjust the key pad and check holder so the final design will be as efficient and comfortable to use as possible.

Source: W. McQuade, "Easing Tensions between Man and Machine," *Fortune,* March 19, 1984, p. 66. Photograph produced with permission of M. L. Abramson.

to the workplace where people must interact with machines—which are products too.

Human factors engineering considers the relationship between the physical and mental characteristics (capacities and limitations) of people and the jobs they do and/or the machines they operate. Much of the research in this field has been done by the military— especially the Air Force—to scientifically design the cockpit environments (seats, instrument panel, levers, windows, and so on) of supersonic fighter aircraft so that pilots can perform their tasks efficiently and with minimum fatigue. For example, "The cockpit of the P–51 fighter of 1940 had 21 instruments for the pilot to watch; by the time the F–100 came along in 1965, that number of instruments had multiplied to 46. In the 1980 F–15, so much information pressed upon the pilot that twice that number of dials probably could not handle it. The ergonomic solution has been to install, in addition to the basic 33 dials, five small cathode-ray tubes around him that keep changing, highlighting only information pertinent to the instant."[5]

However, human factors engineering is also used in the design of many other products, machines, and working environments. "Kodak has 40 ergonomists who do everything from helping to make copiers and cameras user-responsive to studying work practices in its factories."[6]

Few would dispute that today's automobiles are more comfortable, easier to drive, have better visibility, and have better-arranged "cockpits" than cars of the 1960s. This is not by chance. Engineers design automobiles these days after careful consideration of human's skeletal structures, their range of vision, hearing capabilities, strength, and their ability to respond to emergencies—such as moving the foot from the accelerator to the brake. The new stoplight mounted at the rear-window level on 1986 autos

resulted from ergonomic studies. They are easier to see and thus can reduce rear-end collisions.[7]

This is also true in the design of machines and working environments. Automatic machines have their levers, instruments, and buttons designed and positioned so that operators can easily monitor the machine's progress, load and unload it, and be protected from excessive fumes, heat, and noise which might result from the process.

In offices, noise-reducing baffles, properly designed desks, chairs, office equipment, and soft background music are the result of human factors engineering considerations.

Much effort these days is being put into the design of videoscreens and keyboards for computers to reduce eyestrain, aches and pains, fatigue, and stress caused by sitting for extended periods at these machines.[8]

Review Questions

1. How is job enlargement related to job enrichment?
2. Compare and contrast different variable work scheduling arrangements. Which seem to be best (or worse) under different circumstances?
3. How widespread is the reluctance to try to improve jobs? How can a job analyst who is supposed to improve jobs win people to a cooperative viewpoint?
4. "I try to find the one best way to do every job," says a method study analyst. Discuss this statement.
5. How can an analyst do motion study work for jobs which have not yet been done? Why would this be necessary?
6. How can a process chart be of any help to a job analyst?
7. Can micromotion study ever be justified? Justify your answer.
8. What is human factors engineering, and how is it used in job design?

---

[5] For an excellent discussion of ergonomic applications in the 1980s, see W. McQuade, "Easing Tensions between Man and Machine," *Fortune,* March 19, 1984, pp. 58–66.

[6] Ibid., p. 58.

---

[7] Ibid.

[8] Ibid.

Questions for Discussion

1. Are not the possible gains from improving manual jobs really quite limited? Aren't the truly large gains the ones which can come from mechanization? Discuss.

2. The Arc Company makes typewriters which it sells for $140.00 and which sell at retail for $200.00. Foreign imports of lower-price, lower-quality typewriters have been cutting into the company's sales, so the president tells a job analyst to "knock $20 out of the cost per typewriter so we can produce a model which will compete." How should the analyst go about doing this?

3. In the purchasing department, the introduction of preassembled sets of purchase order forms reduced the order preparation time of the typists by one third. Yet after two months, there was no visible evidence of any cost reduction. What problems may be present here?

4. The use of task forces, or productivity improvement committees, is supposed to make supervisors more receptive to suggestions by "outsiders" about how to improve the work in their departments. Will it really work this way? Discuss.

5. At the Pennsylvania Steel Company the people doing chipping work on castings were told by the supervisor to squirt oil on the castings so that they could see better what they were doing. The workers said that squirting oil from a can was not in their list of job duties, and they refused to do it. After a three-day layoff as a penalty for their refusal to do the work assigned, the workers filed a grievance asking for pay for the time off, claiming that the layoff was improper. What should the arbitrator decide? Why?

6. "I fill in for the boss whenever she isn't around." How should this situation be handled so far as job evaluation is concerned?

Problems

1. Place five piles of paper before you, then assemble sets of five in order, and staple them. Make a chart of the method you used. If you had to do this by the thousands, what improvements in method can you suggest? Develop an improved method, and estimate the percent savings.

2. The Champion Company's advertising department sends out thousands of direct mail pieces annually. A big item is a five-page booklet which is hand assembled, stapled, and inserted into a mailing carton. Last year this job took 2,000 hours of clerical time. Next year the volume will be 2½ times as much.

Harry Trolley, the methods analyst, is asked to see what he can do to improve the job. Here are his time estimates for the present method.

Element	Minutes per 100 Booklets
Assemble five sheets	5.46
Stack five sheets	4.92
Inspect assembled sheets	6.67
Staple	7.21
Shape carton	6.04
Insert into carton and aside	4.32
Replenish pages	1.47
Replenish cartons	2.39
Total	38.48

Trolley estimates that by installing a fixture costing $800, he will save .02 minute per booklet of the assembling element and another .02 minute of the stacking element. He also expects to save half of the replenishing time by having a materials handler preposition the pages and cartons in a special rack costing $100. The handler's time is not important in solving this problem since he is on the job anyway. Clerical time costs $5.00 an hour.

Disregarding coffee breaks and other time out, what is the yearly output using the present method? How much will the proposed method save (if it will save anything) during the coming year? If the new method saves money, how long will it take to get back from savings the money spent for fixtures? Does it appear that Trolley has exhausted the savings possibilities?

3. On machine M, it takes .32 minute to unload a product from the machine and to load in the next part to be processed and .95 minute to machine the product. On machine N, it takes .24 minute to unload and load and .85 minute for the machine to do the same work. Machine operating costs are $10.00 and $8.00 per hour, respectively. The operators of both machines earn $5.50 an hour.

   a. Devise a plan with one operator running both machines. Each machine is automatic, once it is started. But the machines do not stop automatically when they finish their operations; the operator must be there to stop them. A worker can, however, stop and unload a machine and then attend to the other machine before loading the first one. Machine unloading time is one fourth of the unload and load time.

b. As opposed to having two operators, one running each machine, how much will the company save (or lose) by the plan in *a?* How much operator idle time is there under each plan? How much machine idle time?

4. It costs $7.20 an hour to operate a retort to impregnate wood with a fire-resistant chemical. The impregnating time (during which the retort is closed) is 38 minutes. It is possible to use 1, 2, 3, or 4 people working as a crew to change loads. The changing time is 33, 22, 17, and 15 minutes, respectively, depending on the size of the crew. The workers have other work to do while the retort is closed, so there is no need to be concerned with them except during load changing times.

a. What size crew is best if the workers are paid $7.50 an hour?

b. How much bonus could the company afford to give the workers if they reduced the changing time by 10 percent?

5. The Dix Construction Company is building a parking lot and has to cut away a hill and use the dirt to fill in a lower spot. It will be necessary to use a power shovel to scoop up the dirt and dump trucks to haul it. Here are the estimates of how long this operation takes:

	Minutes
Load truck	5
Travel to dump area	5
Dump load	1
Return	4

a. This is a big job, and the power shovel costs money, so it is desirable to keep it busy. To do this, how many dump trucks will be needed?

b. What is the most economical combination if the

shovel costs $40.00 an hour and the trucks $22.00 an hour? Use a chart if it would be helpful.

6. Blinks Armored Car has a number of high-volume coin counting and wrapping machines. They provide this service to hundreds of banks and other customers. Being semiautomatic, the machines require a machine operator to do the following on the Susan B. Anthony dollar counting and wrapping line:

	Minutes
Unload machine of wrapped Susan B. Anthony dollars	.2
Load machine hopper with SBA dollars	1.7
Machine counting and wrapping time	7.0

Several machines are counting and wrapping Susan B. Anthony dollars, and since the machines are semiautomatic, an operator can operate several machines. They are so close together that the time it takes to go from one machine to the other can be neglected. The machines do not, however, stop after they have finished their operations; the operator must be there to take out the finished pieces.

a. How many coin counting machines can a person operate? Draw up a worker-machine chart showing how your plan works, or make a tabulation of consecutive times showing what the operator is doing all the time.

b. Suppose that in answer *a* you have to concern yourself with costs, and suppose that a worker costs $.2 a minute, and machine idle time costs $.15 a minute. The object is to minimize costs. Is the answer still the same? Show your analysis.

c. Is the answer any different if the machines stop automatically after completing their operation, thus freeing the worker from having to be there the moment the operation is finished?

d. If there were a large number of coin counting machines, is there any way to eliminate the idle time of both machines and workers?

Case 25–1 _____

The time study analyst has had a request to set a production standard on a new job done on milling machines. In line with his usual practice, he observed the operator perform the operation several times before starting to write down the times.

On similar jobs, it is normal for the operator to fasten several pieces into the machine together and machine them all at the same time, much as a person might cut several pieces of paper at the same time on a paper cutter.

This was not the way the operator did it, however. He placed one piece carefully and did the cutting operation on it, and then continued to the next pieces but one at a time. The analyst asked the operator to put them in six at a time, but the latter refused, saying that this was the way he did the operation, and this should be the way to be covered by the standard. The analyst called the supervisor and told him that he could not set the standard unless the job was done as it should be done.

The supervisor smiled and said: "Come on, Stan, give us a real study. You know you should mill six at a time." Whereupon the operator replied rather heatedly: "Look here, who is being time-studied? You or me?"

What should be done? Who should decide work methods?

Case 25–2 _____

The city's sanitary department has hired you as an analyst to evaluate different ways to use trucks and workers to collect trash in the city and to charge for their service. There are several alternatives, but the ones which seem to be of most interest are as follows:

1. Replace the rear-loading compacting trash trucks (which require a driver and two laborers) with newer side-loader trucks with special brakes and remote controls which are designed to operate with one person who drives and loads.

2. Provide residents free of charge with special trash containers which they must wheel to the curb on their pickup day. (Trash is currently picked up from the back yard or garage if residents pay an extra $2 per month.) Equip existing rear-load or newer side-loading trucks with devices which pick up and empty these special containers into the trucks.

3. Provide residents with free, heavy-duty plastic trash bags which must be placed at curbside on pickup day.

4. Continue to pick up trash from backyards and garages, but charge each resident extra, depending on the number of cans, the distance the collector has to walk, and whether it is steep or level.

a. Can you think of any other alternatives or variations on the alternatives presented?

b. What information would you need to collect before you began your analysis?

c. What kind of "behavioral" problems should be considered in your analysis?

d. (Optional) Visit a local sanitary department or private trash hauler, and get their opinion on the alternatives presented.

Chapter 26

Managing Job Safety and Health

We have had, for over a hundred years, legislation providing for some kind of financial payment to workers injured on the job. But for most of that time the employer was not liable if the injury resulted from an accident caused by the worker's own carelessness or that of a fellow worker. Now the employer is fully liable, no matter the circumstances, even to the point of being liable if the worker injures himself while violating the company's safety rules.[1]

Not only is the employer financially liable for injuries, but also for job-caused impairment to health. Until very recent years, this area of employer liability—health impairment—was very small compared to liability for accident-caused injuries. But in the 1970s and 1980s, health impairment claims became much more common. These will be discussed later in this chapter.

Obviously, almost every manager of every kind of organization wants the employees to have safe working conditions.

Nonetheless, people still are injured on the job, so the effort to reduce accidents becomes an unending responsibility of production and operations managers. Actually, on a relative basis, factories, stores, and most places of employment are quite safe places to work. Statistically

speaking, life is safer on the job than off—more people are injured at home than at work.

However, as long as there is even one accident which causes human suffering, it is one too many. Accidents cost in both human suffering and in money—so worker safety is a high priority to consider in job design.

THE INJURY HAZARD

The total working population in the United States is a little over 95 million people. Of these 95 million, some 5 to 6 million suffer some kind of work-related injury or illness every year.[2] Half of those injured (about 1 in 30 of those working) miss one day or more of work as a consequence of their injury. A third or more of those who miss a day have to spend one day or more recuperating in bed.

Injury Hazard by Industry

Industries vary a great deal in their injury records. Banking, communications, petroleum refining, and retailing are the safest (see Figure

---

[1] A good history of safety legislation over the last hundred years is given in *Safety Standards* magazine for July–August 1973.

[2] The U.S. Department of Labor reports that there are some 6 million work-related injuries and illnesses each year. The National Safety Council reports 8 million injuries, of which only half require medical attention and the unjured worker does not miss as much as one day of work.

FIGURE 26–1
Days Lost to Accidents per 100 Full-Time Employees in 1980 *(industry averages)*

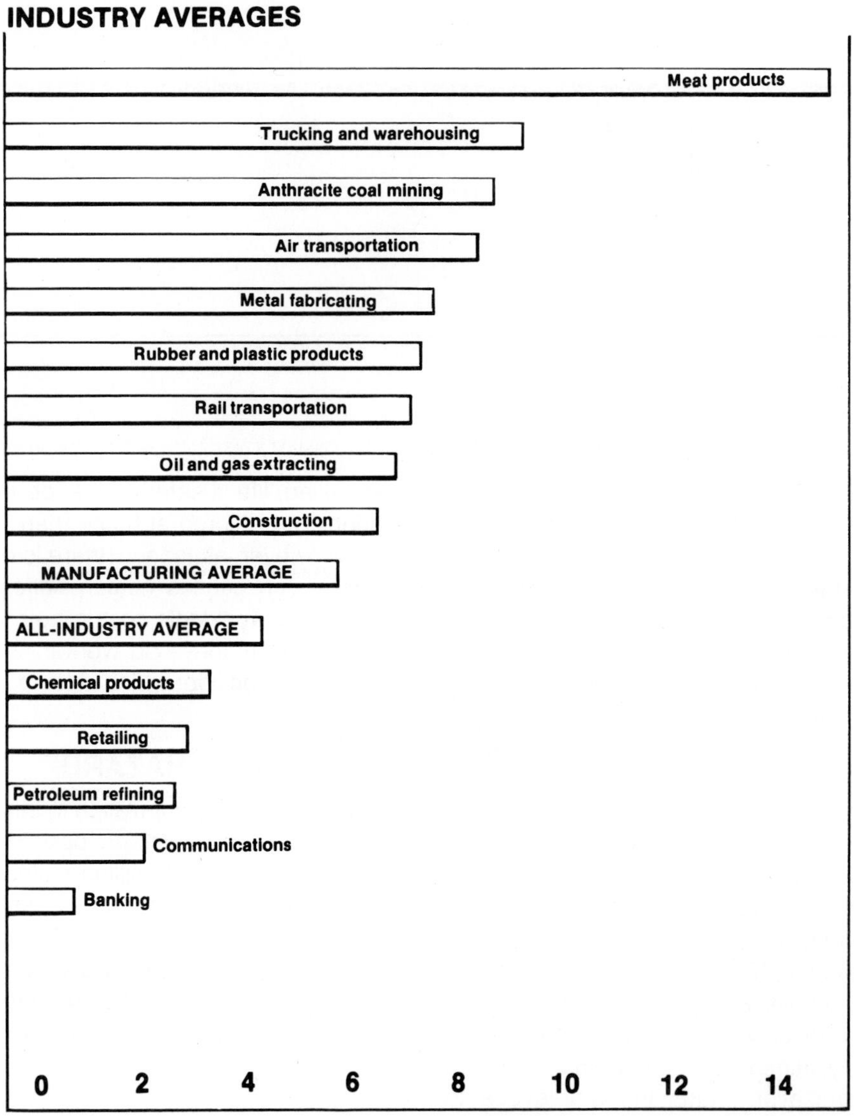

INDUSTRY AVERAGES

Industry	Days lost
Meat products	
Trucking and warehousing	
Anthracite coal mining	
Air transportation	
Metal fabricating	
Rubber and plastic products	
Rail transportation	
Oil and gas extracting	
Construction	
MANUFACTURING AVERAGE	
ALL-INDUSTRY AVERAGE	
Chemical products	
Retailing	
Petroleum refining	
Communications	
Banking	

```
0     2     4     6     8     10     12     14
```

Source: J. Main, "When Accidents Don't Happen," *Fortune,* September 6, 1982, p. 64. Data obtained from the Bureau of Labor Statistics. © 1982, Time, Inc. All rights reserved.

FIGURE 26–2

Group	Number of Deaths	Deaths at Rate of 1 per:
Trade	1,300	17,100 (safest)
Manufacturing	1,800	13,500
Service	1,700	11,300
Government	1,700	9,100
Transportation and public utilities	1,500	3,400
Agriculture	1,900	1,800
Construction	2,600	1,800
Mining and quarrying	500	1,600 (most dangerous)

26–1) with less than three lost workdays per year per 100 employees—the standard way injury rates are measured. At the other extreme, meat packing, trucking and warehousing, and coal mining have the highest incidence with rates of eight days per 100 employees per year.

Fatality Hazard by Industry

Work-related deaths are about 13,000 a year (or 1 in every 7,000 people working). This contrasts with 23,000 deaths from accidents in the home. The work-related deaths are spread among industrial groups as shown in Figure 26–2.

The 66 million people who work in trade, manufacturing, and service are working in the safest places. The 14 million people who work in the mining and quarrying, construction, agriculture, transportation, and public utilities industries are in far more hazardous occupations.

Within these figures is one subset which is important. Over one third of all of these deaths are auto and truck accident deaths. They are not "on-the-job" deaths in the sense of occurring at a regular workplace. Improvements in job safety conditions will not reduce this kind of fatality.

Another important subset in these statistics is the low total for manufacturing. To many of us, "work-related deaths" generates a mental picture of factory operations. Yet only 14 percent of worker deaths occur in manufacturing. Making

factory jobs safer will have little impact on the 13,000 total. Improvement must come everywhere if much is to be accomplished.

Injury Hazard Trends

Both accident and death rates have generally gone down year by year for many years. This had been brought about by the constant efforts of managers to reduce them. Federal legislation, particularly the Occupational Safety and Health Act, which took effect in 1971, with its strong penalties for unsafe working conditions, no doubt stimulated even more the effort which managers had been putting into job safety before that law was passed. Astonishingly though, since the passage of OSHA, accident rates have been rising from a low of 3.2 in 1972 to a high of 4.2 in 1979. The rate for 1980 was 3.9. Some think that the younger, accident-prone work force of the 1970s caused it, or that more accidents were reported due to OSHA's enforcement, or that people are abusing the workers' compensation benefits by filing for claims that may not be justified.[3]

THE COSTS OF ACCIDENTS AND HEALTH IMPAIRMENT

The human suffering caused by accidents is itself enough to justify the constant effort of managers

---

[3] J. Main, "When Accidents Don't Happen," *Fortune*, September 6, 1982, p. 64.

to try to reduce them. In addition, the monetary costs are high—but their magnitude is impossible to estimate accurately.

First, there is the cost of the working time lost by injured workers. Some 40 million worker-days are lost each year by the 5 or 6 million of our 95 million employed people who are injured. But this is only a small part of the total costs. There may also be property damage. But, most significant are the costs of interruptions to the work of others, the time others spend with injured workers, the cost of first-aid facilities, and the cost of doctors, nurses, personnel department employees, and others. And there is all of the record-keeping and investigating and recording and reporting of accidents, filing payment claims, and so on.

The National Safety Council estimated that work accidents cost $23 billion in 1978. Of this total, $10.6 billion was for visible costs, including medical costs of $2.5 billion, insurance and administration costs of $3.9 billion, and $4.2 billion in lost wages

Other costs, which included the value of time lost by other workers and such things as accident reporting costs, etc., amounted to another $10.6 billion. An additional $1.8 billion cost was caused by fire damage.

In the United States, workers' compensation benefits are paid to workers injured on the job. In case of serious injuries, the total costs of a single case can run into many thousands of dollars. Workers' compensation laws are state laws and differ from state to state. But in nearly all states the payments are made from taxes paid by employers. Those employers which have the highest accident rates pay higher tax rates. (The laws usually specify the payment to be made for each kind of injury, and the injured employee may not sue for more.) Since these costs can easily be 4 percent of the payroll, there is a considerable cost reduction incentive to managers to provide safe working conditions for employees.

DuPont is a case in point. Their successful safety program is credited with saving them more than $26 million in 1980. (See Figure 26–3.)

The Occupational Safety and Health Administration is also active in promoting and policing safety. If OSHA inspectors find unsafe conditions, the agency can assess fines. Employees may also file complaints with OSHA charging that conditions are unsafe. It is even possible for the Secretary of Labor to order a factory or service establishment to close down if it has dan-

FIGURE 26–3
Safety Is Profitable at Du Pont

Pierre Samuel du Pont, founder of the American branch of the family, set an example of top management involvement in safety in 1817 by leaping from his sickbed at the age of 77 to help put out a fire in a powder mill. Today, at the regular Friday meetings of Du Pont's top management in Wilmington, safety is always the first item on the agenda. The pattern holds throughout the company—safety comes first. Everyone understands that "a job will not be done unless it can be done safely," says James Kearns, a general manager of the textile fibers department. Supervisors and managers realize that without a good safety record, they just won't get promoted.

Du Pont's safety efforts reap enormous savings. In U.S. plants in 1980 the company had 129 accidents that caused workers to lose time from the job—an annual rate of .12 accident per 100 workers, or $\frac{1}{23}$ the National Safety Council's average rate for all manufacturers. Had Du Pont's record been average, the company would have spent more than $26 million on additional compensation and other costs, using the Safety Council's estimate of $9,400 for the average cost of a disabling accident. That's 3.6 percent of Du Pont's profits. To make up the difference, in view of the company's 5.5 percent net return on sales, Du Pont would have had to increase sales by nearly $500 million. That seems reason enough to be fussy about safety.

Source: J. Main, "When Accidents Don't Happen," *Fortune,* September 6, 1982, p. 68. © 1982 Time, Inc. All rights reserved.

gerous working conditions which are not remedied. The law even allows, in extreme cases, for managers who knowingly permit a seriously unsafe condition to exist, to be fined or even put in jail. Such laws have been in effect in England and France for some time but they have only been in effect in the United States with the passage of OSHA legislation in 1971.

MANAGING SAFETY AND HEALTH

The overall responsibility for carrying out organizational responsibilities for the safety and health of employees rests largely with the production or operations manager of the organization. But this is a specialized area which needs the attention of a specialist. Consequently, nearly all large organizations have safety engineers and medical people who manage the health and safety of others. All of this work normally comes under the general direction of the industrial relations director. In addition, most companies can utilize the extensive safety engineering staffs of their insurance companies. Insurers have a high stake in preventing accidents and often require companies to conform to their safety and health standards before they will sell them insurance.

These specialists are responsible for discovering hazardous conditions and working with industrial, maintenance, and machine design engineers to correct unsafe or unhealthful conditions. They are also responsible for keeping up to date on new safety regulations and standards and for record-keeping and accident reporting. They develop and manage organization-wide health and safety programs, and they watch over heating, lighting, ventilation, and good housekeeping. Typically, these programs are ongoing and include worker safety training programs and the proper orientation of new workers from the safety point of view. They also handle such things as the publication of "accident-free days to date" statistics.

Physical examinations for job applicants aid in health safety in that existing disabilities are unearthed, thus helping to place people where these disabilities will not be aggravated. And, periodic physical exams are often given for "preventive" health maintenance purposes. What may have been an appropriate job for a worker may no longer be true because of changes in his or her health or in the job.

Exercise and Wellness Programs

Some companies suggest individually tailored programs of physician-monitored exercise in company-provided or public recreational facilities. The objective of these "wellness" health programs is to help upgrade the physical well-being of the organization's employees and to reduce stress in their executives.[4] Their objective is to reduce absenteeism, improve productivity, and reduce the effects of cardiovascular disease (heart and lung ailments) for everybody, but especially for key executives.

One firm, Intermatic, Inc., of Spring Grove, Illinois, has gone so far as to pay their employees a bounty of up to $4 for each pound of excess weight they lose and to pay them a nice bonus if they quit smoking for a year. The company's objective is to increase the health and physical fitness of its employees and, indirectly, to increase their productivity.

Coors Breweries has a fully outfitted "wellness center" staffed with exercise physiologists and the latest equipment for their employees.

THE HAZARD IN THE JOB

It usually takes a combination of hazardous conditions and carelessness on the part of human beings to cause accidents. An oily floor does no harm in itself. Most people who walk on an oily floor do not fall; but, when many people habitually walk on oily floors, falls are almost certain to occur. Cleaning off the oil would help, but extra care on the part of those who must walk

---

[4] See "How Companies Cope with Executive Stress," *Business Week*, August 21, 1978, pp. 107–8.

on them would also prevent most of the possible accidents.

Although hazardous conditions cannot always be eliminated, often they can be. The first step in their elimination is the recognition that they exist. Many situations are obviously dangerous—a piece of material projecting into a dimly lighted aisleway, for example. Other situations, just as hazardous, are nor obvious but will be revealed by an analysis of accident statistics.

A list of accident hazards in factories, including the less obvious ones, would be lengthy. It would include slippery floors and steps, the use of ladders and scaffolds, protruding materials, unguarded fast-moving machinery—particularly belts, gears, and cutting tools, dies, and drill presses—flying particles from grinding wheels, and slivers from lathes, chippers, and so on. It would include unguarded balcony edges, stairwells, elevator shafts, low-hanging overhead conveyors or other objects, handling heavy materials, trucks with heavy loads, narrow aisles, blind corners, and employees smoking where there is a fire or explosion hazard. In addition, in many companies, there are dangers from high-voltage electricity, molten metals, high temperatures, chemicals, irritating fluids, noxious fumes, various kinds of dust, burns, fires, and explosions.

Many hazards are within the job itself. Metal pieces shaped by forming dies usually have to be placed precisely into the dies by hand. Punch presses, too, need to have the part positioned exactly. Welding is another activity where workers have to hold pieces while the operation is being done. In all of these cases, operators need first to place the piece in position and then keep their hands out of the way. The danger is that they will not get their hands out of the way before the machine operates.

It is easy to be too negative toward managers who do not eliminate every hazard. People fall down stairs; so stairs are a hazard. Workers using ladders sometimes miss the step and fall and hurt themselves. And on the consumer front, nearly 1,000 bicycle riders are killed in accidents each year; so bicycles are hazardous, almost as much so as motorcycles. People burn themselves on hot stoves. And skiers twist their knees and ankles and break their legs.

There is a hazard in every one of these situations; yet, there is little that a manager of a manufacturing or a service organization can do to prevent hazards such as these from causing accidents. Both governmental regulators and the general public rarely seem to appreciate the impossibility of eliminating all hazards on jobs, and those related to jobs, and to consumers' use of products. The best that managers can do is to take the most effective preventive measures possible.

The problem of safety is not one problem but many. Hazards are so different and so varied that a "contingency" (it all depends) approach must be taken.

MAKING WORKING CONDITIONS SAFE

Safe working conditions are management's responsibility. The degree of safety found in any plant is a matter of machine design, plant layout, lighting, good housekeeping, good maintenance, and the provision and *use* of safety guards and equipment.

Machine designers have for years been putting more and more moving parts under cover. This trend seems to have been motivated partly to improve the appearance of the machine by presenting smooth curved surfaces to the eye and partly by the desire to make it safer to operate. Today machinery buyers are often insisting on safety features being built into machines in addition to those required by safety regulations.[5]

Better and better equipment is being made for what used to be dangerous work. Acid burns and lung damage from fumes in electroplating have been materially reduced over the years. Dust explosions in flour mills, food processors,

---

[5] See "Buyers Must Insure OSHA Compliance," *Purchasing*, April 26, 1977, pp. 43–45.

and candy companies are almost unknown. In steel mills, burns from molten steel have almost disappeared. The availability of better equipment is largely responsible. Portable saws, drills, grinders, brushes, and the like, and their grounded extension cords now provide much better protection than before.

Plant layout and good lighting are also important to safe working conditions. Narrow aisles with blind intersections can cause accidents to industrial truck drivers, as can poorly lighted aisles and workplaces. The slope of ramps used by industrial trucks should not exceed a 10 percent grade. Pipes, conduits, drains, valves, heaters, fire apparatus, and so on should be located where they are convenient for repair or access but are out of the way of ordinary traffic.

Floors, stairs, and ramps must be kept free of water, oil, and grease. Floors, if subjected to liquids, should be provided with proper drainage. Materials, containers, scrap, trash, and other obstructions should be put in places where workers will not stumble or slip on them and where trucks will not bump into them and knock them over. In the winter, loading docks, receiving platforms, and aisles in outside storage yards should be cleared of ice and snow.

To remain safe, a plant must be well maintained. Worn machinery is not always dangerous, but worn materials handling equipment, crane cables, hoists, elevators, industrial trucks, conveyors, storage racks, or electrical wiring can be very dangerous. Most of these situations are as dangerous to maintenance employees themselves as they are to others, if not more so.

In spite of all that can be done to create safe working conditions, there will still be a few situations which cause some people to have accidents. Aisles cannot always be straight, and it is impossible to remove all posts, overhanging projections, and stepdowns. Such hazards should be painted a bright color to make them noticeable. Alternating diagonal orange and black stripes are sometimes used. Convex-shaped mirrors suspended from the ceiling at an angle permit workers and truckers to see if anything is coming around blind intersections of aisles. Steps or sloping floors which might cause falls can be coated with an abrasive non-slip covering. All of these practices help reduce accidents.

SAFETY EQUIPMENT

Safety equipment can be of many kinds. Perhaps the best is equipment which is fastened onto or built into machines, thus making an accident difficult. Machine guards are of many types, depending on the machine. Motors, driving belts, gears, and electrical control panels are encased or are in wells surrounded by guard rails. Transparent shields cover grinding wheels. The whole wheel is sometimes encased. Rotary saws, except for the cutting section, are covered. Punch presses are equipped with protection devices such as a sweep arm or an attached glove or arm shackle. With the downstroke of the punch, the sweep arm clears the operator's arms from the punching area. The glove or shackle is fastened to the machine in such a way as to draw the worker's hands back from the machine as the punch descends.

Shears, brakes (sheet-metal bending machines), and other sheet-metal equipment are required by law to be provided with guards. Forming presses for shaping metal are equipped with electrical control buttons which the operator must be pushing as the die descends. There is a button for each hand and both must be pushed simultaneously while the machine operates. They are located away from the die to ensure that the operator's hands are in the clear.

Safety push buttons are especially helpful where two or more workers operate a machine, since, without them, one worker might start the machine's stroke before the others are clear. Sometimes forming presses are equipped with barrier "doors" which have to close and interlock, keeping the operator's hands out, before they will operate. Some of these machines are equipped with electronic or even ultrasonic sensors which will stop the machine if the operator's hands get into the danger zone.

Safety devices on machines frequently pose difficult problems for designers. First of all, safety guards must protect the worker. Second, they should not slow down the machine's operations very much because slower operations increase operating costs. Furthermore, if a safety device slows down the work too much, the worker, particularly if he is working on piecework, will try to circumvent it. (He tapes down the push buttons or removes the sweep arm or doesn't wear the glove or shackle.) Third, if serious accidents are possible, even though highly improbable (as in "calendering" in the rubber, linoleum, and plastic film industries) the safety device, if tripped, must be designed to stop high-speed equipment instantly.[6] It must also be located so that it would be tripped almost instantaneously should a worker get caught in the rolls.

Chemical and electroplating processes often give off noxious fumes and vapors. Other operations are extremely dusty. Most of the hazards to employee health can be eliminated by providing hoods, canopies, or ducts over the operation to convey the fumes and dust away by an exhaust fan.

A second type of safety equipment is the kind that is fastened to or worn by the worker. There are safety glasses, goggles, and hoods for welders. Rubber aprons, gloves, and boots are used by electroplaters. Leather gloves are needed for many operations where sharp, rough, hot, or cold materials are handled. Shoes with nonslip soles should be worn where floors are slippery. "Safety" shoes, having a steel toe cap, are a protection for heavy materials handlers. Respirators worn over the nose and mouth to purify the air are used for spray painters and workers in extremely dusty places. Ear plugs or ear muffs protect the hearing of workers where the operations are noisy.

Almost without exception, most workers do

not like to wear protective devices. The devices are usually uncomfortable to wear, and most workers consider them to be nuisances. Where the injury hazard is slight, and, when the protective equipment is uncomfortable to wear, the company usually has to insist that nonuse carry a penalty of discharge.

A third type of safety equipment is needed in case of a disaster, particularly fire. In wooden buildings, overhead sprinkler systems are required by law. A water tank to supply water and to maintain water pressure in case of a fire may also be required. Fire extinguishers (sometimes automatic ones) and fire hoses should be provided at numerous locations in the building. In most factories several types of fires are possible. Fire may be caused by defective electrical wiring, or oil, explosive fumes and dusts, or other combustibles. Since fires of different kinds respond to different treatments, different types of fire extinguishers are needed. For example, burning oil or magnesium cannot be extinguished by water. An appropriate type of extinguisher is needed for each type of fire.

ACCIDENT PREVENTION: THE HUMAN ELEMENT

Most accidents involve both unsafe conditions *and* unsafe human practices. In past years the National Safety Council reported that unsafe acts occurred in almost 90 percent of all accidents. Although the NSC no longer makes this statement, there is no reason to believe it has changed. (Goodyear Tire reports 92 percent.) The installation of safe machines, safety guards, and so on is not enough to reduce accidents very much. It is hard to keep a 22-year-old forklift driver from driving his truck too fast around the plant. Nonetheless, workers must work safely because it seems to be human nature always to expect accidents to happen to someone else. It is difficult to instill a safety attitude in people because they continue to take chances and accidents continue to happen.

Years ago, smoking during work hours by

---

[6] "Calendering" is a rolling operation in which materials are squeezed between closely set rollers.

factory workers was often forbidden in most factories. Now, it is forbidden, as a rule, only where it creates a fire hazard or in confined spaces where it might annoy nonsmokers. In spite of possible fire hazards, however, workers sometimes do smoke in restricted areas. The company *must* enforce its no-smoking rules where safety is involved.

Most managers recognize that carelessness contributes to most accidents, so they try to educate workers in safety matters. Workers should be told of the hazards and shown how to work safely, but, for the most part, educating workers in safety is a matter of developing a safety-conscious frame of mind rather than teaching them specific things to do. Safety consciousness can be fostered by the way in which warnings of hazards are phrased. One company found that it was more effective to say, "Even 240 volts can prove fatal—660 volts here!" instead, of "Danger, high voltage."

Accidents are depressing, and workers do not like to think about them. Quoting statistics and showing pictures of accidents or injured workers rarely impresses workers with the need for safety because they dislike listening to, or looking at, these materials.

The fact is that relatively few workers do get hurt. Naturally, therefore, it is hard to "sell" safety to them. Various schemes are used to encourage employees to work safely. Shop rules usually require that goggles and other safety devices be worn where conditions warrant caution; sometimes the penalty for failure to do so is discharge.

Some companies have tackled the problem of safety education through union-management safety committees. Sometimes they make any injured worker, upon returning to work, a safety committee of one in his or her department to look over the department for hazardous conditions and practices and report them.

The company paper should give special recognition to accident-free departments. Sometimes a "dunce prize" is given to the department having the last accident. It is retained and has

to be displayed at the department entrance until another department has an accident; then that department must display it. Safety competition should never, however, be permitted to become so intense that minor injuries are unreported and untreated just to preserve the record.

Posters and cartoons displayed on bulletin boards and in the company paper are effective in safety education. Sometimes they can be made humorous without being grisly. Workers look at these posters and laugh, but they do look and, as a result, probably think a little more about working safely. "How-to-do-it" and "how-not-to-do-it" posters are less interesting than humorous posters and, of necessity, must be quite elementary. "Misery" posters, aimed at making the reader aware of the grief that can come from unsafe acts, tend to stir up fear, which many people think does not cause workers to work more safely. Besides, they emphasize the *results* of unsafe acts rather than the acts themselves.

Accident records show that some workers are more accident-prone than others. Putting them on the safest jobs lowers the accident rate. However, it is rarely possible to detect accident-proneness among job applicants. By the time they have worked long enough to establish an accident record, a lot of damage has been done. Reassigning accident-prone workers to safer jobs is not, therefore, a quick way to reduce the accident rate.

THE OCCUPATIONAL SAFETY AND HEALTH ACT

The Occupational Safety and Health Act, which took effect in 1971, imposed much stiffer safety regulations than had applied before. It also extended the coverage of existing laws to almost everyone working, including those in the construction industry, who had been omitted before.

This law (OSHA) set up the Occupational Safety and Health Review Commission in the Department of Labor to handle all safety matters. OSHA inspectors have the right to enter plants to see if unsafe practices are going on.[7] And, although the agency has far too few inspectors to do the inspection part of their work very effectively, the very existence of OSHA has improved conditions in many places.

In its early days, OSHA was guilty in the issuance of quite a few orbitrary and not very logical regulations. Ice in drinking water for employees was banned. So were full round toilet seats, and so were all protective railings which were not exactly 42 inches high. And there were others. Such rulings, collectively, put almost everyone in a violation position and lost a great deal of public support for the good that was supposed to come out of the new law. As a result, Congress ordered that these nuisance standards be gotten rid of and (in 1978) 928 "nit-picking" safety rules (about 10 percent of all rules) were revoked. Some of the early rulings have also been modified because of economic hardships, especially to smaller companies. Under the Reagan administration, OSHA seems to have become even more reasonable. OSHA is concentrating on high-accident industries and less on those with good safety records. First, regulations covering the keeping of workers' hands out of dies made it almost impossible for them to do their work, and at the same time made almost all of the equipment in the nation in violation. To conform with the regulation, the required modifications would have cost anywhere up to $35,000 per machine. The costs of die-made products would have skyrocketed, and many small employers would have been forced out of business.

Within OSHA one of the main departments develops standards while another department enforces regulations. Inspectors, if they find a violation, issue citations (like traffic tickets). In flagrant cases there can be fines and court orders closing down the operation. Fines can be as much as $1,000 a day until the condition is corrected.

NOISE

In the 1970s noise reduction became part of the spillover from the new emphasis on both safety and environmental improvement. Industry had not been unaware of noise as a problem, and factory designers had done much to reduce it, but most were still noisy places. The setting of standards for allowable noise levels on the job is one of OSHA's responsibilities.

Interestingly, noise is not always considered disagreeable. Many people like the loud roar from their motorcycles or automobiles. They like the feeling of power that seems to go with it. And, indeed, rock music concerts have sometimes been measured at 125 decibels.[8]

Although we know that long exposure to excessive noise will ultimately impair a person's hearing and that workers exposed to high levels of noise are several times more likely to develop high blood pressure than those in quieter environments, we don't know much about the levels of noise that do harm. Noise affects some people more than others. Also, most people's hearing deteriorates as they get older even when they have not been overly exposed to noise. And, unfortunately, the harm which might be caused in younger people working in noisy surroundings usually does not show up until they are older.

OSHA regulations regard exposure to average noise levels of 90 decibels or over for eight hours or longer as probably injurious to most people. As a rule of thumb, if a work area is too noisy for comfortable face-to-face conversation, it probably is a hazardous noise level. OSHA regulations do not prohibit higher noise intensities but limit a person's exposure time to them. Figure 26–4 lists the restrictions and relates them to familiar noise levels. Figure 26–5 shows the regulations graphically. the government's Environmental Protection Agency (EPA) has also set a noise limit for factory operations

---

[7] A 1978 U.S. Supreme Court ruling requires OSHA inspectors to obtain a search warrant if the company insists upon it. In practice, however, few firms insist.

[8] Noise is measured on a logrithmic scale in terms of decibels, which are a measure of sound intensity. Thus, a sound of 70 decibels is 10 times as loud as 60 decibels. Eighty decibels is 10 times as loud as 70 decibels, and so on.

FIGURE 26–4

Decibel Level and Exposure Limits for Selected Noise Sources

Source of Noise	Decibels above the Start of Hearing	Maximum Daily Exposure (hours)
Painful noise	130	0
Jet engine at passenger ramp	115	¼
Riveting, chipper, planer, circular saw	110	½
Textile loom, screw machine, subway train passing station	105	1
Noisy factory, punch press, blast furnace	100	2
Jack hammer, grinder	95	4
Lathe, motorcycle, Niagara Falls	90	8
Very loud radio in home, spinner, lathes	80	—
Average street or factory noise	70	—
Typical office	60	—
Quiet office	50	—
Quiet home	40	—

even lower at 85 decibels. OSHA and EPA are not in agreement on this point.

Companies must limit noise exposure to the levels indicated in Figures 26–4 and 26–5 or else supply workers with ear plugs or ear muffs or reduce the time exposure. Workers, however, often refuse to wear plugs or muffs. Employees who are continually exposed to an average of 85 decibels must be given hearing tests annually.

FIGURE 26–5

Legally Permissible Noise Limits for Employee Exposure

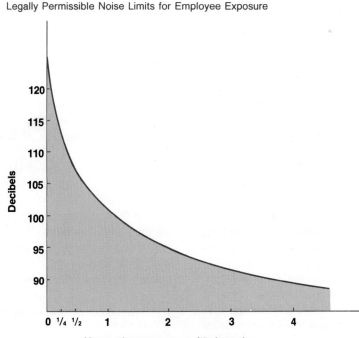

Hours of exposure permitted per day

Noise Control Methods

Noise is merely air vibrating at frequencies which the human ear interprets as sound and which is undesirable. So vibration and noise are related. Vibration and noise can't be eliminated altogether, but they can often be "damped," "sponged up," reduced, or confined to limited areas, thus reducing harmful effects. Noise from old and worn equipment can be reduced by putting in new and better-fitting bearings and parts. Noise from impacts made by stamping dies is difficult to control, so it is best to locate these machines off by themselves. Vibration from heavy equipment can be minimized on the ground floor by mounting heavy machines on separate foundations with small spaces between the foundation and the regular floor.

On upper floors other methods have to be used. Many kinds of vibration isolators are used. Machine mountings are made of springs, rubber, felt, cork, and other elastic materials. Suspension arrangements are also sometimes used. These methods of vibration control are in addition to vibration reducers built into the equipment itself. In the machines, vibration and noise may be reduced by pads, snubbers, bumpers, flexible joints, shaft seals, and other means.

Noise and vibration may be airborne, structurally borne, or may be transmitted by diaphragms. If the source of the noise can't be eliminated, damping methods will have to be directed at the means by which the noise is conveyed. Baffles, curtains, and acoustically covered walls will reduce airborne noise or vibration. Flexible mounts will reduce the amount conveyed by the machine structure. Heavy concrete masses with their high inertia reduce vibration. If walls and ceilings tend to act as diaphragms transmitting noise, soundproofing acoustical materials will help.

All of these noise reduction methods cost money, and it has been estimated that meeting OSHA levels could cost nearly $15 billion. The ultimate cost could double if the Environmental Protection Agency is able to enforce its proposed 85-decibel standard.

These cost estimates may be on the high side. Armstrong Cork reports that it can bring a medium-sized metal-working plant's noise level down to 85 decibels for about $20,000. Armstrong sells a "Noise Control Package," which consists of strategically placed hanging wall panels, noise protection screens, wedge-shaped sloped noise absorbers, baffles, and vibration damping tile.[9]

HEALTH IMPAIRMENT

In the past, safety concern was almost wholly directed at reducing accidents, with little attention being directed at job-induced health impairment. There were, however, a few exceptions, such as in the case of silicosis, which caused lung damage to coal miners, radium burns of workers putting illuminated numbers on clock dials, and lead poisoning in the paint industry.

Now, however, with more years of experience and better detection research relating cause and effect, health hazards are being found in more places. Many of these had gone unrecognized before because so many situations cause health impairment only over a long time period of exposure.

It is now known that there are health hazards, including a great incidence of cancer, among workers who work with polyvinyl chloride, asbestos, certain insecticides, and in the coke-making part of the steel industry. Hazards have also been found in the use of beryllium and other chemicals.

Since some of the disabilities are so slow developing and since people not associated with these industries also have cancer and other of the job-related impairments, it is difficult to evaluate the various hazards. The hazards in the making of polyvinyl chloride seem, however, to be well established, and its manufacturing processes are now closely regulated.[10] In addition,

---

[9] Reported in "Sponging up Plant Noise," *Factory,* August 1975, pp. 25–27.

[10] The health problems in this industry are reported in Paul H. Weaver, "On the Horns of the Vinyl Chloride Dilemma," *Fortune,* October 1974, pp. 150 ff.

NIOSH (OSHA's health department) estimated that coke-oven workers were 10 times more likely to get lung cancer than other steelworkers; the risk of asbestos workers was one in five before safeguards were installed.[11]

OSHA personnel have been trying to find out what levels of exposure are dangerous so that standards can be set to confine exposure to safe hazard limits over a period of time. At the start, since the cumulative effects of long-time exposure to small amounts of a hazard are not known, the initial standards may be overly stringent. These can be relaxed if long experience indicates that they are overly restrictive. By the early 1980s several hundred standards related to job-induced health hazards had already been set. These include regulations covering the manufacture and processing of such items as chloroform, mercury, sulphuric acid, carbon monoxide, silica, and even cotton dust.

The Costs of Health Impairment Protection

The costs of health impairments caused by working conditions have, in the past, been much less than the costs of injuries from accidents, but they are going up more rapidly. Impairments are usually uncomfortable and sometimes seriously so, but working-age people seldom die from them. The costs of individual cases of health impairment sometimes continue for a long time so individual cases can easily cost more than most accident injury cases.

Two other developments have increased their total costs even more. First, workers who develop arthritis, lower-back pains, high blood pressure, migraine headaches, alcoholism, and any number of other ailments have been blaming their jobs for the ailments. (Air traffic controllers are vocal on this point.) And it is true that conditions can be caused by or made worse by the stresses of life, including working conditions. Requests for extra compensation based on such

claims are not always approved, but they are approved often enough to contribute to the rapid rise in the costs of health impairment.

Second, former employees, now retired, sometimes claim that their present disabilities—often of the kind associated with growing old—were caused by job conditions years earlier. These claims, like those of present employees, are often approved—again increasing the costs of health impairment.

Financial Liability

Employers are financially liable for accidents and for many work-induced illnesses. Injured workers are usually paid by workers' compensation.

The amount of the compensation is spelled out in each state's law in the form of money awards per week for each kind of injury. More serious injuries call for larger weekly payments and for more weeks, perhaps up to several years, and in some cases, for life. Workers' compensation laws specify the payments that workers are entitled to and at the same time they usually do not allow lawsuits for higher amounts.

The erosion of the value of compensation benefits because of inflation has made most of them quite inadequate. There always seems to be a lag in adjusting the amounts of the awards upward fast enough to keep up with inflation. Furthermore, the amounts of compensation vary a great deal from state to state. Most states pay about two thirds of the injured worker's wage up to maximum, with a range from $112 per week in Mississippi to $942 per week in Alaska.

In recent years, the low payments and prohibition against suing the employer have generated a flood of lawsuits directed against the manufacturer of the machine or process on which the accident occurred. Many of these lawsuits have resulted in very high awards, which in turn has skyrocketed the costs of insurance. Some small companies have gone out of business because they can no longer buy insurance at reasonable rates.

Obviously, under these conditions it is easy

[11] See Denise Brookman, "Gearing up to a New OSHA," *Purchasing*, April 26, 1977, pp. 32–39.

to appreciate that employers who manufacture equipment are just as anxious as OSHA commissioners to eliminate hazards.

Review Questions

1. Classify the kinds of safety equipment commonly used in industry.
2. What kinds of safety devices are there to keep people's hands out of the die in stamping machines?
3. Who is commonly responsible for managing safety and health in an organization?
4. Are accident prevention programs generally effective in reducing accidents? What makes good programs work?
5. What are the general powers of OSHA? Has this changed in the middle 1980s?
6. What is the current noise standard which is being enforced by OSHA?
7. How can noise be controlled in industry?

Questions for Discussion

1. Should producers of consumer products and of machinery be liable for potential hazards? Discuss.
2. How far does a company's responsibility extend in the matter of safety for workers? Does it cover the workers being required to use safe methods? Or does it stop with the company providing safe working conditions?
3. How can an employer get workers to do their work safely? What problems must be solved?
4. What causes accidents: hazards or people? Discuss.

5. Does a person who is hurt while disobeying company safety rules get workers' compensation benefits? What is the logic behind this practice?
6. Can an injured worker covered by workers' compensation sue anyone? Discuss.
7. In a landmark Supreme Court decision, OSHA inspectors are now required to obtain a search warrant prior to visiting if companies insist. Would you insist? Discuss.

Problems

1. Visit a local manufacturing organization (or service), and write a brief report on their job safety and health program. How do they manage this function, and what is their attitude toward OSHA?
2. Brown Manufacturing must decide which kind of safety device to install on a new metal stamping machine which is being installed. These devices are required to ensure that the operator's hands are out of the die area during the machine's stamping cycle. They have narrowed their choice to three alternatives: double button system (each hand must push a button to activate the machine); arm shackles which jerk hands out of the die area before the machine cycles; and the ultrasonic system which senses hands if they are in the danger area and stops the machine cycle. The per machine cost of these three devices and the cycle time per part for the three parts made on the machine vary as follows:

Device	Cost per Machine	Cycle Time per Part by Type (minutes) A	B	C
Double button	$200	.1	.3	.05
Arm shackles	75	.15	.4	.1
Ultrasonic sensor	800	.05	.2	.1
Percent of parts made on these machines		30%	50%	20%

Which device should they install? Are there any "behavioral" problems which should be considered in this problem? If you need more information in order to solve this problem, what information do you need?

Case 26–1

A sheet-metal shear at the Treadway Company had no guard on it and, therefore, was dangerous, making it possible for people to lose their fingers. The state safety inspector ordered Treadway to install a safety shield and control buttons so that the workers could not operate the shear unless they had their hands out of danger.

A year and a half later, Bill Gott, an employee, lost three fingers in the still unprotected shear. The safety inspector had not been back in the interim and, in the ordinary course of events, wouldn't have been back for at least six months more. Shortly after the safety inspector's visit, Jack Combs, a former machine operator, had been made supervisor of the department. He said he'd never heard of the safety engineer's order.

What allows such things to happen? Suggest a remedy.

Case 26–2

After a company appointed a safety engineer, accidents went up to a new high, so the personnel department interviewed the supervisor with the worst records to see what was happening. Here are some of the answers. "Safety? That's not my job anymore. Safety's the safety engineer's job. He'll get the credit, so let him work for it." What should be done at this point?

Case 26–3

"My foreman is a fair guy but pretty slow with a hospital pass. If you cut your finger and yell for relief, he hands you a Band-Aid. You could bleed to death before a relief man arrived. He hopes that you'll let it go and that he won't have to get a relief man or report having an accident. Same thing with a headache or a cold. He'll give you an aspirin and tell you that it will make you feel better soon. He doesn't want you going to the hospital. He goes against the labor contract all the time, because he isn't supposed to refuse a man a trip to the hospital."

This report comes to you, the safety director. What do you do?

Case 26–4

The Evans Company has a program which encourages their employees to improve their physical fitness, stop smoking, and lose weight. The employees are given an extra half hour at lunch for an exercise class and are paid a bonus for losing weight and if they stop smoking. Some employees really like the program and some say it discriminates against them. Should they keep it? Why? Why not?

Chapter 27

Work Measurement and Standards

Standards are highly desirable for almost every kind of organized work. Managers need to have some idea of how long work will take, how many employees will be needed, and what it will cost. Only with this information can they make intelligent decisions about schedules, facilities, people needed, costs, and selling prices.

Holiday Inns needs to know how long it will take to clean a room after a guest leaves. American Airlines needs to know how long it will take to unload the baggage when an airplane lands or to serve food and drinks during flight. Smith-Corona needs to know how long it takes to assemble a typewriter, and U.S. Steel needs to know how long it takes to make a steel rail.

In all of these cases, managers need to have some idea of the time it takes to do things. They measure the time that work usually takes and set standards so they can plan. But they don't stop there. After the event, they check to see if the standard was met. If it took longer than the standard called for, then it probably cost more than it should have and used up some of both the time and money needed for other activities.

The first use of standards, then, is for planning and deciding what to do and what not to do and what things will cost. The second use is to compare what does happen with what is supposed to happen.

This leads to a third and very important part of a manager's responsibilities: The comparison between actual and expected will usually show a number of discrepancies. Most of the time the plan, the standard expectation, is not accomplished in all respects. Reasons for the discrepancies are then investigated by managers and remedial actions taken. Most of this kind of analysis falls in the realm of budgetary control.

Here we are interested in the standards themselves and how to set them. Sometimes reasonably good standards can be set just by looking back at what has been done in the past. Holiday Inns, American Airlines, Smith-Corona, and U.S. Steel can use historical performance data to obtain answers to the questions we posed.

Yet setting standards for work by using actual historical performance may not be a very good way to do it. The time taken to do things in the past includes the method used as well as the casual pace so often found in unorganized work. Unless the job has been studied and a good method determined, the time taken in the past is probably more than it should be.

Properly set production standards specify

the time it should take to do work when it is done in the best way. These standards can be set only after the job has been analyzed and the best way determined and timed when performed by a normally proficient worker.

But, developing production standards will not automatically ensure that operations will be more effectively controlled. Managers do not always use all of the managerial tools, including production standards, which are at their disposal. Furthermore, production can be accomplished without standards. Workers working on machines and materials will produce something. They will produce products, but without standards they will rarely produce as much as they would with standards. Finally, desirable as it is to have production standards, some kinds of work are not susceptible to measurement. Thus, standards based on output, time taken, and other quantitative measurement, cannot be set. Instead, other, more subjective standards must be developed.

The discussion here will be centered on production standards as they are set and used in both factory and repetitive service operating situations. These same techniques can be adapted and used for determining standards in offices, banks, and services provided by governmental units.

In factories, production standards are most often set by time study methods with a stopwatch being used to time the work. In many companies the end product, the time standard, is used in setting piece rates for pieceworkers.

Production standards and time standards are the same thing. One says that a worker should do the job 20 times in an hour, and the other says that the job is a three-minute job. Occasionally, when a standard is stated as a quota, the quota actually represents the quantity of production needed in a given period of time in order to keep unit costs down to the level used in setting selling prices.

There are also other important reasons for developing standards. Many companies, which do not use piecework incentives, use time study and set up time standards. And conversely, a few companies which use incentives set their time standards without using time study.

Aside from piecework, production standards are needed to determine what work should cost, to estimate the cost of new jobs, and to determine what it costs to do work in alternative ways. Standards are needed to know how much work machines can turn out, and for scheduling work as well as for setting quotas for machine-paced work. They are also required for assembly line balancing (Chapter 22), and as inputs to break-even analysis, capital investment analysis, simulation, queuing, and other methods described later, such as capacity planning, shop loading, and linear programming.

CONCEPT OF A PRODUCTION STANDARD

A production standard embodies a concept of normality and reasonableness. Almost all jobs can be done fast, or slow, or in between. The idea of a standard implies determining a particular rate which is reasonable and expected. Other performance is then regarded as better than standard or poorer than standard. The process of choosing and deciding normal times is implicit in standard setting, and this implies that judgment must be used. Standard setters cannot escape having to judge normality as they try to set fair and reasonable standards.

To illustrate how important this is, we might consider the simple task of walking a mile. If several men were to walk a mile, some of them would finish before the others. Perhaps the fastest man would finish in 15 minutes, the slowest man would take 30 minutes, and the others would be spread out in between, with most men taking 19 or 20 minutes. (A time of 20 minutes [3 miles per hour] is somewhat leisurely for most people.)

If it were cold weather or if rain were threatening, the average time would probably be less. The men would have an incentive not to dawdle. The same would be true if those who finished the mile in 20 minutes or less were to get a reward; probably almost everyone would make it and be rewarded. But, if only those who finished in less than 16 minutes were to be rewarded, fewer of the men would make it. A person has to hurry to walk a mile in 16 minutes, and to some of the men the incentive might not be enough to cause them to hurry this much.

Several points are involved here which are pertinent to setting production standards. The casual workaday pace of people differs, and their best performance capabilities also differ. So does their response to incentives. Furthermore, performances differ both because of chance variations (some of our walkers might have had to wait for traffic or a traffic light) and the effort a person is willing to exert. A person can go faster or can slow down, as he or she wishes. All of these variations exist in production jobs. The time it takes workers to do jobs varies for similar reasons.

It might seem that the proper way to set production standards would be to see how long a job takes and use that time as the standard. But the time observed would depend wholly on who was observed and the performance during the period of observation. Returning to our walkers, the one we happened to pick to observe might be the one who walked a mile in 15 minutes or it might be the one who took 30 minutes. Of course, neither 15 nor 30 minutes would be reasonable to use as a standard. More certainty of reasonableness is needed than just accepting the observed time as the standard.

The next step to improvement in standard setting would seem to be to see how long a job takes on the average—over several performances and with several workers. This method is much better than using the time taken on one performance as the standard. Yet it is still not perfect as a standard-setting procedure because the workers observed might all be fast (or slow),

and, if this is so, their average time would not be a reasonable standard. If the workers observed were all very good, an average of their times would not allow enough time for the standard.

Using the average of the observed time is also an imperfect solution because workers have control over their work pace. If the time a worker takes is to become the standard, he would be working against his own best interest if he performed the task in his minimum time. It would only be human nature for him to slow down and stretch out the time during the observation. Furthermore, he might gain a few friends among his co-workers if he did aid in achieving loose, easy to meet, standards. However, the surprising thing is that workers do not always slow down when standards are being set. There is enough slowing down, however, to make it unwise to accept observed times, even an average of several observed times, as being reliable for standard-setting purposes.

It becomes necessary, therefore, not only to gather data on how long it takes to perform jobs but also to "pace rate" (judge the normality of) the performances observed. If 10 men were observed walking one mile and they all did it between 15 and 17 minutes, their average would be about 16 minutes, but this average is better than normal and should be rated as such by the standards setter. The pace rating should indicate that this is, let us say, 125 percent of standard. Thus the standard, when it is set, will allow more time than the 16 minutes actually taken; in this case 1.25 as much time, or 20 minutes in total.

Or, at the other extreme, the men observed could have walked very slowly and averaged, perhaps, 25 minutes. If this were so, the standard setter's pace rating should be below 100. This time, when he calculates the standard time, it should be something less than the average of the times observed. If their performance was rated at 80, then .8 of the time observed will become the standard, and $.8 \times 25 = 20$ minutes.

Again, a 20-minute mile would be regarded as the standard.

As we said, it is necessary for the standards setter to judge the normality of the pace observed, but the concept of normal is somewhat abstract. It should be the pace, or time, that it would take an ordinary, experienced worker to do a job while applying himself in a normally diligent fashion (but not his pace when he is really pressing himself).

This concept of normality is particularly important where wage incentives are used because the production standard is the basis on which a worker's bonus is calculated. If a job is regarded as a five-minute job, then the worker is expected to perform the job 12 times in an hour before he starts to earn a bonus. Production of 15 units would earn him a 25 percent bonus. Should six minutes be regarded as the standard time, however, the worker would get a bonus for all production in excess of 10 an hour. If he could produce 15 units, he would get a 50 percent bonus. Thus, the *reasonableness* of the standard is very important.

NUMBER OF CYCLES TO TIME

Production standards are usually set by a standards setter (a time study engineer) who watches the operator doing the work and records how long it takes him to do each part of the job. When the operator finishes his job, he repeats it on another unit of product, and this goes on and on. If the analyst watches only a few work cycles, he gets a fairly good idea of how long the job takes, yet his findings are not as reliable as they would be if he watched a larger number of cycles. One question, therefore, is how many cycles are enough to provide reliable figures rather than just happenstance averages which might differ from typical job averages.

For the moment we will overlook the possibility that the worker slows down while being studied. Most companies want the calculated time

value to have a 95 percent probability or more—of being within 5 percent of the true average of observed times. To achieve this level of accuracy, tables are available for analysts to use. These tables specify how many work cycles to study in order to provide the desired reliability. Westinghouse uses the table shown in Figure 27–1.

It is, of course, very important to observe enough cycles so that enough times are recorded to provide reliable averages. Yet the standards setters should not mislead himself by thinking that many recordings will of necessity give him a more accurate average time to use as the job standard. If the worker slows down, he can slow down almost as easily for many cycles as for a few, in which case the average of his times will be an average of poor performances. Thus, there is little safety in large numbers of observations. The analyst will still have to rely on his pace-rating adjustment in order to set a proper standard.

FIGURE 27–1

	Number of Cycles per Year		
	10,000	1,000–10,000	1–1,000
Cycle Time	Number of Cycles to Study		
8 Hours	2	1	1
3	3	2	1
2	4	2	1
1	5	3	2
48 Minutes	6	3	2
30	8	4	3
20	10	5	4
12	12	6	5
8	15	8	6
5 Minutes	20	10	8
3	25	12	10
2	30	15	12
1	40	20	15
.7	50	25	20
.5 Minutes	60	30	25
.3	80	40	30
.2	100	50	40
.1	120	60	50

NEED FOR TIMING JOBS
BY ELEMENTS

As was suggested, it might seem that the way to time a job would be to look at the clock when the job starts and again when it ends. The elapsed time is the time it takes to do the job. But even apart from the pace-rating problem, this is too simple a method to give accurate results.

In order to get accurate results, it is necessary to consider the separate parts of each job and to time each part even though the parts add up to the whole. When the analyst considers the job part by part (he calls these parts *elements*) and watches the worker do the entire job several times, he discovers two things. First, he finds that the time the worker takes to do each part of the job varies and, second, that the subparts of the job are not always performed exactly the same way every time the worker does the operation.

If the analyst timed the job only on an overall basis, he may never know about either of these things. Or, if he noticed them, he wouldn't know what to do about them. So, in order to determine a proper standard, he needs to develop a list of the job elements and to time them separately.

Recording the times for each element's performance helps the analyst get a better idea of how long each regular job element takes and its variability among cycles. The time study analyst needs to consider this variability when he makes his choice of the time to use as the element's observed time.

Writing down separate element times also helps him arrive at the appropriate time to allow for irregular elements, those which occur only now and then. He needs to know how long they take when they occur, how often they occur, and their variability.

Furthermore, some of these irregular elements will prove to be necessary for the job, but some are likely to be unnecessary. Operators sometimes do extra things that are not part of the regular job in order to add to the job's time. And workers often perform the occasional but necessary parts of the job more often than is required.

Both of these actions by workers make the job take longer than usual during the period of observation. In order to arrive at a proper production standard, the analyst needs to exclude all extraneous elements. Yet, he must be sure to include the time needed to be taken for all necessary but irregular elements according to how frequently they should occur.

PERFORMING THE STUDY

The first thing the analyst does when starting to collect data for determining a production standard is to decide the job's elements—the parts of the job to be timed separately. Next, the analyst writes the element descriptions in sequence on a recording sheet preparatory to recording their times.

This can be seen in Figure 27–2, which is a time study on an operator assembling pairs of roller skates and packing them into cartons. In Figure 27–2 the elements are "Preassemble toe clips," "Toe clips to frame and run on," and so on.[1]

From here on, the analyst writes in the time it takes to perform the elements, usually letting the stopwatch run continuously and recording its reading at the end of each element.[2] In column 1 of Figure 27–2, the numbers 08, 30, 47, etc., are observations from a continuously running stopwatch. Later the analyst subtracts the elements' ending times from their starting times to get the net time for each element. These are the italicized numbers (*8, 22, 17,* etc.) shown in the columns.

In Figure 27–2 the elements succeed each

---

[1] This study was done in a college classroom as a demonstration and with only the skate key for a tool. Obviously, this work would go much faster when done in a factory on a repetitive basis and with appropriate tools used at a properly designed workplace by an experienced worker.

[2] "Snap-back" time study devices are often used which eliminates this step. At the end of each element, the analyst can push a button and the timer returns.

FIGURE 27–2

	Cycle					
	(1)	(2)	(3)	(4)	(5)	(6)
Element			*Time in Hundredths of a Minute*			
Preassemble toe clips	08	136	315	455	647	794
	8	*14*	*16*	*13*	*10*	*13*
Toe clips to frame	30	155	333	476	672	811
	22	*19*	*18*	*21*	*25*	*17*
Assemble front wheels to frame	47	170	347	506†	686	827
	17	*15*	*14*	*(30)*	*13*	*16*
Tighten axle nut and aside	56	180	362	516	695	837
	9	*10*	*15*	*10*	*9*	*10*
Assemble rear wheels to frame	71	193	388*	529	710	854
	15	*13*	*(26)*	*13*	*15*	*17*
Tighten axle nut and aside	82	205	399	542	735‡	863
	11	*12*	*11*	*13*	*(25)*	*9*
Attach frame halves, bolt and nut on	100	228	418	564	755	879
	18	*23*	*19*	*22*	*20*	*16*
Tighten nut and skate, aside	122	253	442	587	781	900
	22	*25*	*23*	*23*	*26*	*21*
Skates, straps, and ankle cushion pads into carton liner		283		620		931
		30		*33*		*31*
Carton liner into and close carton, aside		299		637		953
		16		*17*		*22*

* Picked up wrong piece.
† Received instructions from supervisor.
‡ Dropped nut off axle.
Performance rating for whole job: 110.

other in vertical sequence. Thus, for the first work cycle, element 1 took $\frac{8}{100}$ of a minute, element 2 was finished at $\frac{30}{100}$, element 3 was finished at $\frac{47}{100}$, and so on. When the operator finished the first roller skate, he went right on to the second one, and again the element times follow in vertical sequence. When the second skate was completed, the operator had a pair of skates, so he packed them into a carton, and continued in this way after every second roller skate.

Before leaving the job, the analyst should also record a judgmental pace rating of the operator's performance so that he or she can later make the appropriate adjustment when calculating the standard time. In our roller skate assembly study this rating was 110, which means the operator's pace was judged to be 10 percent faster than normal.

SETTING THE STANDARD

The first step in setting the standard from the raw data is to subtract the elements' ending times from their starting times. This was done in Figure 27–2, producing the actual time that each element took. Again, these times are in italics and are the values used in our example from this point on.

Note there are several readings for each element, and that the individual times vary somewhat. In this analysis we used a simple arithmetic average of the element times observed, except that the times in parentheses were omitted as not typical. (See footnotes in Figure 27–2.)

These averages appear in Figure 27–3 as the *element time* figures. Next, these times were multiplied by how often the element occurs per

FIGURE 27–3

Element	Frequency	Element Time	Time per Pair of Skates
		Time in Minutes	
Preassemble toe clips	2	.123	.246
Toe clips on frame	2	.203	.406
Assemble two wheels	4	.148	.592
Tighten axle nut	4	.108	.432
Attach frame halves	2	.197	.394
Tighten frame nut and bolt	2	.233	.466
Pack two skates into carton liner	1	.308	.308
Insert liner into carton and aside	1	.183	.183
Total average cycle time observed ("selected" time)			3.027
Adjust for performance rating of 110 percent			.303
Normal time			3.330
Add 12 percent for fatigue and personal time			.399
Standard time (in minutes per pair)			3.729

Standard hourly output: 60 ÷ 3.729 = 16.1 pairs per hour
Piece rate at $6.00 an hour: $6.00 ÷ 16.1 = $.37 per pair

unit of output. When our sample study was taken, the analyst timed putting on the skate's front wheels and tightening the axle bolt as different from assembling the back wheels, but these turned out to be identical activities; so, in summarizing the data in Figure 27–3, putting wheels on appears as only one element but is said to occur four times per pair of skates.

After each element's time was multiplied by its frequency, the typical cycle time totaled to 3.027 minutes. This is called the *selected* time. Next, the 110 percent performance rating was used, causing the addition of 10 percent more time and an adjusted time of 3.330 minutes per pair of skates. This is called *normal* time. Finally, we added 12 percent to normal time for fatigue and personal time, resulting in a *standard* time of 3.729 minutes per pair.

The method described here is typical of how time standards are set. Personal and fatigue allowances are sometimes set a little lower, perhaps at 10 percent.

Many jobs, of course, are more complicated than assembling roller skates. If they have several miscellaneous elements that are done inter-estingly, this makes it difficult to determine how much time to allow for them. One way is to take a more extended time study and handle such elements on a proportional basis, as we did with putting the skates into cartons.

This, however, may take a long time to do well because of the infrequency of these elements. Therefore, the analyst may use "work sampling" (explained later in this chapter). If an operator is observed performing miscellaneous elements one fifth of the time and main elements four fifths of his time, it is assumed that miscellaneous elements take one fourth as much time as main elements, and they are therefore assigned one fourth the time of main elements.

MACHINE TIME WITHIN WORK CYCLES

Many machines are semiautomatic; once they are set up and the material is inserted, the machines perform all the operations. All that the operator does is take out the completed product and put in the next one. While the machine works, if there is nothing for the operator to do, there is a question of how the element "wait for machine" should be handled in the production standard. If the wait is short or if the machine's operations need monitoring, "wait for machine" should be listed along with all of the other elements and incorporated into the standard. If a job takes 2 minutes to unload and load and a ½-minute wait while the machine runs, this would result in a 2½-minute production standard.[3] But if unload and load time is 2 minutes and then the machine runs by itself for 10 minutes, this job probably should be considered a 2-minute, not a 12-minute, job. The operator is given other work to do during his idle 10 minutes—possibly operating other machines, inspecting output, or moving materials.

SETUP AND CHANGE TIME

Machines usually have to be "set up" for each job or changed over from the previous job. The tools, tool holders, and material holders, and so on, all must be put in place and adjusted. But before that begins, the old setup from the last job must be torn down and its tools and gadgetry put away. Besides this, the operator usually has to make a trip to the tool crib to return tooling and get the tooling for the new job, and perhaps a drawing. Along the way he rings out on his old job and rings in for his new job—often by inserting his badge in a computer terminal and typing in the job numbers and other information.

However, the setting up of many semiautomatic machines is often done by a setup mechanic who does nothing else. He is usually paid by the hour, so there are no production standards required for tearing down and setting up.

Many workers on incentive pay plans, however, are on jobs where they set up their own machines and then run them themselves. There are three choices (none of which is ideal) of paying for setting up: (1) pay by the hour, (2)

set standards for setting up and pay on an incentive plan, (3) put the setup time in with the machine operating time on a pro rata basis and have one production standard cover both setup and operating the machine.

Pay Hourly

Number 1 (paying for setup at an hourly rate) is somewhat unsatisfactory, particularly if a pieceworker is to be paid his regular job's base rate for it. Since he is not earning a bonus for this work, he feels that his pay is cut while he is setting up. But if he is paid his average earnings, including his usual bonus, while setting up jobs without standards, he may take a rest while doing it. In fact, on his time card he may exaggerate the time the setup takes to boost his earnings.

Incentive Pay Plan

Number 2 (developing standards for the setup jobs) is a better choice, and the best if incentives are used. But, since there may be a wide variety of setups, these standards are slow and costly to determine if identical setups are infrequent. Weeks may pass before the time study analyst can have an opportunity to watch even two or three setups of a given kind. Also, the operator can often use part of the previous job's tooling, so that complete setups are not always required. (A similar problem arises in processing situations, as, for example, in paint mixing. It takes more time to clean the equipment and go from black to white than from white to black because in the former case the equipment has to be cleaned more thoroughly.)

Pro Rata Basis Pay

Number 3 (allowing time for setup on a pro rata basis within the regular rate) is sometimes chosen and is a fairly satisfactory method. It does not solve the difficulty of setting many standards, nor of having to set standards for setups based on very few observations, or of partial setups.

---

[3] This is known as *enforced* idle time and should be measured and documented in the standard. If additional standard work is required in the future, management can simply reduce the enforced idle time in an amount equal to the increase in standard time. This approach can minimize the labor grievances as well as save money.

It *does* avoid having hundreds of standards for setups on the records, but they have to be set anyway before they can be put into the standard for operating a machine on a pro rata basis, so there is no reduction of standard-setting effort.

Including setup time in the standard for operating a machine on a pro rata basis usually works reasonably well if the average quantity of units run at one time doesn't vary a great deal—for example, if a machine requires a minor new setup for every new job—as might occur with a printing press. (The main job is running sheets of paper through the press.) For example, from past experience the analyst knows about how many sheets are usually run each time. Assume the average run is 200 sheets and the operating time for turning out 200 sheets is four minutes. If we assume that it takes two minutes to change to a new job, these two times can be added together, and we find that it will take six minutes to set up and print 200 sheets of paper, or three minutes per 100. This then becomes the standard.

This is fair if the printing runs average 200. But, if the operator gets several orders for 25 sheets, he has to run eight such orders to turn out 200 sheets. He will spend 4 minutes running the machine and 16 minutes changing to new jobs, a total of 20 minutes. Yet, the standard only allows him six minutes' credit and six minutes' pay. On the other hand, if he has a run of 1,000, it takes 20 minutes to run them plus 2 minutes' change time for a total of 22 minutes, but the standard allows 30 minutes.

Thus, including setup time on a pro rata basis may make standards tight or loose if the variability of run length is high, and not evenly distributed around the average used to prorate the setup time into the standard.

PROBLEMS IN SETTING PRODUCTION STANDARDS

Most of the problems in setting production standards center on situations where the analyst has to use judgment. And of these, "pace rating" (also called *leveling*) is probably the most open to question. It is apparent that some particular pace should be thought of as reasonable and that this pace should not be either a worker's best or poorest performance. Yet, it is hard to convince everyone that the end result, the time standard, is correct when they know that the times allowed contain an adjustment reflecting the analyst's judgment of normality.

However, no better way seems to be available than to have the standard setter make such a leveling judgment. Some companies try to refine this by having the analyst make several pace ratings, one for each element, and adjust each element's average time to "normal" before summing up the times to get the job standard. A few companies even try to have their analysts rate every occurrence of every element. This extra effort on their part may produce better standards; yet, the process still requires judgment.

It might seem that the need to judge pace could be reduced or even eliminated by studying all the members of a group and using their average time as the standard. But we have already noted that this is unfair to groups of good workers who turn out more work than a fair standard should call for. And we also noted that such a standard would be equally wrong if it were an average of slow performers. There is the added difficulty that there are often only one or two workers on many jobs. And there is the still greater difficulty that a group of workers who are being studied may all slow down.

Judgment must also be exercised in the matter of how often certain things should be done. An operator may have to stop the operation in order to measure the material, or sharpen a tool, or replace a broken or worn tool. But, how often must he stop the operation to sharpen the tool? When has it become dull enough to need sharpening? This too is a matter of judgment. In some cases, there may be a question of whether certain elements are really needed at all as part of the job—the work might be someone else's work. Again, judgment plays a key part in the setting of standards.

27/3/85

2/4/85

LIMITATIONS TO USE OF TIME STUDY

Production standards can exist and are used in many instances where the work itself cannot be timed. These production standards, however, are only approximations and are rarely as good as time study standards; yet, approximate standards are usually better than none. The weaknesses of time study as a method for setting production standards can be enumerated as follows:

1. An analyst can time only what he can see. This eliminates the timing of the thinking parts of jobs and leaves only manual jobs.

2. If an analyst times a job, it has to be a specific job—with starting and stopping points and separable into units so that it is possible to count how many times it is done. This is difficult to do with, say, the work of a janitor, or plant guard, or with most office jobs.

3. It doesn't pay to set standards for some jobs that are infrequently done. The gain from setting standards for a small job that will be done only once or twice in the future rarely justifies the cost of the analytical work. Standards setting by time study is best applied to repetitive jobs.

4. Nor does it pay to time jobs and set standards when workers do a wide variety of things. A maintenance department carpenter, for example, does too many things to have standards for all of them (his daily work report might be several pages long). Also, it is too costly to verify what he says he did. And when no one checks reports, some workers on piecework may report that they have turned out more work than they did.

5. It usually does not pay to have standards for only part of an operator's work. If it isn't possible to develop standards for all of their work some workers may exaggerate the time they report doing daywork (for which they get paid by the hour) to increase their earnings. A worker may have spent four hours on piecework and four on daywork (not in single stretches of time but intermittently during the day), but he may report three hours of piecework and five hours

of daywork. It looks as if he did nine hours' work in the day (four hours of piecework, done in three hours, plus five hours of daywork) instead of eight. The supervisor is put on the spot and may have to give him nine hours of pay or arbitrarily (although perhaps correctly) cutting his claim of five hours of daywork to four.

6. If quality is hard to define (as in polishing a surface), standards and production incentives may cause quality to fall off. The operator may say that he has done the job well enough when he hasn't.

The analyst should think twice before accepting this criticism of production standards, though. If a worker is on daywork instead of piecework, he might, if allowed, shine a polished surface all day and be proud of the fine job he does. Unfortunately, he cannot be allowed to spend this much time on an operation. Jobs where quality is difficult to define are exactly the places where good production standards, as well as quality standards, are needed.

7. Unions often oppose time study; in that case, and if the union is very strong, it may be able to stop or severely limit time studies. Standards may be set by other methods but not with time studies.

2/4/85

4/4/85

WORK SAMPLING

Work sampling (occasionally called *ratio-relay* study) means observing, at randomly determined time intervals, what sort of work activities are going on so that the proportion of time spent doing each can be estimated. An analyst takes a "tour" through a workplace, say 500 times, over a period of weeks and notes what the operator is doing each time. Perhaps an office secretary might be observed typing 250 times, filing 150 times, telephoning 50 times, and doing personal things 50 times. Thus, 50 percent of her time is spent on typing, 30 percent on filing, 10 percent on telephoning, and 10 percent on other things.

This method can be used to determine how often job elements of factory or office activities occur to provide the information needed to incorporate time for them into production standards. Work sampling can also be used to set complete standards and not just the time for the miscellaneous parts of jobs. Work sampling is also useful for setting production standards for work that is difficult to analyze with time studies—such as most clerical work.

Work sampling is often thought of as a low-cost way to set standards, and this may be true. Yet this is not always true because the job being observed may require a trip by the analyst to the job area for each observation. Also, the observations should be taken at randomly determined times of the day and not be concentrated in the hours when the observer may happen to be near the operation. And, it may take a considerable amount of time to obtain observations. If, for example, 500 observations are required, this means 10 a day for 50 days.

One advantage of work sampling is that it probably represents true-to-life situations. Operators rarely get the chance to dress up their performance to try to mislead the analyst. Against this is the disadvantage that there is no pace rating. In order to set a standard without pace rating, the analyst would have to determine the number of units turned out in a day, or other appropriate measures of output. Both a fast and slow typist might very well be typing 50 percent of the time, but the fast typist types more pages in a day. Thus, the analyst would have to match typing output to each typist included in the work sampling to develop meaningful standards.

A Work Sampling Example

Suppose we wish to estimate the proportion of time that inventory clerks should spend in a stockroom doing various activities—picking orders, putting parts away, checking the book accuracy of quantities on hand, paperwork, transporting parts, walking, and miscellaneous activities, and to use this estimate for setting standards and determining their capacity to handle orders.

Also suppose there are three clerks, and that our work sampling study will observe them during one 15-minute tour within each of eight hours (from 8:00 A.M. to 5:00 P.M., with lunch break from 12:00–1:00 P.M.) for 10 days (3 × 8 × 10 = 240 observations). The time each tour would begin, however, is to be determined randomly, using a random numbers table (see Appendix F). Since there are 60 minutes in an hour, and each tour takes 15 minutes, we want to determine when each tour should begin so that tours do not overlap. As an example of how we would determine when to take the eight 15-minute tours for the first day, we arbitrarily picked the first two random number digits (60 minutes is two digits) in the left-most column of Appendix F, *if* they were 60 or less. Reading down the column, the numbers chosen were 21, (68 skipped) 58, 37 (93, 75, 80 skipped), 24, 59 (63 skipped), 03, 32, 50, and 44. Figure 27–4 shows the form we used, the start times for each tour, and the observations (the check marks) for the first day. Note that we had to discard the 2:03 start time (substituting 32, the next random number) because 1:59 plus 15 minutes would overlap into 2:03. The results show that 58 percent of the time is spent picking parts orders and putting parts away, with the balance spread among the other activities.

Determining the Accuracy of the Estimate

Using statistics, we can determine the accuracy of our observations for a given level of confidence. First, suppose after observing the clerks for all 10 days (240 observations), we came up with the same percentages shown in Figure 27–4. Let us consider only the "picking parts orders" activity proportion of 0.33. If we want to be 95 percent confident of our estimate, we can say that the true proportion of time spent picking orders is within the range given by the following formula:[4]

---

[4] 1.96 is obtained from Appendix C, Section B. The value in the table which corresponds to 1.96 is 0.97500. Since this is a two-tailed confidence interval, 1.0 − .97500 = .025 × 2 = .05; 1.0 − .05 = .95 or 95 percent, the confidence level desired.

$$\text{Range} = \text{Observed proportion} \pm 1.96$$
$$\times \frac{\sqrt{\text{Proportion (1 - Proportion)}}}{\sqrt{\text{Number of observations}}}$$
$$= .33 \pm 1.96 \times \frac{\sqrt{.33\,(1 - .33)}}{\sqrt{240}}$$
$$= .33 \pm .059$$

Thus, with 240 observations, we can be 95 percent confident that the true proportion of time spent picking orders is from .271 to .389, or from 27.1 percent to 38.9 percent of the time.

Now, suppose during this 10-day period, 200 orders were picked during the 80 total hours included in the study. Since 33 percent of the time was spent picking, this means each order picked averaged $(80 \times .33)/200 = .132$ hours or 7.92 minutes.

Next, presume the analyst pace-rated the

FIGURE 27–4
Work Sampling Form and Result for First 8-Hour Day of 10 Days

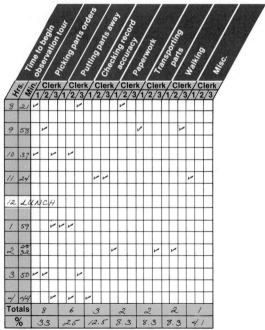

Note: Checks indicate the activity each clerk was doing when observed during each tour.

three clerks' picking efficiency at 90, 100, 105. The first picked 75 orders during the study (37.5 percent), the second 100 (50 percent), and the third only 25 (12.5 percent). A weighted pace-rating factor then would be $(90 \times .375) + (100 \times .5) + (105 \times .125) = 96.87$.

Combining the weighted pace-rating factor with the time obtained from work sampling and adding 12 percent for fatigue and personal time results in the following time standard for picking one order: $7.92 \times .9687 \times 1.12 = 8.59$ minutes.

Thus, if one of the three clerks were assigned full-time to do picking, he would be expected to pick, on the average, 56 orders in a 480-minute workday. Or, if he were assigned 30 orders to pick in a day, this should take 258 minutes, or 53 percent of his workday.

Using our 95 percent confidence interval, we would only expect the number of orders picked per day (if that is all he did) to be below 47 or above 68, only 5 percent of the time:

$$480/(80 \times .389/200 \times 60 \times .9687 \times 1.12) = 47$$
$$480/(80 \times .271/200 \times 60 \times .9687 \times 1.12) = 68$$

If he picked less than 47 orders per day, something is probably wrong with his productivity, and it should be investigated. If he consistently picks more than 68 orders per day, and is on incentive pay, the standard is probably too loose, or his accuracy is poor.

OTHER WAYS TO SET PRODUCTION STANDARDS

Production standards for semiautomatic machines are sometimes set by starting with a machine's maximum output capacity. Something less than this, say 90 percent of capacity, is determined to be the best that can be hoped for. Then a decision is made that even 90 percent of capacity is very good and that this much output merits a bonus, perhaps 25 percent. So 90 percent of the best expected production is regarded as being 125 percent of standard, and the standard becomes $100 \div 125 \times .90$, or 72 percent of capacity. Thus, if a machine could, theoretically, turn out 500 pieces an hour, 450 units would be regarded as maximum production and the standard would be 360 units per hour. A pieceworker who turned out 450 would earn a 25 percent bonus.

Production standards for piecework purposes are often set by direct negotiation between a company's industrial engineers and the union's standards committee. In the shoe and textile industries it is common for these people to sit down together, look over the new patterns, compare them to the old patterns and standards, and thereupon agree on the new standards. This practice, however, would be unusual in other industries.

Another method for setting standards, which is used commonly enough to merit mention, is simple estimation. The foreman or an experienced estimator looks at a drawing or product design and, based on his past experience, estimates how long the work should take. Contractors in the building trades have to do this all the time when they bid on contracts to build houses. And in factories, too, this may be about the best that can be done when it comes to setting a standard for making a complex product such as a custom-made industrial solar water heater.

4/4/85

14/85 ## STANDARD DATA

New jobs are often similar in many respects to old jobs. Often, certain parts of a new job are identical to parts of old jobs. In such cases, using the time values from old standards for the same activities would reduce costs. This situation is common enough that time values for certain activities and sets of movements can be regarded as established data that are available for use in setting the cost of developing new standards.

Such standard data are of two main kinds. One uses job element times from past studies in what is called a *macroscopic* method. The other regards all jobs as collections of very short or minute movements, which can be called a *microscopic* method. Once someone makes a

catalog of their times, no one ever has to do it again—for any job. All anyone has to do is list every movement an operator makes, get the time for each movement out of the catalog, and add the times up.

Macroscopic methods are like building a prefab house: The analyst works with the major elements of a job, just as a prefab house is made from preassembled sections of walls, floors, cabinets, windows, and roofs. Microscopic methods are like building an ordinary house—out of bricks, nails, boards, and glass. Such jobs are made up of little movements: reach, pick up, carry, insert, and so on.

Macroscopic methods are limited to particular operations, such as operating a turret lathe, and they apply to any and all jobs done on that size and kind of lathe. Microscopic methods are universal and can be used for all operations and all jobs which are primarily physical in nature.

Macroscopic Methods

Macroscopic methods use standard data which are often put into formula form and thus can be easily computerized. Often they are put into precomputed tables, and sometimes presented in charts.

Macroscopic methods assume certain elements are constant irrespective of the specific operation on jobs done on the same machine or similar machines. Oiling a machine's bearings takes the same amount of time irrespective of the job the operator is working on. So does blowing or brushing out chips. So does loosening or tightening tool-holder jaws.

Certain other elements are variable. The time it takes to drill a hole, or to plane or grind a surface for example, depends on the depth and diameter of the hole or the size of the area to be planed or smoothed and how much metal is to be removed. The times for the job element vary, *but in a predictable way*. Other elements, such as making spot welds, are constant, but their total time depends on how many times they need doing.

In all of these cases the analyst, by looking at a drawing, can predict the time an element will take on a new job. Most elements are either clearly constant or they are variable. And in almost all cases where an element's time varies, the analyst can determine, by formula, how long it will take. He can then list the times for constant elements and the calculated times for variable elements. Adding these figures produces production standards for new jobs without waiting for them to be done.

Using regression analysis for developing macroscopic standards. A common method used for measuring work and setting macroscopic standards is regression analysis. However, in this application, we observe the relationship between the amount of work done and the time it takes to do it. Figure 27–5 shows a simplified example of the relationship between the number of rooms cleared by custodians and the time spent doing them.[5]

The line drawn through the scatter diagram of dots can be derived using regression (least squares) analysis.

For example, the derived formula might be:

Cleaning time = 2.0 hours + (.167 hours
× Number of rooms cleaned)

If 10 rooms are to be cleaned, it should take 2 + (.167 × 10) = 3.67 hours. (Pace ratings and personal allowances can be considered, but we will not do so here for simplicity.)

But all rooms and other spaces that are cleaned are not the same. Some rooms are larger than others, bathrooms may take more time than offices, and hallways are not even rooms. So, we might use a more complex method—multiple regression—to determine a more accurate relationship for the time it should take to do a variety of cleaning activities. While we will not develop the mathematics of this

[5] This example was adapted from George C. Smith, Jr., *Work Measurement: A Systems Approach* (Columbus, Ohio: Grid Publishing, 1978), pp. 35–44.

FIGURE 27–5
Relationship between Time Worked and Rooms Cleaned

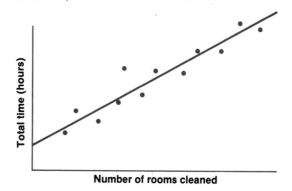

method here, suppose we calculated the following multiple regression formula from a sample set of observations of custodians cleaning offices, restrooms, and hallways:

Cleaning time = .83 + (.2 × Number of offices)
+ (.28 × Number of restrooms)
+ (.00083 × Number of square feet of hall space)

For a janitorial assignment of 10 offices, 3 restrooms, and 3,000 square feet of hall space, it should take:

Cleaning time = .83 + (.2 × 10) + (.28 × 3)
+ (.00083 × 3,000)
= 6.16 hours

Assume that pace-ratings and that fatigue and personal time have been included in the above formula. Since each custodian works an eight-hour shift, the analyst can easily use the multiple regression equation to add rooms or hall space so that the job tasks sum to about eight hours. Several combinations exist, but to fill out the remaining 1.84 hours, the analyst must consider the availability and closeness of offices, restrooms, and hall space.

Suppose two more restrooms are available and several offices are still unassigned, but no more hall space is available. One solution is to add the two restrooms and enough offices to the custodian's duties to build his workload nearer to 8 hours. If we add 6 offices, he will have a workload of 7.92 hours:

$$\text{Cleaning time} = .83 + (.2 \times 16) + (.28 \times 5)$$
$$+ (.00083 \times 3{,}000) = 7.92$$

Standard data such as described here are available for several kinds of jobs—clerical, custodial, bank jobs, and nursing services, as well as for a wide range of factory jobs. These data may be purchased from companies who specialize in developing macroscopic standards through extensive research and experimentation.

Microscopic Methods

In Chapter 25, therbligs—the basic, minute movements which make up all of a person's physical movements—were discussed. They provide the basis for the microscopic method for setting job standards.

Industrial engineers have developed lists of minute human movements (reach, grasp, move hands, and so on) and have also, by using high-speed moving pictures, studied these movements carefully and a set time value for each. Catalogs of times for these minute movements may be purchased, and part of one of these catalogs is shown in Figure 27–6.

The time values shown in such a catalog are listed in very short intervals. Perhaps the best known of these catalogs of times is called *methods time measurement* (MTM). MTM times are shown in TMUs (time measurement units), which are $\frac{1}{100,000}$ of an hour (30 TMUs = 1 second).

To use microscopic methods, the analyst lists the operator's movements in great detail and then looks at a catalog of times to see how long each movement will take. This work is not for the amateur since an operator often is doing one thing with one hand and another with the other. The analyst has to pay attention to which catalog time to use.

Proponents of microscopic methods say that by using these methods an analyst can get very accurate time standards more quickly than by any other means. They also claim that the thorough investigation needed to list the elements of a job causes the analyst to see so many places the job is being done inefficiently that he or she is often able to make numerous improvements.

FIGURE 27–6
Time Values for Therblig "Reach" in TMUs *(.0006 minutes)*

Distance Moved (inches)	Kind of Movement				Case and Description
	A	B	C	D	
¾ or less	2.0	2.0	2.0	2.0	A. Reach to object in fixed loca-
1	2.5	2.5	3.6	2.4	tion, or to object in other hand
2	4.0	4.0	5.9	3.8	or on which other hand rests.
3	5.3	5.3	7.3	5.3	B. Reach to single object in loca-
4	6.1	6.4	8.4	6.8	tion which may vary slightly
5	6.5	7.8	9.4	7.4	from cycle to cycle.
6	7.0	8.6	10.1	8.8	C. Reach to object jumbled with
8	7.9	10.1	11.5	9.3	other objects in a group so
10	8.7	11.5	12.9	10.5	that search and select occur.
15	11.0	15.1	16.3	13.6	D. Reach to a very small object
20	13.1	18.6	19.8	16.7	or where accurate grasp is re-
25	15.4	22.2	23.2	19.8	quired.
30	17.5	25.8	26.7	22.9	

Source: MTM Association for Standards and Research.

MTM standards are usually quite accurate but each one takes a considerable amount of time to set up, even with the catalog of times available. The time required and the cost entailed are serious handicaps in companies where the labor contract requires standards to be set within three days on all new jobs, and this is a common requirement.

To meet this problem, MSD (master standard data), GPD (general-purpose data), and MCD (master clerical data) have been developed—to shorten the standard-setting time. These adaptations of MTM combine sets of therblig data into larger "building blocks"—not as time study elements but large enough to drastically reduce the MTM standard-setting job. Using these building blocks reduces the cost of setting standards and thereby allows its use in more places, including clerical activities.

In some companies, MSD, GPD, and MCD are computerized, which has further lessened the time and cost of setting standards. IBM, not unnaturally, is one of the companies which uses computers for developing standards. The standards setter just lists the code for each basic data time and a computer calculates the standard.

H. B. Maynard and Company, a consulting organization, and the principal proponent of MTM, has also developed a simplified version of MTM which it calls MOST (Maynard operation sequence technique). MOST eliminates much of the time-consuming detail of MTM by working with groups of movements instead of specific individually detailed movements.[6]

Implementing Standards

We have been discussing the matter of setting standards as if the job were complete when the standard is set. Yet, in one sense, this is only part of the job. Standard setting should also include the implementation process. In order for

standards to make their fullest contribution, they have to be accepted and used.

Acceptance begins with the start of the standards development procedure. People should be told ahead by their supervisor that a job study is going to be made. It should be explained that the standards analyst is an expert at what he or she does and that they are experts at doing their job. This develops an expectation that the two of them should work together to develop a fair and honest standard.

After the data are collected, the standards engineer should review the observations with the worker to see if anything was omitted, or if anything should be deleted, and if the frequencies are reasonable. This both improves the accuracy of the data and aids in gaining trust from the worker that the observations are reasonable.

If there are differences, they should be resolved before the standard is set. When agreement is reached, the standard should be reported to the workers.

The standard should be backed up by the detailed record of the work method which it covers. Variations and changes form the work method should be monitored, and new standards set when the method changes.

This approach to standards setting should improve their accuracy, fairness, and acceptability.

8 4 85

Review Questions

1. Why are production standards necessary even in companies not using piecework? What are they used for?
2. Discuss the need to time a large number of work cycles to increase the reliability of the averages of observed work time for setting standards.
3. Why is it desirable to time jobs element by element, rather than the entire job? How will this produce a better standard?
4. Where is judgment usually exercised in setting production standards? Discuss how judgment can be eliminated, reduced, or improved in setting standards?

---

[6] This method is described in Kjell B. Zandin, "Better Work Management with MOST," *Management Review*, July 1975, pp. 11–17.

5. Explain briefly how a time study analyst develops a time standard after collecting the raw data.

6. In practice, time study cannot be used everywhere. Why not?

7. Can production standards be set by work sampling without using a stop-watch?

8. What are the steps in designing a work sampling program?

9. Compare macroscopic and microscopic methods for setting production standards by using standard data instead of time study. How is regression analysis used in applying macroscopic data?

10. "Positive incentives are good; negative incentives are bad." Discuss these statements.

11. What are some of the problems encountered in using piecework? How can they be handled?

12. Incentive plans for people who work on products are more common than for indirect workers. Why? What problems are there in putting indirect workers on incentives? What solutions are there to these problems?

13. Is it true that workers are better off because they receive fringe benefits? Or wouldn't they be better off to take the money cost of the fringe benefits as an added wage instead? Should people have a choice?

Questions for Discussion

1. "Standards cannot be set in service organizations (banks, hospitals, restaurants, insurance companies, police departments, etc.), because service is too subjective." Discuss.

2. When a time study analyst sets a time standard and has a choice of operators to study, should he or she study a good worker? Or whom? Why?

3. What should a supervisor do when one of her workers says that the piece rate is too low and that he thinks it should be adjusted upward?

4. A leading industrial consultant reports that management often permits a standard to be bargained instead of measured. Or it permits workers to do the job their own way instead of the best way. This consultant sees both practices as bad. What is wrong with these practices?

5. Both the United Automobile Workers and the International Ladies Garment Workers unions have time study engineers on their payrolls. Wouldn't this be a big help in deciding upon the reasonableness of disputed standards? The union's and the company's time study analysts could, together, study the job and jointly arrive at a standard satisfactory to both. Discuss.

6. What behavioral problems should an analyst expect from people being timed with a stop watch? From people observed in a work sampling program?

7. The union has fined a company employee for violating the production quantity ceiling the union set on a factory job. The employee seems to have no alternative but to hold his production down and pay the fine, or else quit or be fired. Is this reasonable? Is it legal? Discuss.

8. Why not eliminate across-the-board wage increases? How can they be incorporated into existing piece rates?

9. Would you work harder or less hard if you were a member of a group being paid on a group incentive plan? Why?

10. In most places of employment, women are allowed six-month maternity leave with pay. After the Civil Rights Act was passed several years ago, quite a few men complained that this discriminated against them. What should be done?

11. Women live longer than men (at least five years more on the average), which makes their pensions cost more. To be fair, shouldn't men get larger monthly pensions so as to make their pension costs the same as those for women?

Problems

1. An operator took eight hours to set up a machine and produce 130 bun warmers. For this job, the standard time for machine setup is 50 minutes and 4 minutes per piece per bun warmer.
   a. What was the operator's "efficiency" for the day?
   b. If the operator were working on piecework, and the job has a base rate of $7 an hour, how much money would be earned?

2. What is the time standard for the following job? Add 15 percent for allowances and show the figures. The times shown are continuous watch readings in minutes.

			Cycle					Performance
Element	1	2	3	4	5	6	7	Rating
Get two empty cases	.11		.55		1.05		1.51	1.05
Put part into case	.22	.41	.65	.83	1.16	1.34	1.60	1.15
Fasten parts into position	.29	.48	.73	.97	1.23	1.41	1.82	.95

3. Mary Joyce and Norman Dorian both operate punch presses of the same kind, and both work on piecework. Their base rates are $8.00 an hour (this is guaranteed). The production standards for the four products which they spend all their time on are: product A, 5 per minute; B, 10 per minute; C, 15 per minute; and D, 20 per minute. In one specific week, when they worked eight hours every day, their production records were as follows:

Joyce

Product	M	T	W	T	F
A	1,200		1,500		900
B	3,000	3,000			900
C			900	1,800	900
D		5,400	3,600	3,600	2,400

Dorian

Product	M	T	W	T	F
A	600			1,500	300
B		900	1,200	1,800	3,600
C	5,400	5,400	3,600		
D	4,800	2,400			2,400

a. Calculate the wages, day by day, of these two operators.

b. If both operators work consistently hard, which (if any) of the standards would appear to be out of line? Which are the tight standards, and which are the loose standards?

4. Anne and Bart do the same operation on two similar machines. The machine cost in each case is $8 an hour. Anne produces 120 pieces per hour and is paid $7 an hour. Bart turns out 115 pieces per hour.

a. What is Anne's cost per piece?

b. What would Bart's hourly rate be if his unit cost is equal to that of Anne?

5. Charles and Don each produce 100 pieces per hour, but Charles' rejects are 2 percent as against ½ percent for Don. Rejects are repairable at $.18 each.

a. Each worker is paid a straight hourly rate of $7 an hour. What is the cost per unit of this item for each worker?

b. If you paid each one so that both would have Charles' cost per unit, what would each one's hourly rate be?

6. For purposes of determining the allowance for miscellaneous elements for setting a job standard, the analyst has collected 500 observations from work sampling. These show that the operator was performing the operation 392 times. He was away from his machine 32 times, and 76 times his machine was not running while he adjusted it, measured the output, and did other miscellaneous activities associated with making products. From time study data, the analyst had previously established that just doing the main parts of the operation takes 4.2 minutes.

a. What should the job standard be?

b. Using the work sampling data, what is the 95 percent confidence interval of the proportion of time the operator spends performing the operation?

7. If every stroke were used to turn out products so that a semiautomatic machine could produce 600 units per hour, what would the production standard be if 85 percent of maximum output were regarded as worth a 20 percent bonus?

8. The company and the union are nearing the close of their negotiations and seem about to agree to a $.30 per hour wage increase. The union proposes that the increase be given as an override so that everyone gets the same amount, $.30. Yet the union does not seem strongly opposed to having the raise incorporated into the piece rate structure, provided only that everyone gets an increase of $.30 an hour.

You are given the job of working out a method of incorporating the increase into the piece rate structure. Try to do it so that Brown, White, and Black all get a $.30 raise. Brown works on daywork at $7 an hour. White's base rate is $6.80, but he is on an incentive job and earns $7.05. Black is on a $7.10 base rate incentive job, on which she earns $7.75 an hour. Show the figures to support your recommendation.

9. The following data have been collected to provide a basis for setting up standard data for winding coils in a coil winding department.

Study No.	Core Diameter	Core Length	Length of Wire Wound	Wire Gauge	Winding Time
1	1½"	5"	3,200'	30	2.10 min.
2	½	4	1,500	10	1.60
3	1	4	1,800	20	1.25
4	1¼	5	2,600	15	2.30
5	½	3	1,200	40	.55
6	1	3	1,525	30	.89
7	¾	4	1,475	15	1.27
8	1	5	2,000	25	1.30
9	½	4	1,600	35	.78
10	1¼	5	2,400	10	2.60
11	¾	3	1,500	25	.99
12	½	2	600	40	.42
13	1	4	2,200	15	1.80
14	1¼	5	2,800	20	2.10
15	½	2	1,500	40	.70
16	¼	1	200	15	.50

Using multiple regression analysis, the following equation was developed:

Winding time = .83 + (.175 × core diameter)
  − (.003 × core length)
  + (.0006 × length of wire)
  − (.029 × wire gauge)

a. Using this equation, how much time will it take to wind a coil which will have a ⅜-inch core diameter, a core length of 2 inches, and contain 3,800 feet of 37-gauge wire?

b. Do the same for a coil on a one-inch core diameter, a four-inch core length, and containing 2,200 feet of 12-gauge wire.

10. The fire department wants to estimate the travel time fire trucks take in responding to emergencies. At random times, the following travel times were measured, and corresponding travel distances were obtained from the trucks' odometers:

Observation	Travel Time (minutes)	Travel Distance (miles)
1	1.25	.5
2	2.00	1.5
3	.50	.2
4	5.75	3.1
5	7.50	4.5
6	6.45	3.5
7	3.52	1.7
8	4.50	2.5
9	2.48	1.1
10	3.60	2.3

a. Plot these observations into a scatter diagram, and estimate the relationship between travel time Y and travel distance X. What is your estimate of the average rate of speed of fire trucks?

b. Using least squares analysis (Appendix H), determine a and b for the equation Y = a = bx. Using this equation, what is the average rate of speed of trucks?

c. What other data would you like before you conclusively say that this equation defines average travel time per mile of fire trucks?

d. Can the above estimates be used in developing standards of some kind for the fire department? (Hint: See Chapter 18.)

Case 27-1

Todd Evers' father Jim had worked for the Heavy Duty Truck Company for 25 years. His job as stockroom clerk was not the highest paid job in the department, but he liked the work, and the department head was glad to have so dependable a man and one who knew the stock so well.

After finishing high school, Todd and his parents thought it would be a good idea for him to work a year before he entered college. With his father's help, he got a job at the Heavy Duty Truck Company operating an external grinding machine. The work was piecework, and young Evers quickly became proficient. In less than three months his paycheck exceeded that of his father's.

The father's feelings were a mixture of pride and chagrin. Todd's mother felt very differently, however. When Todd brought home a check larger than his father's for the second consecutive pay period, and it appeared that he would continue to do so, she berated her husband severely. What kind of a husband was he anyway? Through all the years she had lived on his meager earnings. Now she finds that in only three months, their 18-year-old boy can make more than his father. Before long, Jim had to move out of the house in order to have any peace. Jim brought his problem to his foreman.

What is the basic problem? Is it job evaluation: Is it piecework? What should be done both in Jim's case and in the company to prevent similar problems in the future?

Appendixes

Appendix A

Discount Table

Present Value of $1 Received Annually for N Years

	Percent						
	5	10	15	20	25	30	40
Today	1.000	1.000	1.000	1.000	1.000	1.000	1.000
Year							
1	.952	.909	.870	.833	.800	.769	.714
2	1.859	1.736	1.626	1.528	1.440	1.361	1.224
3	1.723	2.487	2.283	2.106	1.952	1.816	1.589
4	3.545	3.170	2.855	2.589	2.362	2.166	1.849
5	4.329	3.791	3.352	2.991	2.689	2.436	2.035
6	5.075	4.355	3.784	3.326	2.951	2.643	2.168
7	5.786	4.868	4.160	3.605	3.161	2.802	2.263
8	6.463	5.335	4.487	3.837	3.329	2.925	2.331
9	7.108	5.759	4.772	4.031	3.463	3.019	2.379
10	7.722	6.145	5.019	4.192	3.571	3.092	2.414
11	8.307	6.495	5.234	4.327	3.656	3.147	2.438
12	8.864	6.814	5.421	4.439	3.725	3.190	2.456
13	9.394	7.103	5.583	4.533	3.780	3.223	2.468
14	9.899	7.367	5.724	4.611	3.824	3.249	2.477
15	10.380	7.606	5.847	4.675	3.859	3.268	2.484
20	12.530	8.514	6.259	4.730	3.954	3.316	2.497
25	14.203	9.077	6.464	4.948	3.985	3.329	2.499
30	15.528	9.427	6.566	4.979	3.995	3.332	2.500
35	16.474	9.603	6.604	4.988	3.997	3.333	2.500
40	17.420	9.779	6.642	4.997	3.999	3.333	2.500

Appendix B

Discount Table

Present Value of $1

	Percent						
	5	10	15	20	25	30	40
Today	1.000	1.000	1.000	1.000	1.000	1.000	1.000
Year							
1	.952	.909	.870	.833	.800	.769	.714
2	.907	.826	.756	.694	.640	.592	.510
3	.864	.751	.657	.578	.512	.455	.364
4	.822	.683	.572	.482	.410	.350	.260
5	.784	.621	.497	.402	.328	.269	.186
6	.746	.564	.432	.335	.262	.207	.133
7	.711	.513	.376	.279	.210	.159	.095
8	.677	.466	.327	.233	.168	.123	.068
9	.645	.424	.284	.194	.134	.094	.048
10	.614	.386	.247	.161	.107	.084	.035
11	.585	.351	.215	.134	.086	.064	.025
12	.557	.319	.187	.112	.069	.049	.018
13	.530	.290	.163	.093	.055	.038	.013
14	.505	.263	.141	.078	.044	.029	.009
15	.481	.239	.123	.065	.035	.023	.006
20	.384	.149	.061	.026	.012	.005	.001
25	.303	.092	.030	.010	.004	.001	
30	.241	.057	.015	.004	.001		
35	.197	.040	.010	.003			
40	.153	.022	.004	.001			

Appendix C

Areas under a Normal Curve

SECTION A

This table shows the percentage of area under a normal curve to the left of a specified number of standard deviations. The percentage of area under a normal curve to the right of a specified number of standard deviations is the complement of the listed percent. For example, the area to the right of −2.4 standard deviations is 100% − 1% = 99%.

Standard Deviations	Percent	Standard Deviations	Percent	Standard Deviations	Percent	Standard Deviations	Percent
− 3.0	.1	− 1.4	8.3	+ 0.2	57.9	+ 1.7	95.3
− 2.9	.2	− 1.3	9.9	+ 0.3	61.7	+ 1.8	96.2
− 2.8	.3	− 1.2	11.7	+ 0.4	65.4	+ 1.9	96.9
− 2.7	.4	− 1.1	13.8	+ 0.5	69.0	+ 2.0	97.5
− 2.6	.6	− 1.0	16.1	+ 0.6	72.4	+ 2.1	98.0
− 2.5	.8	− 0.9	18.6	+ 0.7	75.6	+ 2.2	98.4
− 2.4	1.0	− 0.8	21.4	+ 0.8	78.6	+ 2.3	98.7
− 2.3	1.3	− 0.7	24.4	+ 0.9	81.4	+ 2.4	99.0
− 2.2	1.6	− 0.6	27.6	+ 1.0	83.9	+ 2.5	99.2
− 2.1	2.0	− 0.5	31.0	+ 1.1	86.2	+ 2.6	99.4
− 2.0	2.5	− 0.4	34.6	+ 1.2	88.3	+ 2.7	99.6
− 1.9	3.1	− 0.3	38.3	+ 1.3	90.1	+ 2.8	99.7
− 1.8	3.8	− 0.2	42.1	+ 1.4	91.9	+ 2.9	99.8
− 1.7	4.7	− 0.1	46.0	+ 1.5	93.1	+ 3.0	99.9
− 1.6	5.7	0.0	50.0	+ 1.6	94.3	+ 3.1	100.0
− 1.5	6.9	+ 0.1	54.0				

SECTION B

This table shows the cumulative proportion of area under a normal curve from the left tail to the point indicated by the number of standard deviations above the mean. For example, at 0.0 standard deviations above the mean, the area is .500000; at 1.64 standard deviations above the mean, the area is .94950. To determine areas under the curve below the mean, use the complement of the tabular value. For example, the area under the curve to the left of the mean −1.64 standard deviations is 1.0 − .94950 = .05050.

	.00	.01	.02	.03	.04	.05	.06	.07	.08	.09
0.0	.50000	.50399	.50798	.51197	.51195	.51994	.52392	.52790	.53188	.53586
0.1	.53983	.54380	.54776	.55172	.55567	.55962	.56356	.56749	.57142	.57535
0.2	.57926	.58317	.58706	.59095	.59483	.59871	.60257	.60642	.61026	.61409
0.3	.61791	.62172	.62552	.62930	.63307	.63683	.64058	.64431	.64803	.65173
0.4	.65542	.65910	.66276	.66640	.67003	.67364	.67724	.68082	.68439	.68793
0.5	.69146	.69497	.69847	.70194	.70540	.70884	.71226	.71566	.71904	.72240
0.6	.72575	.72907	.73237	.73536	.73891	.74215	.74537	.74857	.75175	.75490
0.7	.75804	.76115	.76424	.76730	.77035	.77337	.77637	.77935	.78230	.78524
0.8	.78814	.79103	.79389	.79673	.79955	.80234	.80511	.80785	.81057	.81327
0.9	.81594	.81859	.82121	.82381	.82639	.82894	.83147	.83398	.83646	.83891
1.0	.84134	.84375	.84614	.84849	.85083	.85314	.85543	.85769	.85993	.86214
1.1	.86433	.86650	.86864	.87076	.87286	.87493	.87698	.87900	.88100	.88298
1.2	.88493	.88686	.88877	.89065	.89251	.89435	.89617	.89796	.89973	.90147
1.3	.90320	.90490	.90658	.90824	.90988	.91149	.91309	.91466	.91621	.91774
1.4	.91924	.92073	.92220	.92364	.92507	.92647	.92785	.92922	.93056	.93189
1.5	.93319	.93448	.93574	.93699	.93822	.93943	.94062	.94179	.94295	.94408
1.6	.94520	.94630	.94738	.94845	.94950	.95053	.95154	.95254	.95352	.95449
1.7	.95543	.95637	.95728	.95818	.95907	.95994	.96080	.96164	.96246	.96327
1.8	.96407	.96485	.96562	.96638	.96712	.96784	.96856	.96926	.96995	.97062
1.9	.97128	.97193	.97257	.97320	.97381	.97441	.97500	.97558	.97615	.97670
2.0	.97725	.97784	.97831	.97882	.97932	.97982	.98030	.98077	.98124	.98169
2.1	.98214	.98257	.98300	.98341	.98382	.98422	.98461	.98500	.98537	.98574
2.2	.98610	.98645	.98679	.98713	.98745	.98778	.98809	.98840	.98870	.98899
2.3	.98928	.98956	.98983	.99010	.99036	.99061	.99086	.99111	.99134	.99158
2.4	.99180	.99202	.99224	.99245	.99266	.99286	.99305	.99324	.99343	.99361
2.5	.99379	.99396	.99413	.99430	.99446	.99461	.99477	.99492	.99506	.99520
2.6	.99534	.99547	.99560	.99573	.99585	.99598	.99609	.99621	.99632	.99643
2.7	.99653	.99664	.99674	.99683	.99693	.99702	.99711	.99720	.99728	.99736
2.8	.99744	.99752	.99760	.99767	.99774	.99781	.99788	.99795	.99801	.99807
2.9	.99813	.99819	.99825	.99831	.99836	.99841	.99846	.99851	.99856	.99861
3.0	.99865	.99869	.99874	.99878	.99882	.99886	.99899	.99893	.99896	.99900
3.1	.99903	.99906	.99910	.99913	.99916	.99918	.99921	.99924	.99926	.99929
3.2	.99931	.99934	.99936	.99938	.99940	.99942	.99944	.99946	.99948	.99950
3.3	.99952	.99953	.99955	.99957	.99958	.99960	.99961	.99962	.99964	.99965
3.4	.99966	.99968	.99969	.99970	.99971	.99972	.99973	.99974	.99975	.99976
3.5	.99977	.99978	.99978	.99979	.99980	.99981	.99981	.99982	.99983	.99983
3.6	.99984	.99985	.99985	.99986	.99986	.99987	.99987	.99988	.99988	.99989
3.7	.99989	.99990	.99990	.99990	.99991	.99991	.99992	.99992	.99992	.99992
3.8	.99993	.99993	.99993	.99994	.99994	.99994	.99994	.99995	.99995	.99995
3.9	.99995	.99995	.99996	.99996	.99996	.99996	.99996	.99996	.99997	.99997

Appendix D

A Further Discussion of Waiting-line Models

BASIC ASSUMPTIONS

As discussed in Chapter 17, queuing (or waiting-line) models are based on rather complex mathematical and probability assumptions about how and when customers arrive to be served at a service facility; how they wait in line; who is next to be served; the population size of the customers; how long the waiting-line can get before the customers will not join the line; and several other assumptions which relate to who serves and how long it takes. If these assumptions can be reasonably met, then there are a number of queuing formulas which can be used to estimate several characteristics about the situation under study—such as the average waiting time of customers; the average length of the line; the average idle time of servers; and so on.

A common assumption of many queuing models is that the probability that some number of customers $P(x)$ will arrive during some period T is defined by the Poisson probability distribution whose equation is:

$$P(x) = \frac{e^{-\lambda T}(\lambda T)^x}{x!}$$

where λ (the Greek letter lambda) is the average arrival rate per time period T; and e is the base of natural logarithms and is approximately equal to 2.718.

Although it is not necessary to use this formula to solve simple queuing problems, the calculation of a few values of $P(x)$, given values of T and λ, will describe the general shape of the Poisson probability distribution: If customers (people, machines, airplanes, and so on) arrive on the average of four per hour ($\lambda = 4$), and we are interested in the probability of zero through ten customers arriving in a one-hour time period T ($T = 1$), the calculations would be:

P (zero customers arriving)

$$= \frac{(2.718^{-4(1)}) \times (4 \times 1)^0}{0!} = .018$$

$$P(1) = \frac{(2.718^{-4(1)}) \times (4 \times 1)^1}{1!} = .073$$

$$P(2) = \frac{(2.718^{-4(1)}) \times (4 \times 1)^2}{2!} = .147$$

and so on, as shown in Chapter 18 under "Gasoline Station Example."

Plotting these probabilities in Figure D–1 shows the general shape of the Poisson distribution, which has been found to be a common pattern in many real life arrivals of customers. Since the area under the curve has a total proba-

FIGURE D–1
Poisson Probability Distribution

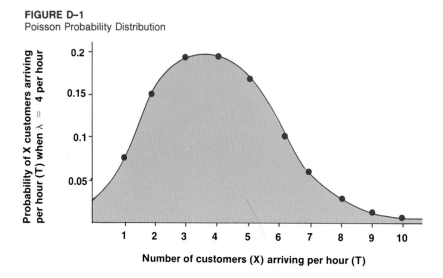

Number of customers (X) arriving per hour (T)

bility of 1.0, the total area under the curve from zero to five, for example, is the probability of five or fewer arriving per hour, on the average—which can be obtained by summing the probabilities for 0, 1, 2, 3, 4, or 5 arriving, which is 0.784.

Likewise, the probability that a server can serve x number of customers in time period T is also assumed to be explained by the Poisson probability distribution.[1] μ simply replaces λ in the Poisson formula.

In summary, the assumptions of the simplest model (Model 1) are:

Single server.

Only a single line may form.

First come, first served (the priority rule for deciding who is served next is called "queue discipline").

Large number of customers (called an "infinite calling population").

The line can get very long ("unlimited line length").

Arrival and service patterns are explained by the Poisson probability distribution, given λ and μ and time period T.

μ must be greater than λ. $(\mu > \lambda)$

Using these assumptions, the equations shown in Figure D–2 can be mathematically derived.

AUTOMOBILE REPAIR SHOP CALCULATIONS (MODEL 1)

As review, mechanics cost $15.00 per hour, the extra server (the stock chaser) costs $4.50 per hour, $\lambda = 4$, and $\mu = 10$, with the existing single server. It is estimated that μ would increase to 12 with the addition of the stock chaser. Under the existing situation, the relevant costs are simply the expected idle costs of the mechanics, which on a daily (8-hour) basis are:

4 per hour × 8 hours × W × $15

Where:

$$W = \frac{1}{\mu - \lambda} = \frac{1}{10 - 4} = .167$$

---

[1] Service *times* are assumed to be explained by the negative exponential distribution, which is the mathematical equivalent of service *rates* (average customers served per time period) being explained by the Poisson distribution. Since the queuing equations presented here require only λ and μ, this relationship will not be explored here.

FIGURE D–2
Formulas for Basic Queuing Models

Model	Solution* Sequence	L Average Number Waiting and Being Served	Lq Average Number Waiting in Line	W Average Time Each Customer Spends Waiting and Being Served	Wq Average Time Each Customer Spends Waiting in Line	Special Equations
1	Any	$\dfrac{\lambda}{\mu-\lambda}$	$\dfrac{\lambda^2}{\mu(\mu-\lambda)}$	$\dfrac{1}{\mu-\lambda}$	$\dfrac{\lambda}{\mu(\mu-\lambda)}$	$\rho=\dfrac{\lambda}{\mu}$
2	ρ,L,Lq W,Wq,Pa	$\dfrac{\rho}{1-\rho}-\dfrac{(N+1)\rho^{N+1}}{1-\rho^{N+1}}$	$L-1+\dfrac{1-\rho}{1-\rho^{N+1}}$	$\dfrac{1}{\mu(1-\rho)}-\dfrac{N\rho^N}{\mu(1-\rho^n)}$	$W-\dfrac{1}{\mu}$	$Pa=1-\left(\dfrac{1-\rho}{1-\rho^{N+1}}\right)\rho^N$
3	$\rho,S,Lq,$ L,W,Wq	$Lq+\rho$	$\dfrac{(\lambda^2 S^2)+\rho^2}{2(1-\rho)}$	$\dfrac{L}{\lambda}$	$\dfrac{Lq}{\lambda}$	$S=\sqrt{\dfrac{\sum\limits_{i=1}^{n}(\bar{x}-x_i)^2}{n-1}}$
4	ρ,Po,Lq L,W,Wq	$Lq+\rho$	$Po\cdot\rho^N\cdot\dfrac{\frac{\rho}{N}}{N!\left(1-\frac{\rho}{N}\right)^2}$	$\dfrac{L}{\lambda}$	$\dfrac{Lq}{\lambda}$	$Po=\left[\sum\limits_{n=0}^{N-1}\left(\dfrac{\rho^n}{n!}\right)+\left(\dfrac{\rho^N}{N!\cdot 1-\frac{\rho}{N}}\right)\right]^{-1}$
5	ρ,Po,Lq L,Wq,W	$Lq+1-Po$	$N-\dfrac{\mu+\lambda}{\lambda}\cdot(1-Po)$	$Wq+\dfrac{1}{\mu}$	$\dfrac{1}{\mu}\left[\dfrac{N}{1-Po}-\left(\dfrac{\mu+\lambda}{\lambda}\right)\right]$	$Po=\left[\sum\limits_{n=0}^{N}\dfrac{N!}{(N-n)!}\cdot\rho^n\right]^{-1}$

* Some formulas require a solution from another formula. This sequence lists the order in which these formulas should be solved.

Definition of variables:
λ = the arrival rate per unit of time.
μ = the service rate per unit of time.
ρ = the utilization proportion of the service facility.
Pa = the proportion of potential customers which will enter the system (Model 2).
Po = the probability of zero arrivals during a given time period.
N = the maximum length of the waiting line, including the one being served (Model 2); For Model 4, N is the number of channels or servers; For Model 5, N is the size of the finite calling population.
S = formula for the standard deviation of a sample.

Thus:

$$4 \times 8 \times .167 \times \$15 = \$80.16$$

If the stock chaser is added, W is:

$$W = \frac{1}{12 - 4} = .125 \text{ hours}$$

and idle mechanics' cost is reduced to:

$4 \times 8 \times .125 \times \$15$

$$= \$60, \text{ or a savings of } \$20.16$$

Since the stock chaser costs an extra $36.00 per day, and only $20.16 is expected to be saved, the stock chaser should not be hired. But, should the stock chaser be hired if a new labor contract won the mechanics a raise to $18 per hour, and because of increased business, the average arrival rate increased to 5 per hour? Average daily idle costs would now be:

$$W = \frac{1}{10 - 5} = .2 \text{ hours}$$

sible. Model 2 has all of the assumptions of Model 1 except that the waiting-line (including the customer being served) is assumed only to be able to grow to a length of N customers. This is also called a "truncated," or "finite waiting-line," model. The formulas for this model are in Figure D–2.

As review, the bank drive-in window can service customers at a rate of 1 every 4 minutes, on the average, or 15 per hour ($\mu = 15$). Customers arrive at an average rate of 12 per hour ($\lambda = 12$). There is only room for 3 cars, plus the car being served ($N = 4$). The bank feels it costs $1.00 each time a customer leaves and parks elsewhere because there is no space to wait. Assuming a 30-hour week, 52 weeks per year, what would be the annual value to the bank of *expanding* the waiting space by 1, 2, 3, 4, and 12 cars? The computations, which we calculated with a computer (all of which are not used in our analysis) are:

Total Number of Waiting and Serving Spaces for Cars (N)

	4	5	6	7	8	16
L	1.563	1.868	2.142	2.387	2.605	3.608
Lq	0.861	1.139	1.396	1.628	1.836	2.813
W	0.148	0.171	0.191	0.209	0.226	0.302
Wq	0.082	0.104	0.125	0.143	0.159	0.236
P_a*	0.878	0.911	0.933	0.949	0.956	0.994
Value	—	$507	$920	$1,222	$1,444	$2,161
Cost	—	$600	$900	$1,100	$1,300	$2,900

* P_a is the proportion of potential customers which will enter the line, because it is not full; $1 - P_a$ is the proportion which will "balk" and not enter the line.

and

$$5 \times 8 \times .2 \times \$18 = \$144$$

By adding the stock chaser, W falls to $\frac{1}{12 - 5} =$ .143 hours, which reduces idle mechanics' cost to $102.96, a saving of $41.06.

BANK DRIVE-UP WINDOW CALCULATIONS (MODEL 2)

As we change the assumptions of Model 1, the calculations become more difficult but not impos-

Since 18,720 customers are expected to arrive annually (30 hours per week × 52 weeks × 12 per hour), we can calculate the value of the expansion alternatives as:

Value = Current

$$\text{cost} - [(1 - P_a) \times 18,720 \times \$1]$$

For the existing situation (space for four cars),

Current cost $= (1 - .878) \times 18,720 \times \$1$
$$= \$2,174$$

Thus, for example, the value of adding one more space ($N = 5$) is:

Value = $2,174 − [(1 − .911) × 18,720 × $1]
 = $507

This amount is the break-even or maximum amount that the bank should pay to add one extra space to achieve a one-year payback. Similarly, the other values, would be the maximum amount they would pay for adding that number of extra spaces to achieve a one-year payback.

A plot of "value" and this cost structure is shown in Figure 17–1 in Chapter 17. It appears that a total of from six to nine spaces would be beneficial, with a total of seven or eight spaces (four or five additional ones) probably being the best trade-off between value and cost, and meeting management's payback period requirement.

FIRE EQUIPMENT DISPATCHING CALCULATIONS (MODEL 3)

Model 3 is similar to Model 1, except the service rate, μ, does not assume a Poisson probability distribution pattern. In fact, it can have any pattern as long as S, the *standard deviation*, of the service *time* can be specified. If the service *time* is constant (no variability) which is the case for many machines which have a fixed cycle, then $S = 0$.

A fire department dispatches its fire engines to fires from alarm headquarters, which is staffed around the clock by a single dispatcher. Assume all of the conditions of Model 1 hold, except that a study has been made of how long it takes the dispatcher to handle each call for service. "Service" here consists of answering the call for service (which only comes from telephones), obtaining the address of the fire, determining which fire trucks to send, and notifying the selected equipment that they should respond to the fire. The arrival rate of "calls for service" is approximated by the Poisson distribution with $\lambda = 10$ per hour, and, from the time study mentioned above, the following service times were observed from a random sample:

Observation*	Service Time in Minutes (X_i)
1	1
2	2
3	1.5
4	3
5	2.5
6	1.5
7	2
8	2.5
9	3
10	1
Total	20.0

* The sample should probably be larger than 10; this small sample size is used to simplify explanation.

The standard deviation of these observations is given by the equation:

$$S = \sqrt{\frac{\sum\limits_{i=1}^{n} (\overline{X} - X_i)^2}{n - 1}}$$

where $n =$ the number of observations in the sample.

First, $\overline{X}$, the average service time, is $\frac{20.0}{10} = 2$, which translates into a service rate (μ) of $\frac{60 \text{ minutes}}{2 \text{ minutes}} = 30$ per hour. The standard deviation, S, is:

$$S = \sqrt{\frac{(2-1)^2 + (2-2)^2 + (2-1.5)^2 + (2-3)^2 \cdots + (2-1)^2}{10 - 1}}$$

$$= \sqrt{.555} = .75 \text{ minutes or } \frac{.75}{60} = .0125 \text{ hours.}$$

In summary:

$$\lambda = 10 \text{ per hour}$$

$$\mu = 30 \text{ per hour}$$

$$s = .0125 \text{ of an hour}$$

Utilizing the equations from Figure D–2:

$$L = .428$$

$$Lq = .095$$

$$W = .043, \text{ or } 2.58 \text{ minutes}$$

$$Wq = .010, \text{ or } .6 \text{ minutes or } 36 \text{ seconds}$$

If $\lambda = 20$:

$$L = 1.427$$

$$Lq = .760$$

$$W = .071, \text{ or } 4.26 \text{ minutes}$$

$$Wq = .038, \text{ or } 2.28 \text{ minutes}$$

FARQUHAR COMPANY CALCULATIONS (MODEL 4)

This model handles the multiple channel, single phase case (see Figure 17–2 in Chapter 17) where all assumptions of Model 1 apply, except that the customer at the head of the single line is served entirely by the server which is next available. The number of servers, N, must be specified, and μ is the rate for each server, which must be equal for all servers (channels). Common examples of this system exist at many post offices and banks. Customers wait in a single line and are served by the first available postal clerk or bank teller.

Farquhar currently has two office copiers, each located in two separate office areas. For each machine, the average service rate, μ, is 15 copying jobs per hour. (A job may be anywhere from one to several hundred copies.) Clerks arrive at each machine with material to be copied at the rate of eight per hour ($\lambda = 8$). Complaints have been made that one machine may be "swamped" while the other one is idle. One suggestion has been to move the two machines to a central area, where the clerks would wait in a single line for the first available machine. However, this would incur additional nonproductive costs for "walking time" of $.225 per order or $3.60 per hour ($.15 \times 2$ machines $\times 8$ orders/hr.) for the entire company. If clerk time is valued at $6.00 per hour, should the machines be consolidated as proposed?

First, for the machines "as is," where:

$$\lambda = 8$$

$$\mu = 15$$

$$N = 1$$

We can use Model 1 equations, since this is really two independent single channel, single phase systems:

$$L = 1.143$$

$$Lq = .610$$

$$W = .143 \text{ hours}$$

$$Wq = .076 \text{ hours}$$

The *hourly* cost of the system "as is," assuming clerks are not idle when they are actually using the machine, is 2 machines $\times$ 8 arrivals $\times .076$ idle hours $\times$ $6 per hour = $7.29.

Putting the machines together, the parameters for Model 4 calculated from the equations in Figure D–2.

$$\lambda = 16/\text{hour (both groups will now arrive at the central location)}$$

$$\mu = 15 \text{ (rate for each machine)}$$

$$N = 2 \text{ (2 servers or channels)}$$

And:

$$L = 1.491$$

$$Lq = .424$$

$$W = .093$$

$$Wq = .027$$

Hourly cost of the consolidation is:

(16 arrivals $\times .027$ idle hours $\times$ $6 per hour)
$$+ \$3.60 \text{ walking cost} = \$6.20$$

The annualized savings, through the consolidation would be:

40 hours/week $\times$ 52 weeks
$$\times (\$7.29 - \$6.20) = \$2,267.$$

MACHINE GROUP SERVICING CALCULATIONS (MODEL 5)

Model 5 is similar to Model 1's assumptions, except that the population of customers is not "infinite," or very large, but "finite," or limited. The dividing line between infinite and finite depends on the values of λ and μ, but as the size of the finite customer population gets larger and larger, the values of L, Lq, and so on produced from Model 5 will eventually be the same as those calculated from Model 1. For this model, we must specify N, the size of the finite customer population.

For our machine servicing example, λ, the arrival rate is for each customer in the finite calling population of five machines. So $N = 5$ and λ is ¼, or .25. This says, on the average, .25 machines arrive each hour, since a "whole" machine arrives, on the average, every 4 hours. The service rate, μ, is every .5 hours, or $1/.5 = 2$ per hour. We must do this arithmetic to put λ and μ into the same time unit—in this case, rates per hour. The values for this situation, which were also produced from the equations in Figure D–2, are:

$L = .832$ (the number of machines, on the average, which are in need of service or are being serviced)

$Lq = .311$ (the number of machines, on the average, which are in need of service)

$W = .799$ (the average time, about 48 minutes, that each machine spends waiting and being serviced)

$Wq = .299$ (the average time, about 18 minutes, that each machine waits to be serviced once it is ready to be served)

The relationship between Wq and W is quite logical. In the above example, $W - Wq = .5$, which is the average service time of a half hour. On the other hand, why is the difference between L and Lq not equal to 1, the machine being served? The answer is that since the probability that there are *no* machines waiting to be served or being served is always greater than zero, then there can be times when the mechanic is caught up or idle. Thus, on the average, the difference between L and Lq will always be a fraction less than 1.

Appendix E

Random Numbers for Monte Carlo Problems*

---

* Described in Chapter 17.

217	590	735	965	276	027	658	289	260	572
686	359	273	366	451	539	308	080	747	416
584	895	372	370	694	623	364	449	416	877
379	668	206	918	238	485	587	543	322	654
933	051	047	945	927	272	310	017	002	807
755	482	252	018	695	273	123	943	518	037
806	672	856	030	043	852	957	768	006	207
242	601	105	033	672	850	951	621	414	904
593	877	679	098	970	840	391	543	174	703
638	780	709	407	697	973	687	859	476	611
39	302	411	195	374	198	057	531	721	508
322	160	509	543	422	523	351	152	617	169
507	794	941	115	728	071	748	679	252	396
447	300	889	181	370	532	608	883	520	539
547	539	210	354	861	025	229	731	141	786
322	810	756	491	869	285	371	709	431	629
536	990	532	133	215	626	463	616	172	135
439	027	759	297	544	890	049	784	156	641
238	273	941	056	196	283	184	154	714	282
709	739	310	685	146	114	027	141	774	229
692	912	670	340	319	116	843	317	396	990
270	999	075	843	918	453	942	797	606	082
054	579	869	187	940	406	743	855	108	135
834	482	068	368	619	539	991	799	920	400
287	594	981	898	433	496	837	673	576	516
943	344	947	996	457	875	060	475	161	741
696	094	870	050	758	332	843	475	933	153
407	272	332	502	258	963	896	467	287	506
120	799	798	761	876	032	477	832	223	404
994	899	118	417	093	298	356	455	145	854

Appendix F

Additional Topics in Linear Programming

In Chapter 18 on linear programming, the text presentation was carried up to the point where an optimal solution to the problem of how many two-door cars and station wagons to schedule was graphically determined. In this appendix, we will demonstrate the use of the simplex method for solving this same problem and discuss some additional topics.

THE SIMPLEX METHOD

In our automobile production example, where we maximized the monetary contribution, we had six unknowns, or variables. Two unknowns were the quantities of the two products: two-door cars and station wagons. These are called "decision variables," because their amounts are the major things we want to determine.

The other four unknowns, called "slack variables," were the capacities of the four departments (stamping, engine, two-door assembly, and station-wagon assembly). Our procedure in the graphic solution was first to solve for the best mix between the two products by determining the number of each kind of car which could be made out of available resources as defined by each corner of the feasible region. So it was possible for us to solve the two equations that formed each corner simultaneously and arrive

at the number of each kind of car to produce. And this, in turn, allowed us to calculate the total contribution at each corner and so find the one which maximized contributions.

In algebra thare is a rule which requires that the number of equations must at least be equal to the number of unknowns in order to obtain a simultaneous solution for the unknowns, if indeed, a solution exists. Yet in our automobile example, even though we had six unknowns and only four constraint equations, we were able to solve this problem by choosing which *two* equations to solve at each corner to find solution values for the *two* unknown automobile quantities. Then, after we had found the optimal solution, we determined each department's slack capacity. Essentially, at each step we were ignoring the other two constraint equations and solving for them later in order to obtain the solution values.

The simplex method solves for all unknowns by choosing at the start of the procedure which two out of the six variables *will* be set at zero, which four variables it will solve for, and which four *may* be zero or a positive number. In this way, we have four equations and only four variables or unknowns (the algebraic requirement mentioned earlier), because two of the variables are, for the moment, set at zero. This allows us to obtain solution values for the other four.

The simplex procedure usually requires the successive solution of a number of different combinations of four of the six variables (the two originally set at zero may come back into consideration, one at a time) in order to find the optimal solution. At each step, the method chooses

Adding slack variables to the other three constraints in a similar fashion gives us:[1]

Maximize:

$$F = \$300\ T + \$400\ W$$

Subject to:

Engine department	$T +$	$1.5\ W + E$		$= 9,000$
Stamping department	$T +$	$.5833\ W$	$+ S$	$= 7,000$
Two-door assembly	T		$+ A_T$	$= 6,000$
Wagon assembly		W	$+ A_W$	$= 4,000$

which four out of the six variables it will solve for and which two are set at zero. Essentially, the simplex method searches through combinations of solutions in a step-by-step fashion until the best solution is found.

Redefining Constraints as Equations

It will be recalled that the four constraints were not really equations, except as defined by the limit lines in the graphic solution. Rather, they were "less than or equal to" constraints, since extra or slack capacity was allowed to occur in one or more departments.

We return now to our original example where one six-cylinder engine was equal to 1.5 four-cylinder engines. For engines, our constraint expression was $T + 1.5W \leq 9,000$. To change this "inequality" constant into an equation, we have to add a "slack variable" to it. The equation for the engine department then becomes:

$$T + 1.5\ W + E = 9,000$$

In this equation, E is the amount of slack capacity (in terms of Ts) that exists in the engine department for any solution. If, for example, $T = 1,000$ and $W = 2,000$, then:

$$1,000 + 1.5(2,000) + E = 9,000$$
$$E = 5,000$$

"F" is the function to be maximized—in this case, the contribution toward profit. E, S, A_T and A_W are the slack variables for each department.

Initial Simplex Tableau

The next step in the simplex method is to set up an initial simplex tableau or matrix. This is shown in Figure F–1, which is a computer printout of the initial tableau, or "iteration" 0. In Figure F–1, the computer redefines the factors in our problem into its generalized program language as follows:

1. The variables (T, W, E, S, A_T and A_W) are now called $X(1)$, $X(2)$, $X(3)$, $X(4)$, $X(5)$, and $X(6)$, respectively, where the numbers in the parenthesis are subscripts (e.g., $X(1)$ is the first variable, $X(2)$ is the second, and so on).
2. Only the *coefficients* associated with each variable are shown under the appropriate X column heading. The zeros in a column simply mean the X variable has a zero value for that constraint equation.
3. The contributions ($\$300$ and $\$400$) are called $C(J)$s, where J is the column number subscript. The zeros over $X(3)$ to $X(6)$ means

---

[1] One other constraint is implied in all linear programming problems: All variables must be greater than or equal to zero.

FIGURE F–1

```
                PROBLEM PARAMETERS
NUMBER OF EQUATIONS    4
NUMBER OF VARIABLES    2
NUMBER OF LESS THAN EQUATIONS    4
NUMBER OF EQUAL TO EQUATIONS     0
NUMBER OF GREATER THAN EQUATIONS    0

            OPTIONS SPECIFIED
SLACK AND ARTIFICIAL VARIABLES WILL BE GENERATED
ALL TABLEAUS WILL BE PRINTED

        PROBLEM WAS INPUT AS FOLLOWS

MAXIMIZE F =    300.0000X( 1) +    400.0000X( 2)
SUBJECT TO        1.0000X( 1) +      1.5000X( 2)     ≤     9000.0000
                  1.0000X( 1) +       .5833X( 2)     ≤     7000.0000.
                  1.0000X( 1) +       .0000X( 2)     ≤     6000.0000
                   .0000X( 1) +      1.0000X( 2)     ≤     4000.0000
```

```
                                            Will Enter Basis                Identity Matrix ▩

PROBLEM   1            ITERATION   0

OBJECTIVE FUNCTION    C(J) =      300.0000      400.0000       0.0000        0.0000        0.0000        0.0000
      C(I)  BASIS            B(I)        X( 1)         X( 2)         X( 3)         X( 4)         X( 5)         X( 6)

   0.0000  X( 3)       9000.0000      1.0000        1.5000        1.0000        0.0000        0.0000        0.0000
   0.0000  X( 4)       7000.0000      1.0000         .5833        0.0000        1.0000        0.0000        0.0000
   0.0000  X( 5)       6000.0000      1.0000         .0000        0.0000        0.0000        1.0000        0.0000
   0.0000  X( 6)       4000.0000       .0000        1.0000        0.0000        0.0000        0.0000        1.0000

Z(J) =                                  0.0000        0.0000        0.0000        0.0000        0.0000        0.0000
SIMPLEX CRITERIA   C(J)-Z(J) =        300.0000      400.0000       0.0000        0.0000        0.0000        0.0000
          OBJECTIVE FUNCTION VALUE      0.0000

Will Leave Basis
```

Source: George A. Johnson.

there is no contribution (or cost) associated with these slack variables.

4. The constant numbers to the right of the equal signs in our equations are under the heading called *B(I)* on the left, where *I* is the constraint row number subscript.

Initial Feasible Solution

The simplex method is a step-by-step procedure which moves progressively from a poor solution to a better and then to a still better solution until the best one is found. But the method requires that it start with a "feasible" solution. And, since at the start it is not known what is feasible, the method always starts from zero. In our case, our starting solution will be to make no two-doors and no station wagons. (We are essentially at the origin, point G, in Figure 18–5.) This program will require no capacity in any department and will produce no contribution. But this *is* a feasible solution, and the simplex method can use it as a starting point in its step-by-step development of the optimal solution.

In order to use this zero program as its start-

ing point, the simplex method requires being told which variables are to be set to zero and which can be more than zero. Since no capacity is required at this point, the slack capacity is available and has a magnitude. The slack variables will therefore not be zero but something greater than zero. Thus, in our initial program, the number of cars and station wagons, the two decision variables, are the two variables which are set at zero. This allows the four slack variables to be more than zero.

Figure F–1 is a computer report of the initial iteration based on this initial feasible solution. Toward the left, the column "BASIS" shows that the initial solution includes the four slack variables, which are now referred to as $X(3)$, $X(4)$, $X(5)$, and $X(6)$. This means, and it is shown by their absence from the BASIS column, that $X(1)$ and $X(2)$ are set at zero.

To the right of the BASIS column is the *B(I)* column with the values for each of the slack variables. Our starting feasible solution is:

$$X(1) = 0$$
$$X(2) = 0$$

$$X(3) = 9{,}000$$
$$X(4) = 7{,}000$$
$$X(5) = 6{,}000$$
$$X(6) = 4{,}000$$

To the left of the BASIS column in Figure F–1 is the $C(I)$ column, which is the per unit contribution of the variables in the BASIS. Since there is no contribution from having slack capacity, these $C(I)$ values are all zero. (In more complex problems, slacks may have costs, which can be factored into the problem by including them as negative values in the $C(J)$ row.)

The total contribution of our initial program will, of course, be zero and is shown to be zero in Figure F–1 by the line at the bottom which says, "Objective function value 0.000." This number is the sum of the per unit contributions in the $C(I)$ column multiplied by the quantities in the $B(I)$ column. We need to know what the process is, because this total will not be zero in later iterations.

$$C(I) \quad B(I)$$
$$0 \times 9{,}000 = 0$$
$$0 \times 7{,}000 = 0$$
$$0 \times 6{,}000 = 0$$
$$0 \times 4{,}000 = \underline{0}$$
$$\text{Objective function value} = 0$$

Improving upon the Starting Solution

The simplex method continues its step-by-step improvements to the starting solution by removing one variable at a time from the BASIS column and replacing it with a new one. Then it resolves the four equations simultaneously and computes the new objective function total. This is all done in a new iteration. In large problems, there may be hundreds or thousands of iterations. In our problem, iteration 1, as well as iterations 2 and 3, is shown in Figure F–2.

This process is repeated one or more additional times until there is no further improvement in the objective function total. At that point, the solution is complete. The variables listed in the BASIS column are the ones which will be used; in our case, they will tell us the quantity of each kind of automobiles to schedule for production. The quantities in the $C(I)$ column will be the per unit contributions of the variables in the BASIS. The quantities in the $B(I)$ column will be the quantities of automobiles to schedule for production.

If $X(3)$, $X(4)$, $X(5)$, or $X(6)$ appear in the BASIS column, this tells us that there is slack capacity in these departments, and the quantity in the $B(I)$ column tells us how much unallocated capacity there is.

The decision as to which variable to remove from the BASIS and which one to bring into the BASIS is determined by a specific set of rules which guarantee, under most conditions, to lead to the optimal solution.

Rule for Choosing the Variable to Enter the BASIS

The rule for choosing which variable to put into the BASIS is to look at the next to last line of Figure F–1 (which is iteration 0)—the line denoted SIMPLEX CRITERIA $C(J) - Z(J)$ and select the largest positive number. (If all numbers in this row are zero or negative, we have arrived at the optimal solution. The BASIS and $B(I)$ columns become the best program to follow.)

In our example, the largest positive number is 400 and is in the $X(2)$ column. This tells us that we are losing more money per unit by not making $X(2)$ items than any other item, so we should put $X(2)$ into the BASIS, and allow it to take on a value greater than zero.

Before going on, however, we should explain how the 400 is computed. In later iterations, the numbers in the SIMPLEX CRITERIA line will not be nice, round and easily understood numbers.

The $Z(J)$ column totals are sums of the products of the numbers in the $C(I)$ column and the corresponding number in the columns for each

FIGURE F–2

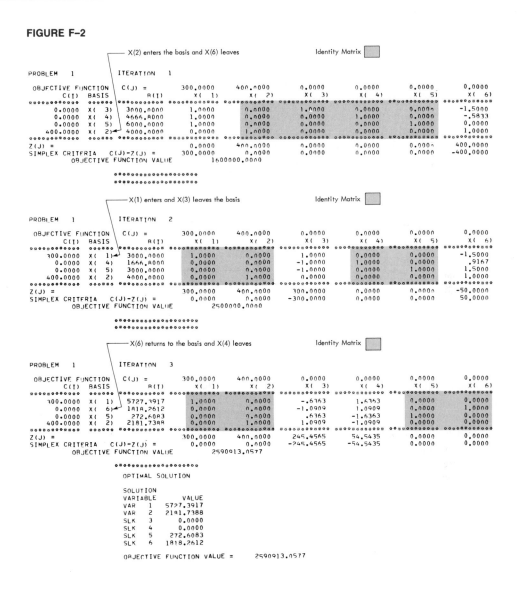

variable. Thus, the $X(I)$ column figure of 0.0000 in the $Z(J)$ row was obtained as follows:

$$C(I) \quad X(1)$$
$$0 \times 1 = 0$$
$$0 \times 1 = 0$$
$$0 \times 1 = 0$$
$$0 \times 0 = \underline{0}$$
$$\text{Total } Z(1) \quad 0$$

Obviously, all other $Z(J)$ totals are also zero in our initial feasible solution.

Now we go to the OBJECTIVE FUNCTION row at the top of iteration 0, and column by column, we subtract the $Z(J)$ figure from the objective function value. The result is the Simplex Criterion value we need. For $X(I)$ calculation is 300 − 0 = 300; for $X(2)$ it is 400 − 0 = 400; for $X(3)$, 0 − 0 = 0, and so on.

Rule for Choosing the Variable to Remove from the BASIS

If $X(2)$, station wagons, is to be put into the BASIS in iteration 1, something already there will have to be removed to keep our system balanced with four unknowns and four equations. The procedure for determining which variable currently in the BASIS must leave is to determine how large $X(2)$ can get before a capacity constraint is met. (Essentially we are moving to the right along the horizontal [wagon] axis in Figure 18–5.)

The question is, which department's capacity do we reach first? It is the wagon assembly's capacity of 4,000 that stops us. This says, at this point in the analysis, that we can make 4,000 wagons, but that in doing so the slack in wagon assembly is used up and will become equal to zero. Since wagon assembly slack is variable $X(6)$, $X(6)$ will leave the BASIS (and will be set at zero by its absence from the BASIS in iteration (1)). $X(2)$ will enter the BASIS and will have a $B(I)$ value of 4,000 units.

The rule, then, to follow for determining which of the current BASIS variables is to leave the BASIS and be set at zero is: Divide each entering variable column coefficient that is *positive and greater than zero* into its corresponding row $B(I)$ value. Of the resulting quotients, the leaving variable is the one which has the *smallest positive quotient*. For our example this calculation is:

BASIS	B(I)	X(2)	Resulting Quotient	
$X(3)$	9,000 $\div$ 1.5	=	6,000	
$X(4)$	7,000 $\div$ .5833	=	12,000	
$X(5)$	6,000 $\div$ 0	=	Ignore	
$X(6)$	4,000 $\div$ 1	=	4,000	←Smallest

The 4,000 for $X(6)$ is the smallest positive quotient, so $X(6)$ will leave the BASIS and be replaced by $X(2)$. The necessary calculations were carried through by the computer, and the results are shown in iteration 1. $X(2)$ is now in the BASIS, and column $C(I)$ shows 400 ($400)

for $X(2)$. The objective function, calculated as described earlier, is now $1,600,000, as is shown in iteration 1 in Figure F–2, a great improvement over iteration 0's total of $0. (Note that this checks with the solution at point E in Figure 18–6.)

Iteration 1 is different from iteration 0 in several ways. There are secondary effects caused by putting $X(2)$ into and taking $X(6)$ out of the BASIS. In particular, putting $X(2)$ into the BASIS, and in a quantity of 4,000, required using up not only all of $X(6)$'s wagon assembly slack capacity, but it also required using up some of the slack capacity in the engine and in the stamping departments. This reduced the slack of $X(3)$, engine making, and $X(4)$, stamping, to 3,000 and 4666.8, respectively. One could say that $X(2)$'s requirements and part of were "substituted" for iteration 0's assignments of the capacity of $X(6)$, $X(3)$, and $X(4)$ to the production of 4,000 wagons. (Note the independent-dependent demand relationship [as discussed in our coverage of MRP] between $X(1)$ and $X(2)$, the end items, and $X(3-6)$, the dependent demand items and capacity requirements.)

Calculating New Rates of Substitution and B(I)s

The coefficient values in the body of each iteration's tableau are really rates of substitution between all six variables and the four which are in the BASIS of an iteration. For example, in iteration 0, the coefficient of 1.5 at the intersection of column $X(2)$ and row $X(3)$ indicates that we can substitute 1.5 units of $X(3)$ capacity (engine department) for 1 $X(2)$ or for 1 six-cylinder engine. And, where column $X(3)$ and row $X(3)$ intersect, the coefficient of 1 simply means that an $X(3)$ is an $X(3)$.

In iteration 0, there is a unique property to columns $X(3)$, $X(4)$, $X(5)$, and $X(6)$. Each column has a single 1, and all other values in the column are zero, and the 1 appears in a unique row. This portion of our tableau is called the "identity matrix," and it always has this structure of 1s and zeros. It identifies for us, or for the computer, exactly which four of the six variables are currently in the BASIS and which two are equal to zero. The four defined by the intersection of 1s in the identity matrix are the same as the four in the BASIS. These variables are shaded in Figures F–1 and F–2.

In iteration 1, the identity matrix has changed. Now it consists of columns $X(2)$, $X(3)$, $X(4)$, and $X(5)$. $X(2)$ has replaced $X(6)$.

We need, at this point, to consider how the new coefficients and the new $B(l)$s in iteration 1 were calculated. These coefficients are really updated rates of substitution.

First, we know what the new identity matrix looks like in iteration 1, because we know which variables will be in the BASIS—$X(3)$, $X(4)$, $X(5)$, and $X(2)$. Figure F–3 shows the coefficient and $B(l)$ portion of iteration 1:

equal to 1, as required by our revised identity matrix.

The old wagon assembly constraint was:

$$\boxed{X(2)} + X(6) = 4,000$$

Since the coefficient of $X(2)$ is already 1, we do not need to revise it. We simply enter the same coefficients into the $X(2)$ row in iteration 1.

At this point our example does not illustrate the procedure fully. Let us suppose, for the moment, that neither $X(2)$ nor $X(6)$ had coefficients of 1. Suppose that, instead, the constraint was: $4X(2) + 2X(2) = 4,000$. With this constraint, we have to turn to the next procedural rule: Divide through each term in the leaving variable's old equation by the coefficient of the new entering variable. Thus:

FIGURE F–3

BASIS	B(l)	X(1)	X(2)	X(3)	X(4)	X(5)	X(6)
X(3)	?	?	0	1	0	0	?
X(4)	?	?	0	0	1	0	?
X(5)	?	?	0	0	0	1	?
X(2)	?	?	1	0	0	0	?

Identity Matrix

Notice that we have placed a 1 in each column of the identity matrix at the correct intersecting row and zeros for the other rows in each column.

The question marks (?) indicate the new rates of substitution and the new BASIS values, which must be recalculated now that $X(2)$ has replaced $X(6)$ in the BASIS. We do this by the simultaneous solution of two equations, *such that* the identity matrix is the one shown in Figure F–3. First, the new equation which redefines the wagon assembly capacity and the quantity of $X(2)$s in the BASIS is revised so that $X(2)$ is

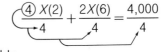

$$\frac{4\,X(2)}{4} + \frac{2X(6)}{4} = \frac{4,000}{4}$$

This yields:

$$X(2) + \tfrac{1}{2}\,X(6) = 1,000$$

These new coefficients of $X(2)$ of 1, (the reason we divided by 4 above was to get this 1), $\tfrac{1}{2}$, and 1,000 would be entered in iteration 1's tableau. Of course, all other variables' coefficients would be zero.

Returning now to our actual problem. We next solve each of the other old equations in turn simultaneously with this new equation, such that the resulting value of the entering variable, $X(2)$, equals zero. Again, this zero requirement is specified by our new identity matrix as shown in Figure F–3.

First, we will solve the new equation simultaneously with the old engine department equation so that $X(2)$ becomes zero:

$$X(2) + X(6) = 4,000 \text{ (new equation)}$$
$$X(1) + 1.5\,X(2) + X(3) = 9,000 \text{ (old equation)}$$

Multiplying the first equation by -1.5 and adding the two equations give us:

$$X(1) + \boxed{0X(2)} + X(3) - 1.5\,X(6) = 3,000$$

$X(2)$s coefficient is now zero. These new coefficients and $B(I)$ values are shown in iteration 1's tableau. The $B(I)$ of 3,000 means that making the 4,000 six-cylinder engines required for the 4,000 station wagons leaves the engine department with enough slack capacity to make 3,000 four-cylinder engines for two-door cars or 2,000 sixes (3,000/1.5).

For the stamping department equation, the simultaneous solution is:

$$X(2) + X(6) = 4,000 \text{ (new equation)}$$
$$X(1) + .5833\,X(2) + X(4) = 7,000 \text{ (old equation)}$$

Multiplying the first equation by $-.5833$ and adding the two equations gives us:[2]

$$X(1) + \boxed{0X(2)} + X(4) - .5833\,X(6) = 4,666$$

As in the case of the engine department, this $B(I)$ of 4,666 tells us that stamping the parts for 4,000 wagons leaves the stamping department with enough slack to stamp enough parts for 4,666 two-door cars or 2,000 six-cylinders ($3,000 \div 1.5$) for wagons.

Finally, the equations for the two-door assembly department are:

$$X(2) + X(6) = 4,000 \text{ (new equation)}$$
$$X(1) + X(5) = 6,000 \text{ (old equation)}$$

Since the two assembly departments are independent, the use of wagon assembly capacity does not affect the two-door assembly department, and its coefficients and $B(I)$ do not change. Thus, these values may be entered directly from iteration 0 to iteration 1's tableau.

The next steps are to recalculate the objective function value and to complete the $Z(J)$ and $C(J) - Z(J)$ rows as before. Notice that in iteration 1's tableau, the objective function is now $\$1,600,000$ ($\$400 \times 4,000$ wagons).

In iteration 1, the largest positive simplex criterion is 300 and is in the $X(1)$ column. This means that $\$300$ contribution will be gained for each $X(1)$ which enters the BASIS (up to some other constraint's limits). In contrast, $X(6)$'s simplex criterion value is -400, meaning that for every unit of $X(6)$ we allow to be put back in the BASIS, there will be a reduction in the objective function value of $\$400$.

Iteration 2

It would seem that no reduction should be made in the quantity scheduled of $X(2)$, wagons, because for every one, up to 4,000 *not* made, a $\$400$ contribution is lost. Yet, if forgoing 1 wagon would allow us to make more than $1\frac{1}{3}$ two-door cars, then we should schedule fewer wagons in favor of two-doors. The simplex method investigates this possibility in iteration 2, which is also shown in Figure F–2.

Since the simplex criterion value for $X(1)$ has the largest positive value (300), it will enter the BASIS in iteration 2. The leaving variable is determined exactly as before and is $X(3)$, the engine department's capacity. This is analogous to moving to point D in Figure 18–5, where we

---

[2] If a $B(I)$ value becomes negative from simultaneous solution, simply multiply each term in the resulting equation by -1 to make the $B(I)$ become positive. This is a requirement in the simplex procedure.

make 4,000 wagons and 3,000 two-doors, utilizing *all* of the capacity of the engine and wagon assembly departments and part of the capacities in the other two departments. These quantities are shown in the $B(I)$ column of iteration 2, as are the revised unused capacities of $X(4)$ and $X(5)$. Iteration 2 also contains the new rate of substitution coefficients and the new identity matrix. These revised $B(I)$ and coefficient values are solved simultaneously as before such that the coefficients in $X(1)$'s column, the variable which replaced $X(3)$, are 1, 0, 0, and 0, as reflected in the revised identity matrix.

Iteration 2 produces an improved objective function value of $2,500,000. But there is now a positive value in the simplex criteria row of $50 for $X(6)$, wagon assembly capacity. This means that for every slack unit of this department's capacity we put back into the BASIS (up to some other department's capacity limit), we will increase the objective function by $50. At this point, we are moving to point C in Figure 18–5, where we make 5,727 two-doors and 2,182 wagons. While the $50 is mechanically calculated following the rules described earlier, an intuitive explanation is in order:

As we move along line segment $D–C$ in Figure 18–5 toward point C, we are *increasing* the number of two-doors and decreasing the number of wagons in the solution. The rate of this substitution as described earlier is 1.5. For each wagon we decrease, we can increase 1.5 two-doors (actually for each six-cylinder decreased, we can produce 1.5 more four-cylinder, which directly affects the quantities of two-doors and wagons). This rate of substitution is shown in iteration 2's tableau at the intersection of column $X(6)$ and row $X(1)$ as −1.5. Here we have a "negative" rate of substitution. This means that for a 1-unit *increase* in $X(6)$ (slack capacity in wagon assembly), we can also *increase* $X(1)$ by 1.5 units. Thus, if we increase the value of $X(6)$ (allow slack capacity to occur) in wagon assembly, this means a reduction in the objective function of $400 for each wagon not produced, but there will be an *increase* of $450 for each

1.5 two-doors that are produced ($300 × 1.5 = $450). These gains and losses net at plus $50 per unit, which is "opportunity cost" of *not* trading some slack wagon assembly capacity to allow more four-cylinder engines to be built, which indirectly allows more two-doors to be stamped and assembled.

Iteration 3

Iteration 3, also shown in Figure F–2, shows the optimal solution for our problem. This is indicated by there being no positive numbers in the simplex criteria row. $X(6)$ returns to the basis and $X(4)$, which is stamping department capacity, leaves, because its capacity is used up. We are at point C on Figure 18–5.

The computer printout shows the optimal program in the BASIS column and the $B(I)$ column, and it is printed separately below. It shows that we should make 5,727 two-door cars and 2,182 station wagons. The objective function value of this program of $2,590,913 is greater than for any other program and checks with our graphic solution to the problem, after rounding.

OTHER USES OF SIMPLEX METHOD ANALYSES

In most cases, the users of the simplex method are seeking solutions like those we have just calculated. The solution to our problem is to schedule 5,727 two-door cars and 2,182 wagons.

The simplex method can, however, be helpful to managers in several other ways. The final tableau in iteration 3, Figure F–2, in fact, shows a number of relationships which managers can use in further decision making. Every number in Figure F–2 has some meaning which can aid in capacity planning and scheduling.

Some, for example, are "shadow prices" and reflect other possible relationships which exist if, for reasons not covered by the problem as stated, the optimum solution is not used. The data provided in Figure F–3, for example, allows managers to calculate the merit of expanding or reducing capacities which set limits to output. These calculations include a process called "ranging."

These data can also show managers how sensitive the problem is to changes in factors and how changes in factors will affect solutions. This is called "parametric sensitivity analysis."

Sometimes, too, managers want to know how to minimize costs rather than to maximize contributions. A modified version of the simplex method can be used here.

These and several other attributes of the simplex method will now be discussed.

Shadow Prices

The values in the simplex criteria row of the final iteration's tableau are called "shadow prices." The ones which are of particular interest are the negative ones of -245.4565 and -54.5435, which belong to $X(3)$ and $X(4)$, the engine and stamping departments slack capacities.

This means, for example, that the opportunity cost of not expanding each additional unit of capacity for the engine department is $245.46. This can be calculated as follows: First, note that the final rates of substitution between $X(3)$ and $X(1)$ and $X(2)$ are $-.6363$ and 1.0909. If we would change the engine department's capacity (in terms of four-cylinder engines for two-door cars) from 9,000 to 9,001, and ignoring for the moment the cost of doing this, we could increase our contribution. This would be possible if we shifted the use of stamping capacity. In our solution there is no $X(4)$, stamping department slack.

But by not making .6363 two-doors, we could produce stampings for 1.0909 station wagons. We would be sacrificing $190.90 (.6363 × $300) by producing fewer two-doors, but we would gain $436.36 (1.0909 × $400) by producing more station wagons, leaving a net gain of $245.46.

In Figure 18–5, this essentially would move the engine department's constraint line to the

right while maintaining the same slope. This would shift point C down and to the right. This shift in point C's location is along the stamping department's constraint line and is directly related to its rate of substitution between two-doors and wagons of .5833, which is the ratio of .6363/ 1.0909.

RANGING

We have just demonstrated the meaning of shadow prices. The $-$245.46 is the per unit opportunity cost for not increasing the capacity of the engine department above 9,000 in terms of two-door cars. (We are still ignoring the possible cost of doing this.) Our question now is, over what *range* of increase would the $-$245.46 opportunity cost apply before we reach some other department's capacity? In linear programming this is called "ranging."

In our case, we could move the engine department's capacity constraint line over to the right (while maintaining the same slope) to point H in Figure 18–5 and would have enough capacity to make 4,667 two-doors and 4,000 wagons. At point H, we would reach the capacity of the wagon assembly department, so that beyond this point the shadow price of $-$245.46 would no longer apply. The engine department's capacity at point H would have to be enough to make 4,667 two-doors and 4,000 wagons (the values at point H can be found by simultaneously solving the wagon assembly and stamping equations). This translates into capacity requirements, expressed in equivalent two-doors of:

$$4,667 + 1.5(4,000) = 10,667 \text{ two-doors}$$

Using Shadow Prices and Ranging for Capacity Planning Decisions

Armed with the shadow price for a limited capacity resource and the range over which it applies, the analyst can calculate the maximum amount that can be paid for increases in capacity. And he or she knows how much capacity can be added in the department without reaching some other department's capacity. Suppose that the capacity of the engine department could be increased only in the increments and hypothetical costs listed in Figure F–4. The relationships would then be:

FIGURE F–4

Capacity (in two-door terms)	Change in Capacity	First Year Cost to Reach this Capacity	Opportunity Cost Avoided	Net Contribution
9,000	0	0	0	
9,500	500	$137,500	$122,730*	$–14,770
10,000	1,000	262,500	245,460	–17,040
10,500	1,500	362,500	368,190	5,690
10,667	1,667†	462,500	409,181	–53,318

* $245.46 × 500.
† Maximum increase before wagon assembly capacity constraint is reached.

Since the only capacity expansion level which produces a positive contribution is the expansion to 10,500, should it be carried forward? Since this solution is for one week's operations, the annual increase in contribution would be $295,880 ($5,690 × 52 weeks). This is an excellent return of 82 percent on the first-year cost investment of $362,500, so the expansion should be undertaken.

A similar analysis can be made with the –$54.54 shadow price for $X(4)$, the stamping department. We will not go through it here, nor will we pursue in detail the interesting problem of how to arrive at the solution if we add the two shadow prices together (–$245.46 and –$54.54 add up to –$300.00). Intuitively, however, it can be seen that the engine and the stamping department capacities of 9,000 and 7,000 are both in terms of two-doors, and the expansion of capacity of one unit in each of these two departments will avoid an opportunity cost of $300, the unit contribution of two-doors.

Parametric Sensitivity Analyses

As an alternative to doing the capacity expansion analysis for the engine department by hand,

most computerized simplex programs compute the range over which each shadow price applies. In addition they also allow us to perform a "parametric sensitivity analysis" of the problem. For example, recall that $X(3)$'s capacity could only be added (because of technical limitations) in increments of 500. Using parametric sensitivity analysis procedures, we simply tell the simplex program first to solve the problem with $X(3)$'s capacity at 9,000, and then to increase it to 9,500, resolve the problem, increase it to 10,000, re-solve, and so on until the range of 10,667 has been reached or exceeded. At each solution point, the final tableau and objective function value would be reported so that they could be compared against the cost of capacity expansion. For problems with many variables, this procedure is essential, not only because the analyst does not have a graphic "picture" to look at, but because the calculations become unmanageable.

Similar parametric sensitivity tests can be done on other $B(I)$ values, $C(J)$ values, and even particular coefficients in the equations. For example, recall our discussion (under "Sensitivity Analysis" in Chapter 18) of changing the process in the engine department so that the new ratio between six-cylinders and four-cylinders was 1:1.25 instead of 1:1.5. Suppose we were somewhat unsure if this was exactly the new ratio between the two. But suppose that we thought the actual ratio would be somewhere between

1:1.2 and 1:1.3. We could perform a parametric sensitivity analysis on this coefficient by beginning it at 1.2, solving, and incrementing it by .01, solving again, successively, until 1.3 was reached.

This would produce 11 solutions which could then be compared to see if the "uncertainty" of this ratio made any difference on the solution mix and upon the objective function. If it didn't, then we would know that the solution is not sensitive to this factor. If it proved to be sensitive, then more analyses could be made to more closely pin down its effect on the results.

COST MINIMIZATION WITH THE SIMPLEX METHOD

Cost minimization can also be done with the simplex method. We will continue using our automobile assembly problem but with certain changes. Recall from our discussion of cost minimization in Chapter 18 that a new process has been developed in the engine department which has changed the four-cylinder and six-cylinder ratio from 1.5 to 1.25. And because of reasons not associated with our problem, management has ruled that the engine and stamping departments should work at their capacity. Overtime is allowed in the stamping department (at an extra cost of $100 per two-door car or equivalent in station wagons), but overtime is not allowed in the engine department where machine maintenance time precludes overtime. The unit costs are $2,000 per two-door and $2,800 per station wagon for all automobiles produced on regular time. Overtime costs apply to all stamping department production in excess of 7,000 cars (in terms of two-doors).

The problem can now be formulated as:

Minimize: $\quad F = \$2,000\,T + \$2,800\,W$

Subject to:
$$T \qquad\quad \le 6{,}000$$
$$W \le 4{,}000$$
$$T + 1.25 \quad W = 9{,}000$$
$$T + .5833\,W \le 7{,}000$$

We have introduced three new things in this problem which require modifications in the simplex procedure. They are: cost minimization; "=" constraints; and "≥" constraints. Minimization requires only a slight change in the procedure, while the incorporation of equality and of greater-than-or-equal-to constraints requires the addition of certain new variables and other modifications.

The major change in the procedure for cost minimization is simply to change the sign of the values in the objective function.

This means that the objective function now becomes:

Maximize:

$$F = -\$2{,}000\,T - \$2{,}800\,W$$

When we *maximize* a negative objective function, it is exactly the same as *minimizing* a positive objective function. Other than this change, *exactly* the same rules for calculating the $Z(J)$ and $C(J) - Z(J)$ rows are used. Additionally, the *same rules* for choosing the variable entering the BASIS (largest positive value rule) and the variable leaving the basis (smallest positive quotient rule) apply. An optimal (least cost) solution has been reached, as before, when all simplex criteria row values (the $C(J) - Z(J)$'s) are negative or zero. The optimal objective function value will be negative rather than positive, however, which identifies it as a cost rather than a contribution.

"Greater Than" or "Equal To" Constraints

Cost minimization problems, however, require some constraints which are either minimum (≥) or equality (=) constraints. If we had only maximum (≤) constraints, the simplex procedure would always produce an optimal solution, which in our automobile production problem, would say to produce *zero* two-doors and *zero* wagons. While this would certainly minimize costs, it wouldn't make any practical sense. The first thing required for handling ≥ constraints is to add a "surplus" variable much as we added a "slack" variable to ≤ constraints. The second thing is to add an "artificial" variable.

The stamping department's constraint is thus transformed from an inequality to an equation as follows:

$$T + .5833W - \text{surplus} + \text{artificial} = 7,000$$

First, let us explain the use of the surplus variable. Suppose, in a solution, that $T = 5,000$ and $W = 10,000$ (assume that the artificial equals zero).

Then:

$$5,000 + .5833(10,000) - \text{surplus} + 0 = 7,000$$

And surplus equals 3,833, the amount stamping capacity is above 7,000. A surplus variable always has a coefficient of -1 in the initial tableau.

The artificial variable is used for one purpose: that is, to form the stamping department's column in the initial tableau's identity matrix and to be in the BASIS in the initial feasible solution. It has a coefficient of 1 and is required, because each identity matrix column must contain a positive 1 and not a -1 as is the surplus variable's coefficient. Additionally, since the artificial variable is placed in the initial feasible BASIS, we want to ensure that it is not in the BASIS in the optimal solution. We ensure this by assigning the artificial variable a very large cost in the objective function. This causes the simplex procedure to regard the artificial variable to be a very costly product. And since we are minimizing costs, it will remove it (and its very large cost) from the BASIS by the time the optimal solution has been reached.[3]

Equality Constraints

Equality constraints also need an artificial variable to form the identity matrix and to be in the

BASIS for the initial feasible solution since they do not have a slack variable. Similarly, we also assign a very large cost to these artificial variables to assure that they will not be in the BASIS in the optimal solution.

Assigning Costs to Surplus and Slack Variables

It will be recalled that in our present problem, we can work overtime in the stamping department at a cost of $100 per unit of capacity above 7,000. We can incorporate this cost automatically into the simplex procedure just by placing this cost in the objective function for the surplus variable. Similarly, if we had wanted to assign a unit cost to idle or slack capacity, this cost could have been added to the objective function for the appropriate slack variable. (We have not done this in our example, because we have assumed, perhaps unrealistically, that slack capacity has no cost.)

Summary of Requirements for Constraint Types

A summary of the requirements for slack, surplus, and artificial variables, and objective function values for the three kinds of constraints is given in the box below.

Computer Solution to Cost Minimization Problem

We solved this problem with our simplex computer program as a cost minimization problem. Figure F–5 shows the initial and last iterations, numbers 0 and 3.

First we should note the $C(J)$ row in iteration 0. $X(5)$ and $X(7)$ are the artificial variables where we have assigned each an arbitrarily large cost of -999999. Also note the -100 cost attached to $X(6)$, the surplus variable associated with using overtime in the stamping department.

---

[3] If an artificial variable is in the BASIS in the optimal solution, this means that there was not a feasible solution to start with, and the constraint to which the artificial belongs is the offending infeasibility.

	Description of Coefficient in Initial Tableau		
Constraint Type	Slack	Surplus	Artificial
Less than or equal to ($\leq$)	1		
Equality ($=$)			1
Greater than or equal to ($\geq$)		-1	1
Objective function coefficient	Cost (negative), contribution (positive), or zero, depending on the problem.	Cost, contribution, or zero, depending on the problem.	Always a large cost (negative value), whether maximizing or minimizing.

FIGURE F–5
Computer Solution to Simplex Cost Minimization Problem

```
              PROBLEM PARAMETERS
NUMBER OF EQUATIONS    4                      OPTIMAL SOLUTION
NUMBER OF VARIABLES    7
NUMBER OF LESS THAN EQUATIONS   2             SOLUTION
NUMBER OF EQUAL TO EQUATIONS    1             VARIABLE      VALUE
NUMBER OF GREATER THAN EQUATIONS   1          VAR   1    6000.0000
                                              VAR   2    2400.0000
         OPTIONS SPECIFIED                    VAR   3       0.0000
SLACK AND ARTIFICIAL VARIABLES WILL NOT BE GENERATED    VAR   4    1600.0000
ALL TABLEAUS WILL BE PRINTED                  VAR   5       0.0000

         PROBLEM WAS INPUT AS FOLLOWS         OBJECTIVE FUNCTION VALUE =   -18759992.0000

MAXIMIZE F =   -2000.0000X(  1) -   2800.0000X(  2) +    0.0000X(  3) +    0.0000X(  4) - 999999.0000X(  5)
           -    100.0000X(  6) - 999999.0000X(  7)
SUBJECT TO
          +   1.0000X(  1) +      0.0000X(  2) +    1.0000X(  3) +    0.0000X(  4) +    0.0000X(  5)
          +   0.0000X(  6) +      0.0000X(  7)                                                        ≤   6000.000
          +   0.0000X(  1) +      1.0000X(  2) +    0.0000X(  3) +    1.0000X(  4) +    0.0000X(  5)
          +   0.0000X(  6) +      0.0000X(  7)                                                        ≤   4000.000
          +   1.0000X(  1) +      1.2500X(  2) +    0.0000X(  3) +    0.0000X(  4) +    1.0000X(  5)
          +   0.0000X(  6) +      0.0000X(  7)                                                        =   9000.000
          -   1.0000X(  1) +       .5833X(  2) +    0.0000X(  3) +    0.0000X(  4) +    0.0000X(  5)
          -   1.0000X(  6) +      1.0000X(  7)                                                        ≥   7000.000
```

•••
•••

```
PROBLEM   2          ITERATION   0

  OBJECTIVE FUNCTION   C(J) =     -2000.0000   -2800.0000       0.0000      0.0000 -999999.0000   -100.0000 -999999.0000
       C(I)  BASIS        B(I)      X(  1)       X(  2)         X(  3)      X(  4)      X(  5)       X(  6)     X(  7)
•••••••••••   ••••••   •••••••••••  •••••••••••  •••••••••••  •••••••••••  •••••••••••  •••••••••••  •••••••••••  •••••••••••
     0.0000   X(  3)    6000.0000    1.0000       0.0000       1.0000      0.0000      0.0000       0.0000     0.0000
     0.0000   X(  4)    4000.0000    0.0000       1.0000       0.0000      1.0000      0.0000       0.0000     0.0000
-999999.0000  X(  5)    9000.0000    1.0000       1.2500       0.0000      0.0000      1.0000       0.0000     0.0000
-999999.0000  X(  7)    7000.0000    1.0000        .5833       0.0000      0.0000      0.0000      -1.0000     1.0000
•••••••••••   ••••••   •••••••••••  •••••••••••  •••••••••••  •••••••••••  •••••••••••  •••••••••••  •••••••••••  •••••••••••
Z(J) =                             -999999.0000 -999999.0000     0.0000      0.0000 -999999.0000  999999.0000 -999999.0000
SIMPLEX CRITERIA   C(J)-Z(J) =  1997998.0000 1830498.1667     0.0000      0.0000 -999999.0000  999999.0000    0.0000
          OBJECTIVE FUNCTION VALUE    -999999999.0000
```

•••••••••••••••••••••••

```
PROBLEM   2          ITERATION   3

  OBJECTIVE FUNCTION   C(J) =     -2000.0000   -2800.0000       0.0000      0.0000 -999999.0000   -100.0000 -999999.0000
       C(I)  BASIS        B(I)      X(  1)       X(  2)         X(  3)      X(  4)      X(  5)       X(  6)     X(  7)
•••••••••••   ••••••   •••••••••••  •••••••••••  •••••••••••  •••••••••••  •••••••••••  •••••••••••  •••••••••••  •••••••••••
 -2000.0000   X(  1)    6000.0000    1.0000       0.0000       1.0000      0.0000      0.0000       0.0000     0.0000
     0.0000   X(  4)    1600.0000    0.0000       0.0000        .8000      1.0000      -.8000       0.0000     0.0000
  -100.0000   X(  6)     399.9200    0.0000       0.0000        .5334      0.0000      .4666       1.0000    -1.0000
 -2800.0000   X(  2)    2400.0000    0.0000       1.0000       -.8000      0.0000      .8000       0.0000     0.0000
•••••••••••   ••••••   •••••••••••  •••••••••••  •••••••••••  •••••••••••  •••••••••••  •••••••••••  •••••••••••  •••••••••••
Z(J) =                              -2000.0000   -2800.0000     186.6640    0.0000   -2286.6640   -100.0000    100.0000
SIMPLEX CRITERIA   C(J)-Z(J) =       0.0000       0.0000     -186.6640      0.0000  -997712.3360     0.0000 -999999.0000
          OBJECTIVE FUNCTION VALUE    -18759992.0000
```

•••••••••••••••••••••••

The initial BASIS values contain slacks $X(3)$ and $X(4)$, the assembly capacities for two-doors and wagons, and the two artificials $X(5)$ and $X(7)$. The first variable to enter the BASIS is $X(1)$, because its simplex criterion value is the largest positive number, and the variable it replaces is $X(3)$.

In iteration 3, and the optimal solution shown at the top of Figure F–5, calls for scheduling 6,000 two-door cars and 2,400 station wagons. Column $B(I)$ in iteration 3 shows us that 400 overtime hours will be needed in the stamping department and that there is still a slack of 1,600 in the station wagon assembly department.

$X(5)$ and $X(7)$, the two artificial variables, have left the BASIS, as planned. The objective function value which minimizes cost is $-\$18,759,992$ (6,000 × \$2,000 + 2,400 × \$2,800 + 400 × \$100 = \$18,760,000). The shadow prices may be interpreted in the same way as described earlier.

Appendix G

Least Squares Formulas and Calculation Procedure

The least squares method is another name for regression analysis and is used to develop estimates of a and b in the equation $Y_c = a + bx$, as explained in Chapter 9. This is called the "bivariate" case of regression analysis, because there are only two variables, Y_c and X. (Multiple regression uses two or more predictor variables to attempt to explain the behavior of Y_c). But here, the only predictor variable is time, the months 1,2,3, through 36.

The Normal Equations

Two equations are used to calculate estimates of a and b, given pairs of historical values of Y and X. They are called the "normal" equations and are:

$$\Sigma y = na + \Sigma x(b) \qquad (1)$$

$$\Sigma xy = \Sigma x(a) + \Sigma x^2(b) \qquad (2)$$

The first term, Σy, is simply the sum of all 36 Ys; n is the number of observation pairs, or 36; a and b are unknowns; Σx is the sum of 1,2,3,4, . . . through 36; Σxy is the sum of each X times its corresponding Y; and Σx^2 is the sum of 1^2, 2^2, 3^2, 4^2, . . . through 36^2.

Figure G–1 summarizes these terms. Substituting these values into our equations:

$$4{,}928 = 36a + 666b \qquad (1)$$

$$95{,}903 = 666a + 16{,}206b \qquad (2)$$

Solving these two equations simultaneously to determine a and b, we multiply equation (1) by -18.5 (because $666/36 = 18.5$) so, when we add equations (1) and (2), the a terms will cancel and we can solve for the b term:

$$-18.5 \, (4{,}928 = 36a + 666b) \qquad (1)$$
$$-91{,}168 = -666a - 12{,}321b \qquad (1)$$
$$95{,}903 = 666a + 16{,}206b \qquad (2)$$
$$\overline{}$$
$$4{,}735 = 3{,}885b$$
$$b = 4{,}735/3885$$
$$= 1.22$$

Then, substituting $b = 1.22$ into equation (2):

$$95{,}903 = 666a + 16{,}206 \times 1.22$$
$$666a = 95{,}903 - 19{,}771$$
$$a = 76{,}132/666$$
$$a = 114.35$$

Thus, $Y_c = 114.35 + 1.22x$

Several statistical measures of the strength of the relationship between Y_c and X are available but are beyond the scope of this text. These methods are discussed in most statistics texts.

FIGURE G–1
Calculations for Bivariate Regression

Demand (Y)	Month (X)	$X \times Y$	X^2
100	1	100	1
128	2	256	4
138	3	414	9
127	4	508	16
112	5	560	25
.	.	.	.
.	.	.	.
.	.	.	.
.	.	.	.
173	32	5,536	1,024
168	33	5,544	1,089
157	34	5,338	1,156
130	35	4,550	1,225
125	36	4,500	1,296
4,928	666	95,903	16,206

Appendix H

Suggested Supplementary Readings

Section One, Overview

Alexander, Tom. "It's Roundup Time for the Runaway Regulators." *Fortune,* December 3, 1979, pp. 126 ff.

DeLooch, James W. "LIFO—Some Important Tax Considerations." *CPA Journal,* March 1978, pp. 38–42.

Epple, Dennis, and Artur Raviv. "Product Safety: Liability Rules, Market Structure, and Imperfect Information." *American Economic Review,* March 1978, pp. 80–95.

Lilley, William II, and James C. Miller III. "The New 'Social Regulation.'" *Across the Board,* January 1978, pp. 33–39.

Nicol, David J. "The Impact of Inflation on Present Value Analysis." *Business Economics,* May 1979, pp. 33–38.

Peters, Thomas J., and Robert H. Waterman, Jr. *In Search of Excellence.* New York: Harper & Row, 1982.

Shih, Wei. "A General Decision Model for Cost-Volume-Profit Analysis under Uncertainty." *Accounting Review,* October 1979, pp. 687–706.

Skinner, C. W. "Manufacturing—The Missing Link in Corporate Strategy." *Harvard Business Review,* May–June 1969, pp. 136–45.

Stobaugh, R., and P. Telesio. "Match Manufacturing Policies and Product Strategy." *Harvard Business Review,* March–April 1983, pp. 113–20.

Weston, J. Fred., and Eugene F. Brigham. *Managerial Finance.* 6th ed. Hinsdale, Ill.: Dryden Press, 1978, chapters 3, 9.

Wheelwright, Steven C. "Japan—Where Operations Really Are Strategic." *Harvard Business Review,* July–August 1981, pp. 69–70.

Section Two, Product Design and Quality Management

Abegglen, James C. "How to Defend Your Business against Japan." *Business Week,* August 15, 1983, p. 14.

Ambler, A. R., and M. H. Overholt." Are Quality Circles Right for Your Company?" *Personnel Journal,* November 1982, pp. 829–31.

"Bendix Shows its System for Automation Inspection." *Automotive News,* February 28, 1983, p. 22.

Blocker, H. J., and H. O. Overgaard. "Japanese Quality Circles: A Managerial Response to the Productivity Problems." *Management International Review,* 2 (1982), pp. 13–19.

Campbell, David R. "How Local Firms Can Document Quality Control." *CPA Journal,* April 1978, pp. 39–43.

Clements, John A. "Interactive Graphics in New Product Quality Assessment Programs." *Quality Progress,* February 1979, pp. 14–16.

DeKluyver, Cornelius A. "Innovation and Industrial Life Cycles." *California Management Review,* Fall 1977, pp. 21–33.

Divita, S. F. "Marketing Quality Control: An Alternative to Consumer Affairs." *California Management Review,* Summer 1978, pp. 74–78.

Gazis, D. C. "Quality Control in OR Literature." *Interfaces,* August 1978, pp. 26–30.

Gray, C. S. "Total Quality Control in Japan—Less Inspection, Lower Cost." *Business Week,* July 16, 1981, pp. 23–44.

Groocock, J. M. "TRW's New Approach to the Measurement of Product Quality." *Management Review,* October 1982, p. 29.

Hayes, R. H., and S. C. Wheelwright. "The Dynamics of Process-Product Life Cycles." *Harvard Business Review,* March–April 1979, pp. 127–36.

Juran, J. M. "Japanese and Western Quality: A Contrast in Methods and Results." *Management Review,* November 1978, pp. 26–45.

Juran, J. M. "Japanese and Western Quality—A Contrast." *Quality Progress,* December 1978, pp. 10–18.

Landvater, John H. "Metric Conversion—A Slumbering Giant." *AMA Forum,* May 1978, pp. 21ff.

Leaman, D. C. "ASQC Quality Control Certification Examinations." *Quality Progress,* August 1978, pp. 17–28.

McLaughlin, Richard A. "Technology: A Faster Pace." *Dun's Review,* August 1979, pp. 77ff.

Obrzut, J. J. "Computers Ferret Out Preferred Fits and Sizes." *Iron Age,* August 7, 1978, pp. 27–30.

"Products of the Year." *Fortune,* December 1982, pp. 42–45.

"Quality and Productivity: America's Revitalization." *Business Week,* November 8, 1982, pp. 19–20.

Savich, R. S., and Thompson, L. A. "Resource Allocation within the Product Life Cycle." *MSU Business Topics,* Autumn 1978, pp. 35–42.

"Small Car War: U.S. Volkswagen Has Problems with Price, Quality and Japanese." *The Wall Street Journal,* February 7, 1983.

Section Three, Production and Inventory Planning and Control

Abegglen, J. C., and A. Etori. "Japanese Technology Today." *Scientific American,* October 1982.

Aberns, Roger. "Basics of Capacity Planning and Control." *APICS 24th Annual Conference Proceedings,* 1981, pp. 232–35.

Alvarez, Ronald. "Purchasing Can Reduce Inventory Investment." *APICS 23d Annual Conference Proceedings,* 1980, pp. 291–93.

Ammer, Dean S. *Material Management and Purchasing.* Homewood, Ill.: Richard D. Irwin, 1980.

APICS *Certification Program Study Guide: Capacity Planning and Control.* Washington, D.C.: APICS, 1980.

Armstrong, J. Scott. *Long-Range Forecasting.* New York: John Wiley & Sons, 1978.

Backes, Robert W. "Cycle Counting—A Better Method for Achieving Accurate Inventory Records." *Production and Inventory Management,* 2d quarter 1980, pp. 36–44.

Baker, K. R., and J. W. M. Bertrand. "A Comparison of Due-Date Selection Rules." *AHE Transactions,* June 1981.

Belt, Bill. "Input/Output Planning Illustrated." *Production and Inventory Management,* 2d quarter 1978, pp. 13–20.

Benson, Randall J. "Can Purchasing Supply Tomorrow's Factory?" *APICS 24th Annual International Conference Proceedings,* 1981, pp. 355–59.

Berry, W. L.; T. Schmitt; and T. E. Vollmann. "Capacity Planning Techniques for Manufacturing Control Systems: Information Requirements and Operational Features." *Journal of Operations Management* 3, no. 1 (November 1982).

Berry, W. L.; T. E. Vollmann; and D. C. Whybark. *Master Production Scheduling: Principles and Practice.* Falls Church, Va.: American Production and Inventory Control Society, 1979.

Biggs, Joseph R., Stephen H. Goodman, and Stanley H. Hardy. "Lot-Sizing Rules in a Hierarchial Multistage Inventory System." *Production and Inventory Management* 18, no. 1 (1st quarter 1977), pp. 104–16.

Blackburn, Joseph D., and Miller, Robert A. "Selecting a Lot-Sizing Technique for a Single Level Assembly." *Production and Inventory Management,* 3d quarter 1979, pp. 42–48.

Bretschneider, Stuart, Robert, Carbone, and Richard L. Longini. "An Adaptive Approach to Time Series Forecasting." *Decision Science,* April 1979, pp. 232–44.

Brongiel, Bob. "A Manual/Mechanical Approach to Master Scheduling and Operations Planning." *Production and Inventory Management,* 1st quarter 1979, pp. 66–75.

Buffa, Elwood S., and Jeffrey G. Miller. *Production-Inventory Systems: Planning and Control.* 3d ed. Homewood, Ill.: Richard D. Irwin, 1979.

Burlingame, L. James, and R. A. Warren. "Extended Capacity Planning." *APICS 17th Annual International Conference Proceedings,* 1974, pp. 83–91.

Carter, Philip L., and Robert M. Monczka. "Steelcase, Inc.: MRP in Purchasing." *Case Studies in Materials Requirements Planning,* Washington, D.C.: American Production and Inventory Control Society, 1978, pp. 105–29.

Cook, Milton E. "Developing a Successful P & IC Training Program." *APICS 23d Annual Conference Proceedings,* 1980, pp. 6–8.

Cox, James F., and Richard R. Jesse, Jr. "An Application of MRP to Higher Education." *Decision Sciences* 12, no. 2 (April 1981), pp. 240–60.

Davis, E. W. *Case Studies in Material Requirements Planning.* Falls Church, Va.: American Production and Inventory Control Society, 1978.

Dempsey, W. A. "Vendor Selection and the Buying Process." *Industrial Marketing Management.* August 1978, pp. 257–67.

Drucker, P. F. "Behind Japan's Success." *McKinsey Quarterly,* Winter 1983, pp. 45–57.

Edson, Norris W. "Measuring MRP System Effectiveness." *APICS 24th Annual International Conference Proceedings,* 1981, pp. 315–18.

Elk, Roger D., and James C. Hershauer. "Extended MRP Systems for Evaluating Master Schedules and Materials Requirements Plans." *Production and Inventory Management,* 2d quarter 1980, pp. 53–66.

Everdell, Romeyn. *Master Production Scheduling.* Washington, D.C.: American Production and Inventory Control Society, 1976.

Fisher, Kenneth. "How to Implement MRP Success-

fully." *Production and Inventory Management* 22, no. 4 (4th quarter 1981), pp. 36–54.

Fisk, John C., and Seagle, J. Peter. "The Integration of Aggregate Planning with Resource Requirements to Planning." *Production and Inventory Management,* 3d quarter 1978, pp. 81–91.

Flosi, Thomas L. "How to Manage an MRP Implementation." *APICS Management Seminar Proceedings,* March 1982, pp. 79–88.

Gallagher, G. R. "How to Develop a Realistic Master Schedule." *Management Review,* April 1980, pp. 19–25.

Graves, S. "A Review of Production Scheduling." *Operations Research* 29, no. 4 (July–August 1981).

Graziano, Vincent J. "Production Capacity Planning—Long Term." *Production and Inventory Management* 15, no. 2 (2d quarter 1974).

Hall, R. W. "Data Accuracy in Material Flow Control." *1980 Conference Proceedings,* American Production and Inventory Control Society, pp. 128–30.

Hall, Robert. "Driving the Productivity Machine: Production Planning and Control in Japan." Falls Church, Va.: American Production and Inventory Control Society, 1981.

Hastings, N. A. J. et al. "Schedule-Based MRP: An Integrated Approach to Production Scheduling and Material Requirements Planning." *Journal of Operations Research,* November 1982, pp. 1021–29.

Hayes, R. "Why Japanese Factories Work." *Harvard Business Review,* July–August 1981, pp. 56–66.

Hoeffer, E. "Supplier Leadtimes Are the Real Inventories." *Purchasing,* February 10, 1983, p. 27.

Hoyt, George. "Effective In-House MRP Training." *APICS 23d Annual International Conference Proceedings,* 1980, pp. 26–30.

Johnson, G. A. *APICS Bibliography.* Falls Church, Va.: American Production and Inventory Control Society, 1981.

Jordan, H. H. "How to Start a Cycle Counting Program." *1975 Conference Proceedings,* American Production and Inventory Control Society, pp. 190–98.

Kobert, N. "Capacity Planning and Inventory Balance." *Purchasing,* March 10, 1983, p. 31.

Kraemer, R. P. "Record Accuracy Through CRT and Bar Coded Data Collection Systems." *1980 Conference Proceedings.* American Production and Inventory Control Society, pp. 90–93.

Kropp, Dean H.; Robert C. Carlson; and James V. Jucker. "Use of Dynamic Lot-Sizing to Avoid Nervousness in Material." *Production and Inventory Management,* 3d quarter 1979, pp. 49–58.

LaForge, R. C. "MRP and the Part-Period Algorithm." *Journal of Purchasing Management,* Winter 1982, pp. 21–26.

Lowere, William M. "Lot Size Rules—A One-Act Play." *Production and Inventory Management* 16, no. 2 (2d quarter 1975), pp. 41–50.

Majewicz, David, and Lloyd A. Swanson. "Inventory Ordering and Quantity Discounts with Time-Varying Demand: A Programming Application." *Production and Inventory Management,* 1st quarter 1978, pp. 91–102.

Mather, Hal. "Too Much Precision, Not Enough Accuracy." *APICS 22d Annual Conference Proceedings,* 1979, pp. 116–19.

Mather, Hal, and George Plossl. "Priority Fixation versus Throughput Planning." *Production and Inventory Management,* 3d quarter 1978, pp. 27–51.

May, Neville. "Shop Floor Controls—Principles and Use." *APICS 24th Annual Conference Proceedings,* 1981, pp. 170–74.

Monden, Y. *Toyota Production System.* Atlanta/Norcross, Ga.: Industrial Engineering and Management Press, Institute of Industrial Engineers, 1983.

————. "Adaptable Kanban System Helps Toyota Maintain Production." *Industrial Engineering,* May 1981, pp. 29–46.

————. "Toyota's Production Smoothing Methods: Part II." *Industrial Engineering,* September 1981, pp. 22–30.

————. "What Makes The Toyota Production System Really Tick?" *Industrial Engineering,* January 1981, pp. 36–46.

Morecroft, J. D. W. "A Systems Perspective on MRP." *Decision Science,* January 1983, pp. 1–14.

Motwane, Aman A. "How to Organize a Production Planning Department." *APICS 24th Annual International Conference Proceedings,* 1981, pp. 347–50.

Naumann, E., and R. Reck. "A Buyer's Bases of Power." *Journal of Purchasing and Materials Management,* Winter 1982, pp. 8–14.

New, Christopher C. "Lot Sizing in Multilevel Requirements Planning Systems." *Production and Inventory Management* 15, no. 4 (4th quarter 1974), pp. 57–72.

Newberry, Thomas L., and Carl D. Bhame. "How Management Should Use and Interact with Sales Forecasts." *Inventories and Production Management* 1, no. 3 (July–August 1981), pp. 4–11.

Papesch, Robert M. "Extending Your MRP System into Your Vendor's Shop." *Production and Inventory Management,* 2d quarter 1978, pp. 47–52.

Pennente, Ernest, and Ted Levy. "MRP on Microcomputers." *Production and Inventory Management Review,* May 1980.

"Preparation: The Key to Successful Negotiation." *Purchasing,* February 1979, pp. 59 ff.

Proud, John F. "Controlling the Master Schedule." *Production and Inventory Management* 22, no. 2 (2d quarter 1981), pp. 78–90.

Schonberger, Richard J. "Clearest-Road-Ahead Priorities for Shop Floor Control: Moderating Infinite-Capacity-Loading Unevenness." *Production and Inventory Management,* 2d quarter 1979, pp. 17–27.

Schonberger, Richard J. *Japanese Manufacturing Techniques: Nine Hidden Lessons in Simplicity.* New York: Free Press, 1982.

Schroder, R. G.; J. C. Anderson, S. E. Tupy, and E. M. White. "A Study of MRP Benefits and Costs." *Journal of Operations Management* 2, no. 1 (October 1981).

Silver, E. A. "Operations Research in Inventory Management: A Review and Critique." *Operations Research* 29, no. 4 (July–August 1981).

Solberg, James J. "Capacity Planning with a Stochastic Flow Model." *AHE Transactions* 13, no. 2 (June 1981), pp. 116–22.

Stratton, William B. "How to Design a Viable Forecasting System." *Production and Inventory Management,* 1st quarter 1979, pp. 17–27.

Steinberg, E.; W. B. Lee; and B. M. Khumawala. "MRP Applications in the Space Program." *Journal of Operations Management* 1, no. 2 (1981).

Steinberg, E.; B. M. Khumawala; and R. Scarnell. "Requirements Planning Systems in the Health Care Environment.'' *Journal of Operations Management* 2, no. 4 (August 1982).

Steinberg, E., and A. Napier. ''Optimal Multi-level Lot Sizing for Requirements Planning Systems.'' *Management Science* 26, no. 12 (December 1980), pp. 1258–72.

Sulsner, Samuel S. ''Basic Shop Floor Control.'' *Canadian Association for Product and Inventory Control,* June 1981, pp. 81–94.

Summer, D. W. ''Computer Forecasting for the Layman (FLEXICAST).'' *Industrial World,* October 16, 1978, pp. 98 ff.

Tersine, Richard J. *Materials Management and Inventory Systems.* New York: Elsevier-North Holland Publishing, 1976.

Ulberg, Merle D. ''Master Scheduling Technique for Rapistan.'' *APICS Conference Proceedings,* 1975.

Vergin, R. C. ''Production Scheduling under Seasonal Demand.'' *Journal of Industrial Engineering* 17 (May 1966).

Vollmann, Thomas E. ''Capacity Planning: The Missing Link.'' *Production and Inventory Management,* 1st quarter 1973, pp. 61–73.

Volsky, Sanford L. ''Purchasing's Inflation Fighter: The Computer.'' *APICS 24th Annual International Conference Proceedings,* 1981, pp. 360–62.

Wantuck, K. A. ''Master Production Planning at Bendix.'' *Inventories and Production Magazine,* July–August 1981, pp. 12–16.

Wassweiler, William. ''Material Requirements Planning—The Key to Critical Ratio Effectiveness.'' *Production and Inventory Management,* 3d quarter 1972.

Wassweiler, William R. ''Fundamentals of Shop Floor Control.'' *APICS 23d Annual Conference Proceedings,* 1980, pp. 352–54.

Waterbury, Robert. ''How Does Just-in-Time Work in Lincoln, Nebraska?'' *Assembly Engineering,* April 1981, pp. 52–56.

————. ''Kanban Cuts Waste, Saves $ with Minimum Effort.'' *Assembly Engineering,* April 1981, pp. 52–57.

Welch, W. Evert. ''Management's Role in Inventory Control.'' *Production and Inventory Management,* 3d quarter 1978, pp. 85–95.

Wheelwright, S. C. ''Japan—Where Operations Really Are Strategic.'' *Harvard Business Review,* July–August 1981, pp. 67–74.

Wheelwright, Steven C., and Spryros Makridakis. *Forecasting Methods for Management.* New York: John Wiley & Sons, 1977.

Wight, Oliver. ''Input/Output Control: A Real Handle On Lead Time.'' *Production and Inventory Management* 11, no. 3 (3d quarter 1970).

Winters, P. R. ''Forecasting Sales by Exponentially Weighted Moving Average.'' *Management Science* 6 (April 1960), pp. 324–42.

Section Four, Special Planning and Control Techniques

Bouman, E. H. ''Production Scheduling by the Transportation Method of Linear Programming.'' *Operations Research,* February 1956, pp. 100–103.

Carlson, Robert C.; John C. Hershey; and Dean H. Krapp. ''Use of Optimization and Simulation Models to Analyze Outpatient Case Settings.'' *Decision Sciences,* July 1979, pp. 412–33.

Hanssmann, F., and S. W. Hess. ''A Linear Programming Approach to Production and Employment Scheduling.'' *Management Technology,* January 1960, pp. 46–52.

Khtaian, G. A. ''Computer Project Management—Proposal, Design, and Programming Phases.'' *Journal of Systems Management,* August 1976, pp. 12–21.

Lee, W. B., and B. W. Khumawala. ''Simulation Testing of Aggregate Production Planning Models in an Implementation Methodology.'' *Management Science,* February 1974, pp. 903–11.

Levy, Ferdinand K., Gerald L. Thompson, and Jerome D. Wiest. ''The ABCs of the Critical Path Method.'' *Harvard Business Review,* September–October 1983, pp. 98–108.

Mize, J. H., and J. G. Cox. *Essentials of Simulation.* Englewood Cliffs, N.J.: Prentice-Hall, 1968).

Moder, J.; E. W. Davis; and C. Phillips. *Project Management with CPM and PERT.* New York: Van Nostrand Reinhold, 1983.

Petersen, Perry. ''Project Control Systems.'' *Datamation,* June 1979, pp. 147–63.

Peterson, Eric. "Project Management Building Block." *Production and Inventory Management* 1, no. 12 (December 1981), p. 25.

Wiest, Jerome, and Ferdinand Levy. *A Management Guide to PERT/CPM.* 2d ed. Englewood Cliffs, N.J.: Prentice-Hall, 1977.

Section Five, Designing Production and Service Facilities

"Automatic Guidance: Making Operations More Efficient." *Modern Materials Handling,* Spring 1978, pp. 52 ff.

Barber, P. J. "The Site Selection Process at Honeywell." *Industrial Development,* November–December 1982, pp. 9–11.

Benson, P. B., A. V. Hill, and T. R. Hoffman. "Manufacturing Systems of the Future—A Delphi Study." *Production and Inventory Management Journal,* 3d quarter 1982, pp. 97–98.

Bolander, Steven F., Richard C. Heard, Samuel M. Seward, and Sam G. Taylor. *Manufacturing Planning and Control in Process Industries.* Washington, D.C.: American Production and Inventory Control Society, 1981, pp. 1–20.

Bylinski, G. "The Race to the Automatic Factory." *Fortune,* February 21, 1983, pp. 52–60.

Carrie, A. S. et al. "Graph Theory and Computer Aided Facilities Design." *Omega* 6 no. 4 (1978), pp. 353–61.

Carroll, Thomas M., and Robert D. Dean. "A Baysian Approach to Plant-Location Decisions." *Decision Sciences* 11, no. 1 (January 1980), pp. 81–89.

Constable, G. C., and D. C. Whybark. "The Interaction of Transportation and Inventory Decisions." *Decision Sciences* 9, no. 4 (October 1978), pp. 688–99.

Fenton, David L. "Industry Gears Up to Save Energy." *Consulting Engineer,* November 1979, pp. 114–19.

"Financial Assistance for Industry." *Site Selection Handbook,* September 1978, pp. 299 ff.

Gerwin, D. "Do's and Don'ts of Computerized Manufacturing." *Harvard Business Review,* March–April 1982, pp. 107–16.

Gold, B. "CAM Sets New Rules for Production." *Harvard Business Review,* November–December 1982, pp. 88–94.

Groover, Mikell P. *Automation, Production Systems, and Computer Aided Manufacturing.* Englewood Cliffs, N.J.: Prentice-Hall, 1980.

Gunn, Thomas G. *Computer Applications in Manufacturing.* New York: Industrial Press, Inc., 1981.

Hall, Robert W. "Repetitive Manufacturing." *Production and Inventory Management,* 2d quarter 1982, pp. 78–86.

Harrington, C. H. "Site Selection: The Distribution Manager Takes on a Bigger Role." *Traffic Management,* December 1982, pp. 37–40.

Herron, David P. "Managing Physical Distribution for Profit." *Harvard Business Review,* May–June 1979, pp. 121–32.

Heskett, James L. "Logistics—Essential to Strategy." *Harvard Business Review,* November–December 1977, pp. 85–96.

Ingersby, T. "New CAD/CAM Entries Have Designs as the Future." *Infosystems,* November 1982, p. 56.

Khumawala, B., and D. C. Whybark. "A Comparison of Some Recent Warehouse Location Techniques." *The Logistics Review,* Spring, 1979, pp. 3–19.

Lasko, Clyde A., and Nick T. Thomopoulos. "Safety Stocks and Service Levels for the Multi-Warehouse Case." *Production and Inventory Management,* 2d quarter 1979, pp. 72–84.

Len, John J. "CAD/CAM—Productivity Tools for MRP Record Accuracy." *APICS 24th Annual International Conference Proceedings,* 1981, pp. 374–77.

Lorenz, J. D., and A. A. Mehle. "Measuring Machine Utilization." *Industrial Engineering,* February 1979, pp. 44–47.

Lusa, J. M. "Manufacturing Systems: Here Comes the Second Revolution." *Information Systems,* June 1978, pp. 53 ff.

Marx, T. G. "Technological Change and the Structure of the Machine Tool Industry." *MSU Business Topics,* Winter 1979, pp. 41–48.

Mehra, Satish. "An Analysis of Energy Conservation in Manufacturing Organizations. *Production and Inventory Management,* 2d quarter 1979, pp. 28–40.

Meier, A. "What Is the Cost to You of Conserved Energy." *Harvard Business Review,* January–February 1983, pp. 36–37.

Millenson, Michael L. "Industry's Own Search for Energy." *Across the Board,* May 1978, pp. 11–19.

Musgrave, W. "Computerized Work Stations." *Dun's Review,* July 1978, pp. 109 ff.

"NC–CAD/CIN Report: A Management Guide to Computer Integrated Manufacturing." *Iron Age,* May 8, 1978, pp. 43–46; June 5, 1978, pp. 45–48; July 3, 1978, pp. 31–38; and July 31, 1978, pp. 73–74.

Schwarz, L. B. "Physical Distribution: The Analysis of Inventory and Location." *AHE Transactions* 13, no. 2 (June 1981).

Senia, A. M. "Air Force ICAM Project Paves the Way for the Factory of the Future." *Iron Age,* January 1983, p. 48.

"Storage/Retreival and Transfer Systems." *Handling and Shipping Management,* January 1983, pp. 77–78.

Thompson, J. "How to Gather the Data You Need." *Modern Materials Handling,* July 1978, pp. 50–56.

Tompkins, James H. "Why Layout Today Demands a Computer." *Modern Materials Handling,* May 1978, pp. 94–98.

"What Management Needs to Know before Picking a Plant Site." Special Business Department Report, *Dun's Review,* October 1979, pp. 14 ff.

Section Six, Managing Productivity

"A Work Revolution in U.S. Industry: More Flexible Rules on the Job Are Boosting Productivity." *Business Week,* May 16, 1983.

Bobbe, R. A., and R. H. Schaffer. "Productivity Improvement: Manage It or Buy It." *Business Horizons,* March–April 1983, pp. 62–69.

Bowen, William. "Better Prospects for Our Ailing Productivity." *Fortune,* December 3, 1979, pp. 68 ff.

Carpenter, W. W. "Developing a Unit of Service to Measure Productivity." *Hospital Financial Management,* July 1978, pp. 14 ff.

Chiles, W. Dean, and Earl A. Alluisi. "On the Specification of Operator or Occupational Workload with Performance Measurement Methods." *Human Factors,* October 1979, pp. 515–28.

Cook, Philip J.; M. W. Jones-Lee; and Bryan C. Conley. "The Value of Human Life in the Demand for Safety." *American Economic Review,* September 1978, pp. 710–20.

Crandall, N., and Leland M. Wooten. "Development of Strategies of Organizational Productivity." *California Management Review,* Winter 1978, pp. 37–46.

"EPA and OSHA May be Paying More Attention to Cost of Compliance." *Chemical Week,* October 11, 1978, pp. 24 ff.

Frost, C. F. "The Scanlon Plan: Anyone for Free Enterprise?" *MSU Business Topics,* Winter 1978, pp. 23 ff.

Golembiewski, R. T., and C. W. Proehl. "Survey of the Empirical Literature on Flexible Workhours: Character and Consequences of a Major Innovation." *Academy of Management Review,* October 1978, pp. 837–53.

Hackman, J. R. "Design of Work in the '80s." *Organizational Dynamics,* Summer 1978, pp. 2–17.

Swartz, R. M. "Use of Standards for Control." *Management World,* October 1978, pp. 32–34.

"They Learn How to Face Emergencies: Dow Plant Tightens Procedures, Prepares Outsiders, Too." *Chemical Week,* July 19, 1978, pp. 45 ff.

Unstot, D. D. et al. "Work Setting and Job Enrichment: An Integrated Approach to Job Design." *Academy of Management Review,* October 1978, pp. 867–79.

"Work-Rule Changes Quietly Spread as Firms Try to Raise Productivity." *The Wall Street Journal,* January 25, 1983.

Index

*This book has been set VideoComp, in 10 and 9 point Spectra
Light, leaded 2 points. Section and chapter numbers are 32
point and 24 point Spectra Bold; section and chapter titles
are 36 point and 32 point Spectra Regular. The size of the
type page is 37 by 48½ picas.*

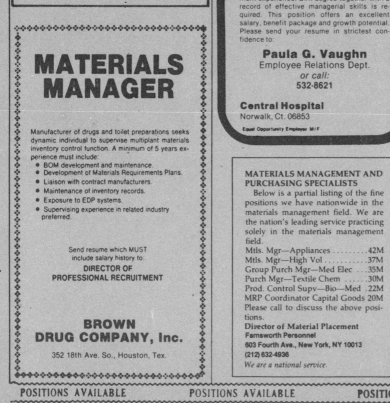